COMMUNITY COLLEGES

Editors
James L. Ratcliff
Stefanie Schwarz
Larry H. Ebbers

Center for Study of Higher Education
Pennsylvania State University

ASHE Series Editor

James L. Ratcliff

ASHE READER SERIES
SECOND EDITION

Pearson
Custom
Publishing

Printed in the United States of America

10 9 8 7 6 5 4 3

Please visit our web site at www.pearsoncustom.com

ISBN 0–536–58571–7

BA 996330

PEARSON CUSTOM PUBLISHING
75 Arlington Street, Suite 300, Boston, MA 02116
A Pearson Education Company

COPYRIGHT ACKNOWLEDGMENTS

Table of Contents

The Students

The Professional Staff

Leadership

Social Role and Future Perspectives

Acknowledgments

A volume such as this does not come to being without the help, guidance, and cooperation of many. It is the compilation of the wisdom, judgment, and fervor of those whose life has been enveloped in inquiry and practice in higher education generally, and community, junior, and technical colleges specifically. As such, it is an invitation to those new to research on the topic to delve into the literate, to taste the controversies, to know the merits and liabilities of these institutions. To join in this feast of inquiry, one must acknowledge all who helped set the table.

First, there are those without whose guidance this volume would never have been possible. Many thanks to Barbara Townsend for her kind and wise recommendations as Editor of the *ASHE Reader* series. The materials contained herein represent the collective judgment of the Advisory Board, whose counsel guided the selection and assemblage of materials.

Advisory Board

Richard Alfred	University of Michigan
Marilyn Amey	University of Kansas
Thomas Campbell	Illinois Central College
Darrel Clowes	Virginia Tech University
Arthur Cohen	University of California at Los Angeles
Rodulfo Garcia	Michigan State University
Elizabeth Hawthorne	Pennsylvania State University
Joann Horton	Texas Southern University
Sylvia Hurtado	University of Michigan
Jesse Jones	Richland College
Steve Katsinas	Oklahoma State University
Ken Kempner	University of Oregon
S.V. Martorana	Pennsylvania State University
Robert Messina, Jr.	Burlington Community College
Terry O'Banion	League for Innovation in the Community College
Jim Palmer	Illinois State University
Laura Rendon	Arizona State University
Ray Taylor	American Association of Community College Trustees
George Vaughan	North Carolina State University
James Wattenbarger	University of Florida
Steven Zwerling	The Ford Foundation

Second, there are those who generously allow us to reprint the source materials. The Association for the Study of Higher Education and the editors of this volume thank the following associations, publishers, and organizations for granting permission to reprint copyrighted materials in this limited edition of the *ASHE Reader on Community and Junior Colleges* and to waive fees whole or in part:

American Association of Community and Junior Colleges
American Council on Education
Change Magazine
Columbia University Press
Community College Review
Community College Services Catalyst
Community/Junior College Quarterly
Community and Junior College Journal
Education and Urban Society
Greenwood Press
Harvard Educational Review
Higher Education
Jossey-Bass
Journal of Higher Education
New Directions for Community Colleges
Review of Higher Education
Research in Higher Education
Routledge and Kegan Paul Press
State University of New York Press
U.S. Department of Education

Special thanks go to Nadine Lamb, who provided the editorial and technical assistance to compile the materials and copyedit the Bibliography.

Finally, a sincere thank you to Maria Rosa Rodriguez, editor of publications/Miami Dade Community College, Wolfson Campus; and Duane Lloyd, Dean of Ellsworth Community College for providing the photographs used on the cover of this volume.

A Note to the Reader

This second edition of the *ASHE Reader on Community and Junior Colleges* is expected to be printed for approximately three academic years, beginning in the Fall of 1994. It is the policy of the *ASHE Reader* series to update the collection of readings included in each *Reader* every two or three years.

A new edition of this *Reader* is anticipated. We would appreciate your comments on the current *Reader* and suggestions for improvement. Specifically, we would like to know which articles, documents and/or book chapters you found particularly helpful, thought-provoking, or informative. We would like to know how you came to use this *Reader* as well, so that future editions can be targeted to your specific needs. Lastly, we ask your help in identifying professional and academic literature which should be included in future editions of this *ASHE Reader*.

Please send your suggestions, comments, and recommendations regarding this *ASHE Reader* to the editor:

> James L. Ratcliff, Director
> Center for the Study of Higher Education
> The Pennsylvania State University
> 403 S. Allen Street, Suite 104
> University Park, PA 16801-5252

Suggestions regarding other topics which could be addressed through the *ASHE Reader* series should be sent to:

> Barbara Townsend, Editor
> ASHE Reader
> Department of Educational Leadership
> Memphis State University
> Patterson Hall 113,
> Memphis, TN 38152

Introduction

In 1994 we have prepared a revised second edition of the *ASHE Reader on Community Colleges*. Much new literature on community colleges has appeared since the publication of the first edition of the *Reader* in 1989. As we reviewed the Community College literature, we were amazed of how diversified community colleges are being portrayed in today's research. Indeed, community colleges make up a large segment of American higher education. Why is it that we are quite comfortable in differentiating between research universities (I and II) and doctoral-granting universities (I and II), but not community colleges? What is it that causes them to be regarded as a group, while we frequently discuss differences among the institutions offering the baccalaureate degree?

These and other questions reaffirm the need to examine community, junior, and technical colleges in the United States. This volume presents articles, book chapters, and papers that reflect the current research and thinking on two-year colleges. Much of this literature considers the institution in isolation. This is not the case with most other research and writing in higher education; it is mostly topical: organization and administration, curriculum, finance, or students. What intellectual or practical justification is there for deviating from the norm of studying the field topically? While there is literature on land-grant colleges and universities, historically black colleges and universities or liberal arts colleges, there are not only whole graduate courses but also complete doctoral programs whose focus is community college education. There are separate leadership institutes, a separate ERIC Clearinghouse, and most recently, a proposed separate assistant secretary of the U.S. Department of Education concerned exclusively with community, junior, and technical colleges.

The *ASHE Reader on Community Colleges* is institutional in focus for several reasons: Clearly, two-year colleges comprise the largest segment of higher education. Of the 3,354 institutions of higher learning in 1994, over one third are two-year colleges. Since 1985 enrollment in public two-year institutions has increased annually, turning sharply upward between 1990 and 1991. Community colleges enroll approximately half of the first and second year students in the United States. One justification, then, for the study of community and junior colleges is simply their number and the size of their contribution to the first two years of college education.

A second rationale has to do with the uniqueness of programs and services. Community and junior colleges provide specific academic, vocational, developmental, and community education programs which, while they may be found in other institutions inside and outside higher education, are the primary domain of the community and junior colleges: the vocational diploma or certificate, the Associate of Applied Arts, the Associate of Applied Sciences, the Associate of Arts, and the Associate of Science degrees.

A third reason for studying these institutions is the people within them. The students often are significantly different in a number of ways: Often they are older. They commute, rather than live in residence. They often are more practically and vocationally-oriented. A greater proportion of the students come to college without strong academic preparation; some enter high school completion and adult basic education programs to remedy these deficiencies. While other colleges and universities have older students, commuter students, students with academic deficiencies, and students who are interested primarily in career preparation, the simple magnitude of their presence in community and junior college classrooms makes them unique.

Just as it can be argued that the mix of students at community colleges is more diverse in background, interest, and ability than most other institutions of higher education, so too can the generalization be made of the faculty and administration. While the majority of introductory and survey courses in the disciplines are taught by community college faculty, these instructors rarely are represented in the academic disciplines and professional societies which guide and unify the fields they teach. The importance of teaching as the primary activity and the lack of emphasis on research and publication divorce community college faculty from their disciplinary base and from the advancement of knowledge; it becomes incumbent on the individual instructor as well as the institution to devise ways to keep teaching faculty involved and engaged in the advancements in their field. This distance from research gives occasion to the discussion of faculty development and renewal which have unique qualities within higher education.

Another distinguishing characteristic of community colleges is their close ties to the social, political, and economic geography of the region. Unlike liberal arts colleges or state universities, most community colleges have specific districts, counties, or areas to serve. Most have elected or appointed boards of trustees drawn from the locale. Advisory committees consisting of local business people, union leaders, and employees can give the community college an opportunity and responsiveness to parochial concerns and conditions uncharacteristic of other forms of higher education.

Thus, the study of community, junior, and technical colleges is a grand inquiry into distinctiveness, identity, and interaction between college and community. Perhaps this accounts for the preoccupation of the literature to describe and analyze the institution in isolation from its sister institutions, the high school and the university. In 1989 when the first edition of the *ASHE Reader on Community College* was published we asked the question: "What's so special about community and junior colleges?" The answer to this rather complex question is still of primary importance today. We think that Clifford Adelman's recent title of a study on Community Colleges gives an answer to the question. Adelman calls the Community College the "American thermometer." This type of institution demonstrates "The Way We Are." Yes, that is why it is important to conduct research on mission, purposes, programs, and services. American culture in large part is formed by Community Colleges—the type of institution which serves almost half of American students today.

Organization of Content

Within this volume, the terms *community college, junior college, technical college,* and *two-year college* are treated as having a commonality. An astute student will note that each term speaks to different purposes, conceptions, and times in the development of these institutions. There are two-year institutions with exclusively vocational-technical missions and there are those with primary aims of providing the first two-years of the baccalaureate degree. There is great variation in the aims, missions, geographical scope, governance, curriculum, students, programs, and services among community colleges. Yet, there has been little examination to date of the extent to which this variation is greater, within community colleges or between them.

As with the previous edition, the *ASHE Reader on Community Colleges* is a collection of readings on a type of higher education institution. In preparing the second edition, we surveyed members of the Advisory Board to determine what new topics ought to be included and what previous topics should be revised. We also asked their opinions regarding the key literature within each topic so as to provide students of higher education generally and of the community college specifically with papers, articles, monographs, and book excerpts that reflect the current knowledge base, areas of inquiry, and issues of discourse in the field. Thus once again, the volume has been topically organized. We have been able to expand significantly the selections contained in this second edition, reflecting the diversity of views and investigations in the field.

The *Reader* is organized into seven sections: (1) History, Philosophy, and Purpose; (2) Organization, Administration, and Finance; (3) Programs and Services; (4) The Students; (5) The Professional Staff; (6) Leadership; and (7) Social Role and Future Perspectives. At the end of each section, we have provided a bibliography for further readings. The suggested reading lists contain the bibliographic recommendations of the Advisory Committee of the *ASHE Reader*. It is not intended to be exhaustive of any topics. For a wider sweep of references in a given area, the reader is advised to turn to A.M. Cohen, J.C. Palmer, and K.D. Zwemer's *Key Resources on Community Colleges* published in 1986 by Jossey-Bass. Unfortunately, no more recent attempt at a comprehensive bibliography has been issued since that date. George Baker and Peggy Tyler completed a brief bibliographic essay as part of *A Handbook on the Community College in America* (1994).

Just as the bibliography in this *Reader* is not intended to be comprehensive, so too the articles included herein are not designed to provide a full and complete picture of the characteristics of the community college. This is not a basic text on the subject. For that, we refer the readers to A.M. Cohen and F.B. Brawer's *The American Community College* (1989) or G.A. Baker's *A Handbook on the Community College in America* (1994). This *ASHE Reader* is designed to accompany such texts in a course or faculty development seminar. It is also an invitation to the reader to reflection, to analysis and to research on the role, function, and contribution of community colleges to American higher education and to the social commitment to access through a differentiated system of colleges and universities.

History, Philosophy, and Purpose

The development of community colleges has paralleled and been supported by the growth of the American research university and the secondary school system in this country. In an historical essay, Thomas Diener traces major linkages between the development of community colleges and changes in workforce education expectations, access, and equity in higher education, the rise of statewide provision for and accountability of higher education, and the commensurate growth in program, purposes, and clientele. In "'First' Public Junior Colleges," J.L. Ratcliff examines the interaction between local college and local community. Three case studies representing three different decades of development (1890s, 1900s and 1920s) illustrate how social and economic issues shaped the support, advocacy, and development of early two-year institutions. He shows how the history of community colleges is part of a larger context of the expansion of the roles and expectations of the educational system and discusses the relationship between the development of junior colleges and the mental measurement movement (precursor to the assessment movement of the 1980s), developmental psychology, vocational guidance and curriculum, and the development of junior high schools. Also, certain progressive legislation, the initiative and referendum particularly, facilitated the growth of two-year institutions.

Edmund Gleazer's "Beyond the Open Door" was one of the most widely read and quoted articles of the 1960s. As president of the American Association of Community and Junior Colleges (AACJC), Gleazer advocated the continued expansion of adult and continuing education, community service and community education functions of community colleges. The article stands as a landmark to the institution's community to adult students and adult development. Michael Brick recounts the history and development of the American Association of Junior Colleges (AAJC), the predecessor organization to AACJC (as of 1992, the American Association of Community Colleges, AACC). In particular, he notes the key role of George Zook and the U.S. Bureau of Education in bringing about the first meeting and conference regarding the role and function of junior colleges. Brick notes the close ties between founding leaders of the organizations, such as James Madison Wood, president of Stephens College in Columbia, Missouri, to the presidents of the University of Chicago (William Rainey Harper) and the University of Missouri (Richard Jesse). He also describes the early activities of the association; its attempts to establish a code of ethics and its committee structure reflected the priorities of the day.

Burton Clark's early (1960) research on San Jose City College lead to a conception that community colleges assisted students in revising their educational goals to better meet their educational preparation and abilities. Dubbed the "cooling out function," Clark's thesis proved a useful rallying point for several critics of the community college. They argued that community colleges served to lower the educational aspirations of lower socio-economic groups by urging them to seek vocational certificates and degrees rather than assisting them to transfer to four-year colleges to complete a baccalaureate program of study. Clark takes on these critics, clarifying what he saw as the parameters of the "cooling-out" function in a subsequent 1980 article reproduced here. Brint and Karabel adapted Clark's "cooling out function" to their own interpretation of the community colleges' contribution to social mobility. They suggest that the distinctive structure of the American education system represents the ideological commitment to social mobility among social classes. They describe how the community college fits into the pattern of institutional differentiation, planned pathways of social mobility, and presumed fluidity within the system—all based on the belief that it is never too late for an individual to find, develop, and capitalize on his or her talents. The article concludes with an examination of such beliefs on the school system generally and the community college specifically. In this way, Brint and Karabel help distinguish the American education system from others and identify the role that community colleges may play in it.

Organization, Administration, and Finance

Community and junior colleges are predominantly public, yet a significant number are private, independent colleges. What is the "community" for Waldorf College, a private junior college? It is the American Lutheran Conference. And what is the community of Shorter College, an historically black junior college? It is the African Methodist Episcopal Church. Public community, junior, and technical colleges are governed in a number of ways. In Washington state, they are governed by a State Board for Community College Education. In Georgia, they are part of the University System of Georgia. Three junior colleges in Colorado are governed locally and are outside the community college system of that state. The University of Toledo and Northern Arizona University have community colleges organized within their structure, while the Pennsylvania State University operates a system of two-year campuses that is separate from that state's community college system. The service areas of public community colleges are defined often by combinations of school districts, by counties, or as wholly independent political subdivisions. Given the murky mix of state and local organization of community colleges, it follows that how community colleges are organized internally varies accordingly.

Richardson, Blocker and Bender give a prototypical description of the internal organization and administration of community colleges. The problems of administration are compounded by the creation of multi-college and multi-campus districts. The role of the chief executive officer, who may bear the title president, superintendent, director, chancellor, or dean, varies according to the legal and organizational structure of the college. Through their discussion, Richardson, Blocker and Bender stress the intimate connections of college and community, of administration and faculty, of college and campus which is often a hallmark of two-year institutions.

The U.S. Constitution left authority for education to the various states of the Republic. The states, in turn, delegated that responsibility to municipalities for elementary and secondary education. Given the varied past and present status of individual community colleges, their legal status is equally difficult to generalize. For public institutions, they are established as a combination of state stature and municipal authority to provide education. State four-year colleges, in contrast, are almost exclusively founded by state statute. Tollefson and Fountain examine the changes that have occurred over the past 25 years in state-level structures and agencies for coordinating community college education. Breneman and Nelson follow with a description of funding status and funding patterns for public community colleges in a number of states. They note that the expanded mission of two-year colleges has budgetary consequences, and they presage the strategic planning, quality assurance, program review, downsizing, and continuous quality improvement initiatives designed to mete out scarce resources across a diversity of educational programs.

In *"Cost Differences: The Amazing Disparity Among Institutions of Higher Education in Educational Costs Per Student,"* Howard Bowen provides a comparative basis for examining the costs of educating students among different types of higher education institutions. He notes that educational costs vary by region. He argues that institutions are less homogeneous by type and warns against making generalizations by type of institution or program.

Richard Fonte's article concentrates on state financial controls over community colleges. He identifies the factors that contribute to budgetary flexibility, budget form and expenditure accountability, tuition and revenue controls, local budget authority and personnel administration at the local level. Fonte's findings suggest that there are significant differences in the organization and administration of community colleges shaped in part by the nature and extent of state fiscal controls.

Programs and Services

Programs and services vary considerably among community colleges. Again, organization affects curriculum. Technical colleges often exclude the curriculum affording transfer and continuance toward a baccalaureate degree. Community colleges organized within or as part of a university system may exclude strictly vocational programs. Major curricular functions of the community college include the transfer, university-parallel and general education curricula, vocational and career curricula, developmental and remedial programs as well as services, and adult, continuing and community education. Cohen and Ignash address some of these issues in *"The Total Community College Curriculum."* They present results of a 1991 study of course offerings and transfer rates at 164 two-year colleges nationwide. The authors describe the relationship between liberal arts and non-liberal arts enrollment and student transfer by addressing questions such as to what degree liberal arts changed in recent years; what the fastest growing subject area are; or, to what degree college size or locale relates to course patterns. For non-liberal art classes, the researchers concentrate on issues such as how much of the community college curriculum is accounted for by the non-liberal arts, and what percentage of non-liberal arts courses transfer within selected states. One of their major findings is that research universities are more selective in terms of the non-liberal arts courses they accept for transfer.

Whereas the Cohen and Ignash article analyzes the transfer function and the curriculum at the state level, Louis Bender's research examines programs and services from the perspective of state legislature. In his article *"State Articulation Policies: Myth and Realities,"* he emphasizes that no two states can be described the same; nevertheless, researchers, policymakers, and the public media continue to project national norms onto state community colleges and higher education systems because they falsely assume uniformity. Bender outlines functions of community colleges as well as of state systems and then describes differences between institutional interests and student interests. Sotello and Turner then take up the issue of transfer. Their research concentrates on describing the complexity and difficulty of two- to four-year college transfer. They demonstrate with the results of a comparative study that the transfer process for Hispanic and white students differs significantly in three California community colleges. Sotello and Turner illustrate that community colleges within the same system can have radically different success rates for white and Hispanic students. The authors particularly point out the impact of interinstitutional linkages and networks on articulation and transfer.

In *"The 2 + 2 Tech-Prep/Associate Degree Program: 1 Making Winners of Ordinary Students,"* Dale Parnell advances the notion that the majority of studies, commissions, and reports on school reform do not effectively address the educational needs of the average 50 percent of students in the general education curriculum. These students are neither college preparatory nor vocational in their secondary school curriculum. Their high school curriculum has no focus, structure, or goals.

Parnell's solution is to build a two-year high school technological curriculum articulated with a two-year community college program.

Some researchers argue that over the past decades there has been a significant decline in the transfer function of community colleges. During their early years community colleges thought of themselves more as colleges than now. As McGrath and Spear underline, from the 1900s through the 1950s such programs accounted for 60 to 70 percent of total enrollment, and transfer rates often served as measures of institutional success. In *"The Remedialization of the Community College,"* McGrath and Spear take up the issue of the evolution of the remedial function. The authors particularly outline that over the past decade a gradual replacement of rigorous academic practices with remedial programs occurred in the Community college setting. Especially for an adequate preparation of nontraditional students there has to occur substantial transformations in their conceptions of education and in their conceptions as learners. Nontraditional students must be exposed to an environment for academic success.

In a recent presentation to the Community College Counselor of Connecticut, a Development Guidance and Counseling Model for student services in the community colleges was offered. Carroll and Tarasuk illustrate how this model can be integrated into the existing student service structure. They review historic trends and recent confusion and changing focus. The authors emphasize that differentiated roles and individual planning as well as guidance and responsive services are essential for effective program management.

Interorganizational arrangements between community colleges and other organizational types provide the community with effective services. In his article *"The Community College as a Catalyst For Economic Development,"* Cantor points out that the coordinating role is often achieved through a partnership of a community college with an "umbrella" organization consisting of representatives of multiple community-based organizations. As a result of his study, Cantor emphasizes that these kinds of interorganizational arrangements have proven successful in creating new organizations as well as new partnerships.

The Students

Perhaps, the largest database of postsecondary educational attendance is the National Longitudinal Study of the High School Class of 1972 (NLS-72). While NLS-72 describes students who completed their secondary education over two decades ago, it does give a rich portrait of those who went on to college, where they attended and what they studied. Clifford Adelman has examined the NLS-72 college transcripts, describing the enrollment patterns of community college students in the study. Adelman finds no cooling out function apparent among these students. Student failure to earn a degree was due to "neither poor academic performance . . . nor . . . a plot by community colleges to flunk out unpromising 'transfer track' students." Instead, he proposes the community colleges serve "occasional learners"—students who drop in to mill around or to gain specific knowledge but not students who seek and attain degrees. A profile that emerges is that a majority of students served by community colleges are not seeking degrees as their primary reason for attendance. He calls for closer, more careful analysis of what students take at the community college and how that impacts their lives.

Rendon and Nora describe recent research on Hispanic community college students. Hispanic students attend community colleges in disproportionately high numbers relative to the total student population but have lower college-going and college-completion rates. Hispanic students who have clear, concrete, and realistic educational goals are more likely to persist in their studies. Having concrete goals was found to be of greater significance in college completion than was the extent to which the students were academically or socially integrated into the college environment and interacted with faculty and fellow students. All forms of financial assistance (Basic Educational

Opportunity Grants, Supplemental Grants, National Direct Student Loans, and College Work Study Programs) were found to have a strong positive influence on college-completion and persistence; the heavy reliance on the student contribution to the costs of a college education (as compared to state general aid to higher education) appeared to influence attrition among Hispanic students.

Richardson finds that more than half of the entering community college students lack the basic skills to do college-level academic work. African-American, Latino-American, and Native American students rely on community colleges as their access point to higher education to an extent greater than the population as a whole. The prevailing model for assisting students lacking basic skills is a deficiency model; remediation is the primary institutional mechanism for raising student abilities to minimum standards. As an alternative, Richardson advocates an achievement model that challenges faculty and staff to create educational environments were student diversity is valued and individuals are encouraged to build upon their strengths rather than their weaknesses. To do this, institutions must take stock of their institutional climate and must effectively manage college cultures.

Weis examines the attitudes and behaviors of African-American students attending an urban community college. She argues that their behavior reflects an ambivalence toward schooling reflective of their position in a class-oriented and racist society. These students embrace and reject their education at the same time. They drop in and out of school, arrive late to class, exert minimal effort toward learning, and use drugs extensively. This, she believes, illustrates their futile attempts to assert their independence from the community college as an institution within a class-bound and discriminatory society; at the same time, these students repeatedly return to the community college as a means of social and economic advancement. The end results are twofold. First, few students graduate and, second, the educational experience tends to reinforce rather than diminish deeply rooted race and class antagonisms. The picture that Weis provides suggests serious problems and issues relative to the effectiveness and efficacy of community college programs and services for urban African American students.

Given Weis' relatively dismal portrait of students and campus climate within an urban community college, it is not surprising, then, for Maxwell to find students within a metropolitan area migrating to suburban community colleges. Within an 11 college metropolitan district, he found that younger students and those seeking to transfer and complete a baccalaureate were more likely to travel greater distances, avoiding the urban community college for the suburban one. While race or personal safety were not predominant reasons why these students sought the suburban campus, that the college offered "the courses that I want and need" and had "a good program in my areas of interest" were cited as primary criteria for college choice (p. 245). Maxwell did not find "white flight"—white-seeking fleeing predominantly African-American or Latino-American populations; instead, he found talented and academically ambitious students of all races and ethnicities seeking the suburban community college. Maxwell's research underscores the fact that there is not one community college. Rather, community colleges vary significantly in the students they attract and the programs and services they offer; this variation in turn affects the extent to which the college does or does not serve Adelman's occasional learner student population.

From this section's readings, it should be clear that the community college continues to serve the historically underrepresented in higher education.11 In the 1980s and 1990s, this means racial and ethnic minorities, as well as displaced workers, homemakers, and the underprepared. In the concluding article for this section, Laura Rendon and Terri Mathews call for reform and renewal of community college. They claim that "the community college is the more important vehicle of opportunity to attain a college education." Yet, they also find mounting evidence that access and opportunity, "the very elements on which community colleges were founded, may now be in jeopardy." Rapidly, the country is evolving from one educational system to two, where suburban high schools and community colleges offered enriched educational programs for advancement and where urban counterpart institutions provide weak educational experiences emphasizing obedience, deference, routine, and mechanical learning. They offer specific suggestions, guidelines and elements for the reforms they see as so crucial to maintaining the educational opportunity on which this country has prided itself.

The Professional Staff

The view on the level of quality of faculty and staff at community colleges is rather diverse. Some argue that community college faculty take pride in their commitment to teaching. They view the ideal faculty member as a concerned, dedicated, and effective teacher. The emphasis primarily focuses on how teaching takes place, not on what is taught. Others argue that the quality of teaching is deteriorating over the past decade. McGrath and Spear carry this notion further and state that recently a weak and disordered intellectual culture has emerged among faculty in two-year colleges. The authors point out that community college faculty routinely express difficulty understanding their students and themselves as well. Taking a dynamic approach to change this notion, the authors outline ideas which could lead towards a new faculty culture. A powerful academic culture can be created and sustained only by a faculty that is itself organized according to academic and intellectual rules of discourse and decision.

Opp and Smith concentrate their research on *"Minority Recruitment Programs at Two-Year Colleges."* A study was conducted to provide current institutional data on the number and percentages of underrepresented minorities among full-time faculty at two-year colleges. The research concentrates on options of academic administrators concerning a number of barriers to university faculty recruitment, and to determine the characteristics of successful recruitment programs. Some of the major findings demonstrate that a positive predictor of larger percentages of underrepresented faculty was whether the vice-president of academic affairs himself/herself was an ethnic minority. Respondents at institutions with low numbers of minorities were more likely to agree with the statement that minorities have difficulty fitting in socially with the community.

In his article *"The Scholarly Activities of Community College Faculty"* Palmer asks an essential question that touches basic principles of overall faculty involvement: "How active are community college faculty members in scholarly work outside of classroom teaching?" So far, few national surveys have addressed this question. Palmer formulates the question by concentrating on institutional support received by faculty for work on scholarly products, barriers to faculty scholarship, as well as faculty attitudes towards scholarship. He concludes that scholarship in the community college is a touchy issue. For example, college leaders need to articulate a broad definition of scholarship and assure faculty that an institutional emphasis on scholarship will not be constructed with a publish or perish framework.

The field of study plays a fundamental role in the renewal of community college faculty. New knowledge is not necessarily generated from research alone. Ratcliff points out that it comes from a base of the field of study. In his article *"Scholarship, the Transformation of Knowledge, and Community College Teaching,"* the author demonstrates that by thinking about the teaching process, we generate new ideas, conceptualizations, and approaches within the field of study. Especially engagement in the literature of the discipline enriches teaching and stimulates a culture of inquiry that we desperately need in our college classrooms.

Leadership

A current major concern in community college groups focuses on leadership at the institutional or local college level. As Bryant points out in his article *"New Leadership Considerations for Old Realities,"* the American Association of Community and Junior Colleges devotes increased attention to leadership development. Bryant sees one of the main concerns to be the overly autocratic inclinations of community college administrators. The author suggests several points that bear consideration in order to create more responsive community college leadership. He particularly concentrates on understanding concepts that are unique to leadership at community colleges, such as the historic place of faculty in academic areas, new parameters of faculty participation in total college governance, and the open channels of communication between faculty and board. Bryant argues in order to perform strong community college leadership, administrators must share more government responsibilities with faculty.

Focusing primarily on issues that can be directly influenced by actions of the governing board or president, Vaughan explores the ethical dilemmas of leadership in today's community colleges. His central question is "What can be done on our campuses to strengthen the commitment to ethical values?" Vaughan believes that the answer to this question lies, in part, in the desire and ability of community college leaders to create a framework on campus in which ethical values can evolve and be examined. Implicit in creating such a campus climate is the belief that the rules, regulations, and standards of conduct of the college must be in concert with the mission of the college. Whereas Vaughan assesses the ethical responsibilities of leadership, Deegan examines other management factors. Deegan describes the community college presidents' perception of the effectiveness of major management concepts related to planning, organization, budgeting/ financing, staffing, and evaluation. The author argues that there will be no simple management fix for issues facing community colleges in the 1990s. While management on an individual campus can be viewed as an art, Deegan nevertheless stresses that the use and impact of management concepts in community colleges can provide a useful concept for understanding the effect of change. The author highlights these ideas with the presidents' perceptions on institutional problems facing them and their perspectives on the future.

In "What We Know About Women in Community Colleges: An Examination of the Literature," Susan Twombly uses feminist phase theory to analyze the literature on female community college students. Her findings suggest that thinking about women has been largely compensatory and bifocal, focusing little on the value of women's experiences. Thinking about women was found to have changed little over the last twenty years.

Social Role and Future Perspectives

Mission and purpose of the community college are currently widely discussed among institutional researchers. Darrel Clowes and Bernard Levin provide an examination of community college missions. The authors state that the academic transfer program at the community college is atrophying. The curriculum at all nonselective institutions is becoming increasingly occupationally and technically oriented. This results in a transfer function that is dominated by occupational curricular structures. But one also has to point out that Community Colleges offer many students an alternative route to achieving a baccalaureate degree. In his article "The Community College at the Crossroad: The Need for Structural Reform," Kevin Dougherty analyses data on these institutions to see how effective they are in helping students to transfer. The author argues that present reformers need to keep in mind the comprehensive nature of the community college and be sure that their reform proposal will preserve rather than diminish the services it offers students. The researcher particularly concentrates on analyses of data on community college students' transfer to four-year colleges. His findings demonstrate that these students receive fewer bachelor's degrees than other college entrants. The author proposes rather large reforms such as transforming community colleges into four-year colleges or making them two-year branches of universities. Dougherty sees this reform process as an open-end experiment.

Oromaner proposes that a more comprehensive view of the community college would emerge if a sociology of knowledge perspective toward analyses of that institution were adopted. The author does not look directly at the community college, but rather at those who write about it and their conceptions. In *"Insiders, Outsiders, and the Community College: A Sociology of Knowledge Perspective,"* Oromaner outlines his ideas of applying Robert K. Merton's discussion of "insiders" and "outsiders" to the often conflicting images of the role of the community college. At present, outsiders are not likely to receive rewards for publishing in community college journals. At the same time, insiders are not likely to publish in outsider journals. Oromaner suggests that one way to change this is by having outsiders publish the journals. Gatekeepers of appropriate journals could have an impact if they were to solicit manuscripts from members of the other group. For future research this change could then result in a broader and more profound base for interdisciplinary research on community colleges.

The *Reader* concludes with Vaughan's statement on *"The Path to Respect."* The author argues that Community Colleges will achieve their full potential as institutions of higher education only when scholarship occupies a prominent climate on campuses that promote scholarship as well as teaching. Vaughan emphasizes that the instructor himself/herself must develop scholarship that he/she can communicate to students as well as to faculty and the overall community.

HISTORY,
PHILOSOPHY, AND PURPOSE

Growth of an American Invention: From Junior to Community College

THOMAS DIENER

The Age of the College—from the founding of Harvard through the Civil War.

The Age of the University—from the 1870s through World War II.

The Age of the Junior and Community College—from the 1960s through the last decades of the 20th century . . . and beyond?

Is this an accurate way to categorize American higher education? Does it help us understand some fundamental changes in the structure and mission of higher education in the United States? In broad strokes, this schema delineates major emphases in American higher education and points to underlying social transformations crucial to the development of our nation. In the beginnings of our country, men of learning, wealth, and power pushed for the creation of colleges and universities to serve private and public purposes. For the private good, they yearned for a college education which would mold the character of young men and give them the classical learnings then thought to be so essential to a cultivated and elegant gentleman. For the public good, this prescribed classical curriculum served very well to prepare the young male citizen for responsible leadership in government and the professions of law, medicine, and the ministry.

These early colleges, designed primarily on the basis of European and English progenitors, wore familiar garb: a prescribed and classical curriculum generally of four years in length. They served familiar faces: those of young men often from the families of the elite and affluent. They served a familiar purpose: to transmit the body of knowledge and values deemed important in those days to the potential leaders of the oncoming generation. The popularity of these colleges was extremely high. Their presence served an emerging society in important ways. They meant leadership for these shores could be educated here. They stood for the growing strength of the colonies. And, these seats of learning, spurred by the spirit of the Revolution, became important symbols for new peoples creating a new land. At one and the same time they stood for the creation of a new political entity, a new nation (unity), and for the diverse religious and social values so vital to immigrants to these shores (pluralism).

Rumblings of change, however, were reverberating throughout the world. Discoveries in the natural sciences, the forces of industrialization, urbanization, and immigration, rising equalitarianism, the increasing secularization of society—all these and many more forces were producing a new nation with special opportunities for personal advancement. The United States of the late 19th century was moving toward a more cohesive and centralized society. The ties of the railroad, the

3

lines of the telegraph, the advent of the airplane and automobile were more than man-made creations. They symbolized the shift of this country from a collection of hunters, pioneers, and small farmers into a more interdependent and urban society; they stood for an era of large industrial and business enterprises . . . and a nation preparing to step into the 20th century and the dawning of the technological age.

It was time for a change in colleges, too. The fervent boosterism of earlier days had produced a plethora of tiny, often isolated higher education institutions, many of which were hardly worthy of the lustrous names they gave themselves. Some critics of the day looked to other shores, looked to the roots of the new American society and its educational enterprises, seeking enlightenment for reform in the United States. Especially attractive was the German university (indeed, the whole of the German educational system pleased many, too!) with its emphasis on scholarship, faculty specialization, and research. Here was an educational enterprise fit for the times—an enterprise of knowledge production, not just knowledge transmittal. The spirit of the scientific approach which urged delving into all corners and dimensions of our world, the belief that rational inquiry could and would not only drive out ignorance but provide new ways to solve human and social problems, this mental set toward human manipulation and domination of the environment fit hand in glove with the argument advanced by many that a university, German style, should be built atop many colleges spread about the nation.

The view from abroad was not the only alternative. Another version of what American higher education might become sprang from efforts to mechanize, indeed industrialize, not only our cities but our farms. For example, passage in 1862 of the Morrill Act, calling for the establishment in each state of higher education institutions dedicated to instruction in agriculture and the mechanic arts, helped crack the monopoly the Middle Ages-based classical curriculum held on American higher education. True, this act did not completely transform the curriculum in an instant, nor did it totally obliterate the traditional and classical courses. But the seeds of change were planted with vigor. And they grew rapidly.

From it eventually came new kinds of faculty with vocational interests, with research interests, with interests in reaching out to the people of their states and regions and helping individuals and groups work on problems and issues affecting their work and their communities. From it eventually came new courses in the social sciences, in natural science, in agriculture, engineering, and business. These courses tended toward the practical, presenting learning which might be applied in emerging vocations, which met immediate needs of the society. From it eventually came new structures for learning. Graduate and professional schools were initiated, experiment stations created. Schools of science were launched, often to be incorporated into developing university structures, sometimes to become independent, freestanding universities of science and technology.

The land-grant movement was not the sole instigator of collegiate change. Other forces, in and out of higher education, were also prompting the transition from College Era to University Era. Professionalization of the faculty with an emphasis on knowledge production, development of an elective system by which undergraduates could exercise more control over their programs of study, the development of business and industry-allied professions and, concomitantly, programs of education for these professions, the emerging public junior high school and high school, increased emphasis on vocational training and engineering education, the creation of complex business and industrial enterprises, some spanning the nation in their influence and organization, increasing currents of power flowing to the federal government with its consequences for national intervention in education—these several trends illustrate the broad scope and complex nature of the changes in the social fabric of our nation and its educational agencies. Thus, the Age of the University drew its strength from both the transformation of American society and the international as well as national concepts of what higher education might be.

The Age of the University in the United States produced (as supporters of the German university concept had so hoped) a grand array of scientific investigations. Scholarship and inquiry advanced in the natural sciences, in medicine, in the social sciences, in the humanities, in agriculture, engineering, and business and commerce; scarcely a field of human endeavor was exempt from the analytical review of the university researcher-teacher. The knowledge explosion of the 20th century was aided mightily by the American university with its rapidly expanding force of highly trained specialists, its laboratories and experiment stations, and its sophisticated means for designing and managing complex research efforts. Indeed, World War II and, in its wake, the rebuilding of Europe and Japan, along with the requirements of the developing nations of the world, further accelerated the dramatic growth and influence of higher education in the United States, especially the research-oriented university.

In view of this scenario, is it presumptuous to now speak of an Age of the Junior and Community College? One which might follow the Age of the University? One which might mark a major new era of educational development in this country? Let us examine this unique development in the United States.

The configuration of the first junior colleges is not known precisely. Courses taught, faculty characteristics, organizational structure, and many other features remain largely a part of a hazy, time-dimmed past. Yet, as one reviews carefully the actual and proposed changes in American education, by very late in the 19th century one can discern certain fundamental issues emerging which would constitute characteristics or themes of the junior college: the debate over the definition, nature, and scope of secondary education; the promulgation of the associate degree; university efforts to separate general from specialized learning. For example, in view of the earlier growth of numerous small, usually private, colleges on the American scene, by the late 19th century the recently established U.S. Office of Education and its Commissioner of Education saw the plight of many of these institutions and began to call for reorganization of American higher education and for stronger evidence of quality collegiate-level instruction. By the early years of the 20th century, the U.S. Office of Education even dared identify a few standards which a "real" college must meet. Attempts to publish a list of these "real" colleges were quickly quashed by strong political as well as educational forces.

By the second decade of the 20th century, colleges were dropping some of their years of instruction (often for lack of students in the upper classes rather than as any genuine attempt to be educational pioneers), high schools were adding 13th and 14th years to their curricula, technical or vocational schools were also attempting some collegiate-level instruction, and a few major universities had redesigned their undergraduate programs to draw distinctions (at least on paper) between the "junior college," or first two years, and the "senior college," or last two years of a four-year liberal arts baccalaureate program. Regional accrediting agencies had begun the tedious task of sorting out collegiate from precollegiate, secondary from higher education. Later years brought even more diversity to the "junior college" ranks—university two-year extension centers, temporary federally supported emergency college activated during the depression of the 1930s, two-year finishing schools primarily for young women, federally established colleges (e.g., in the Canal Zone and, much later, the Community College of the Air Force), normal schools for teachers, privately owned two-year colleges, and, of course, the comprehensive community colleges.

One reason the junior college in the United States has been difficult to understand is that it has taken on so many forms of sponsorship and control. Is the junior college a high school and a part of secondary education? Is it collegiate and a part of higher education? Is it a unique educational enterprise standing apart from both of these worlds yet, at the same time, able to link them in new and constructive ways? Answers, at times cool and rational, at times rendered with some passion, have been offered in the affirmative to all three of these questions. While debates over definition and organizational form have waxed and waned, leaving not a few educators and probably most citizens perplexed (if concerned at all with these issues), a core of functions began to emerge, a core which, in the main, helped determine the essence of a junior college.

Certainly early on, the concept of the junior college as a shortened version of a regular or four-year liberal arts college held great attraction. Thus, the two-year college offering the freshman and sophomore courses seemed most advantageous. The courses were a known commodity, they served a good purpose in supplying young citizens with what many educators regarded as the basic general liberal education, and, best of all, with careful monitoring, students could transfer these course credits to a senior college or university, at which point they would begin their specialized or professional studies. To a lesser extent, the provision of a general education useful to many citizens was an early junior college function; to a greater extent, the intent to provide a college transfer program—one which provided the two-year general education component of a four-year liberal arts program—was a legitimate, indeed laudable, function. To this day these first two functions continue as important parts of junior and community college work.

Another function, guidance and counseling of students, also has a long history in the junior college. If students were enrolled in these institutions but expected to actually complete their work elsewhere, the college had responsibilities to help those students succeed at the junior college and move smoothly to the university. So, directly related to the early instructional program was a complementary noninstructional activity, that of student guidance.

As the junior colleges of the United States grew in number and importance another basic function emerged. This one had to do with the emerging employment needs of our nation. As the country became more heavily industrialized, as business and commerce expanded, the need for trained technicians, accountants, and clerical personnel increased rapidly. Even women who might spend their time as homemakers needed, some felt, to have education beyond the high school, education in the domestic and homemaking arts. Some early junior colleges began their work as technical and vocational colleges. More likely an institution beginning as a junior college would add vocational programs to its existing transfer programs. The vocational or job training function became, especially by the 1930s, an important portion of the mission of many junior colleges.

Following World War II the junior college expanded still further its basic set of functions. Beyond the general education, transfer, guidance, and vocational education functions, society was demanding greater access for all citizens to higher education, greater opportunity for technical and job skill learning, greater availability of programs and services for adults, not just the youth of our nation, and institutions which not only were locally controlled but drew their inspiration, their spirit for being, from their clientele. The clientele, as the century progressed, tended more and more to be "the public"—thus *public* schools and school districts, *public* colleges, and even specially created *public* junior college districts were established.

Services to adults in the community did not mean sacrificing those original and more traditional functions; it meant adding a new range of services. It also meant opening the collegiate door to more women, to blacks, hispanics, and other minority members, to working men and women who needed to upgrade their job skills or broaden their avocational interests, to retirees and those making mid-life career changes, to citizens interested in the economic or cultural or political development of their community.

The other wing of this new function—community service—might include some of the aspects of adult education named above, but it also meant more. It was a way by which the junior college, a product of the community, became a means for the community to examine itself, its strengths and weaknesses, its aspirations. So the college engaged in community surveys, formed education-community or education-work councils, and initiated other means by which the local community analyzed its political, economic, educational, or cultural needs. In turn, the junior college also became a central figure in community discussions on how to create a new future, how to solve some of its problems. This attitude of participation in community life and development, this proactive stance toward not only individual learning but community reformation, left outmoded the name and concept of the junior college.

Finally, the junior college became known for the development and provision of remedial or compensatory education. Given the post-World War II "open door" philosophy of admissions to education, two-year institutions attracted a wide range of human talent—including many students who aspired to higher education but did not have the requisite academic preparation (oftentimes despite the award of a high school diploma). Older adults as well as younger students saw the junior-becoming-community college as a ready point of access to higher learning. The colleges, in turn, found themselves struggling to take virtually all learners, regardless of educational level or competence, and prepare them for advanced study.

Difficult task that it was, the fast-changing junior college ventured into these rarely charted educational waters. These new community colleges abandoned the traditional notion in higher education that quality was defined by the high numbers of persons denied admission or the high rate of academic failure among those admitted. The concept of adding value—taking the learner where he or she is and promoting tangible academic success—became a mission, a hallmark, of the two-year community college movement.

The public, two-year, comprehensive community college (called by a variety of names, including technical college and junior community college) became the dominant model, the mid-20th-century model, of the junior college. A number of private junior colleges survive today. So do large numbers of institutions whose primary focus is on career training. But the predominant modern form of the junior college is the public community college, regardless of name, whose mission embraces all of the functions just described. That is the institution most often found in our large urban centers, most often serving the first-time and minority college student, most often the major two-year-college supplier of educational services to persons and communities in the late 20th century. The impact of the community college by the 1980s is dramatic and massive: it enrolls over one of every three students in American higher education and over half of all entering freshmen.

What forces supported and nourished this growth of the junior and, later, the community college? First, much of American education in the 19th and early 20th centuries was enamored with ideas coming from the rising tide of industrialization and free enterprise. The United States, land of opportunity, gave public and private entrepreneurs alike the chance to succeed. Faith in the efficacy of education was a leading light in the building of the nation. So colleges and universities sprang up, especially in the 19th century, very quickly and very frequently. A kind of social Darwinism was at work, prompting one and all to have a go at starting a college. Americans responded with vigor and pride. Those institutions which met the challenge survived. Survival was the measure of quality.

At the same time, the movement toward efficiency in business and industry was making its inroads in education, too. Many of the reformers in higher education saw the excesses a policy of complete laissez-faire would bring—a breakdown in adherence to standards of excellence and an extreme and deleterious dedication to growth and expansion. Whether from a desire to espouse quality education or efforts to shut off competition (or both), early university reformers of higher education like William Rainey Harper of Chicago, David Starr Jordan at Stanford, and Alexis Lange at California urged reorganization to bring about efficiency and eliminate waste. Their efforts helped promote the junior college as a social and educational device prompting efficiency and order. Efforts to reshape and restyle the American university were important in creating a climate, and indeed a form, for the junior college. The undergraduate college in some cases was divided in half to create a junior college and senior college. While more active as an idea than in actual practice, this concept had powerful repercussions in giving credibility to the notion of junior (general) versus senior (specialized) education.

The weakening and demise of many of the four-year colleges launched in the 19th century also added strength to the call for higher education reform. Many colleges were struggling for existence, had limited facilities and faculties, and, often, scarcely any students in the junior and senior classes. Regular colleges were, in fact, often junior colleges. The more efficient use of resources prompted educational leaders such as Philander Priestly Claxton, U.S. Commissioner of Education in the second decade of the 20th century, to urge weak senior colleges to become stronger institutions by shedding the last two years of course offerings and becoming authentic junior colleges.

The public high school was another force supporting the growth of the junior college. The Kalamazoo case of 1874 established the principle of supporting public education with public monies. The rapid increase in public high schools laid the foundation for further expansion of educational opportunities. Pride in their communities and their high schools motivated educators to look for additional ways to serve their eager new constituencies. The lure of university leaders eager to push onto and into the secondary school curricula the so-called general education of the freshman and sophomore years of college was hard to resist. Particularly in California and throughout the midwest, the early 20th century saw numerous examples of high schools pointing proudly to their new plans and programs which offered the 13th and 14th grades to qualified students.

Hand in hand with this rise of the secondary school was a change in the structure of employment opportunities. Early in the 20th century technological developments adopted by American business and industry created fewer jobs for unskilled youth. Machines were displacing workers in large numbers. These changing job requirements demanding more highly skilled workers gave impetus to the work of the junior college. Many youths enrolled in vocational courses in high school. But this training was often insufficient or outmoded; prospective workers needed more adequate preparation for the new jobs being created in business and industry. The training needs of the U.S. economy provided a strong push for the establishment of technical junior colleges and the inclusion of technical and business programs in the curricula of existing junior colleges.

National and regional agencies and procedures were still another force guiding the emergence of the junior college. The U.S. Office of Education was never an accreditation agency, but its reporting standards, with rare exception, helped frame definitions of junior colleges as institutions of higher education, not secondary education. So, too, did the early efforts of the American Association of Junior Colleges. More powerful in their effects were the efforts of regional and state accrediting agencies charged with the responsibility of insuring some semblance of quality in educational institutions. The regional agencies—in particular, educators attempting to police their own institutions and offerings—viewed the emerging junior college movement as just that—primarily a college-level course of study and not a high school. Although often housed in high school buildings, early policies of regional accreditation agencies were quite explicit in outlining how junior college programs were to be separate and distinct from secondary school programs.

Lastly, a major drive in the United States—the extension of educational access to more and more citizens—was of special import for the development of the junior (by now becoming a community) college. A movement in American higher education has been *from* the notion of college-as-fortress *to* one of college-as-service-provider. What has transpired in the development of common schools and the secondary schools, the provision of increasingly diverse programs and services for an increasingly diverse student body, has been mirrored in higher education. The junior college, at first a copy of a portion of the elitist university, began to widen its course offerings. It expanded in its types of students served. The inclusion of vocational programs and daughters as well as sons of blue-collar workers began the transformation of the junior college to the community college.

The great surge of transformation, however, awaited the consequences of the cataclysm of World War II (and resultant education boom energized by the GI Bill) and the pricking of the national conscience in such events as *Brown vs. Board of Education*, the civil rights movement of the 1960s, and the leadership of Martin Luther King, Jr. The political pull for expanded educational opportunities for the poor, the disadvantaged, and minorities came strongly and principally from many federal sources: legislation, elective orders, and federal task forces, all urging the expansion of American higher education to serve new clientele. The community college was proposed as a major entry point for the growing masses of American citizens who wished advanced education beyond the high school. The push for expanded educational opportunity came as women, minority groups, the handicapped, those with little or no prior experience with higher education, those seeking middle management and technical jobs surged forward in search of higher education credentials. Thus, the concept of the open door college, or democracy's college, became the means by which access to educational opportunity was established for all Americans. The two-year community college was the chief vehicle by which this was accomplished. The open door college was committed to all graduates of the American high school, to offering a wide variety of educational programs, and to serving the fast growing numbers of a diverse student body.

Was the coming of the community college an unblemished achievement? Was its influence all for the good? Were there no laws in its concepts and execution of its programs? Some critics maintain that the community college tried to be all things to all people. In good economic times perhaps society could afford to offer something of everything to everyone. When economic hard times strike, what must give way? Would the traditionally free or low tuition fees remain free or low, thus serving the poor? Would adult programs or community services not carrying traditional academic credit be eliminated? Would the community college become simply a technical school?

What of academic standards? Is it a service to provide an open door for the admission of virtually all who would seek entrance to higher education only to have that open door become a revolving door—easy in, easy out? Has easy access and the attempt to provide educational opportunity actually been a ruse by which academics have been able to lower their expectations for student performance? Or inflated their grades to make higher education not only accessible but painless and failure proof? And if lowered standards have prevailed, what does this mean for businesses and industries and our nation as a whole, which rely on increasing levels of job expertise and citizen skills?

Are the community colleges simply educational systems for the further manipulation of the poor, the minorities of our society, our lower socioeconomic class citizens? Are they a hoax appearing to offer access and opportunity when in fact offering mediocre training for dead-end jobs? Are they a pacifier to divert the attention of the poor and disadvantaged from their lot in life and prepare them to labor contentedly in the lower echelons of a technological world? Materials toward the end of Part IV of this book raise serious concerns about the capability of these institutions to extend quality educational opportunity and cast doubt on their future directions and vitality.

The evidence is mixed. The scholar must be cautious in framing a response to these troublesome questions. Perhaps some builders of the junior and community college movement saw it more as a way of keeping unsullied the halls of the university (that is, of excluding the poor, minority persons, and women) than as a democratic device for the uplifting of large sectors of our population. Some community colleges have promised more than they could deliver; misleading statements of intent have damaged sincere attempts to work with disadvantaged learners. Academic standards of quality have at times been diluted and grades inflated as a way of coping with the flood of new students in community colleges.

Upon long reflection, however, and after careful review of all the evidence (collected here as well as that found in many other places), I believe the two-year college movement stands for more victories than defeats, more successes than failures. The junior and community college is an important American invention which, despite imperfections, was and is remarkably effective. While all of American higher education has broadened its vision of who should be taught what and how, the community college has been the principal way by which the United States, in the post-World War II era, has in fact offered valid and expanding educational opportunities to increasing portions of our citizenry.

What trends have been evident in the 20th century development of the junior and community college?

Certainly the locus of control has swung sharply from private to public control. The early junior colleges usually were private, and they remained the dominant model of organization really until World War II (although the public sector enrolled the majority of two-year college students by the 1920s). This had many implications for the two-year college movement, first, by helping establish junior colleges as part of higher education rather than as part of secondary education. Secondly, though, it meant the early planning and perpetuation of a more traditional and standard collegiate curriculum. The emergence of the public two-year college signaled a greater sensitivity to a greater diversity of students and the need for a more comprehensive curriculum.

Another trend was the enlargement of the curriculum from an early reliance on the standard freshman and sophomore or general education college offerings to an increase in vocational and career-oriented courses and programs. American societal and business needs were changing rapidly; the two-year colleges began to offer more and more opportunities for job training and retraining. Increasingly, learners were workers first, students second.

Coincident with this change in American job structure and requirements was a rising expectation on behalf of civic education. Being a good citizen, and trying to define what that entailed, was a priority matter for the early 20th century in the United States. Public schools were struggling with this concept, and the junior college was seen as a part of the educational apparatus by which active citizenship was defined, instilled, and inspired. The role of the community college in the American-ization of post-Vietnam War immigrants indicates this is still an important function.

The trend first toward local establishment and control of the junior college and more recently toward more state-wide coordination and control is of great importance. The early literature of the junior college makes almost sacred the theme of local control. And, indeed, part of the genius of the movement was that it sprang from a variety of environments and was dedicated to meeting those particular local needs. That theme is still strong today. Late in the 20th century, however, the move toward centralization in many areas of our society is also strong. The economics of recession forces states to look very closely at the use of scarce resources and plan for greater coordination and, in many places, control. Statewide systems of community colleges have tempered the educational individualism and localism of an earlier day.

Along with the rest of the nation, junior and community colleges have moved to town. Urbanization has directly affected two-year institutions. The mid-century decades have seen not only the development of state systems of colleges but a rapid increase in massive, metropolitan, multi-campus systems. Like the colleges and universities ahead of them, junior colleges tended to begin in rural and small-town settings. By the late 20th century, the people and, therefore, large community college enrollments were in the large urban and suburban areas of the United States.

The community college movement has made a distinct turn from single purpose institutions to colleges with a range of purposes and programs. The first junior colleges saw the transfer function as their sole purpose—serve the university and serve it well by careful preparation of students for study in the junior and senior years. That noble purpose was useful but limited. As the junior college concept matured so did its view of its mission (to educate persons for jobs, to serve adults, to enroll part-time students, to provide community services, to be a "second chance college," to offer guidance and counseling services, to be a point of educational access for women and minorities). Consequently, the junior college has become a multi-purpose institution.

Along with this expansion in purposes has emerged a change in student clientele and campus climate. Even today remnants remain of some early junior college notions of elitism. Small enclaves still exist where a classical curriculum is taught to a carefully screened and selected group of students. By and large, however, the drive toward egalitarianism in American society has pro-duced a wide variety in students and their learning environments. The community college and its faculty serve the widest range of student ages, abilities, and interests of any institution in American higher education. It represents the American-built opportunity for a greater variety of individuals to develop and cultivate their talents and skills more fully than any other educational institution. It is the setting in which part-time, low-income, and working citizens enjoy equal educational opportunity with their full-time, middle-class, and affluent counterparts. The community college is truly the "people's college" for it serves young and old, educated or illiterate, U.S. citizen, immigrant, refugee, or international student, Ph.D. holder or seeker of a G.E.D. (high school equivalency certificate). And it serves all these clientele by design.

Lastly, the modern community college faces issues of accountability not dreamed of by its pioneers. Little was done to hold early American colleges accountable for their programs and services. Governing boards, presidents, and faculties went about their business secure in the knowledge that they, especially the faculty, knew what was important to be taught. Even the lay board, a distinctive feature of American higher education, did little to determine educational programs and courses. The college, in the person of the faculty, held sway.

Then came the business and industrial revolution of the late 19th century, the surge of public education in the early 20th century. Employers, students, farmers, minority groups, women, workers, unions, civic organizations, and others pressed higher education more closely for relevant and practical and technological programs. As the public paid more of the educational bills, had more sons and daughters enrolled, became more and more vocal and concerned about educational services, the cry for accountability grew louder.

Consumer groups, accrediting agencies, federal bureaus, civil rights activists, and modern concepts of goal-oriented management helped create an aura in which the public community college not only could but should reveal its means of organization, program development, financing, and control. Beyond that, accountability meant actively pursuing and using a range of citizen, employer, and student representatives to help develop institutional policies and service.

Perhaps this is the most American feature of this American invention: that the community college is of the people, by the people, and for the people. It arises from the aspirations and faith of the people of a locale or state; it holds itself open to rapid change; it adapts and reshapes its organization and offerings in response to changing societal needs.

Is consideration of an Age of the Junior and Community College useful in a study of the history of American higher education? I believe it is. The American college, as a model, is still lively; so is the American university. Together their members constitute major segments of a higher education enterprise admired and imitated around the world. But the transformation of American secondary and higher education in the last 100 years has produced a new institution—the junior and community college. The American college and university have been joined by a third major type of institution, enlarging and expanding the mission and scope of American education beyond the high school. I believe we see now that the advent of the Age of the Junior and Community College signaled the opening of another and distinctive chapter in the evolutionary development of American higher education.

"First" Public Junior Colleges in an Age of Reform

JAMES L. RATCLIFF

Background and Perspective

Education is basically reformist in orientation. Educators' interest in how people and institutions change is based on their desire to improve the content, processes, and organization of education. The evolution of community and junior colleges is a case in point. These institutions evolved as part of an effort to improve upon the structure and efficiency of higher education [28, 57, 60]. Along with the advent of the state university, the two-year college represents an American innovation in the reform of the structure of higher education.

The rise of the public two-year colleges was concurrent with other great educational reforms and innovations of the late nineteenth and early twentieth centuries: the junior high school, the mental measurement movement, the progressive education movement, manual training and vocational guidance, compulsory secondary education, and the application of scientific management to educational administration. These changes, in turn, were part of a great surge in social reform spanning from the 1890s into World War I. This impetus for reform set the tone of politics within the majority of American social institutions during the twentieth century [34]. Historians have come to regard social reform in three major periods. First, there were the agrarian uprisings against the industrialization of the nation, best exemplified by Populist politics and the 1896 Bryan presidential campaign. The second reform era was that of the Progressives, extending from 1900 to World War I. The third was the New Deal era of the 1930s. Each of these periods possessed unique characteristics, which influenced both high culture and mainstream society and which extended beyond the specific agendas of Populist, Progressive, Republican or Democratic parties [27, 34].

Between the Progressive and New Deal periods were sandwiched the 1920s. This decade has often been viewed by post-New Deal historians as an unfortunate interruption in the beneficent adaptation of reform. For these historians, the stock market crash in 1929 only reconfirmed the failure of the political conservatism of the 1920s, leading to the collapse of our economic and social institutions. More recent interpretations identify the 1920s as a time when "common values and common beliefs were replaced by separate and conflicting loyalties" [49, p. 425]. Similar to our own day, the twenties were a time of interest group advocacy and the ascendancy of the middle class over immigrant, labor, and ethnic minorities. It was also one of the great periods of growth in numbers of public junior colleges.

The public junior college emerged from the Populist era more as an idea than as a reality. According to Koos [44, p. 2], there were no public junior colleges in 1900. By the end of the Progressive Era (in 1919), there were only 6 public two-year colleges. According to Campbell [13, p. 223], by the end of the 1920s, that number had grown to 258! These statistics, examined in isolation, might lead one to the conclusion that the junior college was a product of a conservative rather than a reformist political tradition. Further examination of the development of these colleges is needed, however, to ferret out the social, economic, and political conditions that favored or hindered their development. Such an examination begins with a consideration of those circumstances held in common by these first public junior colleges.

In most states, the first locally supported, public two-year college faced certain obstacles to establishment and organization that were unique. First, the support of various interest groups within the municipalities had to be developed and marshalled. Second, the support necessary for the passage of state legislation to enable the establishment of two-year colleges had to be garnered. Third, relations needed to be established with neighboring four-year institutions to enable students to transfer credits earned at the new college.

The thesis of this article is that the first locally supported, public two-year colleges overcame these obstacles without the benefit of legal, financial, or institutional precedent within their states. Private colleges did not face comparable legal and financial hurdles; four-year institutions did not face comparable articulation issues in their founding; and junior colleges that were formed as branch campuses of universities, that were reorganized from normal schools, or that were developed as part of a state system of higher education, did not confront comparable need for local citizen support and effort in their establishment. For these reasons, the founding of the first locally supported, public junior college provides a unique opportunity to examine the nature of local and state support for the establishment and development of higher education.

Reported here are preliminary findings of a larger investigation of the relationship and influence of external and internal forces on the founding of selected colleges. Those studied were the first public junior college in states where locally controlled institutions were initiated. The present investigation is limited to the years immediately preceding the college founding and the initial years of operation. These colleges were identified through the combined listing of Eells [23], Koos [44] and Campbell [13]. The research objective was derived from current literature on strategic planning and management in higher education [52], which suggests a decisive influence of external forces and events on the direction, operation, and reform of higher education.

Causes and Influences of Educational Reform

How do such reforms in higher education occur? It may be tempting to attribute educational reform to educational (rather than political, economic, or social) factors. Such attribution gives credence to the importance and prominence of the profession and the field of study. Likewise, it may be reassuring to educators to discover that educational leaders were at the forefront of change within higher education. Thus, when it is reported that the faculty gained widespread control and influence over the curriculum and the colleges in the 1960s, an "academic revolution" is proclaimed [36]; when little impact is sensed from college administrators in the 1970s and 1980s, lack of effective leadership is lamented [43]. Given the reformist orientation of education, it should not be surprising that educational change is often attributed to educational movements and their leaders.

In a review of community and junior college literature, Reid [61, p. 143] noted "two interesting positions which seem to be major assumptions in virtually all the reporting of this movement: (1) that the movement is best explained by the great man theory, and (2) that the community junior college grew in response to cultural changes." The contemporary relevance of Reid's observation is illustrated in Deegan, Tillery and Associates' recent book [20, p. 4]: "Propensity for change in the community college resulted primarily from: (1) a lack of certain academic traditions during its formation years; (2) the diversity of local communities that nurtured the colleges; and (3) the effectiveness of local, state, and national advocates in shaping a new institution." Books that were most highly regarded by community college presidents and professors of community college education described the development of college ideologically rather than historically. In a previous review of literature, this author [57] found that all but two of these books were written during a span of fourteen years (1960-74). They were not actually histories of the community-college movement but did contain brief chronological descriptions with numerous historical inferences and interpretations. The other two books (Eells, [23]; Koos, [44]) also were not historical works, but were treated as such by the authors of the more current works [76, pp. 16-17].

Koos' and Eells' interpretation of the community-college movement was shaped by the sources of their information: college catalogs, questionnaires, and articles appearing in the prominent literary and educational journals of the day [44, pp. 16-17]. These two researchers turned to the words of the prominent contemporary higher educational leaders—William Rainey Harper, David Starr Jordan, William Watts Folwell—to discern the purpose and direction of junior-college development. Their early historical interpretations dissonantly portrayed the community-college movement as a popular, democratic educational reform advocated and lead by elitist university presidents who sought to cast off the burden of educating the lower division of the baccalaureate. However contradictory that interpretation may seem, it rests upon a single explanation of historical causation—the "great man" theory.

Typified by the Hellenic and Victorian historians, the "great man" theory holds that great leaders are primary and direct causes of historical events. Such a view tended "to give insufficient weight to the role institutions play in forming the ideas of leaders, in structuring the problems they faced, and in molding the solutions they might attempt and achieve" [66, p. 31]. Research on college establishment and founding attributed the development of early junior colleges to great men, such as William Rainey Harper at the University of Chicago. Alexis Lange at the University of California, and Henry Tappan at the University of Michigan [26, 28]. Such research failed to yield information on the complex of social, political, and economic relationships that existed between college and community.

Research Questions

The purpose of the research presented in this article was twofold: a) to determine the social phenomena associated with the founding of first publicly supported two-year colleges in three states, and b) to compare and contrast the development of these colleges in light of the social phenomena accompanying their founding. Certain basic questions directed the historical investigation: (1) How did the colleges originate and what were their antecedents? (2) What factors lead to the establishment of the colleges? (3) Which conditions, factors, or persons influenced their development?

Methodology

This study was a comparison of local, institutional histories. The investigation generated three case histories within the macrocosm of concurrent state and national events in order to analyze, compare, contrast, and explain [29, 66]. My approach was not intended to isolate the colleges, as has been the case in those investigations which have sought the "first" junior college [23, 31, 77]: rather, my intent was to interrelate historical phenomena using perspectives drawn from related social sciences. The procedures followed specific steps: (1) the selection and delimitation of the study of each case; (2) the accumulation, classification, and analysis of source materials; (3) the ascertainment of facts based on corroborative evidence; (4) the formulation of tentative interpretation of facts; (5) the synthesis of the interpretation of the cases in a logical, organized form; and (6) the comparison of facts of the case with those of the other cases.

The following primary sources were used in this exploratory investigation: (a) newspapers, and (b) college publications. Secondary sources were also consulted: (a) histories of the higher education in each state, (b) histories of local and state politics and society, and (c) pertinent journal articles and dissertation research.

The three cases chosen were Saginaw Junior College (reportedly est. 1895 in Michigan), McCook Junior College (est. 1926 in Nebraska), and Springfield Junior College (est. in 1917 in Massachusetts). These colleges were founded in three distinct time periods; their respective dates of establishment were separated by roughly ten years. The chronological separation of cases afforded analysis of those factors the three colleges had in common and those factors that were unique to each case.

A Junior College in Saginaw?

In the course of this investigation, it was discovered that one of the colleges selected for examination never really came into existence! At least, it never came into existence within a four-year period of when it was reported to start! Although no college materialized in Saginaw during this period, the historiography of this fictitious event is intriguing and instructive.

Andrews [1], Brooks [7], Brush [9], Dunbar [21], Eells [23, p. 53], and Hines [32] reported that there was an upward extension of the East Side High School in Saginaw, Michigan, to incorporate college-level work. Directly or indirectly these authors seemingly based their information about Saginaw on Gray's 1915 study of the junior college in California [30]. That Saginaw was Michigan's first public junior college experiment was contradicted (but not disputed nor disproved) by Rieske [62]. Curiously, these above claims failed to be substantiated by either an extensive review of the local Saginaw paper from 1 October 1894 to 31 July 1898 or by the report of the school superintendent, A. S. Whitney, which showed no student enrollees beyond grade 12 at the high school from 1891 to 1896 [80, p. 6].

Michigan is often regarded as a pioneer state in the development of two-year colleges. Texts frequently mention Henry Tappan's advocacy of the reorganization of higher education along the German model, by which students would be admitted to the university at the fourteenth grade [17, 22, 49, 70, 75, 76]. In 1882 the University of Michigan adopted a plan of instruction, called "the University system," which differentiated the general education function for the first two years of college from the more specialized study of the junior and senior years [33]. These three events— Tappan's presidency, the curricular distinction between upper and lower divisions, and the upward extension of the curriculum of Saginaw's East Side High School—were not related.

Tappan was an unpopular president during his eleven-year tenure at Michigan from 1852 to 1863. He was dismissed from office twenty years before Michigan adopted the University system and thirty-two years prior to the first alleged junior-college experiment (in Saginaw). The primary purpose of the 1882 curricular reform was to allow the more able students at the University of Michigan the opportunity to engage in independent study and reading rather than to encourage transfer students from five- and six-year high schools [21, p. 143]. The heavy demands placed on faculty to direct the independent study and reading under the 1882 curricular reform contributed to its abandonment in 1901.

Eells [23, p. 53] and Andrews [1, p. 514] claimed that in 1895 Saginaw's East Side High School began to offer freshman college work in Latin, algebra, trigonometry, English, and history. No evidence was offered by either author to corroborate this claim. A review of the *Saginaw Evening News* coverage of school board meetings and minutes, and the high-school graduation lists from October 1894 to 31 March 1896 failed to substantiate their claim. Although the *News* covered such items as the purchase of storm windows for the schools, teachers' salaries, and the addition of 9th-grade courses in English, history and French, no mention was made of the upward extension of the high-school curriculum to include the first year of college. Eells [23, p. 53] also claimed that by 1897, eight students with such work had graduated at the university in three years after entrance. Again, evidence of this was either lacking or was inaccurate. It was a common practice among universities of the time to grant incoming students advanced standing and credit for subjects upon which they could pass an examination. In fact, students from Saginaw schools did perform well at the University of Michigan; in 1894 there were eighty Saginaw graduates enrolled at Ann Arbor [73]. If the Eells' claim that students from Saginaw were granted advanced standing was correct, the fact alone still would not substantiate the founding of a formal junior-college organization within Saginaw schools.

The review of secondary literature pertinent to the alleged Saginaw experiment raised serious questions about the quality of scholarship in prior research on community-college development. The wording used in each of the aforementioned descriptions of the supposed Saginaw six-year high school was nearly identical; the sources were either not documented or they were from a single, secondary source (either Gray [30] or Brush [9]. The thesis that "great man" Tappan had planted the seed for curricular reform at Michigan that was to manifest itself twenty years later, and that that 1882 University of Michigan reform stimulated the founding of a junior college experiment some thirteen years later is, at best, historically cavalier. That this erroneous tale should pass without scrutiny through major literature on the topic generates doubt about the validity and reliability of historical descriptions of other aspects of the community junior-college movement.

Was the social, political, and economic climate conducive to founding a junior college in Saginaw in 1895? Throughout the period preceding the U.S. presidential election of 1896, the controversy over bimetalism and "free silver" raged. The national economy was expanding rapidly, but the economic policy of the Cleveland administration was monetarist; the amount of money in circulation was determined by the amount of gold held by the federal government. This produced the effect of holding constant or devaluing fixed assets, such as property values. Under such circumstances the price for borrowing money or issuing bonds was high. The net effect of economic factors was inhibiting upon the growth of public education.

The civic and economic leaders of Saginaw viewed the school system and other public services as assets to the continued growth of the community. Technological advances in motorized transportation, improvement of roads and waterways, and the discovery of a nearby energy source, coal, made the long-term future of Saginaw seem bright, in spite of the recession gripping the economy in 1895-96. There was widespread support for education beyond high school in the community, through extension, the YMCA, support of denominational colleges, a professional school and proprietary education. There was strong and regular communication between Saginaw school officials and the University of Michigan and the University of Chicago—two institutions of higher education where the lower division and upper division work had been organizationally separate in the curriculum. Also, educational leaders of Saginaw were reformist in outlook; they had been active in introducing developmental educational psychology to the teachers and in seeking more efficient and productive means of organizing the course of study. Seemingly, the social, political, and educational climate of Saginaw seemed conducive to the advent of a junior college.

Saginaw citizens were informed of William Rainey Harper's system of colleges and academies to be affiliated with the University of Chicago. An article in the *Saginaw Evening News* portrayed the plan as primarily denominational: "Baptist colleges and academies are preparing to come under the wing of the University of Chicago" [18]. And the story did not discuss the prospect of upward extension of the public high school to form such colleges. The Saginaw school system reduced, rather than expanded, services during the recession years of 1894-96. The limitations placed on expansion of services were products of the monetary policies of the Cleveland administration, and those economic barriers did not recede until the end of the recession and the presidential election of 1896.

The First Public Junior College in Massachusetts

The first public junior college in Massachusetts was founded in 1917 in Springfield. The Springfield population had jumped from less than eighty-nine thousand in 1910 to over one hundred thousand inhabitants by the end of 1914. Manufacturing firms were locating in this western Massachusetts trade center. The *Springfield Daily Republican* reported that the capital investment in Springfield industries increased 59 percent from 1910 to 1915, and that during the same period, total salaries and wages paid by Springfield employers expanded by 36 percent [19]. A former resident of Springfield, who returned in 1916 after being away for fifteen years, noted the extensive building and renovation along Main Street, the numerous new parks, and the new residential sections guided in their development by the city planning commission. Although the Springfield economy, like that of Saginaw, had languished during the 1892-96 recession, it had recovered handsomely during the Progressive era prosperity [16]. The growth in business and population translated into enrollment growth at the high schools [3].

A major political item for Springfield in 1916 and 1917 was the revision of the city charter. Since there was no home-rule bill in the state the debate over the revision of the Springfield city charter was conducted in the state legislature. Part of that debate involved the separation of the school board from the municipal government. The problem of having the school board report to the mayor's office was illustrated in 1916. In that year, the school board, afraid of losing good teachers due to low salaries, had recommended a pay increase. The city finance committee and the mayor's office opposed the pay increase. The fight between the school board and the mayor extended into the spring of 1917, when the board was to consider the proposal to establish the junior college. The city-charter bill in the legislature would give the schools the power to buy land, erect buildings, and effect salary scales without consulting the city council [15]. But in 1917, the school board was not free to turn to the voters for a tax increase, and the city was not free to turn to the voters to revise its character to give the school board greater discretion in decision making. A second political fight ensued among legislators over the form of the revised charter: the city-manager form of government versus the federal charter form. In 1917 the Union for a Progressive Constitution proposed amendments to the state constitution that would incorporate the initiative and referendum processes in the government of the Commonwealth. In 1917 Springfield did not have access to the political reforms of direct democracy, the initiative and referendum—to raise teacher salaries, to raise taxes, or to build support for educational reforms.

In the year prior to the founding of Springfield Junior College (SJC), 1916, the Board of Education established four junior high schools. This innovation was intended to provide a logical exit point for those students who were more attracted to the jobs and wages of the local industry than to continuing their education; secondary education was still seen as elective rather than compulsory in Springfield. Then too, the three high schools—Commercial, Technical, and Central—were crowded. The school board reasoned that, as three year (rather than four-year) high schools, the crowded conditions could be eased. There were also educational reasons for the junior high school. The Board, the junior high principal, and the teachers espoused the developmental belief that children in these grades should be taught differently than those in either the elementary schools or the high schools. The first junior high school began as one teacher's educational experiment in 1898-99, was continued throughout the Progressive era, and was institutionalized across the Springfield school system in 1916. Springfield's State Junior High School even included a remedial program to assist those students who had failed one or two subjects in their high school entrance examination [18]. These were progressive reforms.

Springfield schools, administrators, students, and teachers were recognized for educational excellence on a number of occasions. In 1916 President E.M. Hopkins of Dartmouth presented a trophy to Springfield's Central High School for high scholarship in secondary education and an award to the three Springfield high schools for excellence in the applied arts [65]. Also that year,

Harvard awarded Central High School a Phi Beta Kappa trophy because its students won the highest honors on the Harvard entrance examinations. William C. Hill, principal of Central High School, was elected as president of the New England Association of Teachers of English [24], and the following year he became the first dean of Springfield Junior College. Superintendent Van Sickle served with Columbia Professor George Strayer on visitation and survey teams to other public school systems. Strayer asked Van Sickle to receive and review the reports of educational innovations in school systems, including the 1914 report of the Grand Rapids, Michigan school system. In that year Grand Rapids began Michigan's pioneer public junior college experiment. Superintendent Van Sickle also well evidenced his commitment to progressive educational philosophy and to the mental measurement movement through his work with Professors Strayer, E. L. Thorndike, and E. P. Cubberly on the "Committee on Standards and Tests for Measuring the Efficiency of Schools or Systems of Schools" of the National Council of Education [69]. Springfield schools and educators were professionally active and involved in the educational reforms of the day.

During 1917 the school board received a number of requests for evening classes for adults. The local machinists' union requested classes in technical subjects [2]. Salesmanship was added to the evening curriculum at the request of several Springfield employers. The curriculum, first initiated in 1897, offered subjects parallel to those of the day high schools, plus technical and commercial courses, a high school preparatory department, and classes for the foreign-born [25]. The formation of junior highs relieved the overcrowding in the high schools and made it possible for the school system to respond to requests from community and labor groups for adult and evening classes. When the school board established the first public two-year college in the state the following year, it too was part of the developmental and progressive framework of the city school system. Located in the Central High School building, Springfield Junior College would not have been possible, physically or philosophically, without the educational reform and articulation enacted between the junior high and high schools.

Springfield Junior College was an upward extension of Springfield Central High School. William C. Hill, principal of Central High also served as dean of the college. Prior to the formation of SJC, Central High had a small number of students who chose to remain for an additional year of post-high-school college work, which was accepted at colleges and universities in the area through their admissions testing practices [14].

Unlike the introduction of the four junior high schools, the junior college received little publicity or public promotion. Without fanfare, the board of education established a junior college department in Central High School in April 1917, with college-level work to begin the following September [39]. Principal Hill presented the idea to a meeting of graduating seniors in May 1917 [37]. Prior to the beginning of the new school year, the *Daily Republican* also provided citizens with a description of the purpose and success of California junior colleges [12]. During that spring, the school district had been engaged in a battle with the city council over raising taxes to increase teachers' salaries. During that debate, the cost efficiency of the school system was questioned by the opponents of tax increases. Given the negative effects of this salary debate on a tax-conscious public, perhaps Superintendent Van Sickle did not want to call attention to the upward extension of the high school as yet another expansion of services. Then too, the newspaper was increasingly taken with stories of World War I and the growing American involvement in it. While the junior high schools had been the subject of a number of articles in the *Daily Republican* in 1916, including a feature story in a Saturday edition, the junior college was only mentioned three times in all of 1917, the year of its founding; and those stories were small, back-page articles.

The public junior college in Springfield was preceded by the Y.M.C.A. college (often referred to as "Springfield College" in the local papers). The Y.M.C.A. College reportedly had offered a two-year college transfer and technical curricula since 1885; that curricula was lengthened to three years in 1896, and in 1916, again was augmented to four years [48, p. 5]. If the report that the Springfield

Y.M.C.A. College maintained a two-year curriculum in the decade from 1885 to 1896 is correct, then it would predate both Bradley Polytechnic Institute (est. 1897, Peoria, Ill.) and the Lewis Institute (est. 1896, Chicago, Ill.) as an early junior college [23, p. 54]. It would not, however, preempt the claims of Lasell Female Seminary (est. 1851) and Susquehanna University (est. 1858) as the first private junior college [31]. It is not intended here to offer a new candidate for first private junior college; however, based on the experience of this investigation in attempting to substantiate Saginaw as the site of a junior college in 1895, it is perhaps prudent to suggest that further research on the early curriculum of the Springfield Y.M.C.A. College may augment understanding of the early development of junior colleges.

Another predecessor of the public junior college in Springfield was the American International College (AIC), an institution founded by French Canadian missionaries in Lowell (Mass.) in 1894. Originally named the French Protestant College, AIC was moved to Springfield in 1898. It was authorized by the Commonwealth of Massachusetts to confer collegiate degrees and had offered a two-year, college-level curriculum since 1894.

In 1916, AIC reported 172 college students representing 20 different nationalities. It claimed to be the only institution of higher education with the specific mission of educating the foreign-born. The College consisted of three departments: the college, the academy, and the introductory department. The college served those non-English speakers who already had some secondary education and were literate in their native tongue. The academy was a preparatory department "with the same certificate privileges at the great universities" as had the Springfield high school students. The introductory department assisted those immigrants who were illiterate in both English and their native language [79, pp. 1, 9]. The American International College provided yet another previously unrecorded, early example of a private two-year college worthy of further investigation. In this instance, the open admissions policy, commitment to progressive educational principles, service to a special population group, and provision for remedial developmental education were distinctive.

Springfield Y.M.C.A. College and American International College were not the only postsecondary opportunities in the Springfield area. Within a short distance were Mt. Holyoke, Williams, Smith, Amherst, and the Massachusetts Agricultural College (MAC). MAC organized extension classes in Springfield in 1916 and 1917. The enrollment of these colleges and other institutions of higher education throughout New England were devasted by the entrance of the United States into World War I [78].

Applying the "great man theory" to the founding of two-year colleges would lead to a search for a national educational leader of the day to whom the development of SJC could be attributed. The most proximal of such leaders to Springfield was J. Stanley Hall, president of Clark University. Hall, like Gilman at Johns Hopkins, Harper at Chicago, and Tappan at Michigan, was impressed with the German research university and sought to separate upper division and graduate studies from the lower division, which he regarded as more akin to secondary education [8]. Clark University, where Hall was founding president, was devoted solely to graduate studies; it was less than sixty miles from Springfield. Clark was the site of one the earliest master's theses on the junior college [7], evidencing some scholarly interest in the institution. In spite of Hall's prominence in higher education and educational psychology, and in spite of research interest in developmental psychology and institutional reform at Clark University, Hall had no apparent role in fostering the SJC experiment.

External events in another nearby higher education institution proved more influential than any particular educational personage. Just as the formation of junior high school and their articulation with the senior high schools made the formation of SJC possible, the curricular reform at Wesleyan University influenced the early SJC curriculum. In 1908 Wesleyan abandoned its prescribed Latin, arts, and sciences curriculum for a program of study allowing for more free electives [22]. In that new curriculum, there was a clear differentiation between freshman year and the later three years. Previously, the division had been between the first two years and the second two years of the baccalaureate program. In the new (1908) Wesleyan curriculum, only English was a required freshman course.

Thus, the new Springfield Junior College designed a one-year arts and science curriculum that articulated well with Wesleyan's course of study. Under the circumstances, it was clear that the addition of English as a SJC course was advantageous, and limiting the Springfield curriculum to the first year of college facilitated the relationship with Wesleyan. The important point here is not that SJC was "forced" to copy the Wesleyan curriculum. Nothing of the sort occurred; indeed many fine Springfield graduates went to Boston, Harvard, or Dartmouth. Rather, the relevant fact is that Wesleyan was rethinking its curriculum and was making a concerted, direct effort to increase its enrollments. The nature of the curricula reform—toward a freshman year of free electives—was permissive, allowing for articulation with SJC. Curriculum reform at the University had positive effects upon junior-college curriculum development.

Courses of freshman grade were offered at SJC in English, Latin, French, German, history, science, and mathematics. English, Latin, and history were new courses at Central High in 1917. Other courses—French, German, science and mathematics—had previously been taken for advanced credit by high school seniors. Colleges would grant Central High students credit for these subjects after taking an examination and meeting the other college entrance requirements. However, in the junior college curriculum, the content of these courses was altered to better emulate the requirements of the freshman year in colleges.

As Springfield's Central High principal, William C. Hill, wrote:

> The courses will be made up of thirteenth grade pupils: that is to say, pupils who have graduated from high school. The majority will doubtless have completed the regular college entrance requirement, but we shall not bar anyone from a course in Latin or French, for example, if he is well qualified for this course, simply because he has not done the work in mathematics and history required for college entrance. We shall not refuse admittance to these courses if we are positive that they are ready for them, but the pace will be set for college freshmen. We shall have some who do not intend to go away to college. We hope to be able to encourage some, who would not otherwise secure a college education, to make a start and perhaps to complete the four year-course elsewhere later [7, p. 38].

What can be seen from this early quote? First, in initiating the junior college, Principal Hill advocated open access. Students were not barred from admission because they had not completed the prerequisite courses in mathematics and history. Nevertheless, there was a clear sense of academic standards; the courses were intended to be a collegiate grade.

The admissions policy anticipated the entrance of some students who otherwise would not seek a college education. For the decade prior to World War I, there were non-traditional learners. Recall that high schools themselves were fairly new phenomena; many were less than two decades old. In this way, the early junior-college movement was part of the reform and reorganization of both high school and college education. Many students, particularly in New England, attended academies as preparation for college. There were few curricular standards at the time which clearly distinguished secondary from collegiate education. Therefore, the open admissions policy of Principal Hill may be viewed as a logical extension of the university practice of waiving freshman requirements in certain cases and admitting students for advanced courses. Although true open access became a hallmark of the comprehensive community college during the 1960s and 1970s, open admissions policies, nevertheless, may have had their start with early junior colleges, such as Springfield.

The new junior college in Springfield was built on a number of partnerships. First, there were vocational programs. The junior college cooperated with the City Library in establishing a librarian's training program. Likewise, Springfield Junior College cooperated with the High School of Commerce to develop a postsecondary secretarial program. The only part of SIC's curriculum that extended beyond the freshman year was the two-year premedical course of study. From the outset, Springfield Junior College offered vocational and preprofessional studies, and from the beginning many of these courses were developed through cooperative partnerships.

In summary, the economic and demographic environment of Springfield in 1917 was supportive of the development of the junior college. The city was growing in population, numbers of employers, and numbers of workers. The educational leadership of the city was progressive and professionally active. The city had a history of educational reform and innovation. In particular, the creation of junior high schools worked to the advantage of founding the junior college. Politically the city was embroiled in a debate over the revision of the municipal government charter. The actions and decisions of the school board were subject to the review of the city council, and that too had led to political battles. The revision of the form of city government was subject to the approval of the state legislature. The initiative and referendum were not part of the state government and therefore were not available as a means for building public support and approval of educational issues. Although Springfield did launch a successful first junior college, the extreme drain of students from college campuses during the war, the historical preference in New England for private higher education [63], and the lack of a public campaign to promote the junior college inhibited its success and growth.

McCook and the Public Junior Colleges of Nebraska

The local school board of McCook, Nebraska, authorized the establishment of a junior college in 1926 [46]; this was to become the state's first public junior college. There was no law in 1926 which permitted McCook to establish a junior college; likewise, there was no articulation policy at the University of Nebraska permitting the transfer of students from a junior college. In the process of garnering support from other communities across Nebraska for passage of junior-college enabling legislation, a junior-college movement was spawned.

Several reasons were advanced for the founding of the college. The educational and civic leaders of McCook believed that the University of Nebraska located in Lincoln (southeastern Nebraska) was too distant, and that McCook students who wished to remain at or near home were discouraged from attending college [54]. One of their principal arguments for a junior college was that in 1925, fewer than 2 percent of graduating Nebraska high school seniors went on to higher education. This educational rationale was coupled with arguments of the civic and commercial benefits that a college would bring to McCook.

McCook visualized itself as a commercial center for southwestern Nebraska. It was growing in population and there was a commensurate demand placed on school building and expansion [47]. A junior college was seen as an asset, as were the museum, public library, country club, and the completion of rail and highway connections with Denver and Omaha. McCook competed with other towns in Kansas and Nebraska for the routing of the transcontinental highway (U.S. 6) and for a north-south national route (U.S. 83). Such public services as a college, a library, and major transportation links would help differentiate McCook from other rural Nebraska communities and attract people from surrounding communities to shop or to relocate.

Other towns sought colleges as community assets. For example, Beatrice Chamber of Commerce staged a fund-raising and publicity drive to lure Doane College to move its campus in Crete (Neb.) to Beatrice [4]. These actions on the part of other communities were followed carefully by the supporters of the junior college in McCook. But the strongest interest by these rival communities seems to be in public rather than private higher education. Proponents of the junior college idea were active in Norfolk (northeast Neb). Like their counterparts in McCook, they sought data on the success of such institutions in other states and on the processes by which these colleges received initial regional accreditation and recognition of their work by nearby universities. The Reverend P.M. Orr headed the campaign for a Norfolk junior college. He argued that Norfolk citizens spent

$20,000 annually in other cities educating their children. Reverend Orr's campaign was followed closely by the McCook newspapers. In the winter of 1925-26, Fairbury, Norfolk, Scottsbluff, and McCook competed to start the first junior college in the state [40].

The editors of the *McCook Daily Gazette*, H.C. Strunk and Mark H. Knight, sparked the promotion of a junior college in McCook. The paper ran a series of stories on the problems students face in going away from home to college and on the success of junior colleges in other communities. It also profiled Port Huron Junior College (Mich.) and Burlington Junior College (Iowa), and included assurances from Burlington's superintendent that "McCook is ideally located for a junior college" [56]. The *Gazette* series concluded with an article by A.C. Olney, California commissioner of secondary schools, in which he described the rationale and the success of nineteen California junior colleges. Prior to becoming commissioner, Olney had served as founding dean of the first two California junior colleges: Fresno in 1910 and Santa Barbara in 1911 [11, 67].

In December 1925 Superintendent of McCook Public Schools, J. A. True, invited A. A. Reed, the Director of the Extension Division, and Dean W. E. Sealock of the Teachers College at the University of Nebraska to confer with him regarding the establishment of a junior college. Sealock supported the establishment of a junior college in McCook and agreed to serve as a resource person in a McCook town meeting to discuss the merits of a junior college. In that meeting, the dean stated that a junior college was feasible in any town of thirty-five hundred or more, citing Clarinda Junior College (Iowa) as an example [72]. Both Director Reed and Dean Sealock were favorable to the junior-college idea, and later both were instrumental in gaining initial recognition for the McCook Junior College (MJC) curriculum from the University of Nebraska Board of Regents.

Editors Strunk and Knight and Superintendent True also sought the perspectives of the Colorado Superintendent of Public Instruction and of the chief of the higher education division of the U. S. Bureau of Education, George F. Zook, on the merits of establishing a junior college. Zook, a know supporter of junior colleges, restated his belief that "education belongs in the hands of public institutions." Although he cautioned, "it is wrong to establish a college in a small, isolated town," he voiced his support of local control: "state-owned institutions are inferior to those owned by municipalities" [10].

McCook businesses were also unanimous in support of the establishment of a junior college. The Chamber of Commerce endorsed the project and, working in conjunction with the YMCA, offered the upper floors of the new "Y" building as the temporary location for the college. Developers J. E. and Charles Kelly proposed to donate a parcel of land to the school district for the expressed purpose of construction of college buildings. The land was located in an area of town where there was substantial projected growth, and the college building would augment the value of adjacent real estate belonging to the Kellys [6].

The information gathering, mass meetings, and publicity about junior colleges paid off. In their 9 December 1925 meeting, the school board voted to start a junior college the following September. The *Gazette* reported widespread enthusiasm for the new college [6]:

> According to members of the board, the project received more public support than any other project brought before the board in its history. Hundreds of people expressed themselves in favor of the project, and only two are known to have opposed it. The mothers clubs of the city voted solidly for the establishment, and the Chamber of Commerce also unanimously favored it.

The board of education initially planned to seek accreditation through the North Central Association. Subsequent to the board's decision to found MJC, Extension Director Reed assisted Superintendent True in developing a curricular plan that would articulate with that of the University of Nebraska. Dean W. E. Sealock of the University's Teachers College also conferred with Director Reed on the proposed MJC curriculum. In the resulting plan MJC agreed to offer courses of comparable curriculum to that taught by the University; these courses were to be taught by instructors deemed by the University to be adequately prepared. In exchange MJC was to receive full recognition for its work by the Extension Division of the University. The initial curriculum included arts and science and prelaw curriculum for transfer; also offered was a two-year normal school curriculum leading to a Nebraska life teaching certificate [38]. Reed and Sealock presented the plan to the University's Board of Regents and recommended that the MJC course of study be formally recognized; the regents gave their approval to the MJC plan in May 1926. That recognition set the pattern for University recognition of the other junior colleges [74, p. 389]. Throughout 1926 and 1927, the University remained neutral to the junior-college movement in Nebraska and in no way opposed it [42].

The informational and promotional campaign for a junior college in Norfolk resulted in the 1928 establishment of a second Nebraska junior college. Like McCook, the Norfolk board of education conducted an unofficial referendum to determine the sentiments of the townspeople prior to the founding of the college. Since no state law permitted junior colleges at the time, it was especially important to have a clear popular mandate for the institution, for if some taxpayers had wished to bring action against the board to prevent the establishment of a college, they would have won and forestalled the founding. However, the referendum vote in each city showed a large majority of voters in favor of establishment of a junior college [35, 46, 64]. Nevertheless, the supporters of the junior college movement in McCook and Norfolk felt the need for immediate legislative action to legitimatize their actions.

These municipal groups were joined by educational leaders in Scottsbluff. This community in the extreme western part of the state also took steps to formally organize a college, even though enabling legislation had not yet been enacted. Wayne W. Johnson, first dean of Scottsbluff Junior College described its origin:

> Scottsbluff Junior College had its earliest beginnings in 1926 as a one-year post graduate school supervised by the high school principal. In 1929 it was first organized as a two-year school of somewhat doubtful accreditation. After the Nebraska Junior College law of 1921 was passed, the Scottsbluff Junior College was reorganized to conform with the provisions of the law [64, pp. 116-17].

Collectively, the cities of McCook, Norfolk, and Scottsbluff worked actively to secure enabling legislation [64]. In January 1927, state Representative Carson Russell (McCook attorney), Representative Barbour (a Scottsbluff rancher), Representative Yensen (a Gering farmer), and Representative Hansen (a North Platte rancher) introduced a bill "to provide for the establishment and maintenance of junior colleges in school districts of the state having a population of more than 5,000" [53]. The bill was indefinitely postponed on a vote of 51 to 37. An examination of the roll call on this vote indicated that the representatives of McCook, Norfolk, and Scottsbluff were supported by representatives from other towns and counties with similar interests and ambitions: Alliance, Broken Bow, and Nelson, Pierce, Fairbury, and Wathill. Some representatives from Omaha also favored the bill; since 1908 that metropolis had supported its own municipal institution of higher education, the University of Omaha. From the private sector only Calvin French, president of Hastings College, voiced support for the junior college [41]. The majority of those voting to postpone the bill were representatives from communities and counties in which the state university, the four state normal schools, and the private colleges were located.

In 1929 another junior college bill was introduced into the legislature; it was supported by the state superintendent of public instruction, legislators, educators, and citizens from McCook, Scottsbluff, and Norfolk. By 1929 agricultural crop prices had declined and the agricultural economy was heading for the depression that was soon to grip the entire nation. Opponents of the junior college legislation claimed that the local tax base of many communities was insufficient to support the colleges, and that the creation of junior colleges would ultimately compete for the limited resources devoted to the state normal schools and the state university [64]. Speaking against the bill were the representatives from Lancaster county (Lincoln) and the presidents of three private colleges: Midland College in Fremont, Grand Island College, and Nebraska Central College in Central City [35, p. 17]. Competition for resources and students was clearly on the minds of legislators as they again considered enacting a junior college bill.

With the junior colleges at McCook and Norfolk established and the petition for recognition of yet a third college at Scottsbluff before them, the University of Nebraska Board of Regents sought to stem the junior-college movement. They instructed Extension Director Reed to notify the junior-college authorities that work would be recognized for one year only and that such relations would not be continued [75, pp. 11-12]. A 1927 junior-college bill was postponed indefinitely through the leadership of Representative Rolla Van Kirk, attorney from Lincoln (hometown of the University of Nebraska). The 1929 bill also was postponed indefinitely, this time by a narrow margin. The University's Board of Regents countermanded Dean Sealock and Director Reed's advocacy of the 1929 proposed junior-college bill (Senate File NO. 102) and instructed the president of the board and the chancellor of the University to lobby informally against the bill [75, p. 275]. The failure of the Nebraska legislature to pass a junior-college bill in 1927 and 1929 was a result of factionalization and interest-group lobbying among public and private higher education sectors.

At the time of the founding of the first Nebraska junior college, the town of McCook was a prosperous, growing regional trade center. The economic climate was oriented toward expansion and development. The population of the town was increasing rapidly. The construction and paving of major north-south and east-west transcontinental highways spurred the growth outlook for McCook. The business and civic leaders saw improved educational, cultural, and transportation opportunities as positive contributions to the town's development. There was a healthy spirit of competition between McCook, Norfolk and Scottsbluff as these communities actively promoted the junior college idea. This watchful rivalry between the medium-sized communities of Nebraska helped to build an interest group and power base for the passage of junior college enabling legislation in 1931.

The fact that colleges were contemplated and founded prior to the enabling legislation was due to local advocacy and to successful models of junior colleges in other states. In the 1920s Progressive era home rule laws and initiative, referendum, and recall provisions were clearly in place in most states. The referendum was used in the Nebraska communities to develop and marshall political support for the junior-college idea. Local newspaper publicity and the public campaigns of chambers of commerce used progressive political mechanisms to build and effect their political goals. Also supportive of college founding were the accreditation standards set for junior colleges by the North Central Association, the initial benign acceptance of McCook Junior College by the Nebraska Board of Regents, and the helpful support of the Dean of the Teachers College and the Director of the Extension Division. The tone of this rivalry between towns, the later resistance to junior colleges evidenced by legislators from counties with private or public colleges, and the change from acceptance to resistance by the Board of Regents illustrated the interest group politics of the 1920s.

Discussion, Analysis, and Conclusion

In 1893 Grover Cleveland was elected president of the United States for a second time. He abhorred corruption and was enthusiastic about local rule, governmental efficiency, and laissez-faire capitalism. The predisposition to local rule and economy in governmental agencies was favorable to the development of such institutions as municipal junior colleges. However, Cleveland also favored a gold standard and objected to the use of government to improve the commonweal. For example, in 1887 Congress appropriated $10,000 to aid drought sufferers in buying new grain seed. Cleveland vetoed the item, declaring that "though the people support the Government, the Government should not support the people " [27, p. 33]. Traditional liberalism of the day argued against the use of public funds or authority to intercede directly for the social betterment of citizens. At a time when the country's economy was growing and when secondary education was expanding, the amount of money available through debt instruments, such as school bonds, was limited by monetary policies. The early 1890s were marked by economic recession and, like the early 1980s, they were not a time favorable to school expansion and the development of junior colleges. In light of these factors, it should not be surprising to discover that a successful municipal junior college did not materialize prior to 1900. Thus, the erroneous case of Saginaw, Michigan, represented the general social and economic conditions of the early 1890s.

Populism was a revolt against the Cleveland form of liberalism. Populists urged direct democracy; they sponsored the initiative of giving voters the power to legislate over the heads of their representatives, and the referendum, providing voters with a veto over the actions of the legislature. Local initiatives served as the informal basis for establishing the support for junior colleges in Nebraska; the mechanisms of the populists and progressives were in place, and local business and civic leaders were versed in their use. Not so was the case of Springfield. Here, the conflict between school board, mayor and city council hampered support for the public school system. Although the educational reforms of the day supported the advent of Springfield Junior College, the development of the college was inhibited by the absence of the political reforms associated with the period. In Nebraska, the first junior colleges could be viewed as another form of direct democracy in the progressive tradition, taking the wishes of local constituents over the heads of the legislature to set by example the organization and interrelationship of public higher education.

During the 1890s, education was individualistic, Horatio Alger still provided a paragon; education need not be formal—one could still be self-educated. But more importantly, the key to education was seen to be in the will and discipline of the individual. Social institutions, such as schools and colleges could only provide the opportunity. Success was in the hands of the individual. For municipal junior colleges to grow, there needed to be a commensurate public sentiment that civic government had such a responsibility to its citizens.

From the nineteenth-century perspective, one did not create opportunity through municipal agencies. The liberalism of Cleveland relied upon the individual to create the opportunities, no matter how difficult the obstacles. The communities examined in this study evidenced educational reform commensurate with their era; together they reflected a continuum of movement away from the nineteenth-century philosophy of mental discipline toward developmental psychology. In Springfield, the junior high school was seen as a possible exit point into the work force, and secondary education was elective. The tradition of quality private higher education coupled with the drain of men from schools caused by World War I inhibited enrollment growth at the junior college. Nevertheless, the Springfield case evidenced the interrelationship of the mental measurement movement, the application of scientific management techniques to educational administration, and the application of progressive and developmental philosophies of education. In these ways, Springfield was reflective of Progressive-era innovations in educational reform.

In a similar manner, the arguments for the establishment of junior colleges in McCook, Norfolk, and Scottsbluff reflected the politics of the 1920s. Recall the premise that the state university was too far from the home of students in these three towns, thereby discouraging college-going. How far that perspective is from Cleveland liberalism! The notion that junior colleges were assets in the competition between communities for resources, commerce, and development mirrors May's [49] description of special interest group politics in the 1920s. Politically and educationally, the communities and colleges examined exemplified the social phenomena of their era.

The thesis of this article was that the first locally supported, public two-year colleges confronted and overcame certain obstacles. The first of these was that the support of various interest groups within the community had to be developed and marshalled. In Springfield, the political mechanisms for such a campaign were absent; in the case of McCook, educators, local politicians, and the newspaper waged such a campaign. The strength of McCook's campaign in igniting the junior college movement in Nebraska and the relative weakness of Springfield Junior College's public support and enrollments confirms the proposition that interest group support was associated with successful college development.

A second obstacle considered was that of enabling legislation to permit the establishment of public two-year colleges. In Springfield, legislation appeared not to be a consideration; Board of Education approval appeared to suffice. Here, the junior college was viewed as a curricular reform within the school system, not as a new, separate entity. Perhaps the pressure for state legalization was lessened by the fact that most Springfield graduates turned to private higher education for continuation of their studies. The need for a legal basis for junior college founding was far more apparent in Nebraska. Here, the effort was clearly to create a new institution—a separate and additional community asset. The campaign for a junior-college law began less than two years after the formation of the college in McCook. The attempts to pass a Nebraska junior-college law in 1927 and 1929 appeared to be stimulated by a growing reluctance at the University of Nebraska to accept the junior college work and political resistance by the public normal schools and private colleges to the further expansion of the movement in the state. The Springfield and McCook cases illustrated the legalization of the first public junior college was an obstacle only when the founding of such colleges was contested.

A third barrier mentioned at the outset was that relations needed to be established with neighboring four-year institutions to allow the students of the first public junior colleges to transfer credits. In both the Springfield and McCook cases, this was less an obstacle than originally proposed. Springfield's history of excellence in secondary education and the recognition of student work for advanced placement by several prestigious universities assisted in the initial recognition of SJC credits. McCook overcame the articulation obstacle at the University of Nebraska with the assistance of a sympathetic extension director and dean of the teachers college; then too, McCook benefitted from the establishment of accreditation guidelines for junior colleges by the North Central Association. Therefore, acceptance of credits by four-year colleges and universities was neither an obstacle nor a precondition to the establishment of a first junior college.

In each of the cases examined, the local school superintendent was an active, influential educational leader. Close working relationships were discovered between the public schools of Springfield and McCook and nearby universities. Springfield evidenced ties with Columbia, Harvard, Dartmouth, and Wesleyan. McCook had contacts with the University of Nebraska. In Springfield, some reference was made to the growth of junior colleges in California, but no reference was made to Alexis Lange or David Starr Jordan [12]. In McCook, successful junior colleges were profiled in Iowa and Michigan, and the state superintendents of public instruction in Colorado and California were consulted. However, in none of the cases reviewed was direct reference made to William Rainey Harper, Henry Tappan, David Starr Jordan, or any other "great man" identified in previous literature on the development of community colleges.

As time progressed, there were more positive examples of junior colleges to point to as models of college founding. Each of the cases examined here was chosen because they were the first public junior college in their respective states. Nevertheless, Springfield had local models of two-year colleges for two decades prior to the founding of SJC. McCook was able to consult with and point to junior colleges in adjacent states as examples. Modeling seemed to follow contacts within the educational community, within the accrediting association, and through the activities of the U.S. Bureau of Education. As noted, the cases examined failed to support the "great man" theory of junior-college formation; they may better be explained by a composite model of change that incorporates adoption/diffusion, political, and social interaction theories of educational change [45]. Further investigation of the institutional histories of junior colleges may determine the applicability of such change models and may illustrate further the relationship between college foundings and environmental factors. Such investigation of change over time through institutional case histories may provide a more substantive basis for the selection of planning alternatives within a strategic planning paradigm [52].

In this investigation, Saginaw Junior College, reported in previous community college literature, was found not to exist—or at least not to be founded within four years of the alleged date of establishment. In the course of investigation of Springfield Junior College, two earlier two-year colleges were identified that had not been reported in the community college literature. These instances suggest that there may be a paucity of reliable, substantiated information on early junior colleges and the circumstances under which they were established. Apparently, educators writing in this field may need to distinguish more clearly between primary and secondary sources of information and may need to use multiple sources of evidence to substantiate claims of educators to the existence, purpose, and direction of collegiate institutions.

This study examines historically distinct time periods. It was not the purpose of this investigation to provide a basis for generalization about development of all junior colleges, or even all first junior colleges. Rather, it was to explore the reciprocal relationship of college founding and factors in the external environment. In the cases examined, the economy, the civic and business support for public education, and the political environment all influenced the nature of college founding. College founding was related to other aspects of educational reform. It was affected by—and sometimes depended upon—the success of political, economic, and social reforms. The susceptibility of higher education to the social phenomena in the external environment was affirmed.

Wagoner [77] has chided supporters of the community- and junior-colleges concept as being less concerned with historical understanding and analysis, and more concerned with "the identification of antecedents that hold promise of conferring the legitimacy of age on the two-year college" (p. 4). He cautioned against exaggerating historical linkages with significant personages and against appropriating prevailing ideals and rhetoric to affirm the role of the junior community college, arguing that such practices "can obscure its real beginnings and deflect attention from a critical appraisal of its pervading ideology, changing missions, and continuing search for identity and integrity." Wagoner's point was confirmed in this investigation. Linkages with the "great men" of community college education have been overemphasized. In the quest for institutional integrity, historical treatments of junior-college development have devoted excessive attention to its relation to other forms of higher education. Indeed, Cohen and Brawer have suggested that the community-college quest for identity was due to its uncertain place within higher education [17]. The study presented in this article found the cases examined to be part of an impulse for educational reform that was not confined solely to higher education. College founding occurred in an environment sympathetic to developmental psychology, mental measurement, the kindergarten and the junior high school, manual training, and applications of scientific management to public institutions. The cases also illustrate the integral relationship between a college and the sectors of its constituent community. Such examination of social behavior within an historical context can provide an important basis for understanding educational change and reform.

References

1. Andrews, A. "The Development of Junior Colleges in Michigan." *Junior College Journal* 2 (June 1932): 513–17.

2. "Ask for Evening Classes," *Springfield Daily Republican*, 19 January 1917, p. 4.

3. "At School, 15,764 Children," *Springfield Daily Republican*, 3 October 1916, p. 1, 9.

4. "Beatrice Wants College," *McCook Daily Gazette*, 17 November 1925, p. 1.

5. Berkhofer, R. J., Jr. *A Behavioral Approach to Historical Analysis*. New York: Free Press, 1969.

6. "Board of Education Decides to Start Junior College," *McCook Daily Gazette,* 9 December 1925, p. 1.

7. Brooks, E. "The Junior College." Master's thesis, Clark University, 1917.

8. Brubacher, J. S., and W. Rudy. *Higher Education in Transition: A History of American Colleges and Universities, 1636–1976.* 3rd ed. New York: Harper and Row, 1976.

9. Brush, H. R. "The Junior Colleges and the Universities." *School and Society* 4 (2 September 1916): 357–65.

10. "Bureau Chief Approves Idea," *McCook Daily Gazette,* 23 November 1925, p. 3.

11. "California has Junior Colleges," *McCook Daily Gazette,* 21 November 1925, p. 1.

12. "California's Junior Colleges," *Springfield Daily Republican,* 19 July 1917, p. 8.

13. Campbell, D. S. "Directory of the Junior College, 1931." *Junior College Journal* 1 (December 1930): 223–34.

14. "Central High Seniors," *Springfield Daily Republican,* 14 June 1916, p. 3.

15. "Change in Referendum over City Charter," *Springfield Daily Republican,* 11 May 1916, p. 1, 9.

16. "A City Refaced—Some Signs of Springfield's Transition from a Good-sized Town into Metropolis," *Springfield Daily Republican,* 4 June 1916, 2nd sect., p. 1.

17. Cohen, A. M., and F. B. Brawer. *The American Community College.* San Francisco: Jossey-Bass. 1982.

18. "Colleges in a Pool," *Saginaw Evening News,* 10 May 1895, p. 6.

19. "Commerce Grows," *Springfield Daily Republican,* 5 May 1916, p. 1.

20. Deegan, W. L., D. Tillery, and Associates. *Renewing the American Community College.* San Francisco: Jossey-Bass, 1985.

21. Dunbar, W. F. *The Michigan Record in Higher Education.* Detroit: Wayne State University Press, 1963.

22. Dutcher, G. M. *An Historical and Critical Survey of the Curriculum of Wesleyan University and Related Subjects,* Middletown, Conn.: Wesleyan University, 1948.

23. Eells, W. C. *The Junior College.* Boston: Houghton Mifflin, 1931.

24. "English Teachers Coming," *Springfield Daily Republican,* 13 December 1916, p. 6.

25. "Evening High School Plans," *Springfield Daily Republican,* 2 October 1916, p. 5.

26. Gleazer, E. J. *This is the Community College.* New York: Houghton Mifflin, 1968.

27. Goldman, E. F. *Rendezvous with Destiny: A History of Modern American Reform.* Rev. ed. New York: Random House, Vintage Books, 1956.

28. Goodwin, G. L. "The Historical Development of Community Junior College Ideology: An Analysis and Interpretation of the Writings of Selected Community-Junior College National Leaders from 1890–1970." Ph. D. dissertation. University of Illinois, 1971.

29. Gottschalk, L. *Understanding History: A Primer of Historical Method.* New York: Knopf, 1950.

30. Gray, A. A. "The Junior College in California," *School Review* 23 (September 1915): 465–73.

31. Hardin, T. L. "Joliet: Birth of a College." *Community College Frontiers* 4 (Spring 1976): 21–23.

32. Hines, H. C. "The Status of the Public Junior College in the United States." *The Educator-Journal,* 18 (December 1917): 180–86.

33. Hinsdale, B. A. *History of the University of Michigan.* Ann Arbor, Mich.: University of Michigan Press, 1906.

34. Hofstadter, R. *The Age of Reform: From Bryant to F.D.R.* New York: Random House, Vintage Books, 1955.

35. Hughes, K. H. "History of the Public Junior Colleges of Nebraska." Master's thesis, University of Nebraska, 1942.

36. Jencks, C. , and D. Riesman. *The Academic Revolution*. New York: Doubleday, 1968.

37. "Junior College Course," *Springfield Daily Republican*, 1 May 1917, p. 3.

38. "Junior College Curriculum is Adopted by Board of Education," *McCook Daily Gazette*, 21 December 1925, p. 1.

39. "The Junior College in Springfield," *Springfield Daily Republican*, 28 April 1917, p. 8.

40. "Junior College is Boomed over State," *McCook Daily Gazette*, 27 November 1925, p. 1.

41. "Junior College is Natural Development," *McCook Daily Gazette*, 8 December 1925, p. 1.

42. "The Junior College Movement: Land Grant College Heads in Conference," *American Educational Digest* 47 (December 1927): 167, 172–73.

43. Keller, G. *Academic Strategy: The Management Revolution in American Higher Education*. Baltimore, Md.: Johns Hopkins University Press, 1983.

44. Koos, L.V. *The Junior-College Movement*. New York: Ginn and Company, 1925.

45. Lindquist, J. *Strategies for Change*. Berkeley: Pacific Sounding Press, 1978.

46. Lindsay, C. "Junior College Law in Nebraska," *Junior College Journal* 2 (October 1931): 11–15.

47. "Looking Ahead," *McCook Daily Gazette*, 9 December 1925, p. 2.

48. "A Longer Course at Y.M.C.A. College," *Springfield Daily Republican*, 10 September 1916, p. 5.

49. May, H. F. "Shifting Perspectives on the 1920s," *Mississippi Valley Historical Review* 43 (1956): 405–27.

50. Medsker, L. L. *The Junior College: Progress and Prospect*. New York: McGraw-Hill, 1960.

51. "Medical College," *Saginaw Evening News*, 13 June 1896, p. 1.

52. Morrison, J. L., W. L. Renfro, and W. I. Boucher. *Futures Research and the Strategic Planning Process: Implications for Higher Education*. Washington, D.C.: Association for the Study of Higher Education. ASHE-ERIC Higher Education Research Report No. 9, 1984.

53. Nebraska. Legislature, House of Representatives. *House Journal*, H. R. 351, 27 January 1927, p. 314.

54. "One Student in Five to College," *McCook Daily Gazette*, 6 August 1925, p. 1.

55. Price, C. F. *Wesleyan's First Century, with an Account of the Centennial Celebration*. Middletown, Conn.: Wesleyan University, 1932.

56. "Propose M'Cook Junior College," *McCook Daily Gazette*, 4 November 1925, p. 1.

57. Ratcliff, J. L. "Social and Political Dimensions of the Growth of Community and Junior Colleges: An Historiography Essay." Paper presented at the meeting of the American Educational Research Association, New Orleans, La., 25 April 1984.

58. ____ . "The Incomplete Revolution." Paper presented at fall convocation. Central Community Colleges, Grand Island, Neb., 1986.

59. ____ . Should We Forget William Rainey Harper? *Community College Review* 13 (Spring 1986): 12–19.

60. "Red Letter Event," *Saginaw Evening News*, 6 February 1895, p. 4.

61. Reid, H. D. "Phenomena Affecting the Community Junior College in the United States, 1960–1975. "Ph.D. dissertation, Wayne State University, 1978.

62. Riekse, R. J. "Analysis of Selected Significant Historical Factors in the History of the Pioneer Junior College in Michigan: Grand Rapids Junior College, 1914–1962." Ed. D. dissertation, Michigan State University, 1964.

63. Salwak, S. F. "Some Factors Significant in the Establishment of Junior Colleges in the United States (1940–1951): With Special Reference to Massachusetts." Ed. D. dissertation, Pennsylvania State University, 1953.

64. Saylor, G. "Development of the Public Junior College Movement in Nebraska," in G. Saylor et al., *Junior College Studies: Legislation, Finance, and Development of Public Junior Colleges, Contributions to Education*. No. 26. Lincoln: Extension Division, University of Nebraska, 1949.

65. "Schools Honored for High Grade Work," *Springfield Daily Republican*, 23 November 1916, p. 6.

66. Shafer, R. J. (ed.). *A Guide to Historical Method*. Rev. ed. Homewood, Ill.: Dorsey Press, 1974.

67. Spindt, H. A. "Beginnings of the Junior College in California, 1907–1921." *College and University* 33 (Fall 1957): 22–28.

68. "Springfield's Junior High School," *Springfield Daily Republican*, 2nd sect., 5 November 1916, p. 1.

69. Strayer, G. D., chairman. *Report of the Committee of the National Council of Education on Standards and Tests for Measuring the Efficiency of Schools or Systems of Schools*. Washington, D. C.: U.S. Bureau of Education, Bulletin, 1913, No. 13.

70. "Success Assured," *Saginaw Evening News*, 8 June 1895, p. 7.

71. Thornton, J.W., Jr. *The Community Junior College*. 3rd ed. New York: John Wiley, 1972.

72. "Town Meeting," *McCook Daily Gazette*, 23 November 1925, p. 1.

73. "U. of M., Rah, Rah, Rah!," *Saginaw Evening News*, 3 October 1984, p. 6.

74. University of Nebraska. *Board of Regents Record*, 9 (July 1, 1925–March 30, 1926).

75. University of Nebraska. *Board of Regents Record*, (September 30, 1926–June 10, 1929).

76. Vaughan, G. B. *The Community College in America: A Pocket History*. Washington, D.C.: American Association of Community and Junior Colleges, 1982.

77. Wagoner, J. L. , Jr. "The Search for Mission and Integrity: A Retrospective View," in *Maintaining Institutional Integrity: New Directions for Community Colleges*. No. 52. ed. by D. E. Puyear & G. B. Vaughan, pp. 3–15. San Francisco: Jossey-Bass, 1985.

78. "War Cuts Enrollment," *Springfield Daily Republican*, 18 September 1917, p. 4.

79. "Where They Still Believe in 'Americanization'," *Springfield Daily Republican*, 3rd. sect., 21 May 1916, p. 1, 9, lithogravures.

80. Whitney, A. S. "Compare the Figures as to the Schools of Saginaw and Detroit," *Saginaw Evening News*, 15 May 1896, p. 6.

Beyond the Open
Door, The Open College

EDMUND J. GLEAZER, JR.

In the months since "After the Boom" first appeared (*Journal*, December/January 1974) I've been listening to and soliciting attitudes around the field as to where we we're going—not just in reference to community services but to the very essence of community colleges.

If the concept of community services is to broaden from a department of the college or a sector of college activities to represent the total stance of the college, and if the concept of service is to yield to the notion of community *use* of the college as an educational resource for individual and community development, let me propose a framework of a new system and suggest some ways to get us from where we are not to being truly community-based and performance-oriented.

While there are a variety of factors which both stimulate and support the evolution of the community college "beyond the boom"—economics, values toward both community and education, public accountability, demography and touches of enlightened leadership—it would be a mistake to assume that such a major transition will take place without a ripple. As more than 1,000 institutions (1,400 or more by 1980), in settings as different as North Platte and Chicago, become more clearly community-based, more oriented to performance than credentials, they will encounter several strategic questions in their own development.

1. What are the markets within this community? How do we translate community perceptions into our objectives?

2. Given what we've got to work with, what are the program possibilities *outside* the confines of traditional academic practice; what are the operational implications of these?

3. Having thrown away the packaging from "Higher Education," what are the criteria for success? How do we measure output and summarize it for fiscal, legal, and managerial purposes?

4. How suited or adaptable are the current resources—specifically staff and physical plant?

5. If we're to become something different, how accommodating is the current public policy climate in which we operate?

6. What resources and vehicles are available to provide technical assistance in advancing both the concept and effective practice of postsecondary education which is truly community-based and performance-oriented?

The program proposed here is premised on the belief that the suggestion of a third major period of evolution is not only valid but healthy and exciting. A parallel belief is that the transition described above calls for a comprehensive response by the field through the national association—particularly in the light of AACJC's newly articulated mission: "To provide national leadership of community-based, performance-oriented postsecondary education."

My purpose is to propose the shape of such a response and in doing so to enlarge upon some factors which make it timely and appropriate.

What Must Be Done?

Over the last several years there has been very vocal and widespread interest in "staff development." In spite of the somewhat negative implications carried by the label, its importance to people in the field has been reflected time and again at conferences and in surveys like Project Focus. In fact, this issue among all others bubbled up so strongly at AACJC's first national assembly that "New Staff for New Students" was selected as the topic for the second one. The statement from that forum cuts across pre-service and in-service development, stressing the importance of competent standards as a basis for selection and planning, the need for expanding the funds available for staff development, and the need for AACJC to play a pivotal role as a clearinghouse, a lobbyist, and a provider of technical assistance. The tone throughout suggested that the initiative must be taken by the field itself.

In the wake of such an expression of interest it is tempting to accept the mandate and to act, precipitously and single-mindedly, on the issue. To do so, though, would miss the mark on two important counts: first, the relationship between "staff development" and "institutional development," and second, the fact that the "beyond the boom" future will in no way be an easy extension of the past.

The overall effectiveness of a college depends upon many things. Competent staff and adequate funding are certainly critical, but they are insufficient for enduring effectiveness. Two other elements which are extremely powerful are (1) the organizational structure—allocation of authority and responsibility, formal framework, communication processes, work roles; and (2) the climate that develops as people work together—goals, constraints, group relationships, and leaderships. Nothing of lasting value will come from an effort to develop staff compentence unless it is accompanied by an equally vigorous effort to ensure that organizational structure and climate keep pace with individual development.

In a sense institutional development is really both a context for staff development and a mission-related strategy for carrying it out. At its best, it includes not only training and education, but operations research, planning and goal setting, and team building around situations that are both real and consistent with what's on the horizon.

Meeting the Future on Five Fronts

The words "mission related" are key. Sensing that a new era is at hand, the real challenge for AACJC is to give specific assistance to member institutions as they seek to establish new missions and mobilize resources behind them. This assistance ought to take the form of five highly interrelated programs to help answer the questions posed above.

First: Advancement of the practice and theory of community-based, performance-oriented postsecondary education through a pattern of projects, e.g., the 1974 Assembly and Project of '76 (to be reviewed later).

Second: Research on the measurement of output and the use of such measurements in planning, budgeting, counseling, and evaluation.

Third: Analysis of the legal and policy climate in which "community colleges" function.

Fourth: Development of the "new staff for new students."

Fifth: Establishment of a field-based research and development network to provide vital national linkages and pursue the programs described above in given localities.

The burden for the effectiveness of such an ambitious effort rests heavily with the kind of coordination possible through the last of these. In a sense, it represents the hub of the total program; each in turn, though, merits closer inspection.

Promoting the Concept

"What does the name community college stand for?" I asked in "After the Boom." "No issue presses more heavily upon people in the field than this one. How we define our business is . . . basic to almost everything else."

One very useful point of departure was offered by Senator Harrison Williams of New Jersey when he introduced the Comprehensive Community College Act of 1969. He said that "these institutions have demonstrated their *potential* (emphasis added) to respond to society's changing needs in ways that bring improvement to the community." Alan Pifer, president of Carnegie Corporation, speaking at the 1974 AACJC Convention, sounded a similar note and proposed that objectives often perceived as secondary be given new priority:

"Other institutions will have a part to play, of course, but I see the community college as the essential leadership agency. Indeed, I'm going to make the outrageous suggestion that community colleges should start thinking about themselves from now on only secondarily as a sector of higher education and regard as their primary role community leadership. . . . Not least, they can become the hub of a network of institutions and community agencies—the high schools, industry, the church, voluntary agencies, youth groups, even the prison system and the courts—utilizing their educational resources and, in turn, becoming a resource for them."

The very phrase "community-based, performance-oriented, postsecondary education" is market oriented. It posits the existence of an over-16 population which is ready and able to "buy in" to self development. We are beginning to recognize that the market is considerably larger than what tradition has led us to expect. Within current confines alone, we know that if every "housewife" took one "course" (anachronistic terms, both of them) every other year, the impact would be an instant tripling of 1972 enrollments. Outside those confines it is mind boggling to think of the market represented by the "learning force" at large.

Item: The post-war babies now 26 years old will be the market for postsecondary education through the year 2000.

Item: In only 26 years, half of the population will be 50 years of age or older.

Item: A recent survey by the Ontario Institute for Studies in Education indicated that most adults spend about 700 hours a year at anywhere from one to half-a-dozen "learning projects" *outside* higher education.

Item: Approximately 11.2 million adults (ages 18 through 60), exclusive of full-time students, are now engaged in learning experiences sponsored by non-educational institutions such as labor unions, private industry, museums, professional and trade associations, and governmental agencies. That number is larger than all students now enrolled in colleges and universities.

Zero education growth? Hardly. But the community college is by no means without competition. Many others recognize training and education as one of the growth industries in the decade ahead. Proprietary schools alone have grown from a scant 500 correspondence schools in 1960 to an impressive 12,000 today. The American Society for Training and Development reports that 475 of its members have budgets of $500,000 and over. There are dozens of organizations breaking into the conference and seminar business.

For better or worse, most of those who see a share of this market are prevented by their traditions from playing a thoroughly opportunistic role. The community colleges are no exception. Stated in the extreme, the kind of community education that excited Senator Williams is still a "cottage industry" barred from rapid development by both old and new categories—adult education, extension, community services, continuing education, nontraditional studies, lifelong learning, and even higher education.

To put our own house in order and be prepared to compete effectively, we must move swiftly to chart the dimensions of community education. Granted, every community is unique; dimensions will always differ. We are now, though, in a kind of prescience period where there is no context for either determining the differences or making useful generalizations about dealing with them. In response, the next few years need to be marked by a concerted and unified effort to chart what's possible, extend what's available, and develop a supportive framework for it all. Some of the immediate steps implied are:

Identify and collect current practices. There is obviously a great deal happening right now, some of it on a trial-and-error basis. AACJC needs to bring together the practices which place more emphasis on "community" than "college."

Determine patterns and trends. "We see through our categories." The promising activities of today must be subject to close scrutiny to determine principles and general guidelines. We need to know what seems to work, and under what conditions.

Define operational problems. Using traditional college resources in nontraditional ways places a new set of demands on the institution. We need to know what they are so as to factor appropriate ways of responding into both planning and training.

Develop specific skills and techniques. Given a trend to community-based postsecondary education, there are a variety of areas where the state of the art needs to be advanced: defining the community, analyzing its interests, getting citizen participation, promoting a new program, or playing the role of the "broker" in drawing on community resources. While some of these can be adapted from current practice, others need to be developed *de noveau*.

Stimulate the expansion of community education. Using the baseline data generated initially, we need to systematically extend community education. "Systematically" here implies the conscious stimulation of markets (senior citizens) and programs (allied health) through the judicious use of seed money. Stimulation should also be provided via the 1974 Assembly topic: Community-based education.

Objective I: By the close of the bicentennial year we should have a coherent and very visible theory regarding the role of the community college in community development.

Extending Output Measures

Writing in *The Center Magazine* in January 1973, Robert M. Hutchins warned that "a large, conspicuous, elaborate system on which the hopes of so many are pinned cannot hope to escape attack in a period of distress unless it can show that it has intelligible purposes and is achieving them." Though he was referring to the entire field of education, his remarks are particularly appropriate for community colleges. Fred Hechinger, writing in the *New York Times* a few days ago, criticized American higher education for turning away from intellectual issues to concentrate on housekeeping and bookeeping. Recent television documentaries about higher education, he noted, have handled the subject as if it concerned the rescue of backrupt railroads. Stating that "educational leadership—demoralized by present fiscal problems and terrified by a future of declining enrollments—lacks the spirit and the voice to draw public attention to questions of substance," Hechinger calls for a new sense of educational purpose as vital to the nation's progress.

As we specify purposes beyond the traditional confines of "higher education" the necessity of being able to work toward objectives becomes more evident. Without the benefit of some measurement of results other than the production of degrees or the accumulation of credits we are highly limited in taking full advantage of our present momentum. Let us briefly consider why.

Objectives serve a two-fold purpose: Before the fact they provide the basis for resource allocation; after the fact they provide the basis for evaluation. If the purpose of evaluation is to be anything but punitive (or cumbersome, as its innocuous best), it must be based on the relative success in achieving objectives that do not reduce all performance to an hour of academic credit. This applies whether the evaluation is of students, staff, programs, management, or whole institutions. Unless we can in some way measure performance we have no way of answering the question "who benefits; who pays?"

There has been a great deal of interest recently, and some excellent groundwork, in utilizing cost benefit analysis in postsecondary education. In spite of the excellent work underway in organizations such as WICHE, ETS, and the Illinois Community College Board, though, the passion for analyzing costs far outstrips the mileage gained in measuring output. While this situation endures the entire resource allocation picture in our field will remain static. Funding formulas, staffing patterns, pricing policy, curriculum planning, and the establishment of institutional priorities are all limited by credit-as-output logic. The corollary, of course, is that new ways of defining results will either come from the evolving experience of the field or will be created, out of justified necessity, by the legislative analysts.

The attempt to measure outcomes in education has traditionally met with a great deal of resistance. It always raises the spectre of reducing the drama of human development to an impersonal calculus, or making irrelevant comparisons among personnel, programs, or institutions. While these misgivings are not without basis, they are more extreme than they need to be. For one thing, only the most obtuse technocrat is unaware of the limits of quantification. In matters of planning, though, it can be one of the educator's best devices when order of magnitude is at issue. And in our field, magnitude is at issue. What is more calculating than what Ivan Illich calls "the hidden curriculum of schooling" which dictates that "each citizen must accumulate a minimum quantum of school years to obtain his civil rights"? By the same token, what is more liberating than the 1971 ruling by Chief Justice Warren Burger (Griggs v. Duke Power Company) that any school degree required or test given to prospective employees must measure "The Man for the Job," not "The Man in the Abstract"? Herein lies the essential rationale for becoming more "performance based."

If I and others are right in our predictions, the people in our institutions will become more vocal in their conviction that they can make a manifest difference in the lives of individuals and the communities in which they live. Rather than being defensive in the face of pressures for accountability, our field and the Association should take the offense in discovering and making use of the various ways in which that difference can be recognized. Some of the immediate steps which seem necessary are:

Get a picture of the state-of-the art and work-in-progress by drawing together current research and practice. AACJC needs to maintain not only cognizance but a contributor's and coordinator's relationship with advances in the measurement of output. We need to:

Systematically try it by placing a "measurement-of-outcomes" component on all experimental projects.

Stimulate research on the measurement of output in the affective domain and other areas which do not lend themselves to easy quantification.

Develop an expanding data bank on comparative costs, benefits, operating ratios, and the like for use in institutional planning and training.

Develop a set of planning parameters for community colleges moving toward a greater orientation community.

Develop specific skills and techniques for the effective use of outcome measures: developing objectives that have operational utility, translating student interests into specific objectives, summarizing and analyzing specific results for managerial purposes.

Objective II: Before the beginning of 1979 we should have broken the credentials monopoly by opening up not only alternative routes to credentials, but the matter of alternative credentials themselves.

Reconsidering Public Policy

In commissioning the second Newman Report, Elliot Richardson asked: "How can national policy and federal programs be altered to take into account the problems pointed to in the first Newman Report?" Those who have read Newman's "Agenda for Reform" are undoubtedly impressed with how he rose to the occasion and are encouraged by how supportive it is of emerging values in the community college field. At the same time, though, those who believe that community colleges are significantly different from the rest of higher education sense the need for a comprehensive treatment of community colleges in particular from the standpoint of public policy. At the federal level the deadline for such a treatment occurs in less than two years when current legislation expires.

Beyond that, though, community college operations are largely conditioned by accrediting procedures and enabling legislation from the state capitols. The fact is that on the whole the entire array of laws and policies governing community colleges view them as followers in higher education rather than "leaders in community development." As this latter role becomes more essence than adjunct, we must ask ourselves in detail how well the policy climate accommodates our intentions. In no other way will we be able to take an active role in its inevitable change.

In a 1970 paper on "The Learning Force," Stan Moses of the Educational Policy Research Center at Syracuse rejected the notion that American education was carried out in a three-layer hierarchy running from primary school through graduate school. This, he said, represented the "core," but overlooked a "periphery" in which over 60 million adults pursued learning activities very important to their lives. His purpose was to challenge the monopoly which the educational establishment has over public policy and public resources.

Continuing education ranked low in the goals inventory conducted as part of the Project Focus. With many such programs having to "pay their own way," one has to wonder if the policy climate has dictated the low priority given to continuing education. At the present, lifelong learning cannot compete with full-time undergraduate education on its own terms.

Present policy has other problematic dimensions. Some of the more effective programs in community colleges are organized around occupations in which completion is *not* a requirement for job entry. As a result, the top 10% in auto mechanics (for example) show up on the attrition figures at mid-program. Some state laws discriminate against vocational students or "defined adults," or make it difficult at best for the college to open its doors in the evening. Such practices present their own "access barriers." For example:

Mississippi: No reimbursement for students before eight o'clock in the morning and after four in the afternoon. No reimbursement for other than full-time students.

Texas: No reimbursement after 12th class day.

Kansas: According to a president, "Legislators tend to think of the community college as a junior college." Accordingly: (a) there is no financial assistance for community service activities—they must be self-sustaining; (b) a college is required to limit its endeavors to college transfer, and state aid is limited to 64 semester hours except for nursing and engineering; (c) there are continued attempts to place colleges under the control of board of regents—the same board that has responsibility for state colleges and universities.

As our institutions do, in fact, become more sensitive to their total communities and more oriented to performance, the challenge is to simultaneously develop forms of public support and accountability based on the image of differentiated institutions reaching out to serve increasingly diverse clientele. Some of the immediate steps implied are:

Commission an interpretive analysis of public policy and the community college, touching on the linkages from enabling legislation through institutional governance to management and operations in the college.

Monitor all experimental projects, specifically in community education, for the impacts of law and policy on both planning and implementation.

Compare the impact of varying state and regional policies through the placement of similar projects in different policy climates—ultimately through a field-based network.

Develop specific skills and techniques for dealing with the legal and policy picture. These should equip cadres of field practitioners to deal with legislative analysts on an equal footing.

Objective III: By the time current legislation expires we should be prepared to help forge a public policy which accommodates our momentum "beyond the boom."

Developing All the College Staff

Let us first establish the paramount importance of staff development. To begin with there is the obvious economic fact that staff accounts for nearly 75% of all the resources in the field. Beyond that, staff contributes the only resource capable of transformation. "Money and materials are depleted, equipment is subject to the laws of mechanics. It can perform well or badly but never more efficiently than it was originally designed to do. Humans alone can grow and develop. Therefore it is essential that this resource be used as fully and as effectively as possible."

Overshadowing all other observations, though, is the fact that it is ultimately the staff, and specifically the faculty, who do the work of the college. Bearing in mind the relationship cited earlier between staff development and institutional development, then, what would be some of the characteristics of an effective development thrust?

It should be mission-related. There are several implications here. Development for the sake of development will never be effective or well supported. Aside from the fact such efforts translate poorly into action and results, there is good reason to believe that expanded capabilities without a definitive outlet increase frustration and job turnover. Terry O'Banion makes reference to an interesting survey of new faculty on the type of information most desired as part of their service training. As a point of departure, most wanted such things as goals of the college, objectives of their departments, and objectives of the courses for which they were responsible. They were asking, in other words, "staff development for what?" One has to wonder who needs development in such circumstances. The irony is that such faculty groups are frequently given workshops on writing objectives and setting goals.

The absence of an orientation to purpose also gives staff development the trial-and-error, patchwork look. Without a sense of intended impact there is a tendency to "buy-in" to fads and ride favorite hobby horses without any way of recognizing disappointment or inconsistency. This is also the case in pre-sevice development. This stage of preparation is so critical that it needs to be strongly guided by the purposes of both the individual and the "buyer"—the community college field. Too often, pre-service preparation has been more obviously guided by the purpose of the preparing institution.

In all fairness, though, the field's best defense is to answer some questions with compelling clarity. "What is the mission of the community college?" "Who is it to serve?" "Is it to be defined in terms of the conventional academic model or something different?"

Ultimately, it should be team-oriented. Considerable research has shown that the basic work group is the strongest influence upon job satisfaction, performance, absenteeism, and turnover. Yet we have historically "developed" people individually and in stratifications and have created adversaries by default. Doing the job in an institutional setting has substantial advantages, but requires grass roots action and administrative support. The development of individual skills or abilities at one level may do little to increase the chances of getting something done.

This principle doesn't preclude the use of experiences of an educational nature which stratify the field ("presidents only"). One of the chief reasons why groups fail to function well together is that they have inadequate problem-solving procedures. Individual development can go a long way toward providing a broadened conceptual framework of enhancing skills. The point is simply that these efforts should be viewed as a means to developing the effectiveness of the team.

There are also pre-service implications here. We usually develop administrators and faculty along separate tracks, allowing them to become "team" over crises and negotiation tables. We must expand the effort to build pre-institutional teams during the didactic stages of their preparation.

It should be widely available. This field boasts nearly 1,200 institutions, 9,000 trustees, 16,000 "managers" and over 200,000 faculty. O'Banion reports that two years ago only 4% of the existing staff members benefited from the in-service portion of EPDA. While the impact of staff development needs to be far more widespread, it would have taken an increase of more than $17,000,000 to expand the impact to just 25% of those on the job. While there is no substitute for the double-occupancy-log, we've got to substitute communication for transportation where possible, take advantage of economies of scale available by regionalizing, and develop approaches to peer and self instruction.

It should be able to expand. Closely related to the need for a widely available approach to staff development is the recognition that our field will grow over the next decade. For example, the number of presidents, deans, vice presidents, and department chairmen will double by 1980. If faculty turnover continues at the rate of 16% per year, the *need* for development should expand at more than twice the *rate* of natural growth in the field. While it might be reasonable to expect some third party assistance, the field needs to be building a means for financing and delivering on the demands imposed by its own growth. Staff development is a cost of doing business—a line item in the budget.

Objective IV: By the close of the decade we should have a delivery vehicle for meeting the staff/ institutional development demands in our field which is capable of operating without third party financing.

Research and Development

There will obviously be need for many partners in the enterprise: the universities, private research organizations, public and government authorities, and the multitude of independent consultants who work on various aspects of the community colleges' developmental needs. Ownership, though, both actual and conceptual, should remain in the hands of the community college field itself. In anticipation of our probable development "beyond the boom" we need to firmly establish the capacity to generate, integrate, and disseminate new insights and practices.

Many of the immediate needs can no doubt be filled by the university community. However, O'Banion reported the current graduate education builds in biases that run contrary to the community junior college. It is critical to ask how reasonable and appropriate it is to expect the graduate schools to radically change their ways to meet the exigencies of our field. On the other hand, we may consider the appropriate staff development responsibilities of the community colleges with specified technical assistance from universities and other such resources.

The related point to bear in mind is that we need a mechanism—not a model, not a sample community college to export to all parts of this land. Based on the diversity in our "market" the field needs many vehicles for development, an identified network of available resources and the capacity to pick up the broad issues on the horizon.

Objective V: We should move to designate as many as half-a-dozen developmental centers around the country, co-located with existing community colleges and similar in concept to the medical school.

They would serve as a locus for all activities described above, providing services to community colleges in their region. Collectively they would constitute a mechanism for "on-line" communication between the field and AACJC. The form of the charter can perhaps best be understood by augmenting a description from the Association of American Medical Colleges:

They provide the setting for the training of a broad range of educational occupations. They are the site for the development and demonstration of new programs and modes of instruction, and exert a strong qualitative effect upon community education in their programs. They conduct research on both the measurement of educational impact and the policy climates in which they function. They continue, as in the past, to be major providers of community education in their own right.

Consider the possibilities for internships or residencies in such settings. Consider the experimental possibilities from bases of operation as diverse as Appalachia and metropolitan Washington. A typical center might be involved, directly or through sub-contract, in the following: pre-administrative internships and residencies in which incumbents would be required to provide management training and consulting services on a performance basis, individual study programs, team development processes, field conference and workshop services, diagnostic services and institutional research, experimental community development programs, public policy research, research on measuring output, and production of publications.

The implementation problems, not only for such a network but for the entire program are considerable indeed. We are in fact, though, passing through another major era in development with impressive opportunities if we seize them.

The Assembly

The Assembly topic for 1974 will be community-based, performance-oriented education. So far, some hearings have been held trying to elucidate the topic and identify some of the critical questions which need to be addressed. What we've found is that we're not really well prepared to approach the topic. We have no operationally useful definition of community education, no good examples, little baseline data, too much "credit" orientation, and a fear of performance criteria.

What is the proper strategy? What *other* community-baed organizations can be usefully involved in our Assembly? Perhaps most importantly, what outcomes should we look for from such an Assembly and how can we get them?

The Bicentennial

Earlier, I alluded briefly to Project 76. Basically, this would be a matter of the 1,000 community colleges in the country getting their communities engaged in "town meetings" on the future of America and their communities.

I see this as being critically important for two reasons:

1. It gives us an opportunity to demonstrate our potential for making an impact on the lives of people and the communities in which they live.

2. It gives us a vehicle for bumping our institutions more squarely into the center of their communities.

As "leaders in community development," can we help people determine what are the "critical choices for Americans," or critical choices in our area? Can we provide initiatives for people to sit down together and identify issues, needs, goals, strategies for raising the quality level of community life? What kind of community do we want?

Presuming we will have such a project, how can we take advantage of it "for marketing analysis?" How can we use the project as a basis for planning and promoting the overall direction of community colleges? Can we train "town hearing" people for the communities in which there is no community college?

These are immediate opportunities. I commend them to you.

From *Forum and Focus for the Junior College Movement*

MICHAEL BRICK

The Junior College Idea

There was an air of excitement in Louisville, Kentucky in March, 1960 as delegates gathered for the annual meeting of the American Association of Junior Colleges. The excitement was engendered by the fact that this was the fortieth-anniversary convention of an Association which many had thought would not last out its first year. Also, many of the delegates knew that a momentous announcement was going to be made concerning a financial commitment by the W. K. Kellogg Foundation to the AAJC.

The junior college movement had come a long way from the days of the late nineteenth and early twentieth centuries when the junior colleges had little status generally, and even less recognition from other educational institutions. By 1960 the junior college movement was one of the fastest growing and most talked about developments in the field of higher education. The Association representing these junior colleges was taking its place as a powerful spokesman dedicated to the promotion of the junior college idea. How and why did all this growth take place?

One of the distinguishing features of American higher education is its diversity. A variety of forms of educational institutions has unfolded since the founding of Harvard in 1636: liberal arts college, technical institute, state university, land-grant college, professional school, normal school, teachers college, state college, municipal college, and, most recently, the junior college. Each arose as a response to the failure of existing institutions to meet the demands for a new or additional type of educational experience.

The development of the junior college as a response to the educational demands of society was in the same vein as the development of state universities and land-grant colleges which arose to meet changing educational demands. The difficulties overcome and the successes achieved by educational institutions in the nineteenth century paved the way for the acceptance of the junior college idea by the public and by local and state legislatures.

American higher education today represents the end product of interaction between the Western European university heritage and the native American environment. From these processes of transplantation and continuous adaptation have emerged the aspects of academic culture which we have come to recognize as characteristically American.

Socio-Economic Forces and the Development of the Junior College Idea

Four basic social and economic forces led to the junior college idea: (1) equality of opportunity, (2) use of education to achieve social mobility, (3) technological progress, and (4) acceptance of the concept that education is the producer of social capital.

Equality of Opportunity

Equality of opportunity has long been an ideal and a principle of the American people. Although the principle does not go back to the beginning of the English settlement, it did gain support at an early stage along the northern Atlantic seaboard.

As early as 1642, the Massachusetts Bay Colony made it obligatory upon all parents and masters to teach their children and apprentices to read and understand the principles of religion and the capital laws of the country, and to give them training "in some honest lawful calling, labour or employment, that may be profitable for themselves, or the Country."[1] Five years later, the General Court of the Colony passed a law requiring all communities of the Colony to erect and maintain schools for the children who would not otherwise be educated. This "Deluder Satan Act" of 1647 was a precedent for universal education, state enforced and financed by imposition of taxes.

The purpose of such laws, of course, was not to train people for democratic dissent. However, literacy itself is a demonstrable danger to tyranny.

The leaders of the early national period fostered the concept of equality of opportunity. George Washington felt keenly the need for expansion of the colonial educational effort.[2] Thomas Jefferson firmly believed in the paramount importance of careers freely open to all the talented. He was devoted to the principle of universal schooling and stated that "the ultimate result of the whole scheme of education would be the teaching of all the children of the State reading, writing and common arithmetic. . . ."[3] Jefferson's views are taken for granted today, but when they were written they expressed a revolutionary doctrine—a belief that every potential citizen should receive at least a minimum of formal instruction.

This unique character of the American way of life has been repeatedly emphasized. Lincoln in his first message to Congress declared that "the leading object of the Government for whose existence we contend is to elevate the conditions of men; to lift artificial weights from all shoulders; to clear the paths of laudable pursuit for all; to afford all an unfettered start and a fair chance in the race of life."[4] Frederick Jackson Turner, the historian of the West, summed up the case as follows: "Western democracy through the whole of its earlier period tended to the production of a society of which the most distinctive fact was freedom of the individual to rise under conditions of social mobility. . . ."[5]

It may be that the West has been more a myth than a reality in its influence on American thought. The romantic West, the democratic West lose both romance and democracy on closer scrutiny. Even if there were no strange elixir of freedom in the air—and indeed, there were often more agues and miasmas—established patterns of status and prestige were less fixed, and social fluidity somewhat more real in the early West. In the Midwest the principle that every child must be given educational opportunity was firmly established by the middle of the nineteenth century.

In the twentieth century, the ideal of equality of opportunity culminated in the report of the President's Commission on Higher Education which proposed the immediate abolition of all barriers to educational opportunity.

> American colleges and universities must envision a much larger role for higher education in the national life. They can no longer consider themselves merely the instrument for producing an intellectual elite; they must become the means by which every citizen, youth, and

adult is enabled and encouraged to carry his education, formal and informal, as far as his native capacities permit.[6]

Social Mobility

Closely associated with this ideal of equal opportunity is the concept of using education to achieve social mobility. The first campaign for free public elementary schools, waged under the generalship of leaders such as Horace Mann in Massachusetts, Henry Barnard in Connecticut, and Thaddeus Stevens in Pennsylvania, was won by the middle of the nineteenth century. But this was only the first phase of the struggle. Before it was over came the attempt to extend the system upward by providing free secondary education, and finally many states and municipalities established universities and colleges where higher education was virtually free to their citizens.

A survey conducted for *Fortune* by Elmo Roper in 1949 showed that "eighty-three percent of all the people would want a son of theirs (if they had one) to go to college, sixty-nine percent want college for their daughters." Of those who wanted their son or daughter to go to college, sixty-six percent gave as their chief reason for sending a son to college, "preparation for a better job, a trade, or profession, greater earning power." The corresponding figure for daughters was forty-eight percent.[7]

A group of sociologists stated the basic fact this way:

> Still believing that their children should rise and seeing in the secondary school and college the principal avenues of mobility, the people sent their children to secondary school and college. The American people learned what the people of older cultures have learned, that the schools are the social elevators in a hardening social structure.[8]

Jesse P. Bogue, a leader in the junior college movement indicated that a democratic society needed well-educated people, and he was convinced that the majority of the American citizenry were determined to have it so. "To write this belief into public policy," said Bogue, "has been one of the longest and hardest fought battles for social welfare."[9]

Education through the twelfth year is almost universal. The next logical step was to provide for the junior college years. Robert M. Hutchins, president of the University of Chicago, in 1931 stated that it would become the usual thing for high school graduates to attend a junior college near home. William II. Kilpatrick, in a valedictory address upon retirement from the faculty of Teachers College, Columbia University, prophesied that "The Junior College bids fair to become well nigh universal."[10] In 1947, junior college leaders predicted that by 1970 at least 50 percent of our youth of college age would be enrolled in the junior college.[11]

Thus the public junior college represents a natural extension of the public school system, and a partial realization of the democratic ideal that secondary school and college education should be available to everyone.

Technological Progress

Given impetus by the Civil War, business expansion and industrialism gained a dominant role by the beginning of the twentieth century. The virtual completion of the national railway network, tremendous increases in productive capacity, and a great outpouring of material goods marked the physical aspect of the conquest. Concomitant factors included an increase in urbanization with its attendant social problems, a shift in the locus of political and economic power, and an increasing awareness from a diverse camp of critics of a growing challenge to democracy.

Between 1865 and the present, a major element in American social thought defined itself. This element was "the business way" which held as principal ideas: (1) material success comes as the reward of superior virtue, (2) there is an insignificant amount of social injustice in the existing society, (3) the fittest and best survive the tests of our society, and (4) wealth tends to be socially benevolent. The business way, which had conquered the economic sphere almost completely and which influenced politics, sought also to win the mind of America. A varied and considerable group of men and institutions helped to define the business pattern of thought: Andrew Carnegie, William Graham Sumner, James McCosh, William McGuffey, Horatio Alger, Elbert Hubbard, Herbert Hoover, the Chamber of Commerce, and the National Association of Manufacturers. Buttressing their arguments by appeals to religion, science, political economy, psychology, anthropology, sociology, and the patience of the common man, they created an atmosphere from which President Calvin Coolidge could draw inspiration for his dictum: "The business of America is business."

Educators as well as businessmen led the way in reshaping educational patterns in America. Charles W. Eliot at Harvard was an example of the new educational leader. Business influence on boards of trustees of academic institutions began to increase.[12]

Discussions of educational objectives reflected the needs of an expanding industrial civilization. The issue of practical versus classical offerings in the college curriculum was argued. There were new demands for training at both professional and technical levels. Demands that education become more practical increased.

The developers of educational programs kept in mind the expansion and direction of industry and business. Industry demanded better-trained personnel. A developing technology was not only producing goods that called for highly skilled labor but was also changing the nature of the economic scene. Important for the junior college movement was the fact that the fields of endeavor which were expanding required for initial entry an educational background comparable to that provided by the junior college. New occupations developed: laboratory technician, medical secretary, dental secretary, aviation mechanic, junior accountant, engineer's assistant, and scores of other mid-level or semiprofessional occupations. Every advance in technology reduced the need for unskilled labor, including that of children and youth of school and junior college age. At the same time technology opened employment opportunity for those who had training beyond high school.

The increasing diversity in the educational requirements of jobs in the work force is well presented in the "Rockefeller Report" published in 1958. The report states that

> One of the striking features of contemporary life is the growing range and complexity of the tasks on which our social organization depends. The reasons for this lie in the explosive route of technological change and the increasing complexity of our social organizations.[13]

The report reveals that certain selected skills and occupations with high educational requirements that in 1910 accounted for 32.8 percent of the labor force, in 1957 accounted for 47.6 percent. The trend will accelerate in the years ahead, aided by automation and the discoveries of research.[14]

Coincident, then, with the expansion of our industrial system, the college for the few became the college for the many. The former was largely the privilege of the elect, the latter the assumption of a birthright secured by the extension of the notion of natural equality from a political to an educational sense. Society demanded from the colleges and universities curricula nearly inclusive enough to invite every type.

Education As Social Capital

After 1940 a profound change took place in the public attitude toward higher education. Social interest in higher education equalled or transcended the interest of the individual and his family. Higher education is now looked upon as a producer of social capital, with awareness that the national well-being is linked to the development of the nation's human resources.

Every thoughtful American is aware of the growing importance of higher education in American life and culture. The reasons are easy to find. In addition to the technological advances already discussed, great attention is being given to the conquest of space, the exploitation of the vast resources of the seas, and the search for breakthroughs in the field of medicine. The emergence of the United States as a world power and the concomitant assumption of the mantle of world leadership have added grave responsibilities of government.

American scientific advances and growing world responsibilities have created an unprecedented demand for college-trained men and women. The American people have come to understand that their national security and welfare depend fully as much on their human resources as upon existing productive capacity and natural resources. They have come to understand that men and women increase in value both to themselves and to society when they are educated. Thus in the public mind higher education has ceased to be an individual matter. It is now the producer of social capital.

Educational Forces and the Junior College Idea

The junior college is intimately related to the entire American educational enterprise. Studies of the junior college's origin and history demonstrate that this institution is descended from the secondary school on the one hand and from the college and university on the other. The secondary school founders of the junior college hoped to extend the educational opportunity of youth through two additional years. The colleges conceived the new institution as chiefly a selective agency to restrain all but the strongest of the rapidly increasing numbers who sought admission to the college and university, thereby providing partial relief to the overburdened parent.

The Public High School Movement

The public high school was neither an accident nor a diabolic scheme of professional educators. It emerged in response to the economic and social demands of a society. The American high school rose from lowly origins in the 1820s to dazzling heights by the twentieth century. What accounted for this growth? Some of the answers to this question also explain the later development of the junior college.

The high school was to be many things to many people. As Wesley points out in his history of the National Education Association, for the colleges the high school was a preparatory school; for the state it was a training ground for democracy and citizenship; for parents it was a prolongation of education within reach of the parental roof; and for the proclaimers of equality it was the people's college.[15]

An important factor in explaining the rise of high schools was the presence of growing numbers of colleges which enlarged the distance between themselves and the elementary schools. This gap had to be filled. While the colleges would have preferred traditional academies to untried high schools, they saw no chance of getting them in the West and exerted some help in the establishment of high schools, giving up their preparatory departments as high schools arose to fill the void.

As the high school developed, arguments arose as to the nature of this institution which were closely related to the arguments that raged over the functions of the junior college when that institution emerged. At the St. Louis meeting of the National Education Association in 1871, Newton Bateman, state superintendent of public instruction of Illinois, examined the question of the state's obligation to support high schools. The state, according to Bateman, should provide common schools for all and high schools and universities for all that want them. The university lifts up and challenges the high school, and the high school provides perpetual incentive toward high standards in elementary schools. To deny a high school and college education to the poor would perpetuate the barriers between the indigent and the affluent; it would create an aristocracy of learning to aggravate that of wealth. Such a restriction seems to say to the children of the poor: "Thus far, but no farther."

Even though the evolving high school grew rapidly in enrollment, broadened its program, adjusted itself to community conditions, and gave less attention to college requirements, the theory of its function did not develop correspondingly. The evolving high school encountered some opposition because next to endowed academies it seemed raw and crude. The high schools had no traditions and were feared by denominational academies and private schools as a threat to their existence. The colleges feared that their control over courses and programs would be impaired and college faculties looked upon high schools as a threat to scholastic standards.

A long educational war was waged by the colleges and the high schools in the definition of function for the emerging public high school. The alternatives for the high schools were either educational independence or subservience to colleges. High schools generally tried to avoid domination by the colleges because they felt they had a different mission. They were to educate citizens, train workers, disseminate culture; they were to serve society and not the colleges; they were the people's college and not the college's preparatory school. Most colleges, in contrast, held that high schools should be preparatory schools, for they sincerely believed that a high school that served a college was better than one that developed its program for other purposes. Definition of purpose for the high school is still an oft-debated issue today at the meetings of the NEA.

The public high school, then, became established as the pattern of secondary education in this country. What the public high school had done was to democratize secondary education. As more students attended and graduated from high school, there was a corresponding increase in the number who sought a college education. In some high schools "postgraduate" courses were established for those students who because of location or cost lacked the opportunity for college work.

The process of high school elongation had begun.

High School Stretching

One of the first states to start the stretching process was Colorado. The high school of Greeley, Colorado, for example, added an extra year of work, the thirteenth grade, in the 1880s.[16] A few years later, in the 1890s, the University of Michigan accepted one year of college work by students from the stronger high schools. By 1895, the East Side High School of Saginaw gave freshman college work in Latin, algebra, trigonometry, English and history.[17] By 1897, eight students had graduated from the University of Michigan in three years, "after doing a year's work beyond the four-year high school course of study in the East Side High School."[18]

Another early high school venture into the area of postgraduate work was the plan at Goshen, Indiana, where two years' work was added to the curriculum. In August, 1904, the local paper carried a notice announcing that beginning in September, the Goshen High School would offer a postgraduate course "that shall be equivalent to and accredited as one year's work in the best colleges and universities. . . . If sufficient numbers shall enroll for the first year's work the course will be extended to cover two years." Arrangements were finally made with the University of Chicago to accept the work for advanced standing.[19]

Nearly all such experiments were eventually abandoned. But in a few cases, as at Joliet, Illinois, the plan to extend the work of the secondary school resulted in the establishment of a separate junior college. Joliet not only claims to be the first public junior college but also illustrates the informal beginnings of the junior college movement.[20]

Junior colleges developed similarly in other parts of the country. J. Stanley Brown, superintendent at Joliet, reported in 1904 at the Conference of the Academies and High Schools affiliated with the University of Chicago that Philadelphia, Muskegon, Saginaw, St. Joseph, Goshen, Joliet, and eighteen semi-public institutions in different sections of the country were working out the six-year plan, giving collegiate work in connection with the high school.[21] As early as 1907 at the University of Missouri, the annual conference of teachers in accredited schools recommended giving college credit for one or two years of college level work done in high schools of larger cities. Eells, professor of education at Stanford University, blamed the matter of expense for preventing the high schools from taking advantage of the plan until 1915, when Hannibal, Kansas City, and St. Joseph, Missouri, organized junior colleges in connection with their high schools. Other institutions that began such work early included both Crane and Lane High Schools in Chicago.

Public institutions were not the only ones to become enamored of the stretching process. The earliest instance of postgraduate work being added to the high school is to be found at Newton, Maryland, where the first Catholic college in what is now the United States was founded in 1677. According to Eells, it might be called the earliest junior college, since in addition to secondary work it carried its students into the freshman year in college. Its students who wished further education were then sent to St. Omer's in Belgium to complete their studies. By the 1930s many academies, seminaries, and finishing schools added two years of junior college work to their courses of study.

California accepted the additional two years of high school most rapidly. The passage by the state legislature in 1907 of a measure authorizing high schools to offer higher educational services, which some were already offering, was the first such major development. The law provided that the board of trustees of any city, district, union, joint union, or county high school could prescribe postgraduate courses of study for the graduates of its high school or other high schools. This legislation was merely permissive and did not provide support to districts undertaking such service.

The California state legislature took the next important step in 1917 when it passed a bill providing for state and county financial support for junior college students on the same basis as for high school students. This legislative action was secured by the determined efforts of interested secondary school people, guided and directed by firm leadership from the state department of education.[22]

In 1921 California took another step forward with legislation providing for the organization of an independent junior college district with its own board, budget, and operating procedures. The junior college flourished in the favorable climate of California.

Thus very strong motivation for the junior college idea came from the high schools themselves.

The State University

From its inception the junior college idea received encouragement and direction from the colleges and universities. The new institution was christened "junior" and in its early infancy bore unmistakable evidence of the relationship which its name implied. The junior college inherited a number of characteristics from the four-year colleges and became practically a replica of the first two years of the regular college.

Not only have the ideas of university leaders contributed to a definition of the primary purpose of the first two years of college, but the development of the state university idea helped redefine education in America. The American liberal arts college as it existed in the mid-nineteenth century was not adequate to the needs of a rapidly changing society. The liberal arts college had done its job well but in terms of the few rather than the many. Growing secularism, the subsequent development of industry, and the emergence of science called for changes in the educational pattern.

While the state university idea found literary expression in the seventeenth and eighteenth centuries, it was not until the nineteenth century that the university itself was fully developed. The rising state universities were characterized by the conviction that the recipients of higher education should not be an intellectual elite, but should be "all citizens capable of benefitting from such training."[23] As it was taking shape in the mid-nineteenth century, the state university idea assumed that a democratic social order required education on every level and that all had an equal right to higher education.

Closely related to the belief that all citizens should have an opportunity for higher education was the idea that the curriculum of a state-supported institution should reflect the professional and practical needs of the citizens. Economic and technological developments were transforming American society and economy and demanded specialized skills. Faced with these social demands for a more functional type of higher education than that being offered by the traditional liberal arts institutions, a few college presidents in the 1820s and 1830s spoke out against the educational *status quo.*

James Marsh of the University of Vermont, Eliphalet Nott of Union College, Philip Lindsley of the University of Nashville, and others attempted to introduce into the classical curriculum applied courses in the arts and sciences. The publication in 1842 of *Thoughts on the Present Collegiate System of the United States,* by President Francis Wayland of Brown University, reflected the ideas of those dissatisfied with the classical curriculum. Wayland denounced the program of the old-time college as ill-suited for equipping young men with the skills most needed in the everyday life of banking, milling, canal-making, bridge-building, and farming. The classical curriculum, Wayland contended, did not provide society with the techniques indispensable to its further material and moral progress.

In the main, the western state universities did not immediately adopt these much needed practical programs, partly because the faculties were liberal-arts oriented. It was only when the Federal Government in 1862 made land grants for the support of agricultural and mechanical education that the movement gained momentum. "Even thereafter," says Curti, "the battle, whether against the wily politicians, the indifferent farmers, or the champions of classical education, was won only after countless skirmishes."[24]

The Land Grant College

Into the pre-Civil War period the American nation was still clinging to the Old World for its thinking and precepts. However, forces already at work in the first half of the nineteenth century would, when channeled, eventually lead to the establishment of a new type of collegiate education. Charles and Mary Beard, describing these pre-Civil War forces, found that "all in all the epoch of 'Jacksonian democracy,' the 'era of the common man' the 'fabulous forties,' and the 'fermenting fifties,' was a time of dramatic mental activity and creative thinking in respect of everything human."[25]

Into this booming new civilization came the land-grant college movement. The changes it brought about in American higher education undoubtedly prepared the way for the eventual acceptance of the junior college idea. The questions raised by the establishment of the land-grant colleges in the nineteenth century were the same that junior college leaders debated in the twentieth century. Can the "liberal" and "practical" in higher education be successfully combined? Should post-high school education be limited to an educational elite or include all those who can profit from advanced study?

As the land-grant college curriculum developed, subjects were introduced and taught on the basis of their practical value. The concept of training for citizenship in a democratic society was also part of the program. By giving some measure of dignity to the vocations pursued by many Americans, the land-grant colleges helped pave the way for the acceptance of vocational training by higher educational institutions. The "new education" was partly responsible for breaking the concept of the fixed and prescribed classical curriculum.

Criticism of the land-grant colleges was both favorable and disparaging. Noah Porter, on assuming his duties as president of Yale in 1871, spoke of the "breeze of public interest and public criticism which is now blowing so freshly through the halls of ancient learning,"[26] and Andrew D.

White, president of Cornell University, speaking of the land-grant colleges, was to claim "in all the annals of republics, there is no more significant utterance of confidence in national destiny out from the midst of national calamity."[27]

Unfavorable criticism, however, came from many quarters. Isaac Roberts, a professor at Cornell, reported:

> When the Press announced one fall that a large number . . . had entered the Freshman class, a leading denominational journal declared that 300 "fresh recruits for Satan" had entered this "Godless college." Another journal called it "a school where hayseeds and greasy mechanics were taught to hoe potatoes, pitch manure and be dry nurses to steam engines."[28]

To sum up, a unique system of higher education evolved through the years in response to societal demands. This kind of evolution marks the development not only of the American state university system and the land-grant colleges, but also of the junior college movement. By disrupting the traditional classical liberal arts curriculum, by being committed to the concept that the state and the nation prosper in proportion to the development of the individual, by democratization of higher education through their belief that intellectual capacity and achievements are not confined to the wealthy and privileged, by their insistence on the equality of studies; by all these, the land-grant colleges broke the monopoly of the classical colleges and the stranglehold of the fixed and prescribed curriculum. They contributed a program and philosophy to American higher education from which the junior colleges borrowed heavily.

The Community Concept

The attempt to implement the concept of equal opportunity for all has led to growing enrollments in the colleges and universities of the country. Such growth, together with the demands of society for a greater variety of trained personnel because of changing technology, has led to a new dimension in higher education. This new dimension is a growing concern about the quality of community life, shown by the growing attempts to meet the needs of the community through higher education.

The idea of a college dedicated to meeting people's needs is not new to Americans. The American state university has had a good deal to do with fostering and furthering the ideal of service to the needs of the community. In the early twentieth century, the University of Wisconsin realized the ideal of service to all the needs of the community. Wisconsin's President Charles R. Van Hise, in his inaugural address of 1904, indicated that Wisconsin was to be an institution for all the people of the state. The University would be a "watchtower," taking an active part in improving society and serving as an essential instrument of public service.[29]

The rise of state universities was paralleled by a movement for democratic higher education in the urban areas of America. The municipal university was created to provide higher education for the people of the cities at public expense. As early as 1847 the Free Academy of the City of New York, later to become the City College of New York, was established, and its course of studies had "especial reference to the active duties of operative life . . . the laboring class of our fellow citizens may have the opportunity of giving to their children an education that will more effectually fit them for the various departments of labor and toil, by which they will earn their bread."[30] Other municipal universities developed, the net result of which was to accelerate and broaden the movement for democratic higher learning.

An added impetus to the developing concept of the community and education working together came with the growing number of adults who sought learning of all kinds. Education was conceived as a continuing process in which the junior college was seen to be especially qualified to render service.

"In addition to preparatory and terminal curricula," said Earl J. McGrath,

> the junior colleges can offer a third type of instruction which will be in great demand in the near future. Such instruction may be described as casual or service courses. . . . The junior colleges, enmeshed in the warp and woof of the community which sustains them, and untrammeled by tradition, are admirably equipped to offer this casual or service type of adult education.[31]

The acceptance by the junior colleges of a community function led to the emergence of the junior college as a community-serving educational institution. This concept went much deeper than the earlier one which thought of the junior college as a local institution designed to provide the community's youth with transfer and terminal curricula.

Community service is a rather recent development. There is little in the literature prior to 1930 which reveals this new conception of the junior college. A series of catastrophic events during the Depression, World War II, and more recently in America's assumption of world leadership, changed the characteristics of the junior college that had emerged in the early 1900s.

The very nature of the young and flexible junior college made possible a closer integration of campus and community without violating hallowed traditions. The opportunity of junior colleges during World War II to work closely with industry, business, and the military in the development of tailor-made programs to meet war training needs helped establish a new pattern. The development was accelerated by the report of the President's Commission on Higher Education. Using the term community college for the first time, the report indicated new potentialities:

> Whatever form the community college takes its purpose is educational service to the entire community, and this purpose requires of it a variety of functions and programs. It will provide college education for the youth of the community certainly, so as to remove geographic and economic barriers to educational opportunities and discover and develop individual talents at low cost and easy access. But, in addition, the community college will serve as an active center of adult education. It will attempt to meet the total post high school needs of its community![32]

. . .

Development of the Junior College

The history of the growth of the junior college has been similar to that of other educational movements. A few junior colleges appeared; their programs and methods were imitated in other localities; and each one tried to prove that it was just as good as its rival in some neighboring city. They had to secure recognition from state universities and then win approval of some agency concerned with standards or accreditation. Both of these forces combined to compel this new institution to conform to the model of the traditional college. Here and there, in various sections of the country, a few daring souls ventured to do the unconventional by supplementing the "preparatory" or academic curriculum with a few terminal programs.

The first genuine example of this new educational species was probably Lewis Institute, founded in Chicago in 1896. Later it merged with Armour Institute of Technology and is now the Illinois Institute of Technology. While the claim of Lewis Institute was challenged in 1920 by the president of Bradley Polytechnic Institute, who declared that his institution was the first in America to be founded as a junior college when it undertook the junior college program in 1897, most historians of the junior college movement accept the claim of Lewis Institute.[44] Monticello College, in Alton, Illinois, has also claimed to be one of the early junior colleges, but this contention is hard to sustain. Russell T. Sharpe, president of Monticello College, seems to believe that the original three-year program given by Monticello was not a junior college program.[45] Still another claim has been made by Susquehanna University, in Pennsylvania, which, as the Missionary Institute of the Evangelical Lutheran Church, opened its doors for instruction on June 14, 1858.[46]

It is generally accepted that the first public junior college was organized at Joliet, Illinois, under the leadership of J. Stanley Brown, who was inspired and encouraged by William Rainey Harper. While various authorities cite 1902 as the year of the founding of the Joliet Junior College, Elbert K. Fretwell, Jr., favors 1901 as the initial year of the college.[47] No matter what the founding date was, by 1920 the junior college idea was definitely rooted in educational programs and was being implemented through the establishment of a variety of junior colleges.

In 1900 there were no public junior colleges in the United States and only eight private junior colleges.[48] By 1961 there were 678 institutions, of which 405 were public and 273 private. Enrollment rose from 100 students in 1900 to 748,619 in October, 1961.[49]

Table1
Growth in Number of Public and Private Junior Colleges (1900—1960)

Year	Number of Colleges			Percentages of Public Colleges
	Total	Public	Private	
1900–1901	8	0	8	0
1915–1916	74	19	55	26
1921–1922	207	70	137	34
1925–1926	325	136	189	42
1929–1930	436	178	258	41
1933–1934	521	219	302	42
1938–1939	575	258	317	45
1947–1948	651	328	323	50
1952–1953	594	327	267	55
1953–1954	598	338	260	57
1954–1955	596	336	260	56
1955–1956	635	363	272	57
1956–1957	652	377	275	57.8
1957–1958	667	391	276	58.6
1958–1959	677	400	277	59.1
1959–1960	663	390	273	58.8

Source: Edmund J. Gleazer, Jr., "Analysis of Junior College Growth," *Junior College Directory,* 1961, table 6, p. 41.

From the beginning the junior colleges were urged to see their functions as broad rather than narrow. They were increasingly urged to become local institutions that would open their doors to the young and the old. The junior colleges grew in numbers and in influence as they developed a pragmatic educational program based on the needs of the whole community rather than on the exclusive needs of students who planned to take their first two years of liberal arts courses in them.

Table 2
Junior College Enrollments, 1900–1960

Year	Total	Public	Private	Percentage Public
1900–01	100	0	100	0
1915–16	2,363	592	1,771	25
1921–22	16,031	8,349	7,682	52
1925–26	35,630	20,145	15,485	57
1929–30	74,088	45,021	29,067	61
1933–34	107,807	74,853	32,954	69
1938–39	196,710	140,545	56,165	71
1947–48	500,536	378,844	121,692	76
1951–52	572,193	495,766	76,427	87
1952–53	560,732	489,563	71,169	87
1953–54	622,864	553,008	69,856	89
1954–55	696,321	618,000	78,321	89
1955–56	765,551	683,129	82,422	89
1956–57	869,720	776,493	93,227	89.2
1957–58	892,642	793,105	99,537	88.8
1958–59	905,062*	806,849	98,213	89.1
1959–60	816,071*	712,224	103,847	87.3

*Cumulative Total. This total includes all students and gives some indication of the number of different people served by the college during the entire year.

Source: Edmund J. Gleazer, Jr., "Analysis of Junior College Growth," *Junior College Directory,* 1961, table 7, p. 42.

An Evolving Agency of Democratic Education

The junior college, offering two years of education beyond the secondary school, is a product almost entirely of the twentieth century. The junior college idea, however, is the result of centuries of philosophical and institutional struggle which influenced all American education and developed an educational system with characteristics not to be found anywhere else in the world.

During the past three centuries higher education in the United States has developed a variety of forms. Among these have been the New England hilltop college, the state college and university, the land-grant college, the municipal college or university, and the junior college. As these various types of institutions evolved, one feature characterized all of them: the concept of democracy. The American, because of his culture, changed the traditional system which he brought with him from the Old World. As a result of this transformation, the American people broadened and democratized these forms so that more and more individuals might have an opportunity to secure postsecondary training. They also increasingly sought to make higher learning both cultural and practical, more closely related to the daily concerns of the average American. Through the years there developed a growing demand for a form of schooling that would make provisions for those persons whose occupational, social, and economic level brought them somewhat above the training available within high school limits, yet somewhat lower than that of the four-year college graduate.

From the struggles to achieve equality of opportunity and to broaden the scope of higher education, the junior college idea was born. The idea took root in the soil of America's cultural, economic, and political heritage. It fed and grew on such concepts as equal opportunity for all and the desire to eliminate financial, geographical, and social barriers to higher education. It was nurtured by such educational leaders as Henry A. Tappan, William W. Folwell, David Starr Jordan, and William Rainey Harper, until by 1920 the junior college was accepted as an academic institution capable of offering the first two years of an approved baccalaureate program.

Between 1920 and 1945 another strain was added to produce a new hybrid form. At least two junior college leaders urged general acceptance by the junior colleges of an emerging trend, that of terminal and semiprofessional programs. Lange insisted that the first concern of the junior college "is with those who will go no farther." President William H. Snyder of Los Angeles Junior College established in 1929 fourteen terminal semiprofessional curricula at his institution.

Since World War II the junior college has emerged out of the mixture of these various strains as an institution which aims to meet the needs of the people in the locality in which it functions. In historical perspective, the junior college has become an institution which still offers the first two years of college education, but has added vocational curricula and an adult education program.

Notes

1. William Brigham (ed.), *The Compact with the Charter and Laws of the Colony of New Plymouth* (Boston: Dutton and Wentworth, 1836), pp. 270–71.

2. Letter to John Armstrong, April 25, 1788, in John C. Fitzpatrick (ed.), *The Writings of George Washington* (Washington, D.C.: U.S. Government Printing Office, 1939), XXIX, 467; letter to Roger Booke, governor of Virginia, March 16, 1795, in Worthington Chancey Ford (ed.), *The Writings of George Washington* (New York: G.P. Putnam & Sons, 1892), XIII, 53.

3. John Dewey, *The Living Thoughts of Thomas Jefferson* (London: Cassell & Co., 1941), pp. 115–16.

4. Special session message to Congress by Abraham Lincoln, July 4, 1861, in James D. Richardson, *A Compilation of the Messages and Papers of the Presidents, 1789–1897* (Washington, D C.: United States Government Printing Office, 1898), VI, 30.

5. Frederick Jackson Turner, *The Frontier in American History* (New York: Henry Holt & Co., 1920), p. 266.

6. President's Commission on Higher Education, *Higher Education for American Democracy* (New York: Harper & Brothers, 1947), I, 101.

7. "Higher Education," *Fortune*, XL (September, 1949), Supplement, 1–16.

8. W. Lloyd Warner, Robert J. Havighurst, and Martin B. Loeb, *Who Shall Be Educated?* (New York: Harper & Brothers, 1944), pp. 48–49.

9. Jesse P. Bogue, *The Community College* (New York: McGraw Hill Book Co., 1950), p.4.

10. *Junior College Journal*, V (December, 1934), 134; VIII (April, 1938), 341.

11. C.C. Colvert, "A Half-Century of Junior Colleges," *Junior College Journal*, XVII (February, 1947), 247.

12. Richard Hofstadter and C. DeWitt Hardy, *The Development and Scope of Higher Education in the United States* (New York: Columbia University Press, 1952), pp. 32–33.

13. Rockefeller Brothers Fund, *The Pursuit of Excellence: Education and the Future of America* (Garden City, N.Y.: Doubleday & Co., 1958), pp. 6–7.

14. *Ibid.*, pp. 7–8.

15. Edgar B. Wesley, *NEA: The First Hundred Years* (New York: Harper & Brothers, 1957), p. 60. The paragraphs that follow in regard to high school developments are based on Wesley, *NEA*, pp. 61, 63, 70.

16. Tyrus Hillway, *The American Two-Year College* (New York: Harper & Brothers, 1958), p. 36.

17. Walter Crosby Eells, *The Junior College* (Boston: Houghton Mifflin Co., 1931), p. 53.

18. A.A. Gray, "The Junior College in California," *School Review*, XXIII (September, 1915), 465–73.

19. Waldo L. Adams, "The Junior College at Goshen, Indiana," *Junior College Journal*, IV (November, 1933), 74; Victor W.B. Hedgepeth, "The Six-Year High School Plan at Goshen, Indiana," *School Review*, XIII (January, 1905), 19–23.

20. See Elbert K. Fretwell, Jr., *Founding Public Junior Colleges* (New York: Bureau of Publications, Teachers College, Columbia University, 1954), pp. 9–21.

21. Information relative to the early development of junior colleges is based on Eells, *The Junior College*, pp. 55–58.

22. Will C. Wood, "The Junior College," *Second Biennial Report of the State Board of Education of California* (Sacramento: 1916), pp. 163–64.

23. Merle Curti and Vernon Carstensen, *The University of Wisconsin* (Madison: University of Wisconsin Press, 1949), I, 22. The following paragraphs on curriculum change follow Curti and Carstensen, I, 26, 29.

24. Curti and Carstensen, *The University of Wisconsin*, p. 29.

25. Charles A. and Mary R. Beard, *A Basic History of the United States* (New York: The New Home Library, 1944), p. 245.

26. W. Carson Ryan, *Studies in Early Graduate Education* (New York: The Carnegie Foundation for the Advancement of Teaching, 1939), p. 5.

27. Cornell University, *Account of the Proceedings at the Inauguration*, October 7, 1868, p. 6.

28. Quoted in Edward Danforth Eddy, Jr., *Colleges for Our Land and Time* (New York: Harper & Brothers, 1956), p. 73.

29. John S. Brubacher and Willis Rudy, *Higher Education in Transition* (New York: Harper & Brothers, 1958), p. 163.

30. John S. Diekhoff, *Democracy's College* (New York: Harper & Brothers, 1950), p. 9.

31. Earl J. McGrath, "The Junior College of the Future," *Junior College Journal*, XV (February, 1945), 266–67. McGrath was then dean of administration and professor of education at the University of Buffalo.

32. President's Commission, *Higher Education for American Democracy* I, 67–68.

44. Frederick Eby, "Retrospect and Prospect," *Junior College Journal*, VI (March, 1936), 279; James M. Wood, "Twenty Years' Progress," *Junior College Journal*, X (May, 1940), 511; Leonard V. Koos, "Rise of the People's College," *School Review*, LV (March, 1947), 142.

45. Letters to Jesse Logue, executive secretary of the AAJC. March 26, 1957 and April 4, 1957. AAJC Archives.

46. Saul Sack, "The First Junior College," *Junior College Journal*, XXX (September, 1959), 13.

47. Fretwell, *Founding Public Junior Colleges*, p. 11.

48. Jesse P. Bogue and Shirley S. Hill, "Analysis of Junior College Growth," *Junior College Journal*, XX (February, 1950), 318.

49. Edmund J. Gleazer, Jr., *The 1962 Junior College Directory* (Washington, D.C.: American Association of Junior Colleges, 1962), p. 27. See Tables 1 and 2 for detailed data.

Foundation and Development of the American Association of Junior Colleges

The catalyst that led to the establishment of the American Association of Junior Colleges was a conference of junior college representatives called by the U.S. Commissioner of Education, P. P. Claxton, in 1920. Dr. George F. Zook, specialist in higher education for the U.S. Bureau of Education, was in charge of the two-day meeting held June 30 and July 1 in St. Louis, Missouri.

Thirty-four members were present at this initial conference. More than a third of them were from Missouri; twelve other states were represented. President James M. Wood of Stephens College, Columbia, Missouri, was chairman of the meeting; Martha M. Reid, dean of William Woods College, Fulton, Missouri, was secretary.[1]

At the time of this initial conference there were probably 175 institutions in the entire country that might be designated as junior colleges. Their programs were diverse and their status often uncertain. The junior college had never been heard of in many places. Some looked upon it as a sort of last stand before the weak four-year college passed completely from the scene. Others dubbed it a "glorified high school."[2]

The past forty-two years have seen many significant changes. The number of junior colleges has increased at such a rate that attendance at AAJC meetings today runs well over 350. During these years the American Association of Junior Colleges has gained recognition and status as spokesman and as leader of the junior college movement.

Founding the AAJC

Nineteen twenty saw many forces at work which led the Bureau of Education to call a junior college conference.

Forces for an Organization

There was James Madison Wood. By 1920 he was the moving spirit of the junior college movement. Wood, who was influenced greatly by William Rainey Harper, had assumed the presidency of Stephens College in Missouri in 1912, when it was almost a dead institution—a four-year college with a preparatory school attached to it and a total enrollment of 137 students. He convinced the Board of Trustees that he could save the institution by cutting off the bottom two years of the high school and the top two years of the college. By 1920 Stephens was a national success; Wood had made the junior college idea work successfully there.[3]

One reason for the conference in 1920 was the desire of Wood to bring together educators who were interested in furthering the junior college idea. He was anxious to find out if other struggling small colleges might be willing to try his Stephens program. Wood probably had a permanent organization in mind, but more important at the time were the national problems of developing an understanding of the junior college and of finding some means of saving many of the marginal colleges.

There was also Zook. He was aware of the nationwide problem of hundreds of struggling colleges about to give up the ghost. Zook was also aware that there were many national education associations and even more sectional and state education associations that were discussing questions affecting the future welfare of education in the United States. Very few that had been formed, however, were discussing the functions and the future of the junior college. It occurred to Zook and to the Commission of Education that it would be desirable for the Bureau of Education to "call a meeting of representatives from the junior colleges of the country for a full and frank discussion of their mutual interests and problems."[4]

The influence of Wood and Zook was instrumental in securing the organizational meeting in 1920. Wood's claim to the title of "Mr. Junior College" was validated when St. Louis, Missouri, in the home state of Stephens College, was chosen for this meeting. Another factor that brought about the St. Louis meeting was the provision for accreditation in higher education, which began in the 1890s but did not begin to press the colleges until the first decade of the twentieth century. Accrediting associations set up standards and began to apply them. Whether or not one was on the accredited list was public information and could be enough either to save or to destroy marginal institutions.

For many colleges, a national organization was an ark of safety. Prior to the formation of the American Association of Junior Colleges the only hope junior colleges had for success was to have a friendly university indicate that it would accept transfer students. But such salvation was neither recognition nor accreditation—it was often charity. The formation of the AAJC offered a possibility for a national organization that could achieve respectability and win recognition for the junior colleges. Inviting four-year college educators to address the Association became policy at the annual meeting of the AAJC. The purpose of the invitations was to stimulate interest in the two-year college movement and to lend respectability to the organization.

The Association was born, then, out of the necessity to define and interpret the essence of the junior college and its potential. A great many people who ran the junior colleges did not understand the place of their institutions in the American educational pattern. Others, who understood, realized that they had to gain recognition. The needs were enough to bring people together to form an organization that would perform such functions.

Definition, leading to recognition, leading to status: this was the primary objective of the AAJC in the 1920s and the 1930s.

The Organizational Meeting, 1920

Zook, who took a leading role in the development of the American Association of Junior Colleges, said on many occasions that it took a good deal of courage to face the heat of midsummer in St. Louis in 1920, and "no little faith that the then vaguely defined institution called the junior college had a future sufficiently important to justify a conference."[5]

Thirty-four educators from twenty-two junior colleges located in thirteen states and the District of Columbia evidently had sufficient faith as they gathered on June 30 in the hot, muggy weather of St. Louis. Zook opened the conference and then introduced Wood, who spoke on "The Function of the Junior College" and acted as chairman for the remainder of the two-day meeting.[6]

Wood raised some interesting questions regarding the junior college that were illustrative of the differences of opinion which existed in 1920, and exist even today, about the nature of the junior college. Wood recommended a reorganization of education in America to allow for a four-year junior college and the awarding of a baccalaureate degree. He suggested reforms in curricula that would fit the needs of students rather than the needs of faculties to teach their specialties.

Others took issue with Wood and indicated that they would not like to see any degree granted to junior college graduates and that the junior college should merely concentrate on offering sixty hours. H. G. Noffsinger, "a quiet gentleman from the hills of Virginia, who didn't say much but thought a great deal," president of Virginia Intermont College at Bristol, remarked that he did not want to see the B.A. degree granted to junior college graduates but would like to see an Associate in Arts degree awarded to those who finished the two-year program.[7]

Another theme at this first meeting was the relationship of the junior college to the secondary school and to the period of later adolescence. Several junior college administrators stressed that the freshman and sophomore years of the standard college course "are in subject matter much more of a continuation of the high school than a beginning of the specialized courses of the junior and senior years of the standard college course." David MacKenzie, dean of Detroit Junior College, differed and insisted that the high school and the junior college were different institutions. Some references—premonition of future debates—were also made to community functions and to the importance of providing vocational education.

A highlight of the conference was the presence of Commissioner Claxton. In his address he stressed that a national reorganization of education "would permit the secondary schools to continue their work to the completion of the general education in the school and the first two years of college."[8] Claxton saw the role of the junior college as that of a selective agency for the "higher institutions" and also as a means of preventing the state universities from being swamped with freshmen and sophomores.

Delegates to the St. Louis conference decided to organize a national association of junior colleges. Martha M. Reid read the report of the Committee on Permanent Organization, which had been appointed by Wood. The report recommended a meeting of the organization of junior colleges be held in Chicago in February, 1921; that those junior colleges that were accredited by "recognized accrediting agencies" be admitted to membership; and that MacKenzie be nominated for president, T. W. Raymond for vice-president, and Miss Reid for secretary-treasurer.[9] The conference approved these proposals and levied a five dollar fee on each institution represented. The fee was to be used by the officers to promote and advertise the next meeting.

Thus the AAJC was born. It received support and approval from those in attendance because they saw the need for such an organization to provide professional leadership and direction for the junior college movement. Or perhaps it received approval because, as Zook said with tongue in cheek, the heat reduced everyone to a common mass so that they were all of one mind. "No one in the conference had the energy to object to anything on the program," said Zook, "including the report of the committee which recommended the formation of the new educational organization to be known as the American Association of Junior Colleges. You are entitled to this explanation as to the manner in which this organization got underway."[10]

Why didn't the junior colleges join with other higher education institutions instead of starting their own national organization? The junior college had not become fully defined. The junior college leaders felt that they had the job of self-definition of their role in American education and this could only be done within their own organization.[11]

Definition and Standards

At the first annual meeting of the AAJC held in 1921, a formal constitution was adopted. The early meetings of the AAJC labored to define the junior college. The speakers at the first official meeting attempted to interpret this newcomer, which meant different things to different people.[12] Committees were appointed at the second meeting, in Memphis, Tennessee, to project an image of the junior college to accreditation societies and to the public. The AAJC defined the junior college as "an institution offering two years of instruction of strictly collegiate grade."[13]

At Memphis the Association also adopted its first standards dealing with definition, admission, graduation, equipment, faculty, support, and recognition. These goals were intended as a statement of aims, something toward which institutions could work; they were revised in 1925 and again in 1929.

Several of the early meetings of the Association were occupied with long and earnest debates on standards. Most junior colleges were anxious to maintain quality at least as high as that required by regional or state accrediting agencies. However, some of the standards imposed particular hardships on junior colleges. For the first two or three years after the organization of the AAJC, accrediting agencies insisted that junior colleges be separate from the high school. This was difficult for those junior colleges that had grown out of the high school organization. At the fourth annual meeting, Lewis W. Smith of Joliet spoke against the standard, insisting that there was no fundamental distinction between the junior college years and the senior high school years.

The adoption of standards by the Association in the 1920s did not mean that the AAJC was becoming an accrediting agency. In fact, from its inception the AAJC consistently avoided the function of accreditation. Arguments against the Association's assumption of this responsibility included:

1. The limiting effect which the time-consuming work of accreditation would have on the primary purpose of the AAJC—to study the professional problems associated with junior colleges.

2. The inability to assume the heavy cost of setting up and operating the machinery needed for accrediting institutions.

3. The existence of agencies supplying such service.

The Code of Ethics

As the junior college movement grew, institutions vied with one another to enroll paying students. This was especially true of some private junior colleges which utilized various means, some of them questionable, to attract students.

At the seventh annual meeting of the Association in 1927, Lucinda Templin of the University of Missouri protested inequitable tuition reductions, inaccurate advertising and publicity statements about their own and competing institutions, and unorthodox campaigns conducted by field secretaries.[14] Although the need for a code of ethics was quite evident, nothing was accomplished until 1934, when Richard G. Cox was appointed chairman of a committee to study the problem.

The fifteenth annual meeting in 1935 adopted a statement of principles of "Code of Ethics." The code required that statements and publications be accurate and truthful, that students known to have made formal application for enrollment at another school not be solicited, that all schools and representatives refrain from making derogatory remarks of any kind relative to any other college, and that, with certain exceptions, schools adhere to the published charges set forth in catalogues.[15]

Organizational Structure and Leadership

The founders of the AAJC faced so many obstacles when they started that it was no wonder that at times they doubted whether it would succeed at all. With no tangible inducements except the appeal of professional obligation, it was often difficult to persuade institutions to pay their membership dues. Finances were always a problem, and in the early organizational years there were sharp discussions and arguments over raising dues from $10 to $15 per year. In addition, there were divisive feelings between private institutions and public institutions. Diversity in types of organizations made more problematic than funny Walter Eells' classic statement that "the only way you knew whether an institution was a junior college was when it defined itself as such."[16]

The "Power Structure"

Analysis of the "power structure" of the AAJC indicates that a small group has guided the destiny of the organization since its establishment. Evidently, this is the pattern in the development of voluntary associations.[17] During the 1920s the early executive secretaries and a handful of ex-presidents ran the affairs of the Association. Campbell, Wood, and Noffsinger were the leaders; Zook and Leonard Koos were the major speakers. The presidents of private junior colleges influenced the direction of the Association.

As the 1930s came to a close, the influence of private colleges began to wane. Private junior college representatives to AAJC meetings questioned whether their problems were receiving proper consideration by the national organization. Public junior college presidents, particularly from California, suggested that private junior colleges had too much to say in the councils of the AAJC.

For the sake of unity, efforts were made to democratize the power structure of the AAJC. This resulted in representation according to geographical location and balance between the private and public junior colleges in assigning leadership positions. A small group still controls the policy making of the Association. But since 1945 the executive powers have been defined and a hierarchy of executive officers, rather than a group of informal leaders, "run the show."

Structural Forms

Constitutional developments. The first constitution of the AAJC was adopted at the first regular meeting in 1921. The purpose of the Association stated in it was:

> to define the junior college by creating standards and curricula, thus determining its position structurally in relation to other parts of the school system; and to study the junior college in all of its types (endowed, municipal, and state) in order to make a genuine contribution to the work of education.[18]

On March 4, 1939, the AAJC adopted a revised constitution which changed the stated purpose of the organization. It declared:

> the purpose of this organization shall be to stimulate the professional development of its members, to promote the growth of junior colleges under appropriate conditions, to emphasize the significant place of the junior college in American education, and to interpret the junior college movement to the country.[19]

The growth of the Association made it necessary to revise the 1939 constitution. A 1943 revision effort failed because of World War II. In 1945, following the resignation of Eells as executive secretary,[20] a new committee of twelve members from ten different states was appointed to draft a constitution. It presented a new constitution for approval at the annual meeting in January, 1946, and secured the membership's approval.[21] In its presentation, the committee pointed out that it was not a document designed to guard or protect any one group, "but it must govern all groups in the AAJC."[22]

The guiding principle of the reorganization under the new constitution was decentralization of the activities of the AAJC, with wider participation by the members. The flow of authority came from the membership to the elected and appointed officers rather than from the central authority down to the members, if any of the functions formerly performed by the central office in Washington were placed in the hands of various committees.

The University of Chicago was still interested in the junior college movement and offered its resources to the AAJC. The Executive Committee of the Association accepted the office space, the editorial services, and a cash contribution from the university.

The support given to the AAJC by the W. K. Kellogg Foundation and the new functions assumed by the central office warranted a new look at the structure of the AAJC. In the spring of 1962 a committee to revise the constitution began its work.[23]

Incorporation. The AAJC was incorporated on April 4, 1944, under the laws of the District of Columbia. The incorporators, as authorized at the annual meeting of the Association at Cincinnati in January, 1944, are the president, the vice-president, and executive secretary.

The principal advantages of incorporation were lending dignity to the organization; insuring permanency of succession under the corporate name; relieving the members and officers of personal liability; giving the organization legal standing in any necessary court procedures; facilitating such business transactions as those involved in the management of investment funds; and prescribing the process of dissolution of the organization and disposition of its remaining assets, if and when the dissolution might occur.[24]

The Board of Directors. The original constitution of the AAJC provided for a six-man Executive Committee of which the president was ex-officio member and chairman. Two members were elected at each annual meeting of the Association and were to serve for a period of three years. The Executive Committee determined policy for the Association. It cooperated with the president in planning and executing the program for the annual meeting.

The constitution of 1946 defined the structure of the present Board of Directors. It consists of the president, the vice-president, the immediate past president, and one director from each of six regional areas. The board is elected by a majority of the active members present at the annual meeting. It appoints the executive director, sets his salary, duties and term of office. The board approves all members of the Association and is required to report its actions for review by the Association delegates at the annual meeting.

* * *

Committees and Commissions

From the very beginning of the AAJC, committees have been an integral part of the administrative structure of the organization. The national office, however, has performed most of the work of the AAJC. An analysis of the "power structure" of the AAJC prior to 1946 indicates that a small group guided the destiny of the organization after its establishment, a not unusual situation in professional organizations. The early executive secretaries and a handful of ex-presidents "ran the show."

However, committees are devices that have enabled the AAJC to carry on important services inexpensively. Wesley has listed other reasons for having committees.

> Why appoint a committee? Because it stops the debate. Because it postpones the issue. Because it seems like a solution. Because it provides time for consideration. Because it shifts responsibility from the whole group to designated individuals. Because some persons want to be appointed. Because it is a way of securing free service. Because it is kind of representative democracy.[51]

It is not surprising that the AAJC, following the pattern of earlier associations, quite early began to create a growing number of committees to deal with a widening range of activities.

At the seventh annual meeting, in November, 1926, the Association authorized the incoming president to appoint a research committee. Lewis W. Smith, president of Joliet Junior College, became chairman, and Wood and George F. Winfield, president of Lon Morris College in Jacksonville, Texas, were made members. The task of this committee was to contact individuals, institutions, and organizations that might undertake studies on junior colleges. It conducted many research studies in the junior college field. In 1928 the University of Chicago, at the request of the committee, surveyed the offerings of elementary economics at junior colleges. Another study conducted by the research committee analyzed attitudes of junior college graduates. In 1939, the committee sponsored a study on the function of administrative officers.

In 1933, Smith asked to be relieved of further work on the research committee. W. W. Carpenter of the University of Missouri replaced him. In his report to the fourteenth annual meeting, Carpenter and his fellow committee members indicated that the job of the research committee needed clearer definition.[52] This need also plagued other early committees of the Association. Clarity of purpose, however, could not be achieved because the members of the committees lacked the funds to hold meetings. Inability to consult except by mail caused overlapping as well as wasted effort.

The reorganization of the AAJC that occurred in 1946 involved overhauling the committee system. The purpose was to enlist participation on the widest possible basis of all sections of the country in research and service. Committees were composed of representatives of the junior colleges in all sections of the country. Membership rotated so that widespread interest would be created and "the genesis of ideas and projects kept close to the grass roots of the Association."[53] The new reoganization successfully halted the movement that threatened to divide the Association.

Five research and service committees were set up, with the vice-president of the Association as coordinator. These committees were slightly altered in 1953 and emerged as Administration, Legislation, Instruction, Curriculum, and Student Personnel.[54] A director of research worked for all of these five committees under the vice-president of the Association and, of course, ultimately under the Board. When Koos retired as professor at the University of Chicago he became the first director of research under this new organization. He was paid by the University of Chicago as part-time editor of the *Junior College Journal* and part-time director of research for the Association. He served in both of these capacities until 1949.

The policy originally set in 1946 was that the research and editorial office was to be located at a university no longer than three years in succession. No doubt this decision was aimed at Koos. The supporters of Eells wanted to limit the influence of Koos and the University of Chicago on the AAJC. The Board of Directors of the AAJC favored living up to this policy, and in 1949 the research editorial offices were moved to the University of Texas. James W. Reynolds, professor of education, became editor of the *Journal*, and C. C. Colvert, professor and consultant in junior college education, became director of research. The universities paid the salaries of the professors who were the editor and the director of research. The cooperating university also paid the half-time salary of the associate editor and associate in research and paid half or more of a secretary's salary.

The University of Texas was once again granted the contract in 1952 even though renewal meant breaking the original policy of the AAJC to hold the research and editorial office at a university no longer than three years in succession. The contract expired June 30, 1955, and the University of Texas decided it wished to terminate the arrangement. The Association discontinued the research office but continued Reynolds as editor with a half-time associate editor and a half-time secretary paid by the Association. Colvert became coordinator of research under the vice-president of the AAJC until 1959, when another reorganization took place.[55]

By the late 1950s dissatisfaction arose over the committee system. The chairmen of the committees reported that they felt that the effectiveness and value of the committee work had lessened in recent years and that the system needed rejuvenation. In July, 1958, at the summer Board of Directors meeting at Estes Park, Colorado, the committee chairmen recommended that the committees be continued as commissions directly responsible to the Board and that each commission be enlarged but maintain regional distribution of membership. The Association adopted a new plan devised by the Board of Directors at the annual meeting in Long Beach, California, in 1959.

There are now five commissions. Each is composed of sixteen members who are representatives from the six regional areas: New England, Middle Atlantic states, Southern, North Central, Northwest, and California. The sixteen members serve three-year staggered terms. A Council on Research and Service, composed of the chairman of each of the five commissions and the chairman of the Editorial Board of the *Journal*, coordinates the activities of the commissions, assists in the promotion of research and service programs, and recommends specific programs suggested by these commissions to the Board of Directors. It also seeks to identify emerging needs for research and service in American higher education with particular emphasis on junior college fields.

In general, the commissions (1) originate ideas, projects and proposals, including estimates of costs, (2) receive suggestions on research and service from the Council on Research and Service, (3) suggest special committees upon the advice of the Council on Research and Service, (4) prepare reports and release findings through the *Junior College Journal*, (5) execute approved plans of research and service, and (6) plan programs for the annual meetings as requested by the Board.[56]

Functions of the Commissions

The Commission on Administration concerns itself with projects in the following areas: administrative practices, organization, and structure; personnel; athletics; library; public relations; finance; and plant facilities and services.

The Commission on Curriculum directs its attention to various aspects of curriculum construction, evaluation, and coordination in junior colleges, such as general education preprofessional education, terminal technical education, adult education, and articulation with high schools and other colleges and universities.

Responsibilities of the Commission on Instruction include the recruitment of teachers, professional education, in-service education, and improvement of instruction.

The Commission on Legislation is assigned responsibility for research and service in such matters as current developments in state and national legislation; evaluation and interpretation of such current developments as are essential to the junior colleges; investigations of issues of a legislative character, and of directives or regulations and the interpretations of these made by governmental agencies; dissemination of these evaluations to the membership in such a manner as the Board may approve; coordination of these activities and information with other agencies of higher education; and recommendations for new legislation.

Research and service by the Commission on Student Personnel are primarily in the fields of admission, testing, guidance, counseling, placement, follow-up for evaluation, student government, curricular activities of students, and technical aspects of student records.[57]

The most important work of the five AAJC commissions is to suggest and initiate research and service projects for the junior college movement. Special funds from the Kellogg Foundation of Battle Creek were given to the AAJC in 1960 to help the commissions perform their tasks.

However, as soon as the commissions began to function, leaders of the Association began to question the relative merits of the system. At the Board of Directors meeting held in Nassau in January, 1961, questions were raised in reference to changes needed so that the commissions might function more effectively. Would smaller commissions be more effective? Should regions be disregarded and leadership for the Association be developed and recruited where available? How could the funds allotted to the commissions be best spent for the greatest service to the Association and to the membership?[58]

To date, no change has been made in the commission system. In addition to questioning the commission system, an attempt was made at the January 1962 meeting of the Board of Directors to do away with the Council on Research and Service and eliminate the position of the chairman of the Council. The motion to eliminate the Council was lost but a motion was passed that the executive director would serve in lieu of the chairman of the council as liaison between the council and the Board of Directors.[59]

* * *

Notes

1. See George F. Zook (ed.), *National Conference of Junior Colleges, 1920, and First Annual Meeting of AAJC, 1921,* Bulletin of the U.S. Bureau of Education, No. 19, Part II (Washington, D.C.: U.S. Government Printing Office, 1922).

2. Doak S. Campbell, "After Sixteen Years," *Junior College Journal,* VII December, 1936, 109.

3. Interview with Doak S. Campbell. former executive secretary of the AAJC, March 30, 1962.

4. Zook (ed.), *National Conference of Junior Colleges,* p. 1.

5. George F. Zook, "The Changing Pattern of Junior College Education," *Junior College Journal*, XVI (May, 1946), 411.

6. Zook (ed.), *National Conference of Junior Colleges*, p. 2.

7. For the various discussions that took place at the organizational meeting in 1920, see Edward M. Bainter, "The Administration and Control of Public Junior Colleges," Merton E. Hill, "Vocationalizing the Junior College," David MacKenzie, "Problems of the Public Junior College," James M. Wood, "The Function of the Junior College," John W. Million, "Advantages of the Junior College," in Zook (ed.), *National Conference of Junior Colleges*.

8. P. P. Claxton, "The Better Organization of Higher Education in the United States," in Zook (ed.), *National Conference of Junior Colleges*, p. 30.

9. Martha M. Reid, "Report of the Committee on Permanent Organization," in Zook (ed.), *National Conference of Junior Colleges*, p. 45. W.G. Bolcom, in 1920 superintendent of schools in Rochester, Minnesota wrote to W.C. Eells on January 17, 1940, indicating that although it did not matter, he was elected the vice president of the temporary organization formed in St. Louis. In another letter, January 26, 1940, Bolcom wrote, "My own opinion is that the Secretary-Treasurer must have confused Mr. Raymond and me. My memory is somewhat hazy in regard to a number of things that took place, but I do remember that . . . I was elected vice-president." Eells papers (in the possession of the author).

10. George F. Zook, "The Past Twenty Years—The Next Twenty Years," *Junior College Journal*, X (May, 1940), 617.

11. Interviews with Doak S. Campbell, March 30, 1962, and W.C. Eells, March 23, 1961.

12. Zook (ed.), *National Conference of Junior Colleges*, part II.

13. *Proceedings of the Second Annual Meeting of the AAJC*, 1922 [p. 2]. AAJC Archives.

14. Lucinda Templin, "The Need of a Higher Code of Ethics in the Administration of Junior Colleges," *Proceedings of the Seventh Annual Meeting of the AAJC*, 1927, pp. 21–26. AAJC Archives.

15. "Minutes and Committee Reports," Fifteenth Annual Meeting of AAJC, *Junior College Journal*, V (May, 1935), 468.

16. Interviews with Doak S. Campbell, March 30, 1962, and Walter C. Eells, March 23. 1961.

17. See Louis Michael Vanaria, "The National Council for the Social Studies: a Voluntary Organization for Professional Service" (unpublished Ph.D. dissertation, Teachers College, Columbia University, 1958), chapter 4; also Stuart F. Chapin and John E. Tsouderos, "Formalization Observed in Ten Voluntary Associations: Concepts, Morphology, Process," *Social Forces*, XXXIII (May 1955), 306–09.

18. Article II, The First Constitution, in Zook (ed.), *National Conference of Junior Colleges*, p. 71.

19. Article II, Constitution of American Association of Junior Colleges, adopted *1939, Junior College Journal*, II (May, 1939), 556–59.

20. See below, p. 42.

21. The 1946 constitution was amended February 21, 1947; June 28, 1952; March 4, 1955; March 8, 1956; and March 4, 1960; but these amendments did not change the organizational structure.

22. James L. Beck, "The New Constitution," *Junior College Journal*, XVI (May, 1916), 436–37.

23. Edmund J. Gleazer, Jr., "Memorandum to the AAJC Board of Directors," April 23, 1962 (mimeographed). AAJC Archives.

24. Walter C. Eells, "From the Secretary's Desk," *Junior College Journal*, IV (May, 1944), 445.

51. Edgar B. Wesley, *NEA: The First Hundred Years* (New York: Harper and Brothers, 1957), p. 292.

52. W.W. Carpenter, "Report of Research Committee to 14th Annual Meeting of AAJC," *Junior College Journal*, IV (May, 1934), 475.

53 "Reports of Research and Service Committees to 29th Annual AAJC Meeting," *Junior College Journal*, XIX (May 1949), 533.

54. Colvert and Littlefield, "A Brief History of the Development of the AAJC," pp. 39–40.

55. *Ibid.*, p. 40.

56. AAJC Student Personnel Commission, "Conference Plan" (December 8–10, 1960), pp. 3–5 (mimeographed). AAJC Archives.

57. Conference Plan, p. 5.

58. AAJC Board of Directors, *Minutes* (January 7–9, 1961). AAJC Archives.

The "Cooling Out" Function Revisited

BURTON R. CLARK

In the mid 1950s, after finishing a dissertation on the character of adult schools (Clark, 1956), I became interested in doing a similar analysis of community colleges. While teaching at Stanford, I spent a summer visiting a number of colleges in the San Francisco Bay Area to explore the feasibility of such research, particularly to weigh the advantages and disadvantages of a case study rather than a comparative analysis of several colleges. I decided to take my chances by concentrating on the college and getting to know it well, looking for connections among the parts of the organization in order to characterize it as a whole. The college I selected was a relatively new one in San Jose that offered entrée and was within easy commuting of Palo Alto. The fieldwork of the study and manuscript preparation during a period of three years or so led to a book and an article published at the end of the decade (Clark, 1960a, 1960b). The book covered the emergence and development of the college. I attended to unique features, but emphasized characteristics that, on the basis of available comparative data, a few side glances, and some reasoning, seemed to be shared with most other public two-year institutions and hence could be generalized—something to lay on the table that could be checked by others elsewhere and might, in explanatory power, be worth their time and effort. I spoke of the character of the community college in such terms as diffuse commitment and dependency on an unselected external social base; pointed to roles it played in the larger educational structure in acting as a screening agent for other colleges at the same time that it opened wider the door to higher education; and suggested that such colleges have particularly sharp problems of identity, status, and autonomy.

Foremost among the generalizations was the "cooling-out" function, a conception that clearly has also been seen by others as the most important conclusion of the study. My purpose in this chapter is to review the concept twenty years later. In retrospect, was it appropriate in 1960? Does it still pertain? How has it been used by others? Since its crucial features are often overlooked, I begin by reviewing the original idea. I then explore the possible alternatives to this particular function as a way of understanding the reasons for its existence. In light of the experiences of our own and other countries during the last two decades, we can better understand the alternatives now than we could twenty years ago. Finally I take up some ways that the idea has been used by others and conclude with a judgment on the value of the concept.

Original Conception

At the outset of the research, cooling out was not on my mind, either as a phenomenon or as a term. As I proceeded in my observations, interviews, and readings of available documents and data, I was struck with the discrepancy between formal statements of purpose and everyday reality. A poignant part of reality was the clear fact that most students who were in the transfer track did not go on to four-year colleges and universities. What happened to them? It turned out that the college was concerned about them, both as individuals and, in the aggregate, as a persistent administrative problem that would not go away. Emerging procedures could be observed that were designed to channel many such students out of transfer programs and into curricula that terminated in the community college. As I observed teachers and students, and especially counselors who seemed central to what was going on, it became clear that such reassignment of students was not easy.

It involved actions that, no matter how helpful, would be felt by many involved to be the dirty work of the organization. This effort to rechannel students could have been called "the counseling process" or "the redirection-of-aspirations process" or "the alternative-career process" or by some other similarly ambiguous term so heavily used in education and sociology. I played with the terms then readily available but all seemed to have the analytical bite of warmed-over potatoes. While I was stewing about how to point a concept, a friend called my attention to an article by Goffman (1952) in which, for various sectors of society, the need to let down the hopes of people was analyzed brilliantly. Goffman used terms from the confidence game in which the aspirations of the "mark" to get rich quick are out-of-line with the reality of what is happening to him or her, and someone on the confidence team is assigned the duty of helping the victim face the harsh reality without blowing his mind or calling the police. Now there was a concept with a cutting edge! So I adopted and adapted it, aware that it would not make many friends in community college administrative circles.

How did cooling out appear to happen in educational settings? Moore has summarized well the argument that I originally put forth.

> The process as described by Clark entails a student's following a structured sequence of guidance efforts involving mandatory courses in career planning and self-evaluation, which results in "reorientation" of the student rather than dismissal. The process begins with preentrance testing, which identifies low-achieving students and assigns them to remedial classes. The process is completed when the "overaspiring student" is rechanneled out of a transfer program and into a terminal curriculum. Throughout the process the student is kept in contact with guidance personnel, who keep careful track of the student's "progress."
>
> The generalizable qualities of cooling out as Clark saw them involve *offering substitutes or alternatives* to the desired goal (here a transfer program); *encouraging gradual disengagement* by having the student try out other courses of study; *amassing objective data* against the preference in terms of grades, aptitude tests, and interest tests; *consoling and counseling* the student through personal though "objective" contacts; and *stressing the relative values of many kinds* of persons and many kinds of talents other than the preferred choice (Moore, 1975, pp. 578-579).

Crucial components of the process that were stressed in the original statement and that I would want to emphasize even more now are that (1) alternatives are provided—the person who is to be denied a desired goal is offered a substitute; and (2) aspiration is reduced in a "soft" consoling way, easing the pain and frustration of not being able to achieve one's first goal and the difficulties involved in switching to and learning to value the offered alternative education and career.

Once I had virtually "seen" the process in operation in one community college it was easy to generalize. After all, the community colleges in general embraced the open-door philosophy and hence were unselective on the input side, while necessarily facing the standards of four-year colleges and universities and being somewhat selective on the transfer/output side. Figures were readily available for all community colleges in California and the nation as a whole that showed how many students entered the transfer track and how many came out of it. And, there was no evidence that community colleges anywhere in the country took the traditional stern approach that students who could not for one reason or another do the transfer work were failures who should be sent away. To the contrary, the attitude expressed everywhere was a generous and open one that the community college should not label students as failures, instead students should be helped as much as possible "to find themselves" and to find courses and career objectives appropriate to their abilities.

Hence a general assertion was warranted: its specific steps might vary, and colleges might or might not be effective in carrying it out, but the cooling out process would be insistently operative in the vast majority of American public two-year colleges. This was necessary given the position of the two-year units in the general educational structure and the institutional roles that had emerged around that position.

Alternatives

One way to enlarge our understanding of this phenomenon is to place it in the context of alternatives. Can it be subordinated or replaced by other ways of proceeding? How could the roles of community colleges be so altered that the process would be unnecessary? Indeed, what has been done at other times and is presently done in other places that reduces greatly the play of this process? Six alternatives come to mind, a set that comes close to exhausting the broad possibilities. As backdrop for these alternatives, let us keep in mind that the cooling out process in community colleges is rooted in (1) open door admissions, a policy of nonselection; (2) the maintenance of transfer standards, an attitude that those who transfer should be able to do course work in four-year colleges and universities; and (3) the probable need to deny some aspirants the transfer possibility and to face the problem of what to do with them.

Preselection

One clear alternative is preselection, either in earlier schooling or at the doors of the colleges. National systems of education continue to select students at the secondary level, indeed to have specialized schools that are terminal. This form of selection remains the model pattern in Europe and around the world, despite the efforts to "democratize" and universalize secondary education in so many countries in the last two decades. The secondary school graduates who qualified for higher education, in the most generous estimates, were still no higher in the early and mid 1970s than 30 percent of the age group in West Germany, 35 percent in Italy, and 45 percent in France (Furth, 1978). Of course, in the United States, automatic or social promotion of students during the secondary schooling has been the opposite of selection, amounting to mass sponsorship. Some selection still takes place, particularly through assignments to curricular tracks within the comprehensive school, but it is minor compared to the dominant international mode. Current efforts to stiffen standards of secondary school graduation in the United States will, if effective, tend to increase preselection.

Naturally, selection can also take place at the doors of community colleges, no matter what the extent of selection at the secondary level. Some minor amount of selection perhaps takes place in some community colleges in certain regions, particularly in the Northeast where the long dominance of private higher education has left a legacy of selection for quality and low regard for the more open-door public institutions.

The greater the selection in the secondary school or at the doors of the colleges, the less need to select within the doors. The gap between aspirations and scholastic ability is narrowed, since a higher threshold of ability is established. Every increase in selectivity reduces the conditions that generate the cooling out process.

This alternative runs against the grain of American populist interpretations of educational justice which equate equity with open doors. The reestablishing of sharp secondary school selection or the closing of the open door is not what most critics and reformers have in mind. But we need to keep preselection in view if we want to understand why countries in the world currently have considerably less need for a cooling out function than the American system of the last quarter-century and the foreseeable future. The traditional injunction is a simple one. If you want to reduce cooling out, keep out the candidates for cooling out.

Transfer-Track Selection

All right, community college personnel can say, we have an open door but we certainly do not have to let every Tom, Dick, and Harry—and their female counterparts—declare him- or herself to be a four-year college student and set sail in the courses that give credit for later transferring. We will stop the "nonsense" of everyone having a chance and, instead, openly select at the doors to the transfer program. Those who appear likely to be latent terminals, if we do not select, will now be manifest terminals from the outset, and hence the need for the cooling out process will be drastically reduced.

This alternative is logical enough, certainly to the academic mind or the conservative critic, and it surely occurs to a minor degree in many community colleges. A quick and honest no at the outset, proponents would say, is better for the student, the faculty, and the institution than a drawn-out, ambiguous, and manipulative denial in the style of cooling out. But, logical or not, this alternative is also not likely to carry the day in American reform. The open-door philosophy is too ingrained; community colleges evermore define their boundaries loosely; almost anyone, part- or full-time, can enroll in courses offering transfer credit; and, besides, students are now in short supply and colleges generally for the foreseeable future will be less rather than more particular.

Open Failure

Perhaps the basic alternative to cooling out is unequivocal dismissal or withdrawal. This response is a classic one, found in the United States in the recent past in the state universities that felt it was politically necessary to have virtually open-door admission but then proceeded to allow the faculty to protect standards and slim the flow of students by weeding out in the first year those "who cannot do the work." Processes of admit-and-dismiss are widely operative in other countries, particularly where the forces pressing for more access are able to block sharp selection at the doors of the system but, at the same time, faculties remain free to flunk or discourage to the point of self-dismissal as many students as they wish in the first year or two.

As pointed out in my original formulation, this alternative is a hard response in the sense the failure is clearly defined as such: it is public, with the student required to remove himself from the premises. It is a rather harsh form of delayed denial— "we have to let them in but we do not have to keep them"—and can be viewed from inside or outside the system as heartless, a slaughter of the innocent. One role of the community college, as the most open segment in the American differentiated system, has been to lessen the need for this response in the state universities and public four-year colleges. The academically marginal and less promising students have been protected from the open-failure form of response by removing them from the settings where it was most likely to occur. Cooling out has been the "softer" response of never dismissing a student but instead providing him or her with an alternative.

This open-failure alternative is also one not likely to carry the day in the United States. Those who are most critical of community colleges do not seem to have it in mind and nowhere does it appear on the agenda of reform. Old-fashioned toughness—"You have failed, so get out of here!"—is not about to be reestablished as a general mode, either in two-year or most four-year colleges.

Guaranteed Graduation

In this alternative we take the social or automatic promotion of students that has characterized much of American secondary education in recent decades and apply it to post-secondary education. As an ideal type, the formulation reads: Let everyone in who wishes to come and let all who persist graduate. In the transfer part of the two-year college, this means let all complete the two years of work, receive the associate in arts or associate in science degree, and transfer to whatever four-year colleges will accept them. Standards are then not directly a problem since students will be allowed to graduate and transfer without regard to scholastic achievement or academic merit. The cooling out effort is no longer required.

This alternative is attractive for many participants and observers, especially those for whom equality is the primary value in higher education to the point of moving beyond equality on access and opportunity to equality of results. It surely is operative to some degree in numerous unselective four-year as well as two-year colleges: once the student is in, the college has a strong interest in seeing that he or she receives a degree. However, this alternative does not serve competence very well and debases the value of degrees, threatening the credibility and legitimacy of postsecondary institutions. It contributes to the inflation of educational credentials whereby individuals must have longer schooling to obtain a certificate of some value. It is a risky road, one for which the dangers have already been spelled out by the experience of the American secondary school and the value of the high school diploma. One may even think of this alternative as a cheating form of equality: Everyone is equally entitled to credentials that have lost their value. Guaranteed college graduation does not solve the paradox—the search for equality defeating its own purpose when it is carried to the point of equal results and statuses (Dahrendorf, 1980). Much of the thrust of the search for equality is to enable people to be freer to choose, which means that institutions and programs must offer a wide range of choices while reducing the barriers that prevent people from having those choices. But equal results, in such forms as automatic passage and uniform certification for all, restrict the opportunities for choice.

Reduction of the Transfer-Terminal Distinction

Another alternative is to reduce the distinction between transfer and terminal as much as possible. Here there are two possibilities. One is to narrow the status gap by enhancing the status of the terminal programs. Community college personnel have worked long and hard at this solution, helped considerably by the specific short-term programs that have high practical returns in well-paying and interesting job placements, for example, fashion designer in New York City or electronic technician in a Massachusetts or California technological complex. Those "life changes" do not look bad, compared to the perceivable returns from a bachelor's degree in English or sociology. But the bulk of terminal programs—centered more at the level of secretarial and mechanical training—are nowhere near that attractive and it remains hard to give them a parity of esteem with what people think a full college education will bring. Prestige ranking of occupations by the general population continues to give sociologists something to analyze, setting limits on how much one can realistically rank the middle-status ones with those of high status.

The second possibility is to blur the distinction, reducing as much as possible the labeling of courses and curricula as transfer and nontransfer, and hence the parallel official and self-labeling of students as on one track or the other. Community colleges have long had courses that serve the double purpose and students who mix the two. There are natural administrative interests within comprehensive schools and colleges to reduce the internal distinctions that divide staff and students, and often raise havoc with morale. Then, too, community colleges have long had the self-interest of wanting to certify who is an appropriate candidate for further education without having clearly designated transfer programs in which the specific courses and course sequences are dictated by the programs and requirements of the four-year institutions.

The transfer-terminal distinction and the meaning of the transfer track have blurred somewhat during the last two decades. Some community colleges manipulate the labeling of courses in order to increase their attractiveness and especially to bolster financial support based on student headcounts in degree-credit courses (Cohen and Lombardi, 1979). Part-time students who come to a college just to take a single course, with no intention of getting credit for it let alone using it toward transferring, are found in transfer courses. "The transfer courses have become discrete. Many students already have baccalaureate degrees and are taking the 'transfer' course in photography to gain access to the darkroom, the 'transfer' course in art to have their paintings criticized, the 'transfer' course in a language so that they can travel abroad" (p. 25). In general, an increasingly diffuse approach to transfer programs has been encouraged by basic trends of the last decade: more part-time, occasional,"non-credit" students; more poorly prepared students—as high as 50 percent of enrollment—with the college staff then having to concentrate on the six Rs of higher education—remedial reading, remedial writing, and remedial arithmetic; more students occupational interest; and a "noncollegiate" drift in community college philosophy toward the organization serving as a community center or even a "community-based" legal entity operating without campuses, full-time faculty, or formal curriculum.

But the blurring of distinctions and meanings has limits beyond which lies a loss of legitimacy of the community college *qua* college. The definitions of college held by the four-year institutions and by the general public still set boundaries and insist on distinctions (that auto repairing is not on a par with history or calculus as a college course.) Again we face an alternative with self-defeating tendencies, one sure to arouse much hostility and stimulate countertrends. The community college will still have to pick and choose among courses as to what is bona fide transfer work and worry about course sequences and the progression of students through them. To eliminate the transfer operations would be to give up a hard-won place in the higher education stream" (Cohen and Lombardi, 1979, p. 27).

Move the Problems to Another Type of College

There remains the most general structural alternative: Eliminate the transfer part of the two-year college, or do away with the community college entirely, or convert two-year into four-year institutions. Then the cooling out function, or one of the above alternatives (slightly modified), would have to occur in a four-year context. After all, most four-year colleges in the U.S. system have relatively open admission, and it need not strain them to open the doors still wider. Some of these institutions have had and still have two-year programs and offer two-year degrees, either terminal or allowing entry to the junior and senior years. Also, two-year programs on the main campus and two years of course work available in extension centers have given even major universities an internal "junior college" operation. And now the increasing competition for students is causing four-year colleges to lower admission barriers and to build the two-year segments.

It is easy to imagine some move in this direction and, amidst the bewildering variety of U.S. postsecondary education, this alternative is surely operative today. But, again, it is not an alternative likely to dominate: the two-year entity is institutionalized and here to stay for the foreseeable future. Then, too, the problems that follow from this alternative are sufficient to block any major development. High among the problems is the reluctance of four-year college and university faculties to support two-year programs and to give them esteem. The evidence has long been in on this point, in the form of the marginal status accorded university extension in the family of university programs and A.A. degrees in B.A.-centered institutions. At the same time the need for short-cycle programs does not lessen. As other advanced industrial societies have been finding out the hard way, in their expansion into mass higher education since 1960, the need steadily grows, from both consumer demands and labor market demands, for a greater differentiation of degree levels rather than a dedifferentiation. Thus other countries have been moving toward short-cycle education. They too are impelled to devise more stopping points, as well as more educational avenues. The crucial structural decision is then whether to put the short-cycle programs within institutions committed to longer programs of higher esteem or to give them to a separate set of institutions. There is no evidence that the first choice is the superior one. In fact, if successful programs depend upon faculty commitment, there is a strong argument for separate short-cycle colleges.

In short, the problem that causes colleges to respond with the cooling out effort is not going to go away by moving it inside of other types of colleges. *Somebody* has to make that effort, or pursue its alternatives.

Use and Abuse of the Idea

The idea of cooling out has received considerable attention in the last twenty years. The original journal article, "The 'Cooling-Out' Function in Higher Education" (Clark, 1960a), has been widely reprinted in books of reading in sociology, social psychology, and education. The term used to name the concept undoubtedly has been eye catching.

Beyond this direct absorption of the idea there have been interesting efforts to extend or revise its use, including the construction of counter or opposite concepts. If students can be cooled out, what about faculty? In an important case study of a new community college in a white ethnic part of Boston, London (1978) argued that the faculty suffered a great gap between their expectations and their reality and had to find ways to console themselves and otherwise handle disappointment. The particular college he studied provided a setting likely to magnify this phenomenon, but, even so, what is starkly revealed in an extreme case can be usefully explored in other cases where it may be more muted and shielded from view. As community college experts know well, the gap between expectations and reality is wider wherever the recruited faculty come from traditional sources and have traditional values and then have to face first-generation college-going students who not only have poor scholastic preparation but want to remain attached to their own traditional values of family and neighborhood.

Then, what about cooling out as applied to particular social categories of students? Moore (1975) interviewed over sixty women in three community colleges and focused attention not on their rechanneling from transfer to terminal curricula but rather on a rechanneling of nontraditional career aspirations for women into traditional choices. In most cases, she reported, the two rechannelings coincided. But not in all, since some original choices were for fields such as data processing that were in the terminal track. Hence she skillfully broadened the use of the idea: "The general concept of cooling out, namely the amelioratory process of lowering and rechanneling aspirations, suits women's career choices as well as it does the transfer process" (p. 580). Her focus on women caused her to explore the role of parents and high school counselors, as well as college counselors and the two-year institutions overall, in pressuring women to move away from choices of nontraditional careers.

Then there is the possible development of reverse concepts; is there a "cooling in" or "warming up" function? There surely is, as community college spokesmen have long maintained. There clearly are students who perform better scholastically than they did in high school and who raise rather than lower their aspirations. They may even begin in a terminal program and are moved by observant personnel or by their own efforts to transfer courses. Baird (1971) explored the aspirations of community college students over time, using survey questionnaire data from twenty-seven colleges and divided the students into *coolers* (lowered aspirations), *warmers* (increased aspirations), and *stayers* (retained original aspirations). He concluded that "contrary to expectation, cooling out occurred seldom, while warming up was relatively common" (p. 163). He pointed to an interplay between high school and college experiences: that coolers (really "coolees"!) had been encouraged by their high school successes to plan for higher degrees, than ran into academic difficulties in the community college and revised their ambitions downward; that warmers had been led by background and high school experiences to plan lower, then succeeded academically in the community college and revised expectations upward. His research had the advantage of a survey covering a large number of colleges and students (over 2,500). But the differences between the groups were small; the results were confusing and hard to integrate; the data centered on self-reported aspirations; the processes of colleges and the actual experiences of students were not observed; and those who were gone by the end of two years were out of the sample.

Without doubt, the most prevalent abuse of the concept of cooling out has been its confusion with casting out. This abuse is not apparent in the serious research literature. Those who have written on the topic have typically observed most of the essential characteristics of the original conception, but I have personally been exposed to it in dozens of conversations and meetings during the years, in such remarks as "she was cooled out" or "don't cool me out" that are meant to refer to a quiet, even devious, effort to simply get rid of or fail someone. Most social science conceptions are liable to a stretching that becomes distorted as they are popularized. One of the major drawbacks to the cooling out terminology is that its catchiness encourages such distortion, all the more readily allowing the idea to slide toward "pop" usage.

Finally, we have the use and potential abuse of the cooling out process in which it is picked up and used in more general analysis of stratification and inequality in society. Here the community college nearly always comes out as a villain, discriminating against the dispossessed, keeping the poor and the minorities away from four-year colleges and universities by letting them in and cooling them out. If this is so, the argument goes, such colleges are then operating objectively as instrumentalities by which the upper classes dominate and maintain privilege. One then need only add a little suspiciousness and the community college is linked to capitalism—at least to American capitalism—with a strong suggestion of a conspiracy in which capitalists construct community colleges to serve their own interests.

In the most carefully constructed argument of this genre, Karabel (1972) has emphasized the large proportions of lower-income and minority students in community colleges. Hence there is a social class difference in who is subjected to the cooling out process, with the community colleges seen as generally operating to maintain the social class system as it is. Karabel points out at the beginning of his essay that this effect is not necessarily intentional; that the two-year college "*has been critical in providing upward mobility for many individuals*" (p. 526) and that measured academic ability is more important than class background in the U.S. in predicting where one goes to college. The main thrust of the argument goes in a different direction. College standards are seen as a covert mechanism for excluding the poor and minorities, serving to justify universities and colleges "as a means of distributing privilege and of legitimating inequality" (p. 539). The community college is essentially a tracking system that is "class-based," *(passim)*—with all the ambiguity on "based." The effort to promote one- and two-year terminal programs is yet another instance of "submerged class conflict" (pp. 548-552), since officials want it while the students do not. And the whiff of conspiracy is strong: "This push toward vocational training in the community college has been sponsored by a national educational planning elite whose social composition, outlook, and policy proposals are reflective of the interests of the more privileged strata of our society" (p. 552). The cooling out process is implicated in all of this, particularly in helping to legitimate inequality by using academic standards in hidden ways to block the upward mobility of the poor and the minorities.

Since Karabel was interested in reform, he concluded with the question of what to do. He suggests that investing more money would not make much difference; that transforming community colleges into four-year institutions would still leave them at the bottom of the prestige hierarchy; and that making the colleges into vocational training centers alone would simply accentuate tracking. The solution he proposes is the grand one of a socialist reconstruction of the entire society: "The problems of inequality and inequality of opportunity are, in short, best dealt with not through educational reform but rather by the wider changes in economic and political life that would help build a socialist society" (p. 558). However, the experiences of socialist societies around the world have hardly been encouraging in their capacity to improve national systems of higher education, including the provision of equal opportunity.

The other major effort in the inequality context, one less carefully constructed, is Zwerling's book, *Second Best: The Crisis of the Community College* (1976). At the time he wrote the book, Zwerling was a teacher at Staten Island Community College in New York City. He was angry at virtually every aspect of the community college, especially the one at which he worked, other than the special programs and approaches in which he and a few colleagues invested their efforts. He portrayed the community college as "just one more barrier put between the poor and the disenfranchised and the decent and respectable stake in the social system which they seek" (p. xvii). He took note of cooling out, devoting a chapter to it as the main role of counseling, and concluded that it helps the college maintain the existing system of social stratification. By means of cooling out, the college "takes students whose parents are characterized primarily by low income and low educational achievement and slots them into the lower ranks of the industrial and commercial hierarchy. The community college is in fact a social defense mechanism that resists basic changes in the social structure" (p. xix). In helping to maintain inequality, cooling out, as he portrays it, works all too well.

Again, what to do? In a mishmash of new directions, Zwerling proposes consciousness raising, in which students are taught more about what is happening to them, thus making them angry and leading them into a process of heating up that will replace cooling out. In addition they should be given more experience in the real world that will help them choose a career. Then, too, they can be helped over "the transfer trauma" by visits to Yale and similar classy institutions. In short, a "student-centered approach . . . offers the possibility that the old cooling out may at last be replaced by a new heating up" (p. 206). But in his last chapter, Zwerling leaves behind such tinkering and moves to the sweeping structural conclusion that if we want a less hierarchical society, we have to restructure the entire system of higher education, beginning with the elimination of the community colleges: "At the very least this would mean *the elimination* of junior or community colleges since they are the most class-serving of educational institutions" (p. 251). All students would enter directly into a B.A.-granting school. In addition, state systems should award a systemwide B.A., instead of allowing individual colleges and universities to award their own degrees of widely different prestige. All this would eliminate "second best," as everyone moved through equated institutions and obtained equal results.

Arguments of this nature have helped fuel an attack on community colleges by those who single-mindedly pursue the value of equality. Those who speak for minority groups are bound to take a dim view of community colleges and demand direct and open access for whole segments of the population to four-year colleges and universities, when they come to believe that "educational equity means nothing if it does not mean equality of educational attainment" (Winkler, 1977, p. 8). They then argue that the concern with equality in higher education should shift from getting minority students into colleges to getting them out as graduates holding bachelor's, doctor's and professional degrees. Any elimination along the way by means of cooling out, dropping out, or flunking out is then suspect as discriminatory, unless it happens in equal portions across social categories.

This shift in the inequality line of reasoning in the U.S. has been little informed by the experiences of national systems elsewhere. Some other nations, particularly France and Italy, have long tried to achieve equal results by means of equated institutions, nationally mandated core and common curricula, and the awarding of degrees by a system-at-large rather than the individual institution. Many systems have long held out against short-cycle institutions and programs, as second best to the traditional universities. But the problems thereby created, as systems moved from elite to mass higher education, have been immense, dwarfing our own in magnitude and making us appear fortunate in comparison. Thus the general drift of painful reform in other advanced systems is toward greater differentiation of types of institutions and degree levels, the introduction of short-cycle programs and degrees, more screening in the first year or two and the breakup of the systemwide degree. The dilemma is still there: Either you keep some aspirants out by selection or you admit everyone and then take your choice between seeing them all through, or flunking out some, or cooling out some. The more other systems get involved in mass entry, the more their problems become similar to ours, including the problem of gap between aspiration and scholastic ability, and the more they must get involved in cooling out or must opt for one or more of the alternatives I have presented.

Conclusion

In the hindsight of two decades, what would I change in the original analysis if I had to do it over again? The most important change would be to have distinguished more clearly between effort and effectiveness in the cooling out process. It is one thing to observe the procedures constructed by colleges and the work they put into cooling out operations, and another to ascertain their effect on students, essentially answering the question whether the effort was effective or not. The distinction was a part of my thinking and writing—appearing in such phrases as "when it is effective"—but should have been clearer. Since I was doing an organizational analysis, I concentrated on the effort side. I had a less clear grasp of the effects, since I was not essentially doing an "impact" analysis, spent much less time with students than with counselors and teachers, and did not systematically interview or survey the students for their reactions. A clearer distinction at the outset could have saved some later confusion about the state of the process. I could also have emphasized a point that naturally follows: The process, no matter how well constructed and operated, it not likely to work smoothly. It tends to become problematic, as individuals and groups to react to it. This heavily problematic nature has been caught in some later research, such as Baird (1971) and London (1978). My own writings undoubtedly contributed to it, since social actors can learn from the results of social science and adjust behavior accordingly.

Then, too, it probably would have helped to have carried the cooling out process one step further: after students move from transfer to terminal programs, or while they are being asked to do so, they often quickly move from college to a job or some other form of withdrawal. This would have hooked cooling out to the enormous attrition of community colleges and suggested a major two- or three-step flow in the denial of hope, lowering of aspirations, and disengagement. But all this would have blurred the sharp focus of the original argument, and I did not have good data on the process of complete withdrawal. You have to stop somewhere, if you want to keep guesses from overwhelming limited information.

One change that I would make if I were doing the research now instead of twenty years ago would be to either do research on, or introduce a major *caveat* about, regional and state differences. We should not expect 1,000 community colleges to operate closely alike in the U.S. system, since our decentralized structure has given primacy to local and state control for community colleges and hence has subjected them more to local and state variations than to national administered uniformity. Then, too, the American system of higher education overall is the most market oriented of the world's advanced systems, with competition a prime element that causes colleges to be uncommonly sensitive to different clienteles, labor markets, and the actions of other colleges. Thus, research today on community college operations ought to take seriously the possibility of considerable variation. At the least, regional differences should be studied, since among informed observers it is well known that New England is a long way from California. The East remains relatively transfer oriented and standards oriented—a setting where tradition, resources, and vested interests have given primacy to private higher education and a resulting institutional hierarchy in which the community college often appears as fifth best, let alone second best. It is then hard for researchers in Boston, New Haven, or New York to imagine the "California model," which has developed in a context where public higher education has long been dominant, community colleges won legitimacy before World War II, and virtually everybody in the hometown, or on the block—including grandma—has gone by the college to take a course. In that type of setting, the colleges have had middle-class as well as lower-class clienteles, suburban as well as downtown locations, and students who qualified for selective institutions as well as those who did not. Now, during the 1970s, the California-type college has moved another step down the road of openness, toward becoming such a diffuse enterprise that its legitimacy as a college, as earlier indicated, may soon become problematic. In this evolution, sequential transfer work has become a minor item, as a share of the whole, buried under huge enrollments of "single-course" students. The California model is more widespread and influential in the nation than that exemplified in the Northeast.

The change in approach that I would *not* make if I had to do the study over again, then or now, would be to extrapolate from my internal analysis of the community college to grand theories about the role of education in society. This is too easy as armchair sociology and too lacking in detailed analysis of connecting links. We especially lack the information and the capacity in the state of the art to compare situations in which the cooling out process operates and those in which it does not, the latter then offering one of the alternatives set forth above. The trouble with the leap to grand theory is that, poorly grounded in empirical research, it is particularly vulnerable to ideology of various persuasions. It also tempts Large Solutions, by others if not the researcher, that have a wide gamut of unanticipated and often undesired effects, outcomes that may do major damage to the less knowing and less powerful actors who cannot get out of the way. Witness the way that problematic research by James Coleman and Christopher Jencks has been used by political forces against U.S. public schools. Contemporary social science has grave weaknesses in application to social policy, and nowhere more so than in educational matters. One has to tread gently, even upon the cooling out process and its obviously unattractive features.

This side of utopia, academic systems, whether in a socialist or capitalist country, will be, in Erving Goffman's large phrase, a graveyard of hope. The graveyard may be large of small, busy or infrequently used, but it will be present. Only the naive do not recognize that with hope there is disappointment, with success, failure. The settings that lead toward the cooling out effort remain, all the more so as democracies open doors that were formerly closed. Any system of higher education that has to reconcile such conflicting values as equity, competence, and individual choice—and the advanced democracies are so committed—has to effect compromise procedures that allow for some of each. The cooling out process is one of the possible compromises, perhaps even a necessary one.

References

Baird, L. L. "Cooling Out and Warming Up in the Junior College." *Measurement and Evaluation in Guidance*, 1971, *4* (3), 160–171.

Clark, B. R. *Adult Education in Transition: A Study of Institutional Insecurity.* Berkeley: University of California Press, 1956.

Clark, B. R. "The 'Cooling-Out' Function in Higher Education." *The American Journal of Sociology*, 1960a, *65* (6), 569–576.

Clark, B. R. *The Open Door College: A Case Study.* New York: McGraw-Hill, 1960b.

Cohen, A. M., and Lombardi, J. "Can the Community Colleges Survive Success?" *Change*, 1979, *11* (8), 24–27.

Coleman, J. S. *Equality of Educational Opportunity*. Washington, D.C.: U.S. Government Printing Office, 1966.

Dahrendorf, R. *Life Chances: Approaches to Social and Political Theory*. Chicago: University of Chicago Press, 1980.

Furth, D. "Selection and Equality: An International Viewpoint." *Comparative Education Review*, 1978, *22* (2), 259–277.

Goffman, E. "On Cooling the Mark Out: Some Aspects of Adaptation to Failure." *Psychiatry*, 1952, *15* (4), 451–463.

Jencks, C., and others. *Inequality*. New York: Basic Books, 1972.

Karabel, J. "Community Colleges and Social Stratification." *Harvard Educational Review*, 1972, *42* (4), 521–562.

London, H. B. *The Culture of a Community College*. New York: Praeger, 1978.

Moore, K. M. "The Cooling Out of Two-Year College Women." *Personnel and Guidance Journal*, 1975, *53* (8), 578–583.

Winkler, K. J. "Graduation, Not Admissions, Urged as Desegregation Focus." *Chronicle of Higher Education*, March 21, 1977, p. 8.

Zwerling, L. S. *Second Best: The Crisis of the Community College*. New York: McGraw-Hill, 1976.

American Education, Meritocratic Ideology, and the Legitimation of Inequality: The Community College and the Problem of American Exceptionalism*

Steven Brint and Jerome Karabel

Abstract. This article examines American education in comparative perspective, suggesting that the distinctive structure of the school system is both an embodiment and a source of the felt fluidity of class boundaries in the United States. Several characteristic features of the American educational system are identified: the avoidance of early selection, the lack of sharp segmentation between different types of institutions, relative freedom of movement both among and within institutions, openness to new fields of study, high levels of enrollment, and the provision of opportunities for educational mobility well into adulthood. The two-year public community college, it argues, is an essential expression of these patterns which, through its very accessibility, reinforces the American ideology that it is never too late for individual talent to reveal itself—and to be rewarded. The article concludes with a discussion of the effects of the nation's distinctive school system on American culture and politics, suggesting that the perceived "classlessness" of American society may in part be a product of its seemingly open and democratic structure of education.

Introduction

The unique system of education that has developed in the United States—a system of which the community college is an integral component—has had a powerful impact on the texture of American social and political life. This impact does not, to be sure, lend itself to precise measurement. Nonetheless, a case can be made that some core aspects of what observers, both foreign and domestic, have referred to as American "exceptionalism"[1]—the egalitarian tenor of daily life, the relative weakness of class consciousness, the felt fluidity of class boundaries, and the persistent national preoccupation with equality of opportunity as opposed to equality of condition—are both embodied in the peculiar structure of American Education—*and* constantly reinforced by this same structure. To understand why this might be so requires a grasp of just how distinctive the American educational system has been in comparative and historical perspective.

Compared to the educational systems of other advanced industrial countries, American education has been characterized by striking levels of openness and fluidity. The first nation to offer access to secondary education to the entire population, the United States was also the inventor of the "comprehensive" high school, where academic and vocational curricula were taught under the same roof. In Europe, in contrast, secondary education was typically divided into separate institutions offering distinct programs of academic, technical, and vocational training. The academic sectors in these systems—in France the *lycée*, in Germany the *gymnasium,* in England the grammar and "public" schools—were attended by only a small proportion of the population and had a decidedly elite character. As recently as 1950, for example, only about five percent of French and German young people—most of them from privileged backgrounds—received academic secondary school diplomas. In the United States during the same period, about 60 percent of young people completed what was admittedly a less rigorous secondary education, and roughly 11 percent of the population graduated from college (Ringer, 1979: 252).

The differences in sheer numbers do not, however, convey a full sense of the depth of the dissimilarities in structure and cultural atmosphere between American and European schools. For it was not simply a matter of more Americans being enrolled in secondary education; what was of greater social and political import was that students of diverse backgrounds were enrolled in the same school. In Europe, the typical pattern was markedly different; secondary students from the same community attended separate schools of sharply divergent statuses, where they studied distinct curricula with students from broadly similar social backgrounds. Moreover, in the elite sectors of the European systems, as Max Weber (1978) noted, a cultural ideal of the classically educated "cultivated man" generally held sway; in such an ideal, with its implicit emphasis on the cultural superiority of the elite over the masses, tended to magnify the social distance between classes that the American comprehensive high school, with its emphasis on the democratic mixing of students in lunchrooms, school assemblies, and extracurricular activities, was expressly designed to reduce.

If the characteristic American pattern of education organization was a unitary one, then the typical European pattern was one of *segmented* schooling—a pattern which Fritz Ringer (1979:29) has defined as "one in which parallel courses of study, are separated by institutional or curricular barriers, as well as by differences in the social origins of their students." American education has not, of course, been free of segmentation; indeed, as George Counts (1922) had already documented in the years after World War I, there has long been curricular tracking by social class *within* American high schools. Nevertheless, the barriers that did exist between the various segments of American education were neither as sharp nor as visible as those in Europe.

One of the most distinctive features of the American education system—and one that is fundamental to its openness—is that it gives students with undistinguished academic records multiple chances to succeed. Whereas in England and many other European countries, allocation to a non-academic track took place as early as age 11 and thenceforth had a virtually irreversible character, the "late-bloomer" in the United States could reveal his or her talents in the high-school years or even later (Turner, 1966). Indeed, in the years after World War II, equality of opportunity in the United States increasingly came to mean that everyone—even those with poor academic records—had a right to enter higher education. As a consequence, as Burton Clark (1985: 315) noted, students emerging from secondary schools in the United States "have second, third, and fourth chances in a fashion unimaginable in most other systems of higher education."

The Community College and American Ideology

The rapid rise of the junior college in the postwar years made the American system of higher education, which already enrolled a far higher proportion of young people than the system of any other country (Ben-David, 1966; Poignant, 1969), markedly more accessible than it had ever been.

From a comparative perspective, what was genuinely new about the community college was not that it charged no tuition or that it made it possible for people to attend college while living at home; after all, many European universities had long been free of charge (indeed, some provided students with stipends for living expenses) and possessed no residential facilities whatsoever. The community college's innovative character resided instead in three of its other features; it offered two rather than four (or more) years of higher education, it provided both academic *and* vocational programs within the same institution, and it was open to the entire population, including adults (and, in some states, even those who had not completed high school).

In a sense, the public two-year college brought to higher education the "comprehensive" model that Americans had introduced to secondary education: universal access, relatively weak boundaries between curricular offerings, and an orientation of service to the entire community. As part of this service orientation, the two-year institution was geographically dispersed so as to provide maximum accessibility; by 1980, over 90 percent of the population was within commuting distance of one of the nation's more than 900 community colleges.

In its very design, the junior college was an expression of the long-standing American pattern of avoiding sharp segmentation between different types of institutions. While the typical pattern in European and other countries has been to draw a sharp line between the "university" and other forms of "postsecondary" education, such barriers have been consciously rejected in the United States. Instead, boundaries between institutions of different types are relatively permeable, with transferable course credits being the "coin" that makes exchange possible (Clark, 1983: 62). Though the community college is the lowest track in America's highly stratified structure of higher education, it nonetheless is connected—through the possibility of transfer with credit—to the system's most prestigious institutions. Thus a student from East Lost Angeles Community College, a predominantly Hispanic institution in a poor urban neighborhood, can in principle transfer to the University of California at Berkeley; in reality, however, only 16 Hispanic students (a rate of well under five percent) transferred to all eight campuses of the University of California in the fall of 1986 (California Postsecondary Education Commission, 1987: 25). Yet even imagining such a move from a British polytechnic to Oxbridge or from a French *institute universitaire de technologie* to the Ecole Normale Superieure conveys a sense of just how different the American system is from some of its European counterparts.

In offering both academic and vocational subjects within the same institution, the community college was continuing an already well-established pattern in American higher education of refusing to create strong institutional boundaries between traditional and newly emerging fields of study. This tradition first became institutionalized in the late nineteenth and early twentieth centuries in the nation's great land-grant universities which were pioneers in introducing such fields of study as agriculture, business, and education. If European universities were slow to integrate into their curricular offerings subjects other than the classical ones of law, medicine, and divinity, the American university eagerly embraced new fields of study such as the social sciences and readily provided training for a wide variety of scientific, technical, and professional occupations (Ben-David, 1966; 1972). The community college extended this pragmatic and utilitarian educational tradition, refusing to exclude virtually any field of study for which there was—or might be—popular demand. And in both community colleges and four-year institutions, students retained the right to change their field of study, sometimes switching from "liberal arts" to "vocational" subjects or vice versa.

Even the seemingly rigid boundary between student and non-student has been eroded by the fluidity of the American system. With the rise of the community college, students could easily enroll in higher education on a part-time basis, often retaining full-time jobs while acquiring student status. In recent years, four-year colleges and universities in search of new student markets have also increased their part-time offerings, following the community college pattern of enrolling growing numbers of adult students. But it is the community college that is the quintessential open-door institution, and the proliferation of opportunities for part-time attendance at any point in the life cycle has powerfully reinforced the belief that it is *never* too late for individual talent to reveal itself—and to be rewarded.

American Education and the Perception of "Classlessness"

From a comparative and historical perspective, the distinctiveness of American education is therefore apparent. What is less clear, however, is what effect, if any, this peculiar structure has had on the political and ideological tenor of American life. While such effects are notoriously elusive, we would like to suggest that they have in fact been present and that their impact has been considerable. Indeed, it is our contention that the perceived "classlessness" of American society is integrally associated with the character of its educational system.

By their very mode of organization, educational systems may tend to promote a sense that the boundaries between social groups are clearly defined and formidable or that they are fluid and easily traversed. In Europe, as noted earlier, systems have historically segregated dominant and subordinate groups in separate institutions, where they instructed them in distinct curricula. Unintentionally or not, such segmented structures are powerful instruments of class socialization, for they are crucibles in which distinctive class cultures may be forged and recreated from generation to generation (Cookson and Persell, 1985). If the effect of segmented systems is to reinforce the level of experienced social distance between groups, non-segmented systems tend to reduce such distance (Ringer, 1979: 267-268). In the United States, the relative lack of such segmentation in both secondary and higher education has highlighted the seeming permeability of class boundaries.

The very structure of the American educational system may thus be seen as both an institutional embodiment of the ideology of equal opportunity and a constant source of reinforcement of it. By avoiding early selection and providing numerous opportunities to show one's talents, the educational system reaffirms the core national belief that any individual, no matter how humble the circumstances of his birth, can rise as far as ability and hard work will take him. In this regard, the provision of opportunities for success well into adulthood is an effective means of keeping hopes for individual mobility alive long after they would have been extinguished in a less open system. Former President of the Carnegie Corporation and Secretary of Health, Education, and Welfare John Gardner (1961: 137) put the matter bluntly: "our principle of multiple chances is not a sentimental compromise with efficient procedures but a measure well calculated to reduce the tensions to which our system is subject."

With everyone, regardless of social origins, given not just one but many opportunities to succeed, the American educational system has been a powerful instrument for the dissemination of meritocratic ideology. For if opportunities for success were made available by the system to all who showed talent and industry, then it followed that failure must reflect a deficiency of individual ability and/or effort (Piven and Cloward, 1980). The message sent out by the schools—a message magnified by the apparent openness and fluidity of the system—was that those who "made it" did so because they had personal qualities that others lacked.

The widespread provision of opportunities for individual advancement through education, a number of prominent educators have argued, was crucial if the masses were to retain faith in the American dream of upward mobility. As the famous anthropologist W. Lloyd Warner, writing in collaboration with Robert J. Havighurst and Martin B. Loeb, put the matter in *Who Shall Be Educated?*:

> The educational system promotes social solidarity, or social cohesion, partly through its provisions for social mobility. A Society has social solidarity when its members believe that they have a substantial common ground of interest—that they gain more than they lose by

sticking together and maintaining intact their political and social institutions. A certain amount of social mobility seems necessary to maintain social cohesion in our class-structured society. The possibility of rising in the social scale in order to secure a larger share of the privileges of the society makes people willing to "stick together" and "play the game" as long as they believe it gives them a fair deal (Warner, *et al.*, 1944: 157).

"Educators," Warner and his colleagues suggested, "should try to adjust the educational system so that it produces a degree and kind of social mobility . . . which will keep the society healthy and alive" (Warner, *et al.*, 1944: 158).

Harvard president James Bryant Conant went even further than Warner in his vision of what a meritocratic system of education could accomplish; for him, the schools, by providing equality of opportunity and thereby avoiding the inheritance of position, would produce a "classless" society. In characteristic American fashion, Conant made clear the "classless society" which he had in mind was compatible with substantial inequality; indeed he explicitly described it in his 1940 article, "Education for a Classless Society," as characterized by a "differentiation of labors with a corresponding differentiation in types of education" (Conant, 1940: 594). One of the fundamental objectives of such a society would be to assiduously avoid the "continuous perpetuation from generation to generation of even small differences." For such intergenerational transmission of privileges "soon produces class consciousness" (Conant, 1940: 598).

A concomitant of these meritocratic ideas is an emphasis on individual mobility rather than group solidarity. Class consciousness has, to be sure, never been especially pronounced in the United States as compared to Europe. Many factors militated against the development of a sense of common fate among the American working classes, including the exceptional salience of racial and ethnic cleavages, the early extension of the franchise to all adult white males, and widespread geographic mobility (Karabel, 1979). Yet among those features of American life hindering the growth of class consciousness must be counted its education system. As it developed over the course of the last century, the American education system—with its rejection of early selection, its openness, its lack of segmentation, its sheer size, and its commitment to the provision of multiple chances to succeed– almost certainly reinforced the national emphasis on individual rather than collective advancement. An institutional embodiment of the national preoccupation with upward mobility, the educational system in its normal daily operations gave renewed vigor to the traditional American belief that, as James Conant (1940: 598) put it, "each generation may start life afresh and. . . hard work and ability. . . find their just rewards." By providing the "ladders of ascent" for which Carnegie (1886; 1889) and others had called a century ago *and* multiple opportunities to climb them, the school infused the American dream of individual advancement with new life.

The enormous emphasis on equality of opportunity institutionalized by the schools has contributed to the relative weakness of class consciousness in the United States in subtle but significant ways. As we noted earlier, the relative lack of segmentation in American education both mirrors and accentuates the apparent fluidity of class boundaries. Moreover, unsegmented schools provide fewer opportunities for the emergence of distinct class sub-cultures than segmented schools. Class-linked modes of dress, speech, and deportment (both academic and non-academic) may, of course, be reinforced by internal divisions within "comprehensive" high schools—a point documented by numerous studies (see, for example, Stinchcombe, 1964 and Macleod, 1987). Nonetheless, it is most unlikely that such schools are as favorable environments for the development of distinct class subcultures as segmented institutions which provide separate and unequal education for students of different class backgrounds. Finally, segmented schooling tends, as Fritz Ringer (1979: 258) has argued to "make social differences seem profound and indelible." By increasing social distance between dominant and subordinate groups, sharp educational segmentation fosters the development of class consciousness.

As one of the most distinctive components of the educational system, the two-year college also contributes to the process of working-class fragmentation, for its very openness to adults transmits the message that it is never too late for the individual to climb onto the ladder of educational mobility and improve his or her position by acquiring additional credentials. Individuals located at the bottom rungs of the class structure thus have an alternative to the strategy of trying to improve their situation through collective action; they can, through ability and effort, use the system of part-time education for adults to rise *from* their class rather than *with* it.

As in other societies, the educational system in the United States plays an important role in the reproduction of inequality from generation to generation. In spite of the apparent openness of the system, a wide body of empirical evidence shows stubborn gaps in educational attainment between students of different social backgrounds and a significant under-representation in the upper tiers of the system of minority students and students from working-class backgrounds (Coleman *et al.*, 1966; Jencks *et al.*, 1972; Karabel, 1972; Bowles and Gintis, 1976; Jencks *et al.*, 1979). The qualities that lead to success in the education system are no doubt partly personal, but they are also to a considerable degree linked to advantages of birth, and especially to family cultural resources (Bourdieu and Passeron, 1977; 1979; DiMaggio, 1982).

In addition to its role in transmitting inequalities, the American educational system may well contribute to the legitimation of these inequalities. The very structure of American schooling has the effect of obscuring the substantial level of transmission of privilege that actually does occur. And it probably does so more effectively than segmented systems on the European model, for the workings of these systems are socially transparent. It is difficult, for example, to miss the social-class implications of the traditional division of British secondary education into secondary modern, technical, grammar, and "public" schools; the class implications of such a system are relatively obvious. In comparison, the American educational system conveys a strikingly democratic appearance through the formal avoidance of sharp and final divisions, the continuous rather than segmented character of institutional prestige hierarchies, and its apparent openness. Overall, the contribution of the American educational system to the reproduction of inequality is relatively opaque. And as a general proposition, it seems likely that the more opaque the mode of reproducing inequalities, the more effective it is likely to be in legitimating these inequalities.

The American educational system and the vast network of community colleges that comprises one of its most distinguishing features may thus be seen as integral elements of a social order that emphasizes individual advancement over collective advancement, personal success over group solidarity, and equality of opportunity over equality of condition. In a way that was not entirely intended, it may also be very important for veiling some of the gaps between American ideals and American practice.

Some interesting comparative evidence exists that indirectly bears on this empirical argument. While the United States is, compared to other advanced capitalist countries, exceptionally generous in its allocation of resources to higher education, it is unusually stingy in its expenditures for social welfare (Heidenheimer, 1973; 1981). In a comparative study of patterns of public expenditure in 21 countries, Wilensky (1975: 7, 122) reports a negative correlation of -.41 between spending for social security and rates of enrollment in higher education; strikingly, the United States ranks twentieth in the former but first in the latter. While there are important exceptions (the Netherlands and Belgium, for example, exhibit high expenditures in both categories), for the majority of countries, one kind of expenditure seems to substitute, to some degree, for the other. Moreover, various studies of the income distribution of the advanced capitalist countries place the United States at or near the very bottom of the list in terms of income equality (Sawyer, 1976; Reich, 1983).

In the United States, the extraordinary level of national resources invested in higher education has helped keep the American dream of individual advancement alive under drastically changed circumstances. But this national preoccupation with inequality of opportunity may be the other side of a relative lack of concern with equality per se—a lack of concern that is a core feature of

American exceptionalism and continues to distinguish the United States from many other advanced societies, where powerful labor unions and working-class parties have been instrumental in the creation of genuine social "safety nets" below which vulnerable individuals may not fall.[2]

Notes

*The research reported here has been supported by grants from the National Institute of Education (NIE-G-77-0037), the National Science Foundations (SOC77-06658, SES-80-25542 and SES-83-19986) and the Institute of Industrial Relations at the University of California, Berkeley. This article is a fully collaborative effort by the two authors and is part of a larger study of American public two-year colleges, *The Diverted Dream: Community Colleges and the Promise of Educational Opportunity in America, 1900-1985*, forthcoming from Oxford University Press.

1. The starting point for most discussions of American "exceptionalism" is the 1906 work by the German sociologist, Werner Sombart, *Why Is There No Socialism in the United States?* Sombart's question has been a lifelong concern of Seymour Martin Lipset (1950; 1963; 1977; 1983) and has also been examined in recent years by Katznelson (1978; 1981), Karabel (1979), David (1986), Howe (1985), and Mink (1986).

2. From a comparative perspective, evidence from a variety of sources suggests that societies with high degrees of working-class organization (as measured, for example, by unionization and/or strength of electoral support for socialist, social democratic, and other left-of-center political parties) tend to have strong Welfare States (Hibbs, 1976, 1977; Cameron, 1978, 1982; Korpi, 1978, 1983, Esping-Anderson, 1984). Within this framework, the relative lack of class consciousness and organization among American workers may be viewed as casually connected to the weakness of the American Welfare State.

References

Ben-David, Joseph (1966). 'The Growth of the Professions and the Class System', in Reinhard Bendix and Seymour Martin Lipset (eds.), *Class, Status, and Power*, 2nd edition. New York: Free Press.

Ben-David, Joseph (1972). *Trends in American Higher Education*. Chicago: University of Chicago Press.

Bourdieu, Pierre and Passeron, Jean-Claude (1977). *Reproduction*. Beverly Hills, CA: Sage Publications.

Bourdieu, Pierre and Passern, Jean-Claude (1979). *The Inheritors: French Students and Their Culture*. Chicago: University of Chicago Press.

Bowles, Samual and Gintis, Herbert (1976). *Schooling in Capitalist America*. New York: Basic Books.

California Postsecondary Education Commission (1987). *Update of Community College Transfer Statistics: Fall 1986*. Sacramento: California Postsecondary Education Commission.

Cameron, David R. (1978). 'Expansion of the Public Economy: Comparative Analysis', *American Political Science Review*, 72(4): 1243–1261.

Cameron, David R. (1982). 'On the Limits of the Public Economy', *Annals of the American Academy of Political and Social Science*, 459(January): 46–62.

Carnegie, Andrew (1886). *Triumphant Democracy*. New York: Charles Scribner's Sons.

Carnegie, Andrew (1889). 'Wealth', *North American Review*, 148: 653–664.

Clark, Burton (1983). *The Higher Education System*. Berkeley: University of California Press.

Clark, Burton (ed.) (1985). *The School and the University*. Berkeley: University of California Press.

Coleman, James S. *et al.* (1966). *Equality of Educational Opportunity.* Washington, DC: U.S. Government Printing Office.

Conant, James Bryant (1940). 'Education for a Classless Society', *Atlantic Monthly,* 165(May): 593–602.

Cookson, Peter W. and Persell, Caroline H. (1985). *Preparing for Power.* New York: Basic Books.

Counts, George S. (1922). *The Selective Character of American Secondary Education.* Chicago: University of Chicago Press.

Davis, Mike (1986). *Prisoners of the American Dream: Politics and Economy and the History of the U.S. Working Class.* London: Verso Editions.

DiMaggio, Paul (1982). 'Cultural Capital and School Success: the Impact of Status Culture Participation on the Grades of United States High School Students', *American Sociological Review,* 47(2): 189–201.

Esping-Anderson, Gosta (1984). *The Social Democratic Road to Power.* Princeton: Princeton University Press.

Gardner, John (1961). *Excellence.* New York: Harper and Row.

Heidenheimer, Arnold J. (1973). 'The Politics of Public Education, Health and Welfare in the USA and Western Europe: How Growth and Reform Potentials Have Differed', *British Journal of Political Science,* 3: 315–340.

Heidenheimer, Arnold J. (1981). 'Education and Social Security Entitlements in Europe and America', in Peter Flora and Arnold J. Heidenheimer (eds.), *The Development of Welfare States in Europe and America.* New Brunswick, NJ: Transaction Books.

Hibbs, Douglas A. (1976). 'Industrial Conflict in Advanced Industrial Societies', *American Political Science Review,* 70(4): 1033–1058.

Hibbs, Douglas A. (1977). 'Political Parties and Macroeconomic Policy', *American Political Science Review,* 71(4): 1467–1487.

Howe, Irving (1985). *Socialism and America.* San Diego: Harcourt Brace Jovanovich.

Jencks, Christopher *et al.* (1972). *Inequality.* New York: Basic Books.

Jencks, Christopher *et al.* (1979). *Who Gets Ahead?* New York: Basic Books.

Karabel, Jerome (1972). 'Community Colleges and Social Stratification', *Harvard Educational Review,* 42(4): 521–562.

Karabel, Jerome (1979). 'The Failure of American Socialism Reconsidered', in Ralph Miliband and John Saville (eds.), *The Socialist Register.* London: Merlin Press.

Katznelson, Ira (1978). 'Considerations on Social Democracy in the United States', *Comparative Politics,* 11(1): 77–99.

Katznelson, Ira (1981). *City Trenches: Urban Politics and the Patterning of Class in the United States.* New York: Pantheon.

Korpi, Walter (1978). *The Working Class in Welfare Capitalism: Work, Unions, and Politics in Sweden.* London: Routledge & Kegan Paul.

Korpi, Walter (1983). *The Democratic Class Struggle.* London: Routledge & Kegan Paul.

Lipset, Seymour Martin (1950). *Agrarian Socialism: The Cooperative Commonwealth Federation in Saskatchewan.* Berkeley: University of California Press.

Lipset, Seymour Martin (1963). *The First New Nation.* New York: Basic Books.

Lipset, Seymour Martin (1977). 'Why No Socialism in the United States?', in S. Bialer and S. Sluzar (eds.). *Sources of Contemporary Radicalism.* Boulder, CO: Westview.

Lipset, Seymour Martin (1983). 'Radicalism of Reformism: The Sources of Working-class Politics', *American Political Science Review*, 77(1): 1–18.

Macleod, Jay (1987). *Ain't No Makin' It.* Boulder, CO: Westview.

Mink, Gwendolyn (1986). *Old Labor and New Immigrants in American Political Development: Union Party, and State, 1875–1920.* Ithaca, NY: Cornell University Press.

Piven, Frances Fox and Cloward, Richard A. (1980), 'Social Policy and the Formation of Political Consciousness', in Maurice Zeitlin, *Political Power and Social Theory.* Greenwich, CT: JAI Press.

Poignant, Raymond (1969). *Education and Development in Western Europe, the United States and the U.S.S.R.* New York: Teachers College Press, Columbia University.

Reich, Robert B. (1983). *The Next American Frontier.* New York: Times Books.

Ringer, Fritz K. (1979). *Education and Society in Modern Europe.* Bloomington: Indiana University Press.

Sawyer, Malcom C. (1976). *Income Distribution in OECD Countries.* Paris: Organisation for Economic Co-operation and Development.

Sombart, Werner (1976). *Why Is There No Socialism in the United States?* New York: M.E. Sharpe.

Stinchcombe, Arthur (1964). *Rebellion in a High School.* New York: Quadrangle.

Turner, Ralph H. (1966). 'Modes of Social Ascent Through Education', in Reinhard Bendix and Seymour Martin Lipset (eds.), *Class, Status and Power.* 2nd edition. New York: Free Press.

Warner, W. Lloyd *et al.* (1944). *Who Shall Be Educated?* New York: Harper & Brothers.

Weber, Max (1978). *Economy and Society.* Berkeley: University of California Press.

Wilensky, Harold L. (1975). *The Welfare State and Equality.* Berkeley: University of California Press.

Suggested Readings:
History, Philosophy, and Purpose

Cohen, A. M. (1985). *Contexts for Learning, the Major Sectors of American Higher Education: Essays.* Washington D.C.: The National Institute of Education in Cooperation with the American Association for Higher Education.

Cross, K. P. and Fideler, E. F. (1989). "Community College Missions: Priorities in the Mid-1980s." *Journal of Higher Education*, 60 (2), 209–216.

Frye, J. H. (1991). "Conflicting Voices in the Definition of the Junior/Community College." ERIC Document Reproduction Service No. ED 337228.

Gleazer, E. J. (1968). *This is the Community College.* Boston: Houghton Mifflin (Chapter 2).

Goodwin, G. L. (1973). "Skeletons in our Closet: The Disturbing Legacy of the Community-Junior College Ideology." *Community College Social Science Quarterly,* 3 (4), 24–7.

Krol, E. J. *The Origins and Evolution of the Two-Year College from Colonial Times to 1950.* Henry Ford Community College, Dearborn, Michigan. p. 41 ERIC Document Reproduction Service No. ED 339–429.

Levine, D. D. (1986). *The American College and The Culture of Aspiration: 1915–1940.* Ithaca: Cornell University Press.

Medsker, L. L. (1960). *The Junior College: Progress and Prospect.* New York: McGraw Hill (Chapter 8).

Nuefeldt, H. G. (1982). "The Community Junior College Movement: Conflicting Images and Historical Interpretations." *Educational Studies: A Journal in the Foundations of Education,* 13(2), 172–82.

Tillery, D. & Deegan, W. L. (1985). *Renewing the Community College, Priorities and Strategies for Effective Leadership.* San Francisco: Jossey-Bass.

ORGANIZATION, ADMINISTRATION, AND FINANCE

Administrative Organization: Chief Executive Officer

RICHARD C. RICHARDSON, CLYDE E. BLOCKER, AND LOUIS W. BENDER

When we speak of the structure of administration in this chapter, we distinguish a part of the institution from the whole. The bureaucratic model previously discussed makes the assumption that everyone in the institution can be fitted into some position within the administrative structure. The implications of this assumption, basically divergent from our own, are evident in the problems of authority and status which consequently appear.

Administrative structure is the most visible aspect of an organization. This is true for a number of reasons. First, the administrative building represents the first contact for most outsiders with the total institution. Second, administration is a coordinating and an implementing activity; as a result, administration becomes a focus through which both internal and external constituencies interact. Third, it is standard practice to attempt to convey the responsibilities of a specific office through a distinctive title. For this reason, an institution will have only one Director of Financial Aid although it may have twenty instructors of English. Both the distinctive title and position in the organizational chart will probably convey that the former is more important than the latter, although this distinction may not be reflected in a salary differential.

The highly organized nature of the administrative structure has contributed to the centralization of power in the hands of administrators. Faculty members, if organized at all, are likely to have a much less tightly defined structure, and the officers within this structure exercise their functions as a secondary aspect of their primary role, the providing of professional services. The same statement can be made for students. While they too have a structure of sorts, it is not well suited to administrative activity. At best, it provides a forum through which their concerns may be formulated and conveyed to other constituent groups.

Because of the differences of organizational characteristics, we will discuss faculty and student structure in Chapter 9 as an aspect of the governance process. But while it is true that faculty structure occurs primarily as a part of the process of governance, faculty members have correctly perceived the power that can be wielded when they are sensitive to the hierarchical control of resources. Consequently, when faculty members organize for collective bargaining, they are likely to devise a structure which parallels the administrative structure in form. There will be an attempt to provide released time to officeholders in the organization, and the active officeholders will seek increasingly to influence and participate in the administration of the institution. The objective of this activity is to provide faculty with greater authority by interposing a secondary bureaucracy (that of the faculty organization) between the faculty members and the primary bureaucracy represented by the administrative structure.

The participative model of governance, which strives to avoid this kind of "aberrant" bureaucratic outgrowth, affects more strongly the overall governance structure of the institutions than it does the administrative structure alone. There are, in the final analysis, certain standards of efficiency demanded by administrative operation which can be achieved most effectively through the use of traditional bureaucratic techniques of organization. Therefore, the administrative structure, part of the participative model, when viewed by itself from the vantage point of the organizational chart, will appear similar to the administrative structure of the traditional model.

Within the structure of administration, it is important that the principles previously identified in Chapter 5 govern relationships among role incumbents. If effective interaction, substantial involvement in decision making, the use of supportive relationships, and management by objectives are not characteristic of relationships within the administrative structure, then we can be assured by our knowledge of the requirement for consistency within a system that such principles will not appear in relationships between the administrative structure and the faculty or students.

We may say, then, that in the institution of higher education there exists a unique constellation of factors which does not correspond to most other types of organization. We have three distinct internal constituencies each with its own structure but interrelated both through functional requirements and through governance structure. While students may be regarded to some extent as clients, or consumers, they also have a relationship different from that characteristic of other social institutions. They are not patients, nor are they inmates. Neither do they consume a product. While faculty members are employees, they are also practitioners of a profession which demands by its nature a relationship to the organization different from that required in the typical business or production enterprise.

The failure of the primary groups involved in college governance (trustees, administrators, faculty, and students) to recognize these differences, while attempting to utilize similarities, has led them to draw certain conclusions about the relationships of faculty and students to the administrative structure which are no longer valid. While we will use the traditional organizational chart as the device for examining the structure of administration, we wish to emphasize our premise that faculty and students, usually certified parts of the structure, are *not* included in the structure as we conceive it. In reference to the circular model previously described, we are dealing exclusively with the sphere of influence labeled administration (7:176–80).

Organizational Graphics

The organizational chart is the most common representation of the structure of our institutions of higher education. Such charts are useful because they provide a portrayal of the positions and functions within an institution as well as the relationship that each position has to others. Organizational charts assist staff members in defining their relationships to the institution as a whole and to one another. At the same time, it is important to understand the limitations of such charts as true indicators of the relationships within a complex organization.

Organizational charts define relationships between positions. In the past, it has been assumed that they also designated status and authority. We have seen from the analysis presented in Chapter 5 that it is no longer safe to make assumptions about authority and status on the basis of the traditional bureaucratic structure. Organized groups of faculty or students may succeed in interposing a secondary bureaucracy between themselves and the primary bureaucracy through use of power politics or collective bargaining techniques. In extreme circumstances, they may through violence succeed temporarily in turning the pyramid upside down. While some may argue that the second example does not truly reflect a loss of status or authority since civil authority exists and can be used to restore the original arrangement, the writers would contend that no institutional administration has survived such a confrontation without incurring losses of personnel from among its ranks.

The organizational chart illustrates the prescribed channels through which the formal media of communication theoretically flow. Presumably, control of the organizational structure implies control over the communication channels. At the same time, it is well known that informal procedures of communication develop and, under certain conditions, act to subvert the prescribed channels. Unless the official channels serve the purposes of all role incumbents satisfactorily, they may easily fall into disuse or, worse, be subject to calculated distortion (13: 8).

The strength of the organizational chart as a representation of administrative structure lies in its ability to convey a concept of the ways in which the institution has chosen to specialize in order to accomplish its objectives. The best organizational structure is one which is responsive to the needs of those who belong to the institution while at the same time promoting the objectives for which the institution exists. Such a structure presumes knowledge of motivational factors related to the satisfaction of role incumbents as well as the careful identification of institutional objectives and planning to relate such objectives to human capabilities.

It is safe to say that few organizational structures actually reflect the conditions identified above. In the first place, one of the most common criticisms leveled at educators is their failure to define objectives clearly. The current emphasis on accountability reflects, in part, a serious effort to force more considered planning with respect to objectives. As previously noted in Chapter 4, most existing organizations pay little heed to the needs of those who are perceived as occupying the lower levels of the hierarchy.

The truth of the matter is that the structures of many established institutions represent not so much the consequences of considered planning as the results of haphazard growth. Positions are added in short-sighted response to problem areas and to the personalities and competencies already integrated into the structure. The organizational chart of an established college not uncommonly reflects the random addition of positions with unusual and sometimes confusing lines of communications in clouded, overlapping areas of responsibility. In new institutions, the structure is likely to reflect similar problems combined with the lack of experienced personnel who keep the machinery operating.

A major weakness of the organizational chart and the structure it reflects is the two-dimensional nature of the representation. An organizational chart conveys only horizontal and lateral relationships. It cannot convey the quality of depth which is characteristic of relationships involving people. Neither can it demonstrate the changes that occur over time. If an organizational chart met all of the conditions previously enumerated and at the same time represented a perfect reproduction of the actual structure, it would be completely accurate only for a brief moment. Almost immediately, the dynamic quality of organizational life would act to change the structure. The chart would become increasingly irrelevant to the reality of organizational life over an extended period of time.

While it is true that all organizational charts are at best distorted representations of institutional interaction, they are nonetheless useful in the study of administrative structure. A comparison of the organizational chart of a structure based upon bureaucratic premises with one influenced by the concepts of participational structure reveals significant differences in such areas as the number of hierarchical levels, span of control, and arrangements for specialization.

Comparison of Bureaucratic and Participational Models

Figure 6.1 represents one method of implementing specialization for a bureaucratic model which has previously been suggested as the most common organizational pattern among two-year colleges. The structure emphasizes unity of command. Each individual reports to only one other

Figure 6.1: Specialization within the Administrative Structure: A Bureautcratic Model

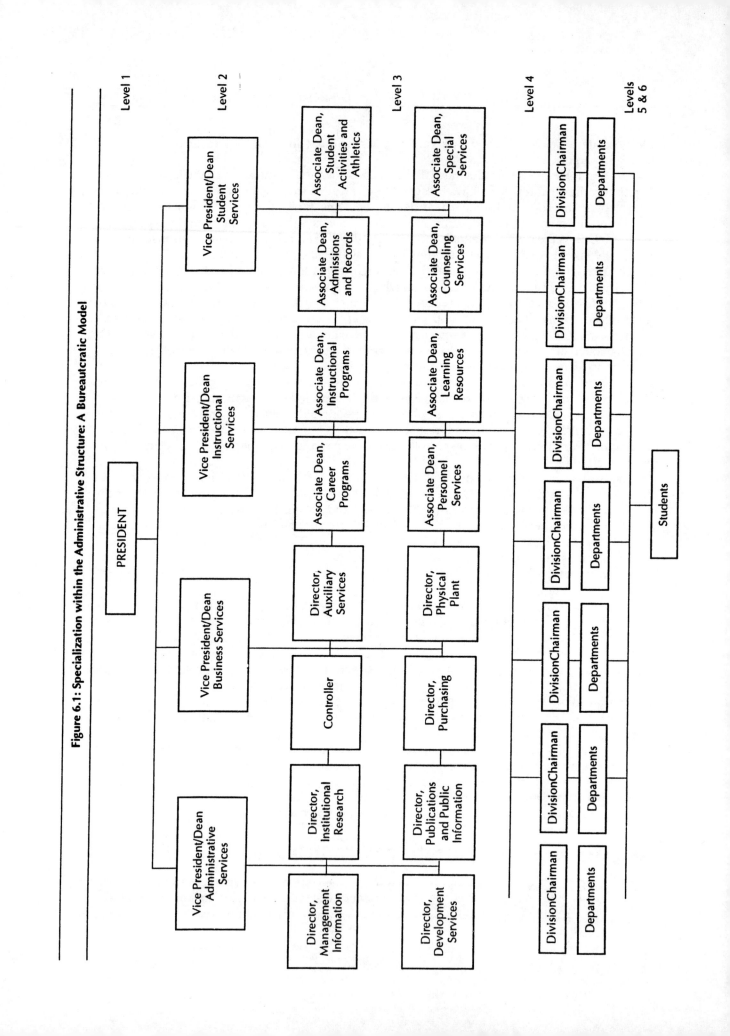

individual within the chain of command. The organization is relatively inflexible since specialization is carefully controlled in both the horizontal and vertical dimensions to avoid overlap wherever possible. Emphasis upon limiting the span of control, as well as upon unity of command, has resulted in six somewhat distinct levels within the organization. While level three is shown in the figure as a staff function and theoretically should not increase the height of the organization, in many organizations this level would represent a line function. In others, the insertion of an executive vice-president could further increase vertical stratification.

The primary focus of this type of organization stresses coordination, since the various hierarchical levels impede communication and consequently limit effectiveness in solving problems related to the initiation of change. Within such an organization, one assumes that faculty and students have their respective positions at the lower levels of the hierarchy. In this regard, we would argue that while Stroup may be right concerning bureaucratic pervasiveness in higher education, we cannot agree that his model is the most desirable alternative. It will be our purpose in the pages which follow to suggest a different approach—the participational model (12:41).

Figure 6.2 provides one arrangement for distributing administrative responsibilities for a participational model. Three levels of responsibilities are defined with four areas of specialization at the second level. The participational model is dynamic and flexible. Each area of specialization is interdependent with all other areas, both vertically and horizontally. Specialization may repeat itself at each level with a somewhat different emphasis since overlapping responsibilities are considered natural and desirable. The multiple channels of communication combined with an attempt to keep hierarchical levels to a minimum encourage two-way communication and problem solving in the organization.

Administrative structure recognizes the existence of faculty and student constituencies which, while related to the structure, are not regarded as a part of it in any hierarchical sense. This type of organization does not manage change through control over the decision-making process, as suggested by Roueche, Baker, and Brownell (8:25–26). Neither is accountability considered primarily or exclusively an administrative responsibility. The principle of unity of command is deliberately violated to improve communication and to encourage a unified approach to institutional objectives by all constituencies.

It has been demonstrated previously that two-dimensional graphics cannot adequately portray the complexity of relationships within an organization. This statement is certainly true with respect to this representation of the participational model. Student Personnel Services has the same need for interaction with Business Services as does Instructional Services. The lines of communication and interaction shown are not intended to convey the implication that these are the only relationships that exist. In reality, each area of specialization must interact and communicate effectively both laterally and between levels with every other area of specialization. It is also important that such interaction and influence flow in both directions since according to our theory, one level or area of specialization within the organization will be able to exercise influence over other levels or areas only to the extent that there exists a willingness to have its own behaviour influenced in turn.

There are no irrefutable arguments that can be presented for four second-level areas as opposed to three or five. In part, the size of an institution as well as its objectives may determine these features of the organization. By the same token, it can be argued that functions assigned to one area of specialization could just as easily be transferred to another. Again, each institution must make its own decisions in these matters based upon an examination of priorities and personnel. The arrangement suggested does provide a comprehensive outline of administrative responsibilities while at the same time demonstrating one logical organization of these responsibilities.

Figure 6.2
Specialization Within the Administrative Structure: A Participative Model

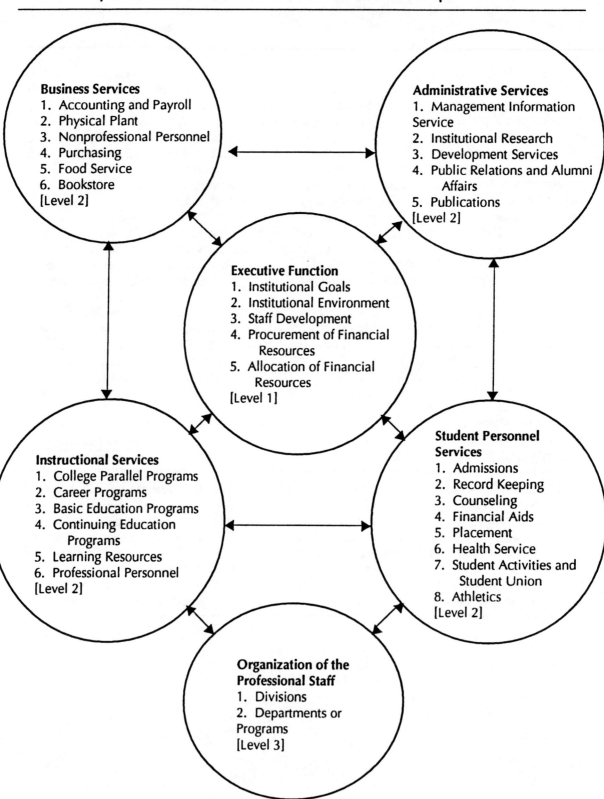

Business Services
1. Accounting and Payroll
2. Physical Plant
3. Nonprofessional Personnel
4. Purchasing
5. Food Service
6. Bookstore
[Level 2]

Administrative Services
1. Management Information Service
2. Institutional Research
3. Development Services
4. Public Relations and Alumni Affairs
5. Publications
[Level 2]

Executive Function
1. Institutional Goals
2. Institutional Environment
3. Staff Development
4. Procurement of Financial Resources
5. Allocation of Financial Resources
[Level 1]

Instructional Services
1. College Parallel Programs
2. Career Programs
3. Basic Education Programs
4. Continuing Education Programs
5. Learning Resources
6. Professional Personnel
[Level 2]

Student Personnel Services
1. Admissions
2. Record Keeping
3. Counseling
4. Financial Aids
5. Placement
6. Health Service
7. Student Activities and Student Union
8. Athletics
[Level 2]

Organization of the Professional Staff
1. Divisions
2. Departments or Programs
[Level 3]

Multi-Institution Districts

There is an unmistakable trend for urban districts to develop more than a single campus. A number of states have chosen to establish two-year colleges as units of a single state system. Even some suburban or rural colleges have added a second campus in preference to developing residence halls when confronted with long distances or geographic barriers. The development of such systems has important implications for our discussion.

Regardless of the degree of decentralization, there are significant differences between a free standing institution and one that is a part of a system. There is little possibility that the degree of autonomy afforded can ever approach the level that is desired by the constituents of a campus. Even in districts that have sought to provide maximum autonomy to campus units by calling them colleges and by providing the chief executive with the title of president, there is still a constant tension accompanied by the ever-present realization that the needs and priorities of the system take priority over the aspirations of the individual units.

Kintzer and his colleagues have discussed in some detail different systems for organizing multi-institutional districts (4). Without becoming involved in the merits of these systems, several points relevant to our analysis can be made. The concepts we will suggest apply to a system whether that system includes a single college or twenty. Their applicability to a unit of multi-institutional system is dependent upon interrelationships between the central administration and units of the system. It would probably not be feasible to develop a participational model for a campus if the system was highly bureaucratic. Since systems depend upon internal consistency for cohesiveness and integrity, all units of a system must have similar forms of interaction at least at points where interfaces occur. Any unit that differs significantly from the norm will create tensions. The impact of these tensions insofar as changing central administration is concerned will depend upon the number of units within the system, their relative size, and the ability of the system as a whole to tolerate diversity and to accommodate change.

A multi-institutional district, like any organization, is more than the sum of the interactions which occur among the individual units and between the units and the central office. In talking about structure, we tend to focus upon relationships between administrators in the central office and those on the individual campuses. While we recognize that the administrators on the various campuses will interact with each other and with central administration, there is far less recognition of the implications of interactions between faculty and student groups among the various campuses and the tendency for such groups to organize themselves in order to exert direct influence on central administration in addition to the indirect influence they exert through their respective campus administrators.

We may say that all of the problems that can be attributed to the bureaucratic structure as an organizational form for the individual college are raised to the nth power in a multi-institutional district with n representing the number of campuses. If the multi-institutional district is to remain responsive to the needs of each locality it serves, the concepts of the participative model assume increased importance. There must be multiple channels through which two-way communication occurs. Competition between units must take place within a cooperative and mutually sustaining frame of reference. Bureaucratic authority must be replaced by the principles of shared authority, and governance patterns must be focused upon the creative resolution of problems and not upon unnecessary coordination.

The highly publicized Newman Report carried the following statement which is closely related to our concern: "The junior college scenario is thus one of transformation of community institutions into amorphous, bland, increasingly large, increasingly state-dominated, two year institutions which serve a number of interests other than that of their own students" (6:74). It is in the nature of all large bureaucratic organizations to become increasingly remote from the needs of their constituencies while at the same time remaining remarkably impervious to change. If the multi-institutional district is to escape this fate, alternatives which go beyond the centralization-decentralization issue will need to be carefully explored. In this process, the participational model has much to recommend it as a starting point.

We have discussed the general nature of the structure of administration and compared two polar approaches to the definition of such structure. We have also suggested that the need for a participational model may be even greater in the multi-institutional district than for a single college. Let us now consider the responsibilities of the chief executive officer.

The Executive Function

The functions of the chief executive officer have been identified by Simon as raising money, balancing the budget, participating in the establishment of institutional goals, working with faculty to create an environment that encourages learning, and recruiting, and maintaining a high quality of faculty. Simon also draws a parallel between the responsibilities of the college president and the top executives in other types of concerns, giving particularly strong attention to the concept of accountability (10: 68–78).

The president's function has had many interpretations, most of which are obsolete. As sometimes sentimental portrayals of what a chief executive officer's life has been in the past, they have value. As a guide for future behavior, they leave much to be desired (11: 9).

If we accept the premise that there is a need for role redefinition, it becomes immediately apparent that the president of the future will need to possess a far greater expertise in managerial competencies and at the same time exercise such competencies in a manner that will make his position far less central to institutional functioning than has been true. Galbraith makes the point that leaders in industry have become far less visible and far less central to many institutional operations than was the case with their predecessors (2:106). Educational institutions, particularly large public ones, in which the bulk of our faculty and students are located, are caught up in a growth process which must parallel in many respects the experience of industry. Presidents will become less visible, less central to the functioning of their institutions; however, this will not necessarily lead to a zero-sum process whereby the chief executive will lose authority and influence equal to that gained by others within the institution. Rather, the president may need to exercise his influence in different causes and in more complex ways.

A central responsibility of the president which relates to everything else he undertakes is the establishment of an institutional environment conducive to learning. The president does not establish such an environment through the force of his own personality so much as he makes possible its development through the ways in which he works with his staff officers and other constituencies of the institution. A president who sets an example by insisting upon clear communication in all directions and who refuses to countenance the use of arbitrary sanctions to enforce administrative preeminence is making a significant contribution to developing one type of institutional environment (1:11).

Equally important is the manner in which he opens access to participation for all who will be affected in establishing goals and formulating policies. To stimulate effective participation, the president must support a policy of open access to information about the institution. He must insist that the roles of administrators be clearly defined and interpreted to all who are affected by their actions. The institution must have a decision-making process which is highly visible, operated without secrecy and susceptible to interaction and influence by all segments of the college community. The stance taken by the chief executive officer on such issues will establish prevailing practice for the entire institution. The credibility of the procedures established by the president for resolving conflict will govern the extent to which they are used by faculty and students. If the president resorts to the use of power or displays arbitrary judgment in his relationships with the faculty, he can expect that the faculty will behave similarly in their relationship with students and administration.

There is the view that the new president of a previously established institution may provoke changes in the institution to move toward greater accountability merely by encouraging a conservative faculty to take advantage of a less authoritarian atmosphere. Failing success through this method, he may use the lever of expressed student concern on the fulcrum of his own leadership to promote student participation in the decision-making process (1: 29).

The president is no longer the supreme arbiter or the power figure in institutional politics. He is a mediator who has a major responsibility, the reconciliation of opposing interests while at the same time preserving institutional goals and directions. Not only must he be able to provide a credible structure through which conflict can be resolved on acceptable terms, but he must also be prepared to recognize when appeal must be made to an external constituency because the problem cannot be resolved internally. It is important that the president avoid advocacy of a particular position. As a mediator, it is his responsibility to seek consensus rather than lock himself into an adversary role. This is not to say that a president should avoid taking positions or that he simply floats on the currents of institutional opinion. It is rather to say that the president must be able to see the advantages and disadvantages of both sides of a position and that he gives clear recognition to the legitimacy of opposing points of view.

The recommended role of a president in the collective bargaining process is illuminating in this respect. Most authorities advise the president to remain strictly aloof from this process, delegating responsibility for administrative participation to a staff officer. There are two very good reasons for this recommendation. First, the president, who may be the person to whom a final appeal for judgment is directed, must not have been previously involved in the bargaining in a way that would void his role as arbitrator. Equally important, however, is a second reason. When the collective bargaining process has been completed, there must be someone within the institution with sufficient moral capital to bring adversaries back into cooperative working relationships and to heal the wounds inflicted further during the adversary process. The president who has been aware of the problems but not closely identified with either of the protagonists occupies such a position.

Even in the absence of collective bargaining the chief executive must recognize the dangers inherent in placing the weight of his office prematurely on one side of an issue. There are very few differences of opinion that develop within a college where institutional objectives are so critically involved that there is no room for compromise. Of course, it is essential that the president recognize such issues but it is equally important that there be firm recognition of his own fallibility. Arrangements must exist to appeal an issue beyond the office of the president when such an issue cannot be appropriately resolved within the institution. In this regard, it is pertinent to make reference to a statement advanced a number of years ago by John Millett (5:241). It was his thesis, and it is ours, that a president can no more operate without student and faculty support than he can operate without board support.

If the president properly recognizes those issues where resolution requires appeal to an external source of reference, it will be no longer necessary to consider him infallible in his judgments. After providing for appropriate review of decisions that create intense institutional antipathies, it becomes possible for students and faculty to have confidence in the processes established by a president without agreeing that he should have the final word on all issues. It is apparent that when appeals are made to an external reference group such as the board, we can expect that under normal circumstances the president's view will prevail. By the same token, if a board is required to deal with too many routine controversies, they must inevitably come to question the effectiveness of their chief executive. In essence, the appeal process becomes the legitimizing machinery through which pressures are brought to bear on all internal constituencies to encourage them to solve their own problems through a mutual give-and-take rather than through power tactics.

The president who can successfully implement the mediating role is in a strong position to reconcile the opposing interests which are inevitably generated by the process of specialization. One of the weaknesses of specialists is that they experience great difficulty in seeing the needs of their area of expertise in relation to the needs of the total institution. The president as generalist must take the broad view and, in addition, must hold in perspective both short- and long-range objectives. Again, the extent to which constituencies are involved in the process of establishing both short- and long-range goals will have a significant impact upon the president's success when working in such areas as resource allocation, without creating unnecessary hostility in the process.

The establishment of goals is a particularly challenging aspect of the president's role. Not infrequently, a president may be selected because he has strong ideas which are consistent with those held by the board of trustees. Many presidents inevitably come to grief in attempting to implement these ideas, for they fail to understand the interdependencies involved in the goal-setting process. Hughes has pointed out:

> The organizational system bears little relationship in fact to the conventional organization chart, which may not represent realistically the way to the achievement of the accompanying goals. This is because organizational units are interactive; that is, people in them interact with each other in ways that are not defined and described by formal "boxes" and lines of authority. Research shows that far more time is spent in lateral than in vertical relationships. In other words, we get our work done not so much through the management principles of authority, responsibility, and accountability, as through negotiations with people in our same level (3:92–93).

If the president wishes to influence a faculty, he must in turn be prepared to be influenced by them. His top priority should be sufficiently different from the faculty's to allow each to support the other in hopes of reciprocation. There are instances, however, when differences are too great and compromise becomes the only answer. While compromises by their very nature create dissatisfaction, it is important for the president to recognize the dangers to the achievement of future goals if the dissatisfaction is not felt rather evenly by all who are involved. A president who cannot compromise effectively is unlikely to endure very long in today's campus conditions. More important, he will not effect lasting change.

The president must be accessible to the various constituencies he serves on a more or less equal basis. This is far more complex than it may seem. The announcement of an open-door policy does not necessarily guarantee accessibility. The president needs to plan his schedule and his activities so that he is in contact with a variety of students and faculty under conditions less formal than an office visit. While it is desirable that he be accessible, care must be exercised to ensure that such accessibility does not undermine staff functioning by short-circuiting the decision-making process. The president is the most visible element in the governance of the institution, and his positive influence in informal situations can do much to promote the appropriate learning environment, while at the same time providing him with important informational inputs that are different from those prescribed in the organizational chart.

Many writers have specified the multitude of tasks which may be carried out by the president. Studies have been done showing the allocation of a chief executive's time spent in such areas as budgeting, fund raising, building construction, and public relations. Such job descriptions and studies have very limited usefulness for the practicing administrator. The emphasis upon particular areas and the amount of time devoted to each are bound to vary with the size of the institution, its direction at a given point in time, the personality and competencies of the president and of other members of his staff, the presence or absence of crises and a host of factors which combine to make each position different in important respects from all other positions. The one thing that the president cannot afford to forget is that he is providing leadership to an organization that involves shifting and complex patterns of human relationships. He must pay attention, simultaneously, to structures and processes, and he must be capable of blending the two so as to encourage successive adaptations to an ever evolving series of challenges. He is not in the business of providing answers, but rather responsible for providing credible leadership in seeking answers, conscious always that the answers will turn out to be parts of new questions.

While the chief executive officer no longer exercises the authority to make final decisions in matters involving substantial differences of opinion, his central position in the communication network contributes to the significant influence of the office in conflict resolution. The role of the chief executive is also central to relationships with external constituencies. To a considerable degree, the effectiveness of the president in his relationships with the board of trustees is both a measure and a consequence of his impact upon other external constituencies. The president cannot escape the close identification of his office with the successes and failures experienced by the institution as a whole.

In the eyes of the local community, the accessibility of the chief executive officer and his interest in community affairs establishes the tone for the entire institution. His comments upon an issue will be regarded by external constituencies as the official position of the institution. This places a major responsibility upon the executive officer to reconcile through his decisions and his statements the emerging norms of a new generation with the prevailing norms of the establishment. The continuing effectiveness of any institution requires that it operate or a least be perceived as operating within the narrow boundaries between established and developing value patterns. While the range of responses that will receive the acceptance of both internal and external constituencies is broader in some areas than others, the limits always exist and a failure by the chief executive to observe them invariably diminishes his moral capital with one group or the other.

Leadership obviously involves departure from accepted norms when the importance of an issue justifies the conflict involved. It is important in the exercise of leadership that the president refrain from taking positions which consistently diminish his credibility with a single constituency, for a failure to maintain a reputation for impartiality is the first step in the loss of confidence, a process which if consummated destroys the ability of the president to continue to function effectively. If, for example, the chief executive lends his support to the faculty in discussions involving salary increases, he may suffer some loss of moral capital with taxpayers. The situation can be balanced by equal insistence upon maintaining productivity and upon accountability.

It should be apparent that the chief executive officer cannot afford to indulge himself in private biases. His view must weigh the concerns of special interest groups in terms of the well-being of the institution as a totality. If he is consistently fair in dealing with both internal and external constituencies, and if his judgment proves sound in predicting the consequences of actions that he recommends, he will retain the respect of all the groups with which he must contend and with that respect the ability to effect compromises which not only resolve conflict but, in addition, offer qualitative responses to the challenges of mission implementation.

The board of trustees represents a microcosm of the publics to which the institution must be interpreted and with which effective interaction must occur. Substantial board reaction against a specific recommendation should alert the president to the probability that similar reactions can be expected from the community. The temptation to assume a favorable vote from the board that resolves the issue should be rejected in favor of careful analysis of the segments of the community that will be affected, as well as ways in which the issue can be interpreted to avoid permanent alienation. In some instances, chief executive officers would be well advised to avoid implementing a plan which has the potential for serious disruption of relationships with external constituencies even if board support can be obtained. The board looks to the president for guidance in foreseeing the probable consequences of specific courses of action in terms of the attitudes of community groups. The board does not have to be misled very often before losing confidence in the president's judgment in this area. Since trustees are seldom representative of the individuals their institutions serve, the overly conservative board may simply be a board that is relying exclusively on its own judgment of probable community reaction because of a lack of confidence in the judgment of the chief executive.

The degree of difficulty experienced by the chief executive officer in influencing a particular constituency will bear a direct relationship to the geographic and political distance between that constituency and the institution. It is this fact that makes it more difficult for institutions operated as parts of state systems or as campuses of a state university to influence and respond to local constituencies. By the same token it is easier for them to influence state and national forces since the organization and magnitude of such systems makes them more visible and accessible at these levels. For this reason it is important for state and university systems to give special attention to procedures for interacting with the local community. In a like manner, institutions operating under the aegis of local control must devise effective coalitions with suitable leadership in order for their views to receive significant consideration at state and national levels.

It is important in terminating our discussion of the chief executive officer to emphasize his role with respect to evaluation and accountability. In its broadest sense, accountability involves nothing more than the assurance that objectives previously defined are being achieved at a satisfactory level within the range of resources available. "Within the range of resources available" implies that these objectives are achieved with participation of all who are linked to them (not in spite of the participation of some, as is often the case). Thus, the dimension of accountability flows in many directions; administrators are accountable to faculty and vice versa. And the president must insist upon evaluation of everything that is done since accountability as a concept is meaningless in the absence of evaluative information.

Summary

Administration organization is highly specialized in order to perform a variety of complex functions with a maximum degree of efficiency. It is highly visible because the prescribed lines of communication within an institution are defined by administrative organization. In the past we have made certain assumptions concerning the inclusiveness and authority dimensions of the administrative organization which no longer seem viable. The assumption that students and faculty are a part of the administrative organization does not seem consistent with the realities of emerging institutional relationships. This is particularly true when we consider the low level positions traditionally assigned to students and faculty by the organizational chart. Faculty and students have successfully challenged the assumptions concerning administrative authority in a number of significant areas. It is well recognized that they have long ignored prescribed channels of communication when it was perceived as being their interests to do so.

When we postulate the participational model as logical successor to the bureaucratic model, it is important to recognize that this alternative changes relationships for faculty and students far more than it does for administrators. Within the administrative structure, the bureaucratic model of organization continues to be viable because it is efficient. At the same time, certain modifications must be made with respect to the assumptions that govern administrative functioning to articulate the structure of administration with internal constituencies. Assumptions concerning the authority exercised by the administrative structure, the concepts of span of control and unity of command must all be reexamined and altered if the bureaucratic structure is to remain functional in a participational setting.

The chief executive officer has the responsibility for controlling the interface which occurs between internal and external constituencies. In implementing this role he must recognize the existence of overlapping areas where prevailing and emerging norms can be reconciled. While leadership may involve departure from the range of decisions that may be within the zone of acceptance for a particular constituency, the chief executive may retain the confidence of necessary groups through limiting the frequency of such decisions and through ensuring the over time the interests of one constituency are balanced against the interest of others.

While the board of trustees represents a microcosm of the community served, interpreting a course of action in such a way that it receives majority endorsement of the board is not the same as reconciling the concerns of community groups reflected by board reactions. The ability of the chief executive to read community attitudes and to avoid compromising board credibility through too frequent controversial recommendations will be a critical determinant in the willingness of board members to initiate new programs. Finally, the effectiveness of the executive officer depends upon his ability to distribute dissatisfaction evenly to the end that all constituencies, both internal and external, retain confidence in his impartiality and judgment.

Notes

1. Cohen, Arthur M. and John E. Roueche, *Institutional Administrator or Educational Leader? The Junior College President*. Washington, D. C.: American Association of Junior Colleges, 1969.

2. Galbraith, John K., *The New Industrial State*. Boston: Houghton Mifflin, 1967.

3. Hughes, Charles L., *Goal Setting: Key to Individual and Organizational Effectiveness*. New York: American Management Association, 1965.

4. Kintzer, Frederick C., Arthur M. Jensen, and John S. Hansen, *The Multi-Institutional Junior College District*. Washington, D.C.: American Association of Junior Colleges, 1969.

5. Millett, John D., *The Academic Community*. New York: McGraw-Hill, Inc., 1960.

6. *Report of Higher Education*. Washington, D.C.: USOE, 1971.

7. Romine, Stephen, "Alternatives to Politicizing Higher Education," *Educational Record*, 52:176–180 (Spring 1971).

8. Roueche, John A., George Baker, and Richard Brownell, *Accountability and the Community College*. Washington, D. C.: American Association of Junior Colleges, 1971.

9. Sammartino, Peter, *The President of a Small College*. Rutherford, N.J.: Fairleigh Dickinson College Press, 1954.

10. Simon, Herbert A., "The Job of a College President," *Educational Record*, 48:68–78 (Winter 1967).

11. Stoke, Harold W., *The American College President*. New York: Harper & Row, 1959.

12. Stroup, Herbert, *Bureaucracy in Higher Education*. New York: Free Press, 1966.

13. Thompson, James D., *Organizations in Action*. New York: McGraw-Hill, 1967.

A Quarter Century of Change in State-Level Coordinating Structures for Community Colleges

TERRENCE A. TOLLEFSON AND BEN E. FOUNTAIN

In the past quarter of a century, community colleges have emerged from the shadow of elementary and secondary education. This is illustrated by examining the changes in state-level community college coordinating agencies as reported in two studies in 1963 and 1989.

A 1963 study by S. V. Martorana found that there were public junior colleges in 38 states (in Blocker, Plummer and Richardson, 1965). In 26 of those, community colleges were coordinated by state agencies for elementary and secondary education. Thirteen states coordinated two-year public post-secondary institutions by means of state boards of higher education or state university boards, whereas only six states had specific state boards or commissions for public junior colleges. The total of the preceding numbers exceeds 38, because some states employed two coordinating agencies.

The 1989 study by Fountain and Tollefson, *Community Colleges in the United States: Forty-Nine State Systems,* published by AACJC's Community College Press, noted that 49 states had public two-year community college systems. This compares with 38 states in 1963. The book draws primarily upon information obtained from state directors of community colleges. The September 12, 1989, issue of AACJC's *Community, Technical, and Junior College Times* records several differences from the 1989 book. This article reflects information contained in the *Times,* where the two sources differ. Today only six states still coordinate public community colleges through state boards of education, compared to 26 states in 1963. These states include Idaho, Iowa, Kansas, Michigan, Oregon, and Pennsylvania (Reinhard, Wisniewski, and Jiminez, September 12, 1989).

Seven states utilize state boards or commissions for higher education to coordinate community colleges, compared to 12 states in 1963. Those seven states are Arkansas, Missouri, Nebraska, New Jersey, New Mexico, North Dakota, and Texas.

Thirteen states were found by the 1989 study to coordinate community colleges through university boards of regents, compared to five states in 1963. Those states are Alaska, Georgia, Hawaii, Kentucky, Louisiana, Massachusetts, Montana, Nevada, New York, Ohio, Oklahoma, South Dakota (with only one "public" tribal community college), Tennessee, and Utah.

Perhaps the most interesting finding in the 1989 study was that the modal group of 22 remaining states had established separate state boards or commissions for community colleges or vocational-technical institutions. The comparison figure in 1963 was six states. States with state boards or commissions for community colleges found in 1989 were Arizona, California, Delaware, Florida, Illinois, Maryland, Minnesota, Mississippi, North Carolina, Rhode Island, South Carolina,

105

Virginia, Washington, Wisconsin, and Wyoming. West Virginia is included in this group based on the *Times'* report that the West Virginia Board of Regents was abolished in July of 1989 and replaced with two boards—one for the university and one for community colleges and four-year state colleges. Fountain and Tollesfon reported a similar structure in 1989 in New Hampshire.

The foregoing comparisons are analogous to looking at snapshot photographs of two different periods in the evolution of the junior and community college movement in America. They do not convey the tremendous struggles in most states that have been overcome to attain the present state systems. Those struggles are still going on in some states.

What of the future? Is it possible to extrapolate the existing trend line and predict with confidence what additional changes will be made in the future? We do not believe so. Because of its brevity, this report necessarily oversimplifies complex situations in many states in both the past and the present. Our comparisons did not show, for example, that both Massachusetts and Ohio once had separate state boards for community colleges and have since shifted the responsibility for coordinating community colleges to state boards of regents, or that two-year branch campuses of state universities are common in such states as New Mexico, Ohio, Pennsylvania, and Wisconsin (Reinhard, Wisniewski and Jiminez, September 12, 1989). Nor have our comparisons indicated the complexities of numerous states with separate state systems for public community colleges and public post-secondary vocational-technical systems in such states as Georgia, Indiana, Minnesota, and Texas. Only the insiders in those and other states, and perhaps not even they, possess the detailed knowledge of their respective social and political milieus to forecast future structural changes with confidence. One last caveat also is in order; it is our observation that structurally similar state community college agencies in different states may function quite differently, based on a host of historical, financial, and demographic variables.

Roger Yarrington said that "... the story is basically a state-by-state story. Each of the stories is different, yet they all have common themes. Taken together they help explain the national development of a new kind of institution, the community college" (1969, p. vii). Yarrington's conclusion in 1969 is still accurate twenty years later, and one common contemporary theme is a nationally dominant post-secondary identity for the community college movement. Barring some totally unforeseen reversal of a strongly established quarter-century trend, community colleges will remain severed from elementary-secondary education. They will either be allied with public higher education or established as distinct post-secondary entities, insofar as state-level coordination is concerned.

Table 1
Changes in State-Level Coordinating
Structures for Public Junior and Community Colleges, 1963 vs. 1989

State	1963				1989			
	None	K-12	BR/HE	BC/JC	None	K-12	BR/HE	BC/JC
Alabama		x						x
Alaska			x				x	
Arizona				x				x
Arkansas	x						x	
California		x						x
Colorado		x	.					x
Connecticut		x						x
Delaware	x							x
Florida		x						x
Georgia			x				x	
Hawaii	x						x	
Idaho		x				x		
Illinois		x						x
Indiana	x						x	
Iowa		x	x			x		
Kansas		x				x		
Kentucky			x				x	
Louisiana		x					x	
Maine	x							x
Maryland		x						x
Massachusetts				x			x	
Michigan		x				x		
Minnesota		x						x
Mississippi				x				x
Missouri		x					x	
Montana		x					x	
Nebraska		x		x			x	
Nevada	x						x	
New Hampshire		x						x
New Jersey		x					x	
New Mexico			x				x	
New York			x				x	
North Carolina			x					x
North Dakota			x				x	
Ohio			x	x			x	
Oklahoma		x	x				x	
Oregon		x				x		
Pennsylvania	x					x		
Rhode Island			x					x
South Carolina		x						x
South Dakota	x				x			
Tennessee	x						x	
Texas		x					x	
Utah	x	.					x	
Vermont	x							x
Virginia	x							x
Washington		x						x

Table 1
Changes in State-Level Coordinating
Structures for Public Junior and Community Colleges, 1963 vs. 1989

State	1963				1989			
	None	K-12	BR/HE	BC/JC	None	K-12	BR/HE	BC/JC
West Virginia		x						x
Wisconsin		x						x
Wyoming					x			x
Total number of states	12	26	12	6	1	7	21	22

"None" means there is no state-level agency, board or commission established to coordinate public two-year colleges.

"K-12" means the state-level coordinating structure for public junior or community colleges is the same one as the structure for public elementary and secondary education.

"BR/HE" means a university board of regents or a board or commission for higher education.

"BC/JC" means a board or commission for public junior, community, and/or vocational technical colleges.

Sources: Martorana (1963) in Blocker, Plummer, and Richardson (1965); Fountain and Tollefson (1989); Reinhard, Wisniewski, and Jiminez (1989).

References

Fountain, Ben E., & Tollesfon, Terrence A. (1989). *Community colleges in the United States: Forty-nine state systems.* Washington, D.C.: American Association of Community and Junior Colleges.

Martorana, S. V. (1963). The legal status of American public junior colleges. In *American Junior Colleges.* Washington, D.C.: American Council on Education (pp. 31–47).

Reinhard, Bill, Wisniewski, Ronita, & Jiminez, Edgar (1989). A look at America's community, technical, and junior colleges. *The Community, Technical, and Junior College Times,* B-7–B-15.

Yarrington, Roger (1969). *Junior colleges: 50 states/50 years.* Washington, D.C.: American Association of Junior Colleges.

The Community College
Mission and Patterns of Funding

DAVID W. BRENEMAN AND SUSAN C. NELSON

Although community colleges have been one of the fastest growing sectors of U.S. higher education in recent years, limited academic attention has been focused on their financing. In the course of preparing a book on that subject for the Brookings Institution, we have tried to blend the economists' concerns for equity and efficiency with the operational problems and issues that confront practitioners and policymakers. This chapter begins with an explanation of the public finance approach that we take as economists. It then discusses some of the state and local issues that we encountered in our conversations with community college leaders and policy-making officials around the country, first in general terms and then in the specific contexts of four of the states that we visited at some length: Florida, Illinois, Texas, and California. The chapter concludes with recommendations for community college leaders to consider.

Economic Analysis

One of the first steps in any analysis is the selection of criteria. As economists, we naturally turned to the standard theoretical tools that our profession uses to examine all kinds of public services: efficiency and equity. Whether the issue is national defense, highways, welfare, or education, econimists use these two criteria to analyze the problem of allocating society's scarce resources between the public and private sectors, as well as within each sector. The study for Brookings takes an economic perspective and hence examines the implications of efficiency and equity for the financing of community colleges.

When applied to publicly provided activities like education, the concept of efficiency offers guidance in determining *what* should be subsidized, while the notion of equity refers to *who* should be subsidized. To economists, efficency means more than just producing something for the lowest cost. An efficient allocation of resources is said to occur if the benefits (both public and private) from the production of some good or service exceeds by as much as possible the total costs (both public and private) of producing it. With the most goods and services in society, an efficient level of production and consumption can be achieved through the operation of the free (nonsubsidized) market, since decisions of individual producers and consumers will take into account virtually all the costs and benefits involved. For activities that produce public as well as private benefits, however, individuals facing a full-cost price will demand too little (from society's perspective) of the good or service. Consequently, an efficient allocation of resources may require subsidies to encourage people to increase their consumption of activities like education. The amount of subsidy should not necessarily equal the total value of the public benefits but should be sufficient to induce a socially optimal level of education.

Applying efficiency considerations to the financing of community colleges suggests that a balance between public and private sources of support seems justified. Starting with the presumption that attending a community college does yield private benefits, it is rational for students, or families, to be willing to pay some tuition. At the same time, since most people agree that there are also public benefits—for example, to the state and local community in having a more educated and trained labor force that increases its attractiveness to business and industry—efficiency also provides a rationale for subsidies from both state and local governments. The diversity of services offered by community colleges, however, leads to different mixes of public and private support. On one hand, activities where the benefits are essentially private should be financed primarily on a pay-as-you-go basis. On efficiency grounds, at least, there is little public interest served by encouraging additional participation in avocational courses such as poodle grooming and macramé. On the other hand, the substantial public benefits from encouraging adults who cannot read or write to take remedial courses argue for complete subsidy, and efficiency considerations suggest that little or no tuition be charged for these activities.

Efficiency is not the only criterion for judging a finance system; equity must also be taken into account. Equity is a more subjective concept than efficiency, so not surprisingly it has been interpreted in a number of ways by economists. Generally, though, it reflects a concern with the distribution of income in society and a concern that poor people have an opportunity for success. Since education is an important component of that opportunity, equity considerations are reflected in the concern that financial barriers not prevent low-income people from furthering their education.

At the community college level, two types of equity issues have emerged. First, there is a broad agreement that some students deserve extra subsidy beyond that suggested by efficiency concerns. Whether this assistance should be provided by lowering tuition selectively with need-based aid or by universally setting it below the level consistent with efficiency remains the subject of heated debate. Second, in states with local support for community colleges, equity concerns are also voiced for residents of poor districts in fashion similar to the school finance litigation that began in California with the Serrano case. Because of variations in district wealth, some communities can support their community colleges more generously and with lower tax rates than can other districts. Although this equity issue is less compelling for a number of reasons at the community college level than at the elementary/secondary level (foremost among them that attending a community college is not required, universal, a necessary right of citizenship), it is one among several considerations that state finance formulas should take into account in distributing state funds to local districts.

Combining the analyses of efficiency and equity suggests that the burden for financing community colleges should be shared by state government, local governments, and the students but that some groups might need additional subsidies. Tuition for students who are not disadvantaged should be set at whatever level is dictated by efficiency concerns, as far below cost as required by the presence of public benefits. Then equity for the disadvantaged could be accomplished by a selective lowering of tuition through student aid. After nearly a decade's experience with large-scale government programs of need-based student aid, the practical arguments against relying on student aid to achieve equity are substantially reduced, particularly if need-based student aid were combined with tuition waivers for special groups like the elderly and the educationally disadvantaged.

The key tuition issue boils down to a political evaluation of the public benefits of what community colleges are doing—of the benefits to society that students will not take into account in deciding whether to enroll. The issue in allocating this subsidy burden between state and local governments depends primarily on the distribution of these benefits between the state and the locality.

The principles of equity and efficiency cannot take us any farther in recommending how community colleges should be financed. Ultimately, the remaining questions are political and philosophical. Consequently, no single best finance formula emerges from our analysis.

This discussion of equity and efficiency does help to focus on the real sources of disagreements over finance. For instance, tension between mission and finance essentially arises from from differing opinions on these efficiency and equity issues, on public benefits, and on who merits extra subsidy. Also, it is not sufficient to argue that community colleges could put $1 million in additional spending to good use in ways that would serve the public. It is necessary to argue that the state or local community would be better off if that $1 million were spent on community colleges than if it were left in the taxpayer's pocket, or if it were spent on other public services like highways or on other educational institutions. The future of community colleges will depend, in part, on how persuasively that case is made to the public.

State and Local Issues

On the basis of site visits to several states and discussions with numerous community college leaders and state and local officials, two general conclusions stand out. First, disputes over financing formulas often disguise fundamental disagreements over purpose, mission, and priorities. Much of the criticism of formulas is misdirected, therefore, because the problems are not technical, but substantive. Second, for practical reasons as well as the theoretical ones noted above, no "single best plan" for financing community colleges exists, and we do not propose one. The unique history and the different functions served by community colleges in the various states militate against a single method of finance being ideal in all cases. The criteria of equity and efficiency, combined with practical operating considerations, do provide guidance, however, in judging some approaches as clearly better than others, and these will be noted briefly.

Policymakers in each state that we visited were embroiled in highly specific debates over financing policy of little relevance elsewhere; nonetheless, several common themes, or issues, emerged from the visits. These common concerns include:

1. Aggregate levels of support, and the concerns that budgets are not keeping pace with inflation and rising enrollments;

2. The balance between state and local support (in states with a local contribution), and how responsibilities should be divided;

3. Equalization of resources among districts with different property wealth (in states with local support);

4. Tuition levels, including what share of costs should be covered by tuition, and the relation to tuition charges in four-year public institutions within the state;

5. Financial support (or lack thereof) for community services and other noncredit activities;

6. Problems surrounding the distribution of state support, including the choice formula (e.g., cost based vs. flat rate), the use of enrollment-driven formulas at a time of slow (or no) growth, and the lack of start-up funds for new programs.

In responding to issues such as these, the states exhibit a bewildering variety of formulas and budgetary procedures impossible to summarize briefly. Although various taxonomies have been proposed to categorize state plans, we have found it useful to consider finance plans as embodying a set of responses to choices that must be made in supporting a community college system. The basic choices that face state and local policymakers in developing a finance plan are: (1) Should the plan be simple or complex? (2) Should it involve public funding from the state only or should there be state and local sharing? (3) If there is sharing, should the state ignore, or attempt to offset, differences in revenue-raising among local jurisdictions? (4) Should program costs differences be considered or ignored? (5) Should tuition cover a specific portion of costs, or should colleges have discretion in setting it? (6) Should only courses for credit be financed or should support be provided for some—or all—noncredit courses? (7) Should the level of state support be linked to that provided to other public sectors of education, or should community colleges be treated in isolation? (8) Should the formula emphasize incentives for low-cost provision of services or simply reimburse colleges for the actual costs incurred? (In addition, there are several administrative and technical choices that influence the allocation funds. Should there be strict line-item control or local discretion to shift funds among among classes of expenditure? Should average costs or some form of incremental costs be used? Should cost parameters be based on systemwide averages (or medians) or should standard costs be used? Should differences in college size (and hence in unit costs) be considered or ignored? Should the formula be based on average daily attendance, weekly contact hours, or student credit hours?)

A state's financing plan can be described rather completely through the answers to these questions, which cover the principal policy decisions that must be made. Analysis and evaluation of a given state plan should focus on the implications of the set of choices embodied in the plan. Examples drawn from four of our state visits illustrate the types of choices made and some of their implications.

Florida. This state's system of community colleges is noteworthy on at least two counts: its strong tradition of local control despite the absence of local financial support and the use of a highly complex system of cost analysis for determining budgets. On the first point, it is commonly asserted that local control requires local financial support, but Florida is an exception to this rule. Local boards, appointed by the governor, exercise considerable policy control over the colleges, and administrators have wide-ranging discretion over the allocation of the budget. It is unclear how secure local control really is should the colleges fall into disfavor with the legislature; nonetheless, Florida currently stands as proof that significant local control is possible in a system that is publicly financed almost exclusively by state government.

The budget for Florida's community colleges is based upon detailed data on program costs in thirty-four fields of study, one of the most elaborate types of such financing currently in use in any community college system. An extensive data base is required for such a system, but states considering a move to cost-based funding should be aware that the level of detail required can be considerably less than that used in Florida. At issue is the trade-off between simplicity and complexity, and a case can be made for limitng the number of cost categories to five or six as a reasonable compromise.

A serious problem experienced in Florida has been the tendency to underestimate enrollments, with the result that unit costs are driven down artificially. These lower costs are then rebuilt into the next year's budget, forcing increased use of part-time faculty and other cost-saving efforts. Now that growth has slowed, it should be possible—and sensible—to shift to prior year enrollments as the budget base rather than to attempt to forecast enrollments.

Texas. This state starkly poses the conflict of values between local decision making and equal educational opportunities regardless of residence. Local communities must vote to create a community college district and are responsible for physical plant construction and maintenance; the state pays for instructional costs, making no distinction in its payments between rich and poor districts. The result is wide disparity in facilities and resources among community college districts in Texas. Dallas and Ft. Worth, for example, strongly support their colleges, providing superb facilities and substantial local tax revenues, while Austin and Houston have not yet voted to authorize a local tax in their districts. Austin Community College has no permanent campus, operating instead out of rented space in downtown Austin and out of buildings converted from other uses. A further difficulty in Texas is that many of the older campuses serve an area much larger than the district's tax base and have not been successful in expanding that base. Because the state makes no attempt to equalize resources among districts, the extremes in resources are probably as great in Texas as anywhere in the country. A state policy that ignores these differences in district resources is hard to justify, unless overarching value is placed on the college as a purely local institution.

Illinois. Although we do not advance a model finance formula, the approach followed in Illinois comes closer to an ideal meeting our criteria—efficiency and equity—than any other state we visited. The state uses a complex formula that incorporates inflation factors, growth factors, program cost differences, an equalization provision recognizing differences in district wealth, and categorical grants for disadvantaged students. Local boards retain important authority, including the power to set tuition. Program costs are collected in five categories—Baccalaureate (college transfer), Business Occupational, Technical Occupational, Health Occupational, and General Studies—and state payments are based on systemwide average costs in each category. This technique rewards efficient operation, yielding a surplus for campuses that keep costs below the average. In a recent change, future budgets will be based on the most recent year's actual enrollments, rather than on forecast levels.

The principal problems under this plan occur because the Chicago district is so much larger than the others. In certain areas, such as General Studies, Chicago produces a large proportion of total instruction in the state, and its costs tend to dominate the systemwide average cost of instruction. The result is a lower state payment than would otherwise exist, hurting smaller campuses that cannot achieve Chicago's economies of scale. One drawback of a plan that operates on systemwide averages is that sharp differences in size and costs will generate inequities among campuses. Consequently, one can foresee a continuing need in Illinois for periodic adjustments to the formula.

California. By far the largest community college state, California has tended to finance its two-year colleges more like elementary/secondary schools than like a part of higher education. The commitment to no tuition reflects this orientation, and California is the only state with such a policy. In our view, many community college leaders in California exaggerate the importance of tuition-free status, ignoring both the experience of other states and the phenomenal growth of federal and state student aid programs. In fact, prior to the passage of Proposition 13, virtually all two-year college activities were fully subsidized, whether for credit, noncredit, or community service. We suspect that these extraordinarily generous subsidies contributed in a small way to the taxpayer revolt in which California leads the nation.

Since passage of Proposition 13, financing of community colleges, as with other social services, has been conducted under near-crisis conditions. The one-year bailout bill replaced with state dollars much of the local revenue that was lost, in a fashion that continued expenditure differences based on district wealth. The new finance plan, A.B.8, does little better, leaving the state in the dubious position of perpetuating differences in local wealth. Attempts at equalization proved politically impossible at a time when total revenues were being cut, and there is a strong possibility that a Serrano-type lawsuit will be filed against the system. Whether the courts will extend the precedent of school finance reform to community colleges is an open—and interesting—question.

Had Proposition 9 passed in June 1980, the required cut in state income taxes coupled with the continuing impact of Proposition 13 would have forced the rise of tuition in all public institutions of higher education in the state, including community colleges. Although Proposition 9 was defeated, the possibility of tuition being required for community colleges in the 1980s remains strong and to resist stubbornly and refuse to plan for it seems to us a self-defeating approach.

The Future

Tension between mission and finance promises to become more pressing in the 1980s as resources for higher education become less plentiful. Institutional leaders will be forced to choose which activities are central to the college and which are of lesser importance. Perhaps the most fundamental choice facing community colleges is whether to emphasize the community-based learning center concept, with an emphasis on adult and continuing education and community services, or to emphasize transfer programs, sacrificing elsewhere if necessary. During the years of greatest growth, such choices were avoided by adhering to the model of a comprehensive community college striving to meet every possible need. Shrinking resources may force the choice between remaining a part of traditional higher education or moving to become a community-based service organization. It may no longer be possible to have it both ways. We conclude with some brief recommendations for community college leaders to consider. First, as noted above, there is a need to set priorities among activities, deciding which are critical to the institution. We did not come away from our state visits with the sense that many colleges had developed a set of priorities for the 1980s, although it seems certain that budgets will be tight. Similarly, there needs to be greater recognition that just because an activity has value is not a sufficient argument for public subsidy. Arguments for support must become more sophisticated and discerning.

Second, too much emphasis is placed on maximizing enrollments, without reference to educational value. Budget formulas during the 1960s and 1970s may have placed a premium on enrollment growth, but enrollment-driven formulas are likely to have deemphasized in the 1980s. Instead, an ability to explain who benefits—and in what way—from enrolling in various courses and programs may be of increased importance. Hence, better assessment techniques must be developed if the case for increased public subsidy is to be made convincingly.

Third, cost comparisons with other public institutions are likely to be misleading and should be avoided. Universities and community colleges are complex institutions, and computations of average cost per FTE student are not very reliable for guiding state resources allocation. The cost structure within community colleges is certainly worth further investigation when focused on comparisons among two-year institutions.

Fourth, we suspect that community service activities will remain largely on a pay-as-you-go basis; rather than bemoan that prospect, efforts should be concentrated on ways to operate with limited   subsidies. Alternatively, it would be perfectly reasonable for a college not to stress activities supported primarily from student fees.

Fifth, discretion is essential in selecting courses in the community service area, even if no public funds are involved. In virtually every state we visited, controversy was raging over some courses being offered by the community college—macramé, belly dancing, cake decorating, poodle grooming, to name but a few. The damage to public relations must be weighed against the value of offering such courses.

Our final observation is that community college leaders in the 1980s must recognize limits, resisting the temptation to spread resources so thinly that quality is lost. This decade provides an opportunity to consolidate gains from the era of rapid growth. As the mission of community colleges becomes more focused and as priorities are determined, it should be possible to reduce tension between mission and finance that we encountered in the states studied. Failing that clarification, the financing of community colleges will become increasingly controversial in the difficult years ahead.

Cost Differences: The Amazing Disparity Among Institutions of Higher Education in Educational Costs Per Student

HOWARD R. BOWEN

Diversity among institutions is a conspicuous and, on the whole, desirable trait of American higher education. Although the word can be used to condone shoddiness, to cover up narrow provincialism, or to excuse shockingly inadequate financial support, in its best sense, diversity enhances the ability of higher education to serve persons of different backgrounds, abilities, and interests. It encourages institutions to invent and try out new programs and methods. It disposes them to tap varied sources of support. In no respect are colleges and universities more diverse than in their unit costs—that is, in the amount they spend per student.

The range of differences in cost per student is astonishing. Some of the variation may be explained by differences in mission. For example, colleges or universities heavily involved in graduate and professional study are likely to have higher costs per student than those concentrating on the instruction of freshmen and sophomores. And those emphasizing the natural sciences, technology, or medicine may have higher costs per student than those concentrating on the humanities and social studies. Cost differences also may be explained to a minor extent by location in urban or rural settings, by location in different sections of the country, and by size of institution. But differences in expenditures remain even when only educational costs are considered and when the institutions being compared seem to have similar missions, location, and size and to be rendering services of similar quality. The extent of these cost differences will be explored in this article.

The Concept of Educational Cost per Student Unit

To begin, it may be useful to clarify exactly what is being measured when the costs of different institutions are being compared. The basic concept is *educational cost*.

Educational cost refers to current expenditures of institutions after excluding outlays for organized research and public service, a *prorated* share of overhead cost attributable to research and public service, and outlays for the operation of auxiliary enterprises such as residence halls, dining facilities, student unions, and teaching hospitals. What remains after these exclusions is current expenditures for the education of students.

A student is the unit of service to which educational cost is to be related. Students are, however, a mixed lot. Some are part-time and others full-time; some are beginners and others are candidates for advanced degrees. To achieve a standardized unit of service, students are counted as full-time-equivalents (FTEs) and weights are assigned to them according to academic level based on estimates of the relative average costs of educating various categories of students. The result of these adjustments is a standardized *student unit* expressed as the equivalent of one full-time freshman or sophomore student.

The basic data for reviewing institutional cost differences were derived from a representative sample of 268 institutions. The institutions were classified as public or private and as research and doctorate-granting universities, comprehensive universities and colleges, liberal arts colleges, or two-year colleges.

Dispersion of Unit Cost

Table 1 presents data on educational costs per student unit for the 268 institutions in the sample. As shown, unit costs differed widely among institutions The maximum unit cost for various types of institutions ranged from three to eight times the minimum unit cost. For all institutions combined, the maximum was nearly ten times the minimum. And the unit cost for third-quartile institutions was one and one-half to two times that for first-quartile institutions. Though the median unit costs for various types of institutions tended to converge, the variance of unit costs among each type of institution was astonishingly wide.

These cost dispersions are corroborated by many surveys made over the past two decades. For example, the National Federation of College and University Business Officers Associations in a report known as *The Sixty College Study* issued in 1960 compared financial data for a nationwide sample of well-known liberal arts colleges. The results reveal wide differences in total educational and general expenditures per student for institutions of comparable size and mission. Similarly, the Carnegie Commission of Higher Education in 1971 assembled data on educational and general expenditures per FTE student for colleges and universities of various types. These figures again reveal striking differences among institutions. Jenny and Wynn, in *The Turning Point* (1972), gathered financial statistics on forty-eight leading private liberal arts colleges for the year 1970–71. They too found wide cost disparities. The range in educational and general expenditures per FTE student varied from $1,552 to $5,135. Comparable findings were reported by Columbia Research Associates in 1971 in a study prepared for the U. S. Office of Education on colleges and small universities (*The Cost of College*) and by McKinsey and Company in 1972 in a study of twelve well-known liberal arts colleges in Pennsylvania (*The Twelve College Cost-quality Study*). Heller and his associates described two "prestige colleges" of roughly the same enrollments with costs of $4,380 and $2,740 per student (Carnegie Commission on Higher Education, *The More Effective Use of Resources*, 1972) and Brinkman in an unpublished manuscript in 1980 estimated instructional costs per FTE student among fifty leading universities ranging from $1,619 to $12,171.

Table 1
Dispersion of educational expenditures per student unit, 268 representative colleges and universities, by type of institution, 1976–77

	Number of insti-tutions reporting	Minimum	First (lower) quartile	Median	Third (higher) quartile	Maximum
Research and doctorate-granting universities						
Public	35	$1,076	$1,758	$2,020	$3,120	$4,786
Private	35	1,517	2,262	3,341	4,528	8,039
Total	70	1,076	1,915	2,677	3,844	8,039
Comprehensive universities and colleges						
Public	32	1,177	1,761	2,025	2,538	3,721
Private	52	1,134	1,893	2,242	2,640	4,249
Total	84	1,134	1,827	2,147	2,615	4,249
Liberal arts colleges, private	65	824	2,546	3,183	3,920	6,492
Two-year colleges						
Public	26	1,102	1,636	1,959	2,859	4,150
Private	23	1,597	1,959	2,736	3,016	6,748
Total	49	1,102	1,791	2,175	2,907	6,748
All institutions (unweighted)						
Public	93	1,076	1,727	2,020	2,848	4,786
Private	175	824	2,149	2,183	3,458	8,039
Total	268	824	1,938	2,545	3,286	8,039

Source: Special tabulation of data from Higher Education General Information Survey, U.S. Department of Health, Education, and Welfare.

Cost Comparisons among Similar Institutions

The degree of cost dispersion shown in Table 1 conceivably could be due to heterogeneity of the various categories of institutions being compared. To explore this possibility, I made an effort to compare costs among small groups of selected institutions that appear to be closely similar. The criteria for selection were: total enrollment; relative commitment to research and public service and to instruction; educational programs; distribution of students among undergraduate, graduate, and professional programs; size of city where located; and Carnegie classification*. Also, my own judgment as to comparability had some influence on the selection. In each group of institutions chosen for close comparability, substantial differences in cost remained (See Table 2).

Similar comparisons were made by Meeth in *Quality Education for Less Money: A Sourcebook for Improving Cost Effectiveness* (1974). He selected at random three pairs of liberal arts colleges for which cost data had been provided in *The Sixty College Study*. Having found substantial cost differences between the institutions in each pair, he then gathered data reflecting the "quality" of the academic environment achieved by each pair of insititutions. Such qualitative differences as he discovered tended to be in favor of the low-cost institutions!

Table 2
Arrays of educational expenditures per student
unit in selected closely comparable institutions, 1976–77

Six major public universities	Five major private universities	Six state colleges (all located in small cities)
Located in large cities or suburbs	Located in large cities	
$2,665	$2,214	$1,194
3,060	3,341	1,762
3,636	4,517	1,936
	4,533	2,067
Located in small cities	Located in small cities	2,133
1,920	4,029	3,430
2,020	5,242	

Six selective liberal arts colleges, located in large cities	Seven selective liberal ares colleges located in small cities
Enrollment: 1,000–1,500	Enrollment: 1,000–1,500
$3,183	$3,137
3,525	3,686
	4,154
	5,223
Enrollment: 1,500–2,000	Enrollment: 1,500–2,000
$2,881	$4,062
3,281	4,079
3,450	4,972
4,228	

Note: These institutions are comparable with respect to total enrollment, relative commitment to research and public service and to instruction, educational programs offered, and mix of students among undergraduate, graduate, and professional levels.

Source: Special tabulation of data from Higher Education General Information Survey. Similar comparisons were made by Meeth in *Quality Education for Less Money: A Sourcebook for Improving Cost Effectiveness* (1974). He selected at random three pairs of liberal arts colleges for which cost data had been provided in *The Sixty College Study.* Having found substantial cost differences between the institutions in each pair, he then gathered data reflecting the "quality" of the academic environment achieved by each pair of institutions. Such qualitative differences as he discovered tended to be in favor of the low-cost institutions!

In another pertinent study, Bowen and Douglass (*Efficiency in Liberal Education*, 1971) made an effort to simulate costs of instruction in a typical selective liberal arts college assuming different modes of instruction. The estimated cost per student course enrollment was about $240 (1970 dollars) when instruction was conducted in a conventional fashion. The authors found that this cost might vary from $134 to $334 by altering the mode of instruction. These changes in cost would come about through moderate changes in such variables as course proliferation, average faculty teaching load, building utilization, and instructional methods. The authors concluded that cost might easily vary in the range of $200 to $300 per course enrollment without noticeable differences in educational outcomes. The important conclusion was that substantial differences in cost do not necessarily connote significant differences in outcomes. That is why the costs for institutions of similar missions and similar levels of quality may differ, and it is why institutions of similar cost may have different educational outcomes.

Cost Comparisons among the States

Another indication of differences in institutional costs is found in comparative figures on average cost per student in the public institutions of the forty-eight contiguous states (see Table 3). (The data were adjusted for differences in consumer prices among the states.)

The five leaders in expenditures per student unit were: Montana ($2,956), District of Columbia ($2,820), Iowa ($2,426), Pennsylvania ($2,325), and Vermont ($2,310). The bottom five were: Connecticut ($1,266), Massachusetts ($1,344), West Virginia ($1,480), New Jersey ($1,544), and Oklahoma ($1,563). Unit costs ranged from $1,266 in Connecticut to $2,956 in Montana, a ratio of 1 to 2.3.

Differences in cost per student would be expected to vary among the states according to the makeup of the several public higher educational systems. For example, states with a large proportion of their students in major universities (New Mexico) might have different costs per student from those with most students in two-year colleges (California). Therefore, I tried to group states with similar proportions of their students in research and doctorate-granting universities, comprehensive colleges and universities, and two-year colleges. It was not easy to find large groups of such states because there is great diversity in the composition of statewide systems of higher education. Nevertheless, in most groups, substantial variations in cost per student occur even among similar statewide systems of higher education. To cite one case, the unit costs were $1,344 in Massachusetts, $1,544 in New Jersey, and $2,130 in New York.

Even if one could select tiny groups of comparable institutions so homogeneous as to eliminate all cost differences, one would not change the reality that the cost of carrying out essentially the same services varies widely among American colleges and universities. The dispersion of costs is astonishingly great—so great that one may reasonably question the rationality or equity in the allocation of resources among institutions of higher education. This state of affairs may be tolerated because so little is known about the relationships between the amount of resources and educational outcomes. The depth of this ignorance is indicated by the almost universal tendency to judge institutional results or quality in terms of inputs rather than outputs and to assume without evidence that more inputs somehow will inevitably produce commensurately greater or better results.

Table 3
Educational expenditures per student unit all public institutions, by states, 1975–76

Alabama	$2,035	Montana	2,956
Alaska	—	Nebraska	1,908
Arizona	1,580	Nevada	1,734
Arkansas	1,892	New Hampshire	1,663
California	1,663	New Jersey	1,544
Colorado	1,761	New Mexico	1,573
Connecticut	1,266	New York	2,130
Delaware	1,930	North Carolina	2,191
District of Columbia	2,820	North Dakota	2,012
Florida	1,935	Ohio	1,832
Georgia	1,794	Oklahoma	1,563
Hawaii	—	Oregon	1,837
Idaho	2,179	Pennsylvania	2,325
Illinois	1,746	Rhode Island	1,998
Indiana	2,063	South Carolina	2,007
Iowa	2,426	South Dakota	1,725
Kansas	1,896	Tennessee	1,988
Kentucky	1,785	Texas	1,981
Louisiana	1,697	Utah	2,083
Maine	1,918	Vermont	2,310
Maryland	1,803	Virginia	1,605
Massachusetts	1,344	Washington	1,592
Michigan	1,969	West Virginia	1,480
Minnesota	1,837	Wisconsin	2,207
Mississippi	2,040	Wyoming	2,116
Missouri	1,754	U.S. all states combined	2,003

Source: National Center for Education Statistics, *Financial Statistics of Institutions of Higher Education, Fiscal Year 1977, State Data*: and *Fall Enrollment in Higher Education 1976*. The index for adjusting the data for differences among the states in cost of living is that of McMahon and Melton, "Measuring Cost of Living Variation," *Industrial Relations*, October 1978, pp. 324–332.

Institutional Differences in the Internal Allocation of Expenditures

Not only do colleges and universities differ widely in their total expenditures per student, they also show great variety in the way they deploy these expenditures among various programs and functions. Certainly there is no one best allocation toward which most institutions tend to converge. Rather, there are numerous and widely divergent patterns of expenditures, even among seemingly comparable institutions. The maximum percentages spent on any function are from two to ten times the minimum percentages, and the percentages for third-quartile institutions generally range from one and one-half to two times the percentages for first-quartile institutions (See Table 4).

Table 4
Dispersion among institutions in the percentage distribution
of educational expenditures among various programs and functions, 1976–77

	Minimum	First quartile	Median	Third quartile	Maximum
Research and doctorate-granting universities, public					
Teaching	41%	53%	59%	63%	72%
Student services	3	4	6	8	11
Scholarships and fellowships	0	5	7	8	11
Academic support	4	6	9	11	15
Institutional support	2	6	8	11	25
Plant operation and maintenance	5	7	9	10	15
Research and doctorate-granting universities, private					
Teaching	36	48	55	60	69
Student services	2	4	5	6	11
Scholarships and fellowships	2	8	10	16	19
Academic support	2	6	7	9	18
Institutional support	5	8	10	13	27
Plant operation and maintenance	5	7	8	10	14
Comprehensive universities and colleges, private					
Teaching	35	43	54	61	68
Student services	2	4	5	6	9
Scholarships and fellowships	0	1	3	5	25
Academic support	3	6	8	11	16
Institutional support	4	9	12	16	27
Plant operation and maintenance	6	11	12	14	20
Comprehensive universities and colleges, private					
Teaching	31	39	44	50	61
Student services	2	6	8	9	18
Scholarships and fellowships	5	9	11	14	30
Academic support	2	4	6	7	15
Institutional support	2	13	17	19	27
Plant operation and maintenance	3	8	9	12	18
Liberal arts colleges, private					
Teaching	22	32	38	41	58
Student Services	2	7	9	11	18
Scholarships and fellowships	10	12	15	45	
Academic support	2	5	7	8	27
Institutional support	5	15	17	23	33
Plant operation and maintenance	5	9	11	13	25
Two-year colleges, public					
Teaching	29	49	56	60	79
Student services	2	5	7	8	12
Scholarships and fellowships	0	0	2	4	5
Academic support	2	4	8	8	16
Institutional support	6	10	17	19	37
Plant operation and maintenance	5	7	10	15	19

Note: Educational expenditures are those related to the education of students; they exclude expenditures for auxiliary enterprises, research, and public service.

Source: Special tabulation of data from Higher Education General Information Survey.

These differences might be ascribed to heterogeneity of the institutions being observed. But when small groups of closely similar institutions were compared, substantial differences in the percentages remain (See Table 5). For example, for six major public universities expenditures for teaching varied from 59 to 72 percent; for six state colleges from 39 to 68 percent; and for thirteen liberal arts colleges from 25 to 51 percent. Similarly, the percentage spent for student services varied from 4 to 7 percent for major private universities and from 7 to 13 percent for liberal arts colleges.

Table 5
Dispersion among selected closely comparable institutions in the percentage distribution of educational expenditures among various programs and functions, 1976–77

	Teaching	Student services	Scholarships and fellowships	Academic support	Institutional support	Plant operation and maintenance	Other
Six major public universities							
Located in large cities or suburbs							
A	68%	4%	5%	9%	8%	7%	—
B	59	9	11	8	7	7	—
C	59	7	8	15	7	5	—
Located in small cities							
D	72	4	2	11	5	7	—
E	63	4	8	12	6	8	—
F	63	6	8	9	4	10	—
Five major private universities							
Located in large cities or suburbs							
G	60	4	15	7	7	7	1
H	49	6	17	13	7	8	—
I	56	7	18	7	7	5	—
Located in small cities							
J	56	5	17	8	5	9	—
K	49	7	17	9	9	10	—
Six state colleges (all located in small cities)							
L	61	2	2	5	11	10	9
M	68	4	3	8	5	13	—
N	65	7	1	8	10	10	—
O	49	6	5	15	8	17	—
P	39	5	3	4	27	10	13
Q	42	9	1	7	13	15	14

Source: Special tabulation data from Higher Education General Information Survey.

* See Radner and Miller, *Demand and Supply in U.S. Higher Education.* New York: McGraw Hill, 1975.

Comparable disparities have been obtained in cost studies of the past. For example, an especially interesting study by Swords and Walwer (*The Costs and Resources of Legal Education*, 1974).

They show that in 1970 the cost per student among the 115 accredited American law schools ranged from $250 to $2,350 with the first quartile at $650, the median at $850, and the third quartile at $1,150. Similarly, Lupton and Moses (*Admissions/Recruitment: A Study of Costs and Practices in Independent Higher Education Institutions*, 1978) show substantial disparities among small liberal arts colleges in cost per matriculant for recruitment and admissions of students.

Concluding Comments

Wide differences among institutions in cost per student have been observed in every study of comparative costs. These differences have been found to persist even when great care has been taken to compare similar institutions, to adjust for geographical differences in price levels, and to adjust and refine the cost data so as to exclude expenditures for research, public service, and auxiliary enterprises, and to standardize student units. What do these differences signify?

One possible answer is that the institutions being compared are actually less homogeneous with respect to the educational programs offered than they seem. This may be especially so at the two extremes: in the case of the major research universities each of which has a considerable claim to uniqueness in the range and characteristics of educational programs, and in the case of community colleges which vary especially in their relative emphasis on expensive vocational programs and less-costly academic programs. But for the many institutions that lie between these extremes, the program differences are likely to be far fewer. In the case of selective liberal arts colleges, they are likely to be minuscule.

There is a serious logical problem, however, in declaring that cost differences are due to differences in program. It is by no means clear whether expensive programs are a result or a cause of high costs. An institution which succeeds in raising ample funds can afford to offer expensive programs. It can offer and even require science, fine arts, or classics, whereas a less affluent institution will tend to steer away from these subjects toward less costly sociology and education. Similarly, a rich institution may have highly developed psychological counseling, art museums, and expensive athletic facilities, whereas a less affluent institution may have to streamline its student services and cultural offerings. Not all high-cost institutions can maintain that their high costs are due solely to the character of their offerings; the historical facts may be the exact opposite. If, however, the high-cost programs have been mandated by a public agency or an accrediting body, or if it can be proven that they are essential to education of high quality, then the claim can properly be made that costs are high because of programs offered. Although the dispersion of costs among institutions would be narrowed (though not eliminated) if comparisons were restricted to institutions having similar assortments of programs, such a procedure would beg the question because cause and effect cannot be clearly sorted out.

The wide differences in cost per student are sometimes justified by citing significant though subtle differences in institutional quality. This argument comes in four forms all relating to the benefits of diversity.

First, it is almost universally argued that the higher educational system, since it is called upon to serve widely varied clienteles, must be diverse. Substantial cost differences are therefore held to be legitimate and even necessary. The widely acknowledged need for diversity does not, however, explain why institutions serving the same or very similar clienteles—for example, selective liberal arts colleges or large state colleges—should exhibit such disparate costs per student. And it does not explain why average costs should be lower in some states than in others even when the states being compared distribute their students among similar assortments of institutions.

Second, it is argued that diversity among institutions is beneficial as it fosters innovation in higher education. The acknowledged benefits from innovation do not, however, explain the substantial cost differences among institutions that are similar not only in size and mission but also in their traditionalism.

Third, it is argued that rich institutions lead the way for the less affluent institutions in showing how to make good use of increasing resources as the funds for all of higher education grow. This argument may go into reverse in a period of declining real resources. In that case, the less affluent institutions may be able to instruct their rich neighbors in how to cope with poverty.

Fourth, it is argued that diversity leading to cost differences among colleges and universities is essential to intellectual and cultural excellence. It is held that there is not enough money or talent to produce such excellence in every institution and that if all institutions were to subsist at the same level of cost per student, the result would be widely diffused mediocrity. The only feasible alternative, it is said, is to concentrate exceptionally talented students and faculty and abundant resources in a few institutions and thus to achieve a few peaks of excellence even at the cost of financial and education poverty elsewhere. But even accepting the importance of special peaks of excellence there is no explanation of the fact that institutions that could be said to have reached the highest peaks of excellence (the Ivy League, for example) operate at widely different costs per student.

Another approach to the puzzle of cost differences relates to academic freedom. It may be argued that academic freedom, which everyone admits is essential on noneconomic grounds, will almost inevitably result in cost differences which appear to reflect uneconomical allocations of resources. According to this argument, since each institution is a semi-independent entity free to gather from all available sources and to exert some control over the use of these funds, costs per student unit will then be determined by the amount of money an institution is able to raise and by the number of student units it chooses (or is required) to serve. If this argument is accepted, cost differences among institutions will tend to be great and indeed will exhibit a quality of randomness. It is as though the unit costs in the 3,000 American colleges and universities were determined by a vast, complicated, and decentralized philanthropic lottery rather than by rational decisions based on the economic allocation of resources.

This apparent randomness is tolerated in part because of a sincere belief that colleges and universities should enjoy freedom of thought and inquiry and therefore should be semiautonomous entities. It is also tolerated because no one knows with any certainty the relationship between money spent and true educational outcomes, and it is perhaps desirable not to have all the educational eggs in one basket. However, many taxpayers, legislators, and donors suspect that wide variance in costs do not necessarily produce correspondingly varying results. The current concern of legislators and donors for cost analysis and accountability is an indication of the uneasiness with which public leaders view this situation and suggests the need for educators to give close attention to evaluation of results.

The data presented in this article provide no obvious standards as to the financial needs for conducting higher education. They tell nothing about the relationship between cost and educational, intellectual, or cultural excellence. They give no clues as to whether high-cost institutions are overfinanced or low-cost institutions underfinanced, nor do they reveal whether the total funds allotted to higher education are excessive or deficient. They point to no single best way to allocate resources within institutions. The data presented raise questions about the financing of education; they do not answer them.

Financial Governance Patterns Among Two-Year Colleges

Richard Fonte

Governance literature in higher education has evolved through a series of methodological phases. The initial phase focused upon comparative and case studies of statewide coordination agencies. Particular emphasis was placed upon analysis of broad legal authorities granted "consolidated governing" boards versus "coordinating boards."[1]

During the second phase, however, the analyses have shifted to reviewing detailed patterns of regulatory control with reduced reference to whether the statewide agency is classified as "coordinating" or "governing".[2]

Curry and Fischer advanced the methodological benefits of analyses focused on "financial governance" characteristics. They defined "financial governance . . . (as) exercised through procedure, rule or regulation of governmental entities outside the formal (statewide agency) governance structure."[3]

This study empirically tested the regulatory conceptual framework theorized by Curry and Fischer. A fifty-state study of regulation of community college systems was undertaken with factor and cluster analysis as the primary modes of analysis. In particular, this study tested whether the Curry and Fischer regulatory constructs and state agency regulatory taxonomy could be empirically demonstrated in the governance patterns of community college state systems. The specific questions for research included:

1. Can discrete state regulatory measures be found to group into broader regulatory factors?

2. Can state systems of community colleges be found to cluster into specific regulatory types based upon underlying regulatory factors?

3. Can community college systems be ranked by the degree of state regulatory control based upon underlying regulatory factors?

Governance Literature

The growth of higher education during the 1960s led to changing relationships between state government and local campuses. The literature frequently sought to prescribe, as well as describe, this relationship.

The reports of the Carnegie Commission on Higher Education, the Carnegie Council on Policy Studies in Higher Education, the Carnegie Foundation for the Advancement of Teaching, and others clearly demonstrate a general prescription for all levels of higher education calling for institutional autonomy from state controls.[4] For community colleges, the focus on institutional autonomy has been coupled with a concern over the impact of state control on local community orientation and mission.[5] The literature also reflects a concern over the regulatory impact of funding approaches and financing procedures for community colleges.[6]

Initially, studies advocated the state coordinating agency in contrast to statewide governing boards as the "desirable" state organizational structure.[7] However, the distinctions have become less than clear between these agencies. Glenny suggested that "the stronger coordinating boards have tended to acquire some of the traditional powers of governing boards."[8]

During the debate over the merits of deregulation in the 1980s, detailed analyses of state financial regulatory controls emerged. Such "financial governance" studies are derived from the body of literature involving both economic regulation and deregulation of the private sector and the regulation of the government sector to assure public accountability.[9] A frequent methodology adopted to apply regulatory analysis has been the case study approach systematically centering on distinct categories of regulations such as purchasing, tuition setting authority, and expenditure controls.[10]

The literature has also provided increasingly sophisticated approaches to analyze the regulatory environment of state higher education systems. Three such designs by J. Fredericks Volkwein and Denis Curry and Norman Fischer and a precursor study by Walter Garms were especially significant in the development of this research effort.[11] Volkwein's study represented the first empirical analysis of the degree of state financial and personnel control over local institutions. Volkwein developed a sixteen-item scale to differentiate state regulatory environments for research universities along an unsegmented continuum of flexibility and control of financial and personnel regulation measures. Volkwein grouped states by "high," "medium," and "low" regulatory environments. This research did not attempt to demonstrate, however, the existence of specific regulatory "types" with particular underlying regulation patterns as defining characteristics. Such a framework was advanced by Curry and Fischer, who developed a taxonomy of four "types" ranging from the most regulated to the least regulated.[12] These models included the (1) "state agency," (2) "state controlled," (3) "state-aided," and the (4) "free market" model. Curry and Fischer's framework is characterized by strong operational definitions for each type based on specific levels of regulatory application (ranging from high to low state controls) on eight measures. The regulatory categories were: (1) Budgeting, (2) Expenditure Oversight, (3) Accountability, (4) Tuition and Fees, (5) Financing Options, (6) Salary Administration, (7) Enrollment Policy, and (8) Program Review.

The Curry and Fischer typology presented a new approach to conceptualizing governance. While structural models of state governance are suggested, they represent precisely defined combinations of regulation. While the typology has had the potential for broader application, the framework has not been tested through any empirical research. This study provides such an analysis.

In a work that represents a precursor of the efforts of Curry and Fischer, Garms developed the first state regulatory taxonomy differentiating community college systems based upon "planned" versus "market" economic principles. His continuum of types identified two planned economy model types, "centralized control" and "decentralized control," and several "mixed model" types characterized by the existence of a financial and control partnership between the state and local institutions.[13]

Both the governance models and the regulatory and budgetary definitions suggested by Garms paralleled closely the types and measures conceptualized by Curry and Fischer. Since Garms proposed that such distinct regulatory types could be identified within the community college sector of higher education, this study attempts to verify this proposition.

Methodology

A survey of state financial controls over community, junior, and technical colleges was undertaken utilizing, as the base, Volkwein's scale of flexibility and control. Questions were adapted from Volkwein and modified for application to the two-year college environment. Additional questions were drawn from the Curry and Fischer checklist of regulation levels and the models of community college financing developed by Wattenbarger, Starnes, and Mercer.[14] A mailed survey with follow-up phone interviews was undertaken of all community college state agency directors. The survey was mailed twice with a three week interval. A 100 percent response was achieved detailing regulatory practices including the nature and intensity of use of various regulatory measures. Sixty-two state systems of two-year colleges were identified, since several states had multiple systems.

Twenty-nine measures of state regulation were included in a six-page survey. The respondent was asked to select for their state the applicable level of state control for each measure described through a series of separate sentences:[15] Each state response was scored for every item, ranging on a scale of high (10) to low (0) regulation.

Through factor analysis the study identified underlying regulatory constructs contained in factor scales. The final regulatory constructs were developed by alternative trial and error combinations, testing particularly, the conceptual framework of regulatory categories of Curry and Fischer. The final combinations included in the regulatory constructs represented the least number of derived factors meeting the Kaiser criterion eigenvalue of 1.00. That is to say, other alternative combinations identified a greater number of regulatory constructs. An aggregated scale score was created for each state on each factor construct.

A single, summary state regulation score was also developed through a second round of factor analysis, which was required because of data limitations caused by analyzing twenty-nine variables with only sixty-two cases. The second round of factor analysis was based on weighted mean scores from the factors derived through the first round. This analysis was used to test the existence of a single overall regulatory factor, as suggested by Volkwein, and to develop an overall regulation score for each system.[16]

The identification of state regulatory "types" was determined through the use of cluster analysis. The analysis of state regulatory types started with the mean scores for each of sixty-two state systems on each identified underlying regulatory construct. Cluster analysis was used to find "similar" groupings of state systems based upon the score of the construct regulatory variables. The analysis utilized and contrasted two methods of clustering, "Average linkage" method and the "Ward's minimum within-group variability method" in determining the appropriate number of cluster "types."[17]

Findings

Factor analysis identified six underlying constructs, involving twenty-six of the original twenty-nine variables. The construct variables developed through factor analysis were: (1) Budgeting Flexibility, (2) Budget Form, (3) Expenditure Oversight, (4) Tuition and Revenue Control, (5) Local Authority, and (6) Personnel Administration. Table 1 details the results of the six factor analyses including the variance accounted for by each of the factors and the titles of underlying regulatory measures. The last column compares the six factors and the underlying measures to the five factor construct. proposed by Curry and Fischer. In those instances when an underlying regulatory measure was not proposed by Curry and Fischer as part of their suggested five-factor construct, the underlying regulatory measure is labeled as "no comparison" on the table.

The six constructs of regulation identified through this study confirm key elements suggested in the conceptual framework of Curry and Fischer.[18] While these writers suggested the existence of five comparable regulatory categories, this study found six factors that cover the same regulatory measures.

Table 1
Regulatory Control Constructs Results of Factor Analysis

Identified Factors and Defining Variables		Related to Curry and Fischer Categories
Factor #1—BUDGETING FLEXIBILITY	Load	
Standard State Budget Instructions	.72	Budgeting
Changing Expenditures after Budget Approval	.60	Budgeting
Year End Balance Use	.51	Expenditure Oversight
(variance explained 58.2%)		
Factor #2—BUDGET FORM	Load	
Nature of Budget	.72	Budgeting
Use of Category Funding	.72	no comparison
(variance explained 76.3%)		
Factor #3—EXPENDITURE OVERSIGHT	Load	
Pre-audit of Expenses	.92	Expenditure Oversight
Check Issuing Authority	.81	no comparison
Budgetary Detailing-Positions	.80	Budgeting
Budgetary Detailing-Dollars	.74	Budgeting
Travel Controls	.73	Expenditure Oversight
(variance explained 71.0%)		
Factor #4—TUITION AND REVENUE CONTROL	Load	
Tuition Setting Authority	.73	Tuition and Fees
Tuition Revenue Control	.66	Tuition and Fees
Auxiliary Revenue Control	.49	Tuition and Fees
(variance explained 59.2%)		
Factor #5—LOCAL AUTHORITY	Load	
Local Bd. Budget Approval	.89	no comparison
Selection of Local Board	.84	no comparison
Taxing Authority	.79	Local Financing Authority
Hiring of President	.69	no comparison
Capital Authority	.58	Local Financing Authority
State v. Local Share of Financing	.57	Local Financing Authority
(variance explained 61.1%)		
Factor #6—PERSONNEL ADMINISTRATION	Load	
Position Control all Positions	.86	no comparison
Faculty Position Control	.85	no comparison
Non-Faculty Salaries	.82	Salary Administration
Non-Faculty System of Classification	.80	Salary Administration
Non-Faculty Position Control	.86	no comparison
Faculty Classification System	.78	Salary Administration
Faculty Salary Setting	.75	Salary Administration
(variance explained 71 %)		

Broad factors of TUITION AND REVENUE CONTROL and PERSONNEL ADMINISTRA-TION were established containing variables with an extremely close relationship to the Curry and Fischer conceptual framework. PERSONNEL ADMINISTRATION, however, was found to contain additional underlying regulatory measures beyond those proposed by Curry and Fischer. Regulation measures involving personnel position controls were added through factor analysis to the construct of PERSONNEL ADMINISTRATION. The original design had included only salary-setting authority and personnel classification system authority These additional measures had been suggested throughout the regulation literature and were found empirically to relate to a single broad construct.

Rather than a single budgeting factor as suggested by Curry and Fischer, the study found two factors, one for BUDGETING FLEXIBILITY and a second for BUDGET FORM.

The BUDGETING FLEXIBILITY factor involved regulations either limiting or permitting institutions to change expenditures after the budget approval, regulations involving the retention or return of year-end budget balances and whether or not standard state budget instructions were followed in the institutional budget development process.

The BUDGET FORM factor involved the method of budget calculation and distribution. One underlying regulatory measure included the nature of the state budgeting approach, e.g., formula-driven or non-formula. The second underlying regulatory measure focused on any restricted purposes funding used in budget distribution, notwithstanding whether the state did or did not use a formula.

Certain regulatory measure variables relating to degree of budget detail over dollars and personnel were found to be statistically related to the EXPENDITURE OVERSIGHT factor rather than to either factor involving the budget. This finding differed from the expectation of Curry and Fischer. In this case and in several others, factor analysis seemed to group variables by the underlying purpose of the regulatory measure, rather than by a subject area category such as budgeting. The EXPENDITURE OVERSIGHT factor, however, was found to contain regulatory measures involving the level of state involvement in the pre-auditing of expenses and state travel controls as hypothesized by Curry and Fischer.

Curry and Fischer had advanced a dimension focused on local institutional authority relating exclusively to local financing power. Factor analysis confirmed a LOCAL AUTHORITY factor with broader characteristics. That is, rather than relating only to financing matters involving local taxing power, state financing share and local capital authority, a factor was established that also included presidential hiring authority, and the selection process of local board members and their budget power. This broader dimension was developed through testing for compatibility in a single factor with the three additional variables stressed as key local authority elements within the literature of community college regulation and control.[19]

The sixty-two state systems were ranked by the six measures along with a composite index of financial control. These data results were used in the cluster analysis. The cluster analysis findings provide empirical support for differentiating state systems of two-year colleges on a continuum of financial and personnel regulation as suggested by both Curry and Fischer and Walter Garms.[20] Cluster analysis supported the existence of three distinct regulatory types containing forty-six of the sixty-two systems.[21] Type A had eighteen systems,[22] Type B, twelve systems[23] and, Type C had sixteen systems.[24] The allocation of the state systems to each of these clusters in the continuum is outlined in Table 2.

The composite regulatory scores for each of the three major regulatory types comprising forty-six state systems are contained in Table 3. Types A and B represented the "strong state regulation" types, while Type C can be distinguished as a low regulation type. The overall regulation scores of both the "strong" regulation types differed significantly from the low regulation type. Moreover, these same two "strong" regulation types were found to have regulatory scores significantly greater than the mean on the measures of Expenditure Oversight, Revenue Control, Local Authority and Personnel Administration Controls. The "low" regulation scores were significantly below the mean on these same measures. Table 3 details differences by each regulatory measure for the three types.

Table 2
State System Regulation Types

Continuum of Regulation

← "High" Regulation ---------------------------- "Low" Regulation →

Type A (18 sys) "Strong" Regulation Direct Control	Type B (12 sys) "Strong" Regulation Indirect Control	Type C (16 sys) "Low" Regulation
Alaska	Alabama	Colorado L
Arkansas CC	Colorado ST	Idaho
Arkansas UCC	Florida	Illinois
Connecticut CC	Louisiana CC	Maryland
Connecticut T	Louisiana UCC	Michigan
Delaware	Minnesota	Mississippi
Georgia	New Hampshire	Missouri
Hawaii	Oklahoma LTAX	Montana
Kentucky	South Carolina	Nebraska
Nevada	Virginia	New Jersey
New Mexico	W Virginia CC	New York CUNY
North Carolina	W Virginia UCC	New York SUNY
Oklahoma NOTAX		Ohio CC
Oklahoma UCC		Oregon
Rhode Island		Pennsylvania
Tennessee CC		Vermont
Tennessee TECH		
Washington		

Detailed profiles of each regulatory type were developed to demonstrate the parallel relationship between the empirically identified types and those advanced conceptually by Curry and Fischer and Garms. These profiles contained in Table 4 include percentage application of specific levels of representative regulatory techniques. Although the differences in regulatory application are not necessarily statistically significant, they provide heuristic description that enhances our understanding of the major regulatory types.

The analysis demonstrated that Types A and B, while both exercising strong levels of regulation, can be distinguished among themselves by regulatory techniques as well as from the "low" state regulation, Type C.

Characteristically, Type A, labeled STRONG DIRECT CONTROL systems, were found to utilize direct expenditure controls. By contrast, Type B systems, labeled STRONG INDIRECT CONTROL, made greater use of restrictive budgetary measures, particularly non-formula funding. This finding confirmed a major contention made by Curry and Fischer and also Walter Garms.

Table 3
Regulatory Types Differences in Regulation Usage

Cluster Type	n	Overall Reg Score	Budget Flexibility	Budget Form	Expenditure Oversight	Tuition/Revenue	Local Authority	Personnel Administr.
A	18	6.00	3.66	5.92	5.19	4.50	6.61	4.07
B	12	5.85	3.96	7.36	4.28	3.56	6.60	4.25
C	16	1.63*	1.25	3.96	0.71*	0.69*	2.37*	0.56*
Average		4.09	2.69	5.83	2.84	2.88	4.70	2.47
F Prob		0.00	0.11	0.00	0.00	0.00	0.00	0.00

Boxed score means were found to be significantly different from starred means on the basis of Tukey T a posterior test. Only significant differences between major cluster types are highlighted on the table.

Table 4
Regulatory Cluster Types Application of Representative Regulation Techniques*

	Regulation Types		
	Strong		Low
Regulation Category/Regulation Technique	A	B	C
	%	%	%
1. BUDGET FLEXIBILITY			
Flexibility in budget after state allocation			
lowest level—complete flexibility	50.0	58.3	81.3
2nd lowest level—great flexibility	27.8	8.3	12.5
State Budgeting approach for Higher Education			
highest level—treated as "state agency"	33.3	25.0	6.3
2. BUDGET FORM			
Nature of funding technique			
highest level—non-formula	22.2	41.7	12.5
2nd highest level—cost-based formulas	66.7	58.3	43.8
3rd highest level—flat-rate formulas	5.6	0	37.5
Use categorical funding	50.0	66.7	25.0
3. EXPENDITURE OVERSIGHT			
Pre-audit of purchase by state			
highest level—most purchases	22.2	8.3	0
2nd highest level—some purchases	22.2	41.7	0
lowest level-no purchases	27.8	41.7	100.0
Position allocation detail in budget			
highest level—great detail	38.9	33.3	6.3
lowest level—no detail	27.8	50.0	93.8
4. TUITION AND REVENUE CONTROL			
Tuition setting authority			
highest level—state sets tuition	33.3	50.0	0
2nd highest level—multi-campus system sets	50.0	33.3	12.5
3rd highest—shared state-local	16.7	16.7	12.5
lowest level—local institution sets	0	0	75.0
Control of tuition revenue			
highest level—state controls general fund	33.3	8.3	0
2nd highest level—cc system/multi-campus	33.3	25.0	12.5
lowest level—institutional control	33.3	66.7	87.5
5. LOCAL AUTHORITY			
Local budget approval			
higher level—no local bd role	50.0	41.7	6.3
2nd highest level—advisory role only	16.7	33.3	0
lowest level—local bd approves budget/expend	22.2	25.0	68.8
Selection of local board			
highest level—no local board	50.0	41.7	6.3
2nd highest level—locally appointed trustees	11.1	8.3	43.8
lowest level—elected boards	5.6	0	50.0
Local taxing authority			
highest level—no authority	22.2	16.7	0
lowest level—local authority taxes	5.6	16.7	56.3
State v. local financing			
highest 1/3—state financed (67-100%)	88.0	66.7	0
highest 1/3—state financed (33–66%)	12.0	33.3	87.5
lowest 1/3—state financed (0-32%)	0	0	12.5

Table 4
Regulatory Cluster Types Application of Representative Regulation Techniques*

Regulation Category/Regulation Technique	Regulation Types		
	Strong		Low
	A	B	C
	%	%	%
6. PERSONNEL ADMINISTRATION			
Position control over all positions			
highest level—state imposed controls	38.9	25.0	0
lowest level—no controls	22.2	50.0	87.5
Non-faculty salary administration			
highest level—state imposed	27.8	58.3	0
lowest level—no controls	44.4	33.3	87.5

*Representative techniques were selected for each factor. These techniques were generally the highest "loading" in factor analysis. Moreover, not all levels of each technique are reported on this table, but only the most relevant.

Strong Direct Control (A) systems were characterized by the highest regulatory scores (5.2/10) on Expenditure Oversight among all systems. In fact, twelve out of eighteen systems scored in the highest third of regulatory application of Expenditure Oversight. This included "higher" regulatory applications of pre-auditing practices, and mandatory budgetary detailing of personnel and dollars than the twelve Strong Indirect Control (B) systems. For example, pre-audit of "most purchases," the highest regulatory level, was exercised by 22.2 percent of Strong Direct Control (A) systems, and only by 8.3 percent of Strong Indirect Control (B) systems. In fact, 41.7 percent of Strong Indirect Control state systems were not subject to any external pre-audit.

As would be expected, the sixteen separate systems classified Type C, "low" state regulation, had an extremely low regulatory score on the Expenditure Oversight measure. In fact, no systems were subject to pre-audit of their expenditures and fifteen of sixteen systems did not have positions designated within the budgets.

In the regulatory category of personnel administration overall scores were high and comparable for both high regulation types. However, Strong Direct Control (A) systems made greater use of position control measures, while Strong Indirect Control (B) states utilized more indirect, salary-setting measures. Among the "low" regulation, Type C, very limited regulation was exercised with "complete institutional autonomy" exercised by over 80 percent of the systems for personnel.

The regulatory measure focusing on budgetary calculations showed considerable differences by regulatory type. Strong Direct Control (A) systems had a lower score than Strong Indirect Control (B) systems (5.9/10 versus 7.4/10) on this measure of regulation. This indicated less frequent use of non-formula budgeting and restrictive purposes distribution. Instead, there appeared to be greater use of cost-based formula budgeting in twelve out of eighteen (A) systems. By contrast, for Strong Indirect Control (B) systems there was a strong use of non-formula budgeting (41.7 percent). Among the "low" regulation, Type C, formula funding was even more predominate at 87.5 percent of all systems. This confirmed the contention of Curry and Fischer and also Walter Garms.

Considerable state control was exercised over Tuition and Fee setting for both strong regulation types. The authority to set tuition, for example, was held by either the state or by a "multi-campus system above the individual campuses" in 83 percent of the situations. Strong Indirect Control (B) systems, however, demonstrated greater flexibility in the institutional retention of tuition and fee dollars, 66.7 percent, than Strong Direct Control (A) systems, 33.3 percent. The "Low" regulation, Type C systems exercised limited state controls over Tuition and Fees (0.7/10.0). Local tuition setting authority was found in 75 percent of the systems, and retention of local tuition revenue "at the institutional level" in 87.5 percent of the systems.

A relatively high state regulation score was found on the Local Authority measure for both major "strong" types. Elements most influencing this score were the limited local budgetary authority of local boards and the weak nature of the local boards. In many cases where local boards existed, they had only advisory budgetary power. Among "low" regulation, Type C systems, genuine Local Authority (2.4/10.0) was exercised by local institutions with autonomous budget authority and local boards of either locally elected trustees (50 percent) or locally appointed (43.8 percent) trustees.

The Low Regulation (C) type also differed from both strong regulatory types by having smaller percentages of their overall financing attributable to state dollars. No "Low" Regulation (C) system was in the highest third of state-financed systems. In fact 87.5 percent were found in the 33 percent to 66 percent range of state financing.

Conclusion

The findings provide empirical support for differentiating state systems of two-year colleges utilizing summary measures of financial and personnel regulation. The study found that twenty-six discrete state regulatory measures can be grouped into six broader regulatory factors. More-over, community college systems can be ranked and compared by the degree of state regulatory control based upon broader underlying regulatory factors. The study demonstrated that analysis focused on "financial governance" characteristics can assist the classification of two-year systems.

The results also confirm that the fiscal and personnel regulatory measures used by Volkwein with research universities can be successfully applied with some modification for an analysis of two-year colleges. The data, therefore, provided evidence to generalize the use of his measures to two-year colleges.

Moreover, the six constructs of financial and personnel regulation identified through this study verify empirically key elements suggested in the conceptual framework of Curry and Fischer. Whether the six regulatory categories would apply to sectors of higher education other than two-year colleges, however, requires further research.

Moreover, the policy debates for two-year colleges involving revisions in funding plans and the benefits of financial deregulation should be assisted by the development of six summary measures of financial regulation. Policymakers are provided with summary measures of twenty-six separate financial and personnel control techniques. These constructs should clarify and focus the policy debates in these areas. They represent constructs that can be easily understood by legislators, state agency personnel and others engaged in the debate of these topics.

The study also demonstrated that community college systems can be found to cluster into three specific regulatory types based upon the six standard underlying regulatory factors. Moreover, state systems can be differentiated along a continuum of control ranging from high to low regulation. The identification of specific regulatory types suggests that governance literature focused on distinguishing between "consolidated governing" boards and "coordinating boards" could be enriched by consideration of "financial governance" characteristics. Further research is, however, necessary to confirm whether it is possible to generalize these regulatory types to other sectors of higher education.

Finally, the study's three major financial regulatory "types" correspond to the three regulatory groupings as suggested by both Curry and Fischer and Walter Garms. That is to say, that the study confirmed the existence of "types" as originally hypothesized by these writers. Moreover, the mix of regulatory measures and the emphasis of each type was supported in the findings. The STRONG DIRECT CONTROL, Type A, parallels the Curry and Fischer "state agency model" and Garms' "Centralized control-planned economy model" and the regulations suggested for these models. Likewise, the STRONG INDIRECT CONTROL, Type B, resembles closely the Curry and Fischer "state, controlled type" and the Garms' "Decentralized control-planned economy model." Low REGULATION, Type C, follows the Curry and Fischer "state-aided" type and the "mixed economic control" model of Garms.

Notes

1. L. A. Glenny, *Autonomy of Public Colleges: The Challenge of Coordination* (New York: McGraw-Hill, 1959); Robert Berdahl, *Statewide Coordination of Higher Education* (Washington, D.C.: American Council on Education, 1971).

2. James Mingle, ed., *Management Flexibility and State Regulation in Higher Education* (Atlanta: Southern Regional Education Board, 1983); J. Fredericks Volkwein, "Campus Autonomy and Its Relationship to Measures of University Quality" (Paper presented at the Association for the Study of Higher Education Annual Meeting, San Antonio, Texas, 1985).

3. Denis J. Curry and Norman M. Fischer, "Public Higher Education and the State: Models for Financing, Budgeting, and Accountability" (Paper presented at the Association for the Study of Higher Education Annual Meeting, San Antonio, Texas, 1986).

4. Carnegie Commission on Higher Education, *Priorities for Action: Final Report of the Carnegie Commission on Higher Education* (New York: McGraw-Hill Book Company, 1973); Carnegie Council on Policy Studies in Higher Education, *The States and Higher Education: A Proud Past and a Vital Future* (San Francisco: Jossey-Bass Publishers, 1976); Carnegie Foundation for the Advancement of Teaching, *The Control of the Campus: A Report on the Governance of Higher Education* (Princeton, N.J.: Princeton University Press, 1982); Edward S. Gruson, *State Regulation of Higher Education in a Period of Decline* (Cambridge, Mass.: Sloan Commission on Government and Higher Education, 1979).

5. S.V. Martorana and J.L. Wattenbarger, *Principles, Practices, and Alternatives in State Methods of Financing Community College* 32 (University Park, Pa.: Center for the Study of Higher Education, Pennsylvania State University, 1978).

6. Lawrence Arney, "A Comparison of Patterns of Financial Support with Selected Criteria in Community Junior Colleges" (Ph.D. dissertation, University of Florida, 1969); J.L. Wattenbarger and P. Bibby, *Financing Community Colleges 1981* (Gainesville, Fla.: Institute of Higher Education, University of Florida, 1981); J.L. Wattenbarger and P.M. Starnes, *Financial Support Patterns for Community Colleges, 1976* (Gainesville, Fla.: Institute of Higher Education, University of Florida, 1976); J.L. Wattenbarger and Sherry L. Mercer, *Financing Community Colleges 1987* (Gainesville, Fla.: Institute of Higher Education, University of Florida, 1987); J.L. Wattenbarger and Sharon L. Mercer, *Financing Community Colleges 1988* (Gainesville, Fla.: Institute of Higher Education, University of Florida, 1988).

7. Glenny, *Autonomy of Public Colleges*; Berdahl, *Statewide Coordination*.

8. L. A. Glenny. *State Budgeting for Higher Education: Interagency Conflict and Consensus* (Berkeley: Center for Research and Development in Higher Education, University of California, 1976).

9. Heather J. Haberaecker, "Factors Influencing The Degree of State Fiscal Regulation of Public Universities" (Ph.D. dissertation, University of Michigan, 1987); Fred Thompson and William Zumeta, "A Regulatory Model of Governmental Coordinating Activities in the Higher Education Sector," *Economics of Education Review* 1 (Winter 1981): 27–52.

10. Mingle, *Management Flexibility;* James A. Hyatt and Aurora Santiago, *Incentives and Disincentives for Effective Management* (Washington, D.C.: NACUBO, 1984).

11. Volkwein, "Campus Autonomy"; Curry and Fischer, "Public Higher Education"; W.L. Garms, *Financing Community Colleges* (New York: Teachers College Press, 1977).

12. Curry and Fischer, "Public Higher Education."

13. Garms, *Financing.*

14. Wattenbarger and Starnes *Financial Support Patterns;* Wattenbarger and Mercer, *Financing Community Colleges 1988.*

15. For example, a measure involving the disposition of year-end balances asked the respondent to indicate whether in the event of an ending balance, dollars were returned to the state or retained at the local level. A measure regarding the nature of state budget process asked respondents to differentiate state funding approaches along a continuum of non-formula, cost-based formula and flat-rate formula budgeting. Table 4 in the results section provides usage percentages of specific regulatory measures at various descriptive levels of the survey.

16. The second factor scale was developed through a second round of factor analysis because of the inappropriateness of conducting factor analysis when the number of cases (that is, only 62) was *not* at least 10 times the number of analyzed variables (which was 29). It was necessary, therefore, to break the data reduction effort into two parts. The initial six factors, the maximum permitted by the data limitations, were identified through six separate factor analyses developed by alternative trial and error combinations. A second round of factor analysis was based on weighted mean scores from the six derived factors. This second round supported the existence of a single overall regulatory factor.

17. Factor Analysis is considered a "heuristic" technique. For this reason, the analysis utilized and contrasted two methods of Clustering, the "Average linkage" method and the "Ward's minimum within-group variability method" in determining the number of cluster types identified through the grouping of state systems. The "Average Linkage" or "average distance" method is the most frequently used method in social science analysis and is the default method of the SPSS program. This study, therefore, considered the "average linkage method" as the presumptive choice, but examined the results of "Ward's method" as a possible alternative.

    Both methods utilize the "proximity measure" of Squared Euclidean Distance which measures the distance between two cases as the sum of the squared differences between the values of the clustering variables. The "Average Linkage" or "average distance" method uses a minimizing between-group distance measure based upon the average of all distances between pairs, while the "Ward Method" focuses on the minimum variance between clusters. Both methods produce relatively compact clusters. See Maurice Lorr, *Cluster Analysis for Social Scientists* (San Francisco: Jossey-Bass Publishers, 1983).

18. Curry and Fischer, "Public Higher Education."

19. Jessie P. Bogue. *The Community College* (New York: McGraw-Hill Book Company, 1950); Clyde E. Blocker, Robert Plummer and Richard C. Richardson. *The Two Year College: a Social Synthesis* (Englewood Cliffs, N.J.: Prentice-Hall, 1965); Barbara E. Taylor, *Working Effectively with Trustees: Building Cooperative Campus Leadership.* ASHE-ERIC Higher Education Report, no. 2 (Washington, D.C.: Association for the Study of Higher Education, 1987); Charles H. Polk, Vaughan A. LaCombe and Jeanne Goddard, "Trustee Selection: Who Gets What, Who Pays," *Enhancing Trustee Effectiveness* (San Francisco: Jossey-Bass Publishers, 1976); E.J. Gleazer, Jr., "Who Decides." *The Two-year College Trustee, National Issues and Perspectives: Special Report* (Washington, D.C.: Association of Governing Boards of Universities and Colleges, 1972); William Meardy, "They Killed 'Community'," *ACCT Advisor* 17 (January 1987): 2; Robert Harrell, "The Virginia Community College System—A State System that Works," *ACCT Advisor* 17 (March 1987): 2.

20. Curry and Fischer, "Public Higher Education"; Garms, *Financing.*

21. The sixteen remaining systems were found to group in four minor clusters that can be generally linked to the major clusters based upon an examination of the cluster analysis statistical results. A three-system cluster containing Iowa, Ohio technical colleges and Ohio community colleges contained within universities, was found to be linked to Type C. An additional small cluster continuing the four systems of Arizona, Kansas, New Mexico independent community colleges and Wisconsin technical colleges was also found to be related to Type C. Seven state systems including California, Texas, Utah, Wyoming, North Dakota and the two-year colleges in Indiana were found to be most closely related to Type B. A very distinct two-system cluster containing Maine and Massachusetts was also identified.

22. Type A contained several states that included more than one system of community colleges. Arkansas independent community colleges and also community colleges contained within universities were found in Type A. In Connecticut and Tennessee both the community colleges and technical colleges clustered in Type A. In Oklahoma, community colleges contained within universities were found in Type A along with two-year colleges that have no independent taxing authority.

23. Type B included multiple systems in Louisiana and West Virginia that contained community colleges within universities and independent community colleges. The Oklahoma two-year colleges that had independent taxing power were found to cluster as part of Type B. The state administered community colleges within Colorado were included as part of Type B.

24. The Colorado independent community colleges with separate tax power were included in Type C. Both the SUNY and CUNY systems in New York were found as part of Type C. The independent community colleges within Ohio were found as part of Type C.

Suggested Readings:
Organization, Administration, and Finance

Alfred, R. L. (1978). "Coping With Reduced Resources."*New Directions for Community Colleges*, No. 22.

Amey, M. J. and Twombly, S. B. (Winter 1992). "Re-Visioning Leadership in Community Colleges." *The Review of Higher Education*, 15 (2):125–50.

Breneman, D. W. & Nelson, S. C. (1981). *Financing Community Colleges, an Economic Perspective.* Washington D.C.: Brookings Institution.

Brint, S. & Karabel, J. (1989). *The Diverted Dream: Community Colleges and the Promise and Educational Opportunity in America. 1900–1985.* New York: Oxford University Press.

Brint, S. & Karabel J. (Fall, 1989). "The Community College and Democratic Ideals." *Community College Review*, 17 (2), 9–19.

Brubacher, J. S. & Rudy, W. (1976). *Higher Education in Transition, an American History.* New York: Harper.

Carnegie Foundation for the Advancement of Teaching (1989). *Tribal Colleges: Shaping the Future of Native America.* Princeton, N.J.: The Foundation.

Cohen, A. M. (1985). "The Community College in the American Educational System." In Clifford Adelman (ed.). *Contexts for Learning.* Washington, D.C.: National Institute of Education.

Cohen, A. M. & Brawer, F. B. (1989). *The American Community College.* San Francisco: Jossey-Bass.

Dziech, B. W. (Summer 1992). "Prisoners of Elitism: The Community College's Struggle for Stature." *New Directions for Community Colleges*, 20 (2), 1–106.

Frye, J. H. (1992). *The Vision of the Public Junior College, 1900–1940*. New York: Greenwood Press.

Garms, W. (1981). "On Measuring the Equity of Community College Finance." *Educational Administration Quarterly*, 17 (2), 1–20.

Garrett, R. L. (Summer 1992). "Degree of Centralization of Governance of State Community College Systems in the United States, 1990." *Community College Review*, 20 (1), 7–13.

Goodwin, D. (1989). *Postsecondary Vocational Education*. National Assessment of Vocational Education Final Report. Volume IV.

Orfield, G. (1992, November). *State Higher Education Systems and College Completion*. Final Report to the Ford Foundation, University of Chicago.

PROGRAMS AND SERVICES

The Total Community College Curriculum

ARTHUR M. COHEN AND JAN M. IGNASH*

The liberal arts as a focus of study derive from the belief that human knowledge and societal cohesion are grounded in rationality. In the earliest American colleges, this doctrine gave rise to a curriculum centering on philosophy, languages, science, and rhetoric. Subsequently, the liberal arts were codified in academic disciplines in the universities and expanded as new ways of organizing knowledge came to the fore. When community colleges were founded early in the twentieth century, they installed the liberal arts, gradually modifying them in accordance with shifting fashions of academic organization and with attention to the capabilities and interests of their students. Despite frequent attempts to shift the curriculum toward studies more directly vocational, the liberal arts, with more than half the enrollment, remain the centerpiece of community college studies.

The Center for the Study of Community Colleges (CSCC) has examined the liberal arts in community colleges nationwide in a series of studies that began in 1975 with a grant from the National Endowment for the Humanities. Since then, CSCC staff have studied various other subsets of the liberal arts as listed:

Date	Sponsor	Number of Colleges in Sample	Curricula Reviewed
1975	NEH	156	Humanities
1977	NEH	178	Humanities
1978	NSF	175	Sciences and Social Sciences
1983	Ford	38	All liberal arts
1986	Carnegie	95	All liberal arts
1987	Ford	109	Fine and Performing Arts
1991	NCAAT	164	All liberal arts

These studies have tallied one or a combination of such variables as the relative magnitude of each academic discipline, enrollments, class size, number of colleges offering the various courses, faculty goals, programmatic patterns, student interests, and the prevalence of remedial instruction and advanced courses. The findings of the CSCC studies have been reported in numerous papers, many of which are summarized in *The Collegiate Function of Community Colleges* (Cohen and Brawer, 1987). This paper reports the findings of the 1991 study.

However, the 1991 liberal arts study is only part of CSCC's entire effort to study the curriculum. In 1992, for the first time in the 16 years CSCC has been studying the community college curriculum, the center tracked the non-liberal arts segment of the curriculum, as well. This portion of the curriculum, accounting for only one-fourth or less of the total community college curriculum well into the 1950s, now accounts for 43 percent of the total credit curriculum. In addition, courses in this segment of the curriculum, once considered "terminal" education designed to lead directly to employment and not applicable for baccalaureate credit, now are often offered for transfer credit. Clearly, the non-liberal arts have grown in terms of proportion of the curriculum offered and as an avenue to further study. The second half of this paper reports the results of CSCC's Non-Liberal Arts Study.

The Liberal Arts

Methodology

The data for the liberal arts study were obtained from 164 community colleges throughout the United States by randomly sampling the colleges listed in the 1990 *Directory of the American Association of Community and Junior Colleges*. The sample was approximately balanced according to size with 51 small (less than 1500 students), 56 medium, and 57 large (more than 6,000 students) colleges in the set. Because a special effort was made to include the colleges that were participating in the National Center for Academic Achievement and Transfer's partnership grant program, the sample was tilted somewhat toward colleges that enroll higher proportions of underrepresented minority-group students.

Catalogs and class schedules for spring 1991 were obtained from the colleges, and course sections in the liberal arts were counted and tallied according to the coding scheme used in the prior studies. The scheme divides the liberal arts curriculum into six major disciplines—humanities, English, fine and performing arts, social sciences, sciences, and mathematics and computer sciences. These six disciplines are further divided into 55 broad subject areas. For example, the sub-subject area "French" is part of the broad subject area "Foreign Languages," which is part of the "Humanities" discipline. For a course section to be listed, the class schedule had to designate a meeting time and place; laboratory, independent study, cooperative, apprenticeship, and field-work classes were not included.

To code each liberal arts course at the appropriate proficiency level, definitions for remedial, standard, and advanced courses were used. "Remedial" applies to any compensatory, developmental, or basic course which is below college-level proficiency and which typically does not carry college transfer credit. "Standard" courses are "first-tier" or "introductory" courses which have no same subject-area prerequisite for enrollment and which carry college graduation or transfer credit. "Advanced" courses carry a prerequisite in the same or a related field as a condition for enrollment.

After coding and tallying 59,205 liberal arts classes into the appropriate sub-subject areas, a random sample of every tenth section under each broad subject area was pulled. The colleges were asked to provide either second-census or end-of-the-term enrollment figures for this sample. The number of sections that had been canceled in each subject area was also noted. Enrollment and average class size figures were then calculated, based on the 164 colleges, and extrapolated to the population of 1,250 U.S. community colleges. Finally, the scheduled course sections in the remainder of the curriculum were counted in order to determine an approximate ratio of liberal arts to non-liberal arts offerings.

Research Questions

The study provided data on many aspects of the liberal arts curriculum, and, together with the earlier CSCC studies, was used to plot trends in the various subject areas. Additional data that were available from a complementary study of transfer rates in 52 of the 164 participating colleges and IPEDS data on the ethnic composition of the student body in all the colleges made it possible to answer a number of questions:

- How have the liberal arts changed in recent years?

- What is the fastest-growing subject area?

- Does college size or locale relate to course patterns?

- How does a college's liberal arts curriculum relate to its transfer rate?

- Does the curriculum differ in colleges with higher or lower minority student enrollments?

- To what extent does the curriculum reflect a college's graduation requirements?

How Have the Liberal Arts Changed in Recent Years?

In general, the liberal arts have expanded. In 1991, they accounted for approximately 56 percent of the curriculum, up from 52 percent in 1986. Very little of this expansion can be traced to innovation or new course designs; most resulted from higher proportions of students enrolling in traditional liberal arts classes.

With few exceptions, the liberal arts reveal remarkable stability. Many of the subject areas continue to be offered by nearly all (90 percent plus) of the colleges: history, literature, political science, English, economics, psychology, sociology, biology, chemistry, math, and computer science. Total enrollments in these subjects reflect their dominance. (See Table 1.) However, the ubiquity of the offerings and the enrollment figures mask certain changes.

Foreign languages, detailed in the section on ESL below, are offered by less than 90 percent of the colleges, but their enrollments, tripling between 1978 and 1991, are exceeded only by English and math. In that same 13-year interval, enrollments in psychology, biology, physics, chemistry, and math doubled, but those in literature, history, and political science changed only negligibly. Therefore, although some basic subjects continue to be offered nearly everywhere, the overall number of students taking them shifts markedly.

Other changes were seen in special-group and remedial studies. CSCC staff coded such courses as "Women's Literature," "Afro-American History," and "Sociology of Mexican Americans" in Group Literature (offered by more than half of the colleges), History of Special Groups (offered by more than one-third of the colleges), and Sociology of Particular Groups (offered by one-fourth of the colleges), respectively. Ethnic studies, coded only if it was listed as a separate course or program, was found in only 10 percent of the colleges. Thus, the CSCC findings should not be compared with those reported by Levine and Curreton (1992), who tallied each special-group course as "Ethnic Studies" or "Women's Studies."

Table 1
Total Student Enrollment Figures and Average Class Size for All Liberal Arts Areas

Subject	Enrollment	Average Size
ENGLISH	1,317,400	21
FINE AND PERFORMING ARTS		
Dance	27,600	16
Music	95,800	11
Theater	19,600	14
Visual Arts	151,700	11
HUMANITIES		
Art History/Appreciation	84,700	28
Cultural Anthropology	31,100	30
Fine and Performing Arts		
(History/Appreciation)	29,900	28
Foreign Languages	460,700	20
History	396,500	31
Interdisciplinary Humanities		
(includes Cultural Geography)	94,200	35
Literature	120,900	23
Music History/Appreciation	65,600	27
Philosophy and Logic	143,200	29
Political Science	249,000	29
Religious Studies	14,300	35
Social/Ethnic Studies	13,400	26
MATHEMATICS AND COMPUTER SCIENCES		
Advanced Mathematics	87,700	20
Applied Math/Technology-Related	41,600	18
Computer Science Technology	147,200	23
Introductory and		
Intermediate Mathematics	766,100	24
Math for Other Majors	99,700	23
Statistics and Probability	69,000	27
SCIENCES		
Biological Sciences (including Agriculture		
Science/Natural Resources)	405,500	26
Chemistry	130,200	20
Earth and Space Sciences		
(includes Environmental Science)	85,100	32
Engineering Sciences & Technology	102,200	15
Geology	24,100	24
Integrated Science	43,400	27
Physics	80,100	19
SOCIAL SCIENCES		
Anthropology	28,000	23
Economics	173,500	27
Geography	19,500	24
Interdisciplinary Social Sciences	30,100	20
Psychology	455,100	30
Sociology	256,300	31

Remedial studies remain prominent in English and math (See Table 2). Approximately 30 percent of the class sections offered in English are at the remedial level, down from 37 percent 15 years ago, and the percentage of remedial math classes dropped by half from 32 to 16 percent. These changes resulted not because the incoming students were better prepared, but because math labs have become more widespread; the CSCC study did not count enrollments in lab courses. Furthermore, much of the remedial English instruction is taking place in tutorial settings and in courses coded as "College-Level Introductory Composition," but which may be taken repeatedly; Florida's College Level Academic Skills Test requirement, for example, has stimulated much of the latter.

Table 2
Percent of Colleges Providing Remedial,
Standard, and Advanced Courses in the Six Major Discipline Areas

Discipline	Remedial	Standard	Advanced
English	89	99	84
Fine & Performing Arts	0	83	75
Humanities	1	97	80
Math & Computer Science	65	98	86
Science	5	100	87
Social Science	0	98	59

Percent of Remedial, Standard, and Advanced Course Offerings in Each Major Discipline Area

Discipline	Remedial	Standard	Advanced
English	30.5	49.7	19.8
Fine & Performing Arts	0.0	62.8	37.2
Humanities	.1	82.5	17.4
Math & Computer Science	15.9*	62.2	21.9
Science	1.0	67.6	31.7
Social Science	0.0	85.8	14.2

*Self-paced, individualized, and lab courses were not counted. A large number of remedial math courses were self-paced, individualized, and lab courses, which explains the low remedial math percentage.

Intracourse shifts undoubtedly have been occurring, as well. Certainly few, if any, instructors are teaching "U.S. History to 1877" in the same fashion they once did; the texts and syllabi have been modified to account for the contributions of women and minorities. But if the course carries the same title, it is coded as the same course.

What is the Fastest-Growing Subject Area?

English as a Second Language (ESL) is far and away the fastest-growing area in community colleges. In fact, the phenomenal growth in foreign languages (from 5 percent of the entire liberal arts enrollment in 1986 to 8.5 percent in 1991) is due solely to the continuing rise in ESL. ESL represented 30 percent of the foreign language enrollments in 1983, 43 percent in 1986, and 51 percent in 1991 when 244,306 students were enrolled. The percentage of colleges offering ESL grew from 26 in 1975 to 41 in 1991. Among the colleges offering ESL, 58 percent offered from one to 25 sections, 36 percent offered from 26 to 100 sections, and the remaining 6 percent offered more than 100 sections. Some of the colleges offering large numbers of ESL sections are listed below:

College	Number of ESL Sections Offered
Yuba College, Marysville, CA	70
Pasadena City College, CA	71
Community College of Philadelphia, PA	83
San Jose City College, CA	89
Miami-Dade Community College (South Campus), FL	152
Passaic County Community College, Paterson, NJ	160
Harry S. Truman College, Chicago, IL	243
El Paso Community College, TX	429

ESL takes many forms. At El Paso Community College, programs in ESL and English for Special Purposes (for advanced students) were available, as well as bilingual education programs which offered instruction in content areas in Spanish. A sample of classes taught bilingually included organizational behavior, U.S. history since 1865, and medical terminology. Miami-Dade Community College separates acronyms for its ESL programs to clearly designate which courses count toward graduation requirements (labeled ESL in the course catalog) and which do not (labeled ENS—English for Non-Native Speakers). Miami-Dade also maintains a Bilingual Institute for Business and Technology, where students can learn technical terminology in both English and Spanish.

All the large colleges offer classes in English language instruction to both ESL and English as a Foreign Language (EFL) students—that is, to both U.S. citizens and immigrants whose native language is not English, as well as to foreign students. Passaic County Community College maintains separate ESL programs for foreign students and for U.S. immigrants and citizens. Most colleges with sizable ESL populations offer special bilingual/ESL services to Limited English Proficiency students to help them succeed in regular coursework. Harry S. Truman College offers ESL-TV for Spanish-speaking adults. Many large campuses maintain bilingual assistance centers for students whose native language is Spanish, but few have established centers for students whose native language is not Spanish.

ESL students from numerous language groups sometimes represent substantial proportions of the college's population, as at Passaic County Community College, where 35 percent of the students take some form of ESL. The Gujarati-speaking population at Passaic is second only to the Spanish-speaking ESL population at the college. At the Community College of Philadelphia, ESL students come from 56 countries; 21 percent of the students are Vietnamese, 17 percent are Spanish, and 14 percent Russian. At Harry S. Truman College, 60 percent are Russian. Thirty-six percent of Pasadena City's ESL students speak some dialect of Chinese as their first language. And at Yuba College, the Hmong students have only recently fallen behind Spanish-speaking ESL students as the largest language group.

With almost a quarter of a million students occupying seats in ESL classes at community colleges across the United States, and with these numbers expected to increase, many policy implications loom. For example, since 60 percent of ESL sections are offered for beginning or intermediate-level students, the time it takes a student to complete a degree program will grow as more students spend more time studying English to prepare for degree-credit classes. In just five years, ESL has jumped a full 70 percent of its share of the total liberal arts curriculum. Its impact on the overall instructional program has yet to be traced.

Does College Size or Locale Relate to Course Patterns?

A perennial problem in comparing rural colleges with urban colleges and small colleges with large colleges is that few rural colleges are large, and few urban colleges are small; therefore, any differences that appear may be related to size or to locale, or to both. The distribution of colleges in the CSCC sample points to the pattern: only three of the small colleges were in urban settings, and only two of the large colleges were in rural areas.

Nevertheless, it is possible to make some comparisons. As noted in Table 3, college size is only modestly related to general curriculum patterns. With the exception of a tilt toward science at the smaller colleges and toward humanities at the larger ones (an effect of the numerous sections of ESL), rounding error may account for the small differences shown.

Table 3
Liberal Arts Curriculum by Size of Institution*

Size of Institution	Percent of Liberal Arts Curriculum Which Is:					
	English	Fine Arts	Humanities	Computer Science	Science	Social Science
Small	22	10	21	18	18	12
Medium	23	08	22	21	14	13
Large	23	10	25	18	13	11

* Totals exceed 100 percent because of rounding.

The curricular differences that may be attributed to college locale can be computed by viewing just the medium-size colleges. But as Table 4 demonstrates, few differences appear except for the greater percentage of Humanities courses (again ESL-dominated) at the urban colleges. Thus like college size, locale is not substantially related to the distribution of liberal arts courses across the curriculum.

Table 4
Liberal Arts Curriculum at Medium-Sized Colleges by College Locale

Size/Locale of Institution	Percent of Liberal Arts Curriculum Which Is:					
	English	Fine Arts	Humanities	Computer Science	Science	Social Science
Medium Rural	23	9	19	20	15	14
Medium Suburban	22	9	21	23	13	12
Medium Urban	23	8	25	19	14	12
Full Sample	22	9	24	20	14	12

Does the availability of remedial or advanced courses vary? The curriculum at the medium-sized rural colleges includes a smaller percentage of remedial courses and a larger percentage of advanced courses. The rural institutions offer three sections of advanced courses for every remedial section offered, while suburban institutions offer 1.9 and urban institutions offer 1.4 advanced sections for every remedial section. For the overall sample, the ratio is 2.2 advanced sections for each remedial section. These differences are more pronounced than those based on size, and they suggest some real differences in the curricular structure. As Richardson and Bender (1987) have argued, urban institutions apparently *do* devote a greater proportion of their curriculum to remedial studies, and, consequently, a smaller proportion to advanced level courses.

The availability of specialized courses in certain disciplines varies even more markedly. Smaller institutions cannot offer as many total class sections as the medium and large institutions. What choices do they make? Table 5 displays the subject areas offered. The larger the college, the greater the likelihood of its offering courses other than basic general studies requirements. From art history to statistics, the ratio of colleges providing specialized classes drops as college size decreases, with the most pronounced differences evident in cultural anthropology, cultural geography, dance, earth/space science, fine arts appreciation, and geology. Differences of this magnitude are not evident when the medium-sized colleges are compared on the basis of location.

In summary, the major liberal arts disciplines are evenly distributed across all community colleges, regardless of size or setting, suggesting that students seeking a general education can obtain basic courses anywhere. Finding advanced courses and courses in specialized subject areas is a different matter. Students at large community colleges have a wide variety of subjects to choose from, but students at smaller colleges and those in rural areas may have fewer choices.

Are Curriculum and Transfer Rate Related?

If, as conventional belief has it, the liberal arts are provided primarily for students expecting to transfer to baccalaureate-granting institutions, then that curricular area should be more prominent at colleges with higher student transfer rates. To test that proposition, CSCC staff matched the data from the curriculum study with the findings from a study of transfer rates that CSCC was conducting simultaneously. The definition of transfer rate was: The number of students who entered a community college in fall 1986 with no prior college experience and who completed at least 12 college credit units there, divided into the number of that group who matriculated at a senior institution by spring 1991. Fifty-two colleges participated in both the curriculum and transfer studies. For comparison purposes, ESL was removed from the liberal arts data set because it is not a typical transfer-related curriculum.

To test the relationship between the proportion of liberal arts courses in the total curriculum and transfer rates, the means for both liberal arts ratios and transfer rates were derived, and the colleges were placed into low and high categories. Colleges with liberal arts ratios at or above the mean were placed in the high category, those below were placed in the low category. Similarly, colleges with transfer rates below the mean were placed in the low category, and colleges with transfer rates above the mean were placed in the high category. Similarly, these categories were cross-tabulated. Findings were that among those colleges with transfer rates below the sample mean, 69 percent were also below the mean for the proportion of liberal arts offerings at the college. Among those colleges with transfer rates classified as high, 63 percent were high in liberal arts offerings. (These were statistically significant relationships at the .05 level.)

A second analysis compared the ratios of remedial, standard, and advanced courses with the college's transfer rates. No significant relationships were found. Thus, while the proportion of liberal arts courses at the colleges appears to be related to transfer, these differences are less apparent when analyzed by course level.

Does the Curriculum Differ at Colleges with Higher or Lower Minority Student Enrollment?

A perennial issue in the analysis of community colleges is the extent to which they assist or retard their students' progress toward the baccalaureate. Because most of the minority-group students

TABLE 5
Percentage of Community Colleges
Offering Liberal Arts Classes, by Institutional Size

Course	Small	Medium	Large
ENGLISH	98	98	100
FINE AND PERFORMING ARTS			
Dance	6	24	40
Music	42	73	90
Theater	26	51	60
Visual Arts	57	86	97
HUMANITIES			
Art History	57	88	91
Cultural Anthropology	15	37	83
Cultural Geography	6	24	40
Fine & Performing Arts			
History/Appreciation	19	41	74
Foreign Languages	70	88	98
History	83	92	98
Interdisciplinary Humanities	26	42	71
Literature	81	93	98
Music History/Appreciation	51	71	86
Philosophy	55	68	95
Political Science	83	86	98
Religious Studies	13	25	26
Social and Ethnic Studies	8	3	31
MATHEMATICS AND COMPUTER SCIENCES			
Advanced Math	68	88	98
Applied Math	38	56	72
Computer Sciences	77	92	98
Introductory & Intermediate Math	96	98	100
Math for other Majors	62	85	93
Statistics	50	83	98
SCIENCE			
Agriculture and Natural Resources	17	17	19
Biological Sciences	85	97	100
Chemistry	79	97	100
Earth/Space Science	19	44	81
Engineering	45	80	97
Environmental Science	15	10	26
Geology	21	33	69
Integrated Sciences	34	41	62
Physics	74	86	98
SOCIAL SCIENCE			
Anthropology	17	22	59
Economics	87	93	98
Geography	28	42	57
History/Sociology/Phil. of Science	2	5	7
Interdisciplinary Social Sciences	21	32	50
Psychology	96	98	100
Sociology	83	97	100

who pursue higher education begin at a community college, and because the students who start there seem less likely than native university students to progress toward the baccalaureate expeditiously, numerous analysts have contended that college policies and procedures are detrimental to that progress (see, for example, Astin [1977] and Pincus and Archer [1989]). The curriculum that the colleges provide frequently is criticized for its emphasis on vocational studies; Brint and Karabel (1989) and Grubb (1991), in particular, cite the vocational studies emphasis as a major contributor to the students' failure to gain higher degrees.

If these contentions have merit, then the curriculum at colleges with high proportions of non-white students should reflect a distinct bias away from the liberal arts. To test that proposition, CSCC staff ran a correlation using the percentage of liberal arts courses offered and the percentage of non-white students. The correlation yielded a positive relationship (.32) that was significant at the .05 level. This correlation indicates that the larger the non-white student population, the larger the number of liberal arts course offerings. As for the curriculum level, the analyses demonstrated no significant relationships between the ethnic composition of a school and the percent of remedial, standard, and advanced courses in the liberal arts curriculum.

Based on these findings, the contention that colleges with high proportions of minorities tend to offer fewer liberal arts classes is not supported. In fact, the colleges with higher percentages of minorities offer more liberal arts courses. The ratio in a few colleges is startling. At Atlanta Metropolitan College (GA), 91 percent of the student population is non-white, and 79 percent of the curriculum is devoted to liberal arts. At Borough of Manhattan Community College (NY) non-white students account for 91 percent of the population, and liberal arts courses account for 71 percent of the curriculum. In comparison, colleges with smaller percentages of non-white students, such as Williamsburg Technical College (SC)—36 percent, and Triton (IL)—28 percent, have percentages of liberal arts curriculums that fall below the mean.

However, noting that ESL was coded under liberal arts and that a community college with a large non-white population may offer more ESL classes than a college with a smaller non-white population, another correlation was run with ESL sections extracted from the percentage of liberal arts courses offered. Although it was not significant, the correlation continued to reveal a positive relationship (.19). Therefore, even while controlling for ESL, the contention that the colleges with high proportions of minorities tend to offer fewer liberal arts classes still is not supported. Even with ESL taken out of the liberal arts, the percentage of liberal arts courses offered at Atlanta Metropolitan and Borough of Manhattan Community College remained above the mean—68 percent and 60 percent, respectively. Ethnic minorities do have access to liberal arts curricula and college-level courses.

Still, it appears that the larger the percentage of non-white students, the lower the transfer rate. At the colleges with a low percentage of minority students, 57 percent had low transfer rates; at the colleges with large numbers of minority students, 85 percent had low transfer rates. Therefore, while a higher concentration of minority students at community colleges is related to more liberal arts course offerings, it also is associated with a lower transfer rate. Whatever the reasons, they should not be attributed to the curriculum. Vocational-course tracking cannot be blamed.

Are Graduation Requirements Related to Enrollments in Liberal Arts Courses?

American community colleges enroll 5.1 million students and award 450,000 associate's degrees each year. Clearly, most students leave without completing degree requirements. Some obtain occupational certificates, many transfer to other institutions, and many more follow other pursuits for awhile, displaying the intermittent attendance pattern that Adelman (1992) documents.

Even so, how much do graduation requirements relate to course enrollments? To test this question, the catalogs for 40 colleges in the sample were reviewed to determine curriculum requirements for the associate's degree. Some slight differences were found among requirements for the various types of associate's degrees (arts, science, applied science, etc.), but for the most part, the basic course patterns were similar. The percentage of community colleges requiring specific subject areas is shown in Table 6, along with the number of students taking classes in those areas.

Except for ethnic studies and its manifestation in courses in the history, sociology, and literature of special groups (offered by fewer than half the colleges), all the disciplines required for graduation are present at nearly all the colleges. This is no surprise, since these often-called "general education" courses have represented the curricular canon from secondary schools through the lower division of universities since early in the century. Computer literacy, a subject area that has grown rapidly in the past 20 years, and the even more recent ethnic studies, are the only contemporary additions. They are required by 11 percent and 8 percent of the colleges, respectively, and their relatively low enrollment figures reflect the lack of degree requirements in these areas.

TABLE 6

Subjects	Sub-subject	Colleges Requiring One or More Courses for Graduation	Number of Students Nationally
English Composition		97%	1,317,400
Humanities (excluding ESL)		88%	704,800
Math		97%	1,064,100
Physical Education/Health		74%	NA
	Computer Literacy	11%	147,200
	Ethnic Studies (separately organized programs only)	8%	13,400
Science		94%	768,400
Social Studies		98%	NA
	U.S. Government	26%	249,000
	U.S. History	34%	396,500

The Non-Liberal Arts

That the non-liberal arts have flourished in recent years is due to a variety of factors. As the CSCC Non-Liberal Arts Study demonstrates, a high percentage of non-liberal arts courses in many subject areas transfer directly to four-year institutions. This factor may be paramount in underscoring the "validity" of the non-liberal arts, since students are not foreclosing their options for further studies through the pursuit of study of the non-liberal arts. A second factor is that of prestige. As many professions require increased years of study as a condition for employment, the status of those professions rises accordingly. Non-liberal arts education therefore need not be viewed as education leading away from the baccalaureate degree.

Methodology

Two major objectives drove the Non-Liberal Arts Study. The first was to quantify the proportion of the curriculum devoted to the non-liberal arts, while the second was to discover the percentage of non-liberal arts courses that transfer to four-year institutions. Because the Non-Liberal Arts Study was the first of its kind conducted by CSCC, a taxonomy had to be developed. Based largely on the "Taxonomy of Academic and Vocational Courses for Less-than-4-Year Postsecondary Institutions" (Grubb, June 1987), a CSCC taxonomy was developed for the non-liberal arts courses using ten major discipline areas: Agriculture Technology, Business and Office, Education, Engineering Technology, Health, Home Economics, Marketing, Technical Education, Trade and Industry, and Other.

The same 164 community colleges that participated in the 1991 National Liberal Arts Study also participated in the Non-Liberal Arts Study. Once the taxonomy was developed, CSCC staff coded non-liberal arts courses using the same course schedules that had provided the data for the liberal arts study. Thus, the ratio of liberal arts to non-liberal arts portions of the curriculum could be established. All policies and constraints used in coding the 1991 liberal arts study applied to the subsequent Non-Liberal Arts Study. The same criteria for identifying remedial, standard and advanced courses applied, as did the same injunction against coding classes without definite times and meeting places.

Since the Non-Liberal Arts Study is a baseline study, the finer gradations of subject categories were not established as they were in the liberal arts studies. Some explanation is necessary, therefore, concerning specific subject areas included under each of the ten broad discipline areas.

The Non-Liberal Arts Taxonomy

As stated above, the CSCC non-liberal arts taxonomy divided this portion of the curriculum into ten major discipline areas. Some areas of potential overlap between the liberal arts and the non-liberal arts did occur, however, as in the areas of agriculture and engineering. For these areas, staff developed strict guidelines to differentiate between potential areas of conflict. An example of a liberal arts agriculture course is "Plant Science," while a non-liberal arts agriculture technology course might be entitled "Agribusiness and Crop Production."

The major categories and specific course areas for the non-liberal arts are as follows:

Agriculture

Horticulture, agribusiness and crop production, forest products and other agriculture products, agricultural sciences, renewable natural resources, animal health technology, nursery operation

Business and Office

Accounting, taxes, business and management, secretarial and related (filing, typing, shorthand, 10-key calculations), labor law, will, trusts and estate planning, legal assistant, other business and office, airline ticketing and reservations

Education

Early childhood education, physical education instructor courses, coaching, children's literature, nanny courses, math, music, or art for teachers, courses for future instructors of the emotionally and mentally challenged

Engineering Technologies

(Most of this category was coded under the Spring 1991 Liberal Arts Study.) Engineering courses that were too occupationally oriented to be coded in the liberal arts were coded under non-liberal arts. These non-liberal arts engineering courses focus on engineering principles such as "Analog or Digital Fundamentals," "AC/DC Current," or "Ohm's Law," as well as more practical subject matter. Examples: "Avionics" (theory of flight and practical aspects of flying an airplane) or "Industrial Electricity."

Health

Nursing, health sciences, allied health, CPR, emergency technician, nutrition, marriage and family counseling courses, drug counseling, working with juvenile delinquents, dental assisting, corrective and rehabilitative physical education or other physical therapy for the physically challenged

Home Economics

Home economics, sewing, cooking, preserving foods, home interior decorating, all home economics courses which are not focused on trade and industry and which are intended for one's personal use at home

Marketing and Distribution

Real estate, fashion merchandising, salesmanship, auctioneering, advertising design layout, purchasing textiles

Personal Skills and Avocational Courses

Physical education, freshman orientation, introduction to the library, parenting, fashion color analysis, career and life planning, self-appraisal courses

Technical Education

Computer software applications (word processing, spreadsheets, database programs, networking, desktop publishing—all *non-programming* computer applications); protective services including fire, police and law enforcement, lifeguard, and military science courses; communication technologies including journalism, TV, newspaper reporting, radio announcing, photo journalism, and other mass media courses, graphics and offset printing; commercial photography

Trade and Industry

Construction; automotive; aviation engineering (concerning the manufacture of airplanes); surveying; drafting including CAD/CAM; other mechanics and repairers; welding and precision metal; other precision production; transport and materials moving; consumer/personal/miscellaneous services including cosmetology, upholstery; hospitality industry courses including culinary arts and wines; pattern design and many apparel construction courses; travel and tourist agent

Other

Social services program training courses, library cataloging procedures

How Much of the Community College Curriculum Is Accounted for by the Non-Liberal Arts?

The Non-Liberal Arts Study revealed that slightly more than 80 percent of the for-credit non-liberal arts curriculum was accounted for by only four discipline areas: Business and Office, Personal Skills and Avocational Courses, Technical Education, and Trade and Industry (See Table 7). Physical education accounted for more than 90 percent of the courses coded under Personal Skills, while computer software applications was the largest category of courses coded under Technical Education.

Five discipline areas accounted for only a small portion of the nonliberal arts credit curriculum, accounting altogether for just under 10 percent. Few courses were coded in the areas of Agriculture (1.2 percent), Education (2.5 percent), Engineering Technology (.2 percent), Home Economics (.2 percent), Marketing and Distribution (3.4 percent), and Other (.2 percent). Several of these categories deserve some explanation.

Table 7
Number of Sections and Percentage of Non-Liberal Arts Courses Offered

Discipline	Number of Sections Offered	Percentage of Non-Liberal Arts Sections	Percentage of Total Credit Sections
Agriculture	529	1.2	.5
Business and Office	11,156	24.6	10.7
Education	1,147	2.5	1.1
Engineering Technologies	889	2.0	.9
Health	4,641	10.2	4.4
Home Economics	106	.2	.1
Marketing & Distribution	1,523	3.4	1.5
Personal Skills & Avocational Courses	8,643	19.1	8.3
Technical Education	8,229	18.1	7.9
Trade and Industry	8,420	18.6	8.1
Other	77	.2	.1
TOTALS	**45,360**	**100.0**	**43.4**

For the Agriculture and Engineering categories, courses were coded under both liberal arts and non-liberal arts. Courses that were more theoretically based and less oriented toward a specific occupation were considered liberal arts courses. In the liberal arts study, both the Agriculture and Engineering categories showed precipitous declines between 1986 and 1991, but the reasons for their declines are different. In 1986, agriculture courses accounted for 1.2 percent of the total liberal arts curriculum, while in 1991, the percentage fell to .1 percent. But when *all* agriculture courses are tallied in both liberal arts and non-liberal arts categories, they still account for only a small proportion of the total 1991 curriculum (.6 percent). At least a partial explanation for the decline is sampling error. In national samples of 10 percent to 15 percent of all community colleges, sampling error has an exaggerated effect for subject areas in which few sections are offered. For example, only 18 of the 164 colleges in our sample offered *any* liberal arts sections of agriculture in 1991. In all, 75 sections of agriculture were found among the 59,205 liberal arts sections that were tallied. These figures are too small to be reliable.

A decline in the number of engineering courses was also evident; in 1986, engineering courses accounted for 5 percent of the liberal arts curriculum; in 1991, that figure was only 2.5 percent. The proportion of engineering courses falls even further when it is considered as part of the total curriculum (2.3 percent), rather than as part of the liberal arts curriculum alone. At least part of the decline in the number of engineering courses may be attributed to two kinds of "category shifts" in the coding of these courses. First, computerized graphics courses often are offered at today's community colleges by several departments and may appear as "Visual Arts" in fine and performing arts departments, as well as in engineering departments. College catalogs do not always clearly differentiate which type of graphics course is being described. The coding of graphics courses, therefore, may have "shifted" from one category to the next between the 1986 and 1991 liberal arts studies, thereby affecting the overall Engineering category tallies. Also, all CAD/CAM courses were considered computer software applications courses, coded under Technical Education. This may have been a second factor contributing to the low percentage of courses coded under Engineering.

Another non-liberal arts area that requires some explanation is Home Economics. Very few "true" home economics courses were found, since many sewing and tailoring, food preparation and food preservation, and interior decorating courses were oriented more toward training students in consumer service areas than toward providing skills to be used in the home. Only courses in baking, cooking, and sewing for one's personal use *at home* were included under Home Economics. Classes such as pattern design, fabrics, wines, culinary arts, and refrigeration for restaurants often were clearly Trade and Industry classes, as judged by both course titles and course descriptions. Nutrition classes often were coded under Health, while parenting classes were tallied under Personal Skills and Avocational Courses. Using this narrowly defined taxonomy, the category of Home Economics all but disappeared, accounting for only .2 percent of the non-liberal arts curriculum.

The last category requiring explanation is Education. This category included courses for those intending to teach. The great majority of classes coded under Education were early childhood education courses, while a few were fitness instructor training courses.

What Is the Ratio of Liberal Arts to Non-Liberal Arts Courses?

For the spring 1991 National Liberal Arts Curriculum Study, 59,205 liberal arts course sections were tallied by CSCC staff, while in the subsequent study of the non-liberal arts, 45,360 sections were tallied. A total of 104,565 course sections were coded in the two studies. A 56.5 percent to 43.4 percent ratio of liberal arts to non-liberal arts courses resulted.

A possible explanation for the lower percentage occupied by the non-liberal arts stems from the way in which courses were coded. As noted earlier (in the Methodology section), a definite time and meeting place had to be listed in order for a course to be coded. Thus, laboratory courses, clinicals, practicums, field experience, independent study, and self-paced or modular classes were not included in the tallies for either the liberal arts or the non-liberal arts. Since laboratory classes occur with greater frequency in many non-liberal arts subject areas, their omission may account at least partially for the lower proportion of non-liberal arts courses. Laboratory classes are popular especially in many nursing and allied health programs, in technical education program classes (such as computer literacy and data processing), and in trade and industry subject areas (such as auto mechanics and cosmetology). In the liberal arts, however, fewer laboratory classes are offered. The largest liberal arts subject area offering laboratory classes is most likely music, where "applied" music classes (often private lessons) were considered laboratory classes and therefore were not coded. Some laboratory classes are also offered in the hard sciences and in foreign language classes, though separate foreign language laboratory classes have declined in popularity and, overall, few sections are offered.

What Does the Total Curriculum Look Like?

Table 8 presents the percentage breakdown of the total curriculum by major subject area, providing a description of the percentages accounted for by the six liberal arts and the ten non-liberal arts discipline areas that account for the total credit curriculum:

Table 8
Number of Sections and Percentage
of Total Curriculum, by Major Discipline Areas

Discipline	Number of Sections	Percentage of Total Curriculum
Agriculture (Non-Liberal Arts)	529	.51
Business & Office	11,156	10.67
Education	1,147	1.10
Engineering Technologies	889	.85
English	13,327	12.75
Fine & Performing Arts	5,671	5.42
Health	4,641	4.44
Home Economics	106	.10
Humanities	14,034	13.42
Marketing	1,523	1.46
Math and Computer Sciences	11,176	10.69
Personal Skills & Avocational Courses	8,643	8.27
Sciences	8,031	7.68
Social Sciences	6,966	6.66
Technical Education	8,229	7.87
Trade & Industry	8,420	8.05
Other	77	.07
TOTAL	104,565	100.0

What Percentage of Non-Liberal Arts Courses Transfers?

As a second component of the Non-Liberal Arts Study, course transferability rates[1] were calculated for the states of California, Illinois, and Texas. Because any course at a community college is likely to be accepted for transfer credit by some in-state, four-year institution, transferability rates were calculated from community colleges to two specific types of four-year institutions—a "flagship" research university and a comprehensive college or university.[2]

In order to create a uniform basis of comparison between states, "transferability" was defined as course-to-course transfer equivalencies, rather than as "program" or "block" transferability of courses between institutions. Transferable courses were those which carried credit to four-year institutions in one of four categories: (1) general education credit; (2) general elective credit; (3) specific course credit in a major field; or (4) major field elective credit. The goal was to discover which courses a student could count on transferring to four-year institutions—even if that student had only taken a few community college courses.

Not all officials in the different states, however, think of transfer in terms of specific "course" transfer—that is, the transfer of a specific community college course for either general or elective credit at a particular four-year college. An example may illustrate the differences. Officials in states such as Florida, for example, prefer to consider transfer in terms of "degree completer" patterns. Community college students are strongly encouraged to complete an associate's degree (or 60 credits in a specified program) before transferring with junior-level standing to a four-year institution. Therefore, obtaining specific course transfer guides for Florida community colleges would be problematic.

Since the method for determining course transferability differs among states, a "generic" methodology for collecting this data for the three states involved in the study was not possible. In California, course transferability was recorded explicitly in the college course schedules; in Texas, articulation officers at the community colleges provided the data; in Illinois, transfer guides were obtained from the state postsecondary agency and were used to calculate percentages of courses in each of the ten major nonliberal arts areas that transfer to four-year institutions. The results for the states of California, Texas, and Illinois are presented below.

Which Non-Liberal Arts Courses Transfer in California?

The system for assessing course transferability in California was fairly simple. State mandate obliges community colleges to list in their catalogs or schedules which courses will transfer to one of the state's two public higher education systems—the University of California (UC) system (with nine campuses) and the California State University (CSU) system (with 20 campuses). Some community college schedules and catalogs list which individual campuses within the systems will accept a specific course for transfer credit, while others merely list course as acceptable for transfer somewhere within the UC or CSU systems. Thus, determining transferability was easy, since catalogs and schedules clearly designated individual course transferability.

Table 9
Transferability Percentages of
California Non-Liberal Arts Courses (N=30)

Transfer Subject Area	CSU	UC
Agriculture	64.5	21.0
Business & Office	61.0	23.0
Education	70.6	5.6
Engineering Technology	62.6	5.7
Health	54.3	16.3
Home Economics	47.1	12.9
Marketing & Distribution	70.3	1.6
Personal Skills & Avocational Courses	88.0	76.7
Technical Education	52.8	11.0
Trade & Industry	35.7	3.7
Other	94.1	35.3
Overall Transferability	61.7	28.9

Thirty California community colleges participated in this phase of the Non-Liberal Arts Study. Not surprisingly, the findings for California indicated very different transferability rates from the community colleges to the UC-system research universities and to the state comprehensive universities (the CSU system). Within the UC system, only courses within the area of Personal Skills and

Avocational Courses transferred in high numbers (76.7 percent), largely because of the extremely high percentage of Physical Education courses which transferred. In fact, the Personal Skills subject area accounted for 26.5 percent of the non-liberal arts curriculum for California, a full 7.4 percentage points higher than the national percentage of 19.1 percent.

Transferability percentages to the UC system fell markedly after the 76.7 percent high for Personal Skills courses. The next highest transferability rate for California community colleges was for courses categorized "Other" (35.3 percent). The small percentage of total California courses coded under this category, 17 courses out of 12,632 (.1 percent), however, make this category too small to be reliable. All other subject areas yielded transferability percentages at or below 23 percent.

Within the state comprehensive university system, however, 61.7 percent of all community college courses transferred, with a range from 88 percent in Personal Skills courses to 35.7 percent in Trade and Industry courses. In both the CSU and UC systems, Trade and Industry courses held among the lowest rankings in percentage of transferable courses. If Trade and Industry courses were the only non-liberal arts courses considered, then some merit might exist in the charge that the transfer function denies students who take non-liberal arts courses access to four-year degrees. But taken as a whole, the non-liberal arts show remarkable transferability to the state university system and challenge the notion that students who take courses in these fields are "cooled out" of baccalaureate degree programs. Nevertheless, there may be some truth in the proposition that a status difference does exist among the various non-liberal arts subjects. For students enrolled in Trade and Industry programs, for example, baccalaureate degrees certainly appear less accessible.

Which Non-Liberal Arts Courses Transfer in Texas?

Eleven Texas community colleges participated in the transferability component of the non-liberal arts study. Transfer articulation coordinators at these colleges provided written transfer agreements designating courses as transferable or non-transferable to the flagship research institution in Texas, the University of Texas at Austin, and to one of two state comprehensive universities, Stephen F. Austin State or Southwest Texas State University.

Table 10
Transferability Percentages
of Texas Non-Liberal Arts Courses (N=11)

Transfer Subject Area	Research University	State Comprehensive University
Agriculture	16.0	28.0
Business & Office	30.3	41.0
Education	17.4	50.0
Engineering Technology	0	0
Health	6.8	7.4
Home Economics	NA*	NA*
Marketing & Distribution	39.4	43.9
Personal Skills & Avocational Courses	99.8	100.0
Technical Education	56.2	71.1
Trade & Industry	5.8	5.8
Other	NA	NA
Overall Transferability	35.3	41.6

*These sections were coded to provide reliable data.

The results for Texas are surprising in that the overall transferability rate, as well as rates for a number of individual subject areas, are quite close. A mere 5.3 percentage points differentiate overall transferability rates between the state's flagship research institution and two state comprehensive universities. This pattern is quite different from that of California.

In Texas, each community college has separate transfer agreements with each four-year institution (unlike California, which lists *systemwide* transferability). Still, this difference does not account for the discrepancy between the California and the Texas data.

Further study of transferability in Texas yielded an interesting case study in which data was obtained on transferability percentages from one community college to 15 four-year institutions in the state, two of them private (See Table 11). The statistics are for courses offered (not sections) and are not directly comparable to other statistics in this study. The percentages do illustrate, however, differences among institutions that accept courses from one community college.

Table 11
Percentages of Courses That Transfer from Lee College

	All Courses Offered	Non-Liberal Arts Courses
Public Four-Year Institution		
East Texas State University	92.9	92.2
Lamar University	41.6	21.2
Sam Houston State University	45.7	27.5
Southwest Texas State University	97.4	97.3
Stephen F. Austin State University	46.9	28.9
Texas A & M University	36.9	16.2
Texas Tech	14.2	5.5
Texas Woman's University	62.9	50.8
University of Houston-Clear Lake	28.8	15.8
University of Houston-Downtown	52.8	33.8
University of Houston-Main	93.3	93.5
University of North Texas	73.2	64.4
University of Texas-Austin	40.6	21.6
Private Four-Year Institutions		
Baylor University	12.7	2.5
Houston Baptist University	11.6	6.5

Several findings deserve comment. First, the two private universities have much lower transferability rates than all but one of the public institutions. Second, the wide disparity between transferability rates to the four-year institutions (from a high of 97.4 percent for all courses offered to a low of 14.2 percent) may be accounted for by two factors influencing articulation agreements: the proximity between the two- and four-year institutions and the ability of the community college articulation officer to build a relationship with a university's transfer coordinator. Lee College (in Baytown) is a considerable distance from the four-year institution where it has its lowest transferability rate (14.2 percent) at Texas Tech (in Lubbock). And third, the differences between transferability of all courses offered and just the non-liberal arts courses range from 20.7 percent to .4 percent. In one instance, the non-liberal arts actually transfer at a slightly higher percentage than all courses offered (93.5 percent to 93.3 percent at the University of Houston-Main). Overall, the differences between transferability rates of all courses offered and those of non-liberal arts courses only do not appear to be significant.

Which Non-Liberal Arts Courses Transfer in Illinois?

Three Illinois community colleges provided data on non-liberal arts transferability to Illinois State University and to the state's flagship research institution, the University of Illinois at Urbana-Champaign. Transfer guides were obtained from the Illinois Community College Board and were used to calculate transferability percentages. The findings reflect California's pattern of much higher transferability percentages to the state university than to the four-year research institution (See Table 12).

Table 12
Transferability Rates of Illinois Community Colleges (N=3)

Community College	Illinois State University	University of Illinois—Urbana-Champaign
Black Hawk	79.0	79.0
Triton	79.2	79.2
Wilbur Wright	92.7	92.7

The degree to which the various non-liberal arts subject areas transfer also follows a pattern similar to that of California, although the pattern in Illinois is more pronounced. The University of Illinois research university showed higher selectivity than the University of California system in accepting non-liberal arts courses for credit (15.9 percent and 28.9 percent, respectively), and Illinois State University displayed a considerably higher transferability rate for non-liberal arts courses than did the California State University system (80.4 percent and 61.7 percent, respectively). Two subject areas in Illinois that yielded different results, however, were the high percentage of Trade and Industry courses that transferred to Illinois State University (86.9 percent) compared to the percentage that transferred to the California State University system (35.7 percent) and the comparatively low transferability rate of Personal Skills courses (largely physical education courses) to the University of Illinois (49.5 percent). For several subject areas, data was too sparse to report. Also, data for Illinois should be considered preliminary, since only three community colleges furnished complete data for analysis.

Table 13
Non-Liberal Arts Transferability Rates in Illinois Community Colleges (N=3)

Transfer Subject Area	Illinois State University	University of Illinois—Urbana-Champaign
Agriculture	100.0	0
Business & Office	78.7	30.9
Education	92.9	17.9
Engineering Technology	100.0	0
Health	29.8	.9
Home Economics	NA	NA
Marketing & Distribution	91.5	0
Personal Skills & Avocational Courses	89.2	49.5
Technical Education	97.2	7.3
Trade & Industry	86.9	4.8
Other	NA	NA
Overall Transferability	80.4	15.9

What General Patterns Are Discernible from the Transferability Data?

Similarities exist in the overall transferability patterns for Illinois and California, although substantial differences also emerge between the two states in transferability percentages for specific disciplines. The following general observations are possible: (1) research universities are considerably more selective in their acceptance of non-liberal arts courses for transfer credit; (2) personal skills and avocational courses tend to transfer at a high rate, largely because of physical education courses; (3) trade and industry courses do not transfer at a high rate, except to Illinois State University; (4) health occupations courses also tend to have comparatively low transferability rates.

The overall pattern for Texas, however, is considerably different than for the other two states. Both Texas's state universities and its flagship research institution seem to accept non-liberal arts courses for transfer at much more similar rates (41.6 percent and 35.3 percent, respectively). This difference is perhaps best revealed by the following figures, which compare transferability data from Texas and California.

Figure 1
Texas Transfers: Non-Liberal Arts Project, 1992

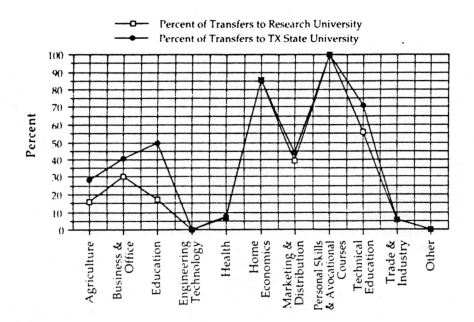

Figure 2
California Transfers: Non-Liberal Arts Project, 1992

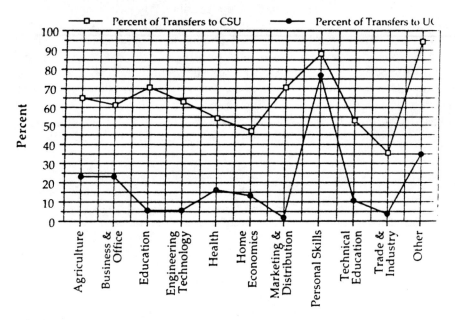

Summary

This paper has reported the findings of the most recent of a series of studies of the liberal arts curriculum at American community colleges. Findings were that overall, the liberal arts have expanded from 52 percent of the total curriculum in 1986 to 56 percent in 1991. This probably resulted less from the introduction of new courses or course requirements than from an increase in the proportion of students pursuing the first two years of baccalaureate study. The enrollment figures show the continued dominance of traditional general education courses: English composition, introductory math, psychology, history, and political science. The most notable shift in the curriculum was in foreign languages, where, fueled by a notable jump in ESL enrollments and in the number of colleges offering ESL, the foreign languages share rose from 5 to 8.5 percent of all liberal arts classes.

Relationships between the liberal arts curriculum and college size, location, minority student enrollment, transfer rate, and graduation requirements were analyzed. Colleges in urban areas were found to offer higher percentages of remedial courses, thereby confirming a generally accepted notion. College size related to course patterns only in the provision of specialized classes: the larger the college, the more likely that a class in, for example, dance or cultural geography would be found. (A similar relationship appeared in earlier studies.) A community college must enroll quite a large number of students in order to support specialized classes in many fields.

The finding that a college's transfer rate is positively related to the percentage of liberal arts courses it offers was no surprise; the liberal arts are basic to traditional baccalaureate studies. But there was no relation between the percentage of advanced courses offered and the college's transfer rate. One explanation may be that as CSCC found in a parallel study of transfer rates, the "median student" transfers after completing approximately thirty units. Thus, half of transferring students do not stay at the community college long enough to enroll in advanced or sophomore-level courses.

The finding that the proportion of the liberal arts curriculum is greater at colleges that are above the mean in terms of the percentage of minority students enrolled refutes the widely held contention that the minorities are tracked into vocational programs—that is, unless those programs require their matriculants to take large numbers of liberal arts classes (nearly all of which carry university-transfer credit). The lack of a significant relationship between a college's minority student ratio and the percentage of its curriculum devoted to remedial, introductory, or advanced courses also suggests that the reasons for the minority students' lower transfer rate cannot be attributed to the curricula the colleges provide.

For the non-liberal arts, general findings indicate that courses in trade and industry do not transfer at high percentages, but personal skills and avocational courses do (largely because of physical education courses). The second major finding is that research universities are more selective in terms of the non-liberal arts courses they accept for transfer. This is especially true in California and Illinois, but less so in Texas. The third finding concerns the overall transferability of non-liberal arts courses. Since most non-liberal arts courses do transfer (except for trade and industry courses), the concept of "terminal education" should be laid to rest.

The non-liberal arts data will be analyzed further and compared with other data recently compiled by CSCC. One set of tabulations will relate the non-liberal arts data to the college student transfer rates. Questions to be addressed in further analyses include whether community colleges with differing patterns of ethnicity and student transfer rates display different non-liberal arts curricular patterns. Further analyses will provide a more complete picture of how the total curriculum functions at American community colleges.

Notes

*Additional analyses and contributions to this report were made by William Armstrong, Chuch Brinkman, R. David Cartwright, Shannon Hirose, Melissa Mellissinos, and Barry Vanderkelen.

1. Throughout this paper *transferability* will refer to course transferability from community colleges to four-year institutions while *transfer* will refer to student transfers.

2. Research Universities I and Comprehensive Universities and Colleges I were defined in this study using the definitions in the Carnegie Foundation's *A Classification of Institutions of Higher Education* (1987), p. 7.

References

Adelman, C. (February 1992). *The Way We Are: The Community College as American Thermometer.* Washington, DC: U.S. Government Printing Office.

Astin, A. (1977). *Four Critical Years.* San Francisco: Jossey-Bass, Inc.

Brint, S. & Karabel, J. (1989). *The Diverted Dream: Community Colleges and the Promise of Educational Opportunity in America, 1900–1985.* New York: Oxford University Press.

Cohen, A. M. & Brawer, F. B. (1987). *The Collegiate Function of Community Colleges.* San Francisco: Jossey-Bass, Inc.

Cohen, A. M. & Brawer, F. B. (1989). *The American Community College* (2nd Edition). San Francisco: Jossey-Bass, Inc.

Grubb, Norton. (June 1987). "The Postsecondary Education of 1972 Seniors Completing Vocational A.A. Degrees and Certificates." U.S. Department of Education: MPR Associates for the Center for Education Statistics. LSB-87-06-26.

Grubb, N. March. (April 1991). "The Decline of Community College Transfer Rates: Evidence from National Longitudinal Surveys." *Journal of Higher Education,* 62(2): 194–222.

Levine, A. & Cureton, J. (January/February 1992). "The Quiet Revolution: Eleven Facts About Multiculturalism and the Curriculum." *Change* 24(1): 25–29.

Pincus, F. & Archer, E. (1989). *Bridges to Opportunity: Are Community Colleges Meeting the Needs of Minority Students?* New York: Academy for Educational Development and College Entrance Examination Board.

Richardson, R. & Bender, L. (1985). *Students in Urban Settings: Achieving the Baccalaureate Degree.* Washington, DC: Association for the Study of Higher Education.

State Articulation Policies: Myths and Realities

LOUIS W. BENDER

No two states can be described as the same; yet, researchers, policymakers, and the national and local press continue to promulgate national norms, generalizations, and claims that mislead or deceive because they assume uniformity. Size, geography, economy, and demographics, as well as dissimilar education governance structures, are important determiners of each state's postsecondary education delivery systems and their relationships. The individual differences of each state cannot be overemphasized. Three aspects of such differences illustrate the variety of contexts for transfer and articulation between lower-division and upper-division institutions.

Two-Year Institutions. The term community college often is the generic descriptor found in the popular press as well as publications of national organizations to refer to all types of public two-year institutions as though they are one. This simplistic technique is appropriate in many cases; however, it is quite misleading in regards to transfer and articulation issues, particularly when national norms or averages are reported. For example, New Hampshire has a system of six vocational-technical colleges, while Alabama has technical colleges, junior colleges, and community colleges making up its system of public two-year institutions. West Virginia has both community colleges and "community college components" of four-year state colleges, while Indiana has branch campuses of universities, vocational/technical colleges, and Vincennes University, a public two-year institution acknowledged as the only true "community college" in the state. Georgia and Tennessee have both junior colleges and technical institutes, while Connecticut, Minnesota, and Nebraska have community colleges and technical colleges. It would be ludicrous to discuss transfer and articulation issues as though these various types of two-year institutions were a single model. Some of the policies discussed in this report are more relevant to one type than another type of two-year institution.

State System. Some states have consolidated governing boards responsible for all public postsecondary institutions, resulting in state policies that apply to all levels and types of institutions in the system. Georgia and Massachusetts are examples of such states under boards of regents, while comparable systems are governed as university systems in Alaska and Hawaii. At the other end of the continuum, a few states essentially have "non-systems," where local determination predominates as a result of little or no system authority at the state level (Pennsylvania, Vermont, and Maine are examples). The origin, nature, and scope of state policy will be quite different even though state legislatures may perceive they are calling for comparable policies.

State Traditions. An important difference needing amplification for this national study is the individual differences in traditions, values, and philosophy in relation to transfer and articulation efforts. Florida is credited by many authorities as exemplary in the comprehensiveness of its transfer and articulation policies and practices. Florida's universities and community colleges hold a keen sense of "system" even though the nine universities are under a single state-governing board of regents while local boards govern the 28 community colleges. A constitution-based State Board of Education (the only remaining colonial practice of its members being the governor and elected cabinet members) is responsible for all levels of education. Policies and procedures identified by community colleges or universities typically are approved or adopted by the state board for all public institutions. The Florida Legislature also plays a prominent role, making statutory provision for various transfer and articulation matters, which results in statewide implementation. This top to bottom authority/power configuration seems repulsive and unacceptably intrusive to many outside the state, yet to most Floridians it is workable and successful.

California, with quite similar transfer and articulation policies and practices, functions from a different perspective. The tradition and philosophy of voluntary participation and a bottom-to-top authority flow seems to be present in California, where the legislature is encouraged to fund incentives or pilot projects in fostering transfer and articulation practices. Part of the reason may be the fact that the University of California System derives its authority from the constitution (similar to the University of Michigan, the University of Minnesota, and Ohio State University) and therefore can be as autonomous or cooperative as it wants to be. As revealed later in this report, the legislature's attitude appears to be shifting toward prescriptiveness.

The California Postsecondary Education Commission plays a key role in maintaining public, legislative, and institutional visibility and attention on transfer and articulation by monitoring and reporting student flow patterns in annual reports, carrying out ongoing studies and analyses of transfer and articulation, and promoting the transfer function among the public segments and independent institutions of California. A quite different orientation can be seen in several Middle Atlantic and New England states where the historic traditions and values of private colleges and universities reflect a strong institutional autonomy ethic even among the public colleges and universities. There is little sense of "system" in such states as Pennsylvania, Virginia, Connecticut, and Vermont, where state planning and coordinating agencies are little more than advisory bodies.

Frederick C. Kintzer, a recognized authority on transfer and articulation, attempted to categorize articulation agreements among states based on the level or origin of authority. While helpful, such classification does not communicate the complexity of traditions. His typology lists Illinois as a state where articulation is legislatively mandated as is the case in Florida. Yet, Illinois is more like Michigan or North Carolina in that interinstitutional cooperation comes primarily from voluntary institutional participation in a statewide association rather than from governmental agencies. However, even the players vary; the Michigan Association of Collegiate Registrars and Admissions Officers plays a central role in transfer and articulation policy formulation in that state, while representative faculty are utilized in North Carolina and Illinois.

As a consequence, it is necessary to examine each state within the context of its socio-political, economic, and educational characteristics. The issue of state-mandated as opposed to voluntary participation has many origins.

Trends and Issues Concerning Transfer and Articulation

Historically, two- and four-year college transfer and articulation matters were primarily an institutional rather than a state concern. The tradition of institutional autonomy and the central role of a faculty in determining the content and performance requirements of each degree program were accepted by society as appropriate since higher education was viewed as "a privilege." The primary players in articulation efforts before the 1960s were admissions officers and registrars. Societal requirements and attitudes have changed since the 1960s, with higher education now being deemed "a right" and a requirement for an increasing portion of our population to develop its capacity to the fullest. During the 1980s the primary players were transfer/articulation officers carrying out an ombudsmanship role. In many states the evidence is clear that faculty-to-faculty groups will be the key players in the 1990s if transfer and articulation problems are to be seriously and successfully addressed.

Voluntary/Localized versus Mandated/Statewide

Research has verified that the majority of two-year college transfer students will apply to a nearby baccalaureate institution. The ideal, therefore, would be for such institutions to work together cooperatively to facilitate the movement of students from one institution to the other. As the case studies in Part II of this report demonstrate, such local articulation programs are possible and are successful. Unfortunately, there are too many cases in too many states where the public two-year and four-year institutions do not cooperate, sometimes actually being adversarial competitors.

The 1980s may well be described by history as the decade when transfer and articulation shifted, at least for public institutions, from the hands of local educational policymakers to state-level public policymakers. In 1989, the year this study was carried out, legislatures in 13 states considered bills or passed resolutions related to transfer and articulation. Perhaps more important for educators is the shift toward prescriptiveness in legislative mandates, thus communicating to faculties an intolerance of perceived abuses to the interest of the student and the taxpayer.

Illustrative of this trend is the Oregon legislative charge in House Bill 2913, which directed the State Board of Higher Education and State Board of Education jointly to develop general education requirements and agreements enabling associate of arts graduates of Oregon community colleges to meet lower-division general education requirements of four-year public institutions in that state. A subsequent charge from the legislature (July 10, 1987) required the joint committee of the two state boards to (1) propose a set of general education requirements for transfer students; (2) establish a common course numbering system for lower-division courses offered by institutions of the two segments; and (3) "propose systems and procedures that insure the enforceability of the agreements reached."

The 1989 General Assembly in Arkansas charged its State Board of Higher Education with developing a minimum general education core for baccalaureate degrees "which shall transfer freely among all state institutions." The 1989 Ohio Legislature required the Board of Regents in that state to establish a study commission

> to make formal recommendations to the Governor and 118th General Assembly regarding implementation of a statewide student credit-hour transfer agreement to address the articulation problems associated with students transferring from state-assisted technical and community colleges to state-assisted universities (Section 5, 5.B. No. 268).

The legislative sentiment toward requiring improved transfer and articulation can be seen in the language of a 1985 law of the Colorado Legislature when assigning responsibilities and authority to its new Commission on Higher Education. It reads:

> The commission shall establish, after consultation with the governing boards of institutions, and enforce student transfer agreements between two-year and four-year institutions and among four-year institutions. Governing boards and institutions shall conform to such agreements and to commission policies relating to such agreements. Such transfer agreements shall include provisions under which institutions shall accept all credit hours of acceptable coursework for automatic transfer to another state-supported institution of higher education in Colorado. The Commission shall have final authority in resolving transfer disputes (Section 23-1-107, HB No. 1187).

Other state legislative budget amendments or resolutions signal an identifiable shift of authority for transfer of credits—which once solely resided with departmental faculties in the name of academic integrity and institutional autonomy—to state-level bodies and agencies.

Why are legislatures taking action that is contrary to the tradition of institutional autonomy and voluntary articulation arrangements? Analysis of testimony of legislative hearings and legislative committee reports reveals a perception in many states that students are being treated unfairly when transferring from one institution to another. The general public and their elected representatives perceive publicly sponsored or supported postsecondary institutions as a system of interdependent and complementary elements that fit together as a whole, not as different, competing elements. Education is viewed as a process, not institutional forms or types. As a consequence, legislative testimony often is directed toward the unfairness to transfer students and to taxpayers when both must pay the price of repeating coursework already successfully completed or when students are required to take more courses than the native students in the same degree program.

Institution-Interest versus Student Interest

A reading of state policies reveals an attitudinal posture in some cases that offers clues, if not insights. Legislative resolutions dealing with transfer and articulation will, almost without exception, reflect a concern for the student's interest, sometimes to the detriment of traditions or values cherished by colleges and universities. In sharp contrast, the interest of institutions can often be found in the wording of statements or the composition of state articulation groups. The North Carolina Joint Committee on College Transfer Students, sponsored by the North Carolina Association of Colleges and Universities and used by the university system as the articulation policy making forum, declares

> these statewide guidelines for collegiate articulation in North Carolina are unique among the states in America. Prepared voluntarily for voluntary use by representatives of colleges and universities which carefully guard and value their academic independence, the guidelines represent a recognition of the importance of common reference points which autonomous institutions may use in considering the admission of and the granting of credit to transfer students. The development and general acceptance of the guidelines stand as a major achievement in academic cooperation (*Guidelines for Transfer*, p. 2).

The policy of The University of Wisconsin System (a governing board) was an exception that deserves to be quoted. Its undergraduate transfer policy includes the following declaration in the introduction:

> Mobility is a common human phenomenon. This is true among students in higher education. For several reasons—a change in major, a family move, the economic and familial necessity of attending college close to home—students are frequently faced with the need to obtain their collegiate education from two or more institutions. In response to these types of needs, The University of Wisconsin System welcomes transfer students from other accredited colleges and universities and from institutions within the system. Thus, a conscientious effort has been made by the UW System to create a student-oriented transfer process. The foremost goal is a policy that provides a strong focus toward serving students and strives to treat continuing and transfer student in the same way on program issues (e.g., degree requirements and program changes and notification) [June, 1989].

Another example of institutional-interest in contrast to student-interest can be found in the purposes and actions of state-level intersegmental bodies, whether called councils, committees, or boards. Representatives from the various segments typically make up the membership of these bodies, which are expected to address problems and issues of transfer and articulation whether identified by students or institutions. When baccalaureate representation is greater than two-year representation, institutional interest will supersede student interest. Examination of agendas and findings of such bodies often reveals interesting contrasts. Some are empowered only to provide advisory findings while others are empowered with binding authority. Usually, products of the advisory groups maintain or champion the institutional prerogative, while intersegmental groups with binding authority typically evidence student-interest priorities. Furthermore, agendas are quite different for those states where such boards are primarily intended to address grievances and problem issues in sharp contrast to those states where the body proactively quests to facilitate improved articulation.

Precursors of Legislative Concern

What has caused governors and legislators to become so interested in transfer and articulation? Editorials and testimony reviewed during this study revealed three different sources. First, *A Nation at Risk* and similar national reports calling for educational reform have resulted in many state legislatures mandating the strengthening of academic programs at both secondary and postsecondary levels. Requirements for English, math, science, and foreign language in high school college-preparatory programs have resulted in additional admissions requirements for the freshman class of public four-year institutions in many states. In many cases, general education requirements have been modified or increased by the same institutions. As a consequence, problems, real or imagined, with transfer students have been identified. In some cases, the root of the problem has been communications between institutions, while in other cases major philosophical differences have surfaced.

A second precursor of legislative concern is the compelling demographic changes in many states, prompting an expectation that colleges and universities will proactively reach out to underrepresented ethnic minority groups and assure access to and opportunity for completion of the baccalaureate degree, the gateway to the professions. Since minority groups disproportionately enroll in two-year institutions, there is an understandable desire by the public and its elected representatives that transfer and articulation result in increased representation of these groups in the upper-division baccalaureate institutions. For example, as early as 1974, the California Legislature passed a resolution calling upon the public segments of higher education to assure minority student initiatives. The Ford Foundation has also played a significant role in promoting attention and action in improved transfer opportunities for ethnic minority students, which has influenced many states to revisit their transfer and articulation practices.

A third and increasingly visible pressure grows out of the demand of graduates of applied associate degree programs for baccalaureate opportunities. The rigor of many contemporary non-transfer technical programs requires students whose preparation would qualify them to pursue a baccalaureate degree. Graduates of applied associate degree programs in health, business, technologies, and service fields are increasingly transferring to baccalaureate institutions. The national press has seldom reported on this phenomenon. Perhaps it is due to the fact that little is known about this population or their problems in the transfer and articulation process, although several states are beginning to act on this serious matter.

Major State Policies and Practices

Nearly every state can certify it has a policy statement on transfer of credit for students moving from two-year to four-year institutions. Some are general and essentially affirm the autonomy of individual institutions in determining the conditions for the transfer and award of credit. Pennsylvania and New Hampshire are states with such policies. An official in Ohio observed that the Board of Regents articulation/transfer policy "guidelines" had been on the books since 1977 but had never been implemented. As previously observed, the Ohio General Assembly included a provision in its 1989 biennial budget bill calling for action on articulation problems associated with student transfer. The New Mexico Legislature passed similar legislation in 1988. Concern for assuring equal access, equality of treatment of students, and enhanced quality are reflected in the prescriptive nature of state legislatures that previously had been tolerant toward concepts of institutional autonomy and self-determination.

State Articulation Agreements

Association Degree Recognition: The associate in arts degree (AA) is the universally accepted credential for programs designed to prepare students for upper-division baccalaureate study. In spite of AACJC's 1984 associate degree policy statement, which was intended to obtain adoption of common associate degree designations to facilitate uniformity and standardized meanings, considerable variation still exists. Many states designate the AA as the degree for those with a general education foundation and a social science emphasis, while the associate in science degree (AS) denotes programs with math and science emphasis. Florida uses the AA for both such programs. The associate in science in Florida is the applied degree, which most states recognize by awarding the associate in applied science degree (AAS). It is understandable that confusion often exists over the meaning and relevance of the various designations. The Missouri Coordinating Board for Higher Education promulgated guidelines for student transfer and articulation in 1987 that succinctly and clearly define the nature and purpose of each degree designation. These guidelines could assist many states in their articulation efforts.

General Education Requirement: Concern for a prescribed course of study insuring that all graduates possess a common core of college-level skills and knowledge is at the heart of the articulation debate in many states. The argument usually focuses on who defines the program. One of the most active states in focusing upon the general education transfer curriculum, California experienced a significant change in 1989 when the University of California segment for the first time delegated to the community colleges the responsibility for designating which courses meet the requirements for a new transfer core curriculum adopted by UC, the California State University, and California Community Colleges. Georgia, Oklahoma, and Tennessee prescribe the basic general education core that must be honored by the upper-division institution. Oklahoma also recognizes the associate degree:

> If a student has completed an associate of science or associate of arts degree, the lower-division general education requirement of the baccalaureate degree shall be the responsibility of the institution awarding the associate degree, providing the general education requirements specified herein are met. If, for any reason, a student has not completed an associate degree program prior to his or her transfer to another institution, the general education requirements shall become the responsibility of the receiving institution. However, the receiving institution will recognize general education credit for all transfer courses in which a reasonable equivalency of discipline or course context exists, with the courses specified as part of general education at the receiving institution, provided that there is an appropriate correspondence between the associate degree and the baccalaureate degree being sought (State Regents for Higher Education, March 1987).

The number of credit hours required as part of the general education core vary from a minimum of 16 credit hours in Iowa to 37 credit hours in Oklahoma.

Three models of general education programs are described by the Missouri guidelines, including competency-based programs, topical or thematic programs, or distributional programs. The preponderance of general education requirements in state articulation agreements would be of the distributional program model.

Course Credit: Delaware and Rhode Island transfer policies call for transferability of all courses between the public institutions of the states. A systematic review of courses by appropriate faculty of course content and proficiency requirements is used for development of a matrix of course credit for all programs offered by the institutions.

Course Comparability

Some legislatures have sought the equal and fair treatment of transfer students by calling for determination and promulgation of course equivalencies, which requires faculty participation.

Common Course Designation Systems: Florida probably has one of the most comprehensive and operationally efficient common course numbering and designation systems. Groups of faculty from the nine universities and 28 community colleges worked as task force groups throughout system development in the 1970s. During the 1980s, faculty groups worked to keep the system (which is fully computerized and online) up to date and current. A problem confronting this activity has been the occasional external pressure of some national accrediting bodies insisting that all professional instruction be at the junior and senior levels. Faculty teams working on the course numbering system have been forced to make compromises on the assignment of numbers, which has resulted in transfer students having to repeat courses completed as introductory coursework at the community college. The American Assembly of Colleges and Schools of Business was identified as one of the accrediting agencies that has created such a problem. (The New Jersey Institute of Technology case study in Part II provided further illustration.) The Florida common course numbering system has been expanded to include vocational/occupational courses and has been made available to independent colleges and universities, thus further facilitating transfer of community college students to upper-division institutions.

Nevada has developed a common course-level numbering system for all system institutions to facilitate student advisement and registration. All community college transfer courses follow a statewide course designation with equivalent university lower-division courses. The system also includes numbering for developmental courses, which are non-transferable.

In Colorado, common course designators for academic transfer courses were developed during the 1989–90 fiscal year by the Colorado Community College and Occupational Education System. The initial goal was to promote commonality across the two-year college system in order to assure more accurate content of courses when providing transfer information to the four-year institutions. A similar strategy is being carried out in Alabama under the leadership of the chancellor of the two-year college system.

A quite different approach is used in California, where course articulation is not predicated on an effort to determine "equivalency," but rather upon "comparability." The California Articulation Number (CAN) System does not attempt to have common course designation and numbering; instead, it requires an institution to designate those identically numbered CAN courses that are acceptable "in lieu of" its own designated courses. Articulation agreements to accept one course "in lieu of" another are usually based on content covered during a comparable period and require a written agreement between two or more institutions to accept and use a specific course completed on the sending campus to meet a course requirement at the receiving campus. Each campus retains and uses its own course number, prefix, and title and then adds the appropriate prefix and CAN when it has qualified the course through written articulation agreements with at least four other institutions, including one each from the two upper-division segments.

Course Equivalency Guides: Use of course equivalency guides to assist in the advisement of students and the transfer process is fairly common. In some states legislative action requires all institutions to maintain updated equivalency guides as a result of legislative action, while voluntary efforts are carried out intersegmentally or within segments in other states. Determination of equivalency practices varies and often offers evidence of faculty or institution attitudes. While joint participation of two-year and four-year faculties is a growing trend, in a few states the prerogative for equivalency determination is the sole province of departmental faculties of upper-division institutions, who carry out a judge and jury function by ruling on course syllabi submitted to the baccalaureate institution by the two-year colleges and apparently without benefit of conferral or collaboration with faculty of the two-year college.

State-Level Transfer/Articulation Bodies

An important mechanism for bringing about collective and continuing efforts to improve transfer and articulation statewide is the provision for a representational body concerned with all aspects of articulation and transfer of students and with positive articulated practices among the institutions. Such bodies vary in nomenclature, authority, and title among states. The Articulation Council of California, while state-supported, is voluntary, with membership drawn from the various segments of the public system as well as from the private sector. Its agreements are non-binding but have been effective as guidelines in most cases.

Similar voluntary coordinating groups responsible for articulation grievance referral beyond the campus level can be found in Arkansas, Maryland, Massachusetts, and Washington. In North Carolina, the voluntary Joint Committee on College Transfer Students, sponsored by the North Carolina Association of Colleges and Universities, includes both the public and independent sectors.

More legislative authority is vested in such coordinating bodies in Florida, Illinois, New Jersey, New York, and Colorado. Florida's Articulation Coordinating Committee is appointed by the Commissioner of Education and its recommendations can become directives under the rule-making authority of the state board or through legislative action. Membership of such groups traditionally has been confined to institutional representatives; however, New Jersey's Transfer Advisory Board includes public representatives as well.

Comprehensive Student Data and Information Systems

Several states have developed computerized student academic advisement systems to aid in counseling and guidance. Florida's on-line advisement and articulation system (SOLAR) provides students with an academic plan according to their selected major and upper-division institution. The system is used in the high schools for advisement also. A similar microcomputer-supported system in California is known by the acronym ASSIST (Articulation System Stimulating Interinstitutional Student Transfer). It provides information on transfer admission requirements, course recognition and comparability, as well as information on support services available at each institution. Some states, including Delaware, Nevada, and Rhode Island, have developed manual rather than computer-assisted systems.

Few states maintain the kind of comprehensive student data bases to monitor student flow and performance that would aid in improving transfer and articulation. Information on applications, transfer admission, credits recognized or rejected, or on transfer student performance, persistence, and academic status are often unavailable and sometimes known but not shared. A separate discussion of this topic and proposed ideal model developed by William Odom, deputy executive director of the Florida Division of Community Colleges, concludes Part I of this report.

Ethnic Minority Groups and the Transfer Function

A California legislative resolution in 1974 (ACR 151, Hughes) called for higher education institutions to reach out to underrepresented ethnic minority groups and identified transfer and articulation as mechanisms for assuring access and opportunity for a multi-cultural citizenry. In the early 1980s the Ford Foundation sponsored several research projects on access and transfer of minorities to the upper-division baccalaureate programs as well as a series of community college-based transfer opportunity program projects. A 1987 AACJC publication, *Transfer: Making It Work,* described the critical areas addressed by the Transfer Opportunity Project and listed other philanthropic foundation minority initiatives.

Regrettably, too few states have encouraged articulated collaborative efforts between two- and four-year institutions in increasing the number of underrepresented minorities who are baccalaureate-degree seekers. Incentive and outreach programs seldom encourage baccalaureate institutions to focus on two-year colleges as a separate level for motivational, bridge, and guarantee programs for minorities. As a result, the secondary school often is the focus of both the two-year and baccalaureate institutions in a competitive rather than collaborative mode. Most state incentive programs are directed toward segmental rather than intersegmental efforts.

New Jersey has instituted a Challenge Grant Program with priorities given to ethnic minority student initiatives involving identification, motivation, and articulated programs by the two- and four-year institutions. Several of these initiatives have involved 2 + 2 transfer agreements. Both the State University of New York and the City University of New York systems have grant programs to encourage two- and four-year consortia projects that promote programs and services to underrepresented ethnic minority groups. California has also provided funds that could be used collaboratively to serve ethnic minority students.

Arizona, Florida, Illinois, and New York have scholarship programs that reserve awards for minority transfer students. Arizona and Florida also provide outreach program funding for both intersegmental and segmental work with secondary schools in minority identification and recruitment programs. Several 2 + 2 + 2 agreements have "intent" language to emphasize underrepresented minority groups.

Studies on minority community college enrollments, transfer rates, and baccalaureate completion rates have increased state policymakers' attention to underrepresentation. Illinois has been especially active in promoting the concept of minority student baccalaureate achievement through transfer. The Illinois Board of Higher Education included the following strategies in a 1989 working paper:

To provide encouragement of, information about, and assistance in transferring, baccalaureate institutions should

- Assign baccalaureate-major advisers to feeder community and junior colleges with high proportions of minority students to advise prospective minority transfer students regularly on course requirements.

- Adopt the concepts contained in the "Articulation Compact."

- Offer admission and financial aid awards and provide transfer credit evaluations to transfer students early and in the same communication.

- Provide a special orientation program, designed with input by previous transfers, for community and junior college minority transfer students beginning at the community/junior college before transfer and continuing at the baccalaureate institution after transfer.

- Establish summer bridge or transition programs to orient and accustom entering minority transfer students (and their parents/spouses) to the institution's academic expectations and campus life.

- Establish a mentorship program for minority transfer students with faculty members or more experienced peers.

- Build student networks by creating smaller communities of identification within each college to serve as a home base for counseling, advising, tutoring, and meetings of study groups, clubs, and organizations.

To assure appropriate academic standards, baccalaureate institutions should

- Provide annual, detailed information on the progress of minority and other transfer students to feeder community and junior colleges.

To assure equal treatment of transfer and native students and to accommodate non-traditional minority students, baccalaureate institutions should

- Hold registration for transfer students on feeder community and junior college campuses or bring community and junior college transfer students to the campus to register at the same time as native continuing students register.

- Allocate sufficient residence hall space for community and junior college transfers, including single parents, and encourage on-campus living the first term after transfer.

- Provide child care services for children of students during all hours that classes are held on campus.

Dorothy Knoell, a preeminent authority on transfer and articulation, has proposed a new conceptualization of articulation as "collaboration" in the two-year and baccalaureate segment for recognizing joint cooperative responsibilities to achieve critical social goals. Collaborative efforts in correcting underrepresentation of ethnic minority groups represent a significant and worthy goals. (The Los Rios case study in Part II provides an excellent illustration of initiatives directed toward underrepresented groups.)

Articulation of Career Education Programs

Maine's six vocational technical institutes were designated "colleges" during 1989, thus joining New Hampshire, Minnesota, Wisconsin, and several other states that have recognized the increased rigor and academic background needed for training programs for the paraprofessional, mid-management, and technician middle manpower spectrum. As the programs have been upgraded, pressure has developed for degree-granting authority. Some states authorize such institutions to award the associate in specialized technology (AST) or the associate in specialized business (ASB) degrees, which typically include not less than 20 percent of coursework in general education and 75 or 80 percent of the work in the area of specialization and related coursework. Other institutions have increased the general education component to approximately 40 percent, typically found in the associate of applied science degree programs. In many states the occupational applied programs are expanding the general education component. As graduates of such programs have sought opportunity for baccalaureate degrees, transfer and articulation problems have developed. (The New Jersey Institute of Technology case study in Part II provides an in-depth illustration of articulated applied programs.)

In 1986 the California Legislature called on its Postsecondary Planning Commission to study and make recommendations on 2 + 2 + 2 articulated career education programs. The Texas

Legislature in 1987 assigned responsibility for the former vocational technical programs to the State Coordinating Board, charging it with incorporating such programs under the Texas Modified Core Curriculum policies. And the Indiana General Assembly directed the State Commission for Higher Education in 1988 to study the compliance of the assembly's mandate that all state universities and the vocational technical college system enter into articulation agreements to facilitate transfer of credits for courses in the associate degree programs, to be effective in 1989–90.

Oregon transfer policies recognize up to 24 credit hours from vocational technical courses as "general electives" and promote 2 + 2 program articulation in the occupational fields. The Iowa Board of Regents policy recognizes up to 16 hours of vocational courses for transfer. Nevada's common course numbering system provides for occupational courses in the applied associate degree programs, the same as in Florida.

Making Articulation Work

A review of all state policies and practices reveals a diversity of programs and services that, if operative, would result in two-year college students' unimpeded movement through upper-division institutions with full recognition and credit for all successfully completed coursework and with their assimilation into the student body with the least possible dislocation or trauma. Furthermore, the ideal relationship of two-year and four-year institutions would be collaborative rather than articulated efforts. Recommendations of the Joint Committee for Review of the Master Plan for Higher Education of the California Legislature in its March 1989 report could serve as model policies for every state. When declaring the transfer function as the central institutional priority of all segments of higher education, the Joint Committee recommended the following:

- The state shall guarantee by statute a place in postsecondary education for all qualified California students who wish to attend. All students who successfully complete the transfer curriculum at the community college level shall be guaranteed by statute future enrollment as upper-division students at the University of California or at the California State University. The grade point average required of all transfer students shall be the same within each segment regardless of their original eligibility, and all such students shall be treated equally with continuing students for admission to the programs and majors of their choice.

- Eligible students who have applied for freshman admission to campuses of the University of California or the California State University and who are not admitted to the campus or college of their first choice may choose to pursue their lower-division coursework at a designated community college. These students are guaranteed upper-division admission to the university campus and college of their first choice if they successfully complete the transfer curriculum, including a prescribed course of study and requisite grade point average, at the designated community college.

- Every community college district shall develop formal transfer agreements guaranteeing upper-division enrollment in specific majors for community college transfer student, regardless of initial eligibility, with at least three campuses of the University of California and the five campuses of the California State University, such agreements to be phased in over a period not to exceed January 1, 1992. The community college districts are encouraged to develop such agreements with as many campuses of the two university segments as feasible. The Board of Regents of the University of California and the Board of Trustees of the California State University shall insure that all campuses of their respective segments participate in the program. Such agreements shall specify the prescribed course of study and requisite grade point averages which shall guarantee entrance to the program of the student's choice. The community college districts and the university campuses shall develop coordinated counseling services so as to facilitate these transfer agreement systems.

- The governing boards of each of the segments are strongly encouraged and expected to develop programs of concurrent enrollment and concurrent student membership across segmental lines, so that community college transfer students are afforded the rights and privileges of matriculating university students.

- The Board of Regents of the University of California and the Board of Trustees of the California State University shall ensure that individual university campus enrollment plans include adequate upper-division places for community college transfer students in all undergraduate colleges and that each undergraduate college on each campus participates in developing articulation and transfer agreements with community colleges.

- The University of California and the California State University shall require students who are not regularly eligible for admission as first-year students (other than those admitted under special provisions) to complete the intersegmentally developed transfer core curriculum or its equivalent at a community college. University admissions offices can make exception to this rule under compelling circumstances. Those students who do complete the required courses with the requisite grade point average shall then be assured access to the California State University or to the University of California as transfer students with full degree credit for that coursework.

- The Board of Regents of the University of California and the Board of Trustees of the California State University shall declare as policy that students from historically underrepresented groups shall be afforded priority in transfer admissions decisions and shall design policies intended to facilitate their success in achieving transfer.

- The Board of Governors of the California Community Colleges, the Regents of the University of California, and the Trustees of the California State University, with appropriate consultation with the academic senates of the respective segments, shall jointly develop, maintain, and disseminate a common core curriculum in lower-division general education for the purposes of transfer. Such a core curriculum is to be designed and agreed to by January 1, 1990, with full implementation on the following academic year.

- The Board of Governors of the California Community Colleges shall have the authority and responsibility to guarantee that all community college students have access to courses that meet the lower-division baccalaureate degree requirements of the California public universities. The Board of Governors, with the cooperation of the Regents of the University of California and the Trustees of the California State University, shall insure that all students are clearly and fully informed as to which community college courses and units are transferable and that requirements in the community colleges correspond to the requirements for, entry to, and success in, upper-division university coursework.

- The governing boards of the University of California, the California State University, the California Community Colleges, and the Association of Independent California Colleges and Universities, and the State Board of Education shall be accountable for the implementation of formal system-wide articulation agreements and comparable courses numbering systems within and among the segments.

- Every community college campus shall maintain transfer counseling centers or other counseling services intended to counsel, advise, and monitor the progress of community college transfer students.

- The governing boards of each of the segments are strongly encouraged and expected to develop new programs of outreach, recruitment, and cooperation between and among the three segments of public higher education, to encourage and facilitate the successful transfer of students between the community colleges and the universities.

- The Governor and Legislature shall provide the financial support necessary for the community colleges and the two public university segments to offer comprehensive transfer programs and supporting services essential to an effective transfer function.

- The chairs of the governing boards of the three public segments of higher education shall present annual comprehensive reports to the Governor and Legislature on the status of transfer policies and programs and transfer rates, indicating outstanding problems of or obstacles to effective intersegmental articulation and coordination.

- The California Postsecondary Education Commission shall advise the Governor and the Legislature biennially as to: (1) the performance of all three public segments of California postsecondary education with respect to the goals and objectives of these recommendations regarding transfer; (2) the effective transfer rates between the different segments; (3) the adequacy of state support for these programs; and (4) further recommendations regarding the operation of these programs.

- The Governor and the Legislature shall monitor the success of the segments in achieving their targeted enrollment levels and in implementing these reforms. A substantial failure to implement reform, to achieve the 60/40 ratio by the designated dates, or to significantly improve the transfer rate of historically underrepresented groups, shall precipitate legislative hearings to show cause why specific budget allocations should not be withheld pending full implementation of these goals and reforms.

An array of policies, practices, and mechanisms identified during this study are intended to facilitate a student's mobility from one institution to another in achieving his or her educational goal while at the same time respecting the responsibility of each institution in determining the nature and form of programs to achieve its mission and reason for being. The following outline of articulation programs and practices illustrates the levels and areas of effort taking place within different states at this time.

Articulation Programs and Practices Identified During the National Articulation Study

I. State Level
   Legislative
           Mandates
           Budget Provisos
           Resolutions
   State Planning and Coordination Agencies
           Master Plan Policy/Recommendations
           Transfer/Articulation Studies
           Transfer Student Flow and Performance Reports

Sponsor State Articulation Working Groups
Leveling and Other Comparability/Equivalency Initiatives
Minority Student Incentive Policies
Program Review Articulation Requirements
Sponsor Conferences and Workshops
Intersegmental Coordinating and Policy Bodies
Articulate Core/General Education Requirements
Grievance Resolution
Promote Program Articulation
Segmental Boards and Agencies
Segmental Common Course/Core Requirements
Segmental Data and Information Systems
Segmental Common Calendars and Reporting Formats
Segmental Minimum Admissions Requirements
Segmental Limited Access Program Policies
Promote Intersegmental Programs
Statewide Voluntary Professional Groups Concerned with Transfer/Articulation
President's Deans' Councils (Both Inter- and Intrasegmental)
Transfer/Articulation Officers
Faculty Representatives (Including Disciplines)
Professional Associations

II. Regional Activities
Professional Voluntary Groupings
Regional Coordinating Councils
Regional Meetings and Workshops
Regional Consortia Projects

III. Institutional
Admissions
Upper-division Entry Comparable to Freshman Services
Joint (Guaranteed) Admissions
Orientation and Preregistration Services
Placement Testing
Common/Electronic Transcripts
Prompt Transcript Assessment and Reporting
Financial Aid Provisions
Transfer Student Services
Recruitment
Counseling/Advising (Manual or Computer-Assisted)
Transfer/Articulation Officers
Transfer Centers
Common Catalogs
Visits/College Fairs
Curriculum
Faculty-to-Faculty Articulation Activities
Articulated 2 + 2 Agreements
Articulated Acceleration
Dual Credit
Advanced Placement
CLEP

> Credit by Exam
> Concurrent Enrollment
> Other Articulation Activities
> Joint Programs
> Joint Use of Facilities
> Cooperative Outreach Programs
> Collaborative Activities

In the final analysis, however, making transfer and articulation work is dependent upon the willingness, commitment, and attitudes of people at the institutional level. People must know each other, communicate with each other, respect each other, trust each other, and work together. President-to-president and faculty-to-faculty relationships have resulted in clearer understanding of the different institutional missions and institutional cultures making up a state's system of postsecondary education. Two-year college faculty have come to realize university faculty members do care about students and are committed to teaching and learning. University faculty simultaneously have discovered that their two-year college counterparts are current in their disciplines and are committed to scholarship. A shared commitment to helping students, the common central purpose of all sincere faculty, can and does come from joint articulation efforts.

Institutional leaders, especially chief executive officers, set the direction and tone by serving transfer students and working with other institutions. (See the University of Central Florida/ Valencia Community College and Texas case studies in Part II for illustrations.)

The Baccalaureate View: Baccalaureate interests in the transfer/articulation debate are typically directed toward quality. Some question the quality of preparation provided by community colleges as well as the quality of performance and persistence of their product. Differences among two-year colleges and differences in the characteristics of their entering students make most state two-year college systems vulnerable to question, skepticism, and doubt. The nature and quality of faculty and staff of the colleges and the emphasis placed on the transfer function in comparison to the occupational programs, developmental programs, and business/industry services compound baccalaureate institutions' concerns.

The ability of two-year institutions to verify lower-division collegiate-level courses together with standards of rigor are important in satisfying the baccalaureate view. Admittedly, some of the ultra-conservative baccalaureate traditionalists will not be convinced; however, the public and its legislative representatives will be.

Two-Year College View: Concern that transfer students are treated the same as native students, coupled with resentment of heavy-handed, condescending attitudes from upper-division institutions, are often found in testimony and comments of two-year college representatives in the debate. Anecdotal evidence is offered for each but often lacks verification.

Two-year colleges simply do not know enough about themselves, their programs, the experiences of their transfer students, and the resultant need for self-corrective action. Two-year colleges in each state must make a commitment to improving systemwide information about transfer and articulation as well as be willing to address internal weaknesses.

State Policymaker View: There is a growing frustration with reported transfer student inequities and injustices resulting from institutional competition, dissension, and uncooperativeness. It would appear that legislatures, reflecting public sentiment, are becoming increasingly intolerant of traditions, structures, and attitudes of academe that place institution interest above the importance and worth of the student.

The long-term response to this view will be a movement from articulation practices to collaborative practices between and among the public institutions in each state.

Recommendations

The Congress

It is recommended that Congress study the injustice to federal financial aid recipients and the cost to taxpayers of state-supported institutions that require such recipients to repeat coursework at receiving institutions that already had been successfully completed at the sending institution. Using the constitutional "welfare clause" authority, Congress should enact legislation that would deny federal funds to states that do not correct such injustices.

It is also recommended that Congress determine whether regional or professional accrediting bodies violate the rights of federal financial aid recipients when imposing requirements that are essentially barriers to transfer and articulation between two-year and four-year programs. (Only one regional accrediting agency was identified in this study as treating transfer and articulation in the same manner as affirmative action policies.)

The AACJC

It is recommended that the AACJC Board of Directors promote the importance of the transfer function by a planned national program that systematically focuses upon critical areas of transfer and articulation. It is proposed that 1991 be designated the "Year of Transfer and Articulation" in order for activities to be high-lighted and the nation to become involved. AACJC-affiliated councils could contribute to their regional and state activities throughout the year.

It is further recommended that three specific areas be addressed during the Year of Transfer, including: (1) the transfer function and opportunities for underrepresented ethnic minority groups; (2) the transfer function and career education programs; and (3) moving from articulation to collaboration programs.

It is recommended that AACJC institute a program of identifying and reporting exemplary transfer and articulation practices comparable to those included in Part II of this report.

The State Legislatures

It is recommended that state legislatures require statewide intersegmental and segmental reports on transfer and articulation activities to insure that legislative intent and priorities for fairness to students and taxpayers are achieved.

It is also recommended that legislatures provide incentives for appropriate transfer/articulation/collaboration efforts of two-year and four-year institutions for increasing the participation of underrepresented minority groups.

It is further recommended that legislatures provide funds for the development of comprehensive student data systems and insist upon all institutions sharing information among and between segments as well as with the legislature and the public.

Finally, it is recommended that state legislatures determine whether state financial aid programs are being violated by institutional practices or requirements of accrediting agencies that would require comparable corrective action as recommended for Congress at the national level.

Suggested Readings

Listings of all policy, study, and procedures sources for each state used in this study cannot be made due to the limitation of space and the variation in citations. Many states provided xeroxed copies of material related to the study. Selected publications are referenced below based on direct value to this study or judged worthy of use by states seeking helpful information on transfer and articulation.

Handbook for Articulation Task Forces 1985–86. Irene Wright, Facilitator, Academic Program Articulation Steering Committee. State of Arizona.

Transfer Policies of Arkansas Colleges and Universities. Arkansas Transfer Advisory Committee. January, 1988.

California Faces . . . California's Future: Education for Citizenship in a Multicultural Democracy. The Final Report of the Joint Committee for Review of the Master Plan for Higher Education. March, 1989.

Handbook of California Articulation Policies and Procedures. Intersegmental Coordinating Council. 1989.

Strengthening Transfer and Articulation Policies and Practices in California's Colleges and Universities: Progress Since 1985 and Suggestions for the Future. California Postsecondary Education Commission. 1987.

Progress in Implementing the Recommendations of the Commission's 1987 Report on Strengthening Transfer and Articulation. California Postsecondary Education Commission. 1988.

Transfer and Articulation with Four-Year Colleges and Universities. A Report by the Board of Governors of California Community Colleges. March 9–10, 1989.

Articulating Career Education Programs from High School through Community College to the Baccalaureate Degree. A Report to the Governor, Legislature, and Educational Community in Response to Assembly Bill 3639 (Chapter 1138, Statues of 1986). California Postsecondary Education Commission. December 14, 1987.

Reaffirming California's Commitment to Transfer: Recommendations for Aiding Student Transfer from the California Community Colleges to the California State University and the University of California. California Postsecondary Education Commission. 1985.

Transfer, Articulation, and Collaboration Twenty-Five Years Later. A Report of a Research Project Funded by the Ford Foundation. By Dorothy M. Knoell. American Association of Community and Junior Colleges, 1990.

Transfer Information System Feasibility Study. Colorado Commission on Higher Education. November 1988.

Articulation Study: The Role of Florida Community Colleges in Articulation. Florida State Board of Community Colleges Task Force on Articulation. September, 1988.

Transfer Study: A Five-Year Study of Students Transferring from Illinois Two-Year Colleges to Illinois Senior Colleges/Universities in the Fall of 1979. Illinois Community College Board by Authority of the State of Illinois. May, 1986.

Performance Audit Report: Transferring Courses to Regents' Universities. A Report to the Legislative Post Audit Committee by the Legislative Division of Post Audit. State of Kansas. January, 1986.

Student Transfers from Community Colleges to Baccalaureate Institutions in Michigan. Preliminary Report by Maureen T. Neal, Community College Services Unit, Higher Education Management Services, prepared for the Michigan State Board of Education. February, 1988.

Credit Transfer: Guidelines for Student Transfer and Articulation Among Missouri Colleges and Universities. Missouri Coordinating Board for Higher Education. October, 1987.

Articulation and Transfer: A Compendium of University Initiatives. By Dympna Bowles, Director of Articulation, and Cerisa Mitchell, Associate Director of Articulation, Office of Academic Affairs. The City University of New York. 1987.

Report of the University Articulation Task Forces. Office of Academic Affairs. The City University of New York. 1988.

Guidelines for Transfer: Recommendations of the Joint Committee on College Transfer Students. University of North Carolina. 1987.

Recommended Transfer Programs Guide 1987–1989: Update. Oregon State System of Higher Education.

South Dakota Postsecondary Collegiate Articulation Committee Report. July 1989.

A Study of the Role of Community Colleges in the Achievement of the Bachelor's Degree in Washington State. Washington State Board for Community College Education. January, 1989.

Policy on Inter-College Transfer and Articulation Among Washington Public Colleges and Universities. State of Washington Higher Education Coordinating Board. February, 1986.

Intercollege Relations Commission Information Booklet. A Commission of the Washington Council on High School/College Relations. 1986.

Transfer Information System Project Definition. The University of Wisconsin System, January. 1989.

It Takes Two to Transfer: Relational Networks and Educational Outcomes

Caroline Sotello and Viernes Turner

The fact that the United States higher education system has a transfer process distinguishes it from systems in much of the rest of the world. In *The Higher Education System,* Burton Clark (1983) notes that there is a high degree of articulation and permeability in the U.S. system compared to that in other countries. We can take pride in the opportunities the transfer process offers students for access across colleges and universities as we attempt to better understand and improve it.

Transfer and "The Complexity of Joint Action"

Current literature suggests that the complexity of the transfer process may impede community college students from getting their baccalaureate degrees. Watkins (1990) cites Palmer saying that transferring "is a tough bureaucratic task" (p. A37) for students. Michael A. Olivas (1979) notes that "negotiating transfer constantly appears to be an impediment to baccalaureate completion by students. . ." (p. 177). Organizational theorists Pressman and Wildavsky (1973) document the fact that organizational processes often look simple and straight-forward, but they are actually extremely complicated and can break down at any number of steps in the process.

Current literature also suggests that interinstitutional cooperation, which is essential to successful articulation, faces barriers. These barriers include: differing cultures in two- and four-year colleges, such as mission emphasis (community vs. knowledge generation) and functional priority (teaching vs. research) (Richardson & Bender, 1987); self-interest, which dictates, for instance, improved articulation when there are too few high school graduates to maintain desired enrollment, and deteriorating articulation when personalities clash (Richardson & Bender, 1987); a choice by community colleges to vocationalize themselves (Brint & Karabel, 1989); and the tendency of four-year colleges to see community college students as "not as good as" (p. A38) their students (Watkins, 1990).

Moreover, difficulties in the transfer process work against minority students because they "are so overwhelmingly clustered in two-year institutions" (Olivas, 1979, p. 177). Richardson and Bender (1987) say that articulation worked reasonably well from the perspectives of universities and suburban community college administrators, but much of current practice appears to impact adversely on inner city colleges and the heavy minority student populations who attend them.

A study by this author addresses the potential effects of interinstitutional relationships on transfer. Relational networks may be one of many factors contributing to the differential implementation of transfer policies among two- and four-year colleges.

Study Description

This paper is based on a 1986 qualitative case study of the transfer process for Hispanic students and non-Hispanic white students in three California community colleges. Given limited space, a thorough review of study methodology and findings cannot be presented here. Further discussion of this research can be found in "A California Case Study: Organizational Determinants of the Transfer of Hispanic Students From Two- to Four-Year Colleges in the Bay Area" (Turner, 1990).

Comparative Case Study Approach

In order to generate hypotheses about community college organizational factors (structures and routines) that may explain differential transfer rates by college, an exploratory, multi-site case study was conducted of three California community colleges in the Bay area with varying transfer rates for Hispanics and non-Hispanic whites. Semi-structured interviews, observations, document review, and student surveys were used to collect data on community college structures and routines from the perspectives of staff, faculty, Hispanic students, and non-Hispanic white students.

Hispanic students targeted for study are of Mexican-American descent. In order to obtain comparable study sites, attempts were made to control for Hispanic student population attributes (e.g., student socioeconomic status), community college size (total college enrollment), percent of Hispanic student enrollment, geographical location, and proximity to a four-year college. All three sites are in the mid-sized group of California community colleges. Enrollments range from 7,000 to 11,000. All are suburban community colleges located in close proximity to a four-year college and to a highly-populated Hispanic community. Hispanic study participants are predominantly from low-income families, and report smaller incomes and larger family size than non-Hispanic white students participating in the study.

Colleges selected for the study exhibit low, high, or discrepant transfer rates when compared to system-wide transfer percentages, for Hispanic and non-Hispanic white students. College Low has an 18% transfer rate for non-Hispanic white students and an 11% rate for Hispanic students. College High has a 39% transfer rate for non-Hispanic white students and a 34% rate for Hispanic students. College Discrepant has a 43% transfer rate for non-Hispanic white students and a 19% rate for Hispanics. This compares to a system-wide transfer rate of 39% for non-Hispanic white students and 20% for Hispanic students. There is no community college with a low transfer rate for non-Hispanic white students and a high transfer rate for Hispanics.

Interviews conducted with community college articulation officers suggest that there may be a set of routinized networks encasing individual community colleges in a web of transfer or non-transfer opportunities.

Interinstitutional Linkages: It Takes Two to Transfer

Student movement from two- to four-year colleges is assisted by the articulation of curriculum from one level to the other. Articulation officers from both college levels arrive together at articulation agreements which the four-year schools use to grant course credit for classes taken at the community college. Articulation officers at College High and College Discrepant also work with feeder high schools to articulate high school courses with community college courses. High school credits can then be used to fulfill community college requirements.

Articulation officers interviewed for this study are part of the counseling services department. At all community college study sites, the articulation function (at most, a half-time assignment) is handled by the student services area rather than the instructional administration area.

Informal interactions between two-year and four-year college representatives, as described by community college articulation officers, seem to have an impact on the institutional transfer process.

Impact of Social Networks

According to the California Master Plan for Higher Education, transfer work at a community college theoretically transfers to all four-year colleges. The plan assumes an educational market exists such that one can move from any given community college to almost any four-year program. However, informal networks appear to actually drive the transfer process. Mark Granovetter (1985) argues that there is a strong effect of social context on seemingly rational choices. He states:

> The main thrust of the "new institutional economist" is to deflect the analysis of institutions from sociological, historical, and legal argumentation and show instead that they arise as the efficient solution to economic problems. The mission and pervasive functionalism it implies discourage the detailed analysis of social structure that I argue here is the key to understanding how existing institutions arrived at their present state. (p. 505)

> Perhaps this web of interaction is mainly what explains the level of efficiency, be it high or low, of the new organizational form. (p. 502)

Granovetter's work helps explain the findings of the study discussed in this paper. All three California community college sites appear to be embedded in informal but routinized networks of curricular relationships with four-year colleges which differentially affect the opportunity for student transfer.

First, study interviews reveal that some community colleges acquire status as transfer schools and others do not. Four-year colleges seem to respond more favorably to curricular articulation with community colleges which have a high student transfer rate than those having a low rate. Kanter (1977) has documented a preference by individuals for "socially similar" individuals. This study suggests that the same phenomena may extend to organizational interactions. The status accorded colleges with low transfer rates influence how four-year institutions respond to them, as these comments made by articulation officers illustrate:

> College Low: "Some [four-year colleges] don't think their staff time is of use because we don't send them many students. For example, I've sent five letters to a [four-year university] and they've never responded."

By contrast, College High and College Discrepant articulation officers make these remarks:

> College Discrepant: "[One four-year university] is very active in communicating with community colleges in establishing course-by-course agreements. [We have agreements] with [this four-year university's] biology, math, engineering, and physics departments."

> College High: "The four-year institutions are making a stronger pledge to be available. . . . [Four-year college representatives] usually came [to College High] once in the spring of the year. [A state college representative] now comes three times. . . ."

Second, interview comments suggest that the transfer status of a community college may, in part, be perpetuated by the historical relationship of the two-year college with the four-year colleges already in its network of transfer options. Thus, some community colleges have specific connections with and serve as feeder schools to specific four-year colleges. The following remarks by community college articulation officers elaborate on these interinstitutional linkages:

College Low: "[We] contact individual campuses for course-by-course articulation. . . . [There are] no articulation agreements with all California State Colleges or University of California campuses because we don't send anyone to some of the campuses, like [four-year state college]. At [this four-year state college] we don't have course-specific agreements, just general education agreements."

College Discrepant: "We don't have [articulation agreements] with a lot of campuses. There are some campuses that we have a lot of difficulty with in terms of 'is your course equivalent to my course?' I spend more of my time on campuses where most of our students go—campuses that are very close and that I can telephone, such as [near-by four-year university]."

College High: "[We] do concentrated articulation with nearby colleges. . . . These colleges would be the ones I would concentrate on first simply because that's where our students tend to go."

Faculty, students, and other staff affiliated with the different study sites also make the following comments further elaborating on the transfer status of their college and its historical relationship with four-year colleges:

College Low: "Our students are crippled by not having a collegiate identify . . . Recently, there was an attempt [in district] to make [College Low] a vocational school. Transfer courses would not be offered."

"We're not just a night school. I'm not going to feel that I've done a good job unless I feel the word is out."

College Discrepant: "We have a good rate of transfer. If the student chooses a [four-year] college program that has a long-standing articulation relationship with [College Discrepant], then fewer problems may be encountered . . . if the student follows the pattern, there is no problem."

"I went to [four-year college]. I had high grades but not adequate financial assistance. They recommended that I come to [College Discrepant] and then transfer . . . Students come here assuming they are going to transfer."

College High: "[College High] is one of the better junior colleges around. [Four-year state university] has classes that I can take here. I want to transfer to [four-year state university]."

"They [four-year colleges] come from all over the area to recruit [College High] students."

The transfer network (ties between two-year and four-year colleges) seems to be routinized at each college. In other words, once a successful connection is made between a four-year and a two-year college, that connection is strengthened by communications between the articulation officers. Students then successfully use this connecting bridge, further strengthening ties. Other potential ties may not be pursued.

The choice of a community college may amount also to the choice of the four-year college. Theoretically, all choices are open to students, but are all choices equally probable? Perhaps it is easier for students to transfer to schools that already have strong ties with the community college they are attending. Rogers and Kincaid (1981) and Kanter (1977) refer to homogenous communication and relational networks as being self-sealing and self-reinforcing. Following this line of thought, it may be that transfer institutions and non-transfer institutions are embedded in a transfer or non-transfer network which is also self-sealing and self-reinforcing. Counselors, other students, and faculty may encourage students to transfer to well-articulated colleges because students can go there with little or no trouble. The transfer process may become institutionalized, and even if unconscious, reinforce the present connections and the potential trajectory of students. This phenomenon can be related to Merton's discussion of "The Matthew Effect in Science" (1968). He argues that "the rich get richer at a rate that makes the poor relatively poor" (p. 62) partly as a result of a social network process.

The transfer status of a community college is perpetuated not only by individual differences in student capability, but also by the historical relationships between the two- and four-year colleges and by the propensity of four-year colleges to respond more readily to community colleges with good transfer records than to those with low records. Therefore, community colleges may not be a "stepping stone" to all four-year colleges as the California Master Plan for Higher Education proposes. Moreover, to the extent that low-transfer community colleges have high minority enrollment, minority students may be more limited in transfers to four-year colleges than are non-minorities.

Interinstitutional Relations and Community College Transfer: Implications and Conclusions

Higher education practictioners at both two- and four-year institutions need to be aware of the potential effects of institutional linkages on student transfers in general and particularly on minority student transfers. More work needs to be done to determine the nature and potential impact of community college linkages to four-year colleges and to the workplace as well as to the surrounding community. If institutionalized linkages between two- and four-year colleges exist systemwide, and if low-transfer community colleges have a high concentration of minorities, these linkages may have a differential effect on the transfer of minority and majority students.

To equalize transfer opportunities for all community colleges, old routines must be consciously changed, not only at the individual level, but at the organizational level as well. Faculty, staff, and "transfer-knowledgeable" students may discuss and promote a wide array of four-year) college options to new students, while college representatives (both two- and four-year) can be opening, developing, and strengthening a wide array of interinstitutional ties. Even those college sites reporting relatively high transfer rates noted that curricular and other interinstitutional ties should be strengthened.

More college resources could be allocated to the crucial articulation function. Articulation officers quoted here have a heavy student counseling workload, and some also coordinate and advertise campus visits by four-year college representatives. This staffing pattern makes it difficult for articulation officers at low-transfer colleges to establish linkages with four-year colleges or for their counterparts at higher-transfer colleges to broaden their linkages.

In addition, the instructional administrative arm of the community college could share the articulation function with the student services staff. Since the goal of articulation is to link curriculums, it might be strengthened by more faculty participation. Successful articulation efforts with high schools and four-year colleges described by College Discrepant take place with high faculty participation from all the educational institutions. If the instructional administrative arm did share the articulation effort, student services staff could continue to have a coordinating role.

Finally, four-year postsecondary institutions may need to expend more resources in outreach to "low transfer" and/or high minority enrollment community college sites. Although it may not be cost-efficient for four-year colleges, more resource expenditure may be justified in order to assist community colleges with low transfer rates to expand transfer horizons for their students. As one community college president explained, "This year we ran classes even if the enrollment was low just to maintain our presence in the (Hispanic) community . . . We want to prove that there is a [college] commitment to the community. It's view toward long-range goals versus short-range goals."

These suggestions are supported by recommendations Cohen (1988) makes to facilitate transfer, which include: faculty exchange, dual student admission, coordinated student support services, communication between staff members, and increased formalization of state-level policies to guarantee university admission at the junior level for community college students.

While community college relational networks appear to have an impact on the transfer process, colleges which enjoy a high transfer status should also assess whether that status equally benefits various racial/ethnic groups *within* the college. College Discrepant, for example, has a good overall transfer rate. However, there is a wide discrepancy of transfer between majority and minority students.

Changes in the articulation process described here will require breaking well-established interinstitutional routines. This will take time and focused, sustained effort.

References

Brint, Steven & Karabel, Jerome. (1989) *The diverted dream: Community colleges and the promise of educational opportunity in America: 1900–1985.* New York: Oxford University Press.

Clark, Burton R. (1983). *The higher education system: Academic organization in cross-national perspective.* Berkeley, CA: University Press.

Cohen, Arthur M. (1988, Summer). Degree achievement by minorities in community colleges. *The Review of Higher Education, 11*(4), 383–402.

Granovetter, Mark. (1985, November). Economic action and social structure: The problem of embeddedness. *American Journal of Sociology, 91*(3), 481–510.

Kanter, Rosabeth M. (1977). *Men and women of the corporation.* New York: Basic Books.

Merton, Robert K. (1968, January 5). The Matthew effect in science. *Science, 159 , 56–63.*

Olivas, Michael A. (1979). *The dilemma of access: Minorities in two-year colleges.* Washington, DC: Howard University Press.

Pressman, Jeffrey L. & Wildavsky, Aaron. (1973). *Implementation: How great expectations in Washington are dashed in Oakland.* Berkeley: University of California Press.

Richardson, Richard & Bender, Louis W. (1987). *Fostering minority access and achievement in higher education.* San Francisco: Jossey-Bass.

Rogers, Everett M. & Kincaid, D. Lawrence. (1981). *Communication networks: Toward a new paradigm for research.* New York: The Free Press.

Turner, Caroline S.V. (1990, Fall). A California case study: Organizational determinants of the transfer of Hispanic students from two-year to four-year colleges in the Bay area. *Metropolitan Education, 6,* 1–124.

Watkins, Beverly T. (1990, February 7). 2-year institutions under pressure to ease transfer: Critics say unneeded complexity deters many minority students. *The Chronicle of Higher Education,* pp. A1, A37–A38.

The 2 + 2 Tech-Prep/
Associate-Degree Program:
Making Winners of Ordinary Students

DALE PARNELL

. . . there is surprisingly little attention given to "ordinary people" in the school reform reports. There is the clear implication that the rising tide of mediocrity is made up of an embarrassing number of ordinary people, and if we want to return excellence to education, we better go out and find more excellent people.

K. Patricia Cross, Harvard Graduate School of Education

The heart of the message we have heard from parents, students, politicians, and policymakers is this: *Give us more structure; give us more substance in our educational programs. Help us develop the confidence that materials and scaffolding of our educational structures match the real-life needs of all our students.*

One of the most recent reform reports points a finger of guilt at the colleges and universities for some of the breakdown in educational-program structure and substance. A distinguished panel of higher-education leaders forthrightly states the problem:

As for what passes as a college curriculum, almost anything goes. We have reached a point at which we are more confident about the length of a college education than its content and purpose. . . . Electives are being used to fatten majors and diminish breadth. It is as if no one cared, so long as the store stays open.

One consequence of the abandonment of structure by the colleges has been the abandonment of structure in the schools. The decline in requirements is contagious, and in the absence of system in national educational arrangements, articulation between secondary and higher education has been allowed to break down. The result is a loss of rigor both in the secondary and in the collegiate course of study. That loss of definition and rigor has encouraged the false notion that there is such a thing as effortless learning, a notion that finds expression in curricular practice and student behavior. As the colleges have lost a firm grasp on their goals and mission, so have the secondary schools. [Association of American Colleges 1985]

The requirements listed for most college degrees look more like a treaty among warring nations than a coherent vision of what it means to be an educated person.

In many ways the associate degree is aimed at maintaining community college comprehensiveness and seeking balance in the curriculum. The associate degree is not only central to the mission of the community, technical, and junior college, but it is also a quality-control issue. Colleges have suffered unintended negative public relations from well-meaning but semi-literate individuals who take a college class or two and then go to the university or to an employer and say, "I am a student of the Community College."

We simply cannot allow the debate about the importance of the liberal arts and the practical arts to degenerate into an either/or argument. They are both important and balance is needed. Educational excellence must be defined in terms of connectedness and applicability, particularly for that sixty to seventy percent of the population who do not work as well, nor as effectively, when dealing only with the abstract. The liberal arts and the practical arts absolutely need each other.

Students in vocational-technical education programs must meet the same basic skill requirements as any other student seeking the high school diploma. But, it must be quickly pointed out that a course in business-letter writing can be rigorous and help students demonstrate writing skills. A course in business mathematics can also be rigorous and help students master computing percentages or applying statistical methods. An applied-physics course can be rigorous and help students master essential academic knowledge through practical experiences. Balance, connectedness, and continuity are key words in any reshaping of the curriculum aimed at improving the education of the middle quartile of students.

Research and experience tell us that students work better with goals; indeed, so do we all. Yet there is a lack of clarity in what high schools and postsecondary institutions expect of their students. Furthermore, there is poor communication between these two educational entities. Even more serious, there is a subtle but stubborn provincialism that suggests that program *articulation*, the careful building of bridges between high schools and colleges, and program *evaluation*, the careful measure of program success or failure, are extraneous to the primary mission of either group.

The national reports have given only cursory attention to the need for continuity in learning, forgetting all the dangerous lessons that the business world has learned of late—what happens when the left hand does not really understand what the right is about? The indicators are not difficult to find.

The concern that high-school students are still not concentrating on developing the "new basics" has been confirmed in a study by the National Center for Educational Statistics. The study found that students are not taking recommended loads in such basic subjects as mathematics, science, and computer science. Interestingly, in the twelfth grade, the senior year, fewer courses were completed in these targeted areas than in any other high-school year, even though these seniors were below recommended program guidelines.

High schools generally do not have a good sense of how their students perform once at college or in the work world, as the colleges and universities, with rare exception, do not keep them informed. Community colleges, who often must deal with students who have failed to reach their own or others' expectations upon high-school graduation, are particularly lax in letting high schools know how their former students are doing.

Generally speaking, although the high-school courses a student takes do not seem important in getting him or her into a community college, they may be absolutely critical to success once the student is there. Yet, there is precious little communication to high-school students from the community, technical, and junior colleges about college *exit* requirements and the recommended high-school preparation related to these exit and program-completion requirements.

In *The Third Wave* Alvin Toffler describes our future world in terms of waves of change. The first wave of change was the agricultural revolution, which took a thousand years to develop. The second wave brought on the industrial revolution, over a mere 300 years. A technology-driven third wave is sweeping the world in a few decades and affecting almost every aspect of our lives.

Robots are invading our factories. Electronic mail is becoming a standard communication device. Disease detection and prevention have been greatly improved. Superspeed air travel is now commonplace. The videocassette recorder is becoming a part of the home entertainment center and was the hottest Christmas sales item of 1984. Laser technology, genetic engineering, and computer literacy are becoming common phrases in everyday communications. Odetics, Inc., a southern California high-technology firm, has just announced the development of Odex II, a computerized mobile robot, both agile and strong. It is not only capable of climbing on the back of a pickup truck but is also capable of lifting the truck. This six-legged wonder can tackle jobs in such high-risk areas as nuclear power plants, stifling mine shafts, or burning buildings. In the initial development and production phase of this robot many engineers and scientists are required. But when 50,000 of these robots are being produced a year, the commercialization of technology will require many technicians for the manufacture, operation, programming, and repair of these machines.

Research on the organic computer, or "biochip," is a growing priority for some genetic engineers, chemists, mathematicians, and molecular biologists. Can we grow computer circuitry in biology labs from living bacteria producing powerful microprocessors? If it can be done, future computer circuits will be designed from groups of organic proteins the size of molecules that will serve as microscopic memory and switching devices, with the ability to more or less assemble themselves.

The Office of Technology serving the Congress of the United States lists communities across the country that are considered "hotbeds" of technology development: Huntsville, Alabama; Phoenix, Arizona; San Diego, California; Los Angeles, California; Santa Clara County, California; Colorado Springs, Colorado, Brivard County, Florida; Orlando, Florida; Chicago, Illinois; Montgomery County, Maryland; Lowell, Massachusetts; Minneapolis-St. Paul, Minnesota; Albuquerque, New Mexico, Portland, Oregon, Philadelphia; Philadelphia, Pennsylvania; Oak Ridge, Tennessee; Austin, Texas; San Antonio, Texas; Salt Lake City, Utah; Burlington, Vermont; Seattle, Washington; Milwaukee, Wisconsin. Futurists tend to agree that the next twenty to thirty years will be a time of explosive progress. Robert Weinstein states:

> Like it or not, our educational institutions have little choice but to change with the times. Either that or be left in the wake of untold technological breakthroughs. Many schools obstinately cling to the past, while others are busy designing curriculums to meet the needs of tomorrow. Yet, it's only a matter of time before even the most reactionary open themselves up to what lies ahead. If our educational system can no longer train and educate our young for the jobs of tomorrow, education has little relevancy. (Weinstein 1983)

Training and education have become integral to most broad-technology workers whether they be nurses, law-enforcement officers, electronic technicians, aircraft technicians, computer operators, auto-service personnel, or marketing representatives. IBM now requires each technician, marketing representative, and systems analyst in that large corporation to spend nineteen to twenty days (one working month) in education and training programs. And IBM is not alone in requiring such programs of its employees. Such widely diverse companies as State Farm Insurance, Southwest Forest Industries, Manufacturers Hanover Trust Company, Abbott Laboratories, Central Illinois Light Company, Citicorp, Steelcase Inc., Valley National Bank of Arizona, and Caterpillar Tractor Company all are moving education and training programs into high-priority positions in terms of strategic planning for economic growth. California Superintendent of Public Instruction Bill Honig has summed up the challenge for schools and colleges this way: "Don't be misled by advocates of a low-tech future. These modern Luddites have historically underestimated the extent and pace of change in the economy. They cite only a portion of the data from the Department of Labor; neglecting statistics that demonstrate substantive growth in jobs requiring high levels of preparation. They are out of step with the people who are hiring our graduates" (1985).

It is estimated that thirty billion dollars is spent annually by U.S. public and private employers for employee education and training programs. This figure does not include costs for training in the military. The Department of Defense estimates that some fifty billion dollars is spent on education and training per year when all DOD education and training costs are included. Public and private employers are concluding that that competencies and related performance of the work force are the major factor in determining the economic and social health of their enterprise.

Clearly, more and more secondary schools and community colleges are waking up to the reality of shifting the curriculum to match a technological world:

> The growing pervasiveness of technology—and the certitude of ongoing technical advances—demands that we provide our young people with the solid base of scientific knowledge they will require. It is not only those who create technology who should have a competency in math and science. Those who use technology should also have a degree of understanding about the tools they use. They must also be able to adapt to changes in technology and the new skill requirements they bring with them. (Young 1985)

It is absolutely imperative that high schools and colleges, particularly community, technical, and junior colleges, become aggressive in examining, developing, and sustaining quality educational programs to serve that great host of Americans who keep this country working.

> *Who will keep our airplanes flying—*
> *our water flowing—*
> *our electricity charging—*
> *our hospitals operating—*
> *our trains tracking—*
> *our computers clicking—*
> *our cars running—*
> *our laws enforced—*
> *our goods and services sold—*

in a society saturated at every level with technology and information? I breathe a little prayer each time I climb on an airplane: Dear Lord, I just pray that the air-frame and power-plant technicians that serviced this plane had excellent education and training programs—and that they enjoy their work!

> Today, graduating high-school seniors can either go right to work, pursue a formal college education, or attend technical school or junior college. In the future we can look forward to new options. Community colleges, for one, will have a lot more credibility than they have today. Although they will still be regarded as interim programs for those unsure of what they want to do with their lives, the community colleges of the future will work closely with the community and industry, thus having a much stronger identity. Industry leaders and teaching staffs will put their heads together to devise curriculums that provide real jobs for graduating seniors. . . . For a growing number of young people, a two-year associate degree or possibly a company- or union-sponsored training program makes more sense. (Weinstein 1983)

The prediction that community colleges of the future will work closely with employers has already come true. *Three out of four community, technical, and junior colleges now report their participation in one or more employer/college partnership arrangements.* Has the time arrived to take the next step in establishing formal community college program partnerships with high schools? How about establishing a new four-year tech-prep/associate-degree program of cooperation between high schools and community, technical, and junior colleges?

Many academically talented secondary-school students have been well served over the years by the college-prep/baccalaureate-degree program, and that work must continue with even greater vigor and attention. But the ordinary students, the middle fifty percent of the high-school student population, have not been served so well. Some eleven million students out of the forty million now enrolled in elementary and secondary schools will not even graduate from high school. Many of these drop-outs will find their way to the community college within a few years without the requisite preparatory background.

It should be underlined at this point that the college-prep/baccalaureate-degree program remains one of the priority programs for the community college. More and more recent high-school graduates are experiencing a cost-effective and excellent undergraduate two years in a community college. *In case study after case study students report they experienced the best teaching of their college careers in the community college.* More students must be encouraged to continue on through the community college and to complete the baccalaureate-degree program. Community colleges are working diligently and must continue to do so to provide a first-rate program leading to the baccalaureate degree. But the traditional college-prep/baccalaureate-degree program is not the focus of this book, even though it remains a top priority in the work of the community college.

Assumptions of the Tech-Prep/Associate-Degree Program

The tech-prep/associate-degree program advocates taking a step beyond the current and usually cosmetic high-school/college partnership arrangements into *substantive* program coordination. The program seeks a middle ground that blends the liberal arts with the practical arts without diluting the time-honored baccalaureate-degree/college-prep track. A closely coordinated four-year (grades eleven through fourteen) liberal-technical education program will provide more room for an electives program than can be achieved in unconnected years.

The program targets are (1) the middle quartiles of the typical high-school student body in terms of academic talent and interest, and (2) the mid-range of occupations requiring some beyond-high-school education and training but not necessarily a baccalaureate degree. The tech-prep/associate-degree program rests on the following assumptions:

1. Additional program structure and substance are required for most high-school students.

2. Continuity in learning is an important and often vital ingredient for student success.

3. Community, technical, and junior colleges have generally failed to give clear signals to high-school students and their parents about what constitutes an exemplary high-school preparatory program, particularly to those students headed for technical-education programs.

4. The most growth over the next fifteen years will occur in those occupations requiring some postsecondary education and training but less than a baccalaureate degree. Professional and technical workers are expected to replace clerical workers as the largest occupational group. (Pyatt 1985)

5. Most of the emerging (and some of the older) technical-education programs cannot be completed adequately in two years, particularly if the student has had inadequate secondary-school preparation. Excellent liberal/technical-education programs require more time. Furthermore, high schools report little technical education is going on at that level.

6. The junior and senior years of high school can be better utilized by many students. The senior year in particular has sometimes been seen as a waste of time for some students.

7. The current twenty-seven-percent high-school drop-out rate can be reduced if students understand the "why" of their learning as well as the "how." This means a breaking down of the walls between vocational and academic education. The largest volume of dropping out of high school occurs between grades ten and eleven. This volume can be reduced if students see a focused alternative-learning program that connects the curriculum with real-life issues.

8. Focused learning motivates more students than does unfocused learning.

9. The associate degree is becoming an increasingly preferred degree by employers for entry into many mid-level occupations.

10. Secondary schools must be preparatory institutions for *all* students and not just for college-prep/baccalaureate-degree-bound students. Students must be better prepared to take that next step, whatever that step may be.

11. Standards of excellence must be developed for all programs, particularly for the middle quartiles of students.

12. Guidance programs must present all high-school students with a curricular program whose goals are clear. The guidance program must also be prepared to help students shift their goals from time to time. Aimlessness is one of the plagues of secondary-school and college students: goals must remain within clear vision of the student.

13. High-school and college faculty and administrators can coordinate their programs and can communicate more effectively when a clear signal is given from the policymakers that there is a policy demand upon the system.

14. Neither the current college-prep/baccalaureate-degree track nor the traditional vocational-education job-specific track will adequately serve the needs of a majority of the students in the future, while a general-education track serves the needs of none. Placing all students in a theory-based baccalaureate-degree program, as recommended in so many of the reform reports, fails to recognize the tremendous individual differences in student abilities, aptitudes, learning speeds and styles, and backgrounds.

Here are some facts to ponder when considering the tech-prep/associate-degree program:

- Fifty-five percent of entering freshmen in all of higher education now begin their college careers in community, technical, or junior colleges.

- Eighty-three percent of the current adult population do not hold bachelor degrees.

- Twenty-seven percent, or one out of four students, do not complete high school. This means that some ten to eleven million will not complete a high-school program unless changes are forthcoming.

- As reported by the high-school graduates in the National Longitudinal Study of the class of 1980, programs of study completed were

Academic (college)	—	37%
Vocational	—	19%
General	—	42%
Unreported	—	2%

- Nearly two-thirds of the high-school drop-outs come from the general-education program.

- The Southern Regional Education Board reports that fewer than one percent of the high-school students in vocational programs are involved in technical-education programs. To remedy this situation, the SREB advocates that high schools, postsecondary institutions, and employers together should develop 2 + 2 programs in which a planned four-year curriculum connects the last two years of high school with two years of postsecondary study along with planned, on-the-job learning. The planned curriculum would include both academic and technical courses.

- The American Electronic Association report entitled "Technical Employment Projects, 1983–87" indicates that the electronic industry will need sixty percent more technicians by 1987 than were employed in 1983. That means 115,000 new electronic technician jobs will be needed by 1987, in addition to other worker replacements.

- The twenty fastest-growing occupations in 1982–1995 all prefer postsecondary education and training, e.g., computer science technician, office machine service technician, engineering technician, banking and insurance personnel. Only two of the twenty require a baccalaureate degree for entry.

- Private-sector employment growth in the future will be in companies with fifty or fewer employees.

- The associate degree is becoming the preferred degree for entry into many technician occupations.

- American private-sector business and industry spends an estimated thirty billion dollars a year on the education and training of eleven million employees.

- All who will be in the work force by the year 2000 are alive today.

- A recent Penn State University study indicates that ninety percent of entering college students in 1982 and 1983 expect a B average in college. Sixty-one percent estimated they would study fewer than twenty hours per week.

- The same Penn State study found that eighty percent of entering college students said they knew little or nothing about their choice of major.

The Tech-Prep/Associate-Degree Program: A Liberal-Technical Education

The four-year 2 + 2 tech-prep/associate-degree program is intended to run parallel with and not replace the current college-prep/baccalaureate-degree program. It will combine a common core of learning and technical education and will rest upon a foundation of basic proficiency development in math, science, communications, and technology—all in an applied setting, but with the tests of excellence applied to these programs as well as others.

Beginning with the junior year in high school, students will select the tech-prep program (even as they now select the college-prep program) and continue for four years in a structured and closely coordinated high-school/college curriculum. They will be taught by high-school teachers in the first two years, but will also have access to college personnel and facilities when appropriate. Starting with a solid base of applied science, applied math, literacy courses, and technical programs, the high-school portion of the career program will be intentionally preparatory in nature. Built around career clusters and technical-systems study, such a tech-prep approach will help students develop broad-based competence in a career field and avoid the pitfalls of more short-term and narrowly delineated job training. *It is the responsibility of the high school to open up the world for the high-school student rather than close it down through narrow and specific job training.*

Based upon locally developed agreements, the tech-prep/associate-degree program can be developed with many options for the student. The high-school experience can be primarily in the liberal arts, leaving the technical education for the postsecondary school years. The reverse of this pattern can also be developed, depending upon high-school equipment and facilities. The usual scope and sequence of the tech-prep/associate-degree program would indicate leaving the highly specific areas of the technical-education program for the latter two years. However, it is not so important where, or even when, the student gains the required learning. What is important is that the student see the program spelled out and see the "gestalt" of the entire four years.

This high-school tech-prep program must dovetail with specific technical education programs on the postsecondary level. More intense technical specialization will be developed at the college level, always in tandem with broad technical competence and broad educational competence aimed at working in a wide-technology society. The community college technical-education programs include law enforcement, nursing, electronics, computers, business, marketing, entrepreneurship, agriculture, electron microscopy, construction trades (usually in cooperation with the apprenticeship program), mechanical technologies, and many others.

It is anticipated that one result of this program will be the enhancement of the associate degree so that it will become the preferred degree for employers seeking to fill a broad range of mid-level occupations. As a result of employer demand, many students are now seeking the associate degree as a preferred career development goal. Over 400,000 of these degrees were awarded in 1984 and the trend is upward.

Making the Partnership Work

The tech-prep/associate-degree program will require close curricular coordination. Most of all, it will require high-school and community college leaders and faculty members to talk regularly with one another and with employers.

The tech-prep/associate-degree concept provides a dramatic model for educators wishing to avoid slippage and loss of continuity in learning. Most important, it brings program structure and substance to the ordinary student.

- Students will develop sound basic skills and knowledge.

- Students will obtain first-rate technical-education preparation.

- High schools will motivate more students and perhaps lose fewer students between grades ten and eleven because they can see a future—a "why" for their efforts.

- Colleges will gain better-prepared high-school graduates.

- The tech-prep/associate-degree program will encourage more high-school students to continue their education in meaningful ways.

- Employers will gain better prepared employees to work in a wide-technology society.

The history of cooperative and coordinated program articulation between high schools and community colleges would not even fill a slim book. But there are signs that progress is being made. The National Commission on Secondary Vocational Education program gives its stamp of approval to the tech-prep associate-degree program:

Secondary and postsecondary levels must also coordinate their programs. The "tech-prep" curriculum being developed in some communities between high schools and community colleges illustrates how this can be done effectively. The program is solidly based in applied sciences, applied math, literacy courses, and technical programs. The high-school vocational-education part of the program covers clusters and systems—electrical, fluid power, business,

and mechanical. Study in such clusters and systems eases the transition to technical education programs in community colleges and other postsecondary institutions (National Commission on Secondary Vocational Education 1984).

Figure 19
The Current Typical Comprehensive High-School Program Enrollment

College-Prep Baccalaureate Degree Program	General Education Program	Vocational Education Program
37%	42%	19%
of the students	of the students	of the students

It must be understood by all concerned that the tech-prep/associate degree is flexible enough
to meet the needs of a great diversity of human talent. There can be many options for students
within this program depending upon student strengths and weaknesses, faculty expertise, and the
facilities of the participating institutions. Following are some options:

Figure 20
The Future Typical Comprehensive High-School Program Enrollment

College-Prep/Baccalaureate Degree Program	Tech-prep/Associate Degree Program	Vocational Education/ High School Diploma Program
1/3 of the	1/3 of the	1/3 of the
high school student	high school student	high school student
body	body	body

The number of students choosing each major will vary greatly from high school to high school and a common
core of learning must undergird all programs.

Figure 21
Tech-Prep/Associate-Degree Options

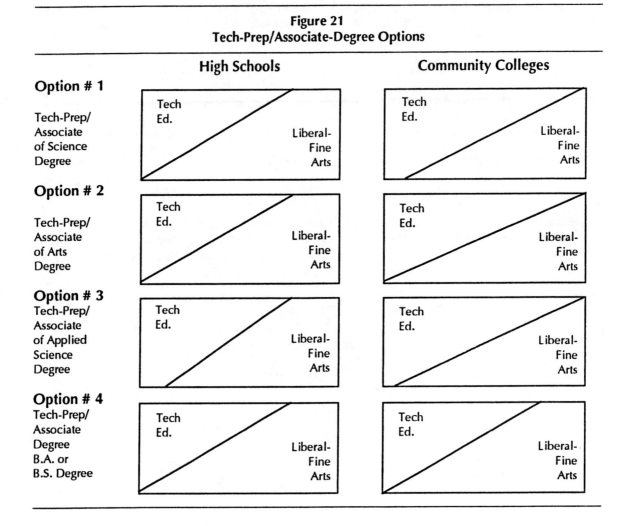

A major challenge for the tech-prep/associate-degree program is the development of a rigorous program in applied science and math. In this regard the State Directors of Vocational Education, representing some thirty-two states, retained the Center for Occupational Research Development in Waco, Texas, under the leadership of Dan Hull, and the Agency for Instructional Technology, under the leadership of Bennie Lucroy, to develop a new high-school applied-physics course called Principles of Technology. The goals of this course are to help students learn technical principles and concepts, improve science and mathematics skills and knowledge, and provide hands-on laboratory experience for technicians. Principles of Technology is now being field-tested in classrooms across America and will be available for general use in the 1985-86 school year. Video tapes and instructional manuals are being prepared to supplement the instructional materials to be utilized in 169 classes per year over the two years of grades eleven and twelve. Fourteen units of study form the foundation for the course, each focusing upon the scientific principles that are the foundation of today's technological developments:

1. Force
2. Work
3. Rate
4. Resistance
5. Energy
6. Power
7. Force Transformers

8. Momentum
9. Energy Converter
10. Optical Systems
11. Transducers
12. Time Constants
13. Vibrations
14. Radiation

These units deal with these principles as they apply to mechanical systems, fluid systems, thermal systems, and electrical systems.

The Principles of Technology course of study is an applied-physics course based upon the time-honored principles of physics but dressed in the clothes of modern technology. After viewing several of the video lessons, this writer has concluded that this is an information-rich and an experience-rich science curriculum which will motivate ordinary students to learn more physics than they might learn in a traditional theoretical-physics course of study. *The curriculum of the future must so integrate the instructional program that students can easily connect what they are learning with real-life issues.*

In general, though, change comes slowly to a school or college curriculum. If you don't believe that, ask John Saxon, math-textbook author and junior college math professor. His request for space to continue advertising his new algebra textbook was refused by *The Mathematics Teacher*, a journal for math teachers, because the editor thought his advertising had become too inflammatory. The state textbook commission refused to approve his algebra textbook despite enthusiastic praise from math teachers such as Barbara Stross, a Portland, Oregon, high-school math teacher, who states about the Saxon approach: "This is what teachers dream about. . . . It's a combination of measurable academic achievement and a blossoming of confidence, pleasure and excitement in learning and practicing math" (Armbrister 1985).

Saxon's theory is simple. He is convinced that ordinary students not only can learn complicated mathematics, they can also enjoy it; math anxiety is produced by textbooks that are too stilted and too theoretical. Essentially the Saxon math-teaching approach focuses on practice and repetition while it helps students understand the "why" of their learning. According to Saxon, "Algebra is a skill like playing the piano . . . you do not teach a child the piano by teaching him music theory. Van Cliburn and Vladimir Horowitz practice. This is the way skills are mastered" (Armbrister 1985).

After some fourteen years of pushing and crusading, the Saxon algebra textbook is becoming widely used in junior and senior high schools across the country and ordinary students are learning algebra.

Jaime Escalante, a Bolivian immigrant who came to the United States twenty-one years ago unable to speak English, was honored at the 1985 convention of the American Association of Community and Junior Colleges as the distinguished faculty member of the year. Escalante completed an associate degree in electronics technology and a bachelor's degree in mathematics in order to pursue his first love—teaching. He chooses to work in a joint-appointment teaching assignment between the inner-city Garfield High School and East Los Angeles College.

Escalante's goal is to make math winners out of ordinary students, and his students have experienced extraordinary success in the advanced placement calculus examination. Sixty-three of his high-school math students received advanced placement credit in 1984. He anticipates that more than one hundred will receive college credit in 1985. This success is so astounding that the Educational Testing Service retested several of the students; the results were the same.

John Saxon and Jaime Escalante are symbolic of many other teachers in America who are proving on a day-to-day basis that ordinary students can experience excellence in learning as long as they are taught by those who understand one important concept: "Education has two roles. Its first is to prepare our young to be productive members of society. That means skill training and preparing people for the jobs of the future. Education's second purpose is more general, and that is to prepare young people—regardless of their eventual career choices—to understand the society in which they live" (Young 1985).

Meeting the Nation's Career Needs

The following lists reflect a growing trend in America today: the increasing number of occupations that require more than four years of high-school training but less than a baccalaureate degree. Those high schools and colleges which have articulated programs are best suited to meet the needs of America's work force, both now and for the future.

Some Occupations Related to the Physical Sciences

High-school graduation usually necessary or recommended	Two years of college of apprenticeship or specialized school usually necessary or recommended	Four or more years of college usually necessary or recommended
Construction helper	Aviation inspector	Aerospace engineer
Construction laborer	Aerospace technician	Anesthesiologist
Cook	Airborne and power plant technician	Anthropologist
Electrotyper and stenotyper	Brick mason	Archaeologist
Electroplater	Broadcast technician	Astronomer
Electronic assembler	Carpenter and contractor	Astrophysicist
Guard	Computer programmer	Biochemist
Janitor and custodian	Computer operator	Cartographer
Laundry and dry-cleaning operator	Chef	Chemist
Machine operator	Drafter	Civil engineer
Truck driver	Engineering technician	Computer engineer
	Electrician	Electrical engineer
	Electronic technician	Environmental scientist
	Electron microscopist	Food and drug analyst
	Graphic artist technician	Geographer
	Heating and air-conditioning technician	Geologist
	Inspector	Geophysicist
	Instrument and appliance repair technician	Industrial engineer
	Nuclear engineer	Mechanical engineer
	Law technician	Metallurgical engineer
	Law enforcer	Meteorologist
	Machinist	Petroleum engineer
	Millwright	Pharmacologist
	Nuclear technician	Physicist
	Plumber and pipefitter	Quality control engineer
	Quality control technician	Safety engineer
	Robotics technician	Traffic engineer
	Sheetmetal technician	

Science technician
Tool and die maker
Travel agent
Systems analyst
Welding technician

Some Occupations Related to the Life Sciences

Animal caretaker	Agricultural technician	Agronomist
Custodian	Agricultural business-	Anthropologist
Dog trainer	person	Athletic trainer
Farmer	Biomedical equipment	Audiologist
Florist	technician	Bacteriologist
Gardener	Cytotechnologist	Biologist
Gamekeeper	Dental ceramist	Botanist
Groundskeeper	Dental hygienist	Curator
Hunting and fishing	Dental lab technician	Dentist
guide	EEG technician	Dietician
Lab assistant	Electrologist	Entomologist
Medical secretary	Fingerprint classifier	Food and drug
Museum worker	Fish and game warden	inspector
Nurse, aide	Food service supervisor	Forester
Nursery manager	Forestry technician	Health educator
Orchardist	Greenskeeper	Horticulturist
Orderly	technician	Industrial
Recreation worker	Health inspector	hygienist
Taxidermist	Histologic technician	Landscape
Waiter and waitress	Inhalation therapist	architect
	Medical lab worker	Medical librarian
	Mortician	Microbiologist
	Nurse, assoc. degree R.N.	Nurse, B.A.
	Nurse, practical	Occupational
	Ornamental horti-	therapist
	culture technician	Optometrist
	Occupational therapist	Physical therapist
	assistant	Physician
	Paramedic	Podiatrist
	Radiologic technologist	Psychologist
	Respiratory therapy	Public health officer
	technician	Recreation
	Recreation assistant	director
	Water and waste	Taxonomist
	treatment technician	Sanitarin
		Teacher/Professor
		Veterinarian
		Zoologist

These ten mythical help-wanted ads typify the shift that futurists predict for the nation's job market, changes that are bound to affect the education and training of the work force of the future.

Geriatric Social Worker: Inner-city private nursing home, immediate opening for capable, reliable person. Must be L.P.N. or have equivalent education. Salary $16,000 to $22,000 depending on experience. References required. Equal Opportunity Employer. Associate degree preferred with broad education background.

Laser Process Technician: High-technology firm needs dependable, experienced laser techni-cian. Should have two years related laser cutting machine experience or will train. Flex time and day care available. Job sharing and shared dividends. Salary $16,000 to $25,000 nego-tiable. E.O.E. Associate degree preferred with solid math and science background.

Genetic Engineering Technician: Positions available for both process technicians and engineer-ing technicians. Relocation. Must have two years technical education and training. Addi-tional education paid by company. Moving expenses paid by firm. Company will buy your present home. Salary $20,000 to $30,000. E.O.E. Associate degree preferred with broad science background.

Battery Technician: Large oil firm needs five technicians with previous experience in fuel cells or high-energy batteries. Shift work, O.T. available, dressing rooms and private locker, discount on all corporate products. Education and managerial training available. $15,000 to $20,000. E.O.E. Associate degree preferred.

Staff Assistant: County tax assessor needs dependable executive secretary skilled in use of word processor and microcomputer. Must have good interpersonal skills with ability to remain calm in conflict situations. Salary range: $16,000 to $24,000. E.O.E. Associate degree preferred with broad educational background.

Electronic Technicians: Small electronics company needs dependable and broadly educated technician. Must be knowledgeable of fluid power systems, mechanical systems, as well as electrical systems. Flex time available. Company stock plan available. Salary $18,000 to $28,000, negotiable. E.O.E. Associate degree preferred.

Police Officer: City of Serenity needs police officer who has completed an associate degree law enforcement training program or is graduate of a police academy. Excellent communication skills required. Preference in point system will be given to those candidates able to communi-cate in Spanish. Salary $20,000 to $30,000 with excellent fringe package. E.O.E.

Nurse: General Hospital needs dependable registered nurse for alternating shift work. Must have good interpersonal skills as well as technical nursing competencies. Salary range $18,000 to $25,000 with excellent fringe benefits package. E.O.E. Associate degree preferred.

Marketing Representative: Small computer-related firm needs dependable individual with sales education and training or equivalent experience. Must be knowledgeable of computer systems and electronics. Some on-the-job education and managerial training available. Asso-ciate degree preferred. Salary begins at $18,000 with additional commission based on sales volume. E.O.E.

Bookkeeper: Small business needs bookkeeper with experience in automated bookkeeping systems. Must have two years technical education and training with associate degree pre-ferred. Flex time and day care available. Salary $18,000 to $25,000.E.O.E.

The Tech-Prep/Associate-Degree
Program in Action

Several community college and high-school systems are beginning to talk about and experiment with the 2 + 2 tech-prep/associate-degree program or similar articulation arrangements. Two such programs come from Newport News, Virginia, in the east and Bakersfield, California, in the west.

Virginia

Under the leadership of Thomas Kubala, President of Thomas Nelson Community College in Virginia, the leaders of the Peninsula Public Secondary Schools and the Peninsula Vocational-Technical Center came together with the leaders of the community college to establish a four-year technical-education curriculum designed to prepare technicians for new advanced-technology occupations such as electronic and telecommunication technicians. The emphasis was placed upon a comprehensive and coordinated tech-prep/associate-degree curriculum spanning grades eleven through fourteen.

Figure 22
Postsecondary Curriculum Structure—General Philosophy

SPECIALITY AREA	• Six courses selected for specialization in appropriate HI-Tech area	SPECIALIZATION
TECHNICAL CORE AREA	• Electricity • Electronics • Mechanics • Electromechanics • Materials • Fluids • Thermics • Graphics • Controls • Computers	COMMON CORE
BASIC SKILLS AREA	• Mathematics • Science • Communications • Computer Literacy • Socioeconomics	

Source: Leno S. Pedrotti, "Redesigning Vocational Curricula—Postsecondary Curriculum Design Guidelines," Presentation at the American Vocational Association/Center for Occupational Research and Development Regional Workshop, Harpers Ferry, West Virginia, May 3–4, 1983.

The aim of the program is to develop master technicians who are broad educated. An interdisciplinary approach to technician education is utilized as well as a competency-based (CBE) component. The secondary-school program develops basic proficiencies in mathematics, applied sciences, communication skills, and trains students to apply these basic disciplines to tools, materials, processors, controls, and energy-conversion systems.

The program is designed so that students can progress smoothly from the preparatory high-school level to a specific, yet flexible, technician program at the community college. The community college program consists of three parts: a common core of learning, a technical core of learning, and several specialty sequences. Figures 22 through 25 are models for the structure of a postsecondary program.

The initial target population for this technician program included the senior-high-school students who were enrolled in the occupational areas of the Clerk Typist and Related Occupations, Mechanical Drafting, and Machine Shop. The faculty, counselors, and administrators of the participating institutions who were responsible for the above-mentioned program areas were also directly involved in the program.

Schools	Number of Students Involved
Hampton City Schools	1500
Newport News City Schools	2400
Poquoson City Schools	136
Williamsburg-James City County Public Schools	164
York County Public Schools	300
Peninsula Vo-Tech	100
Thomas Nelson Community College	500
Total	**5090**

A written agreement was executed between the community college and the other participating schools. A sample of such an agreement follows:

Articulation Agreement

This agreement is made between Thomas Nelson Community College and Hampton City School Division.

We hereby agree to the following:

1. Participating instructors at the secondary and postsecondary level will formally adopt and teach from a list of competencies (task list) based on job entry-level task requirements. Criteria for evaluation and recording levels of competency will also be formally adopted.

2. Prior to the beginning of each academic year, a meeting will be scheduled to review each occupational area and amend, as necessary, the occupational task lists, grading systems, recording forms, and objective reference tests or criterion-referenced measures to establish levels of competency. The directors of vocational education of each participating school division and the Virginia Peninsula Vocational-Technical Educational Center, the appropriate division chairman at Thomas Nelson Community College, program heads, supervisors, and teacher representatives (as required) will attend.

Figure 23
Postsecondary Technology Curricula

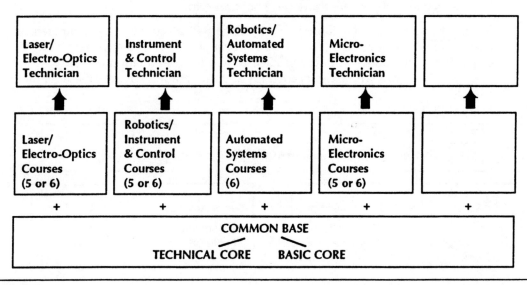

Source: Pedrotti.

Figure 24
Postsecondary Curriculum Model for Robotics/Automated Systems Technology

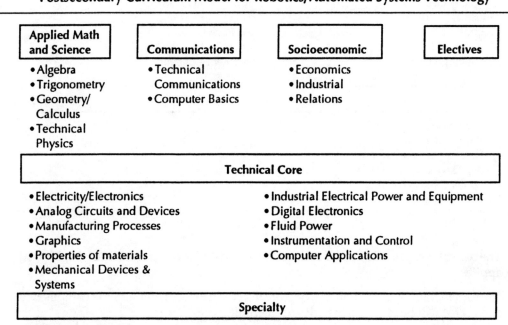

Source: Pedrotti.

3. The school division will maintain a competency record for each student which identifies areas and levels of task achievement. This record will become a part of the student's official record and will be forwarded to Thomas Nelson Community College as part of the student's high-school transcript.

4. Credit at Thomas Nelson Community College will be granted for competencies mastered at an achievement level of 3.0 or better on a scale of 0-4, as defined in the respective instructional resource guides, providing continuation of study in the program area begins within two academic years after graduation from the secondary school.

Figure 25
Postsecondary Curriculum Model for Computer Technology

| Applied Math and Science | Communications | Socioeconomic | Electives |

- Algebra
- Trigonometry
- Geometry/ Calculus
- Technical Physics

- Technical Communications
- Computer Basics

- Economics
- Industrial
- Relations

Technical Core

- Electricity/Electronics
- Industrial Electricity
- Graphics
- Properties of Materials
- Mechanical Devices

- Electrochemical Devices
- Heating and Cooling
- Fluid Power
- Instrumentation and Control
- Computer Applications

Specialty

- Circuit Analysis
- Digital Fundamentals
- Active Devices and Circuits
- Analog Devices and Systems
- Computer Circuits and Programming
- Digital Computers

Source: Pedrotti.

5. The college will provide a list of courses for which advanced credit (in total or in part) applies.

6. No examinations will be required for granting credit for achievement of a competency and no fee will be required for advanced credit.

7. All participating new faculty and administrators, full-time and part-time, will have training in competency-based education and will receive orientation on the articulation process described herein.

8. This agreement will be reviewed annually as stated in number two above and, in addition, will be reviewed by the President of Thomas Nelson Community College and the Superintendent of Hampton City School Division, or their designees, every three years.

President   Superintendent of
Thomas Nelson   Hampton City Schools
Community College

Date _____   Date _____

California

With the assistance of an employer's advisory committee, the Kern High School District and the Kern Community College District have developed a 2 + 2 tech-prep/associate-degree program in agriculture education. Business education coordination is also under development.

These two districts serve most of Kern County, California, and both have had agriculture programs for years. Kern County is one of the top three productive agriculture counties in the U.S. Agriculture accounts for about twenty percent of the wages and salaries earned in that region. The modern agribusiness enterprise finds itself in need of trained technicians in agriculture mechanics and in the application of computer science to production and marketing. Other needs relate to the training required in the use of chemical fertilizers, insecticides, and soil analysis.

The agriculture employers have been most critical of the high-school and college programs on two points: (1) they noted a significant lack of congruence between what is taught and what the agriculture industry needs, and (2) they were outspoken about the lack of communication within the educational institutions and with the agricultural employers of the county. With that impetus from the employers, the Boards of Trustees of the Kern High School District and Kern Community College District passed a joint resolution authorizing the formation of a joint advisory committee to make recommendations to the two districts with respect to the development of an agricultural instructional program that would be coordinated from high-school through community college level.

Under the leadership of Jim Young, Chancellor of the Kern Community College District, and Don Murfin, Superintendent of the Kern High School District, and key faculty members, along with the motivation of key agribusiness leaders, a 2 + 2 tech-prep/associate-degree program has been developed in Agriculture Business, Crop Science, Mechanized Agriculture, and Ornamental Horticulture. One of the interesting aspects of this program is the awarding of a competency certificate at the conclusion of each of the four years of study.

Other interesting features of this program include:

- A four-year emphasis on communication skills
- A four-year emphasis on mathematics and problem solving
- A greater depth of training in technical skills
- Work experience opportunities as a result of job entry-level proficiencies
- An integrated introduction to the humanities and a common core of learning.

Figure 26
Kern High School District and Kern Community College
District Organizational Model

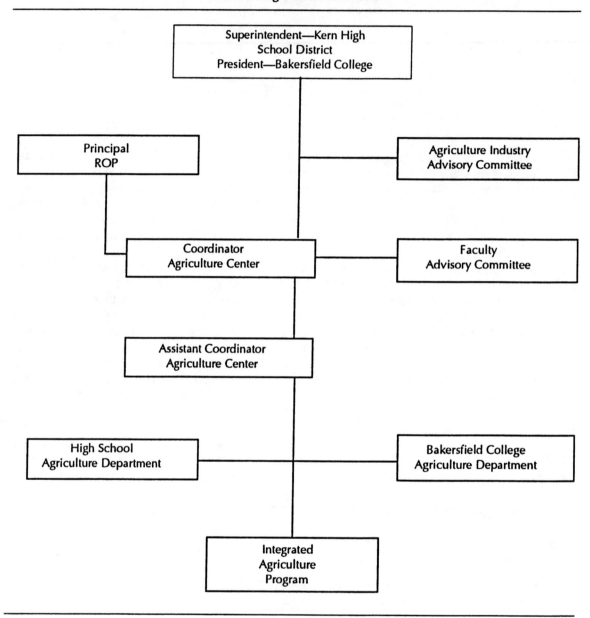

Figure 27
Kern High School District and
Bakersfield College Agriculture Business

GRADE 11 FALL		GRADE 12 FALL		GRADE 13 FALL		GRADE 14 FALL	
Courses	**Site**	**Courses**	**Site**	**Courses**	**Site**	**Courses**	**Site**
American History	HS	American Government	HS	English-Composition (3)	BC	*English-Technical	
English	HS	English	HS	Humanities(3)	BC	Writing (3)	BC
Mathematics	HS	Conversational Span	HS	Ag. Bus. 5–AG.		Behavioral Science (3)	BC
Physical Science or		P.E. or Elective	HS	Agriculture Law	BC	Physical Fitness	BC
Chemistry	HS	Technical Math (3)	C	Acctg. 53A Intro. to		Ag. Bus. 7–Calif.	
Typing/Comp. Intro.	ROP	AG. Bus. 3–Ag. Mkt.		Accounting (3)	BC	Agriculture Law	BC
Ag. Bus I–Intro. to		& Econ. (3)	BC/C	Elective (3)	BC/C	Elective (3)	BC/C
Cal. Ag. (3)	BC/C						

GRADE 11 SPRING		GRADE 12 SPRING		GRADE 13 SPRING		GRADE 14 SPRING	
Courses	**Site**	**Courses**	**Site**	**Courses**	**Site**	**Courses**	**Site**
American History	HS	American Government	HS	English-Speech (3)	BC	Humanities (3)	BC
English	HS	English	HS	Ag. Bus. 6–Ag. Labor	BC	Fine Arts (3)	BC
Mathematics	HS	Conversational Span	HS	Relations (3).		Mngt. 59 Personnel	
Physical Science or		P.E. or Elective	HS	Physical Fitness (1)	BC	Management (3)	BC
Chemistry	HS	Technical Math (3)	C	Acctg. 53B (3) to		Elective (3)	
Typing/Computor.	ROP	AG. Bus. 4–Ag. Mkt.		Accounting	BC	Elective (3)	BC
Ag. Bus 2–Ag. Bus.		& Farm Mngt. (3)	BC/C	Elective (3)	BC/C		
Management (3)	BC/C						

Certificate of competency in typing	High School diploma and/or certificate of competency in agriculture	Certificate of competency in the use of computers in agriculture	Associate of science degree in agriculture business

Diploma/Certificate/Degree

SUGGESTED ELECTIVES

AN. S. 1–Intro. to Animal Husbandry	CRP.S. 4–Advanced Trees & Vines	Bus. A. 1A–Principles of Accounting (3)
AN. S. 2–Beef Production	MECH. AG. 1–Intro. Agric. Mech.	Bus. A. 1B–Principles of Accounting (3)
AN. S. 3–Sheep Production	Mech. Ag. 2–Ag. Equipment Set & Oper.	Acctg. 54–Payroll Accounting (3)
CRP. S. 1–Principles Crop Production	Ornamental Horticulture 2–Nursery	Acctg. 3–Tax Accounting
CRP. S. 2–Alfalfa & For. Crops	Mgmt.	Bus. A. 18A–Business Law (3)
CRP. S. 3–Trees & Vines	Ornamental Horticulture 3–Plant I.D.	Insur. 21–Principles of Insurance (3)
	Orn. Hort. 4–Plant Identification	

*Courses to be designed

Where courses will be taught (site):
Agriculture Center–X
Bakersfield College–BC
High School Campus–HS
Regional Occupational Program–ROP

No. of college units indicated in: ( )

Figure 28
Kern High School District and
Bakersfield College Agriculture Business

GRADE 11 FALL		GRADE 12 FALL		GRADE 13 FALL		GRADE 14 FALL	
Courses	**Site**	**Courses**	**Site**	**Courses**	**Site**	**Courses**	**Site**
American History	HS	American Government	HS	English-Composition (3)	BC	English	BC
English	HS	English	HS	Humanities (3)	BC	Behavioral Science (2)	BC
Mathematics	HS	Conversational Span	HS	Crop.S 3—Trees &		Physical Fitness (1)	BC
Physical Science or		P.E. or Elective	HS	Vines	C	Crop.S 5—Weed	
Chemistry	HS	Technical Math (3)	C	Ag. Bus 2—Ag Bus		Control	C
Typing/Comp. Intro.	ROP	Crop S1—Prin of		Management (3)	BC	Crop.S 6—Soils (3)	C
Ag. Bus I—Intro. to		Crop Production (3)	C	Elective (3)	BC/C	Elective (3)	BC/C
Cal. Ag. (3)	BC/C						

GRADE 11 SPRING		GRADE 12 SPRING		GRADE 13 SPRING		GRADE 14 SPRING	
Courses	**Site**	**Courses**	**Site**	**Courses**	**Site**	**Courses**	**Site**
American History	HS	American Government	HS	English-Speech (3)	BC	Humanities (3)	BC
English	HS	English	HS	Crop.S 4—Ad Trees		Fine Arts (3)	BC
Mathematics	HS	Conversational Span	HS	Crops & Vines	C	Physical Fitness (1)	BC
Physical Science or		P.E. or Elective	HS	Mech Ag 6—Farm		Crop.S 8—	
Chemistry	HS	Technical Math (3)	C	Fabrication	C	Entomology (3)	C
Crop.S 7—Irrigation (3)	C	Crop.S 2—Alfalfa &		Elective (3)	BC/C	Mech Ag. 3—Farm Power (3)	C
Mech Ag. 2—Equip		For Crop (3)	C	Elective (3)	BC/C	Elective (3)	BCC
Ser & Opr	C						
Typing/Computer Intro	ROP						

Certificate of competency in typing	High School diploma and/or certificate of competency in field crops production upon completion of grade 12 spring semester	Certificate of competency in tree and vine crops at the end of grade 13	Associate of science degree in crop production certificate in agronomy

Diploma/Certificate/Degree

SUGGESTED ELECTIVES

Agriculture Business 3—Agriculture Marketing & Economics
Agriculture Business 4—Accounting & Farm Management
Agriculture Business 5—Agriculture Computers
Agriculture Business 6—Agriculture Labor Relations
Animal Science 1—Introduction to Animal Science
Mechanized Agriculture 4—Farm Engines

Mechanized AGriuclture 5—Fluid & Pneumatic Power
Mechanized Agriculture 7—Farm Tractors
Mechanized Agriculture 8—Farm Small Engines
Ornamental Horticulture 1—Plant Propagation
Welding 1—Oxy/Acetylene
Welding 538—ARC

Where courses will be taught (site):
Agriculture Center–C
Bakersfield College–BC
High School Campus–HS
Regional Occupational Program–ROP

Figure 29
Kern High School District and
Bakersfield College Mechanical Agriculture

GRADE 11 FALL

Courses	Site
American History	HS
English	HS
Mathematics	HS
Physical Science or Chemistry	HS
Ag. Bus 1—Intro to Cal. Ag (3)	C

GRADE 12 FALL

Courses	Site
American Government	HS
English	HS
Conversational Span	HS
P.E. or Elective	HS
Technical Math (3)	C
Mech Ag. 3—Farm Power (3)	C

GRADE 13 FALL

Courses	Site
English-Composition (3)	BC
Humanities (3)	BC
Mech Ag 5—Fluid & Pneumatic Power (3)	C
Welding 538—ARC (3)	BC
Auto 1—Basic Auto (3)	BC/C
Elective (3)	BC/C

GRADE 14 FALL

Courses	Site
English-Technical Writing	BC
Behavioral Science (3)	BC
Physical Fitness (1)	BC
Mech. Ag. 7—Farm Tractors	C
Elective (3)	BC/C
Elective (3)	BC/C

GRADE 11 SPRING

Courses	Site
American History	HS
English	HS
Mathematics	HS
Physical Science or Chemistry	HS
Mech Ag. 1—Intro to Ag Mech (3)	C
Ag. Mech 2—Equip Ser & Opr (3)	C

GRADE 12 SPRING

Courses	Site
American Government	HS
English	HS
Conversational Span	HS
P.E. or Elective	HS
Technical Math (3)	C
Mech. Ag. 4—Farm Engines (3)	C

GRADE 13 SPRING

Courses	Site
English-Speech (3)	BC
Mech Ag 6—Farm Fabrication (3)	C
Mach Shop 1—Elem (3)	C
Elective	BC/C
Elective (3)	BC/C

GRADE 14 SPRING

Courses	Site
Humanities (3)	BC
Fine Arts (3)	BC
Physical Fitness (1)	BC
Mech Ag. 8—Farm Small Engines (3)	C
Elective (3)	BC/C

Certificate of competency in service and operation upon completion of grade 11, spring semester	High School diploma and/or certificate of competency in entry level farm mechanics	Certificate of competency fabrication and repair	Associate of science degree in mechanized agriculture

Diploma/Certificate/Degree

SUGGESTED ELECTIVES

Agriculture Business 2—Agriculture Business Management
Agriculture Business 5—Agriculture Computers
Animal Science 1—Introduction to Animal Science
Crop.S 1—Principles of Crop Production
Crop.S 3—Trees & Vines

Crop.S 6—Soils
Crop.S 7—Irrigation

Crop.S 8—Entomology
Ornamental Horticulture 4—Plant Identification
Automobile 102 B—Automobile Engines Machinery
Machine Shop 53D—Advanced Machine Shop
Mechanical TEchnical 59A—Basic Hydraulic Fluid Mechanical
Welding 1—Oxy/Acetylene
Welding 74—Tig and Mig

Where courses will be taught (site):
Agriculture Center–C
Bakersfield College–BC
High School Campus–HS
Regional Occupational Program–ROP

No. of College untis indicated in: ( )

Figure 30
Kern High School District and
Bakersfield College Agriculture Business

GRADE 11 FALL		GRADE 12 FALL		GRADE 13 FALL		GRADE 14 FALL	
Courses	Site	Courses	Site	Courses	Site	Courses	Site
American History	HS	American Government	HS	English-Composition (3)	BC	English-Technical (3)	BC
English	HS	English	HS	Humanities (3)	BC	Behavioral Science (3)	BC
Mathematics	HS	Conversational Span	HS	Orn.Hort. 4—Plant		Physical Science (3)	BC
Physical Science or		P.E. or Elective	HS	Indentification (3)	BC	Orn.Hort. 6—Landscape	
Chemistry	HS	Technical Math (3)	C	Crop. S 6—Soils (3)	C	Cont./Maint. (3)	BC
Ag. Bus. 1—Intro. to		Ag. Bus. 2—Ag. Bus.		Mech Ag. 1—Intro to		Crop.S 7—Irrigation (3)	C
Cal. Ag. (3)	BC/C	Management (3)	BC	Ag. Mech. (3)	C	Mech. Ag. 6—Farm	
						Fabrication (3)	C

GRADE 11 SPRING		GRADE 12 SPRING		GRADE 13 SPRING		GRADE 14 SPRING	
Courses	Site	Courses	Site	Courses	Site	Courses	Site
American History	HS	American Government	HS	English-Speech (3)	BC	Humanities (3)	BC
English	HS	English	HS	Orn. Hort. 5—Land		Fine Arts (3)	BC
Mathematics	HS	Conversational Span	HS	Design (3)	BC	Physical Fitness (1)	BC
Physical Science or		P.E. or Elective	HS	Crop.S 8—Entomology (3)	C	Orn. Hort. 7—Turf	
Chemistry	HS	Technical Math (3)	C	Mech. Ag. 2—Ag. Equip		Management (3)	BC
Orn. Hort. 1—Plant-		Orn. Hort. 3—Plant		Ser. & Oper. (3)	C	Mech. Ag. 4—Farm	
Propagation (3)	BC	Identification	BC	Ag. Bus 3—Ag Marketing		Engines (3)	C
Orn. Hort. 2—Nursery				& Economics (3)	BC	Ag. Bus. 5—Agriculture	
Management (3)	BC			Elective (3)	BC/C	Computers (3)	BC
						Elective (3)	BC/C

Certificate of competency in plant care and maintenance	High School diploma and/or certificate of competency in nursery management upon completion of grade 12 spring semester	Certificate of competency in landscape design	Associate of science degree in ornamental horticulture and/or certificate or competency in landscape maintenance/turf

---

Diploma/Certificate/Degree

SUGGESTED ELECTIVES

Agriculture Business 4—Accounting & Farm Management   Mechanical Agriculture 5—Fluid & Pneumatic Power
Agriculture Business 6—Agriculture Labor Relations   Welding 1—Oxy/Acetylene

---

Source: Kern Community College District

Where courses will be taught (site):
Agriculture Center–C
Bakersfield College–BC
High School Campus–HS
Regional Occupational Program–ROP

No. of college units indicated in: ( )

The Dallas County Community College District in Dallas, Texas, has been working for several years on coordinating the community college vocational-education programs with feeder high-school programs. Program articulation guides have been published in the following areas:

Auto mechanics   Building trades-carpentry
Child development   Digital electronics technology
Drafting and design technology   Legal assistant
Office careers   Medical lab technician
Welding technology   Ornamental horticulture
Auto body technology   technology

These guides identify the competencies a student must possess to receive credit for specified courses in the community colleges.

There is much activity across the nation directed toward program coordination. The Illinois State Board of Education has spent considerable effort over the past two years in attempting to clarify the relationship between the secondary and postsecondary vocational-education delivery systems. By July 1, 1987, regional secondary-school systems and the community colleges must meet and define articulation agreements and/or cooperative arrangements.

For many years the Hagerstown Junior College in Hagerstown, Maryland, has maintained program-coordination agreements with feeder high schools in the areas of business education/ secretarial science, licensed practical nursing/associate-degree nursing, distributive education/ cooperative education. Three different types of procedures are followed in assessing competence: advanced placement, awarding college credit, and challenge examinations. Students following the articulation agreements have been tracked as they complete the associate-degree program. They make higher grades than those not following the articulation program, and they tend to complete degree requirements earlier.

Finally, Sacramento City College President Doug Burris (now serving as Los Rios District's Vice Chancellor) and Sacramento City Unified School District Superintendent Tom Guigni have created the Sacramento City College-Sacramento City Unified School District Articulation Council. The Council is composed of administrators, including deans of instruction from each segment, who meet monthly. Special articulation committees work in the following areas: English; English as a Second Language; Counseling Services; Occupational Technology; Math, Science, and Computers; Core Assessment. Soon to become involved are Humanities, Fine Arts, and Social Sciences.

Four objects were set for the project: to integrate the two systems' curriculum; to develop a core assessment/placement model; to plan an articulation program for instructional programs and students services; and to disseminate information about these activities. Some accomplishments of the council thus far:

- A process to exchange course outlines, teaching materials, faculty rosters, and educational films

- Curriculum guides for teachers and students

- Articulation agreements which specify student competency levels

- An inter-institutional directory of English teachers.

Additionally, the Sacramento articulation project has been regarded as a vehicle for assessment and research on student performance and learning problems, as well as colloquium for teachers. The Articulation Council has extended the college's comprehensive assessment testing program to selected groups of students in the high schools, evaluated the results, and formed a permanent Research and Evaluation Committee.

Figure 31
Dallas County Community College District—Student Profile

DALLAS COUNTY COMMUNITY COLLEGE DISTRICT
DIGITAL ELECTRONICS PROGRAM ARTICULATION STUDENT PROFILE

School _____

Verification Signature _____

School Official

Date _____

Student's Name _____ Birthday _____ SS# _____

Address _____ City _____ State _____ Zip _____

Please transmit student profile to college registrar as soon as it is ready for evaluation.

	Date	Instructor's Signature
1. DC Circuits		
Introduction to Electricity		
1.01 - Define terms of sketch symbols for terms related to electricity		
1.02 - List major characteristics of a substance which governs its conductance		
1.03 - Describe creation of a potential difference		
1.04 - List possible effects of applying a potential difference to a conductor		
1.05 - Describe an element		
1.06 - Draw schematic symbol for a battery and label polarity of terminals		
1.07 - List most common causes of laboratory accident and ways to prevent them		
1.08 - List general precautions to prevent lab accidents		
1.09 - List steps to take if lab partner receives electrical shock		
1.10 - Practice good safety habits and correct laboratory procedures		
Voltage, Current, and Resistance		
1.11 - Define and sketch lab and formula symbols for voltage, amperage, and resistance		
1.12 - Describe electron current flow and conventional flow philosophies and state difference between them		
1.13 - List the 4 factors affecting conductor resistance and state how each affects the resistance		
1.14 - Prepare for reading resistors		
1.15 - Read values of 10 resistors		
1.16 - Identify linear and nonlinear portions of a scale		
1.17 - Identify value of picket		
1.18 - Define knob terms		
Scientific Notation and Metric Prefixes		
1.19 - Convert numbers		
1.20 - Complete test on number forms		

continued

	Date	Instructor's Signature
1.21 - Define and write symbol for metric prefix terms		
1.22 - Read 20 standard four-banded color-coded resistors		
1.23 - Write standard color code for resistors		
Ohm's Law and Power		
1.24 - Calculate 20 Ohm's Law problems		
1.25 - Enter number into calculator		
1.26 - Perform mathematical operations with calculator		
1.27 - Predict effect on the unknown quantity		
1.28 - Convert schematic drawing into working circuit		
1.29 - Define "polarity" and list effects of incorrect polarity on voltmeter		
1.30 - List and use techniques for avoiding meter movement damage when using VOM		
1.31 - Read 6 voltage values from a VOM Scale		
1.32 - Pass test on VOM reading		
1.33 - Define and identify a series circuit		
1.34 - Describe behavior of voltage, current, and resistance in a series circuit		
1.35 - Pass test on unknown values of series circuit		
1.36 - Define terms related to series circuits		
1.37 - Construct a series circuit with ammeter and read current value		
Introduction to Parallel Circuits		
1.38 - Pass test on unknown values of parallel resistance		
1.39 - Define terms related to parallel circuits		
1.40 - Describe the 3 laws governing parallel circuits		
1.41 - Calculate total resistance values of circuits with unlike resistors		
1.42 - Calculate total resistance of parallel circuit with two unlike resistors		
1.43 - Calculate total resistance value of circuit with several resistors of the same value		
1.44 - Calculate and measure value of resistance, current, and voltage		
Parallel Circuit Analysis		
1.45 - Describe behavior of voltage, current, and resistance in a parallel circuit		
1.46 - Pass test on unknown values of parallel circuits		
1.47 - Calculate and measure total resistance of circuit		
Parallel-Series Circuits		
1.48 - Define and identify parallel-series circuit and series-parallel circuit		
1.49 - Reduce parallel-series circuit to one equivalent resistor		
1.50 - Reduce circuit to single resistor, and draw each equivalent circuit		
1.51 - Calculate all voltage and current values for each reduced circuit component		

continued

	Date	Instructor's Signature
1.52 - Calculate all unknown values in parallel-series circuits		
1.53 - Measure resistance, voltage, and current at any point in parallel circuit with four or more branches		
Series-Parallel Circuits		
1.54 - Reduce series-parallel circuit to one equivalent resistor		
1.55 - Reduce circuit to one equivalent resistor, showing each reduced circuit		
1.56 - State values of current and voltage for each resistor in original circuit		
1.57 - Calculate all unknown values of series-parallel circuits		
1.58 - Identify switches		
1.59 - Define terms related to series-parallel circuits		
1.60 - Connect two-way and three-way switching arrangements		
Voltage Dividers and Power		
1.61 - State the 9 formulas for power in a DC circuit		
1.62 - Write lab and formula symbols for power in electrical circuit		
1.63 - Define "one watt of electrical power"		
1.64 - Define and perform, with a calculator, "squaring a number" and "square root of a number"		
1.65 - Pass power test		
1.66 - Calculate voltage, current, and resistance for all parts of circuit and prove calculations		

Source: Dallas County Community College District
The student must complete the 66 core (*) competencies.

The Remedialization
of the Community College

DENNIS MCGRATH AND MARTIN B. SPEAR

Histories are stories we tell one another. With them we try to understand ourselves, to sustain our traditions and institutions, sometimes to raise doubts and disappointment, to urge new direction. History is written many times, from different points of view, with different plotlines and different meanings.

The movement for democratic education also has not a single history, but many. The most familiar "insider" history tells the heroic tale of the triumph of open access. Other versions highlight the ironies of history. For them, the most important plot device is the unnoticed motivation, or unintended consequence—"cooling out," for instance. Usually such alternative histories coexist peacefully, since they emphasize and try to explain different features of the evolution of educational institutions (Brint and Karabel, 1989; Cohen and Brawer, 1982). Only in times of crisis will an institution be forced to choose among its histories, to discover or rediscover a guiding myth.

So our own history of community colleges is only one among many that might be written. What it tries to make sense of is less the formal and quantitative features of open access than its qualitative, experiential, and cultural features. Our plot finds rigorous academic practice moving from the center to the periphery at community colleges. Replacing it at the cultural center, encouraged by institutional arrangements, and progressively legitimated in the theories and the rhetoric of community college pioneers, are pale remedial practices—which is why we call our story "the remedialization of the community college."

The Decline of the Transfer Function

During their early years community colleges thought of themselves more as colleges than they do now; "university parallel" programs were much more central in their youthful self-definition. From the 1900s through the 1950s such programs accounted for 60 to 70 percent of total enrollment, and transfer rates routinely served as a critical measure of institutional success (Eells, 1931; Medsker, 1960; Lombardi, 1979). Nor was success hard to find. In a famous study, Knoell and Medsker followed 7000 community college students who transferred in 1960 to a variety of four-year institutions in ten states. Within three years of transferring 62 percent of those students received bachelor degrees; and the researchers confidently predicted that at least 75 percent ultimately would graduate (Knoell and Medsker, 1965).

Since three-quarters of all entering students typically declared an intent to transfer, Knoell and Medsker's research seemed to certify that the community college mission of access could be

217

realized without danger of eroding academic standards. Community college graduation rates compared favorably with those of most traditional four-year colleges—even when the large community college commitment to career education was factored in. The place of the rapidly growing community college as an integral part of higher education appeared secure: local high school graduates could be provided with the first two years of college work at low financial cost and, apparently, at no academic cost. That idea has proven remarkably durable. Even in those places where the transfer function has virtually collapsed, it remains a prominent part of the story colleges tell themselves and their students. It recalls a time when community colleges in fact as well as in word promoted smooth movement between high school and university.

During community colleges' "junior college" phase, university parallel programs were the exemplary programs, in relation to which other curricular areas defined themselves. The present formal curricular and departmental organization of colleges are relics of that time when the transfer program was clearly distinguished from career, technical, and remedial programs. Similarly, if informally, the laments about declining standards also draw sustenance from the memory of when the rigorous academic practices of university lower-division courses were the models of excellence. When teachers look back, they recall, or seem to, a time when classes were taught differently, or students were better. But what these common memories really signal is just that the liberal arts university parallel program once occupied a more important cultural position than now.

The initial success of the transfer function was attained with the most traditional population of students community colleges have yet seen. Subsequently, transfer rates dipped precipitously, even to single digits in some areas. Although no well-developed national data base on the transfer process exists, the information that is available is enough to suggest the magnitude of the problem. Arthur Cohen and Florence Brawer estimate that fewer than five percent of full and part-time community college students transfer with junior status to four-year institutions (Cohen and Brawer, 1982); Kintzer and Wattenbarger found declining transfer rates in six of the nine states with large community college systems (1985). The decline has been most pronounced for minority students. Since more than forty percent of all black college students and more than fifty percent of all Hispanic college students are enrolled in community colleges, this represents a very important decline in real opportunity for those groups (Wilson and Melendez, 1984:10).

The traditional university parallel program is no longer the primary transfer vehicle. Occupational and technical programs issue more than half of all community college degrees, and significant numbers of students from those programs transfer to four-year institutions (AACJC, 1979). Community colleges no longer assume that career program students are less likely to transfer than those enrolled in liberal arts courses; almost any vocational program may now represent itself as satisfactory preparation for transfer.

This greatly complicates the problem of the academic culture of community colleges, because it makes it more difficult to decide what sorts of academic practices ought to be expected in any particular program. At the most mundane level, research on the transfer problem shows that students from terminal career programs, what were once the most important contrast to transfer programs, may actually transfer at rates higher than university parallel students. More significantly, students' apparent preference for career programs that are also transfer programs strongly implies that recovery of the transfer function cannot take the form of strengthening liberal arts sequences in the university parallel curriculum. So many "transfer students" are now in career programs that it is now hard to miss what was always the case: a successful transfer function depends less on what specific courses students take than on the strength of the classroom, on the closeness of the fit between the academic culture of the community college and that of the university.

Success with the early cohorts of relatively traditional transfer students encouraged colleges along a path from which they have never wandered. On both sides of the transfer relation, community college and university faculty and administrators came to conceive an appropriate transfer track as one that duplicates the university curriculum—what is called "articulation." Community college transfer curricula once were "university parallel." They attempted to reproduce the university lower-division curriculum with students who really were not much different from university students. Over time "university parallel" shaded into the somewhat weaker "articulation," in which the central concern is with course matching between institutions. The virtue of these was that they provided direct, formal measures for transfer courses and programs. So, even when nontraditional students began crowding community college classrooms, curricula could remain formally parallel and courses articulated—whatever the educational reality might be. Thus was transferability of courses retained even while transferability of students became a national crisis.

Fascination with articulation makes it extremely difficult to raise important questions about the nature of the preparation that community colleges offer to transfer students. Whether the dominant aspect of a transfer program was to approximate or duplicate the university lower-division, or to prepare students, by whatever means, to undertake upper-division work was a matter never really debated, never really thought open to debate. The traditional way was assumed to be the correct way—even for nontraditional students. Perhaps the road not taken, that excellent preparation may not be "parallel" preparation, deserves a second look, but the widespread decline of the transfer function has not elicited such a reexamination.

Formal course comparability remains what everybody looks for in a transfer program; "articulation" is the criterion by which they are evaluated by students, faculty, and counselors at both the community college and the receiving institution, and by registration and admissions officers at both institutions. Whatever the substantive reality may be, the more a transfer curriculum is just like (or is said to be just like, or maybe just aspires to be just like) what is offered, or is said to be offered, in the first two years at the local university, the more highly it will be regarded by everyone.

The profusion of qualifiers suggests how deeply problematic that really is and has always been. Articulation agreements based on comparability of course content can't penetrate very deeply; surely they are too weak a device, are the wrong sort of device, for ensuring the fit between the academic cultures of community college and university. Even if the long-suppressed question of whether it is a good idea for students to be doing the same sorts of things at both institutions, that courses should be in that sense equivalent, should be taken as settled, formal course articulation can't be the mechanism for accomplishing it.

Formal equivalencies, decided through the proxy of course descriptions, hide more than they reveal. They cannot specify what really goes on in the classroom—behind the same syllabus may lurk rigorous or anemic practices, strong or weak expectations, traditional pedagogy or the most striking innovation. By ignoring those critical aspects of the academic culture, by not being able to notice them, articulation agreements provide the structural framework within which the cognitive level of the academic culture can spin downward.

Faculty know that the relations between formal representations of courses and programs, say as they appear in college catalogs but also in course outlines, reading lists and syllabi, and what actually goes on in the classroom are frequently, and perhaps usually, of the most tenuous sort. Only the most rigidly structured disciplines, mathematics being the best example with the hard sciences following, are exceptions to this principle and they not always. The more common pattern is for individual faculty members, whether led by personal eccentricity, by strenuous efforts to improve students' success, or by outcome of classroom negotiation, to modify courses so that they gradually come to bear little resemblance to the official catalogue descriptions. Stipulating course comparability in the face of that natural movement—something state departments of education, or legislatures, will occasionally try—is bound to be a somewhat surreal and arbitrary exercise that unfortunately masks substantive diversity and cultural *disarticulation* in the name of a formal articulation.

As community colleges follow the logic of articulation, they mimic features of "equivalent" university courses. The opening for innovation on the academic side of the transfer problem is small; consequently, efforts to strengthen the transfer function typically treat it from either an administrative or student services perspective, with solutions proposed as one would expect for problems so framed.

For administrators, the transfer problem looks like a matter of maintaining the formal integrity of community college courses and programs within the higher education hierarchy. Formally negotiated articulation agreements are the favored device for achieving that, and are still frequent enough to be thought the rule. But problems in some regions have been so severe as to prompt bureaucratic and even legislative interventions. Florida has gone the furthest, by legislating a statewide system of common course numbering and common transcripts for all public community colleges and universities. Several other states, including California, have reinforced articulation agreements by establishing central offices to facilitate cooperation among institutions. Multicampus systems sometimes establish a central office to coordinate and facilitate transfer; for instance, CUNY assists in coordinating articulation among senior institutions and community colleges in the system (Donovan, 1987).

Formal institutional efforts to smooth transfer rarely influence classroom and curricular activities. In fact, they don't even try. They are designed to protect and legitimate current courses and programs rather than change them. Any problems about transfer are conceived as falling not on teaching faculty, but on the student service staff, particularly counselors. Student service professionals are not primarily academics. They are carriers of a social service ethos which drives them to think about the transfer problem in terms of either the social and psychological needs of students or their inability to cut through the bureaucratic thicket of higher education. Students lack information about financial aid, application deadlines, or course articulation; they are fearful and need support; they experience "transfer shock"; they have too many family and job responsibilities.

Those concerns have given rise to a wide range of student services. Many institutions have established transfer offices and have designated transfer information officers to advise students and to assist with articulation problems. Some schools coordinate counseling and advising with area high schools and major four-year receiving institutions in order to improve continuity of service. Laney College, for instance, works with counselors from the Oakland Public School District and the University of California system. South Mountain Community College cooperates with Arizona State University in a comprehensive orientation program. Miami-Dade Community College has been the leader in utilizing computerized information systems to improve student advisement with its Advisement Graduation Information System; many institutions now routinely provide microcomputer access to transfer information for their counseling staffs (Donovan, 1987).

Administrative efforts to ensure the transferability of courses, and student service initiatives to supplement academics with enriched counseling and advising—these surely count as energy well-expended, although not unqualifiedly so. They play strongly to the ways that students conceive their own transfer process (primarily in terms of their not "losing" credits), as well as to the advertising and mythology of community colleges, (primarily that community colleges offer the "same education" but at bargain rates). Certainly, it is astonishing that the weakening of the transfer function, which originally served to establish the academic legitimacy of the community college, has so often met with student service interventions, rather than with attempts to reinvigorate academics. The redefinition of relations between community colleges and universities in administrative and student service terms has been an important mechanism by which university parallel programs were displaced and the difficult educational issues about the academic role of community colleges forced underground.

This was permitted to happen because a different problem commanded the attention of the community college. By the 1970s many of the nontraditional students who entered through open doors were "underprepared." Nobody really understood how these students might be incorporated into the traditional academic culture; so the academic culture itself was changed. Theorists worked to develop new conceptions of education for these students, conceptions which were often opposed to those of university parallel programs.

In *Fostering Minority Access and Achievement in Higher Education* (1987), Richardson and Bender describe the displacement of the university parallel curriculum in this way: "the preoccupation with remediating from 60 percent to 90 percent of their entering students, along with the need to provide social services, and with the need to prepare their clientele for immediate employment, leaves [community colleges] with little energy and few resources to offer challenging transfer programs to those who enrolled with the ultimate intent of earning a baccalaureate degree" (1987:3). In their view, colleges neglected transfer programs while focusing on more pressing matters. Actually, what may have started as neglect ultimately became a matter of principle. Colleges began self-consciously to devalue traditional academics as they evolve from junior colleges to comprehensive community colleges. More and more being a "teaching institution" came to mean being a remedial institution.

The Evolution of the Remedial Function

The era of open access saw the construction of hundreds of new two-year institutions and state systems—nontraditional institutions for nontraditional students. As large numbers of academically underprepared students began to fill their classrooms, community colleges struggled to redefine their mission and articulate it to other educators, state agencies, and legislators. The distinctive language of remediation that developed decisively affected the ways colleges talk about their students, and about themselves—what they are as institutions, their societal mission, and their role within the higher education system. However, that is something best seen in retrospect; early on, few of the now familiar categories of remediation were available and certainly none of the programs.

As with the comprehensive high school, what "inclusion" has always implied for the community college is the proliferation of functions and services. Community colleges had to balance very different roles: transfer, remediation, vocational training, and community service. Each of these embodies different conceptions of the social and educational mission of the community college. As in the earlier "great school debates," waves of theory, criticism, and counterargument served as symbolic politics in which arguments about pedagogical practice held place for suppressed issues about the role of schooling in influencing poverty and the class structure.

For colleges to develop the characteristic remedial strategies, they first had to shake themselves loose from what was then the conventional wisdom, "compensatory education." That notion was introduced into educational discourse following World War II and had gained substantial legitimacy when the Elementary and Secondary Education Act of 1965 authorized billions of dollars to encourage schools to focus on underprepared, "culturally deprived" low-income and minority children. If children of the poor were to perform at levels comparable to middle-class children, schools would have to find ways to "make up for the debilitating consequences of discrimination and poverty," to compensate for the cultural deprivation of a home environment which did not support education (Chazen, 1973:35). Compensatory education regarded children's sociocultural experience as cumulative, and consequently favored early interventions such as Get Set and Head Start. Nevertheless, in the inner cities' compensatory, "motivational" programs sometimes appeared as late as high school.

Despite very visible achievements, compensatory education was criticized both from the educational left and right, and made little headway in higher education. While the charge of "cultural imperialism" from the left would eventually contribute to the shattering of the decades-old consensus concerning the value of public education, from the perspective of colleges the criticism from the right was more pressing.

Compensatory programs seemed to threaten colleges' traditional sense of mission. By defining the educational problem in terms of the social and cultural experience of students, they redefined schools as social or community action agencies, rather than as educational institutions. In contrast, remediation offered neutral scientific and technological categories in place of controversial cultural or political ones. As the language itself suggests, remediation works on a medical model: specific weaknesses are diagnosed, appropriate treatments prescribed, and the learner/patient evaluated to determine the effects of treatment (Clowes, 1982:4). By concentrating on specific academic "deficiencies" of individual students, rather than on large social inequities, remediation nestled comfortably within the traditional education/social mission. By committing to remediation over compensatory education, community colleges avoided the troubling issue of cultural disarticulation, which compensatory education had at least noticed, in favor of the more manageable and ideologically comforting idea that nontraditional students lacked discrete mechanical "skills" which might be improved through application of an appropriate educational technology.

Although institutions rushed to redefine themselves by reference to remediation for underprepared students, by the early 1970s important lines of criticism were already well-established. One line of criticism raised social and cultural issues again in a new way, and questioned whether community colleges really functioned to maintain inequalities of social class. For the first time the claims of access were challenged by concerns about opportunity. Whatever else community colleges do, they also helped isolate traditional colleges and universities from the growing group mobility. Arthur Cohen and Florence Brawer also explicitly-offered a liberal response to the social goals of the left critics, arguing that no form of schooling can "break down class distinctions . . . or move entire ethnic groups from one social stratum to another" (1982:353). In this way, they tried to release community colleges from direct reliance on any particular social or political agenda. Community colleges were to be ideologically neutral, concerned only to enhance educational opportunity to broader segments of the population.

But when the critics examined the educational effectiveness of what colleges were actually doing with underprepared students, they found conventional and mostly ineffective programs. Students whose previous academic performance was marginal or failing were encountering either regular college coursework for which they were clearly not ready, or replays of what they had already failed at. Remediation helped those on the borderline of acceptable academic performance; but, as Cross remarked, "We have not found any magic key to equality of educational opportunity through remediation" (1976:9). Remedial efforts operated on the fringes of higher education, in what were only partly legitimate vestibule programs, and had not penetrated into the instructional core of colleges.

In John Rouche's first national study of remedial programs, he found only limited commitment to remediation. Reviewing programs in the late 1960s, he noted that, "as many as 90 percent of all students assigned or advised into remedial programs never completed them . . . little wonder that critics of community colleges soon referred to the open-door policy as a 'revolving door policy'" (1968:48). Most remedial programs consisted mainly of watered-down versions of regular college-level courses, housed within regular academic departments and taught by faculty with little preparation and little commitment to remediation. Rouche and Cross both applauded the comprehensive programs that were developed in the 1970s as distinct improvements on that picture. The new programs offered a broad range of educational services and teaching strategies, had a volunteer teaching and counseling staff, and were often housed within separate divisions of remedial education (Rouche, 1973). They offered a glimpse of the coming "instructional revolution" needed for colleges to be educationally effective. In Cross's sanguine assessment remediation "started as a simple approach to equality through lowering the access barriers . . . turned into an educational revolution involving all of higher education. The revolution has reached the heart of the educational enterprise—the instructional process itself" (1976:9).

According to its advocates, the instructional revolution would be based on "mastery learning," individualization of instruction, and new learning technologies. Starting with remedial programs, where the sense of crisis was acute, the revolution in pedagogy was imagined as spreading throughout community colleges, and then to the other sectors of higher education. Community colleges were to be the distinctive vanguard institutions of the instructional revolution. Their large commitment to the difficult project of remediation would force them to innovation, and their success would encourage others to follow. Change of this magnitude would call for ruthless single-mindedness. Familiar classroom practices such as lectures and group discussions probably would be replaced in the great effort to enhance student achievement. As Arthur Cohen put it: "[given the] aim of engendering minimum, fundamental achievement in all students all the instructional processes are then directed toward bringing students to this goal" (1969:22).

For improved educational practice these theorists drew from cognitive psychology, which seemed to them to suggest that instruction ought to be radically individualized. Things like programmed and computer-assisted learning, with their emphasis on self-pacing, active participation, clear and explicit goals, small lesson units, and frequent feedback, were especially recommended. These practices would enable even students with a prior history of failure to achieve success by leading them through carefully graduated learning sequences, from the simple to the complex, the speed of movement and difficulty of task always geared to the present capabilities of each student.

The "educational effectiveness" theorists—Cross, Rouche, Cohen, Brawer—saw themselves as encouraging community colleges to become "achievement-oriented" institutions. Following the precepts of the instructional revolution, at last community colleges could offer a realistic promise of educational achievement to the vast majority of their students. They spoke from within the great tradition of Progressive education which attempted to develop a science of instruction and to place it at the service of incrementalist social reconstruction. However, with the emergence of so-called developmental programs in the 1970s, community colleges turned away from the path projected by the Progressives. They were torn by competing impulses, by alternative visions of the precise nature of their mission with underprepared students.

The Developmental Drift

The educational effectiveness movement was the work of theorists and policymakers; what came to be called "developmental education" was more the diffuse creation of a multitude of active classroom instructors whose experience disposed them away from educational technologies, and more generally, away from primarily cognitive understandings of remediation. Developmental educators argued that the familiar remedial concern of bringing students "up to college level" in their "basic skills" was only part, and maybe not the most important part, of what the community college ought to be doing for the students that were overflowing the remedial classrooms.

Advocates of developmental education did not define themselves in the tradition of Progressive education, with its model of cognitive psychology informing an ever improved practice. Instead, they portrayed the goal of their efforts in terms of the ideal of a fully developed, multifaceted self that successfully integrates the cognitive and the affective aspects of personality. Frequently, developmental educators looked to the psychological theories of Jerome Bruner and Jean Piaget for support. From them they drew the notion of developmental stages, of readiness to acquire concepts and skills. From the humanistic psychology of Carl Rogers and Abraham Maslow they took an emphasis on the importance of empathetic communication in promoting personal growth, the need for teachers to fully accept student individuality and nurture it. The vocabulary of remediation began to look cold and unfeeling. The talk of "educational technology," "intentional learning," and "the teacher researcher" was rejected at the ground level in favor of notions like "developing the whole person," and "helping students understand themselves and their lives."

The shift from remediation to developmental education happened quietly, without rancor or debate. Since they rely on such utterly different accounts of college mission, of proper classroom goals and methods, perhaps that is surprising. Indeed, often each explicitly defined itself against the other, portraying itself as trying to accomplish different ends by different means and for different reasons. More often, however, the two camps talked past each other, and, in any case, lacked any institutional means to articulate and settle their differences. What finally happened was that the alternatives merged institutionally, and appeared to merge theoretically. Developmental goals—developing personal consciousness, changing affective styles, encouraging social competence, enriching the lives of students, their families, and their communities—were no longer clearly distinguished from the remedial goals of ameliorating skill deficiencies. In the 1970s and 1980s programs began to describe themselves as "remedial/developmental," and pursue a peculiar blend of cognitive and personal development goals.

Remedial categories continue to guide admissions testing and placement, and entrance and exit criteria for precollege courses. Those are all described in terms of the mastery of writing, reading, and computational skills; and, of course, precollege programs are dominated by reading, writing, and mathematics courses. Developmental understandings deeply shape the way faculty actually teach those courses, however, and what they value about them. When teachers share stories, they are less often about how students have increased their academics skills, than about how "one of my students now reads to her children," or how another "registered to vote for the first time." Teachers in developmental programs are extremely concerned with issues of students' self-esteem, their personal growth, and feelings of autonomy; counseling is a critical element in those programs. As one observer notes: "Counseling is considered almost a panacea in that it is supposed to give high-risk students the extra attention they need" (Moore, 1981:20).

The affinity between developmental programs and the student service function commonly results in institutional alliances between developmental faculty and counseling staff. Richardson and Bender notice that since the counselors have an ambiguous relation to the academic function, those alliances are not entirely benign. "On the negative side, the existence of a special cadre of staff [student services] who see themselves as protectors of the open-door philosophy for the underprepared has produced fewer academic solutions than desirable. . . the rift between academic and student service staffs. . . can erupt into conflicts that stymie efforts to deal with the issues of academic quality and standards" (1987:49). Counselors often oppose the imposition of academic standards; according to Richardson and Bender, they think of themselves as student advocates. As the cryptocounseling stance of developmental instruction established itself throughout the community college, the counseling staff was tremendously reinforced by an energetic and committed developmental teaching faculty. Since they were now trusted colleagues rather than wary adversaries, long-standing, latent tensions between academics and student services became even more deeply submerged. Both jobs, it appeared, could be accomplished without compromise.

The confusion of function of remedial/developmental programs accelerated the weakening of the academic culture of the community college. The new programs lacked the clarity of vision of either the purely remedial or purely developmental, although they appropriated much of the vocabulary and many of the practices of each. The important point is that in remedial/developmental programs cognitive and affective achievement are not clearly distinguished, and are actually allowed to drift together.

Inevitably, the mixing of the "hard" outcomes proposed by remediation, with the softer ones of developmental programs, made the hybrid "medial/developmental" programs notoriously difficult to evaluate. The fact that few students ever successfully made the transition from the special precollege programs into the regular curriculum was not taken to show those programs to be failures; instead, such programs could be defended as encouraging and facilitating the full mental, moral, and emotional growth of students whose lives might be enriched by their coming to know, to appreciate, and ultimately to express themselves fully as members of society and as members of their social and racial group. If the universally dismal outcomes of precollege programs no longer produce a sense of crisis, it is because developmental "social service" goals have eclipsed the traditional cognitive objectives of higher education.

The broad processes by which community colleges have been remedialized are clear enough although the particulars of the story differ from state to state and even from college to college. Carried by and proselytized by a committed faculty, remedial/developmental understandings and practices spread from precollege programs both vertically and horizontally, even into university parallel programs. That process is encouraged by institutional practices that effectively scatter underprepared students everywhere. Academic policies may reduce core course requirements and restrict prerequisites. Admissions, testing, and registration policies may produce somewhat haphazard placement. Funding formulas and financial aid policies often encourage rapid movement from precollege programs into regular college courses, or concurrent placement in them. And, of course, counseling and advising almost always puts very high value on maximizing student choice. Of those common policies some are freely chosen, others are forced on institutions. Taken individually, and certainly in combination, they result in extreme heterogeneity of the classroom: almost any student may be registered in almost any course.

In the era of open access, even declared transfer-oriented students look underprepared to faculty, and are in fact drawn from the lower quintiles of the public high schools. They are considered college level only because so many of their fellow students are even less well-prepared. When the illiterate, the somewhat literate, and the literate, sit side by side in the community college classroom, the distinction between remedial and "regular" students, and between the remedial/developmental function and the traditional academic function, will be blurred or even obliterated. A very vigorous academic culture, constituted by the social and intellectual practices of the academic disciplines, might have resisted these powerful tendencies. However, at community colleges, unlike universities, academic disciplines have only a very weak status—for example there are no upper-division courses, and often few sophomore level courses. Disciplines might have relied on university conceptions of academic rigor, but when transfer relations with universities were finally interpreted in terms of the bureaucratic concern of articulation, community college courses were cut loose to follow their natural paths. As it turned out that path was away from discipline-specific concerns and toward generic conceptions of instruction.

From remediation and the educational effectiveness movement, faculty took a vocabulary for describing underpreparedness. Some prescriptions they found congenial, such as careful sequencing, and breaking complex ideas into simple elements; but they stopped short of adopting the full range of educational technology. They also began to use the vocabulary and exemplary practices of developmental programs. The result of this dual movement was the reshaping of the typical classroom, and more globally, of the entire academic culture. What came to predominate was a mixture of a mechanical "skills" activities, and information retrieval—which taken together are what Richardson calls bitting—with a social service mission of individual affective development.

Pedagogy and Ideology

What is troubling about the remedialization of community colleges is the extent to which it seems to reinforce the left's critique of community colleges, that under the banner of providing enhanced educational opportunities they unintentionally help perpetuate the dual structure of American education which works to deny meaningful social mobility. What becomes of students is largely a matter of how their education shapes them; that in turn depends on what settings and practices they encounter and engage. The history we have sketched has seen the weakening of both faculty and student expectation about what counts as rigorous academic work. Intellectual activity became debased and trivialized, reduced to skills, information, or personal expression—for students who look to education as their chief hope of advancement. The remedial and developmental practices that now largely constitute the academic culture of community colleges are far too weak to elicit the powerful transformations needed to really make a difference in students' prospects.

We have earlier argued that nontraditional education is best thought of in terms of cultural disarticulation. This provides a novel way to understand the precise nature of the two-tiered structure of American education. Of course the "two tiers" reflect and help sustain the racial and class divisions of American society. Partly, they are able to do this because they are very different cultural enterprises, striving through their practice to form students in particular ways. Ironically, the educational practices offered to children of professionals at four-year colleges and universities are tougher, more rigorous, and denser than those offered to the nontraditional students for whom education means the most.

Notice, for instance, the very different status of language in the academic programs, and the lives, of more traditional students at more traditional sorts of schools.[1] For them, reading and writing is not a matter of mastering semantic, syntactic, and orthographic correctness, as in remedial programs. Nor is it a matter of students being provided with unfettered opportunities for intellectual, aesthetic, moral growth, and "finding their own voices," as in developmental programs. For traditional students, academic reading and writing is part of a style of life that is rich and meaningful beyond the classroom. Academics is for them a system of progressive initiation into various communities of discourse. Similarly, in community-based literacy programs students' progress with language and thought is usually firmly anchored in what are real world problems, dilemmas, and possibilities (Kozol, 1985).

Not so for remedial or developmental students. For them language and thought are rules to be mastered, so divorced from any meaningful use that one of the great concerns among their teachers is how to find or create appropriate adult materials at grade school levels. Semesters, possibly years, of what has to seem to them to be drudgery will precede any useful and significant outcomes for them. If traditional students had to engage in countless, essentially pointless exercises before their real engagement with academics could begin, their retention rates might begin to approximate those of remedial students and far fewer bachelor's degrees would be awarded.

The developmental solution to the debilitating apathy associated with dictionary exercises and mechanical drills is to embed skills instruction within various genres of personal expression. Thus, little reaction papers, opinion papers, journals, and personal narratives—thought to be intrinsically rewarding as well as educationally worthwhile—have mostly supplanted repetitious mechanical drills. Both, however, are in striking contrasts to the sorts of cognitive and expressive activities that characterize traditional classrooms, and which constitute the cultural core of the academic and professional world. To put it bluntly, weak academic practices subtly exclude nontraditional students from that world, rather than inviting them into it.

None of the ideological accounts of the mission of the community college, a list of which practically retells their history, acknowledges the full dimensions of the educational challenge of nontraditionality, of the problem of declining intellectual or literacy standards. Since neither educational practices nor proposed outcomes are independent of ideology, or of each other, major pedagogical alternatives have to be thought of as much more significant than the happenstance choice of individual classroom teachers. They are devices by which society molds itself into a certain image. For liberals, educational practices should promote individual achievement in a competitive setting that is conceived as essentially meritocratic; the nontraditionality of students is to be addressed by large social service organizations within the collegiate structure. Vocationalists interpret pedagogy as training—rote memorization, the mastering of a myriad of tasks, and preparation for a specific and delimited role within a rigid professional hierarchy. The social activist tries to counter the "hidden injuries of class" by bringing students to full consciousness as members of an oppressed group so as to promote collective political action to alter the existing social and political arrangements. The triumphant remedial and developmental attempts to reconstruct community colleges draw variously on those familiar competing ideologies, in the sort of eclectic appropriation that ought to signal failure rather than success. But none of the reigning ideologies recognizes the cultural features of nontraditionality. None encourages rigorous intellectual work for nontraditional students. Apparently, powerful intellectual training is to continue to be reserved for an elite; for the second tier, language competencies will be the mechanical, the informational, and the expressive.

If nontraditional students are to be adequately prepared for academic success, there must be substantial transformations in their conception of education and their sense of themselves as learners. Correlatively, nontraditional institutions have to change in ways that allow nontraditional students to experience education as something more than simply memorizing, reciting, expressing, and opining. If this has been hard for colleges to see, it is because pale intellectual practices haven't been entirely accidental. They have been endorsed as reasonable and beneficent, as implied by cutting-edge educational theory, as offering nontraditional students the best environment for academic success. The relation between the academic culture of community colleges and the standard educational theory which supports it is so tight that any substantial reform of practice will require a reform of theory.

Notes

1. We recognize that these are becoming harder to find. One of the consequences of the massive expansion of higher education is that only the most elite colleges and universities have been insulated from the influx of nontraditional students, and they not entirely. Faculty at many middle level universities share the community college experience of trying to recall what traditional education looked like.

References

American Association of Community and Junior Colleges. "Follow-up and Transfer of Two-Year College Students." Washington, D.C.: American Association of Community and Junior Colleges, 1979.

Brint, Steven and Karabel, Jerome. *The Diverted Dream: Community Colleges and the Promise of Educational Opportunity in America, 1900–1985.* New York: Oxford University Press, 1989.

Chazen, M., ed. *Compensatory Education.* London: Butterworth, 1973.

Clowes, Donald A. "More Than a Definitional Problem." *Current Issues in Higher Education,* 1 (1982): 1–12.

Cohen, Arthur M. *Dateline '79: Heretical Concepts for the Community College.* Beverly Hills: Glencoe Press, 1969.

Cohen, Arthur M. and Brawer, Florence B. *The American Community College.* San Francisco: Jossey-Bass, 1982.

Cross, K. Patricia. *Accent on Learning: Improving Instruction and Reshaping the Curriculum.* San Francisco: Jossey-Bass, 1976.

Donovan, Richard A., Schaier-Peleg, Barbara, and Forer, Bruce. *Transfer: Making it Work.* Washington, D.C.: American Association of Community and Junior Colleges, 1987.

Eells, Walter C. *The Junior College.* Boston: Houghton Mifflin, 1931.

Kintzer, Frederick C. and Wattenbarger, J. L. *The Articulation/Transfer Phenomenon: Patterns and Directions.* Washington, D.C.: American Association of Community and Junior Colleges, 1985.

Knoell, Dorothy M. and Medsker, Leland L. *From Junior to Senior College.* Washington, D.C.: American Council on Education, 1965.

Kozol, Jonathon. *Illiterate America.* New York: Anchor Press, 1985.

Lombardi, John. "The Decline of Transfer Education." Eric Clearinghouse, Topical Paper No. 70 (December 1979).

Medsker, L. L. *The Junior College: Progress and Prospect.* New York: McGraw Hill, 1960.

Moore, William M. *Against the Odds.* San Francisco: Jossey-Bass, 1970.

Moore, William M. *Community College Response to the High Risk Student.* Eric Clearinghouse Monograph, 1981.

Richardson, Richard C. and Bender, Louis. *Minority Access and Achievement in Higher Education.* San Francisco: Jossey-Bass, 1987.

Roueche, John E. *Salvage, Redirection or Custody? Remedial Education in the Community College.* Washington, D.C.: American Association of Community and Junior Colleges, 1968.

Roueche, John E. and Kirk, Wade R. *Catching Up: Remedial Education.* San Francisco: Jossey-Bass, 1973.

Wilson, Reginald and Melandez, S. E. *Minorities in Higher Education: Third Annual Status Report.* Washington, D.C.: American Council on Education, 1984.

A New Vision for Student Development Services for the 90s

BRADFORD W. CARROLL AND PAUL E. TARASUK

Introduction

In a recent presentation to the Community College Counselors of Connecticut, a Development Guidance and Counseling Model for student services in the community colleges was offered (Tarasuk & Carroll, 1989). The authors met with a group of Connecticut community college counselors to present the conceptual framework of a K-12 Developmental Comprehensive Guidance and Counseling Model and to demonstrate how this model could be adapted and revised to meet the needs of counselors at the community college level nationally. In addition, a career component of the model used in a community college was demonstrated. The major purpose of this paper is to illustrate how this model can be integrated into an existing student services structure.

Historic Trends

Presently there is a conflict regarding the mission and direction of student development services in the community college (Dassance & Harr, 1989). O'Banion (1989) traces several key student development models that have emerged in the period between 1960 and 1980. One of the more recent offerings proposed in 1983 by the Dallas County Community Colleges (as cited by O'Banion) has a strong developmental core where it is suggested that adult developmental theories be used to carry out all the basic functions of their program. O'Banion further proposed the need for a shift in student services from a "sixties value base" to a new "eighties value base" (p. 10). In the 1960s and 1970s, many student services professionals gave less support to rules and regulations, instead "allowing students to select their own directions without much direct assistance from the institution" (p. 11).

The 1990s will reverse this process and emphasize what O'Banion (1989) calls "quality reformation," in which the above will be strongly challenged and expectations from students will be increased; more controls and structure will be provided by the institution including "assessment and placement, general educations curricula, attendance policies, F grades, and policies of suspensions and probation" (p. 11). Therefore, there appears to be a change from a more student-centered to a more institution-centered model. In addition, the idea of a model based on a developmental theory is nothing new (Creamer, 1987).

This article expands on the foregoing concept and ultimately offers a specific framework in which to organize tasks and more firmly establish the professional role of student development educators. The program will contain a student-centered humanizing process as well as meet and satisfy institutional standards for structure and accountability. The commonly held goal of all counselors is to meet the students' developmental needs. However, this is too vague a concept in today's fiscally conscious educational environment. There is an increasing demand in the community colleges and across the educational spectrum for measurable outcomes (Alfred, 1982). Creamer (1987, 1989) indicates that budgets expand more slowly than service demands, and that there is pressure to create a new model or strategies to allow for a more "frugal use of limited financial resources that leads to equal or better results than are achieved under current practices" (p. 32, 1989).

Recent Changes

Community college counselors in Connecticut and across the nation feel the pressures of a rapidly changing, culturally diverse student population, as well as increasing enrollment and decreasing financial support from their states due to budgetary cuts (Cohen, 1989; Curry & Young, 1989; Dassance, 1984). In a major study of the professional activities of community college counselors, Keim (1988) concludes that there is a trend toward an extremely heavy workload for counselors, increasing administrative responsibilities and decreasing average number of counselors per institution.

In the 1950s and 1960s, according to the mission statement of the American Association of Community and Junior Colleges, community college counselors were employed to meet the needs of students in the areas of personal/social, educational and career/vocational counseling (O'Banion, 1989). These were similar to areas for which senior high counselors were also responsible. Historically, both the community college counselors and the senior high counselors utilized clinically based medical model—focusing primarily on a one-to-one counseling relationship.

During the 1970s and 1980s, community college counselors became important members of the student services team (Dassance, 1984; Payne, 1989). This became necessary because there were dramatic increases in the enrollments of nontraditional students, minority students from the inner cities, part-time students, returning women and displaced workers—students who have been described by Payne (1989) as "academic boat people" (p. 23). There were also growing connections with the business/industrial community (Cohen & Brawer, 1982; Dickens, 1986; Hudesman, 1986; Ostertag, Pearson & Baker, 1986). The community college counselors, by and large, became the recipients of all the additional and ancillary services which were designed to reconcile new institutional pressures with the needs of a newly diversified student population.

Confusion of Role

Ancillary services include many activities beyond the already established personal/social, educational and career/vocational counseling. Additional services include assessment, placement, information dissemination, orientation, study skills, curriculum development, consulting, teaching, disciplining, record keeping, managing and coordinating. O'Banion (1989) confirms this situation in stating:

> ... some historical analysts have reduced the student personnel function to that of maintenance, a process in which a group of caretakers provide a series of services scattered around the campus: financial aid, registration, admissions, student activities, academic advising and so on ... a number of states describe this function as an essential 16 or an essential 37, or an

essential 74. This kind of listing obscures any sort of philosophical considerations for a part of the community college that is in dire need of a strong philosophical base. (p. 8)

Therefore, it is obviously a major concern for community college counselors that they are expected to be involved in a greater variety of services than ever before. Counselors find themselves in a quandary, and role conflict is often prevalent. The current organizational patterns of many counseling programs are based on an ancillary services concept loosely grouped around broad role and function statement (Cohen & Brawer, 1982; Creamer, 1989). Rather than having a proactive, preventative role, in their present state counselors are in supportive and remedial roles; their skills and training are not effectively used and their preventative model based on developmental principles would offer a structured program with a philosophical source.

As far back as 1978, Bordzinsky (cited in Dassance and Harr, 1989) stated, "The student services sector has been primarily a reactive group.... It must become proactive if it is to survive ... it must learn to anticipate and control its environment [or] become extinct" (p. 3). In a similar vein, Dassance and Harr (1989) state that "all too often student affairs have responded to challenges by developing a helter-skelter array of services, often not preceded by thoughtful planning, integration with existing services, concern with proper prioritizations, or institutional collaboration. Such an approach has left student affairs vulnerable to criticism" (p. 21). Likewise, Richardson and Simmons (1989) suggest replacing a homogenized and undifferentiated approach to one with a "more program-oriented arrangement" (p. 36). Thus it certainly seems as if a model with a specific program would make sense in future planning.

A Change in Focus

As the community college counselor in his or her student services role continues to attempt to become "all things to all people," confusion occurs, thus leading to a high level of frustration for the counselor. The traditional clinical model of counseling appears no longer viable. A model based on a developmental approach and committed to lifelong learning for all students needs to be emphasized (Gleazer, 1980). This would mean a shift from the traditional programs and counselor role of the 1960s:

- From working less in individual counseling settings to increased group settings,

- From remediation to prevention,

- From a crisis-based to a planning-based orientation,

- From reactive to proactive services,

- From an unplanned/unstructured approach to a more systematic one that is curriculum based, involving all students with measured results,

- From a medical model of services to an educational model (Gysbers, 1987; Myrick, 1987).

It was evident that the community college counselors in Connecticut were struggling with the same concerns as the K-12 counselors in Connecticut. The K-12 school counselors responded to the concern by launching a K-12 task force sponsored by the Connecticut School Counselors Association (CSCA) and the Connecticut Association for Counseling and Development (CACD). The end result of the task force meetings was the development of written guidelines for Connecticut school counselors to use in developing local K-12 comprehensive development guidance and counseling programs (CSCA, 1988).

Suggested Framework

The conceptual framework of the K-12 Comprehensive Development Guidance and Counseling Program (CSCA, 1988) includes a preface, philosophy, major goals, role descriptions, basic expected services and a program description with K-12 objectives on which to base the curriculum. This is outlined in Table 1 below. To further clarify Table 1, explanatory details of the important features of role description and program components follow.

Table 1

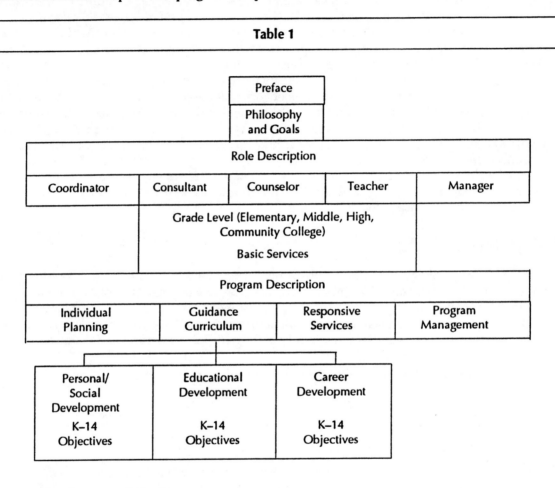

Descriptions of Roles

The counselor as COORDINATOR: integrates resources from the college and wider community to establish a complete network of services for personal/social counseling as well as career development. This could involve a diversity of services ranging from psychiatric referral to internships and full-time employment.

The counselor as CONSULTANT: offers professional expertise to administration, faculty, staff and other college community members on issues ranging from freshman recruitment and orientation programs to retention and dropout prevention.

The counselor as COUNSELOR: provides a broad range of opportunities for problem solving and addressing personal issues in helping students develop as total people in group as well as individual sessions.

The counselor as TEACHER: gives small and large group instruction on topics ranging from drug and alcohol abuse to study skills, time management, and improving one's self concept.

The counselor as MANAGER: plans, implements, and evaluates the overall system necessary for supporting, maintaining, and improving the comprehensive developmental counseling program.

Program Components

Individual Planning: consists of activities to help all students plan, monitor, and manage their own learning as well as their personal and career development. This includes individual appraisal where counselors help students analyze and evaluate abilities, aptitudes, interests, and achievements, resulting in setting specific educational as well as personal and occupational goals. Additional activities include decision-making skill development, values clarification, job-seeking skills, and work exploration experiences.

Guidance Curriculum: provides structured developmental experiences through either classroom or group activities related to career planning, self-knowledge and interpersonal skills. Could include such topics as study skills, human relations training, communication skills, marriage and family living, and stress reduction.

Responsive Services: includes personal counseling in a small group or on an individual basis; consultation, crisis counseling and, when necessary, referral for more serious types of personal issues.

Program Management: plans activities that establish, maintain, enhance, and evaluate the overall program. Includes professional development (updating professional knowledge and skills), staff and community relations, serving on departmental curriculum committees or advisory councils, initiating research projects, grant writing, and training peer helpers.

Consequently, one can visualize how the levels of the model can easily be extended to include grades 13 and 14 and also to achieve objectives to meet the needs of the community college student population. There is a long and well-established history of cooperation between high schools and colleges. Greenberg (1988) emphasizes the need to reassess the fundamental curricular and instructional assumptions of the transition from high school to college. This becomes even more crucial when students entering community colleges are not knowledgeable about career, goals, transfer aspirations and study skills, for example. Closer articulation and collaboration of efforts between the high school and community college community has been recommended by several others (Bernstein, 1986; McCabe, 1988; Mabry, 1988; Stoel, 1988; Van Allen, 1988).

As a way of illustrating how this developmental model could relate to community college student services, the Connecticut community college counselors were asked to brainstorm a list of their roles, duties and services as they related to the four basic program components described above. Table 2 is a summary listing the roles, services and duties provided by this group.

Table 2

Component I—
Individual Planning
Academic—
    Counseling/guidance/advising
Career—
    Counseling/guidance/advising
Student recommendations
Job placement
New study orientation
Placement testing & scoring
Study skills
Re-admission interviews
Transfer advising & counseling
Career information
Retention counseling
Probation
New students (F/T, P/T)
High risk students
Re-entry & adult counseling
Veterans advising
Academic survival

Component II—
Guidance Curriculum
Teaching, career planning, small groups
Workshops
Guest lecturers, presentations
Self-paced academic courses
Program development
Teaching, self-assessment
Job search strategies
Communication skills
Stress reduction
Family living

Component III—
Responsive Services
Personal counseling
Crisis intervention
Social counseling

Component IV—
System Support
(Program Management)
Special services for special needs
(hearing impaired, blind)
Referrals to community resources
Consult with faculty
Attend division meetings
Arrangements of office
Ordering materials
Organizing career room/computer/software
Coordinate and supervise work-
study & other clerical help
Writing of grants
Coordinate peer counseling program
Coordinate tutoring
Training & overseeing faculty advisors/staff
Work on articluation agreements
Professional development
Assist learning disabilities coordinator
Job developments
Admissions information
Community counseling
Supervision of interns
Receptionist
Management tasks
Academic standards
Advising & retention
Supervise budget

It should be noted that the roles, duties and services included under each of the four basic program components above are remarkably similar to the services offered by senior high school counselors as described in the K-12 Developmental Comprehensive Guidance and Counseling Program (CSCA, 1988).

Career Planning Component

A major goal of community colleges is to help students determine appropriate career goals, whether or not such students are recent high school graduates or older returning students who view education as pragmatic and leading to marketable skills (Healy and Reilly, 1989). For such students, career choice and, especially, indecision, become a cause for anxiety. Historically, the vocationally undecided college student has been a challenge to counselors, particularly at the community college level (Lopez, 1983). It is believed that this lack of adequate goals, specifically regarding vocational choice, plays a large part in a student's lack of motivation for college and hence leads to an increase in dropping out.

Among the researchers who have considered this problem are Elton and Rose (1970). They found a major discrepancy in the survival rates of vocationally decided and undecided freshmen. Only 17% of undecided freshmen persisted until graduation, in contrast to 43% who proposed career commitments, even though those commitments might have undergone later change. Grites (1981) contended that it is no surprise that undecided students tend to leave college usually after their freshman year, more frequently that those who have made even tentative choices of majors. Going from decision to doubt and then to another choice appears to be a more stabilizing process than having to no initial direction at all. Otto (1980) asked 500 entering freshmen at Florida Keys Community College to rank in order the importance of goal statements in areas of career, personal, social and cultural development. The most significant goal statements in order of importance were choosing a career; exploring individual talents, skills and abilities; increasing interpersonal skills; and learning more about individually chosen fields of interest.

Thus, a developmental, proactive, preventative model is ideal for a community college population and utilization of this model can be easily demonstrated in the area of career decision making. Specifically, the career choice process can meet our model's program components in individual planning and guidance curriculum (career planning groups or in-class presentations). As this process stimulates personal issues, the responsive services area could also be involved. The counselor could function in the role of coordinator, teacher and counselor. It is most applicable if making career choices is seen as an ongoing developmental process as people enter and exit the workplace, change careers, or return for further education. An explanation of this process follows.

In a study of entering community college freshmen, Carroll (1990) utilized Holland's Vocational Preference Inventory (VPI) as a screening instrument to identify those individuals who are what Holland (1985) calls undifferentiated. A flat or undifferentiated VPI profile suggests an individual will have poor academic achievement, vocational instability and less ability in persisting toward a set goal than a more differentiated student. From a developmental perspective, Holland further suggested that undifferentiated profiles indicate vocational immaturity and difficulty in defining a role within a future occupation.

Students with flat, undifferentiated profiles were randomly placed into experimental and control groups of 45 each. The experimentals received a three-credit course entitled "Self Assessment and Career Planning" during their first college semester, while controls were not treated. Both groups were post-tested at the end of the semester on the VPI for increasingly differentiated or more focused career choice. Also, both groups were compared on variables of school withdrawal and academic achievement.

The three-credit course addressed the vocational or career development dimension, because students entering the course lacked direction and were unable to appraise their talents and life experiences in order to arrive at some initial career goals. Thus, this course was presented as a developmental process in a decision-making format to help students appraise themselves and gain insight and self-knowledge through assessment of past life and work experiences in combination with group sessions, tests and inventories, human relations "games" and role playing. The result was a unique personal profile of interests, skills or aptitudes, values, and personality style that accelerated the vocational development process.

Statistically significant results were found in all areas including degree of increased VPI differentiation and career direction, school withdrawals and academic achievement. Experimentals showed increased differentiation, fewer school withdrawals and significantly higher grade point averages than the control groups. This base of knowledge will allow new life situations to be appraised and added as they are experienced, thereby refining and focusing the choice of one's life work. Other researchers have used a variety of models to provide a career planning process to community college students (Allyn, 1989; Dickens, 1986; Hudesman, 1986).

Carroll (1990) concludes that many community college students enter college with both limited self-knowledge and a sense of how they "fit" or project themselves into the world of work.

Therefore, a developmental model lends itself to addressing these issues because it allows the counselor to be proactive, preventative, planning based, and present in the classroom in a teaching role to become part of the curriculum planning process. Essentially the medical model is replaced by an educational one for service delivery.

Conclusions

It appears that a student services model at the community college which emphasizes a developmental approach is a viable concept. Creamer (1989) states "accomplishable goals must be agreed on, and the goals must have credibility throughout the college. . . . A new model . . . should rest on theories of human development and learning (p. 36). The Connecticut community college counselors have taken the first steps in establishing an action plan as advocated by Gysbers (1987):

1. Decide to change, to take charge of their own destiny;

2. Get organized, establish advisory and steering committees;

3. Select a program structure; and

4. Initiate assessment of the current program.

Gysbers (1987) suggests a nine-step action plan to be completed in a two-to three-year sequence. Dassance (1984) summarizes the need for such a program by stating that student: " . . . services have been particularly vulnerable to budget reductions. . . . Student personnel has struggled to establish its legitimacy within post-secondary education. . . . There is an enhanced awareness of the necessity and value of basing student development practice on human development theory" (pp. 25-27).

References

Alfred, R. L. (1982). Improving college resources through impact assessment. In R. L. Alfred (Ed.), *Institutional impacts on campus, community and business constituencies* (pp. 93–107). San Francisco: Jossey-Bass.

Allyn, D. P. (1989). Application of the 4MAT model to career guidance. *Career Development Quarterly, 37*(3), 280-288.

Bernstein, A. (1986). The devaluation of transfer: Current explanations and possible causes. In L. S. Zwerling (Ed.), *The community college and its critics* (pp. 31–40). San Francisco: Jossey-Bass.

Carroll, B. W. (1990, March). Career indecision: Suggestions for identification and remediation. Paper presented at the Annual Conference of the Connecticut Association for Counseling and Development, Manchester, Connecticut.

Cohen, A. M. (1989) What next for the community colleges? An ERIC review. *Community College Review, 17*(2), 53–58.

Cohen, A. M. & Brawer, F. B. (1982). *The American community college.* San Francisco: Jossey-Bass.

Connecticut School Counselor Association and Connecticut Association for Counseling and Development. (1988). *K-12 Developmental Guidance and Counseling Program.* Hartford, CT: Connecticut School Counselor Association.

Creamer, D. G. (1986, February). A performance standard for community college counseling: Institutional goal attainment. Paper presented at the Regional Symposium of the National Council on Student Development, Orlando, Florida.

Creamer, D. G. (1987). How developmental are community college student personnel purposes? *Community College Review, 12*(4), 27–30.

Creamer, D. G. (1989). Changing internal conditions: Impact on student development. In W. L. Deegan & T. O'Banion (Eds.), *Perspectives in student development* (pp. 31–43). San Francisco: Jossey Bass.

Curry, J. & Young, B. (1989). Trends and issues in student development. In W. L. Deegan & T. O'Banion (Eds.), *Perspectives in student development* (pp. 93–102). San Francisco: Jossey-Bass.

Dassance, C. R. (1984). Community college student personnel work: Is the model still emerging? *Community College Review, 12*(3), 25–29.

Dassance, C. R. (1987, April). National standards for student affairs: Opportunity for renewal. Paper presented at the Annual National Convention of the American Association of Community and Junior colleges, Dallas, Texas.

Dassance, C. R. & Harr, G. (1989). Student development from theory to practice. In W. L. Deegan & T. O'Banion (Eds.), *Perspectives on student development* (pp. 19–30). San Francisco: Jossey-Bass.

Dickens, P. R. (1986). Vocational assessment and exploration for students with special needs in a community college. *Journal of College Student Personnel 27*(2), 181–182.

Elton, C. F. & Rose, H. A. (1970). A longitudinal study of the vocationally undecided male student. *Journal of Vocational Behavior, 1*, 85–92.

Gleazer, E. J., Jr. (1980). *The community college: Values, vision, and vitality.* Washington, DC: American Association of Community and Junior Colleges.

Greenburg, A. R. (1988). High school students in college courses: Three programs. In J. E. Lieberman (Ed.), *Collaborating with high schools* (pp. 69–84). San Francisco: Jossey-Bass.

Grites, T. J. (1981). Being undecided might be the best decision they could make. *The School Counselor, 29*, 41–46.

Gysbers, N. C. (1987, Spring). How to re-model your school guidance program. *Counselor Education and Supervision Spectrum, 11–16.*

Healy, C. C. & Reilly, K. C. (1989). Career needs of community college students: Implications for services and theory. *Journal of College Student Development, 6*(30), 541–545.

Holland, J. L. (1985). *Making vocational choices: A theory of vocational personalities and work environments* (2nd ed.) New Jersey: Prentice-Hall.

Hudesman, J. (1986). Counseling style: Its impact on the academic performance of college students in special programs. *Journal of College Student Personnel, 27*(3), 250–254.

Keim, M. C. (1988). Two-year college counselors: Who are they and what do they do? *Community College Review, 16*(1), 39–46.

Lopez, F. G. (1983). A paradoxical approach to vocational indecision. *Personnel and Guidance Journal, 61*, 410–412.

Mabry, T. (1988). The high school/community college connection: An ERIC review. *Community College Review, 16*(3), 48–55.

McCabe, R. H. (1988). The educational program of the American community college: A transition. In Eaton, J.S. (Ed.), *Colleges of choice: The enabling impact of the community college.* New York: MacMillan.

Myrick, R. D. (1987). *Developmental guidance and counseling: A practical approach.* Minneapolis, MN: Educational Media Corporation.

O'Banion, T. (1989). Student development philosophy: A perspective on the past and the future. In W. L. Deegan & T. O'Banion (Eds.), *Perspectives on student development* (pp. 5–17). San Francisco: Jossey-Bass.

Ostertag, B. A., Pearson, M. T. & Baker, R. E. (1986). Programs for the learning disabled in California community colleges. *Journal of Reading, Writing, and Learning Disabilities International, 2* (4), 331–347.

Otto, A. M. (1980). A study to determine student goals for students enrolled in a community college. Unpublished doctoral dissertation. Nova University, Florida.

Payne, J.L. (1989). The high school/college interface: A new challenge for the community college. *Community College Review, 16*(4), 22–27.

Richardson, R. C., Jr. & Simmons, H. L. (1989). Is it time for a new look at academic organization in community colleges? *Community College Review, 17* (1), 34–39.

Stoel, C. F. (1988). History of the high school connection. In J. E. Lieberman (Ed.) *Collaborating with high schools* (pp. 13–23). San Francisco: Jossey-Bass.

Tarasuk, P. & Carroll, B. (1989, December). Developmental guidance and counseling: Implications for the community college. Paper presented at the meeting of the Connecticut Community College Counselors Association, Waterbury, Connecticut.

Van Allen, G. H. (1988). Two-plus-two programming: A focus on student achievement. *Community College Review, 16*(3), 48–55.

The Community College as a Catalyst for Economic Development: Results of a National Study

JEFFREY A. CANTOR

This article describes interorganizational arrangements—joint efforts characterized by participation of community-based organizations such as community colleges, economic development organizations, governmental agencies (those responsible for job training, economic development, agricultural development, etc.), civic groups, and chambers of commerce. This coordinating role is often achieved through a partnership of a community college with an "umbrella" organization consisting of representatives of multiple community-based organizations. Programmatic activity includes more than single events; these interorganizational arrangements can include multiple programs and a wide array of events. The fact that these arrangements are among community colleges and other community-based organizations lends promise that the joint efforts can be more sustained over time, independent of the success of any single organization, program, or event. These kinds of interorganizational arrangements have proven successful in creating new organizations, new partnerships, and/or nonprofit organizations should the need arise.

Introduction

The relationship between local economic development and education and training has become a topic of increased interest to community and business leadership. This interest results in part from a recognition that our society is becoming too dependent on imported goods and products, and dangerously complacent with illiteracy, and inner-city poverty. Success in economic development for a fuller employment is highly dependent on mutual cooperative efforts between communities and their various public and private institutions. Often overlooked is an uniquely American institution—the community college.

This article reports on a recent study (Cantor et. al., 1989) describing several successful ventures in which the community college serves as a catalyst for both economic development and training. This article describes these findings and provides information by which others can adopt ideas to initiate successful local activities.

239

Background and Need

The community college is in a unique position in the community as it possesses a wide scope of available resources to meet various community needs (Mundhenk, 1988; Charner & Gold, 1987). While rich with educational and training programs, economic development as one of the goals of the community college is not new. The literature is filled with examples of projects, programs, and initiatives involving collaboration between the college and its local business community.

Collaboration between community colleges and other community economic development organizations occurs in various ways. A single project is one basic way, wherein a community college may offer a class to prospective small business entrepreneurs, or a faculty consultant can organize a single customized job training class for an employer. The essential characteristic is that it may only be an isolated event, occurring as infrequently as once in the life-cycle of a firm or during a single semester at a community college.

Community colleges have invested increasing amounts of resources aimed at economic development objectives such as customized job training programs, entrepreneurship "centers," and even related activities such as business assistance services or the operation of incubator buildings for start-up businesses—all which represent programmatic initiatives or commitments that go beyond single events (Burger, 1988; Mihelich, 1988; Charner and Gold, 1987; Holdsworth, 1987; Kingry and Cole, 1985). These organizational or programmatic efforts are more sustained than those at the "event" level, as they are collections of events. However, they are often in isolation of other activities within the community such as industrial recruitment and a need for specific kinds of proactive training and manpower development resources aimed at economic development.

Interorganizational arrangements and collaboratives and practices involving the community college—arrangements which are apart of the infrastructure of the community and thus permanently sustained serve as the focus of this article. Little has been documented about these interorganizational arrangements, even though they are more comprehensive than single practices, projects, programs, or organizations, thus making the community college an indispensable resource and catalyst for economic development in the community.

A Conceptual Framework

To analyze the concept of linkages between economic development and job training, one must recognize that job creation and economic growth initiatives often goes counter to the ways in which these initiatives traditionally have been organized at state and local levels (see U.S. Small Business Administration, 1985; "Small Business Dynamics," 1983; Armington and Odle, 1982; Birch and MacCracken; 1982). Typically, the public policies and services related to these two areas, as well as to a critically important third area—education—have operated as parallel systems (see Figure 1), with:

- Economic development policies being the province of local government and local economic development agencies;

- Job training being administered by corporations as well as by the job training operators sponsored by such related public initiatives such as JTPA; and

- Educational practices being governed by local school systems and postsecondary institutions such as community colleges.

The parallel nature of these systems can produce potential "mismatches" in outcomes. For instance, economic development initiatives, such as the establishment of an enterprise zone, (Mier, 1982; Butler, 1981) may be underway that will eventually reduce the need for certain jobs, even though job training programs are presently placing new employees in those types of jobs. Similarly, the educational practices in place within the community college may not give the appropriate emphasis to academic subjects most relevant to job training or employment needs. To best overcome the potential mismatches, these three systems need to operate as one—hence interorganizationally.

Figure 1
Three traditionally parallel systems

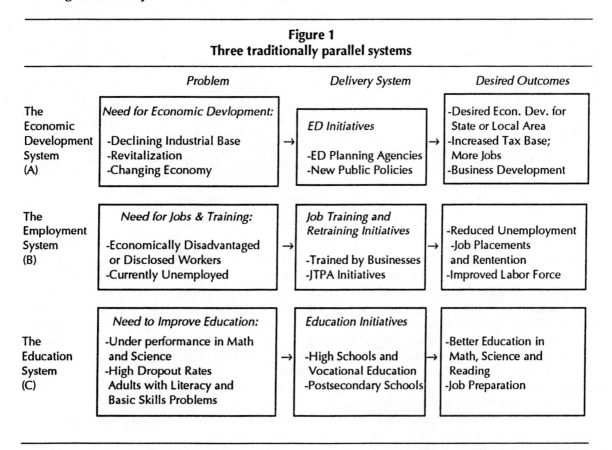

	Problem	Delivery System	Desired Outcomes
The Economic Development System (A)	*Need for Economic Devlopment:* -Declining Industrial Base -Revitalization -Changing Economy	*ED Initiatives* -ED Planning Agencies -New Public Policies	-Desired Econ. Dev. for State or Local Area -Increased Tax Base; More Jobs -Business Development
The Employment System (B)	*Need for Jobs & Training:* -Economically Disadvantaged or Disclosed Workers -Currently Unemployed	*Job Training and Retraining Initiatives* -Trained by Businesses -JTPA Initiatives	-Reduced Unemployment -Job Placements and Rentention -Improved Labor Force
The Education System (C)	*Need to Improve Education:* -Under performance in Math and Science -High Dropout Rates Adults with Literacy and Basic Skills Problems	*Education Initiatives* -High Schools and Vocational Education -Postsecondary Schools	-Better Education in Math, Science and Reading -Job Preparation

A Model for Exemplary Linkages: A Review of the Literature

Economic development is an organized, planned, and cooperative effort between the public and private sectors to improve community economic conditions (Sanders, 1988; Illinois, 1986). Analyses of these activities indicate a process occurring within an area that encourages the revitalization, expansion, and attraction of business and industry, providing increased employment opportunities and enhancing the quality of life; a coordinated, cooperative effort among business and industry, labor, education and government; and a clearly defined role and responsibility for all groups associated with the process. Collaboration and support for economic development is often accomplished by a triangulation of business and industry, economic development agencies (quasi-governmental, state, and local), and community colleges (McNett, 1988). Figure 2 presents an overview of the emerging patterns of collaboration.

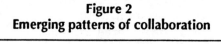

Figure 2
Emerging patterns of collaboration

Economic development collaboratives best occur when maximum cooperation is achieved between all participating organizations, each of whom stands to benefit in some form. It is best controlled at a local level and focused on small business, and without undue duplication of resources (Illinois, 1986). The roles, responsibilities, and unique abilities of each of the organizational entities is useful to understand and analyze.

State/local governmental roles. State government offices of economic development provide technical assistance, site surveys, training for initial or expanding work forces and financial resources for both training and economic development, to municipalities and businesses seeking to promote either relocation or expansion. Municipalities and county government activities include assistance in site location, financial package development, manpower recruitment and training, and assistance in meeting local codes and regulations. The Harford County (Maryland) Department of Economic Development is a good example of a successful local agency.

Quasi-public agency roles. The economic development corporation has emerged over the last two decades at both the regional and local levels. This organization serves a needed role as a nongovernmental service-oriented, and not-for-profit entity often under IRS Code (501 (c) 3) capable of directly matching government services such as economic development planning, with finance and loan packages, job training assistance such as JTPA, and other technical assistance with client business and industry. It markets its region or locality. Very successful organizations have emerged in this capacity such as New Hampshire's Highlander Economic Development Corporation, Kentucky's Bluegrass State Skills Corporation (Zimmer, 1988), and Maryland's Susquehanna Region Private Industry Council (SRPIC) (Ford, 1988). Many of these agencies such as SRPIC emerged out of the need for delivery organizations under the Job Training Partnership Act of 1983.

The role of the community college. A fourth and a very powerful organization involved in the economic development partnership is the community college. This unique organization, once viewed solely as an educational institution, possesses the resources, capabilities, and local community-based avenues and economic interests to serve as a catalyst in overall local economic development, and a very valuable service to business and development, and a very valuable service to business and industry within its area (Mundhenk, 1988). Activities include outreach services such as customized training and on-site college programs for business and industry, faculty consultation, technical assistance (pre-screening and skills assessment of new employees for businesses, consultation in specific disciplines or in business operation, job placement services, and technical library resources), sponsorship of entrepreneurial "incubators" and small business assistance centers, and identification of sources of venture capital funds for small businesses (Kingry & Cole 1985). Community colleges are assuming new and emerging roles in community economic development through expanded institutional missions and goals (Charner & Gold, 1987).

An Expanded Role for the Community College in Economic Development

National trends have been reported in the broad economic development area (Charner & Gold, 1987). Over eighty-five percent of the community colleges promote their involvement in economic development, and one-third have published institutional mission statements referring to economic development. Catalytic and diffusion activity include linkages with economic development agencies to provide technical assistance in the forms of management counseling, resource information, and community supported services. Catalytic activities consist of: (a) linkage with other state and local agencies to support the establishment of new and expanding business and industry; (b) extension of technical assistance to business and industry in the essential managerial functions of planning, organizing, implementing, and controlling; and (c) delivery of job specific entry-level and supplemental customized training.

These kinds of activities are causing community colleges to better define their role in economic development—specifically: (a) their degree of involvement; (b) whether the involvement is active or passive (such as organizing, coordinating, brokering, consulting, establishing, coordinating vs. providing space); (c) whether the involvement should be essentially an internal effort of the college or whether it should concentrate on bridging the gap with already existing economic development efforts; (d) whether the involvement should include personnel or only functions; and (e) whether the college should just serve as a catalyst or also as a performer of identified tasks.

In sum, community colleges cannot simply commit themselves to do economic development, but must cause it to occur (Ohio, 1987; Mundhenk 1986). Community colleges through interorganizational arrangements can effect proactive involvement. Therefore, the paper's primary purpose is to describe and disseminate new information regarding community college collaboratives involving job training and economic development efforts. The conclusions are intended to be a rendition of "what works," and "why," with lessons learned for others wishing to consider similar initiatives.

The Study

Five explanations explaining why organizations collaborate have been prominent in previous research. Organizations successfully collaborate because they derive *mutual exchanges* from each other (Van de Ven, 1976; Levine & White, 1961); or because they are able to increase their *access to external funds of governance opportunities* (Benson, 1975); or are given *mandates to collaborate*, as in a legislated set of functions, where, the creation of the necessary statutes and regulations would alone cause an arrangement to operate; or collaborate because they develop *formal agreements* between each other, specifying the responsibilities of each participating organization (Goodlad, 1975); or collaboration because they have conflicting goals, and the collaboration allows the organizations to mediate their conflicts in a socially approved manner (Hall et al., 1978; Litwak & Hylton, 1962).

Definition of Innovative Collaborative Efforts

The interorganizational arrangement was the primary qualification for an "innovative" collaborative effort between job training and economic development for the purposes of this study. These arrangements demonstrated exemplary and sustained outcomes regarding job creation and job training and placement and involved significant collaboration, coordination, and proactive direction from a community college.

Hypotheses

The study's main hypothesis was that a single coordinating organization (possibly a community college) would be found at the hub of the interorganizational arrangement and that this organization would have been newly formed just for the purpose of combining job training and economic development activities. A second hypothesis was that informal networks—e.g., resulting from overlapping board memberships—were more important ingredients in making arrangements work, compared to formal arrangements among organizations. A hypothesized linkage model (Figure 3) was developed and analyzed in light of data collected. A case study methodology systematically reviewed the data.

Figure 3
Hypothesized linkage model

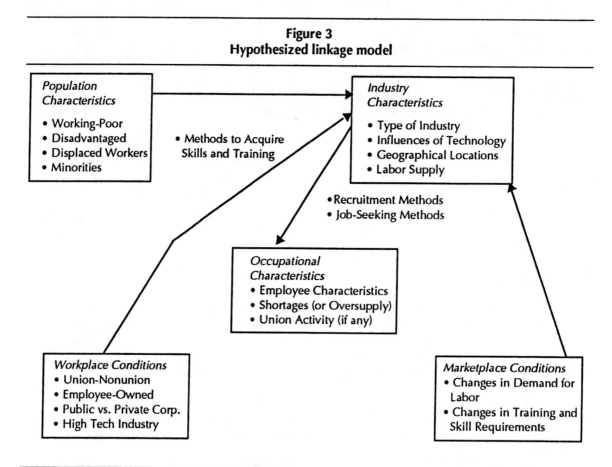

Site Selection Process

Criteria used to select sites for analyses included evidence of linking job training with economic development efforts in order to produce sustained positive outcomes including documentable job creation, successful assistance to small businesses, and a solid record placing entry-level (i.e., JTPA-eligible) persons in jobs. A site had to include the joint actions of two or more service providers (including community colleges) in which either different organizations collaborated or a single organization linked the activities of different service providers. A total of five sites are reported on from this study as follows:

—The Pima County Community Services Agency—the JTPA operating agency (Tucson, Ariz.) and Pima Community College. Pima County, Arizona covers 9420 sq. miles including two Indian reservations. It has a population of 700,000 which includes the major city of Tucson. Involved in this interorganizational collaboration are county and city economic development agencies, the private industry council (PIC), the Tucson Economic Development Corporation, and the Pima Community College, among others.

—The Susquehanna Region Private Industry Council, Inc. (SRPIC) (Havre de Grace, Md.) and Harford Community College and Cecil Community College. Harford County and Cecil County, Maryland, have populations of 163,000 and 70,000 respectively, and comprise the region northwest of the city of Baltimore.

—Greater Grand Rapids Economic Area Team (Grand Rapids, Mich.) and Grand Rapids Community College. This team consists of over 60 public and private organizations in Kent County. Located in western Michigan, Kent county has a population of 485,000.

—The Seattle-King County Economic Development Council (Seattle, Wash.) and Seattle Community College. The city and county have a combined population of 1.2 million—nearly 1/3 of the state's population.

—The Chester County Partnership for Economic Development, Inc., a 501(c)3 corporation comprised of Chester County government and other quasi-governmental agencies serving West Chester, Pa., and local educational institutions including Chester Community College. Chester County, Pa. is a suburban Philadelphia community of 346,000 people. Figure 4 describes the interorganizational arrangements of this site formed especially to address the issues of regional economic development. These interorganizational arrangements are typical of each of the sites described in this study. At each site, either a PIC or another-for-profit corporation assumed the coordinating role for joint interorganizational activities.

Findings

Institutional Arrangements

Each of the site's interorganizational structures was analyzed to address the first hypothesis that new organizations would be formed for the specific purpose of coordinating joint job training and economic development efforts. Figure 5 shows the target organizations in each case. A new organization had been created at four of the five sites, as only Pima county had a central organization in place earlier than 1983. The new organization had not necessarily been created to support joint activities only. In two cases (Grand Rapids, and Seattle-King County) the new organization was started to administer certain programmatic activities, either training or economic development programs.

Figure 4
An example of a typical interorganizational arrangement—The Chester County, PA site

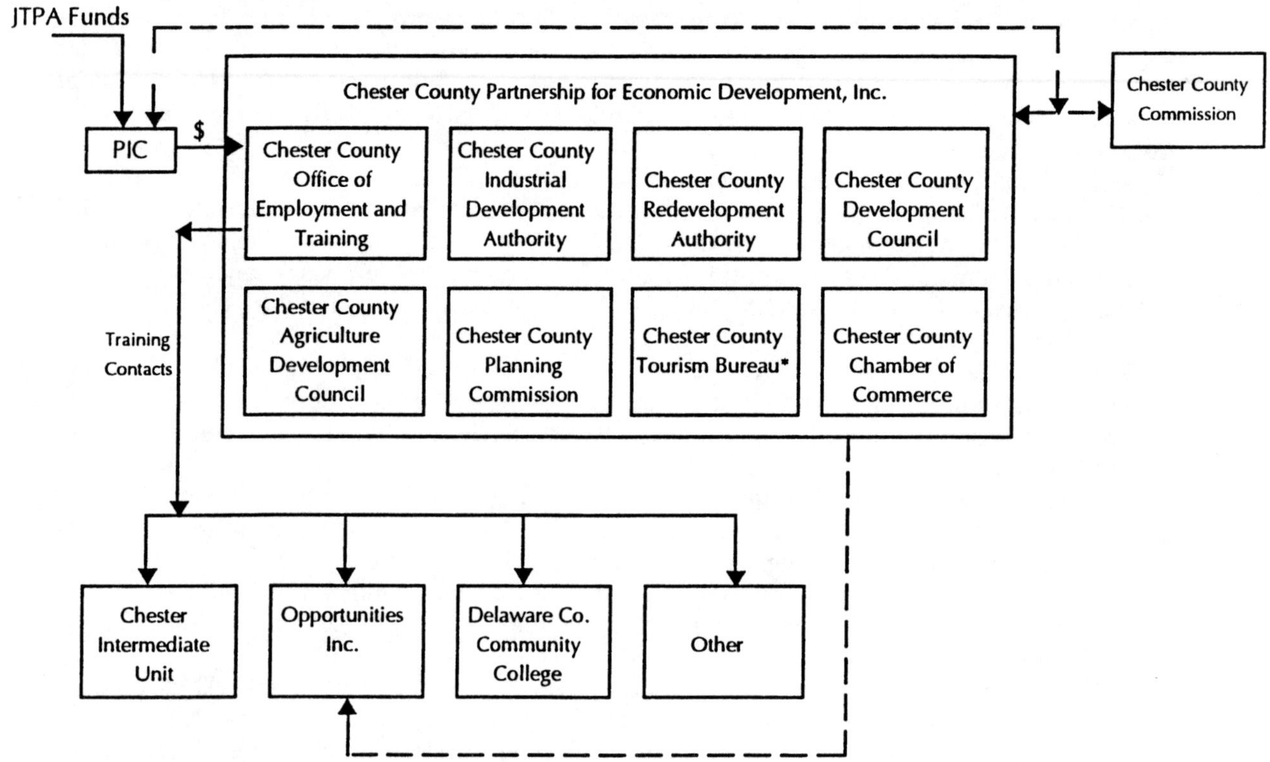

JTPA Funds

Chester County Partnership for Economic Development, Inc.

PIC $

| Chester County Office of Employment and Training | Chester County Industrial Development Authority | Chester County Redevelopment Authority | Chester County Development Council |

| Chester County Agriculture Development Council | Chester County Planning Commission | Chester County Tourism Bureau* | Chester County Chamber of Commerce |

Training Contacts

Chester County Commission

| Chester Intermediate Unit | Opportunities Inc. | Delaware Co. Community College | Other |

*Private, Non-Profit Organization
————▶ -Formal Agreements of Contracts
— —▶ -Overlapping Memberships or Informal Arrangements

Two of the sites had organizations that supported the hypothesis. One was the Susquehanna Region PIC, Inc.—located in Harford and Cecil Counties, Maryland. Unlike most PICs, this one had been founded explicitly for combining job training provided principally through the two community colleges, and economic development efforts, also supported by the colleges. The PIC was precedent-setting in that it also was the first organization to represent a joint effort between two counties including each country's community college—that had not previously collaborated (Figure 4). Finally, the PIC's by-laws included performance-oriented criteria that gave the organization and its staff an innovative, incentive-laden structure despite being a nonprofit organization. In all of these respects, the PIC reflected the type of innovative organization that the researcher thought might be discovered at most of the sites. The other umbrella organization—or "partnership," located in Chester County, PA, whose members consisted of key agencies and the colleges within the county. The partnership was established as a nonprofit organization, allowing it to receive public and private monies. Job training and economic development activities were coordinated at the community college and other training agencies. In this county the PIC served as an advisory body to the partnership. This partnership was the type of innovative organization that the researcher hypothesized might be discovered at most of the sites. (In fact, such a partnership had just been formed in 1988 at a third site—Pima County, Ariz.—which may eventually become responsible for the joint activities.)

Figure 5
Identity of target organizations in each case

	Case 1	Case 2	Case 3	Case 4	Case 5	Case 6
Organization(s) Conbat to the Economic Arrangement	Pima County Community Services Department	Susquehanna Region PIC, Inc.	The Partnership for Economic Development of Chester County, Inc.	Northeast Florida PIC, Inc.	Greater Grand Rapids Economic Area Team (GGREAT)	Seattle King County Development Council
Start Date of Organization	Not a new organization	1983	1984	1984	1984	1985
Other Major Organizations In the Arrangement	Tucson Economic Development Corp. Tucson Local Development Corp.	Two Chambers of Commerce Two Departments of Economic Development	Seven major ED and Job Training agencies in county government (PIC is advisory to JT agency)	Chambers of Commerce and Committees of 100 in five counties	Grand Rapids Area Chamber of Commerce City of Grand Rapids Development Office GRAETC (Job Training Agency—PIC is advisory)	Seattle King County PIC, Inc. Seattle Dept. of Community Development King Co. Dept of Planning and Community Development
Formal Arrangement(s) among the Organizations	• PIC contracts to two ED agencies for ED activities • ED agencies use first source agreements	• PIC contracts to Chamber of Commerce to do ED activites	• PIC contracts to Partnership to do Ed activities • Partnership is umbrella organization; coordinates ED and JT activities of member agencies	• PIC contracts to Chamber of Commerce or Committees of 100 in each county to do ED activities • Extensive first source agreements in one county	• GGREAT contracts to Chamber of Commerce for ED activities • GGREAT contracts to other organizations for ED activities • First source agreements between ED and JT agencies, but does not Include GGREAT	• PIC contracts to EDC for ED activities • PIC enters into formal partnerships with local ED agencies for special projects

Note: Case 4 not reported in this study.

Thus, a single organization appeared to be central to the formal collaborative arrangement at each of the five sites, and in most cases the community college was also an integral part of the formulation of the new collaborative structure. This suggests that new locales may undertake joint job training and economic development efforts without necessarily creating a totally new organization to coordinate these activities, but rather to suggest a new role for the community college to play in serving as a catalyst for integrating other local agencies and activities into such a collaborative.

Core organizations in the formal arrangement. Usually tied to the target organization was a small group of collaborating organizations including the community college. Depending upon whether the target organization was itself a PIC or an economic development agency, the core organizations could include: an economic development agency (whether part of the local government or not); a chamber of commerce or committee of 100 (two or more where multiple jurisdictions were collaborating); and other job training agencies. The actions of these collaborating organizations are usually formally bound through contractual agreements, or as a result of the arrangement itself (e.g., a partnership arrangement).

Job creation outcomes. To assess the effects of the inteorganizational arrangements on economic development (job creation) and training outcomes, each of the sites in coordination with its community college(s) had estimated the number of new jobs created during a given period based upon local data sources. The results showed significant numbers of new jobs created (around 300–500 or more new jobs each) as a result of new business starts, expansions or reallocations. For example, in Pima County, 110 persons were retrained and placed after a Hughes Aircraft layoff in 1988; this was a result of the close coordination between Pima Community College and the PIC. In Chester County, four (4) incubator projects at the colleges in cooperation with the Partnership led to 77 new jobs. Likewise, the SRPIC provided the impetus for business start or expansions accounting for approximately 875 new jobs in the region.

The Effects of Joint Efforts Linking Outcomes with Arrangements

The preceding has indicated the extent to which all sites had similar interorganizatinal arrangements involving a community college(s) which resulted in exemplary job training and economic development-job creation outcomes. This leads to three possible conclusions:

- That the arrangements may serve to produce a long-term and site-specific capability in economic development and therefore are worthy of replication by other community colleges at sites across the country;

- That the strength of the arrangements rests on informal rather than formal ties;

- That the arrangements did have an effect on the outcomes, but that the establishment of a definitive relationship is impossible to create, due mainly to the difficulties of attributing any job outcomes to a particular initiative. Figure 6 summarizes the nature of the joint efforts that were documented.

Overall, the evidence showed that all five arrangements involving community colleges were active in supporting the types of joint efforts that would have plausibly led to some of the job creation outcomes and that would have linked job training outcomes to them. In this sense, although the exact impact could not be assessed, the interorganizational arrangements were considered causally linked to the outcomes.

Figure 6
Examples of joint efforts at each site

	Case 1 Pima County Community Services Dept.	Case 2 Susquahanna Region PIC Inc.	Case 3 Chester County Partnership for ED, Inc.	Case 4 Northeast Florida PIC, Inc.	Case 5 Greater Grand Rapids Economic Area Team	Case 6 Seattle King County EDC
Programs or Projects	First source agreements Roundtables	Long-term marketing campaign Community college adoption of ED objectives (#4)	ED task forces Attracting new jobs to replace loss of Lukens Steel jobs (#7)	ED task force in one county (#1) First source agreements Joint presentations to prospective employers Fundraising drive county (#5) Expansion of voclech in response to ED needs in one county (#6)	Marketing program State-Supported development programs	Program to assist businesses to get Dod contracts (#3) Program to identify local suppliers of goods and services bought elsewhere (#4) Downtown development project (#1)
Small Business (#6)	Use of SBA loans	Small business development center	Four separate Incubator projects (#2) Revolving loan fund Entrepreneurship workshops (#5) Assistance to women-owned business (#4)	Small business center in one county SBA loans Project for dislocated workers to start own business (#2) College consortium to help small business (#1)	Entrepreneurship forum Small business center	Incubator programs Small business center

Number in parentheses, after each vignette, refers to vignette number in each case study.
Note: Case 4 not reported in this paper.

Model Implications

Evidence exists to show that interorganizational arrangements involving community colleges provide an important capability for dealing with economic development over an extended period of time. These arrangements are desirable because they include specific projects and programs, but they go beyond these individual efforts and produce a longer-term capability in economic development.

A first level for analyzing the model is direct and simple, in which joint efforts will hopefully lead to both job creation and job training outcomes. First the economic development activity leads to the creation of new jobs; second, the new jobs are entry-level jobs. Most of the joint efforts cited were intended to follow this model. However, this direct model oversimplifies marketplace reality, as economic development activities are likely to lead to new jobs at entry level and at higher positions.

Planning Model

The direct model can be modified to account for the fact that economic development activities cannot necessarily be implemented immediately in all situations. In some cases, as was encountered in Harford and Cecil Counties, an economic development organization first needed to be established and staffed, and then in turn could plan and implement the economic development activities through its various participating organizations including the two community colleges. In some situations this initial organizational step can be complicated and time-consuming (Pressman & Wildavsky, 1973). Figure 7 describes this planning step in the direct model.

In the Harford and Cecil Counties case an example is development of a small business information and assistance center at Cecil Community College, and the activation of the chamber of commerce in Cecil County, which had not previously been staffed.

Figure 7
The planning model

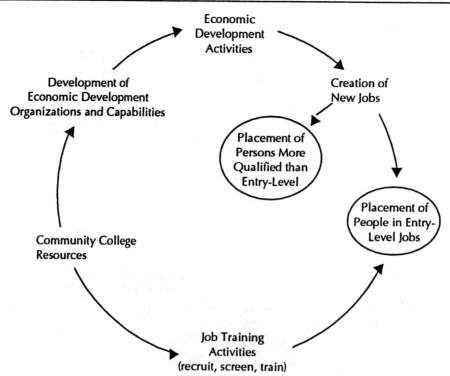

Planning and Development Model

A final additional complication arises as the economic development process can involve an extended sequence of economic development activities over a long period of time, in which job creation may only occur toward the end of the sequence. Figure 8 shows this complication. For a totally undeveloped rural area, as was found in several areas within most of the sites, the relevant economic development activities may include zoning or land preparation activities, infrastructure construction, commercial or residential development, and finally job creation and training. Of course, some jobs (e.g., construction) can be created in support of the development activities themselves; but these are only transitional jobs for the area in question.

Figure 8
The planning and development model

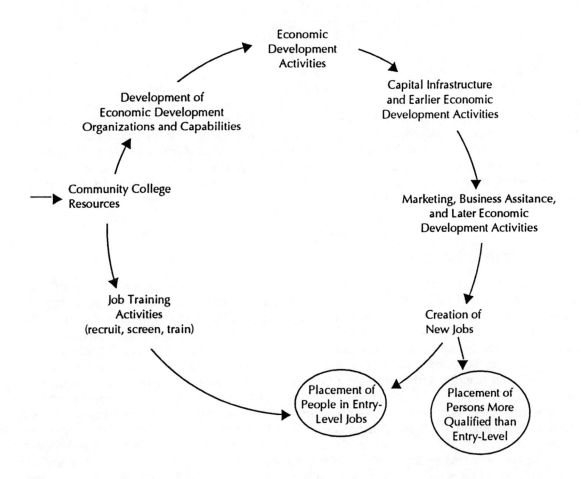

The Community College as a Focal Point for Economic Development

Community colleges can solidify interorganizational arrangements involving job training and community economic development, thus maximizing the resource potential of bringing together the three traditionally parallel local delivery systems—i.e., the economic development system, the job training system, and the education system (see Figure 1).

Progression through these phases of economic development may in fact require a decade or more of time. During such time, the existence of the community college in the interorganizational arrangement is likely to provide the continuity needed to initiate and support the necessarily wide variety of economic development activities. For example, the arrangement can call upon different sources such as college faculty consultation for small business development, and seek project or program support for different phases, depending upon the nature of the need. However, a single project or program alone might be too rigid to sustain this flexibility and adaptiveness over long periods of time.

The ability of an interorganizational arrangement to support a variety of planning and development activities, as might be appropriate for different kinds of communities over time, is a major benefit of the arrangement. Having such an arrangement means that: (a) a site will be able to seek support from a variety of sponsors often through or in conjunction with the community college for a variety of activities, thereby increasing the resourcefulness and adaptiveness of the site; (b) the site also might then be able to progress through an initial, capacity-building phase during which new organizations might have to be created, which would be especially relevant for sites who are just starting economic development activities for the first time; and (c) the site also would be able to implement a diverse array of economic development activities over time, tuned to the advancement of the economic development process, and ultimately leading to job creation outcomes.

Therefore, to the extent that the planning and development model is relevant to a site's needs, or to the extent that economic development is viewed as a sustained process over time, and not just a one-shot effort, the more likely a site will benefit from having an inteorganizational arrangement of the sort found in the five cases studies.

The Importance of Informal Communication Ties in Making Arrangements Work

A final issue was to examine the source of strength of the arrangement. The preliminary hypothesis was that informal networks rather than formal agreements were the important ingredient in making an arrangement successful. The bulk of the evidence supported this hypothesis. The most common agreement was a contractual relationship between a PIC and some other organization commissioned to carry out economic development activities. Only one site, Pima County, had first-source agreements as counterparts to PIC contracts. At the other three sites (Harford and Cecil Counties, Chester County, and Seattle-King County), no first-source agreements existed. Grand Rapids had no PIC contracts for economic development but did have a first-source agreement.

Aside from these contracts for economic development, no substantial interorganizational agreements were found. Further, Chester County's Partnership arrangement was the only umbrella organization in which multiple organizations would be tied together through a membership structure. No evidence existed of other possible forms of agreements such as mandates to collaborate, interagency agreements, or any similar device suggested by the hypothesized motives for interorganizational collaboration. The resulting conclusion was that the working of the interorganizational arrangements could not have depended upon formal agreements.

Richness of Informal Networks. In contrast, extensive examples were found of overlapping memberships among the board members, officers, and other key positions of the various organizations at all sites. Given these overlapping memberships, an important ingredient was the extent of communication among the key individuals at a site, and the degree to which information about job training or economic development was shared. The presidents of both community colleges were principal members of the SRPIC. Interestingly, continuity of board leadership initially considered a critical aspect of successful networks, was not found in two of the five cases (Chester County and Seattle-King County), where annual or bi-annual rotation was the routine practice. While found in other cases, this feature was therefore not considered essential to the overall observation regarding the richness of informal communications. The key individuals appear to stay in contact regardless of the continuity of board leadership.

Conclusions and Recommendations

This study focused on interorganizational arrangements involving community colleges as an innovative way of creating exemplary job training and job creation outcomes. Such arrangements have not been examined closely in the past, and the study therefore attempted to determine the benefits from these arrangements. The major conclusions were that:

- These arrangements were associated with exemplary outcomes at all five sites;

- These arrangements produced important benefits to the sites, primarily in providing for a flexible and adaptive capability for dealing with the prolonged period of time required by the economic development process; and

- These arrangements are therefore recommended as possible mechanisms for other (but not all) sites across the country.

Future Prospects

Further arguments can be made with regard to the advantages and disadvantages of having these arrangements. Among the important advantages, the arrangements may represent a solid first step in producing initial collaboration among the three parallel delivery systems (the economic development system, the employment system, and the education system). At all sites, the arrangements produced (or coincided with) extensive informal communications among the leaders of the organizations in these delivery systems (e.g., local community college, chamber of commerce, and job training agency), regarding possible opportunities for job creation and job training. Service contracts by the JTPA program already meant that the employment system was being linked with community colleges and other key components of the education system; the extension to economic development activities, often a result of further contracts by the PIC to some economic development entity such as a chamber of commerce, facilitated the collaborative pattern even further. In the long run, the separate delivery systems may collaborate even more closely, and this cannot help but create a more effective use of available resources within all three systems. A further advantage evolves from the flexible and adaptive nature of the interorganizational arrangements, and their ability to focus on a broad variety of policy initiatives. Because the arrangements include multiple organizations and multiple activities, they also may be adaptive in surviving unexpected turnover among organizations or programs. In this sense, the arrangements may be providing a forum for communication among the key leaders of a community, independent of specific initiatives. Such a resource is bound to be beneficial to local communities.

The presumed disadvantages also must be considered. The interorganizational arrangement may not be worth the cost and effort if a site's objective is to meet the needs of a specific economic development or job training problem. If such specific problems have been clearly identified, and if the desire is only to deal with them, the initiation of a specific project or program may be the more appropriate (and quicker) response than nurturing the formation of an interorganizational arrangement.

A further suspicion is that this type of interorganizational arrangement may also only work best in small to medium-sized communities. The amount of impact leveraged by an initial economic development outlay from PIC funds, generally $50,000 or less, will be more visible and attract serious attention in such communities. In addition, the arrangements may become too cumbersome and even bureaucratic in larger communities having a multiplicity of organizations, activities, and key individuals.

A final limitation on interorganizational arrangements is related to the interpersonal relationships within the leaders of a community. Where such leaders want to collaborate, the provision of external funds and the availability of program mandates will certainly help to produce strong interorganizational arrangements. However, if such leaders do not want to collaborate or have antagonistic relationships in the past, no extent of external resources or mandates is likely to make an arrangement work.

Summary

Interorganizational arrangements are joint efforts characterized by participation of community-based organizations, community colleges, economic development organizations, governmental agencies (such as those responsible for job training, economic development, agricultural development, etc.), civic groups, and chambers of commerce. Often, the coordinating role is through a partnership or other type of "umbrella organizations" whose board consists of representatives of other organizations, and not just a set of individuals.

Just as a programmatic activity includes single events, interorganizational arrangements can include multiple programs and a wide array of events. The fact that the arrangement is among organizations is associated with the hope that the joint efforts can be more sustained over time, independent of the success of any single organization, program, or event. The interorganizational arrangement can create new organizations, new partnerships, or nonprofit organizations should the need arise.

References

Armington, C., & Odle, M. (1982). Small business—how many jobs? *Brookings Review*, Winter, 1, 1–4.

Benson, J. K. (1975). The interorganizational network as a political economy. *Administrative Science Quarterly*, 20, 229–249.

Birch, D. L., & MacCracken, S. (1982). *The small business share of job creation—Lessons learned from the use of a longitudinal file*. Cambridge, MA: Massachusetts Institute of Technology, Program on Neighborhood and Regional Change.

Butler, S. M. (1981). *Enterprise zones: Greening the inner cities*. New York: Universe Books.

Burger, L. T. (1988). A statewide model for a systematic community college economic development program. *Journal of Studies in Technical Careers*, 19, 157–165.

Cantor, J. A., Yin, R. K., Bateman, P. C., Vaughan, R., Lande, S. & Dain, D. (1989). *Interorganizational Partnerships in Local Job Creation and Job Training Efforts: Six Case Studies*. Final Report prepared for the U. S. Department of Labor, Employment and Training Administration, under Contract no. 99–8–4700–75–064–01. Washington, D. C.: Cosmos Corporation.

Charner, I., & Gold, G. (1987). Building effective business/higher education partnerships for economic development. *Community Services CATALST, XVII*, (1) 20–23.

Goodlad, J. I. (1975). *The dynamics of educational change: Toward responsive schools.* New York: McGraw Hill.

Hall, R. H. et al. (1978). Interorganizational coordination in the delivery of human services. In L. Karpik (Ed.), *Organization and environment* (pp. 293–321). Beverly Hills, CA: Sage Publications.

Holdsworth, R. W. (1987). No shrinking violet. *Community and Junior College Journal, 55*, (3) 24–27.

Kingry, L., & Cole, L. (1985). The role of Oregon community colleges in economic development. *Community College Review, 13*, (2) 11–17.

Levine, S., & White, P. E. (1961). Exchange as a conceptual framework for the study of interorganizational relationships. *Administrative Science Quarterly, 5*, 420–583.

McNett, I. (1988). The development triangle: Community college assistance for economic growth. *Education-Economic Development Series #6*. Washington., D. C.: Northeast-Midwest Institute, Center for Regional Policy.

Mier, R. (1982). Enterprise zones: A long shot. *Planning*, April, 10–14.

Mihelich, A. L. (1988). The community college as economic development center. *Journal of Studies in Technical Careers, 10*, 171–177.

Mundhenk, R. T. (1988). Community colleges as catalysts in economic development. *Journal of Studies in Technical Careers, X*, (2) 107–116.

Pressman, J. L., & Wildavsky, A. (1937). *Implementation: How great expectations in Washington are dashed in Oakland*. Berkeley, CA: University of California Press.

Sanders (1988). Economic development: Commitment, communication, and coordination. *Journal of Studies in Technical Careers, X*, (2) 117–124.

State of Illinois. (1986). *Economic development grant report-Fiscal year 1986*. Springfield, Ill. Illinois Community College Board.

U. S. Small Business Administration. (1985). *The state of small business: A report to the president*. Washington., D. C.

U. S. Government Printing Office. (1983). Small business dynamics and methods for measuring job creation. *In The State of Small Business: A Report of the President* (pp. 61–68). Washington, D. C.

Van de Ven, A. H. (1976). On the nature, formation, and maintenance of relations among organizations. *Academy of Management Review, 3*, 24–36.

Zimmer (1988). Stimulating economic development through job training. *Bluegrass State Skills Corporation Monograph*.

Suggested Readings:
Programs and Services

Andrews, H. A. and Marshall, R. P. (Summer, 1991). "Challenging High-School Honor Students with Community College Courses." *Community College Review*, 19 (1), 47–51.

Bender, L. W. (1990). *Spotlight in the Transfer Function: A National Study of State Policies and Practices.* Washington, D.C.: American Association of Community and Junior Colleges.

Clowes, D. A. and Toroles, D. (1985). "Community and Junior College Journal: Lessons from Fifty Years." *Community and Junior College Journal.* 56 (1), 28–32.

Eaton, J. S. (1984). "Tapping Neglected Leadership Sources." *New Directions for Community Colleges,* 12 (2), 93–99.

Gottschalk, K. (1978). "Can Colleges Deal With-High Risk Proxblems?" *Community College Frontiers,* 6 (4), 4–11.

Grubb, W. N. (1984). "The Bandwagon Once More: Vocational Preparation for High-Tech Occupations." *Harvard Educational Review,* 54 (4), 429–451.

Harris, N. C. and Grede, J. (1977). *Career Education in Colleges A Guide for Planning Two- and Four-Year Occupational Programs for Successful Employment.* San Francisco: Jossey-Bass. (Chapter 4). 64–100.

Knoell, D. M. (1990) Transfer, Articulation and Collaboration: Twenty-Five Years Later. The Report of a Research Project Funded by the Ford Foundation. Washington, D.C.: American Association of Community and Junior Colleges.

McCabe, R. H. (1981). "Now Is the Time To Reform the American Community College." *Community and Junior College Journal,* 51 (8), 6–10.

McCartan, A. (1983). "The Community College Mission: Present Challenges and Future Visions." *Journal of Higher Education,* 54 (6), 76–92.

Moore, K. (1986). "Assessment of Institutional Effectiveness." *New Directions for Community Colleges,* 14 (4), 49–60.

Oakes, J. (May 1983). "Limiting Opportunity: Student Race and Curricular Differences in Secondary Vocational Education." *American Journal of Education,* 91 (3), 328–55.

Palmer, J. C. (Feb/March 1992). "Implementing Student Tracking Systems: Concepts and Issues." *Community, Technical, and Junior College Journal,* 62 (4), 14–19.

Shaw, R. (1989). "Curriculum Change in the Community College" in O'Banion, Terry (ed.), *Innovation in the Community College.* New York: American Council on Education, Macmillan.

Vaughan, G. B. (Spring, 1991). "Institutions on the Edge: America's Community Colleges." *Educational Record,* 72 (2), 30–33.

THE STUDENTS

The Way We Are:
The Community College
as American Thermometer

CLIFFORD ADELMAN

Introduction

Three decades ago, as the distinctive American phenomenon then known as the "junior college" was on the verge of transformation as a type of organization, Burton Clark offered a challenging criticism of its role in our society (Clark, 1960a; 1960b). In his analysis, the junior college played a "cooling out" function. That is, it took whoever entered its doors and tracked them out of the mainstream of social mobility in the United States. It froze their ambitions. It chilled their minds. It iced them with remedial courses. It cut them off from the economic benefits of a society that paid well not only for a Bachelor's degree but for a Bachelor's degree from the right schools that provided the right connections. In an era when those schools and connections meant more than they do today, the junior college was a backwater that reflected but dimly the mission of higher education, and offered, more dimly still, the promise of upward mobility. This happened not by the design of junior college administrators and trustees, but as a by-product of the higher education system. My hyperbolic description of Clark's work notwithstanding, and even though the analysis was drawn from a study of a single junior college in California, Clark was very insightful and credible at the time.

When the Higher Education Act was passed in 1965, there were 654 2-year colleges in the United States, 30% of the total number of institutions of higher education. Two decades later, there were 1,350 2-year colleges, constituting 40% of all institutions of higher education. Very few were called "junior colleges" any more. In 1965, these institutions enrolled 20% of all students at all levels of higher education, including graduate and professional school, and 24% of all first-time college freshmen. Two decades later, the figures were 37% and 44%, respectively (Snyder, 1989). These are official approximate numbers. When a type of institution grows that rapidly in a specific economy or market, its identity and role are likely to change. The climate may even become somewhat warmer. The people who attend may, in fact, define the mainstream.

Most of the growth in the community college sector of U.S. higher education took place in the first decade following passage of the Higher Education Act. The subjects of this monograph, members of the high school class of 1972, graduated from high school toward the end of this steep trajectory. Their use and experience of the community college over the following decade, I propose, can serve as a thermometer of what this institution has become, can tell us, indeed, whether Clark's temperature reading still holds. And to the extent to which people from the Class of '72 who attended community colleges are representative of the Class as a whole, their experience may be emblematic of the ways in which we Americans use other normative institutions such as those of religion and the arts. If so, the accounts laid forth in this study may say much about the way we are.

I. The Question and the Method

This study asks a series of questions about a large group of individuals who associated themselves with a particular type of educational institution, and, through that association, about the role of that institution in our culture. To be sure, this is a limited definition of institutional role. It does not account for the service roles these institutions play in local communities, the economic roles they play in regional labor markets, or the faculties, finances, and governance that influence and shape these other roles (in the matter of community colleges, Breneman and Nelson, 1981). And despite appearances, this definition precludes precise measurements of the economic efficiency of community colleges (Nunley and Breneman, 1988).

Despite appearances, too, this approach to the role of community colleges is not framed in terms of arguments (deriving from Clark's "cooling out" thesis) over whether they promote or hinder access to higher education, whether their principal role is to prepare students for transfer to 4-year colleges, or whether they act as self-interested institutions more than responsive institutions (Folger, H. Astin, and Bayer, 1970; Karabel, 1972; Alba and Lavin, 1981; Cohen and Brawer, 1982; Grubb, 1988; Richardson, 1988; Brint and Karabel, 1989). These issues will inevitably arise, but only after we read the record.

The problem with the traditional arguments about the role of the community college is that they subordinate the experience of individuals to larger constructs of social class and status or economic power. These arguments assume that our lives are characterized by order and continuity, and that whatever happens to us has a clear origin, hence an absolute cause. Details, differences, disorder, and discontinuities are not part of this structuralism, and are often swept under the rug. The possibility that individuals and groups can use institutions in the course of making their own history is not admissible. The possibility that patterns and textures of human experience could tell us more than origins and causes is unthinkable to those for whom the superstructures of class and status are all powerful.

But what if an archaeologist of the 25th century stumbled upon the ancient binary remains of the National Longitudinal Study of the High School Class of 1972 (NLS–72)? This massive archive followed a single generation for 14 years with detailed surveys, included high school records and test scores, and, most importantly, gathered the college transcripts of those who attended any kind of postsecondary institution between 1972 and 1984. Watching individuals leave their traces on this archive over and over again, like a palimpsest, what could that archaeologist say about the community college as an institution? And what could that person say about people who attended community colleges, and the patterns and textures of their relationship to the institution? Indeed, patterns and textures govern this account, not superstructures, despite the socioeconomic vocabulary of "earnings," "occupation," and "educational attainment" that are built into government-sponsored surveys such as those of NLS–72.

The record the archaeologist would discover, of course, is hardly complete. One of the principal artifacts on which I rely, a transcript, contains limited information about what students do in an institution. The transcript does not record extra-curricular activities or non-intellective aspects of maturation that we all hope result from participation in postsecondary education. In this case, transcripts also tell us little about the environment of community colleges (see London, 1978), changing attitudes of community college students (see deArmas & McDavis, 1981), the commitments community college students make to their institutions (Stage, 1988), or student involvement that Astin (1984) defined as the amount and quality of effort students devote to learning—all of which influence student progress and attainment to various degrees.

In these contexts, however, and provided they are accurate,[1] transcripts provide a strong link between the circumstances of individuals and groups prior to postsecondary education and their circumstances, activities, and attitudes after postsecondary education. Not cause, but link. They reflect, too, the links between individual choice behavior and both the constraints and possibilities of the institution. The NLS–72 Postsecondary Education Transcript Sample (hereafter referred to as NLS/PETS) provides stronger links in this regard because it covers 12 years of student history and can trace students across state lines and across temporal gaps in attendance. Studies confined to individual institutions or state systems and for shorter periods of time (e.g., Alba and Lavin, 1981) cannot do this.

Others have used the NLS–72 surveys to analyze the careers of community college students (e.g., Breneman and Nelson, 1981; Anderson, 1981; Velez, 1985; Pascarella, 1986; Nunley and Breneman, 1988), or to understand who attends community colleges within the first two years of high school graduation (Alexander, Holupka, and Pallas, 1987). But the difference between the survey and transcript data is so significant as to call such analyses into question. For example, Cohen (1988) says that only 825 NLS–72 students enrolled directly in community colleges following high school graduation. Tinto (1987) says 815, Velez and Javalgi (1987) say 1,407, and Grubb (1991)—who presumably used the transcripts—never says.[2] I tried to figure out where these figures came from in the survey data, and gave up. The cleaned NLS/PETS transcripts, on the other hand, show 2,867 students enrolling in community colleges at any time in 1972 (and 2,426 in September alone), the year they graduated from high school. The differences in these figures are too great for comfort. Transcripts may be difficult to interpret at times and occasionally are missing key pieces of data, but they neither exaggerate nor forget.

- Who used the community college?

- When (at what distance from high school graduation, for how long, in relation to attendance at other types of postsecondary institutions)?

- What did they study?

- What credentials did they earn both from the community college and other institutions (and when)?

- What happened to them in the labor market?

These are the basic questions of the data into which we are about to plunge.

To make full sense of these questions, it is important to include in the analysis those who did not continue their education at all after high school. Unlike the other monographs in this collection,[3] then, let alone studies produced on both sides of the "cooling out" debate, this study pays attention to what journalistic shorthand calls "non-college youth."

II. The Story Told by These Data

Let's swim through the data, take the temperature readings, then step back and ask what those readings say about the way we are.

Demographics and Attendance Patterns

The question, "Who attends community colleges in our society?"—like the question, "Who goes to church or to museums?"—is not so simple. The question of who attends cannot be divorced from an understanding of how they attend, and I have rarely met a study that addressed this issue in any terms other than full-time/part-time or completed/dropped out.

Because they cover 12 years of the life of a generation, the postsecondary transcripts of NLS/ PETS teach us that there are at least two other ways of describing attendance patterns. The first includes only those people who continued their education after high school, and uses community colleges as the principal reference point. Let's call this framework, the Community College Attendance Pattern.

The second encompasses all students who were seniors in high school in the spring of 1972, and uses credentials earned as its principal reference point. For convenience, let's call this second framework the General Postsecondary Attendance Pattern.

The Community College Attendance Pattern

For purposes of understanding how people attended community colleges, I used a "cascading" logic involving credits earned at different types of institutions, degrees (Associate's and Bachelor's) earned, dates of degrees, and dates of first and last attendance.[4] This logic yielded 10 attendance patterns. For the 12,332 students in the sample whose postsecondary transcript records indicated any earned credits, these patterns are (percentages of students in each category are weighed[5]):

1. Transfer with two degrees.   3.4%

    Students in this group earned both an Associate's degree from a community college and a Bachelor's degree from another kind of institution (4-year college, theological school, 4-year technical college, school of art or design, etc.), and earned the Associate's degree before the Bachelor's. The small number of students who earned the Associate's degree *after* the Bachelor's are in category #10. Students who earned Associate's degrees from 4-year colleges are also in category #10.

2. Transfer With One Degree, the Bachelor's.   3.3%

    Students in this group earned more than 10 credits from a community college but no Associate's degree, and a Bachelor's degree from a 4-year college. They also attended the community college prior to receiving the BA.

3. Transfer With One Degree, the Associate's.   1.7%

    Students in this group earned an Associate's degree from a community college, and more than 10 credits from a 4-year college, but did not complete the Bachelor's degree.

4. Terminal Associate's Degree.   5.7%

    Students in this category earned an Associate's degree from a community college. The few who also attended a 4-year college (prior, concurrent, or subsequently), earned 10 or fewer credits from that type of institution, that is, at best, they were "incidental" 4-year college students.

5. No Degree, 2-Year and 4-Year, Non-Incidental.   2.7%

    Students in this category attended both community colleges and 4-year institutions, earned more than 10 credits from each type, but never earned any degree, Associate's or Bachelor's. They were "non-incidental" attendees at *both* types of institutions.

    Slightly more than half of these students attended the community college before enrolling in a 4-year institution, and, technically, are also "transfer" students. The balance are known in the community college literature as "reverse transfers," that is, they entered the 4-year college first and subsequently enrolled in a 2-year college.

6. No Degree, Non-Incidental, 2-Year Only.   15.6%

Students in this category earned more than 10 credits from a community college, but no AA or BA degree. If they also attended a 4-year college, they earned 10 or fewer credits from that institution, that is, they were "non-incidental" attendees at community colleges and "incidental" 4-year college students.

7. No Degree, Incidental, 2-Year.   7.6%

Students in this category earned 10 or fewer credits from a community college, and no degree. Only 4% of them attended other kinds of institutions as well, but also earned 10 or fewer credits from those institutions.

8. No Community College, but 4-Year College.   49.3%

This large slice of the NLS/PETS sample consists of students who attended only 4-year colleges. Within this group, there are six other patterns of attendance and degree attainment. But since none of them refer to the community college, they need not be elaborated here.[6]

9. No Community College, No 4-Year College.   6.7%

Ninety-six percent of the students in this category attended proprietary trade schools, Area Vocational-Technical Institutes or specialized institutions such as hospital schools of nursing, radiologic technology, etc.

10. Other Patterns.   4.1%

This is a residual category for cases that do not fit in the previous nine categories. Some students in this category, for example, earned Associate's degrees from institutions other than community colleges, and may also have earned Bachelor's degrees. Some earned Bachelor's degrees but took a course or two at a community college—either before or after the degree. Some are missing transcript data (credits, grades, dates of attendance, etc.) that might have placed them elsewhere.

The reader will notice the implicit definition of "transfer" in the logic of this first set of attendance patterns. It is a restricted definition with two components: an earned degree (Associate's, Bachelor's or both) and an earned credit threshold (more than 10). I have previously used the "more than 10 credit" threshold (Adelman, 1990a, 1990b, 1991) to describe those who made a commitment to postsecondary education of at least one semester or its equivalent over a period of 12 years. The threshold was derived from analyses of credit production for the entire NLS/PETS sample, and is applied to commitment at any one type of institution. Under this definition, it is insufficient merely to enroll: you have to make a go of it. A transfer is thus not a transfer unless a sufficient (non-incidental) commitment was made to both types of institutions.

If this definition of "transfer" was loosened by not requiring earned degrees, then some students in the 5th attendance pattern ("No Degree, 2-Year and 4-Year, Non-Incidental") would be included, namely those who entered the community college before they enrolled in a 4-year college.

Comparing the restricted and loosened definitions of "transfer," we find the following total percentage of NLS/PETS students transferring over 12 years:

Universe:	Transfer: restricted	Transfer: loosened
All NLS/PETS (12,599)	8.1%	9.5%
Community college attendees (5,708)	18.9	22.2
Attendees earning more than 10 credits from community colleges (4,115)	25.3	29.5

While transfer is a major concern of the literature and ideology of community colleges, "transfer" is treated here as an umbrella term for textures of attendance involving two different types of institutions, textures that (depending on how one defines the universe of students) cover roughly 30% of community college attendees. As the first set of 10 attendance patterns demonstrates, the "transfer" patterns are significant, but hardly exhaustive.

I will refer to these 10 patterns frequently throughout this study and its tables. But they are somewhat difficult to follow—and not always enlightening—when considering questions broader than community college attendance.

General Postsecondary Attendance Patterns

Particularly when comparing the background characteristics and labor market experience of community college students both to 4-year college students and those who did not continue their education after high school, we need a second way of describing attendance patterns: a seven-category configuration, as follows, for the full NLS–72 sample of 22,652 (percentages, as always, are weighted):

1. Transfer With a Bachelor's Degree.   3.7%

    Students in this group attended both 2- and 4-year colleges, entering the 2-year college first, and ultimately earning a Bachelor's degree. They may or may not have earned an Associate's degree along the way. Those who didn't, earned more than 10 credits from the 2-year college.

2. Terminal Associate's Degree.   4.2%

    Students in this group earned an Associate's Degree from a community college, but no higher degree. Some 22.7% of the people in this group also earned more than 10 credits from 4-year colleges.

3. No Degree/Non-Incidental.   10.1%

    These students never earned any degree, but attended 2-year colleges where they earned more than 10 credits. Some 14.3% of this group also earned more than 10 credits from 4-year schools.

4. Proprietary/Vocational or Incidental.   7.8%

    This category covers students who either attended proprietary/vocational schools only *or* enrolled in 2-year colleges but earned 10 or fewer credits from those institutions. The rationale for putting these two groups together is that, compared with other groups, they both spent very little time in postsecondary institutions. For example, 65% of the proprietary/vocational school students and 61% of the incidental community college attendees were enrolled for less than 6 months over a 12-year period.

5. Four-Year/Other, With Bachelor's Degree.   19.1%

This category covers those who either attended only 4-year colleges *or* whose postsecondary attendance patterns are not accounted for by the other patterns but who earned a Bachelor's degree.

6. Four-Year/Other, Without Bachelor's Degree.   11.3%

This category covers students who met the same conditions as in #5, but who did *not* earn a Bachelor's degree. Some of them earned Associate's degrees from 4-year colleges or specialty schools.

7. None.   43.9%

To the best of our knowledge,[7] these students did not enroll in any kind of postsecondary institution between high school graduation in 1972 and the fall of 1984, when they were 30 or 31 years old.

What do we see in the demographics of the people who continued their education after high school and who fit the various attendance categories described under both the Community College Attendance Pattern and the General Postsecondary Attendance Pattern? The following observations are based on Tables 1 through 4:

- Despite the greater ethnic diversity of the community college student population, blacks from the Class of '72 were far less likely to use the community college in their postsecondary education than Hispanics, and no more likely than whites. This is hardly a new observation (see Alexander, Holupka, and Pallas, 1987; Cohen, 1988). Yet somehow the popular mythology persists that a majority of black college students attend community colleges. That simply was not true for the NLS–72 cohort. Nor does it appear to be true for more recent cohorts (Alsalam and Rodgers, 1991). Observed from a slightly different perspective: of the major minority groups, over time, blacks are the least likely to attend community colleges.

  The reason seems obvious. Some 53% of the black college students in the NLS/PETS sample graduated from high schools in the 17-state southern region (v. 27% of all students in the sample), and most of the Historically Black Colleges (HBCs)—almost all of which are 4-year schools—are in that 17-state region. It has been demonstrated previously (Astin, 1982) that blacks residing in the South prefer to attend HBCs.

- Students from second-language backgrounds exhibited attendance and degree attainment patterns very similar to those for students from English-speaking households. In fact, they were slightly more likely to continue their education after high school (57.5% to 56%).

  These phenomena seem odd for two reasons. First, Hispanics are more likely to attend community colleges than members of other ethnic groups, and, as Table 4 indicates, more than a third of the Hispanics in the PETS sample came from non-English-speaking households.[8] Secondly, among students from second language backgrounds who entered postsecondary education, the proportion from the lowest SES quartile is double what it is among students from English-speaking households. Since community colleges serve a higher percentage of low SES students than do 4-year colleges, we would again expect to find a concentration of second language background students in the community college attendance patterns.

But among the universe of second-language students in the NLS/PETS, only 18% were Hispanic. Three out of four were either white or Asian-American, and their attendance patterns balance out those of Hispanic students.

- Women who attended community colleges were more likely than men to earn terminal Associate's degrees, and less likely than men to use the community college as a way station on the road to the Bachelor's degree. As previously demonstrated (Adelman, 1991), women in the generation of NLS–72 were less likely than men to continue their education after high school, but among those who did continue, women were more likely than men to earn credentials.

- Community colleges served a higher proportion of NLS–72 students from low and (particularly) medium SES backgrounds than did 4-year colleges, but a lower proportion than did proprietary and trade schools (see Table 3). In fact, in terms of socioeconomic status, it was the medium-range student in the Class of '72 who was most likely to attend a community college.

  However, there is no question that the critical community college attendance categories encompassing "no degree" students and terminal Associate's degree students house a higher proportion of people from low SES backgrounds than do other attendance categories (Table 3).

The basic demography (race, sex, socioeconomic status), then, both challenges and confirms popular mythology. This demography may turn out to be slightly different for the next major group in the U.S. Department of Education's longitudinal studies program, the High School Class of 1982, but in ways that only confirm the basic trends noted above. National surveys of total enrollments (Snyder, 1989) show that, by 1986, a majority of minority college students attended community colleges, but this came about principally from further increases in the percentage of community college students who were Hispanic, a dramatic increase in the percentage of community college students who were Asian-Americans (a group that was too small to desegregate in the Class of '72), and a corresponding drop in the proportions of both whites and blacks.[9]

Such cross-sectional enrollment surveys, however, tell us nothing about the more important phenomena of attendance patterns which emerge only over time. We have no idea what kinds of enrollments these may turn out to be. It is for that reason, among others, that we eagerly await the 10-year postsecondary transcript sample for the Class of 1982 (also known as the "High School and Beyond/Sophomore Cohort," the members of which were first surveyed as 10th graders in 1980).

Considered only as a demographic variable, the age at which this cohort attended community college must be inferred from first and last dates of attendance (where known), and assuming an age of 18 in 1972. As Table 5 indicates, well over half the community college attendees had come and gone before they were 22, but 26% (and a slightly higher percentage of women) were enrolled at some time between the ages of 25 and 30.

It may very well be that community colleges serve significant numbers of "older" students, but if so, a large proportion appear to be enrolled in non-credit or continuing education programs. The NLS–72 archive provides survey data on school attendance and status through age 32 (as opposed to age 30 on the transcripts). Some 16.5% of the entire sample indicated enrollment in some kind of school between the ages of 30 and 32 (1984–1986). Of this group, 30% attended community colleges. Of this group, in turn, 39% classified themselves as special students and 31% indicated no degree objectives. Those are large pieces of a small group.

Time of Attendance

The last of the demographic observations leads us to consider the points in their educational careers at which the members of the High School Class of 1972 used the community college.

There are a number of ways to approach the time factor. The first is somewhat limited in coverage but strong as a bench mark: the distribution of Associate's degrees by year of receipt.

Year of Associate's Degrees Earned by High School Class of 1972

Year	All	From Community Colleges	From Other Types of Institutions
		(percent)	
<1974	1.0	1.1	0.8
1974	45.4	44.8	48.2
1975	18.4	18.4	18.2
1976	10.0	10.6	6.8
1977–78	10.7	10.2	13.1
1979–80	7.3	7.6	5.8
1981–84	7.2	7.3	7.2

Approximately three-quarters of those who earned Associate's degrees by 1984, then, did so within 4.5 years of graduation from high school, that is, by the end of 1976. Those who use the community college for purposes of credentialing, it appears, do so at comparatively early points in their lives.

A second way to consider the time spent by students in community colleges is to analyze the gap between dates of first and last enrollment. As Table 6 indicates,

- Incidental attendees (earned 10 or fewer credits) did not take a course one year then come back years later for another course. In other words, whatever they did in a community college, they got it over with quickly. It is not surprising that they were the least likely of all attendance groups to say, at age 26, that they were tired of school.

- Approximately one-third of the non-incidental community college attendees (including AA recipients) were enrolled in community colleges for a period of 40 months or more. That does not mean that they enrolled every semester or that they enrolled full-time. It simply means that the student came back to the institution time and time again. We might call this phenomenon "continuous use."

- Nearly half of those who attended community colleges were enrolled for less than 16 months. Of this group, 30% earned at least 30 credits during that period of time, which is about what one would expect for full-time students; but 40% earned 10 or fewer credits, indicating incidental status.

Taken together, these three patterns indicate that the relationships between most community college students and their institutions were too brief to have much impact beyond the classroom. All the better reason, as we will see, to pay close attention to what people study in community colleges.

A third way to think about the time factor is in terms of the date of entry either to postsecondary education in general (see Table 7) or to community colleges, in particular (see Table 8). As Knepper (1989) has demonstrated, delayed entry does not affect the time it takes to earn a B.A. for those who earn it. But delayed entry does lessen the likelihood that the degree will be earned at all. The NLS/PETS transcript data indicate that, even over a 12-year period, there is a direct correlation between when people enter community colleges and their ultimate educational attainment. In this respect, it bears noting that only among "incidental" community college students do we find a significant percentage who delayed entry to postsecondary education by more than 30 months (see Table 7). For the Class of '72, the later in life one entered a community college, the more incidental one's use of the institution.

In addition, students who were on active military duty at any time between 1972 and 1979 (6.5% of the transcript sample) not only attended community colleges in higher proportions than the entire transcript sample (54.6% v. 42.3%), but also—as one would expect—tended to delay entry to community colleges for two years or more after high school graduation, hence were less likely to earn degrees (see Table 9).[10] Among the military personnel, patterns of attendance by race were the same as for the general population: blacks were less likely to use the community college, Hispanics more likely.

Two-thirds of all those who attended community college by the time they were 30 or 31 years old entered postsecondary education (in any kind of institution) directly from high school, and 80% entered within 18 months of high school graduation (Table 7). But that percentage varied with attendance pattern, and in direct relationship to the level of degree(s) earned. This phenomenon suggests that students on the "transfer" tracks had a fairly good idea when they were seniors in high school that they would transfer, hence did not unduly delay postsecondary entry.

Among *all* high school seniors in the NLS–72 sample, only 9% planned to transfer from one kind of institution to another. But among those who planned to attend 2-year colleges, the proportion with definite or tentative plans to transfer was 53%. And among those who eventually attended 2-year colleges and transferred, the proportion planning to do so as high school seniors was 85%. In general, then, those who plan to transfer—even before they enter higher education—are more likely to do so.

The Role of Aspirations and Plans

Entry to postsecondary education in terms of both time and place involves many choices. Among the conditions and constraints on those choices are the student's own aspirations and plans for further education. Previous analyses invoking the aspirations of NLS–72 students who attended community colleges (e.g., Levin and Clowes, 1980; Velez, 1985; Velez and Javalgi, 1987; Nunley and Breneman, 1988) were concerned principally with the issue of predicting the attainment of the Bachelor's degree, and were based wholly on survey data. But with reference to the transcript data, the distinction between aspirations and plans is complex and revealing, and is presented in Tables 10 and 11.

In the initial questionnaire administered to them as high school seniors, the NLS–72 participants were asked two questions: "What is the highest level of education you would like to attain?" and "What is the highest level of education you plan to attain?" The differences in their responses to those questions are underscored by the actual attainment of this group 12 years later (Table 11), as well as by the percentage in each category of aspiration or plan who entered postsecondary education immediately following high school, that is, who sought to actualize their aspirations or plans as early as possible.[11]

Table 10 presents the differences between aspirations and plans for groups of students by demographic and ability characteristics. As one would expect, there is a continuous down-shifting from aspirations to plans, but the extent and distribution of the shifts are irregular. For example, 54% of all NLS–72 students *aspired* to the Bachelor's degree (I include both the "4-year college/BA" and the "Graduate school" categories here). This percentage drops to 43% when the terms of the question are *plans*. Where does the difference go? What did these 11% of the NLS–72 students plan to do when the Bachelor's degree option was removed?

Roughly a quarter of the students in that group shifted their plans to community colleges, but nearly half dropped their plans for postsecondary education altogether. As Table 10 demonstrates, this pattern differs somewhat by race and socioeconomic status:

- Hispanics in the NLS–72 had consistently lower aspirations than either blacks or whites (43% of Hispanics, 52% of blacks, and 55% of whites aspired to the Bachelor's). When the question shifts to plans, Hispanics lowered their targets by a far more significant amount than either blacks or whites.

- With the shift from aspirations to plans, the community college gains among whites and Hispanics, but not as much among blacks. This phenomenon is consistent with the demography of community college attendance noted earlier.

- Only students in the highest SES quartile maintained plans roughly equivalent to aspirations. Their only trade-off was between graduate school and the BA.

The data on aspirations and plans in relation to SAT/ACT scores demonstrates a greater degree of down-shifting among students in the lower bands, indicating that they are not oblivious to their own general learned abilities. [For purposes of these analyses, ACT scores were converted to the SAT scale.] To the extent to which students scoring above 975 refocused from aspirations to plans, on the other hand, the trade-off was largely between graduate school and the Bachelor's degree.

A closer—and different—look at SAT scores in relation to aspirations and plans reinforces the realism of students' self-appraisal:

Mean SAT Scores by Educational Aspirations and Plans
(standard deviation in parentheses)

Highest Education Level	Aspired	Planned
High school graduate	849 (202)	821 (177)
Voc/trade school	830 (171)	840 (173)
Community college/AA	817 (158)	834 (159)
4-year college/BA	912 (184)	957 (189)
Graduate school	1014 (201)	1049 (212)

In all categories save "high school graduate," the mean scores for the group that *planned* to attain a given level of education are higher than those for the group that *aspired* to that level, that is, there is a better match. Where there is a better match between a student's sense of his/her abilities and his/her educational goals, we would like to think that the student will attempt to actualize those goals as soon as possible. If that hypothesis is true, the relationship between educational *plans* and time of entry into postsecondary education should be direct. Indeed, it is:

Percent of Students Who Entered Postsecondary
Education Directly from High School, by Educational Plans

Highest Level Planned	All NLS–72 Seniors	PETS Sample Only
Graduate school	73.1	82.4
4-year college/BA	71.5	83.3
Community college/AA	45.9	69.4
Vocational/trade school	19.7	50.8
High school graduate	4.1	27.8

The Weak Force of Credentials

What should be obvious from this presentation so far is that the community college did not loom large in either the aspirations or plans of the NLS–72 high school seniors. Only 12.4% of the entire cohort planned to attend a community college, and only 8.5% of the entire cohort (and 14.2% of those who actually attended postsecondary institutions) *planned* to earn the Associate's degree (the principal credential awarded by community colleges) as their highest credential. Another 8.2% (and 15.4% of those who actually attended) planned postsecondary vocational or technical education. While it is true that some proprietary and vocational schools award the Associate's degree, the NLS–72 high school seniors knew the difference between a trade school and a community college.[12]

Not only was the bench mark credential of the Associate's degree dimly visible in the plans of the NLS–72 cohort; it was also a weak force. That is, over time, and compared with the Bachelor's degree, very few people who initially planned to get an Associate's degree actually got it—even in 12 years: 26% versus 55% of those who planned to get the Bachelor's and actually received it. Not only that, but 30% of those who initially planned an Associate's degree never attended a community college at all, and another 15% were but incidental attendees.

Community colleges award "certificates" in addition to Associate's degrees. But only 4% of the NLS–72 community college attendees received such certificates. The recipients tended to be white women who did not earn any other credential or degree, and the most common fields for certificates were secretarial (14%) and allied health/nursing (24%).

What's at issue in this discussion is the certifying function of community colleges in the educational career of this cohort. To what extent are Associate's degrees or certificates awarded by community colleges primary goals of students? To what extent are they consolation prizes? Are the credentials relevant at all to the education of a generation? The transcript data strongly suggest that people attend community colleges principally for purposes that have little to do with earning credentials. The credentialing role of the community college is, in fact, a minor aspect of its mission.

Do the ways in which students use community colleges in this respect say more about the way we are than the popular perception of a credential-hungry society? Does our economic life demand credentials—or something else—from education? These are questions worth pondering, but only after we have learned some more from the NLS–72 archive.

Attendees: Academic Background and General Ability

In order to appreciate what the community college does for the people who attend (depending on how and when they attend), it is helpful to consider what those people bring to the community college in terms of previous education. For this task, the NLS–72 archive contains high school records, high school class rank, and a variety of ability measures.

In addition to providing baseline information against which to set community college coursetaking patterns, general educational attainment, and basic labor market outcomes, these academic background variables, in fact, help explain and refine our analysis of community college attendance patterns.

The data on high school class rank (see Table 12), high school curriculum (see Table 13), and equated SAT/ACT scores (see Table 14) present a complex portrait of community college attendees. It is obvious, first, that those who never continued their education after high school had the weakest backgrounds, no matter what measure one uses. Community colleges may be open-door institutions, but there are many high school graduates who aren't prepared to walk through that door—and who, furthermore, aren't interested in walking through.[13] While the gaps between the high school performance (class rank, SAT/ACT scores) of the weakest group of community college students (the incidental attendees) and the NLS–72 seniors who did not enter postsecondary education at all through age 30 are not great, the differences in curricular backgrounds in math, science, and foreign languages are more noticeable.

The few highly talented students in the NLS–72 simply did not attend community colleges, regardless of socioeconomic background. The data on this issue will no doubt surprise many who have contended that "high ability" students from low SES backgrounds are (a) shunted into community colleges and (b) do not earn Bachelor's degrees (Folger, H. Astin, and Bayer, 1970; Karabel, 1972; Brint and Karabel, 1989; Grubb, 1991; ETS, 1991). Part of the problem lies in the definition of "high ability" or "high talent" (Karabel and A. Astin, 1975) or "high resource" (Alexander, Holupka, and Pallas, 1987). Surprisingly, most of these analyses use a single, aggregate measure of ability or talent, and few of them tell us where the "cut-score" for "high" whatever-it-is lies. That's not fair.

The definition of "high academic resource students" used here involves three measurements, each of a different kind. First, we take the top quartile of performers on a special ability test (a mini-SAT) given to most NLS–72 participants as high school seniors. Second, we use high school class rank, and again take the top quartile. Third, we use high school records and draw in anyone who took *either* more than 5 semesters of math, *or* more than 5 semesters of science, *or* more than 5 semesters of foreign languages (that's a fairly flexible formula). A "high academic resource student" must be in *all three* measurement groups. Only 5% of the entire NLS–72 sample—and 8% of those who continued their education after high school—met all three criteria.

Table 15 lays out who these "high academic resource students" were and what happened to them. It's a small group, particularly when distributed across three SES categories times either seven patterns of attendance or five levels of degree attainment. So the standard errors of measurement are sometimes large, and the comparisons are not always statistically significant. Nonetheless, we can say that the vast majority—nearly 80% of them—never set foot in a community college. Only 7.5% of the entire group of "high academic resource" students came from the lowest socioeconomic quartile—versus 53.8% from the highest SES quartile—and the principal sorting criterion was not the ability test, but the curricular thresholds. No matter how generous the formula, the results demonstrate that low SES students are far less likely than others to take one of the three major elective pieces of a college preparatory curriculum in high school.

What distinguishes all the low SES and high SES groups here is whether they continued their education after high school at all, not where they went to school or what degrees they earned. Some 13% of the high academic resource/low SES students—versus about 6% of the high academic resource/high SES students—did not enter any kind of postsecondary institution by the time they were 30 years old. That turns out to be a statistically significant difference. Of those who continued their education (NLS/PETS), some 72% of the high academic resource/low SES students earned at least a Bachelor's degree versus 80% of the high academic resource/high SES students. That turns out *not* to be a statistically significant difference. In other words, there was no difference in the Bachelor's degree achievement rate of low SES and high SES students of similarly strong academic preparation and ability!

For the entire NLS–72 sample, those who eventually earned degrees of *any* kind brought a stronger background to postsecondary education than those who didn't, and that is no surprise. A higher percentage of transfer students who eventually earned Bachelor's degrees took requisite college preparatory curricula in math and science than did students who attended only 4-year colleges and never earned a Bachelor's degree. Those who earned terminal Associate's degrees brought higher SAT/ACT scores, class ranks, and science and foreign language backgrounds to the community college than the non-incidental students who failed to earn an Associate's degree.

Failure to earn a degree, however, was due neither to poor academic performance in the community college, nor, as Karabel (1972) darkly hinted, to a plot by community colleges to flunk out unpromising "transfer track" students: no one who earned 30 or more credits from a community college but no degree had a GPA less than "C." And since only 9% of community college course enrollments wind up as "Incompletes" or "Withdrawals" (versus 11% for research universities,

12% for comprehensive colleges, and 14% for liberal arts colleges), it is highly unlikely that this group failed to earn degrees due to failure to complete courses and receive a grade (even an "F").

Since the "no degree" attendance patterns cover the largest group of community college attendees, since the time-frame for completion was 12 years (a rather substantial period), and since common sense would indicate that lack of financial aid is not a major cause of withdrawal from low-cost, open-door commuter institutions, we ought to advance some other hypotheses as to why they did not finish a degree program.

This inquiry will take us directly into the curricular experience of community college students. I propose that there are two distinct curricular patterns of those who attend community colleges, but earn no degree whatsoever.

The first—and involving the largest group (about 75%)—is a pattern of coursework with no distinct focus. Grubb (1991) calls this phenomenon "milling around." While for some, "milling around" constitutes a *de facto* completion of high school, for others there is no such goal. And when there are no goals, it is easier to disengage.

The second curricular pattern involves a sufficiently distinct course of study (usually occupational in nature) for students to take from that curricular experience what they think they need for the labor market. The formal credential is not a concern; the subject matter is. Goals apply here, but they can be stated in terms of "sufficient knowledge." If this hypothesis holds, it will reinforce my previous contention that the credentialing function of the community college is not one of its principal missions, and that the way we are has more to do with learning than with pieces of paper.

Indeed, the NLS–72 students who attended community college demonstrate that learning without the currency of credentials drives us more than we think. While that learning may not pay off as much as the credential (as we shall see), it appears to drive us nonetheless.

Coursetaking: The Community College as Provider of Knowledge

Let us follow up this notion, first, by examining Table 16. The table compares the "majors" of those who received an Associate's degree from a community college with those of students who never earned any degree but who did earn at least a year's worth of credits from a community college. The Associate's degree completers obviously include a large percentage (43%) who "majored" in general studies or traditional arts and sciences subjects. Given the fact that 30% of the completers transferred to 4-year institutions *and* eventually earned a B.A., and that the general studies or traditional arts and sciences curricula are more likely to lead to B.A.s,[14] that 43% is in line with expectations.

In examining hundreds of individual records of "no degree" students who earned 30 or more credits in community colleges, however, I could determine a concentration (defined as either a minimum of 15 credits in a single field or allied fields, or two-thirds of credits in traditional arts and sciences curricula) for 66% of them. Of this group, about a fourth "majored" in traditional arts and sciences subjects. Among the rest, courses of study were dominated by occupational fields for which no license or degree is required, for example, business administration, engineering technologies, office support occupations.

The tendency to take from the community college that knowledge of immediate use in the workplace—and without regard to credentials—is illuminated by Table 17, which answers the following question: How much more likely were NLS/PETS students to take a particular course within an attendance pattern largely limited to community colleges versus an attendance pattern involving both community colleges and 4-year colleges? To illustrate the reading of Table 17: a student who attended community colleges in either an incidental, no degree, or terminal Associate's degree pattern is roughly four times as likely to have taken "Technical Mathematics" as a transfer student.

The list of courses with high ratios in Table 17 is dominated by subjects of either just such workplace utility (Technical Drafting, Data Processing, Office Machines), or precollegiate courses in math and English (which are prerequisites to everything else), or courses in the standard curricula of Nursing (Anatomy and Physiology, General Health Sciences), or the Police Academy (General Law Enforcement). In the latter connection, let us remember that the period during which the NLS–72 cohort went to college was one in which institutions of higher education received "Capitation Grants" for nursing students, and the Law Enforcement Assistance Act provided plentiful funding of postsecondary police training. Those occupational training support systems are no longer as generous.

But asking what courses one is "more likely" to take under a given community college attendance pattern produces a different answer from the question of what courses yield the highest percentage of credits earned. Credits are proxy measures for time; and Table 18 presents the courses accounting for the highest percentage of *total time* spent in higher education by students who attended community colleges. Again, I have split the list according to community college attendance pattern. The 43 courses in the left-hand column of Table 18 account for 48.3% of the all credits (hence, all postsecondary time) of those who attended community colleges as either incidental, no degree, or terminal Associate's degree students. The 43 courses in the right-hand column, on the other hand, account for 43.8% of the credits (hence, time) of all those who attended community colleges in patterns involving 4-year college attendance.

Let us note, first, the degree of concentration in the curricular experience of this generation. That only 43 course categories (out of 969 in which community college enrollments were recorded) account for such a large proportion of the total time spent in higher education by community college attendees indicates that those students followed fairly narrow paths through the offerings of the institution. As a guide to interpretation, the median percentage of credits generated by any one course category was less than 0.15%. So to observe a course such as Computer Programming or Medical/Surgical Nursing generating 0.5% of all credits is to observe a significant cut of the postsecondary time of this category of students.

Second, there is a substantial overlap in the two lists of courses: 29 out of 43 appear on both lists (though in slightly different order). The characteristics of the 14 cases for which the lists differ follow from the academic backgrounds of students in the two blocks of attendance patterns, as well as from our previous notion of "workplace utility":

Community College Only	Community and 4-Year College
Nursing: Medical/Surgical	English Literature
Stenography	Developmental Psychology
Secretarial: General	American Literature
Automotive Mechanics	Organic Chemistry
Clerk-Typist	Statistics (Math)
Intro. to Business Admin.	Physical Science: General
Introductory College Math	Philosophy: General, Introduction
Business Math: Arithmetic	Zoology: General, Introduction
Technical Math	Elementary or Intermediate French
Personal Health: General	Physical Education (Education)
Electronics Technology	Bible Studies
Remedial Reading	Geography: Introduction
Data Processing	Finance
Computer Programming	Geology: General

Given the comparatively weak secondary school mathematics background of community college attendees in the no-degree and terminal-Associate's categories (see Table 13), it is not surprising to see the heavy representation of pre-collegiate mathematics in their curricular experience. Community college programs for this generation evidently insisted on both remediation and on mathematics prerequisites for their major occupationally oriented programs.

The 29 courses that appear on both lists, though, are principally introductions to the basic arts and sciences disciplines. In that respect, the community college also seemed to insist on providing at least the rudiments of a general education to a far larger proportion of its students than merely to those who transferred.

The Concept of "Principal Provider"

This presentation of curricular experience raises the question of what type of institution was the "principal provider" of a given curricular content to this generation of students. The question is important from a labor market perspective because if we assume that the knowledge-content of work is determined by the learning people bring to the workplace, we can (a) identify those dysfunctions in work force preparedness that can be traced to prior education, hence, target our educational improvement efforts more precisely, and (b) better match existing college and community college students to the labor market by referring to what they studied. If we need X, we will know better which type of institution is the principal provider; and if we need a better X, we will know which provider to target for improvement efforts.

Of what kinds of knowledge, within fields, is the community college the principal provider to our economy and society?

Table 19 attempts to explore an approach to this question through the concept of enrollment differentials. It takes some illustrative fields, and selects, from within those fields, courses typically offered by *both* 2-year and 4-year colleges in which total enrollments were dominated by the community college. For each course, a contrasting case is offered: another course in that general field for which the community college is not the principal provider. For example, if one were looking for a technical writer, one would more likely turn to the universe of community college students than one would if the job involved creative writing. Likewise for real estate agents as opposed to insurance agents; child care specialists as opposed to family relations counselors, and so forth.

Not all courses, to be sure, are so occupationally specific. Some, however, are tied to occupational curricula, for example, the Engineering Physics course to the Engineering Technologies programs offered in community colleges versus the Engineering Mechanics course frequently taken by Engineering majors in 4-year colleges. But within traditional arts and sciences courses, the community college is a principal player only at the introductory/general level. There is nothing wrong with this: for most of us, the knowledge received through formal education in all areas, save our specialization, is general and introductory. It's part of the way we are.

Labor Market Outcomes: the Emphases of Work

What happened in the labor market to those students from the High School Class of 1972 who attended community colleges? Given the very rich data on the 5th (1986) follow-up survey of the NLS-72, there are many ways to approach the question, and many labor market variables upon which we can draw (earnings, unemployment, industry, etc.) At this point in the discussion, however, I want to focus on two connections between curricular experience and work.

First, let us note the general distribution of occupations held by NLS-72 community college attendees in 1986, presented by attendance pattern (Table 20). "Occupation," to be sure, is not a very informative category of analysis, since what people actually do on the job is more important to our understanding of the relationship between education and work than what people call themselves. Nonetheless, and despite the slipperiness of some occupational categories (e.g., "Managers"), Table 20 not only provides some basic parameters, but also lends strength to the analyses above.

The most interesting group in terms of the overall topic of this paper are the terminal Associate's degree holders. Even though credentialing may not be one of the principal roles of the community college, and the Associate's degree a weak force in the aspirations and plans of students, that degree, nonetheless, is the basic credential for the U.S. community college.

Furthermore, we can be sure that people who earned an Associate's degree from a community college experienced as full a range of community college curricula as the bench mark 60-credits allows (though 70.6% of terminal Associate's degree holders earned more than 60 credits from community colleges). In other words, this group had maximum exposure to the principal provider of its postsecondary education, and without major contamination of curricular experience at another type of institution.

For their present or most recent job, the 1986 survey asked NLS–72 respondents the degree to which they worked with ideas, people, paper, and things. Table 21 presents the responses, by major course of study, of Associate's degree recipients (from community colleges) who were in the college transcript sample and who claimed they worked "a great deal" with ideas or people. Most of the responses fit common sense empiricism. On the assumption that they are working in the general area of their community college concentration, majors in "Protective Services" need to work with the law (ideas) as well as people. Those in business support services work far more with people than with ideas. There thus appears to be a general match between curriculum and work role.

In terms of aggregate rankings, respondents worked mostly with people, followed by paper, ideas, and things, with the spread between people and ideas being 21.4%. These aggregate rankings well reflect the overall role of ideas in the community college curriculum.

But what happens if we focus the same questions only on those who said (in the 1986 survey) that they used their postsecondary education a great deal in their work? Within this group, the proportion who said they worked "a great deal" with *ideas* is 20% higher than that for the entire universe of Associate's degree holders.

What this variation implies is that a community college curriculum dominated by ideas is far more occupationally relevant, has far more actual "workplace utility," than the curriculum experienced by the mass of those who study in community colleges. In fact, the proportion of Associate's degree recipients for whom education was very relevant to work *and* who worked a great deal with ideas is higher than that for Bachelor's degree recipients who never attended a community college (70% v. 63%).

III. College, Church, Museum: Where Are We?

For the past 20 pages or so we have been swimming through a great deal of data, though perhaps (believe it or not) not enough. What does this account tell us about the role of the community college in the lives of a generation? Much of what we have seen confirms previous analyses or imputations from national databases such as the Current Population Surveys of the Bureau of the Census or the Higher Education General Information Surveys. But the transcript data both augment and depart from previous analyses in ways that encourage us to reconfigure the very language we use to describe the mission of the community college, and in at least two ways.

Occasional Institutions

First, the institution seems to function in a variety of what I would call "occasional" roles. In a more common phrasing, it serves individuals for *ad hoc* purposes. While there are regular church-goers and museum habitués, our uses of those institutions are more likely to resemble attendance patterns at community colleges. An institution capable of an occasional role must be very flexible, tractable, and penetrable. That doesn't mean that the institution is friendly, efficient, or effective. In the case of community colleges, it does not necessarily mean that the institution provides quality instruction or guidance, or that it keeps its promises to students. It simply means that the institution easily accommodates a variety of decisions to engage in intentional learning within a formal organization. Governed by the culture of credentialism and its timetable, 4-year colleges are less accommodating.

The students whose records we see in this archive are adults, and their choices to use a particular institution for a particular purpose at a particular time in their lives are intentional, even if the purpose is "milling around." What the community college does is to canonize and formalize the many decisions we make as adults to engage in learning for either limited, highly focused purposes or for general purposes. The community college is thus neither a "terminal" institution (Karabel, 1972) nor a transfer institution. Beyond the "value" of learning (the normative aspect of its existence), its purpose and role is not so easily fixed (Zwerling, 1986). The same can be said of other institutions, for example, churches and museums, that speak a language of values (the normative), but that serve us in very practical, utilitarian ways.

A second version of this theme (and it is qualitatively different from the first) is that the community college functions as an intermediary institution: a waystation or stepping stone or gap-filler for individuals in transit from one status to another, for example, adolescent student to labor market adult, working adolescent to adult student, etc. The universes of the labor market and baccalaureate education, however complex, have far more definite boundaries, rules, and expectations in the lives of individuals than does the community college. While it is hard to infer student motivation from transcript data, it appears that students in all attendance patterns (including "Incidental") knew that the community college would do something for them, would help them get from here to there. Even if they were constrained by geography, family circumstances, poor academic preparation, or socioeconomic status, they seemed to make of the community college what they wanted to make of it. They used the institution for a time, and then moved on.

A third version of this theme casts the community college in the role of "testing ground." That is, the institution provides individuals with the chance to test their tolerance for an interest in postsecondary education. More than half of those whose educational aspirations as high school seniors were limited to the high school diploma eventually attended community colleges, but a third of those people decided that postsecondary education was not for them, and became incidental students.

These variations on the "occasional use" theme reinforce Grubb's (1988) observation that labor market conditions and anticipated rate-of-return are not powerful factors in motivating students to enroll in community colleges. These variations on occasional use also call into question the very idea of "attrition" or dropping out of community colleges.

From their days as seniors in high school through age 30, the community college functioned in the lives of NLS–72 students with a comparatively low degree of imagibility, resulting from its minimal role in credentialing and from the amorphous nature of the Associate's degree. For some students, particularly those whose Associate degree "majors" can be described only as "General Studies" or "Liberal Arts and Sciences," the Associate's degree was but an advanced high school diploma, serving as a warrantee, so to speak, of general learning. There is nothing wrong with that. In fact, given the well-documented decline of the quality of learning in U.S. secondary schools, such programs are necessary, and the community college is one of their principal providers.

The Proximate Institution

The second major theme concerns the populations served by the community college. Given its occasional roles, minimal costs, and ease of access, the community college, by its very nature, can reach a broader spectrum of American society than other types of postsecondary institutions. This reach is augmented by the sheer number and geographical distribution of community colleges.

While recent (1986) data show that the proportion of minority students who are U.S. citizens is higher in community colleges (22.5%) than among undergraduates in 4-year institutions (16.6%),[15] for reasons of proximity to one's primary residence, the community college inevitably will serve the majority more than minorities. Outside the South and parts of the Southwest, for example, rural America is heavily white, and the principal postsecondary presence in rural areas is either the community college or the state college. As Grubb (1988) pointed out, the highest enrollment rate in community colleges in the country is in the state of Washington (22.9% of the eligible population), a state in which over 90% of the population is white, and in which there are 20 community colleges *outside* Seattle, Tacoma and Spokane.

With a little more work, I believe the NLS–72 data can demonstrate an old rule of elasticity of supply: when the only provider is X, X provides to (a) the dominant ethnic population, and (b) to students of all ages. So if the community college, considered nationally, serves an older population (as well as a younger one), it is the result of elementary economics. For the same reasons, the community college winds up serving a higher proportion of white, Hispanic, and Native American students than black students (who will make extra efforts to attend a Historically Black College). We also know that rural populations are more likely to be classified in the low and medium SES ranges than metropolitan populations. So for those who select postsecondary institutions on the basis of proximity, as many students do (A. Astin, Green, and Korn, 1987), community colleges will inevitably be the principal providers, hence will wind up serving a higher proportion of low and moderate SES students than will other types of educational institutions.

In this respect, the community college is not like our religious or cultural institutions. Its "liturgy" (curriculum) is non-sectarian, and there's no need for more than one in town (or county, or city district). From another perspective, while there are variations in that liturgy, they do not depend on visiting exhibits or performers: they are resident.

Indeed, the curricular liturgy of the community college is fairly consistent. We can infer what the community college offers from what students take; what it seems to offer is a combination of specialized curricula in three major occupational fields (allied health, business and business support services, and engineering technologies), and general studies curricula dominated by the social sciences. Students interested principally in either the sciences or the humanities either do not attend community colleges at all or transfer very quickly. Common sense would conclude that there is no way these institutions could offer enough depth in the basic sciences or the humanities to reach the "trapgates" of the fields. The transcripts confirm such a hypothesis.

Within this theme, the transcripts also suggest significant sex stereotyping in curricula pursued, hinting that students were advised into traditional roles (Kirby, 1981; Gittel, 1986). Women who pursued community college *occupational* education in the mid- and late-1970s did so principally in office support services, allied health, nursing, retail marketing, education, and applied arts. These fields accounted for nearly 70% of the occupational Associate's degrees awarded to women in the NLS/PETS. On the other hand, two-thirds of the men who earned occupational Associate's degrees did so in agriculture, business administration, computer-related fields, engineering technologies, protective services, and precision production/repair.[16] This theme is somewhat troubling, particularly in light of the spectacular rise in the overall educational attainment of women over the past two decades.

IV. Defenders and Critics: Reflections on an Old Debate

Having read a good deal of the record, and having reflected briefly on the nature of the community college as both an occasional and proximate institution, let's go back to the debate between the functionalist defenders of the community college and what Dougherty (1987) calls the "class reproduction school" of community college critics. To put it too simply, the "functionalists" say that the community college is the best vehicle for equal opportunity in postsecondary education; their opponents counter that the community college does nothing but perpetuate existing inequalities in American society. Both schools may now take what they wish from the transcripts, but I think the entire NLS–72 database ultimately helps us transcend this unproductive debate.

Hocus-Pocus Research

Three points need to be raised about the research used in the work of both defenders and detractors.

First, I am baffled by the construction of variables and estimates in most of the work bearing on this debate. Without the transcripts, for example, it is nearly impossible to determine precisely who is on a transfer/academic track in a community college and who isn't. What the student responds on a survey form or what he or she tells the registrar is not necessarily what he or she actually does.[17] Without the transcripts, it is nearly impossible to determine who changed from one track to another—and when. Having read, line-by-line, the complete academic records of over 10,000 students in the NLS/PETS, I am not sure that the construct of "track" itself is very helpful. On so many occasions, the community college portions of student records showed individuals starting out with a combination of basic skills courses and introductions to the disciplines and professions, then selecting more and more courses in a given field, as if they were choosing a "major" (and regardless of whether they actually received a degree).[18] This pattern is almost identical to that of students working through the curricula of 4-year institutions (except that, in 4-year institutions there is less work in basic skills and more in introductory college-level skills, for example, students take College Algebra or Finite Math instead of Pre-Collegiate Algebra). From the general to the focused. Should we be upset that community college students do it just like 4-year college students do it? Is this phenomenon properly called "tracking"?

Second, the literature on both sides evidences considerable confusion and outright naiveté concerning aspirations and plans with respect to the "baccalaureate degree." Using a metaphor from the nightly newscasts, the Bachelor's degree is the Dow Jones Industrial Average of U.S. higher education. That is, everybody has heard of it. When people ask "What did the market do today?" they mean the Dow Jones, and that's the answer they get, even though it is not the real answer to their question. What we have done in the semantic shorthand of our culture is to equate "Dow Jones" and "Market." We have done the same with "Bachelor's Degree" and "college Degree," let along "Higher Education Attainment." In fact, in the language and rhetoric of the critics' discourse, "a degree" is shorthand for the Bachelor's.

The Associate's degree, on the other hand, is like the NASDAQ average of Over-the-Counter stocks: virtually nobody knows what it is or how to interpret it. In contrast, the Bachelor's degree is a culturally visible symbol with significant power in public policy. No congressional committee, for example, asks the U.S. Department of Education for trends in production of Associate's degrees. They don't ask for the NASDAQ average: they want the Dow Jones. And what is true for congressional committees is even more true for 18-year-old high school seniors, let alone their parents.

So when we look at "aspirations" we are looking at attachments to culturally visible and powerful symbols, even if those symbols are vaguely understood. Those of us who have administered the Cooperative Institutional Research Program (CIRP) survey to entering college freshmen know that a significant proportion do not understand what various degrees either mean or require.[19] Furthermore, the intensity of one's "aspirations" ranges widely, from casual to committed (Alexander and Cook, 1979). When we look at "plans," on the other hand, we get closer to the individual's sense of his or her realistic options, and these seem to rely less on the most visible and powerful symbol of postsecondary educational attainment in our society. Inheriting their constructs from Clark's (1960a) "cooling out" thesis, none of the defenders or critics bother with this distinction, even though the NLS-72 provides the opportunity to explore it.

Third, when it deals with the economic outcomes of education, the literature is often bizarre. The most notable and persistent of the critics (Karabel, 1972; Karabel, 1986; Pincus, 1980; Pincus and Archer, 1989; Brint and Karabel, 1989) perform hocus-pocus analyses of secondary sources. They take other scholars' studies, state system studies, institutional studies, and census data—all with different samples, different populations, different years (boom or bust), different definitions of variables—utter an incantation, and pretend that it all makes sense. When it doesn't make sense, they challenge their opponents, the defenders of community colleges, to prove that it does make sense. The defenders, in turn, are even more helpless because, as the critics correctly point out, they are trapped by the propaganda machines of organizations that seek increased funding (federal, state, local) for community colleges. When there is money on the table, no one will admit to either flaws or ambiguity in institutional performance. No one wants to look directly at unobtrusively obtained national data.

Measuring Mobility

Lastly, the debate relies heavily on the effects of community colleges, principally in terms of social mobility. But the debate takes place in a comparative vacuum of meaningful effects. That is, with the exception of Monk-Turner's work (1983) based on the National Longitudinal Surveys of Labor Market Experience (another set of archives housed at Ohio State University), none of the studies of this issue analyzed by Dougherty (1987) have truly long-term employment, occupation, or earnings data, let alone information on family formation, home ownership, or anything else that would allow comparison of the SES of children to that of their parents. With the fifth (1986) follow-up, the NLS-72 archive now provides such data, at least through age 32/33.[20] Let's look at some of the variables that would be used in constructing SES ratings for the NLS-72 students at "thirtysomething."

Occupational Plans v. Occupational Realities

There are two ways of considering the occupational distribution of community college attendees at age 32/33. The first, presented in Table 22, selects 31 specific jobs within five broad occupational areas (business, technical, health services, production/operations, and human services). The presentation allows us to see the distribution of groups with specific educational histories across those occupations.

Among business occupations, for example, the distinction between accounts and bookkeepers is notable: the former draws a high percentage of those with Bachelor's degrees and 4-year college backgrounds, the latter draws a moderate percentage of those who either never attended college or never earned a degree of any kind. Terminal Associate's degreeholders tend to turn up in managerial/administrative jobs in manufacturing industries in roughly the same proportion as do former 4-year college students, but that distribution does not hold for managerial/administrative jobs in financial service industries.

While I cannot explain why a comparatively high percentage of transfer students who earned Bachelor's degrees wind up as personnel workers, the direct relationship between terminal occupational Associate's degrees and ultimate occupation stands out clearly in the cases of electronic technicians, health technicians, and nurses.

There are hosts of fascinating relationships displayed in Table 22 that deserve further investigation. My point in laying out a complex picture of occupational distribution in relation to educational background is to indicate that the routes we take from schooling to work are not always linear. In fact, contrary to the claims of both defenders (e.g., Roueche and Baker, 1987) and critics (e.g., Pincus, 1980; Pincus, 1986), attending a 4-year college does not straighten the line between education and work any more than does attending a community college.

A second way of looking at the occupational distribution of students in the NLS-72 cohort at age 32 is with reference to their plans at age 19. This portrait, set forth in Table 23, brings us flush against the contention of community college critics from Clark (1960a) to Brint and Karabel (1989) that community colleges—far more than 4-year colleges—frustrate the ambitions of students who attend. The early critics such as Clark never had the large scale, long-term data of NLS-72, particularly with its transcripts as a sorting mechanism. The later critics seemed to ignore such data or used it without the transcripts. In neither earlier nor later analyses were the kind of data set forth in Table 23 considered.

Table 23 compares occupational expectations at age 19 with occupational realities at age 32 for five groups. The first group consists of community college students who earned more than 10 credits from community colleges but no degree higher than the Associate's. This group, in turn, is split between those who earned no degree whatsoever by the time they were 30, and those who earned either a certificate or Associate's degree. Second, we take 4-year college students who never attended a community college and who earned more than 10 credits from one or more 4-year colleges. They, too, are divided in two groups: those who earned no degree whatsoever by the time they were 30 and those who earned at least a Bachelor's degree. Lastly, we have those students who, to the best of our knowledge, did not attend any kind of postsecondary institution by the time they were 30.

What do we see? First, as a rule, the hopes of youth exceed the realities of age. That's the way we are. No matter where people go to school or what degree they earn (if any), they wind up at age 32 doing something other than what they had planned at 19, and what they wind up doing tends to have less "status." Does this surprise anyone? As teenagers, we dream of becoming Nobel prize winners—or the equivalent; by "thirtysomething" we forget Nobel's first name (assuming we ever knew it) or how he blasted his way into history, and are happy to have steady jobs, to be respected in our work, able to pay the rent, take a vacation, and raise our children well. Is this, as the critics imply, a national tragedy?

In fact, when asked if they were satisfied with the progress of their careers at age 26 (unfortunately, this question was not asked at age 32), 82.5% of those employed said yes. Among those who had "made a go" at postsecondary education, the only feature of personal history that distinguished the most satisfied from the least satisfied was an earned degree of *any* kind, including a terminal Associate's degree from a community college.

Indeed (and secondly), people who do not earn degrees are more likely to wind up in "lower status" occupations than they originally planned than are those who did earn degrees. Does that surprise anyone? What may surprise some is that this phenomenon *applies equally* to community college students, 4-year college students, and students who never went to college. For example, a higher percentage of NLS-72 community college students who earned terminal Associate's degrees wound up in "professional" occupations (26.5%) than 4-year college students who did not earn a Bachelor's degree (20.9%).

Third, the background "noise" of occupational life is commerce, an area that, to the typical 19-year-old, is vast and unknown. We are more likely to fade into this background by the time we are in our early 30s—as managers, administrators, salespersons, and buyers—than we ever imagined, and less likely to invest the considerable time, effort, and energy in additional schooling to become professional workers.

The literature that criticizes community colleges for thwarting the aspirations of their students often uses the occupational category of "manager" as a privileged class. Given the number of people who call themselves "managers" in any survey, the occupation hardly represents an elite. As an occupational category, "manager" covers vast territories, from CEOs to the proprietor of the local dry cleaning establishment to the administrator of the county recreation department's evening programs. It sounds somewhat strained to call the people who inhabit this territory a privileged class. In general, as Table 23 shows, a higher percentage of people wind up in this category than originally aspired to it, whether they went to a 2-year college, a 4-year college, or no college (the only exception involves terminal Associate's degreeholders).

The category, "professional," is also misused in the critical literature. If, at age 19, I say I want to be an actor, am I aspiring to a "profession" in the same sense as "lawyer" or "dentist" or "college professor"? And, given the wages of dinner theaters and regional theaters, is acting an "elite" occupation?

The literature critical of community colleges for thwarting the aspirations of students to become "professionals" never tells us what it means by "professional," nor justifies the putative "professions" as elite or privileged classes. Are schoolteachers members of a profession? You bet! Are they a privileged or elite class? Tell that to the 2.5 million schoolteachers in this country! As Table 23 demonstrates by using three explicit categories of "professionals" (including schoolteachers), *even if* one defines "professions" in terms of those generally requiring a *post*-baccalaureate degree (the NLS–72 category I label "Professional II"), community college attendance has no greater negative impact on occupational aspirations than 4-year college attendance. In fact, in both types of institutions, the more significant determinant of whether one's aspirations to become a "professional" were fulfilled was whether or not one earned a degree. This phenomenon should also surprise no one: what makes professions "professions," in part, is that they require certified, specialized knowledge, and the certification is reflected in the degree.

Earnings

As a component of SES, earnings is a critical variable, and Table 24 presents the earnings of NLS–72 students in their most recent full-time jobs in 1985, by community college attendance pattern. Looking at the 1985 data, there is no clear-cut pattern that would lead us to conclude that community college attendance is a drag on earnings—at least through age 32/33. The highest paid group attended community college, and the lowest paid group did not. This pattern held for men, and women with children (by age 32/33). The greatest differentials between the earnings of men and both groups of women (those with children, and those without children), however, occurred in categories of community college attendance in which no degree was earned. For women who attended community colleges, then, earning a degree had a greater impact on earnings at thirtysomething than was the case for men.

We also note (and Table 26 reveals a similar pattern) that terminal Associate's degreeholders earned less than those who were non-incidental attendees but never earned any degree. This is not a new observation (see, e.g., Pincus, 1980; Nunley and Breneman, 1988). Why does this happen? It happens, in part, because the non-graduate has more years of job experience. But it happens more because a higher percentage of the non-graduates wind up in business-related occupations that, at age 32, pay better than occupations in health care fields dominated by terminal Associate's degreeholders. And it happens even more because women are a majority of terminal Associate's degreeholders, and women are unquestionably the victims of inequities in the labor market that have nothing to do with educational attainment (Adelman, 1991).

Home Ownership

Another potential component of SES is home ownership. In this case, we can examine home ownership rates at age 32 by socioeconomic status at age 18, using college attendance patterns as an intermediate variable. Table 25 does so. If we focus on students who were in the lowest SES quartile at age 18, hence least likely to come from families that owned their homes, we see that the highest rates of home ownership at age 32 were among those who attended community colleges and whose highest degree was the Associate's. The lowest rates of home ownership among this group were for people who attended community colleges, transferred to 4-year colleges, and subsequently earned a Bachelor's degree. Once again, there is no clear-cut pattern. One cannot conclude that community college attendance either hinders or advances the changes of home ownership. The relationship between home ownership and college attendance pattern is, in fact, rather tenuous.

General Economic Mobility

But in terms of economic mobility, the critics have a point that is strongly borne out by the NLS–72 data. Table 26 looks at 1985 earnings, unemployment, and job experience by both postsecondary attendance pattern and SES in 1972. Basically the table answers the question, "What patterns of postsecondary attendance are most likely to minimize unemployment, maximize earnings, and move an individual from a lower to a higher SES category?"

What do we see in Table 26? As Jencks *et al* (1972) observed, SES has a lasting impact on economic status. It takes a lot of work to override one's initial circumstances, whether one starts out in the lowest or the highest brackets. If we focus only on those students who did not continue their education after high school, we see exactly the same economic positions 14 years later. Even with no postsecondary education, as initial SES rises, wages rise, mean years of job experience rise, and unemployment drops. The only postsecondary attendance pattern that consistently overcomes initial economic circumstance is that of 4-year college attendance, whether or not a Bachelor's degree was earned.

This is an unfortunate aspect of the way we are. It is unfortunate in terms of the community college role because so many community college attendees in the NLS–72 sample seemed to use the institution for genuine purposes of learning, irrespective of social outcomes. Their behavior says that intentional learning is ingrained in us, whether that learning is incidental or continuous, whether it is basic general education or occupationally oriented, whether it is undertaken for enlightenment or the acquisition of specific skills. It is an article of our faith that learning ought to be rewarded, and that is one of the major normative messages of educational institutions.

There may be a brighter side to this matter that the account given in these pages does not reach. The most significant work to date on these data (Conaty, Alsalam, James, and To, 1989) uses the transcripts to demonstrate that, with few exceptions, *what one studies* has a greater impact on earnings at age 32 than where one attended college. To be sure, the subjects of the Conaty *et al.* study were the Bachelor's degree recipients; but if the relationships between coursetaking and earnings (controlling for college major, SAT scores, SES, etc.) are significant, then we ought to examine those relationships among community college attendees before we conclude that the normative message of community colleges remains unfulfilled.

V. Is Life So Cold? Concluding Thoughts About the Way We Are

Roughly one-quarter of the NLS–72 generation attended community colleges in different ways, and they represent a more typical segment of the population of high school graduates (race, sex, socioeconomic status) than either those who attended only 4-year colleges, those who attended only proprietary or vocational schools, or those who never continued their education at all. They clustered around the averages of just about everything. What does their behavior tell us about the way we are?

First, that we use major normative institutions for utilitarian purposes and that our relationships with those institutions are more occasional and *ad hoc* than otherwise. We recognize the value of education, but once schooling ceases to be compulsory, we tend to go to school only on our own terms.

Second, that we are more interested in learning, in acquiring new skills, and in completing our basic general education than in advanced credentials, even if those credentials yield greater economic rewards. At the same time, to the extent to which we acquired strong academic backgrounds in the course of our compulsory schooling, we are more likely to complete postcompulsory schooling of any kind, academic or occupational.

Third, while we are genuinely committed to lifelong learning, we nonetheless concentrate formal learning at early stages of our lives. We are children of time and its conventions. We do not easily break from cultural traditions of when to do what. Perhaps we know that the more distant we are from formal education, the more difficult it is to recapture both knowledge and the discipline of schooling.

Fourth, our general knowledge is just that—general and introductory. The time we typically allow for schooling does not permit depth. So we grasp for something particular, something we perceive as related to current or future work. The result is that we may know more about what we do for a living but are less adaptable to changes in the conditions or opportunities of work. If there is a just complaint about what community colleges allow us to do, it lies here (Pincus, 1986).

Lastly, our youthful aspirations and hopes exceed what actually happens to us, no matter what we do in between. Does that mean we should abandon them? If life itself is a "cooling-out" process, does that mean we should spend most of it moping about what could have been or blaming "the system" for what didn't happen to us? Do we adopt the position that only the 1% of the population at "the command posts of the American occupational structure" (Karabel and Astin, 1975), only the movie stars, succeed in our society and that everyone else fails? everyone else is a victim? everyone else doesn't count?

Aspirations and hopes usually translate into effort, and effort makes something better than what otherwise would have been for individuals, groups, and the nation. And while we all gripe about our lives and fortunes, if that's all we do, we freeze ourselves out of efforts to improve the lives and fortunes of our children. The Class of '72 did not throw in the towel. We can't afford to, either.

References

Adelman, C. 1990a. *A College Course Map: Taxonomy and Transcript Data.* Washington, D.C.: U.S. Government Printing Office.

Adelman, C. 1990b. *Light and Shadows on College Athletes.* Washington, D.C.: U.S. Government Printing Office.

Adelman, C. 1991. *Women at Thirtysomething: Paradoxes of Attainment.* Washington, D.C.: U.S. Government Printing Office.

Alba, R. D. and Lavin, D. E. 1981. "Community Colleges and Tracking in Higher Education." *Sociology of Education* 54: 223–237.

Alexander, K. L. and Cook, M. 1979. "The Motivational Relevance of Educational Plans: Questioning the Conventional Wisdom." *Social Psychology Quarterly* 42: 202–213.

Alexander, K. L., Holupka, S. and Pallas, A. M. 1987. "Social Background and Academic Determinants of Two-Year versus Four-Year College Attendance: Evidence from Two Cohorts a Decade Apart." *American Journal of Education* 96: 57–80.

Alsalam, N. and Rogers, G. T. 1991. *The Condition of Education, 1991*. Volume 2. Washington, D.C.: National Center for Education Statistics.

Anderson, K. L. 1981. "Post-High School Experiences and College Attrition." *Sociology of Education* 54: 1–15.

Astin, A. W. 1982. *Minorities in American Higher Education*. San Francisco: Jossey-Bass.

Astin, A. W. 1984. "Student Involvement: a Developmental Theory for Higher Education." *Journal of College Student Personnel* 25: 277–308.

Astin, A. W., Green, K. C. and Korn, W. S. 1987. *The American Freshman: Twenty Year Trends*. Los Angeles: Higher Education Research Institute.

Breneman, D. W. and Nelson, S. C. 1981. *Financing Community Colleges: an Economic Perspective*. Washington, D.C.: the Brookings Institution.

Brint, S. and Karabel, J. 1989. *The Diverted Dream: Community Colleges and the Promise of Educational Opportunity in America, 1900–1985*. New York: Oxford University Press.

Clark, B. 1960a. "The 'Cooling-out' Function in Higher Education." *American Journal of Sociology* 65: 560–576.

Clark, B. 1960b. *The Open-Door College*. New York: McGraw-Hill.

Cohen, A. M. 1988. "Degree Achievement by Minorities in Community Colleges." *Review of Higher Education* 11: 383–402.

Cohen, A. M. and Brawer, F. B. 1982. *The American Community College*. San Francisco: Jossey-Bass.

Cohen, A. M. and Brawer, F. B. 1987. *The Collegiate Function of Community Colleges*. San Francisco: Jossey-Bass.

Conaty, J., Alsalam, N., James, E. and To, D-L. 1989. "College Quality and Future Earnings: Where Should You Send Your Sons and Daughters to College?" Paper presented at the annual meeting of the American Sociological Association.

deArmas, C. P. and McDavis, R. J. 1981. "White, Black, and Hispanic Students' Perceptions of a Community College Environment." *Journal of College Student Personnel* 22: 337–41.

Dougherty, K. 1987. "The Effects of Community Colleges: Aid or Hindrance to Socioeconomic Attainment?" *Sociology of Education* 60: 86–103.

Educational Testing Service. 1991. *Performance at the Top: from Elementary Through Graduate School*. Princeton, N.J.: Author.

Fetters, W. B., Stowe, P. S., and Owings, J. A. 1984. *Quality of Responses of High School Students to Questionnaire Items*. Washington, D.C.: National Center for Education Statistics.

Folger, J. K., Astin, H. S., and Bayer, A. E. 1970. *Human Resources and Higher Education*. New York: Russell Sage.

Gittell, M. 1986. "A Place for Women?" In Zwerling, L. S. (ed.), *The Community College and Its Critics*. San Francisco: Jossey-Bass, 71–80.

Grubb, W. N. 1988. "Vocationalizing Higher Education: the Causes of Enrollment and Completion in Two-Year Colleges, 1970–1980." *Economics of Education Review* 7: 301–19.

Grubb, W. N. 1989. "The Effects of Differentiation on Educational Attainment: the Case of Community Colleges." *Review of Higher Education* 12: 349–374.

Grubb, W. N. 1991. "The Decline of Community College Transfer Rates." *Journal of Higher Education* 62: 194–217.

Hilton, T. L. and Lee, V. E. 1988. "Student Interest and Persistence in Science." *Journal of Higher Education* 59: 510–526.

Jencks, C. et al. 1972. *Inequality: a Reassessment of the Effect of Family and Schooling in America*. New York: Basic Books.

Karabel, J. 1972. "Community Colleges and Social Stratification." *Harvard Educational Review* 42: 521–61.

Karabel, J. 1986. "Community Colleges and Social Stratification in the 1980s." In Zwerling, L. S. (ed.), *The Community College and Its Critics*. San Francisco: Jossey-Bass, 13–30.

Karabel, J. and Astin, A. W. 1975. "Social Class, Academic Ability, and College 'Quality'." *Social Forces* 53: 381–398.

Kirby, E. B. 1981. "Petticoats to Jackhammers: Strategies for Women in Occupational Education." In Eaton, J. S. (ed.), *Women in Community Colleges*. San Francisco: Jossey-Bass, pp. 43–53.

Knepper, P. 1989. *Student Progress in College: NLS–72 Postsecondary Education Transcript Study*. Washington, D.C.: National Center for Education Statistics (CS#89–411).

Kolstad, A. 1987. *NLS–72/DMDC Military Records: Data File User's Manual*. Washington, D.C.: National Center for Education Statistics, (CS#87–383).

Levin, B. and Clowes, D. 1980. "Realization of Educational Aspirations Among Blacks and Whites in Two- and Four-Year Colleges." *Community/Junior College Research Quarterly* 4: 185–193.

London, H. B. 1978. *The Culture of a Community College*. New York: Praeger.

Monk-Turner, E. 1983. "Sex, Educational Differentiation, and Occupational Status." *Sociological Quarterly* 24: 393–404.

Neumann, W. and Riesman, D. 1980. "The Community College Elite." In Vaughan, G. B. (ed.) *Questioning the Community College Role*. San Francisco: Jossey-Bass, pp. 53–72.

Nunley, C. R. and Breneman, D. W. 1988. "Defining and Measuring Quality in Community College Education." In Eaton, J. S. (ed.), *Colleges of Choice*. New York: ACE/Macmillan, 62–92.

Pascarella, E. T. et al. 1986. "Long-Term Persistence of Two-Year College Students." Paper presented at the annual convention of the Association for the Study of Higher Education. ED #268–900.

Pincus, F. L. 1980. "The False Promises of Community Colleges: Class Conflict and Vocational Education." *Harvard Educational Review* 60: 332–61.

Pincus, F. L. 1986. "Vocational Education: More False Promises." In Zwerling, S. L. (ed.), *The Community College and Its Critics*. San Francisco: Jossey-Bass, 41–52.

Pincus, F. L. and Archer, E. 1989. *Bridges to Opportunity: Are Community Colleges Meeting the Transfer Needs of Minority Students?* New York: Academy for Educational Development.

Richardson, R. C. Jr. 1988. "The Presence of Access and the Pursuit of Achievement." In Eaton, J. S. (ed.), *Colleges of Choice*. New York: ACE/MacMillan, 25–46.

Rouche, J. and Baker, G. 1987. *Access and Excellence: The Open Door Colleges*. Washington, D.C.: Community College Press.

Snyder, T. D. 1989. *Digest of Education Statistics, 1989*. Washington, D.C.: National Center for Education Statistics.

Stage, F. 1988. "Student Typologies and the Study of College Outcomes." *The Review of Higher Education* 11: 247–258.

Tinto, V. 1987. *Leaving College: Rethinking the Causes and Cures of Student Attrition*. Chicago: Univ. of Chicago Press.

Tourangeau, R. et al. 1987. *The National Longitudinal Study of the High School Class of 1972: Fifth (1986) Follow-Up Data User's Manual*. Washington, D.C.: National Center for Education Statistics.

Velez, W. 1985. "Finishing College: the Effects of College Type." *Sociology of Education* 58: 191–200.

Velez, W. and Javalgi, R. G. 1987. "Two-Year College to Four-Year College: the Likelihood of Transfer." *American Journal of Education* 96: 81–94.

Zwerling, L. S. 1976. *Second Best: the Crisis of the Community College*. New York: McGraw-Hill.

Zwerling, L. S. 1986. "Lifelong Learning: a New Form of Tracking." In Zwerling, L. S. (ed.), *The Community College and Its Critics*. San Francisco: Jossey-Bass, 53–60.

A Synthesis and Application of Research on Hispanic Students in Community Colleges

LAURA I. RENDON AND AMAURY NORA

Hispanic students have used open access community colleges as their primary passageway into higher education. Roughly 60 percent of all Hispanics enrolled in institutions of higher education are concentrated in community colleges. However, the cohort's flow through what has come to be called the postsecondary pipeline continues to be marked by premature departure (Duran, 1983; Haro, 1983; Rendon, 1982; Olivas, 1979). Expanded Hispanic student enrollments in community colleges have not necessarily been reconciled by increased retention and transfer rates to senior institutions. Studies document that Hispanics are not completing their programs of study and have attained only minimal success moving from lower to upper division programs of study that lead to baccalaureate (Lee, 1985; Wilson and Melendez, 1985; California State Postsecondary Commission, 1985; Astin, 1982). Thus, a question remains as to whether equal opportunity and equal outcomes can be made compatible goals in community colleges.

While the persistence and progress of Hispanic students in community colleges have received limited research attention, a few studies provide both descriptive and inferential information that colleges may use to improve practice and policy. Although community colleges are not research institutions, the design, implementation, and evaluation of models and strategies intended to increase their Hispanic student-holding power may be enhanced through the use of current literature. The relative lack of success that community colleges have had in designing interventions that improve Hispanic retention rates may be partially attributed to the colleges' limited experience using data and information as a base to improve practice and modify policy. Neglecting to employ research may give way to the development of ill-conceived and ill-focused programmatic design and evaluation of student support and curricular strategies which may, at best, become temporary measures yielding limited outcomes. This essay provides community college practitioners a review of the current research literature on Hispanic community college students. Second, the implications of the research and recommendations to improve practice and policy are presented. While relatively few empirical studies are available to analyze the progress of Hispanics in community colleges, review of current research provides indicators that the cohort's persistence and flow from lower to upper division programs of study remains less that satisfactory.

287

Research Portrait of Hispanic Students

Although research related to Hispanic participation and achievement in two-year colleges has generally suffered from inconsistencies in definition, sampling and methodology, a relatively small base of knowledge exists that may provide a sketchy but useful portrait of Hispanic student retention and transfer to senior institutions.

Hispanic Student Retention: Data are available to both confirm and suggest (by the fact that Hispanics are disproportionately enrolled in community colleges) that Hispanics are not progressing well through the postsecondary educational pipeline. In a survey taken two years after 1980 seniors enrolled in postsecondary institutions, 50 percent of the Hispanics were not enrolled in college (Lee, 1985). Further, according to the Commission of the Higher Education of Minorities (1982), one of the most important reasons that Chicanos, Puerto Ricans, and American Indians are underrepresented in graduate programs is their greater-than-average attrition from undergraduate colleges, particularly community colleges.

In a study of seven states where the largest enrollment of Hispanics was found, Haro (1983) discovered "an average college attrition rate for the Spanish surnamed student population of 80.4 percent, compared to 62.3 percent for the majority population." The state of California, which account for nearly one-third of all Hispanic enrollments in higher education (Olivas, 1986), had a five-year college graduation rate of 15.4 percent for Mexican Americans, 34.2 percent for white, non-Hispanics, and a three-year graduation rate of 27.9 percent for Mexican Americans and a 38-percent rate for white, non-Hispanics (The California State University and Colleges, 1979).

The problem of minority and low SES student underrepresentation really begins at the pre-college level. Hispanics have lower high school graduation rates than whites. In 1985, 59 percent of Hispanics graduated from high school, compared to 84 percent for whites (Wilson & Melendez, 1986). Exacerbating this problem is the fact that Hispanic high school graduates are less likely to attend college than whites. About 32 percent of white students attend college, compared to 29.9 percent for Hispanics. Factors which have been found to have an impact on dropout rates and low levels of college participation among Hispanics include: (1) insufficient financial resources, (2) lack of academic integration into their respective institutions, and (3) lack of commitment to educational goals (Nora, 1987). Other factors suggested as having an influence on Hispanic attrition are: poor quality of education at inner city schools, undeveloped study skills, the absence of role models, institutional right to fail policies, declining literacy demands and student lack of academic preparation in reading, writing, and math (Wilson & Melendez, 1985; Rendon, 1982).

Transfer Rates to Senior Institutions: Slippage in the educational pipeline also occurs during student transition from two-year to four-year institutions. Estimates on baccalaureate degree intentions of community college students range from a low of 52 percent to a high of 74 percent (Richardson & Bender, 1986). It is estimated, however, that only 5 to 25 percent actually achieve this initial goal (Richardson & Bender, 1986; Bensimon and Riley, 1984; Astin, 1982). A case in point is illustrated by the state of California, which has the largest number of Hispanics in the largest system of community colleges in the country. In California, community colleges experiencing the largest transfer losses recently tended to be those with very high proportions of Chicano or Black freshman students (California State Postsecondary Commission, 1985; Hayward, 1985). Affirming that the initial intentions of community college Hispanic students rarely translate to reality are figures which substantiate their gross underrepresentation in the share of college degrees earned. In 1980, Hispanics comprised approximately six percent of the United States population. Yet, they earned only 2.3 percent of the bachelor's, 2.2 percent of the master's, 1.4 percent of the doctorates, and 2.2 percent of the first professional degrees (Wilson & Melendez, 1985).

Financial Aid and Retention: Student financial aid has recently received attention as a determinant of student retention. The relationship of financial aid and student persistence, particularly as related to Hispanic college students, takes on a serious nature in light of recent research findings. A study by Olivas (1986) on Hispanic financial aid recipients found that not only were students uninformed about their parents' income, but also that half of all Hispanic students in the study overestimated their actual income. In a separate study on financial aid packaging policies and Hispanics in higher education, Olivas (1985) found that over 60 percent in a representative sample of over 16,000 Hispanic students received only single-source aid and that this one source of aid was "almost exclusively Basic Education Opportunity Grants (or BEOGs, known as Pell grants since 1981)." Even when multiple source aid was awarded to Hispanic students, 95 percent of all multiple sources in the study included Pell grant awards.

These findings, although noteworthy within their own contexts, take on added importance when coupled with recent findings on financial aid and persistence. Studies by Astin (1975), Voorhees (1985), Brooks (1981), and Herndon (1982) have found that student financial aid, such as college work study, has a positive effect on student persistence. However, if Hispanic community college students who may qualify for financial assistance are overestimating actual income on financial forms and being denied financial aid, not only are these students having to bear the disproportionately high costs of a college education, but their chances of succeeding and attaining some form of college credential may be reduced.

Current Findings in Hispanic Student Retention Studies

McCool (1984) conducted a multiple regression analysis on factors which were hypothesized to influence Hispanic student retention in two-year institutions and found that number of credit hours completed, identification of positive and negative reasons for withdrawal, experience, perceptions, and goal selection affected students' ability to achieve educational objectives. "The common factors consistently found to relate significantly to . . . achievement goals . . . were factors seen to be expressions of the students' satisfaction with and commitment to their educational experience."

A recent study of Hispanic transfer students enrolled in six community colleges in Texas, Arizona, and California (Nora & Rendon, 1988) provides additional insights into the student persistence and transfer problem. Findings revealed that 51 percent of Hispanic students indicated they had plans to transfer after earning the associate degree, and 72 percent indicated that transferring was very important. However, the majority of these same students had limited contact with faculty outside of class and did not participate in academic or career counseling, freshman orientation, study skills workshops, or honors programs. Further, the majority of students received little, if any, encouragement to transfer from community college faculty. Thus, it appears that while most Hispanic students want to transfer and attach great importance to transferring, they do not exhibit academic integration behaviors such as maintaining contact with faculty or participating in academic, career, and social activities on campus. This same study found that students with high levels of commitment to attending college and attaining their educational goals had applied to more four-year institutions and had sought more information about transferring from counselors, faculty, friends, four-year institutions and community college catalogs. They also had high levels of social and academic integration. However, students who exhibited high levels of social and academic integration tended to have positive attitudes about transferring and to exhibit transfer-related behavior. In sum, community college students who had higher levels of initial commitments to the institution and their educational goals, higher levels of academic and social integration, and whose parents had higher levels of educational attainment were more likely to have integrated better both socially and academically at their institutions. Of those two-year student populations in the study, ethnic origin was not found to be related to any of the factors in the study.

Two retention studies (Nora, 1987ab) provide recent research-based information on Hispanic student retention in community colleges. Both studies utilize a structural equation model, which uses intent variables with multiple indicators in hypothesized causal models. Nora's (1987a) study tested the hypothesis that high levels of congruency between students and their environments lead to high levels of credential attainment, hours earned, and goal satisfaction. The study was a secondary analysis of an extant data set (Rendon, 1982) of a random sample of Chicago students in three South Texas community colleges.

The major finding from Nora's (1987a) study was that the strongest effect on Hispanic student retention in community colleges was institutional/goal commitments. Neither academic integration (i.e., measures of student perceptions about their academic experiences with faculty, counselors and administrators, as well as perceptions about career preparation opportunities at their institutions) nor social integration (i.e., informal student contact with faculty members, counselors and peer groups) had a significant impact on retention. However, Hispanic students who enrolled in a community college with a strong sense of wanting to attend the college and a strong commitment to their educational goals tended to earn more college hours and credentials.

Fox (1985) has consistently found that high levels of academic integration have more of an impact on persistence than any other variable. Conversely, other retention researchers have found social integration to be more influential (Pascarella and Terenzini, 1980; Pascarella, Terenzini and Wolfle, 1985). Nora's (1987a) findings, however revealed that for a community college Chicano student population, institutional/goal commitments were more significant than academic and social integration measures.

A second highlight from Nora's (1987a) study was that the longitudinal data collected over a four-year period (1977–1978 to 1981–1982) revealed that only 29.91 percent of the Hispanic student population graduated or received some form of college credential. Even though Hispanic students earned enough college credit hours to earn a degree (mean=65.167), fewer than one-third graduated or earned some form of credential.

Student Finances and Retention Rates: A causal model examining the effect of campus-based and noncampus-based financial aid on Hispanic community college student retention was employed by Nora (1987b). Campus-based financial programs included Supplemental Education Opportunity Grants (SEOG), College Work Study (CWS) and National Defense Student Loans (NDSL). Noncampus-based resources were Pell grants. The study example was representative of a total population of 883 first-time Chicano students who were enrolled full-time or part-time n 1982 in a South Texas community college whose characteristics were found to be similar to other community colleges in South Texas.

According to Nora's (1987b) study, the largest effect on Chicano student retention was Pell grants. The second largest effect was produced by SEOGs, CWS and NDSLs; the third largest effect was from GPAs. In sum, Chicano community college students who received higher levels of noncampus and campus-based financial aid were enrolled in more semesters, earned more semester hours, and received some form of college credential. Moreover, Chicano students who received higher levels of campus-based resources earned higher grade point averages. Nora's study substantiates the impact of financial resources on persistence found in other studies (Voorhees, 1985ab) which have indicated that campus-based resources (SEOGs, CWS, NDSLs) have both direct and total effects on retention. As in Nora's (1987a) previous study, this analysis revealed that although the mean number of semester hours earned (mean=55.26) could have indicated that many students earned a community college credential, 82.38 percent did not.

Implications and Recommendations

In summary, the portrait of Hispanic student participation in community colleges remains bleak. Neither retention nor transfer rates to senior institutions suggest that Hispanics have made significant gains in community colleges. Further, Hispanic students may be reducing their retention potential by overestimating their actual income levels. To address irregular participation and achievement levels, community colleges need to utilize available research to modify policies and educational practice.

The facts that social integration has not been found to have a significant effect on Hispanic student retention (Nora, 1987a) and that academic integration does not have the largest impact on persistence suggest that the development of a strong sense of academic and social affiliation with the institution may be secondary to having a commitment to clear, concrete, and realistic goals at an early point of college enrollment. Hispanic students with diffuse goals appear to have a disadvantage over those students with clear institutional/goal commitments.

Further, in both of Nora's studies (1987ab), most students had more than enough college credit hours to enable them to earn college degrees or certificates; yet, less than 70 percent earned such credentials. This contradiction may be explained by the fact that many Hispanic students may be enrolling in community colleges without a clear conception of what their goals are, giving way to weak or nonexistent commitments to attending the institution or achieving a specific educational goal. For others, external preoccupations such as job-related or family problems may preclude students from developing clear goals and/or commitment to studies. Some students may enroll in college for reasons unrelated to earning a college degree. In any case, having unclear goals and weak commitments to achieve them appears to work against Hispanic student retention and ultimate graduation. The implication is that community colleges need to provide assistance and information for students to set firm, clear, and realistic educational goals at an early enrollment point.

To this end, community colleges can provide counseling and advertisement to assist students to explore, sort, and select appropriate career and educational goals. Once these are selected, students may be assisted to choose proper courses and sequences. This process may be facilitated by implementing a faculty advisement program. Students may be assigned to a faculty advisor who can serve as a contact person who can help them shape their goals as well as to become actively involved in the studying and learning process. In the same fashion, transfer students may benefit from being assigned to a transfer counselor who is housed in a transfer center. Transfer counselors can help early identified transfer students with a proper course selection and sequence and the completion of admissions, financial aid housing forms.

Assessment of students, coupled with feedback mechanisms that incorporate frequent interactions with faculty, may serve to provide students with the information they need to make proper course and program selections and to assess their own progress to come closer to achieving their educational and career goals.

With regard to financial aid, one must consider the nature of the Hispanic community college student clientele. Most students come from low socioeconomic status backgrounds and from families where precedent of attending college is not well established. Because both campus-based and noncampus-based resources have been found to have a significantly large impact on retention rates among Hispanic community college students, two-year institutions need to do more than simply meet a student's financial need. The colleges need to develop a comprehensive financial aid advisement program that reaches out to students and their parents before students graduate from high school. Hispanic parents need to understand and appreciate the higher education system as well as its costs and the financial assistance available for their children. Parents can also be educated about completing IRS forms and student financial aid applications in a thorough and timely fashion.

Although receiving financial aid, particularly Pell grants, appears to be a determining factor of Hispanic student persistence, the majority of Hispanic students receiving Pell grants do not necessarily earn degrees. While students identify factors that influence Hispanic student persistence, other unanswered issues lead to the conclusion that more research needs to be conducted on the diverse and complex factors which may be operating to impact Hispanic student retention in community colleges. To this end, community college institutional researchers and scholars may design research studies on Hispanic student sub-groups in selective settings in diverse geographical areas. The future success of Hispanics in community colleges is largely dependent on whether empirical information is available to be used as a base for the colleges to make systemic curricular reforms, and devise academic and student support interventions. Until then, equal outcomes will tend to remain incompatible goals.

References

Astin, A.W. (1975). *Preventing students from dropping out.* San Francisco, California: Jossey-Bass, Inc.

Astin, A.W. (1982). *Minorities in American higher education.* San Francisco, California: Jossey-Bass, Inc.

Bensimon, E.M. & Riley, M.J. (1984). *Student predisposition to transfer: A report of preliminary findings.* Los Angeles, California: Center for the Study of Community Colleges.

Brooks, J.W. (1981). Academic performance and retention rates of participants in the College Work Study Program and recipients of National Direct Student Loans. *Dissertation Abstracts International, 40,* 3440–A. (University Microfilms No. 8023407).

Burkheimer, H.J. & Novak, T.P. (1981). *A capsule description of young adults seven and one-half years after high school.* Research Triangle Park, North Carolina: Center for Educational Research and Evaluation.

California State Postsecondary Education Commission. (1985). *Update of community college transfer student statistics, fall, 1984.* (Commission Report 75–21) Sacramento, California: CSPEC Eric Document Reproduction Service No. ED 256–399.

Commission on the Higher Education of Minorities. (1982). *Final Report on the higher education of minorities.* Los Angeles, California: Higher Education Research Institute, Inc.

Duran, R.P. (1983). *Hispanics' education and background.* New York, New York: College Entrance Examination Board.

Fox, J. (1985, March). *Application of a conceptual model of college withdrawal to disadvantaged students..* Paper presented at the annual meeting of the American Educational Research Association, Chicago, Illinois.

Haro, C.M. (1983). Chicanos and higher education: A review of selected literature. *Aztlan, 14(1),* 35–76.

Hayward, G. (1985). *Preparation and participation of Hispanic and Black students: A special report.* Sacramento, California: California Community Colleges, Office of the Chancellor. (ERIC Document Reproduction Service No. 254 285).

Herndon, M.S. (1982). A longitudinal study of financial aid persistence, dropouts, and stopouts: A discriminant analysis. *Dissertation Abstracts International, 42,* 4736A–4737A.

Lee, V. (1985). *Access to higher education: The experience of Blacks, Hispanics and low socio-economic status Whites.* Washington, D.C.: American Council on Education.

McCool, A.C. (1984). Factors influencing Hispanic student retention within the community college. *Community/Junior College Quarterly, 8,* 19–37.

Nora, A. (1987). Determinants of retention among Chicano college students: A structural model. *Research in Higher Education, 26* (1), 31–59.

Nora, A. (1987b). *Campus-based aid programs as determinants of retention among Hispanic community college students.* Presentation to the American Educational Research Association Annual Meeting, Washington, D.C.

Nora, A. & Rendon, L.I. (1988). Hispanic students in community colleges: Reconciling access with outcomes. In L. Weis (Ed.). *Class, Race and Gender in U.S. Education.* New York, New York: SUNY Press.

Nora, A. & Rendon, L.I. (1988). *Determinants and predisposition to transfer among community college students: A structural model.* Paper presented to the annual meeting of the Association for the Study of Higher Education.

Olivas, M.A. (1986). *Financial aid and self-reports by disadvantaged students: The importance of being earnest.* (Monograph No. 86–90). Houston, Texas: Institute for Higher Education Law and Governance.

Olivas, M.A. (1985). *Latino college students.* New York, New York: Teachers College Press.

Olivas, M.A. (1979). *The dilemma of access.* Washington, D.C.: Howard University Press.

Pascarella, E. (1980). Student-faculty informal contact and college outcomes. *Review of Educational Research, 50,* 545–595.

Pascarella, E. & Terenzini, P.T. (1979). Interaction effects in Spady's and Tinto's conceptual models of college dropout. *Sociology of Education, 52,* 197–210.

Pascarella, E.T. , Terenzini, P.T. & Wolfe, L. (1985, March). *Orientation to colleges as aniticpatory socialization: Indirect effects on freshman year persistence.* Paper presented at the annual meeting of the American Educational Research Association, Chicago, Illinois.

Pascarella, E.T. & Terenzini, P.T. (1980) Predicting freshman persistance and voluntary dropout decisions from a theoretical model. *The Journal of Higher Education, 51* (1).

Rendon, L.I. (1982). *Chicanos in south Texas community colleges: A study of student and institutional-related determinants of education outcomes.* Unpublished doctoral dissertation, University of Michigan, Ann Arbor, Michigan.

Richardson, R.C. & Bender, L.W. (1986). *Students in urban settings: Achieving the baccalaurate degree.* Washington, D.C.: Association for the Study of Higher Education.

The California State University and Colleges. (1979). *Those who stay—Phase II: Student continuance in the California State University and Colleges.* (Technical Memorandum No. 8). Sacramento, California: California State University and Colleges, Office of the Chancellor.

Voorhees, R.A. (1985a). Financial aid and persistence: Do the federal campus-based aid programs make a difference. *The Journal of Student Financial Aid, 15(1),* 21–30.

Voorhees, R.A. (1985b). Student finances and campus-based financial aid: A structural model analysis of the persistence of higher need freshmen. *Research in Higher Education, 22(1)* 65–91.

Wilson, R. & Melendez, S.E. (1986). *Minorities in higher education.* Washington, D.C.: American Council on Education.

Wilson, R. & Melendez, S.E. (1985). *Minorities in higher education.* Washington, D.C.: American Council on Education.

Responding to Student Diversity:
A Community College Perspective

RICHARD C. RICHARDSON, JR.

The rapid growth of community colleges during the '60s and '70s can be traced, in part, to public policy decisions to limit the amount of diversity selective four-year institutions were required to accommodate. Two-year colleges were created to serve as the major access point for populations previously excluded or underserved. Four-year colleges were expected to focus on achievement as traditionally defined. This arrangement has resulted in the concentration of students of color in institutions with the fewest resources from which they are less likely to graduate or transfer than their Anglo counterparts.[1]

The current concern with underpreparation is in large measure a concern about the long-term effects of concentrating a potential underclass in institutions that on the surface appear to be designed to support existing social and economic arrangements. Community colleges are not alone in this dilemma. Wildavsky[2] describes programs originating in the Great Society era generally as failures because they had as their objective changing client behavior and as it turns out, "Human Beings Are Not Very Easy to Change After All."[3] Confronted with clients who refused or were unable to change to conform to Great Society expectations for upward mobility from first-time exposure to higher education, community colleges first sought programs that required no change in clientele and, then, clientele who could be changed, or, better yet, needed no changing.

In the *Diverted Dream*, Brint and Karabel[4] argue an administrative conspiracy as the explanation for the "vocationalization" of community colleges during the '70s and '80s. Wildavsky's perspective offers a more straightforward explanation. By the early '70s it was clear to many community college leaders that continuing concentration on the transfer function with a clientele from which many of the higher-achieving and more academically oriented students had been "creamed" by four-year institutions could only lead to failure rates in excess of those for which they had already been publicly criticized. The development of career programs in which less well-prepared students could succeed was an attractive alternative. Later, as these programs led to increasingly close relationships with business and industry, community colleges had many opportunities to attract already employed workers, a clientele that needed no changing to benefit from the work-related programs their employers helped to establish.

During the '70s, the philosophy of "right to fail" gave students with increasingly marginal preparation the opportunity to attempt any academic course community colleges offered without prerequisites.

The community college emphasis on career programs and a widely publicized surplus of four-year graduates produced among transfer offerings by the late '70s, a "stultifying sameness of a curriculum shrunken to introductory courses."[5] In the early '80s, a pair of NIE-funded studies at two separate universities reached essentially similar conclusions. An institution established to "level up" disadvantaged segments of society had achieved much of its success through leveling down the critical literacy skills required for successful completion of arts and science courses.[6,7]

The preparation of students attending community colleges generally improved in the '70s,[8] but the '80s have been a very different story. By the middle of the past decade, concern about the level of basic competencies and the preparation of students for more advanced work had moved from its ranking as fourth in 1979 to the top concern among community college administrators.[9]

In the last part of the current decade, community colleges have been drawn, often reluctantly, into the assessment movement. The results have confirmed that more than half of entering community college students lack the basic skills required to do credible academic work.[10] In urban institutions the numbers often range from three-fourths to more than 95% of the student body. As assessment becomes increasingly widespread, community college educators, like their K–12 colleagues, find that the idea of making measurement public has outrun their ability to demonstrate student accomplishment.[11] In lieu of approval for extending opportunities, community college leaders now often find themselves responding to charges that the less well-prepared students they increasingly serve are graduating or transferring at levels significantly below those previously attained by a better prepared cohort.

The general issue of preparation cannot be separated from factors of race and ethnicity. Blacks, Hispanics and American Indians disproportionately rely upon community colleges as their point of initial access to higher education. California community colleges enroll 40% of all high school graduates but 80% of all graduates of color.[12] Blacks and Latinos are less well represented among graduates and transfer cohorts than among community college students. In Florida, where 60% of all baccalaureate candidates are expected to begin in community colleges, Blacks constituted 18.7% of the 15–24 year-old population, 17.5% of the high school graduates, 13% of the community college enrollments, and 4.8% of the Associate in Arts degree graduates in 1988. In the same year they represented 7% of the state university system freshmen and earned 4% of the baccalaureate degrees.[13] From these data and studies of information provided by the National Center for Educational Statistics, it is clear that community colleges are a part of the pipeline problem as well as a potential contributor to a solution.

Defining Underpreparation

The way a problem is defined has much to do with shaping the efforts aimed at its solution. Describing the way community colleges relate to their constituencies as strategic marketing rather than offering products, distributing services efficiently or selling existing programs and services, has brought about fundamental changes in the ways leaders think about their responsibilities and in their ways of doing business.[14]

The preparation problem has generally been defined in terms of student deficiencies. The deficiency approach has involved the use of standardized or faculty-developed assessment instruments as the basis for placing students with those advised to enter developmental courses defined as underprepared.

Under the deficiency approach, even the most highly selective institutions enroll students who are underprepared. At UCLA, one of the most selective universities in the nation, there is a large Academic Advancement Program that serves a predominantly minority student population who enter under Student Affirmative Action (SAA) guidelines. The mean high school grade-point average (GPA) for all UCLA entering freshmen in 1986 was 3.76. The mean high school GPA for SAA matriculants was 3.41. At UCLA, students with GPAs that would earn them merit scholarships in many other institutions are identified as underprepared.[15] The matter is further complicated by curricular differences. In some institutions, students who start their mathematics sequence below the level of calculus are considered underprepared.

Researchers at Arizona State interviewed 107 Black, Latino, and American Indian graduates from 10 predominantly Anglo, four-year colleges and universities to determine whether a student's perspective on preparation might furnish an alternative to the deficiency view of student prepara-tion.[16] Many of these baccalaureate graduates had previously attended a community college. The interviews documented in detail incredible stories of motivation, persistence and sacrifice both from students and from their families. More than half of these degree recipients had begun their college careers carrying the label of underprepared.

These students' interviews suggested that preparation involves more than the high school attended and the courses taken. Preparation includes developing accurate expectations about college participation through experiences that approximate college-going. Preparation has cogni-tive, physical, temporal and social dimensions. The need for college students to develop accurate expectations about course content and academic skills is well understood, but substantially less attention is given to the other three aspects of preparation for college-going.

Preparation is directly related to family educational experience. Students with the most de-tailed and accurate expectations came from families with a tradition of college-going. Preparation was also influenced by association with present and past college-goers in school, in the community and in the workplace. Positive role models helped students prepare by providing indirect simula-tion of college-going through the sharing of college experiences.

The beliefs students develop about valued adult roles and the part played by education in structuring access to those roles, a characteristic we labeled "opportunity orientation," represents a second major dimension of student diversity. The reason so many first-generation college-goers attend as adults has to do with the norms for becoming "adult" in the working-class and inner-city communities where they grow up. In many such settings, becoming adult involves getting a job or joining the service, not attending an institution of higher education. As young adults experience educated role models in the military or on the job, they increasingly recognize their own talents and better understand the opportunities afforded by a college degree.

A view of adult status that excludes higher education as an appropriate choice provides an inadequate base for selecting high school courses and leads to indifferent performance in the courses that are chosen. Students with this orientation are most likely to attend college as adults, if at all, and bring with them the liabilities of their previous educational experiences, as well as the challenges of balancing coursework with the demands of a family and a job. The problematic characteristics of more diverse learners are cumulative. Lack of exposure to educated families and rigorous schooling causes preparation deficiencies. These are aggravated by cultural norms that define going to school and attaining adult status as mutually exclusive. The problem would be serious under any circumstances, but it is aggravated by the proportionately greater numbers of Black, Latino, and American Indian students who experience poor preparation.[17]

The interviews identified four categories of student preparation. Group I included graduates who came from educated families, attended suburban or high-performing inner-city schools and always expected to go to college. This was the group who succeeded at places like UCLA despite being stereotyped in some instances as underprepared. Students from this group were very unlikely to attend community colleges. A second large group involved first-generation college students who lacked the detailed preparation of Group I, but who had grown up with strong parental encouragement to build a rewarding life through attending college. Group II identified mentoring, summer programs, and such support activities as tutoring and learning laboratories as critical to their ability to persist. A significant proportion of this group began their postsecondary careers in a community college.

A third, quite small group, grew up in families and communities where the people with whom they associated had not been to college and where they were consistently advised that attending college would make no difference in the opportunities they would subsequently experience. Hampered by a lack of preparation and attitudes that defined college attendance as an inappropriate activity for adults, Group III graduates overcame incredible odds, including negative peer and family pressures. All graduates in this group reported community college experience as part of their degree attainment marathon. A high proportion were employed at the time of the interviews in jobs no better (and in two instances worse) than the jobs they held before entering college, perhaps reflecting the self-fulfilling nature of the prophecy made by their friends and families.

A fourth group, also small, had detailed preparation, but lacked the conviction that a college education would make a significant difference in their lives. Group IV included a number of American Indians who came from reservations where unemployment rates were high and opportunities for professionally trained workers very limited. Several students from this group had attended associate degree institutions.

The characteristics of these four groups illuminate the preparation issue as it is currently defined for community colleges. Group I students are heavily recruited by selective institutions because their admission poses no threat to the way these institutions are currently doing business. Group II students are also heavily recruited, especially by teaching-oriented comprehensive colleges and universities. Even though they require special assistance in making the transition from high school and in coping with the demands of college work, they attend in the traditional full-time mode and are highly motivated. While institutions must make some adaptations to serve them effectively, such changes can often be accomplished by specialized staff, leaving the academic core of the institution free to continue traditional learning practices.

Group III is disproportionately Black and Latino and is concentrated in and around the larger American cities. In a very real sense, no one is anxious to serve this group, if by serving them is meant taking seriously the responsibility for helping them achieve success across the entire range of academic majors. Inner-city community colleges are happy to have them as clients as long as everyone understands that the outcomes for judging institutional success should be social welfare-oriented or preparation for lower level vocational careers. The problem of underpreparation for community colleges is most critically the task of achieving traditional outcomes for students whose diversity in preparation and opportunity orientation make them poor candidates for traditional learning practices.

Group IV is to some extent created by the unique circumstances of life on an Indian reservation. The phenomenon can also be observed among affluent and alienated majority students who have not been persuaded that the quality of their lives depends to any serious degree upon their own exertions.

A Conceptual Framework for Analyzing Preparation Issues

Figure 1 represents a model of the process through which 10 institutions involved in a national study of minority progress to the baccalaureate altered their organizational cultures to respond to the pressures produced by a more diverse student body.[18] When confronted with internal or external pressures to improve participation, institutions reacted in Stage 1 by emphasizing recruitment, financial aid, waiver of admission standards and providing more convenient class offerings. The more diverse students admitted experienced difficulties in meeting academic expectations developed for students with different precollege experiences.

To counter high attrition rates, institutions adopted systematic interventions in Stage 2 to change students so they were better able to cope with institutional expectations. Some of the more multicultural institutions in the study approached a third stage when they adopted strategies to alter the learning environments they provided for more diversely prepared students rather than expecting students to do all of the changing.

Within the model, organizational culture is defined as the assumptions and beliefs shared by members.[19] Adaptation is defined as changes in an organization's behaviors, values and beliefs to maintain or improve relationships with those who control resources.[20, 21] The learning environment consists of the interventions and strategies an institution employs to help students achieve outcomes. The learning environment can be thought of as the observable product of an institution's invisible culture. Administrators and faculty leaders manage culture to ensure that institutions move through the three stages rather than reducing standards, redefining outcomes, or tolerating excessively high attrition.

The model in Figure 1 contrasts open-access institutions and the achievement problems they commonly experience with selective institutions which are much more likely to experience participation problems. However, selective and open-access institutions can experience both types of problems. A racial or ethnic group can be underrepresented in the selective allied health programs of a community college. Conversely, a selective university in an urban setting may have good participation rates accompanied by disproportionately low graduation rates for some groups.

Colleges work with three sets of variables in responding to preparation issues: student characteristics, expected outcomes, and organizational culture. Institutions can limit student diversity through screening out those who lack the skills necessary to achieve specified outcomes within their existing learning environments. They can substitute new outcomes requiring less in the way of preparation or opportunity orientation; or alternatively, the requirements for achieving existing outcomes can be reduced. Finally, they can work to alter the organizational cultures that define the range of student diversity their learning environments serve effectively. Altering organizational culture is the most difficult and time-consuming of the three alternatives, but it is also the one that offers the best hope for augmenting deficiency approaches with alternatives that emphasize achievement.

Institutional Strategies for Responding to Preparation Issues

Community colleges have had substantial success in removing the barriers to participation by previously underrepresented groups. They have also had better success in reducing race and ethnicity-related differences in achievement than many of their four-year counterparts. Important disparities remain, however, and are an important factor underlying much of the current concern about community college outcomes.[22]

In 1986, Blacks were 88% as likely as Anglos to attend a two-year college in the 26 states where they represented more than 5% of the population. A Black attending a two-year college was 85% as likely as an Anglo to graduate. Latinos in the 10 states where they represented more than 5% of the population in 1986 were 68% as likely to attend and 91% as likely to graduate as Anglos. With the exception of a 6% decline in participation by Blacks, all rates remained essentially constant between 1980 and 1986. By way of contrast, Blacks, Latinos, and American Indians, as a group, were only 64% as likely as Anglos to attend a four-year institution in 1986 and only 71% as likely to graduate.[23]

The model in Figure 1 can be used as a tool to help institutions assess the effectiveness of their strategies for responding to student diversity. The first step requires the examination of outcomes over time to determine the relative importance of strategies that focus on reducing barriers, changing students, or changing the learning environment. The outcomes that drive much current debate are graduation and transfer rates. Participation rates also remain important in institutions created to promote equity. While other outcomes might reasonably be considered in any analysis, they cannot substitute for the purposes most closely associated with the policy decision to establish community colleges as opportunity institutions.

Institutions with declining participation rates may discover that changes in the policy environment, including quality initiatives and diminishing student financial assistance, have eroded some of the progress they had previously made in serving underrepresented populations. The strategies for removing barriers to participation are grouped under stage 1 of the model.

Figure 1
A Model of Institutional Adaptation to Student Diversity

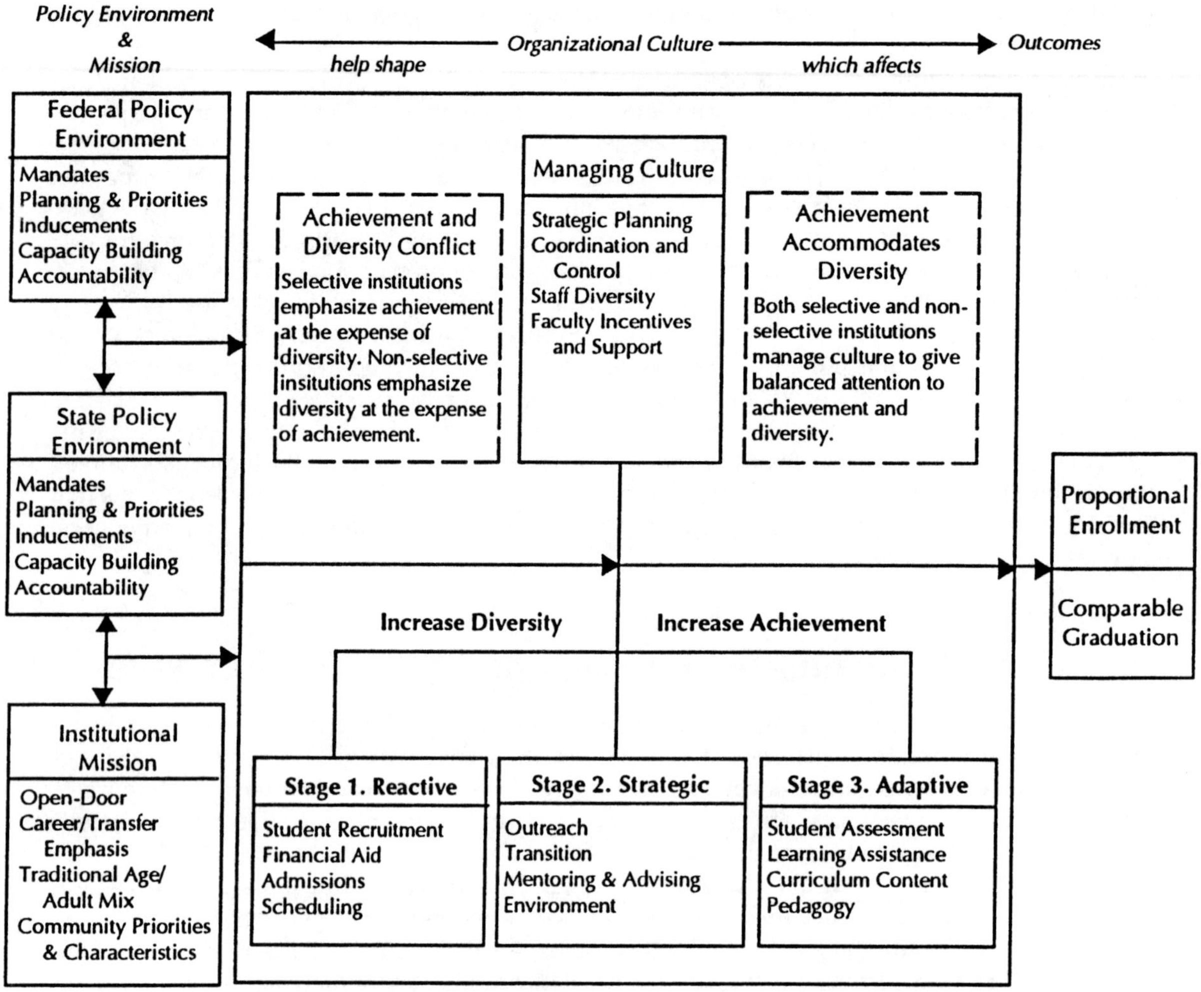

Policy Environment & Mission ← *help shape* ——— *Organizational Culture* ——— *which affects* → *Outcomes*

Federal Policy Environment

Mandates
Planning & Priorities
Inducements
Capacity Building
Accountability

Achievement and Diversity Conflict

Selective institutions emphasize achievement at the expense of diversity. Non-selective insitutions emphasize diversity at the expense of achievement.

Managing Culture

Strategic Planning
Coordination and Control
Staff Diversity
Faculty Incentives and Support

Achievement Accommodates Diversity

Both selective and non-selective institutions manage culture to give balanced attention to achievement and diversity.

State Policy Environment

Mandates
Planning & Priorities
Inducements
Capacity Building
Accountability

Proportional Enrollment

Comparable Graduation

Increase Diversity   **Increase Achievement**

Institutional Mission

Open-Door
Career/Transfer Emphasis
Traditional Age/ Adult Mix
Community Priorities & Characteristics

Stage 1. Reactive

Student Recruitment
Financial Aid
Admissions
Scheduling

Stage 2. Strategic

Outreach
Transition
Mentoring & Advising
Environment

Stage 3. Adaptive

Student Assessment
Learning Assistance
Curriculum Content
Pedagogy

*Student diversity has three major dimensions: (1) preparation, (2) opportunity orientation, and (3) mode of college-going. African Americans, Hispanics, and American Indians share these dimensions with other groups, but are distributed differently as a function of historic discrimination and socio-economic status. Note: Adaptation for community colleges, modified 1/25/90.

Community colleges in Chicago and elsewhere have placed greater emphasis on recruiting from inner-city schools and have established merit scholarships for students of color. Such actions communicate their interest in serving the academically talented as well as those with preparation problems. Many community colleges have also placed renewed emphasis on the transfer sequence, often in collaboration with neighboring four-year institutions. Urban community colleges have adopted multiple admissions criteria for selective allied health programs to ensure enrollments reflective of the racial and ethnic composition of their open-door programs.

Fine tuning Stage 1 strategies may provide help to community colleges in changing the image they present to better prepared students. However, additional emphasis on removing barriers has at least as much potential for increasing the preparation problem as for moderating it. More promising for most community colleges are the Stage 2 strategies that focus on preparation, broadly defined, as a means of reducing the mismatch between institutional expectations and student capabilities.

Community colleges can motivate high school students to stay in school and to take more rigorous coursework through outreach programs of the type offered in Los Angeles and elsewhere. They can strengthen preparation and assist transition through summer programs of the type offered by South Mountain College in Phoenix. They can emphasize mentoring and tutoring to offset limited opportunity orientations in addition to providing extra help for students with nontraditional academic preparation. And they can give special attention to buffering identifiable minority students from the racism that often intrudes from the surrounding community.

It is not sufficient to offer some of these interventions to students who qualify under state or federal equal opportunity guidelines. Community colleges are most often the institution of choice for first-generation college students. Such individuals are, at best, uncertain climbers. Providing them with a ladder with missing rungs is a sure recipe for failure. The institutions most advanced in their use of Stage 2 strategies provide a comprehensive and coherent combination of these interventions to all students on the basis of need rather than race or ethnicity.

Community colleges also need to enhance their competitive position for the first-generation students in the traditional age group most likely to benefit from Stage 2 interventions. One promising approach is the guaranteed acceptance program currently offered in the states of Pennsylvania and Washington. At the Community College of Philadelphia (CCP), students are guaranteed acceptance to the main campus of Penn State in the program of their choice with full credit for all coursework upon completion of the provisions of an agreement they sign at the time they enter CCP. Any attempt to improve advising and remove barriers to trouble-free transfer will improve the appeal of community colleges to better prepared and more serious students.

Stage 2 strategies can be found in abundance in most community colleges. Some improvement in outcomes may result from further refinement, better coordination and making the programs and services more widely available. It seems highly unlikely, however, that race and ethnicity-related differences in participation and achievement, in addition to generally low graduation and transfer rates, can be fully offset by relying exclusively on Stage 1 or Stage 2 interventions. Community colleges will also have to consider Stage 3 strategies for changing their learning environments.

Technology has been (and perhaps remains) the great hope of administrators and state policy officials for changing the learning environment. The results of implementing new technologies have been disappointing, however, largely because technology has had little impact on classroom instruction.[24] Altering the values and beliefs of faculty members so that technology and other forms of pedagogy are used effectively with the students who now attend community colleges, as distinct from those the faculty might prefer, requires changes in organizational culture. Such changes are most likely to occur when Stage 3 strategies are systematically employed.[25]

Student assessment helps to create more manageable learning conditions within the classroom. It may also be used, not necessarily to popular acclaim, to enforce accountability for student learning as in Florida and Texas. Developmental education—reading, writing, mathematics, study skills, test-taking skills, and personal adjustment[26]—represents a major Stage 3 strategy for addressing deficiencies between student preparation and the demands of academic programs. Developmental programs pressure existing faculty practices by demonstrating that under the right conditions underprepared students can persist and achieve at rates that sometimes exceed the performance of better prepared counterparts in the standard programs. For optimum contribution, such programs must be designed to counter the common student perception that they constitute an obstacle separating them from their reasons for attending college.

Curricular and pedagogical change can be powerful strategies for changing culture where faculty are a central part of the decision-making process. While the focus of institutional response to diversity has often involved incorporating the contributions of other cultures through adding courses or changing the content of existing courses, there is also the opportunity to strengthen faculty accountability for transfer programs (as distinct from individual courses)[27] and to bring transfer courses into closer alignment with the offerings of four-year institutions which accept the largest proportion of a college's transfers.

Arguably, community colleges have paid more attention to all three of the stages than their four-year sister institutions. Part of the transfer issue clearly relates to the unwillingness of four-year institutions to match the scheduling adjustments, support services and responsive learning environments routinely provided by many community colleges.[28]

While changing organizational culture represents the most promising long-term approach for dealing with preparation issues, short-term strategies are also necessary to address immediate problems. Two possibilities for exploration are suggested by the experiences of urban schools and university professional schools.

City school districts in Memphis, Los Angeles, and elsewhere have chosen to concentrate resources on helping some students achieve excellence rather than attempting to bring everyone to some minimum level of underachievement. While the results are sometimes demoralizing for those who remain behind in neighborhood schools stripped of their more talented students, the outcomes for those who remain behind are not discernibly worse than before, and the more talented are challenged to develop their full potential. Honors programs in community colleges represent a manifestation of this line of thought. Too often, however, the criteria for participation exclude highly motivated and talented students of color who have been diagnosed by the deficiency model as underprepared.

The Boston University (BU) Medical School recruits college juniors from historically Black colleges and universities in the South. Students are admitted to medical school *as an honor* at the end of their junior year based on grades and instructors' recommendations. No test scores are involved. Students spend their senior year at BU where they earn credits toward graduation from their sending colleges, while concurrently receiving credit for several of the courses required for their first year of medical school. Those who belong to sororities and fraternities at sending colleges are given full membership in related BU sororities and fraternities. At the end of their senior year at BU, they receive a bachelor's degree from the sending institution and enter medical school a step ahead of those who came in through regular admissions procedures.[29] The tech-prep option represents a similar approach by community colleges for career programs.[30]

The BU program and those offered by the public schools in Los Angeles and Memphis are important because they represent radical departures from the deficiency model. The magnet programs identify and build on students' strengths rather than focusing on weaknesses. The BU program provides an alternative for students who would never qualify for admission to a medical school under standard procedures. Both programs make use of the concepts embodied in the model through addressing systematically all three stages of adaptation within a single program. Both the magnet program and the alternative medical school program remove barriers, help students adjust to high expectations, and change the learning environments students experience.

Community colleges are not free to choose between the deficiency and achievement models. Given scarce resources and continuing pressures from students seeking access, they must continue to implement the deficiency model as best they can. Concurrently some may choose to dedicate more of their resources to programs where carefully selected and highly motivated nontraditional learners from underrepresented communities experience an opportunity to achieve excellence. Perhaps the most compelling reason for seeking better balance between deficiency and achievement approaches rests with the contribution of the latter to administrative efforts to alter organizational culture.

The Role of Leadership

As a function of their philosophy and funding, community colleges remain more firmly attached to unrestricted access, job training, community service, convenience and low cost than to such correlates of achievement as intellectual inquiry, the collegiate function, or a generally educated population.[31] While most community colleges display characteristics of all three of the stages depicted in the model, many could improve their outcomes for more diversely prepared students by giving greater attention to Stage 2 and Stage 3 strategies.

How do institutions change to achieve a better balance between the emphasis given to increasing diversity and the attention focused on changing the learning environment to promote higher levels of student achievement? The answer suggested by the model involves the management of organizational culture.

Administrators manage organizational culture through strategic planning, by coordinating and controlling the implementation of plans, by assessing outcomes, by selecting new staff who embody the values and behaviors desired in the changed culture, and by providing incentives and support to existing staff to encourage them to change in desired directions.

The recent efforts of Miami-Dade Community College furnish a case study of how the process operates. Through consensus-building task force activity, the college defined seven shared values related to teaching and learning. These values were legitimated through adoption by the Board of Trustees in December 1987.[32] In a related activity, a second subcommittee, studying the environment Miami-Dade provided for teaching and learning, produced a statement on faculty excellence which was adopted by the board in October 1988.[33]

After reaching consensus on shared values and faculty behaviors related to the attainment of those values, a third subcommittee developed a framework for relating the institution's system of rewards and recognition to the identified values and behaviors. Following extensive discussion and appropriate revisions, the framework was adopted by majority vote of the faculty in April 1989. Concurrent with these efforts to mobilize and empower existing staff, Miami-Dade has worked with the University of Miami to define expectations for new staff and developed a program to ensure new staff develop the values, beliefs, and knowledge necessary for them to become fully contributing members of the Miami-Dade community.

When these efforts are placed in the context of student assessment as mandated by Florida and the learning assistance for which Miami-Dade has long been widely recognized,[34] it is apparent that college leadership has consciously managed the culture to ensure systematic attention to each of the variables that are involved in changing the learning environment. Other community colleges have paid attention to Stage 2 and Stage 3 interventions as well, but most have not been as systematic or persistent in their efforts over such an extended period of time.

Conclusion

The preparation issue is arguably the most important challenge community colleges currently confront. It cannot be neutralized by redefining outcomes so that underprepared students can achieve them. Nor can it be avoided by excluding students who are assessed as extremely high risk. Increasing the numbers who participate without corresponding increases in the numbers who attain outcomes to which the public attaches priority only aggravates the problem. Changing the learning environment, especially that part which is determined by student interaction with faculty members, is the only alternative that offers much hope for long-term improvement.

Approaching the issue of student diversity from the perspective of organizational culture can help institutional leaders avoid the pursuit of strategies that promise diminishing returns. It is organizational culture that furnishes the context within which faculty beliefs and values define teaching and the learning process. It is organizational culture that gives meaning to the concept of underpreparation and defines the appropriate institutional response.

The prevailing community college approach to student preparation issues involves a deficiency model where remediation is emphasized as the dominant strategy for bringing everyone to minimum standards. Needed as well is an achievement model that challenges faculty to design an environment where diversity is valued and individuals are inspired to build on strengths to attain maximum potential. A complicating factor is that the two models need to coexist in most community colleges for the foreseeable future.

The task of implementing achievement models in institutions historically committed to access is, above all, a task of managing culture. While culture management is more time-consuming and difficult than the introduction of technology, it is the only approach through which the faculty who control the nature of the learning environment and its impact on students can be influenced to augment deficiency views and practices. There are emerging models of the way the process works. Efforts to manage culture will be aided by the opportunity to employ new staff as those representative of founding values and beliefs retire in large numbers over the next decade.

References

Anadam, K. "Technology for Education: Promises and Problems" in G. H. Voegel, editor, *Advances in Instructional Technology: New Directions for Community College*, no. 55, Fall 1986.

Astin, A. W. *Minorities in American Higher Education*. San Francisco: Jossey-Bass, 1982.

Augenblick, Van de Water and Associates. *An Examination of the Overall Structure for the Delivery of Public Postsecondary Education in Florida: Final Report of the Structure Committee of the Florida Postsecondary Education Planning Commission*. Denver, Colorado: AVA, January 1990.

Brint, S. and J. Karabel. *The Diverted Dream: Community Colleges and the Promise of Educational Opportunity in America, 1900–1985*. New York: Oxford University Press, 1989.

Cohen, A. M. and F. B. Brawer. *The American Community College*. San Francisco: Jossey-Bass, 1982.

Cross, K. P. and E. F. Fideler, "Community College Missions: Priorities in the Mid-1980s" *Journal of Higher Education*, vol. 60, no. 2, March/April 1989.

Culbert, A. "Early Acceptance and Institutional Linkages in a Model Program of Recruitment, Retention, and Timely Graduation from Medical School" in *Black Student Retention in Higher Education*, edited by M. Lang and C. A. Ford. Springfield, Illinois: Charles C. Thomas, 1988.

Eaton, J. S. *Colleges of Choice: The Enabling Impact of the Community College*. New York: ACE/Macmillan, 1988.

Goodman, P. and J. W. Dean, Jr. "Creating Long-term Organizational Change" in P. Goodman and Associates, *Change in Organizations*. San Francisco: Jossey-Bass, 1982.

Kotler, P. and K. F. A. Fox. *Strategic Marketing for Educational Institutions*. Englewood Cliffs, New Jersey: Prentice Hall, Inc., 1985.

Kuh, G. D. and T. E. J. Whitt. *The Invisible Tapestry: Culture in American Colleges and Universities*. ASHE/ERIC Higher Education Report, no. 1. Washington, D.C.: Association for the Study of Higher Education, 1988.

McCabe, R. H. "The Educational Program of the American Community College: A Transition" in J. S. Keaton, editor, *Colleges of Choice*. New York: ACE/Macmillan, 1988.

Miami-Dade Community College. *Faculty Excellence: Teaching/Learning*. District Board of Trustees, October 1988.

Orwell, G. et al. *The Chicago Study of Access and Choice in Higher Education*. Chicago: University of Chicago Committee on Public Policy Studies, September 1984.

Parnell, D. *Dateline 2000: The New Higher Education Agenda*. Washington, D.C.: The Community College Press, 1990.

Pfeffer, J. and G. R. Salanck. *The External Control of Organizations*. New York: Harper and Row, 1978.

Pincus, F. L. and E. Archer. *Bridges to Opportunity: Are Community Colleges Meeting the Transfer Needs of Minority Students?* New York: Academy for Educational Development and College Entrance Examination Board, 1989.

Richardson, R. C., E. C. Fisk and M. A. Okun. *Literacy in the Open Access College*. San Francisco: Jossey-Bass, 1983.

Richardson, R. C. and H. L. Simmons. "Is It Time for a New Look at Academic Organization in Community Colleges?" *Community College Review*, vol. 17, no. 1, Summer 1989.

Richardson, R. C. *Serving More Diverse Students: A Contextual View*. Denver, Colorado: Education Commission of the States, June 1989.

Richardson, R. C. and L. W. Bender. *Fostering Minority Access and Achievement in Higher Education*. San Francisco: Jossey-Bass, 1987.

Richardson, R. C. and E. F. Skinner. *Achieving Access and Quality: Case Studies in Equity*. New York: ACE/Macmillan, scheduled for release Summer 1990.

Skinner, E. F. and R. C. Richardson, "Making It in a Majority University: The Minority Graduate's Perspective," *Change*, vol. 20/no. 3, May/June 1988.

Roueche, J. E. and G. A. Baker. *Access and Excellence: The Open Door College*. Washington, D.C.: Community College Press, 1987.

Roueche, S. D. and U. N. Comstock. "A Report on Theory and Methods for the Study of Literacy Development in Community Colleges." Washington, D.C.: National Institute of Education, 1981.

Tomlinson, L. M. *Postsecondary Developmental Programs: A Traditional Agenda with New Imperatives*, Report no. 3. Washington, D.C.: School of Education and Human Development, The George Washington University, 1989.

Warren, J. "The Changing Characteristics of Community College Students" in W. L. Deegan, D. Tillery and Associates, *Renewing the American College*. San Francisco: Jossey-Bass Publishers, 1985.

Wildavsky, A. *Speaking Truth to Power: The Art and Craft of Policy Analysis*. Boston: Little, Brown and Company, 1979.

Notes

1. A. W. Astin, *Minorities in American Higher Education* (San Francisco: Jossey-Bass 1982), p. 153. See also R. C. Richardson, *Serving More Diverse Students: A Contextual View* (Denver: Education Commission of the States, June 1989) for an expanded treatment of the effects of the policy decisions of the "Great Society" era.

2. A. Wildavsky, *Speaking Truth to Power: The Art and Craft of Policy Analysis* (Boston: Little, Brown and Company, 1979), pp. 49–53.

3. Cited by Wildavsky as the title of a *Saturday Review* essay by Amitai Etzioni.

4. S. Brint and J. Karabel, *The Diverted Dream: Community Colleges and the Promise of Educational Opportunity in America, 1900–1985* (New York: Oxford University Press, 1989).

5. A. M. Cohen and F. B. Brawer, *The American Community College* (San Francisco: Jossey-Bass, 1982), p. 288.

6. R. C. Richardson, E. C. Fisk and M. A. Okun, *Literacy in the Open Access College* (San Francisco: Jossey-Bass, 1983).

7. S. D. Roueche and U. N. Comstock, "A Report on Theory and Methods for the Study of Literacy Development in Community Colleges," ERIC Document Reproduction Service No. ED211 161 (National Institute of Education, 1981).

8. J. Warren, "The Changing Characteristics of Community College Students" in W. L. Deegan, D. Tillery and Associates, *Renewing the American College* (San Francisco: Jossey-Bass, 1985), p. 60.

9. K. P. Cross and E. F. Fideler, "Community College Missions: Priorities in the Mid-1980s," *Journal of Higher Education*, vol. 60, no. 2 (March/April 1989), p. 211.

10. See, for example, R. H. McCabe, "The Educational Program of the American Community College: A Transition" in J. S. Keaton, editor, *Colleges of Choice* (New York: ACE/Macmillan, 1988).

11. Wildavsky (1979), p. 46.

12. For an extended discussion of this phenomenon and additional references, see R. Richardson and L. Bender, *Fostering Minority Access and Achievement in Higher Education* (San Francisco: Jossey-Bass, 1987).

13. Augenblick, Van de Water and Associates, *An Examination of the Overall Structure for the Delivery of Public Postsecondary Education in Florida: Final Report of the Structure Committee of the Florida Postsecondary Education Planning Commission* (Denver, Colorado: AVA, January 17, 1990).

14. P. Kotler and K. F. A. Fox, *Strategic Marketing for Educational Institutions* (Englewood Cliffs, NJ: Prentice Hall, Inc., 1985) is a standard reference on this topic.

15. R. C. Richardson and E. F. Skinner, *Achieving Access and Quality: Case Studies in Equity* (New York: ACE/Macmillan, scheduled for release Summer 1990).

16. A detailed account of the study and its outcomes appears in E. F. Skinner and R. C. Richardson, "Making It in a Majority University: The Minority Graduates Perspective," *Change*, vol. 20/no. 3 (May/June 1988), pp. 34–47.

17. For a study on the concentration of minority students in urban institutions that lack the resources and diversity of the surrounding suburban areas which contribute to the visibility of minority preparation problems, see, for example, G. Orwell et al., *The Chicago Study of Access and Choice in Higher Education* (Chicago: University of Chicago Committee on Public Policy Studies, September 1984).

18. For a complete description of the model and its development, see R. C. Richardson and E. F. Skinner (Summer 1990).

19. G. D. Kuh and T. E. J. Whitt, *The Invisible Tapestry: Culture in American Colleges and Universities,* ASHE/ERIC Higher Education Report, no. 1 (Washington, D.C.: Association for the Study of Higher Education, 1988).

20. The concept of resource dependence is treated in depth in J. Pfeffer and G. R. Salancik, *The External Control of Organizations* (New York: Harper and Row, 1978).

21. P. Goodman and J. W. Dean, Jr., "Creating Long-term Organizational Change" in P. Goodman and Associates, *Change in Organizations* (San Francisco: Jossey-Bass, 1982).

22. This issue is concisely discussed in F. L. Pincus and E. Archer, *Bridges to Opportunity: Are Community Colleges Meeting the Transfer Needs of Minority Students?* (New York: Academy for Educational Development and College Entrance Examination Board, 1989), p. 1.

23. The graduation rates for African Americans, Hispanics and American Indians are significantly higher in four-year than two-year institutions, but the discrepancies between Anglo and minority participation and graduation rates are less in two-year than in four-year institutions. All statistics are based on ratio comparisons of data furnished to the National Center for Educational Statistics through the Higher Education General Information Survey (HEGIS). Comparisons should be interpreted with caution since more two- than four-year institutions fail to report HEGIS data and many of the missing institutions are located in urban settings. The probable effect of their omission is to understate participation and overstate graduation for the two-year sector.

24. K. Anadam, "Technology for Education: Promises and Problems" in G. H. Voegel, editor, *Advances in Instructional Technology: New Directions for Community Colleges,* no. 55, (Fall 1986), pp. 70–71.

25. This proposition is currently being tested in a Ford Foundation-funded research project being conducted by the author. The project has identified faculty behaviors associated with student achievement in community colleges and demonstrated that these behaviors vary significantly across a random sample of community colleges. Currently, we are examining the relationship between administrative priorities and strategies and the incidence of Stage 3 faculty behaviors. A progress report on this project will be presented at the 1990 meeting of the American Association of Community and Junior Colleges.

26. L. M. Tomlinson, *Postsecondary Developmental Programs: A Traditional Agenda with New Imperatives,* Report no. 3 (Washington, D.C.: School of Education and Human Development, The George Washington University, 1989).

27. One scheme for accomplishing this is described in R. C. Richardson and H. L. Simmons, "Is It Time for a New Look at Academic Organization in Community Colleges?" *Community College Review,* vol. 17, no. 1 (Summer 1989), pp. 34–39.

28. The barriers to transfer imposed by public four-year institutions in urban settings are documented in depth in R. C. Richardson and L. W. Bender, *Fostering Minority Access and Achievement in Higher Education* (San Francisco: Jossey-Bass, 1987).

29. A. Culbert, "Early Acceptance and Institutional Linkages in a Model Program of Recruitment, Retention, and Timely Graduation from Medical School" in *Black Student Retention in Higher Education*, edited by M. Lang and C. A. Ford (Springfield, Ill.: Charles C. Thomas, 1988).

30. For a description of this program, see D. Parnell, *Dateline 2000: The New Higher Education Agenda* (Washington, D.C.: The Community College Press, 1990), pp. 60–61.

31. J. S. Eaton, *Colleges of Choice: The Enabling Impact of the Community College* (New York: ACE/Macmillan, 1988), pp. 3–4.

32. The values identified by the teaching/learning project and adopted by the board were published by Miami-Dade Community College in an undated pamphlet titled, "Values: Teaching and Learning." The introduction relates these values to the development of mission goals, philosophy and operational procedures.

33. Miami-Dade Community College, *Faculty Excellence: Teaching/Learning* (District Board of Trustees, October 1988).

34. See, for example, J. E. Roueche and G. A. Baker, *Access and Excellence: The Open Door College* (Washington, D.C.: Community College Press, 1987).

Elements of Culture

Lois Weis

"Most of these people [students at Urban College] have no basic skills; they can't read or write, can't do math, they don't know Malcolm X, John Coltrane, Bobby Seale, Huey Newton. They just don't know. (. . .) I am continually shocked. My own people can't read, write, and know nothing about their own history. We have no heroes. Our heroes become Abraham Lincoln and the Emancipation Proclamation—all the rest are dead and buried (. . .).

Black people are going back to being slaves. That's why I wear this bracelet [locked]; I don't intend to take it off until we get out of slavery." (An Urban College graduate)

This chapter details elements of black student culture at Urban College. As I will argue, these elements are themselves contradictory: students embrace and reject schooling at one and the same time. Students affirm the process that is education but drop in and out of school, arrive late to class, exert little effort and engage in extensive drug use. The effects of the culture are twofold: (1) an exceedingly low graduation rate per entering class; and (2) the reproduction of deeply rooted race/class antagonisms in the broader society. In the latter case, it is black culture acting in concert with white culture that is linked to the reproduction of fundamental antagonisms.

I will briefly compare elements of black student culture with those noted among the white working class. The comparison rests primarily on Paul Willis's data on working class boys in England and Howard London's data on white working class students in a community college in the United States.[1] Unlike the students in Urban College, those in London's study have fathers who are members largely of what Edwards calls the Traditional Proletariat. These jobs are located within the subordinate primary market; they are better paying than secondary market jobs and involve long-term stable work with prospects for advancement. In the United States they are distinguished from secondary market jobs most fundamentally by the presence of unions.[2]

Willis's "lads" are also of the white manual labor working class. While the fathers of students are engaged in generalized rather than in skilled labor, pervasive wagelessness is not a feature of the class landscape.[3] The English equivalent of the wagelessness and economic marginality noted for Urban College students lies with immigrant groups, particularly West Indians. The lads' economic position is therefore closer to that of London's students than that of Urban College students.

It is noteworthy that white working class students at Urban College (who constitute approximately 30 percent of the student body) do not manifest a culture similar to that noted by London and Willis. While it is difficult to assess the depth of this difference given that I did not study white culture directly, it can be argued that white lived culture in Urban College takes a different shape and form from that noted in previous investigations given that it emerges dialectically in relation to that of the black urban underclass as produced in the college as well as the larger white working class. I will address the reproduction of race/class antagonisms toward the end of the chapter.

Attitudes Toward Authority and Knowledge

One dimension of black student culture at the community college is the affirmation of both the idea of teachers and the content of school knowledge. In contrast, investigators of working class white cultural forms note a distinctly negative attitude toward authority and school knowledge, manifested in incivility toward faculty.

The most obvious dimension of the lads' culture, for example, is "entrenched general and personalized opposition to authority." The lads engage in behavior designed to show resentment while stopping just short of outright confrontation. There is, notes Willis,

> an aimless air of insubordination ready with spurious justification and impossible to nail down. If someone is sitting on the radiator, it is because his trousers are wet from the rain, if someone is drifting across the classroom he is going to get some paper for written work, or if someone is leaving class, he is going to empty the rubbish "like he usually does". . . A continuous hum of talk flows around injunctions not to, like the inevitable tide over barely dried sand and everywhere there are rolled-back eyeballs and exaggerated mouthings of conspirational secrets.[4]

While it is tempting to relate these behaviors to adolescence rather than social class *per se*, it is important to note that adult white working class males in the community college exhibit similar attitudes toward authority and engage in comparable behavior.[5] About a month or so after school opened, students in London's study began injecting *sotto-voce* taunts into classroom lectures and discussions. This opposition took a distinctly class form in that, for the most part, it was done by students in manual training programs and aimed at liberal arts teachers or vocational training teachers who were considered too abstract. Law enforcement students did not harass teachers who were ex-detectives, for example, but they did harass the lawyer who taught legal aspects of police work. Students reacted negatively only in those classes that were "too intellectual," that is, too centered on mental labor.[6]

The case of Urban College students, both male and female, is substantially different. Rather than rejecting the idea of teachers or the content of school knowledge, Urban College students criticize teachers only in so far as they do not encourage what students consider a fair transaction. In return for respect or obedience on the part of students, students expect faculty to share their knowledge. As the following transcriptions suggest, negativity is expressed only in terms of faculty not caring enough or not working hard enough to ensure that students learn. In contrast to the white working class, Urban College students steadfastly affirm what the faculty have to offer—they simply want them to offer it and hold teachers at least partially responsible for student failure.[7]

> *Anthony:* See what it is that, for one thing the instructor—he doesn't present the class to make anyone feel comfortable. He could be a much more influential force in the class if he would emphasize certain things and de-emphasize things that he emphasizes right now. As far as participation, don't be so sarcastic because people that are hesitant to get up in class right now are afraid more so of him than they are of the class.
>
> (. . .) They are afraid of his critical judgment on them as a human being and an individual and a student, instead of him using his influence to make these people feel comfortable.
>
> *LW:* Could you elaborate?
>
> *Anthony:* He would, I imagine, have a much better class, put a greater attendance record and fewer drop out if he would put himself in the position to realize that the students don't have confidence within themselves yet, and a little more personal understanding. (. . .) It's a monotone, monotonous type of class, no fluent conversation, no fluent inter-relationship between the instructor and the student. (a Business Administration student)

* * *

James: I would like to see more dedication on the part of the faculty.

LW: In what sense?

James: There is a vast difference between a pro and a novice in anything. If you are a professional, you take pride in whatever your specialty is; you take pride in doing a good job. The old-fashioned shoe cobbler, he took immense pride in turning out or trying to turn out the perfect pair of shoes. I feel a professional person can look at the situation no different. That you must take pride in whatever you are doing and try to do the best possible job. I feel that any teacher over there should be concerned about his students more than the others, and enough to look down the line and pick the paper a student has achieved and he can see his handiwork in the achievement of the individual students.

When I went to school (. . .) the teacher held the same place of honor and respect that the black preacher did who came to the house on Sunday to eat up all the chicken. Well a teacher held the same esteem that he did. In my household I *had to study and I had to learn, but in exchange for this my teachers were dedicated.* [My emphasis]

LW: When you say that teachers here are not dedicated, what do you mean?

James: (. . .) There may be some who don't have what I consider a dedication, they are just there to get the money. They are not unlike the students themselves [referring to the commonly held notion that many students attend school simply to obtain grant money]. They are there to get paid and they are going to do as less they can. . . . This works to the detriment of the student because what it does is lower standards and makes the person think that they are getting an education when they are not. Then they leave this facility and go some place else; they get a job, go to another school, then they cannot pass the entrance test, or they get in class then they can't maintain because the proper groundwork hasn't been laid over there. . . . I feel that the ones [teachers] who are not dedicated should be held to performance within the scope of their employment. If they cannot perform, then it's about standing aside and allowing someone to assume the position who can. (. . .) I want my teachers to be dedicated in teaching me, not just there to get the dollar. (a Paralegal student)

* * *

[an informal group discussion]

Johnnie: As far as the professors I'd attempt to keep their attendance in line (. . .) because the professors at Urban College tend to just take for granted the students in this school.

(. . .) They take the attitude that the student at this school doesn't really want to learn. He's here for some reason or another other than to learn. "So I'm going to miss this day and I'm going to miss that day."

Claude: It's bias.

Johnnie: (. . .) This is my first semester. I started off with five classes and now I'm presently at four. Out of four classes I have two good instructors that are there when they are supposed to be and the way they go about instructing is compatible. You know, you can really get into it. But I have two other instructors that are hardly ever there; what they teach they don't test on, and they use attendance as their chain on you or something. He says if you don't attend, you don't get a good grade, but if you attend and he's not there, your motivation about getting to this class tends to drop somewhat. You go to class; you break your neck to get there at 9:00 [a.m.] and you go to class and the instructor's not there and he told you you were going to have a test and you studied *all* night—stuff like that.

(. . .) If they [faculty] couldn't handle the job in the beginning they shouldn't have took the job. 'Cuz you can't go out here and get a job in industry and then expect somebody else to do your job 'cuz that's too much for you. You shouldn't be there in the beginning (. . .). You see, a lot of these professors use teaching as a second job or even a third job. There's a lot of good instructors there but they don't apply themselves. I know the students don't either and that has the instructor's motivation drop somewhat. (. . .) I can understand that, but *that is their job* [emphasis mine]. And so far as the students are concerned, they are paying to go to school and if they show up or not, that's their fault.

* * *

Jerome: At Urban College the instructors tend to make that assumption that everybody is on the same footing when they're not. Certain people can't even understand whiteys, so there's a communications breakdown. Then you have a personality clash between some teachers and students. (. . .) You know, I take the attitude you're white, you don't care, you get paid anyway. I know you don't care if I learn. That don't caring attitude—it's transmitted over a period of time. (. . .) Students are off into that, so there's no communication between students and teachers.

LW: (. . .) Could you be a bit more specific?

Jerome: In a sense, like, you have various wealth of people, most of them are people you can categorize as being unemployed, underemployed, social service recipients, you know, uh, poorly educated in the sense that the reading level and the math skills are below par of most high school kids now. So you know that with that knowledge that most instructors up there have, they are still around there with that Harvard school attitude and that's not Harvard. So to me that's cold and impersonal. "I'm going to do my job and fail three quarters of them and the two/three good ones can just slip through," you know. (a Fashion Merchandising student)

The above discussions suggest that Urban College students do not reject the idea of teachers, nor do they question the legitimacy of their knowledge. They are willing to admit that faculty possess worthwhile knowledge and that they, as students, would like to obtain it. Within the context of Willis's teaching paradigm (which is only partially related to a class paradigm), students resent the lack of what they consider a fair exchange.[8] Some students, like Jerome, attribute the lack of a fair exchange to racism. As he states, "You know, I take the attitude, you're white, you don't care, you get paid anyway. I know you don't care if I learn."[9] Even those who are most critical, however, adhere strongly to the notion that the content of knowledge is legitimate. Not only do they see knowledge as legitimate, but they also envision it as power. College knowledge has an immediacy and potency that is readily verbalized; it is not an abstract set of codes or principles but rather leads to personal enhancement and collective improvement directly. This is clear in the interviews with Anthony, Jerome, and James below.

Anthony: [on a Salesmanship class]

[I've learned] how to make a presentation. It made me aware of public speaking. (. . .) It made me aware of "know yourself before you try to sell anyone else."

(. . .) There is a few people in this particular class that are still a little withdrawn. I guess you know from being in the class, a few of them are still sort of hesitant. But now that I know the importance of myself being confident, and confidence to the particular person that I am trying to sell something to, I have no qualms about speaking right out now, because I know not only is it going to benefit me but if there is anyone who I might be working for in this particular field it is gonna benefit them all, and by benefiting them I know it is gonna benefit me.

LW: So that all these sales presentations that people are making in class are useful?

Anthony: (. . .) Public speaking is. *I knew it had a definite importance or it wouldn't be offered in a college level* [my emphasis], but now I have become aware of what it can offer if you are gonna be in this particular field or any field. (a Business Administration student)

* * *

Jerome: [on a Salesmanship class]

No matter what the attitude the instructor has, he is presenting some valid material. You can't fight it nowhere round the world. In the sense that he is giving it out wrong, that might be another thing, but the material *is* valid. There is a reason behind it; you have to be very naive not to see it. (a Fashion Merchandising student)

* * *

James: One of my primary objectives is to write. A man like Mr _____, the English composition teacher, has helped me immensely in this regard. (. . .) Now I want to become a writer because I believe I have something to say and heretofore I have done the same thing that a writer would have to have, giving people advice, counseling them, that sort of thing. But today I would like to put it down on paper so that those who come after me will at least have certain guidelines whereas they can get around the pitfalls I have experience with. And I have had experience with some pitfalls. You can't be out there [the streets] for twenty years without running into these pitfalls and witnessing the effects of these pitfalls.

LW: So you feel that there are specific skills, like writing, that a school like this can give you. Are there other things beside writing?

James: Sure, the law. The law encompasses it all, that people, random people, ordinary people to and fro up and down the street they run afoul of the law because they have had no experience with the law. They haven't been taught or they haven't been trained in the legal aspects of living. I feel that if people did have a basic working knowledge of the law and how the law works, you would automatically have less crime because they would have learned to appreciate the law.

LW: You are saying something very interesting. You said that people don't know the law on the streets and you also said that if they did know the law there would be less crime. Why is that?

James: This is going to lower crime because if a person understands the legal machinery they can protect themselves better, but the law has heretofore been used to victimize certain people who don't know the law. But this other guy knows and you don't know, like you have a (. . .) relationship with the preponderance of the dominance resting with the people who have knowledge of the law and he can work the relationship the way he chooses. So you end up being used in your ignorance of the law, and I have seen this happen countless times. It hasn't happened to me, but I have seen it happen to others.

LW: So you want knowledge to be more evenly distributed?

James: I want it to be universal, because you see, law, contemporary law, man-made law is with us from the cradle to the grave and it is incredulous to me that the system would deny basic legal education to its citizens if you are talking about making better citizens. You have crime because citizens, to a degree, do not want to obey the laws. Now spiraling crime keeps pace with inflation and just as inflation can go into a depression, spiraling crime can go into outright anarchy. All because they do not know; all because way down the line you had the tendency to cancel out respect for the law by keeping the knowledge away from ordinary people.

The point here is that students affirm rather than contradict legitimated knowledge. This goes well beyond merely viewing knowledge as legitimate; students see an immediacy and potency to knowledge and some, like James, argue that it should be shared. He wants to write "so that those who come after me will at least have certain guidelines whereas they can get around the pitfalls I have had experience with. And I have had experience with some pitfalls. You can't be out there [the streets; see chapter 1] for twenty years without running into these pitfalls and witnessing the effects of these pitfalls." For James, knowledge does not represent a commodity to be accumulated and exchanged solely on an individual basis; it is useful primarily in terms of the collectivity. This of course deviates from the middle class model where, as Jean Anyon argues, knowledge is seen as a "possession." In exchange for information, facts and dates, middle class students expect to obtain good grades, acceptance at college, and a good job.[10] While there is certainly some of this among lower class black students (due primarily to a dominant ideology which stresses individual accumulation and exchange), knowledge is also seen in relation to the collectivity.

Chronic Absence

A second cultural element is related to class attendance. For Willis's working class lads, absenteeism signals their generally oppositional stance; their "struggle to win symbolic and physical space from the institution and its rules and to defeat its main perceived purpose: to make you 'work'."[11] Students are adept at managing the formal system and winning space for themselves. The core skill here is being able to get out of any given classroom, thus preserving personal mobility within the school. These actions do not contradict their perceptions of schooling and school authority. London also concludes that high absenteeism among white working class students follows more or less logically from perceptions of the institution.[12]

Urban College students, unlike those of the white working class as described in previous investigations, actively affirm knowledge and the idea of teachers. Criticism of the faculty centers around beliefs that they are not trying hard enough, are not meeting their contractual obligations (showing up to class), or are too impersonal. There is a sense on the part of Urban College students that faculty possess knowledge that is worthwhile. Despite this, the absentee rate at Urban College is exceptionally high. This coincides with the fact that one of the things that the institution attempts to extract from students is regular attendance and a sense of responsibility for such attendance.[13] There is a well-articulated attendance policy which is announced at the beginning of each semester in every class. Students are allowed a pre-determined number of cuts in any given class before their names are struck from class rolls. Attendance qua attendance *counts* and student names are removed from class lists if the maximum number of cuts is exceeded within the first three weeks of school. Students are given "W" or occasionally "F" grades if they exceed the maximum number of cuts during the remainder of the semester. If a student's name is dropped during the first three weeks of the term, he/she is not eligible for grant money that semester.[14] Grant checks amount to approximately $500.00 per term (tuition is also paid) and are distributed about two-thirds of the way through each semester.[15] It is possible for students to receive all "W" grades and still maintain grant eligibility. Over 90 percent of students at the college receive financial aid of this sort.[16]

In spite of the attendance policy and the fact that, generally speaking, students do not overtly reject the nature of knowledge embedded within the institution, the absentee rate is extremely high. Students consistently register for classes, obtain grant money, are given "W" or "F" grades for excessive cuts, and register for these same courses next semester when the pattern is likely to repeat itself.[17] Data presented below for courses offered in the 1979 Fall semester provide some indication of the extent of absenteeism and associated dropout rates.

While these data do not measure absence from class *per se*, the "W" grade, in particular, provides an indication of such absence. Faculty generally give "W" grades to students who stop attending class, although some faculty fail these students. Since "F" and "W" grades are also given to students who attend class regularly but do not complete the course successfully, they must be interpreted with caution.

The high percentage of withdrawals is noteworthy. An average of 30 percent of males and females end up with "W" grades in college courses. The failure rate is also high, and it is only a slight overstatement to argue that close to half the students do not successfully complete any given course (not including those who drop out in the first three weeks). It is only in the Radiologic Technology program, which is the only selective program on campus and is comprised over-whelmingly of white students (see Table 2.4 for estimates of enrollment in curriculum by student race) that this pattern does not occur.[18] Here the failure and withdrawal rates are each less than 5 percent. This is in sharp contrast with mathematics, where 36 percent of the students receive "W" grades in college credit courses and 15 percent fail them. The data are similarly striking for remedial mathematics courses: 31 percent of students receive "W" grades and 15 percent fail.

Table 2.1
Fail and Withdraw in College Credit and Remedial Classes, Fall 1979[a]

Courses	Fail		Withdraw	
	%	No.	%	No.
College Credit				
Mathematics[b]	14.5	12	36.1	30
Science[c]	8.4	34	26.8	109
English	13.0	65	27.3	150
Social Science	8.5	56	25.5	168
Health and Physical Science	3.1	4	30.5	39
Secretarial Science	25.8	86	27.3	91
Business Administration	4.7	32	33.5	227
Paralegal Assistant	7.5	14	21.3	40
Fashion Buying and Merchandising	—	—	28.4	25
General Studies	—	—	28.5	59
Criminal Justice	—	—	44.1	30
Child Care	6.6	11	22.9	38
Radiologic Technology[d]	4.2	1	4.2	1
Remedial[e]				
Mathematics	15.9	34	31.3	67
Business Administration	6.4	3	29.8	14
English[f]	16.0	66	31.2	129

[a]   Figures were calculated on the basis of grade sheets turned in by instructors at the end of the term. All day classes are included in the tabulations. Data are presented for the combined male and female population. An analysis by gender revealed only slight differences. Figures refer to percent of total enrolled in all courses in each curriculum.
[b]   Calculated by curriculum.
[c]   Chemistry, Physics, Biology.
[d]   This program has very few black students due to stringent entrance requirements.
[e]   Students are placed in these courses on the basis of test scores on an examination in English and Mathematics. Many of these classes are graded on a Satisfactory (S)/Unsatisfactory (U) basis. The "F" and "U" grades are consolidated here.
[f]   Over 21 percent of all students enrolled in Remedial English classes received "incomplete."

Absenteeism is further clarified in Table 2.2. Faculty were asked to note the number of students attending their classes "regularly" on 14 January and 1 April 1980. Since the semester does not end officially until the middle of May, the data understate actual attrition per semester.

Data again suggest widespread absenteeism. In remedial courses, teachers estimate that 50 percent of students attend regularly by 1 April, and the situation is only slightly better in college credit classes: 68 percent attend regularly by the same date. My own in-class observations indicate even greater absenteeism than Tables 2.1 or 2.2 suggest. A class in Fashion Merchandising began with close to 35 students; by 14 December between seven and 12 students attended the course. Twelve of an original 32 students were attending Salesmanship by 17 November. Thirty-four students attended a Business Seminar (a remedial course) on 8 February; attendance dropped to between four and 22 by 5 May. *Actual attendance* is even lower than that suggested by data presented in Tables 2.1 or 2.2. It must be kept in mind that this is not simply a measure of class attendance: students who do not attend class do not receive credit for the course.

Chronic absence as well as stopping in and out are distinct elements of lived cultural form among students at Urban College. As the discussions below indicate, students comment negatively on this practice and are quick, like the faculty and administration, to label it a "problem." At the same time, these students are part of the collective culture and engage in the very practices they criticize. Among the students interviewed below, only one (Diane) attends class regularly.[19] James was not allowed to register for courses the following semester because of the number of "W's" on his record. Jerome only occasionally attends class and has been enrolled in degree programs at Urban College and other local institutions on and off for over ten years.[20] Belinda has been at Urban

Table 2.2
Class attendance as reported by faculty, Spring 1980[a]

Courses	14 January	1 April	Percentage retained
College Credit			
English	386	230	59.6
Mathematics	109	74	67.8
Business Administration	532	324	60.9
Science	426	297	69.7
Social Science	275	204	74.2
Secretarial Science	115	82	71.3
Fashion Buying and Merchandising	64	41	64.1
Child Care	69	64	92.7
Radiologic Technology	24	21	87.5
Criminal Justice	78	67	85.9
Total	2078	1404	67.6
Remedial			
English	315	144	45.7
Mathematics	227	125	55.0
Business Administration	72	40	55.6
Total	614	309	50.3
Total College Credit and Remedial	2692	1713	63.3

[a] Faculty were asked to note the number of students who attend "regularly" in each class they teach. Data are presented by curriculum.

College for over four years and has still not accumulated enough credits to graduate. The widespread nature of this practice contributes to an exceedingly low graduation rate per entering class. It has been estimated that of the 827 students admitted into degree programs in the Fall of 1977, only 93, or 11 percent, graduated in May 1979. The figure is somewhat better for the following year: of 527 students admitted in Fall 1978, it has been estimated that 131, or 25 percent, graduated in May 1980. Even assuming a three-year cycle, only 131 of the 827 (16 percent) admitted in the Fall of 1977 graduated three years later.[21]

Jerome: The retention rate of the students is awful now, you know. Were you around in September? The campus was full, you know, you couldn't move around. Now it is like an isolated jungle.

LW: I've noticed that (. . .) Why do people drop out?

Jerome: They lose interest in it. They lose interest in the school. Like what I am saying is, when you sit down and really weigh the advantage, you say now here I am, got two kids, I know I need a job bad but I don't have the skills to get this job. Now school can provide me with some of the skills that I need to obtain a job that will take me up off subsistence, but I don't have time to go to school. My time now has become so valuable that I have to use it wisely to more or less like make sure that everything stay correct at home. So you cannot study with all them problems on your head, you know, knowing where your rent gonna come from, your next food of mouth, not so much your mouth, it's the kids' mouth, making sure they stay warm and healthy, you know. This is the problem.

So, a lot of blacks are eliminated through a whole lot of social mis-errors, not only blacks I would imagine all people—white too (. . .) but it is more pronounced, you can see it better in the black community than you can see [it] in the white, where the average age of the teenage girl at 13, you know, five out of six, you know, got a baby already. You know, it's a lack of training, and definitely, it's no question, clear across the board that it is a lack of home training. Then you get into a deeper psychological sort of thing; people accept the attitude that they just got a position in life, their position is never having any importance into it. They are willing to accept that. (. . .) They just give up. (a Fashion Merchandising student)

* * *

Belinda: Before I came here I drove a cab. There were pimps waitin' on these girls [at Urban College]. I had one guy I drove him around for a whole year; four times a year when the BEOG checks came out. He registered, came to a couple of classes now and then, checks came out and he withdrew. (a Business Administration student)

* * *

LW: Do you get the impression that most of the students here are pretty serious about their work?

Diane: Well I find that it splits. I find that some are very serious and others, they could [not] care less. (. . .)

LW: Why do you think they're here if they're not serious?

Diane: Well I don't know. It's hard for me to understand. Like when grant checks come out classes all of a sudden get very small, and they also get smaller when the work gets difficult and they can't do it, so they drop. (a Secretarial Science student)

* * *

James: I feel that the attendance policy, as it is structured, it is unfair. But at the same time I feel that there are some people who go to the school who should be penalized because they are undertaking fraud, because when you register you sign a contract in order to get the BEOG grant, in that you will attend school etc. etc. Now if you go for a week or two and you don't go back anymore until they hand out the BEOG checks and you go pick up the check and you initiated this knowingly and intentionally, it's fraud and they should be dealt with accordingly.

Now the attendance policy, I think, has a tendency to penalize students who really want to come to class but due to their lifestyle or their problems, or the neighborhood where they live, or problems with children in the household that they [classes] sometimes are missed, and I believe a system could be worked out whereas all of these factors can be taken into consideration, whereas these outright wrongdoers can be penalized.

(. . .) I am almost out of Public Speaking. (. . .) I don't have children, I don't have a wife to go home to, but there are people over there who do and it works to an extreme detriment and it has a tendency to demoralize them and it will drive them off campus. I feel that they should adjust the attendance policy. There are classes that started out with 35–40 people and now they have got about 9 or 12 people. And that shouldn't be. (a Paralegal student)

While students are critical of this practice, they engage in the behavior they criticize. James admits that he is "almost out of Public Speaking," and Jerome rarely attends class, even when he is on campus. Students are far more critical when, as James puts it, "you go pick up the check and you initiated this knowingly and intentionally, it's fraud and (. . .) should be dealt with accordingly." If it is not intentionally fraudulent, students label absenteeism a "problem" but are less harsh in their judgment, locating the source of this problem in the home. Both James and Jerome clearly articulate this. Jerome refers specifically to the "lack of home training" and James argues that the attendance policy as a "tendency to penalize students who really want to come to class but due to *their* lifestyle [emphasis mine] or *their* problems, or the neighborhood where they live, or problems with children in the household that they [classes] sometimes are missed." Unlike that of the working class whites, the behavior depicted here is not *overtly* oppositional and is not linked totally to the institution. Students partially locate the source of this behavior in themselves. This is important, and, as I will argue in later chapters, must be linked to factors within the institution as well as the broader class/ cultural context in which it operates, and the history of black resistance in the United States.

Arriving Late to Class

Even students who attend class often walk in late. They are marked "absent" or "present" depending on a given faculty member's policy with respect to lateness.[22] Some faculty consider a student absent after the first ten minutes of class, while others count a pre-determined number of late arrivals as one absence. Still others consider anyone "present" who comes to class at all, no matter how late. Individual faculty policy appears to exert little impact on this practice since the pattern described in the two classes below is rather common.

Salesmanship class 17 September 1979*

10:00–10:50 a.m.

[Professor takes roll at 10:00]
[only ten people in class—over half the class is missing]

Mr Pierce: (. . .) Full consumption and full production means full employment. We are prosperous so long as goods are bought and sold. As long as goods are bought and sold, everybody is busy working.

[10:10 two women walk in]

(. . .) In a market economy employment is based on full production. This country depends on production and goods being sold. Salesmen are very important for this country. We need salesmen to keep the economy going.[23]

[10:12 one man walks in]

[10:15 another man walks in]

(. . .) In this country we depend on factories doing maximum production. To keep prosperity high, you have to be constantly selling goods. Goods have to be sold. When selling drops off, we go into a dangerous recession. You're all too young to have lived through the first depression. We're now coming into the second, but government takes over. Government hires people to work. Got to find a source of income for people. Government steps in and creates jobs for people. Government doesn't mind since roads are being built; parks are being cleaned up. In our economy which is based upon full production, goods have to be produced, things have to be sold. Keeps economy going.

[10:20 one woman walks in]

(. . .) Salesperson produces profit for self and company. I'm talking about the industrial professional salesperson, not the clerk at the counter; they usually make a fixed wage.

(. . .) A salesman who can build up a following of happy customers will do well and make a lot of money (. . .)

[10:25 one woman walks in]

[10:30 one man walks in]

*Business Organization 21 September, 1979**

9:00–9:50 a.m.

Mr Fitzgerald: Almost was going to forget attendance, can't do that, I'll have the administration after me.

[takes roll]

[many people absent]

[9:05 one woman walks in]

(. . .) We're going to do something different with respect to the quiz. I'll go over the quiz right after you take it.

[9:06 one man walks in]

(. . .) Take all your paper off your desk.

[Quiz administered]

[9:35 one woman walks in]

[9:45 two women walk in]

The practice of walking into class late is widespread. Unlike the case of white working class males, however, this cannot be understood as a deliberate attempt to win symbolic and physical space from the institution and to defeat its main perceived purpose—to make you work. Willis's lads, for example, developed to a fine art the practice of stopping in class before "waggin off," and Paul Corrigan's "smash street kids" behaved similarly.[24] Investigators suggest that among the white working class, absenting oneself from class or being late to class is deliberately and overtly oppositional. It is an overt attempt to gain space within the institution and live one's own culture in direct opposition to institutional culture. While arriving late to class at Urban College is, in the final analysis, an assault upon official notions of time, it does not constitute a direct assault, and, like absence from class, reflects different tensions in located cultural form. I will pursue this point in chapter 3.

Drugs

Cocaine, "horse"[25] and especially marijuana are obtained easily at Urban College. Drugs are an important part of campus life and students often "get high" between classes and attend class "stoned."[26] This is common particularly among men, although women engage in this practice as well. The point here is not that students smoke marijuana (this is exceptionally common among college students in the United States), but that many do so before and after each class and before examinations and quizzes.[27]

The interviews below suggest the frequency of drug-related activities on campus. It is significant that a number of white students resent these practices.

LW: If you could make changes at Urban College, what changes would you make?

Mike: (. . .) Well I think I'd tighten up security. You can get high in any one of the bathrooms and not really get caught.

(. . .) The enthusiasm of the students is the pits. I doubt that any of them open a book. (. . .) The majority of the students get high, and just from my own experience if you get high during the early part of the day, the THC that's in the pot kind of depresses you and you are really not into homework. (a white student)

* * *

George: People are stoned down here [Urban College] a lot. It's part of the culture. In fact, when you shake someone's hand, you often hand them a joint. That means "come out and have a smoke." It's part of everyday life; it's part of the way people socialize —every party, every day. (a Business Administration student)*

* * *

[an informal discussion]

Caroline: They [students] actually sit there and deal in front of everybody. (. . .) They think I'm a teacher since I wear skirts and stuff. I walk into the ladies' room and they yell "flush, teacher" and everything goes down.

Cynthia: I wish there was some kind of fining, something like that. Like if they get caught smoking marijuana they'd get $50.00 taken out of their check. That's the only way you could hurt the students because they're all on BEOG and TAP monies. The only way to hurt them is to hit them in the pocketbook. (two white students)

* * *

Jay: I have a good time [at Urban College]. Maybe it's the way I dress. Being white in an all black school. Maybe it's the way I dress that allows me to be friends with them. I've grown up in the [Italian] ghetto . . . the west side, lower _____ you know, the pits, and you kind of pick up the lingo, you know, it's really slang, "hey bro'," this and that, and I can talk to 'em on their level and I dress like 'em, I *dress*, you know. It's not so bad. I don't get my ass kicked in the bathroom every day.

(. . .) I do smoke pot [marijuana], that helps too in a sense just being with peers in the school (. . .) I feel comfortable. I don't know if I would go out to black bars with them; there's just certain limitations. (a white student)

Jay points out that it "helps" to "smoke pot" since students often share a joint (marijuana cigarette) between classes. This annoys many of the white students since they feel that this detracts from their education. As Cynthia argues, "I wish there was some kind of fining. Like if they get caught smoking marijuana they'd get $50.00 taken out of their check." Obviously this does not characterize all white students since, as Jay argues, smoking pot "helps (. . .) in a sense just being with peers in the school." Drugs are, however, symbolic of a larger struggle between blacks and whites in the institution.

While students engage mainly in the use of marijuana on campus, harder drugs are available and can be purchased with little difficulty.[28] Belinda, a Business Administration student, is employed in the bookstore and makes the following observation:

"I know the game they [some of the students] play. I know the street game. We have pros here. A lot of junkies still. That's why my penny candy goes so well here [in the Urban College bookstore]. You get quick energy and those on heroin want sweets."

While drug use is widespread, only certain individuals sell drugs. An individual *deals drugs* on campus simply to make his or her own life more comfortable. Clifton, for example, a Business Administration student, buys and sells drugs for profit. He considers it a part-time job and visualizes Urban College at least partly as a marketplace—it is a place to sell his wares.

Clifton: [You have to do something] on the side to put away for a rainy day. (. . .) You have to do something . . . . If it was something very harsh you would go to jail because people talk and no way I would do that. It's just a little side hustle. I make fifty, sixty dollars a day. I do all right, better than the average student. I mean, you are a student, you don't have much money and you have to work on the side just to make ends meet, especially if you have an apartment.

The desire for an apartment of one's own and money to purchase consumer items such as clothes, stereos and records ensures a steady supply of drugs on campus.[29] Peddling drugs is simply a way of earning money.

That drugs are part of the very fabric of life at Urban College is further exemplified in the essay below written by a student in an Introduction to Sociology class. Students were asked to interview a person and write about "a typical day." A female student turned in the following essay.

The Nickel Bag Man[30]

Marijuana has become so prevalent in today's society to those users of this drug that it is now no longer a problem to find or buy. Marijuana is used by people of all ages. It has crossed all educational and economical barriers. I will look at a typical day for one seller of marijuana, who will be called C.B.

"I've been a hustler all my life, Baby. Coming from down south where nobody had anything. I soon learned that I had to hustle if I was going to have anything in life before I die. Ain't that what we all want to have, a nice crib [place to live], wear a suit, and have a bad ride [nice car]?"

"You want to know how my day goes don't you Baby?" I get up at 5 a.m. five days a week, and make my way to my slave [place of work] that's Chevy, you know. A man in my line of work has to have a straight slave. The man [police] is always watchin' you. Besides Chevy be a great place to sell my herb. The people on that damn line needs a break from all that bullshit them foremen hand out.

"I leave the plant at 10 o'clock every day to take care of the people who come to the crib to get their bags. At 11:30 I'm on my way back to _____ to work the rest of my shift.

"I'll sell to anybody. I got a few regulars who are about twelve and some are way up there in age. If they got the cash I sell. Most of them only want nickel or dime bags [five or ten dollar bags] though I don't mind that 'cause you make more money nickel and diming it. That's the name of the game make as much money as you can."

"My regulars they trust me, they know I only sell good shit. They can't get to the suburbs where the really good stuff is so they find old C.B. Now, I'm not saying my shit ain't good 'cause it is. But white folks still get the best. Same old story the white man seems to have the best of everything.

"About 7 o'clock I start hitting the spots. A man has got to show his face or he ain't trusted. You know how folks are, if you can't be seen you don't make sales.

"That's how a day goes, ain't nothin' to it. I've got what I need and so does my lady. She takes care of me so I take care of her."

While students do not spend all their time engaged in drug use at the college (although some do just that), drugs are part and parcel of day-to-day existence within the institution. Drug use serves to maintain the collectivity (it is not, for the most part, an individual act),[31] and also serves to distance students from the process that is education. We have here an example of a "lived contradiction": unlike working class white males, Urban College students, both male and female, affirm the idea of teachers and school knowledge. Elements of their own lived culture, however, are contradictory. Students embrace and reject schooling at one and the same time; they affirm the process that is education but drop in and out of school, arrive late to class, exert little effort, and engage in extensive drug use. What are the effects of this culture on student outcomes?

Urban College Outcomes

I pointed out earlier that elements of student culture contribute to an exceedingly low graduation rate per entering class. It has been estimated that of the 827 students admitted into degree programs in the Fall of 1977, only 93, only 11 percent, graduated in May 1979. Even assuming a three-year cycle, only 131 of the 827 (16 percent) admitted in the Fall of 1977 graduated three years later.[32]

These data, while informative, represent an aggregate of black and white student attainment. While the graduation rates of 11 and 16 percent are striking, such figures (which are not tabulated by race) cannot adequately portray success rates of black students relative to white students. Data presented in Table 2.3 represent estimates of Urban College graduates by race. These estimates are based on student residence upon graduation. Since the city in which Urban College is located has distinct black neighborhoods (like most American cities), it is possible to provide such estimates with a reasonable degree of accuracy.[33]

Over 70 percent of Urban College students are black. While I cannot provide data on *actual* attrition by race within each curriculum (such data are not available), data presented in Table 2.3 are suggestive in this regard. Overall it can be estimated that 63 percent of graduates from 1975–8 were white and 37 percent were black. In all fields except two of the Liberal Arts areas (Social Sciences and Humanities) and General Studies,[34] the proportion of white graduates exceeds that of black graduates. This is despite the fact that the institution was designed specifically to serve racial minorities and that black students are in a clear majority in all classes except those associated with the Radiologic Technology program.[35]

Table 2.4 provides estimates of enrollment in curriculum by student race in Spring 1980. These data indicate an exceptionally high proportion of black students in all curricula except Radiologic Technology (17 percent) and Paralegal (50 percent). Business Administration, Child Care, Criminal Justice, General Studies, Liberal Arts and Secretarial Science are over 75 percent black.[36] While it cannot be assumed that the proportion of white to black students was exactly the same in 1975–8 as in 1980, there is no reason to expect the 1975–8 figures to differ substantially from the 1980 figurers. If anything, the college may have enrolled *more* whites relative to blacks in 1980 than during previous years.[37]

The data presented in Table 2.3 and 2.4 suggest strongly that while black students constitute a clear majority in nearly all curricula, they make up a relatively small proportion of those who graduate. This must be linked, in the final moment, to the culture the students *themselves* produce within the institution. It is not simply a matter of the institution creating the outcomes.

The lived culture of students also serves to exacerbate tensions between blacks and whites. While there is little *overt* tension between the two groups (e.g., fighting, racial taunts), black and white students do not, for the most part, mix.[38] There is no question but that students (both black and white), given a generally racist society and a collective response to such racism on the part of blacks, are predisposed to this "apartness" before entering the institution. The culture that is created within the institution, however, serves to reinforce and reproduce these tensions and antagonisms. My goal here is to map culture as it is produced among urban blacks and discuss the response to such culture among white students at the college. This is not to imply that it is black culture that "determines" such outcomes. Clearly this is not the case, since whites produce their *own* located culture in the college which is dialectically linked to both black culture and broader white working class cultural forms. In fact, the shape and form of white culture is somewhat different than that noted by previous investigators of the white working class.[39] Since I did not

Table 2.3
Estimates of Urban College Graduates by Curriculum and Race, 1975–8 (Associate degree only)[a]

Courses	Black %	Black No.	White %	White No.
Security Administration and Loss Control	22.2	22	77.8	7
Liberal Arts—Mathematics	0.0	0	100.0	2
Liberal Arts—Science	41.2	7	58.8	10
Liberal Arts—Social Science/ Human Services	50.0	23	50.0	23
Liberal Arts—English/Humanities	60.0	18	40.0	12
General Studies	57.1	12	42.8	9
Recreation Leadership	100.0	1	0.0	0
Radiologic Technology	2.6	1	97.4	38
Criminal Justice[b]	0.0	0	100.0	1
Child Care	25.0	12	75.0	36
Business Administration	42.7	35	57.3	47
Secretarial Science	30.8	8	69.2	18
Total	37.0	119	63.0	203

[a]   Calculated on the basis of final graduation lists. Student race was estimated from place of residence.

[b]   This is a new program at Urban College.

study white culture directly, however, my intention here is simply to highlight the response of white students to black culture as it is produced in the college, and explore the way in which this culture and white response to it may be linked to the reproduction of fundamental antagonisms. The comments of white students below are suggestive of this process. Students respond most fervently to the issue of absenteeism and dropping in and out.

[an informal discussion]

Caroline: (. . .) I don't like the kids who come to school, get their BEOG, and they don't show up. . . . You don't see them until next semester.

Cynthia: (. . .) I don't think they should be accepted back into school next year. But I understand they have phony proof. That kids were collecting under phony names and stuff. I heard a rumor—you know the machine downstairs that takes pictures—that somebody came in and took a bunch of pictures, they stole them from the machines or something. So they had all this phony proof and came in and picked up [other students'] checks.

Whether that was true or not or whether that was rumor I don't know. But when you first go to school the classroom is completely filled. Now I'm lucky if I have twelve students in the class. My biggest class there's about twenty students. And if there's any kinds of money distributed, after that three-quarters of the class is gone.

* * *

Table 2.4
Curriculum by Student Race, 1980[a]

Courses	Black		White	
	%	No.	%	No.
Business Administration	75.0	39	25.0	13
Fashion Buying and Merchandising[b]	100.0	1	0.0	0
Retail Business Management[b]	100.0	3	0.0	0
Paralegal[b]	50.0	5	50.0	5
Security Administration and Loss Control	0.0	0	0.0	0
Child Care	81.0	17	19.0	4
Criminal Justice	75.0	6	25.0	2
Emergency Medical Technology	0.0	0	0.0	0
General Studies	77.3	34	22.7	10
Liberal Arts	86.1	31	13.9	5
Radiologic Technology	16.7	1	83.3	5
Science Laboratory Technology	66.7	8	33.3	4
Secretarial Science	85.7	12	14.3	2
Total	75.1	157	24.9	52

[a]   Based on results obtained from a questionnaire administered to all day English classes in Spring 1980. Among other things, students were asked to state their curriculum and race. Data presented here do not distinguish between students enrolled in degree or certificate programs.

[b]   These are new curricula at Urban College.

Jennifer: I was in a minority—I was paying for my education. A lot were getting EOP; a lot were getting BEOG (. . .) I *wanted* to be there. I cut my classes here and there but I would generally attend my classes. But there would be some classes where there would be six students in there once the money came in. (. . .) A lot of kids really came out well. They get tuition, spending money, textbooks and transportation, so they were really making money by going to school.

(. . .) You find a lot of people who go to school because it's worth their while. This creates a lot of problems because you get into some of the classes and they really don't give a darn; they don't really want to be there and it makes it really difficult for you sometimes because I was paying enough money where I didn't want to waste the time. But you can't really change something like that. (a Child Care graduate)

*   *   *

Joannie: [I would change] the students themselves. They're here just for the money or they're here just to, you know, to be with their friends. (. . .) I think it's just a big joke with some of the people. They're not here for an education. I was doing some transcripts in General Studies [she is a work study student] (. . .) and there were people who took five courses and passed one. (. . .) One took six and failed all six. It was terrible. They're not here for an education. They're just here for the fun of it all.

LW: (. . .) In Child Care, do you feel this?

Joannie: Yeah, like we have a test, OK. Most of them don't show and then they have an option of taking a makeup. But they even miss the makeup day too. It doesn't bother them.

(. . .) I'm work study. The other students got their grants and I'm still waiting for money from work study (. . .) As soon as the BEOG and TAP come in, they leave. *They cheat me* [my emphasis]. I'm working for my money and it bothers me. (. . .) They're giving the school a bad reputation.

(. . .) My studies here are so easy for me. Child Care doesn't require much from students. It's nothing. I haven't had homework in the last three or four weeks. It's just like high school to me. (. . .) In math I just sit and do my homework in class. (a Child Care student)

Absenteeism is clearly a point of contention. While many black students complain about high absenteeism as well, they do not express the same bitterness as white students and, for the most part, do not feel that *they* are being cheated because of others' absence.[40] Students like James and Jerome, for example, engage in the very practice they criticize. It is significant that white students resent high absenteeism among blacks basically because they feel that it affects *their* education. Joannie argues that "(t)hey're giving the school a bad reputation" and that she hasn't had "homework in the last three or four weeks. It's just like high school." Jennifer states that many students don't "give a darn" and that she resents this "because I was paying enough money where I didn't want to waste the time." While black students often comment negatively on absenteeism as well, there is no comparable sense that others' absence affects *their* chance of success. This is felt very strongly by whites, particularly if they are not receiving money to attend school. The issue of money should not be overstated, however: the majority of white students at Urban College are also grant recipients.[41] As comments below suggest, white students also react negatively to the low level of academic skills and perceived level of effort among blacks.

Julie: There's one thing that really bothers me [about Urban College]. I'm very upset by it. I can't understand why they allow people that don't even know how to multiply 4 times 6 in the school. There's a girl that was in my class and one day I was sitting across from her and she asked me how much 4 times 6 was. I mean that was such a blow. I still can't understand why they let people come in that aren't ready. (a Fashion Merchandising student)

* * *

Barbara: That is the thing that stands out most in my mind—that the majority of people could not read—they just couldn't read. I was very shocked; I just couldn't believe it. (. . .) They couldn't read a page out of a book without it taking them an hour.

LW: (. . .) Did you know white students who couldn't read also?

Barbara: No—there was one girl that seemed to be having a hard time, but I don't know if it's that she just didn't understand what was going on.

LW: Did you feel that this slowed down the classes you were in?

Barbara: Yeah, it did. (. . .) The courses went very slowly, that's about what it came down to.

LW: (. . .) Were your friends black, white or both?

Barbara: The majority were white. I wasn't close with any of the black students.

LW: There wasn't much mixing between black and white students?

Barbara: Not really. (. . .) There wasn't any hostility; it was very casual. You're in your own little cliques. (a Secretarial Science graduate)

* * *

John: In several cases I sat next to people who couldn't spell their name and they were working on their second year of an Associate's degree. (. . .) Most of the time you could walk through the halls without even seeing anybody. It was not an overcrowded school by any means. But two days out of the year (. . .) was what they called "EOP Day." You couldn't move in the school. You could not move because there were so many people swarming. (. . .) It was like somebody opened the doors and people started rushing in. It was certainly an absenteeism school where most of the people there were not there.

(. . .) I would have to say that in large part it was a big waste of taxpayers' money. I don't think that anybody should be paid to go to school if they're not going to go. (. . .) If you're going to go to college you should get *something* out of it and I don't think they did. (a Liberal Arts graduate)

* * *

Jan: I found that I was one of the few people there that actually did any work. (. . .) The other students didn't bother to do the work. (. . .) The work had to be a lot slower. (a Business Administration graduate)

* * *

Dick: The RT [Radiologic Technology] program was an advanced course; in fact you had to take four exams before you could even get into it.

(. . .) The other classes were mostly empty; in fact they were mostly scatterbrain type courses. (. . .) I think Urban College is a below standard school. I think that is because of the socioeconomic level of the community that is supporting the school—that is basically the black community here. (. . .) They lower their standards in order to accept most of the blacks.

(...) A lot of the students come from the south; I think they're getting a free ride. They go and they get all this money from BEOG and TAP and everything else. (a Radiologic Technology graduate)

There is no question but that white students react negatively to elements of black student culture. Many feel that students are there "just for money," that they absent themselves from class after checks are distributed, and that they put little effort into school-related work. As Joannie puts it, they were "there for the money" or "to be with their friends." There is little sense on the part of white students that black students, as a group, are serious about school or that they are serious about trying to get ahead. Dick argues that a lot of the students come from the south and that "they're getting a free ride." He also states that "the American thing is sort of to move up and improve yourself. Basically from what I can see from the southern blacks, they don't care."[42]

White students also feel that many black students do not have adequate basic skills and that this lowers standards. Courses have to proceed more slowly due to high absenteeism, low level of effort and lack of basic skills among blacks. As Dick states, "the other classes [outside the Radiologic Technology program] were mostly scatterbrain type courses." There is a distinct sense not only that students are "getting a free ride," but that, as Jan notes, "students didn't bother to do the work" and "the work [in classes] had to be a lot slower." An important point here is that white students resent black student culture primarily because they feel that it hurts their own personal chance of success within the institution and in the broader society. There is a strong sense on the part of whites that classes are not as rigorous as they might be and they hold blacks responsible for lowering standards.

This tension is exacerbated by the amount of drug use on campus. As Caroline states, "they actually sit there and deal in front of everybody." Cynthia adds that there should be "some kind of fining. (...) Like if they get caught smoking marijuana they'd get $50.00 taken out of their check." White students articulate strong antagonism toward blacks and feel that they suffer in the institution *because* of blacks.

Unquestionably the United States is a racist society and many white students enter Urban College with well-developed prejudices through which their perceptions of blacks are filtered. White students are, nonetheless, responding to actual elements of black student culture as produced within the institution. While whites may exaggerate these elements to some extent given their own prejudices, it *is* true that many blacks drop in and out of class, arrive late to class, exert little effort in school, and engage in activities that otherwise serve to slow the pace of learning.[43] White students are not simply reacting to black students on the basis of long-standing prejudice and stereotypes. Elements of culture are *created* within Urban College and it is these elements that help reproduce and maintain broader race and class antagonisms. Larger antagonisms are not simply "lived out" in Urban College—they are re-created and experienced anew in this particular site. It is this very production of culture (which is, after all, a highly human activity) that serves to polarize further (or at least reinforce existing polarization) blacks and whites. Barbara states "there wasn't any hostility; it was very casual. You're in your own little cliques." In the final analysis, however, despite the lack of overt hostility, deeply rooted antagonisms are re-created within the institution and blacks and whites interact very little.[44]

I have argued in this chapter that the lived culture of black students contributes to low "success" rates in traditional academic terms. I have also suggested that black culture, in concert with white culture, reproduces existing antagonisms in the larger society. Given that the lived culture of black students is in itself contradictory (students embrace and reject schooling at one and the same time), how does it arise? What factors, both within and outside the institution, "determine" the shape and form of student culture? I will explore these issues in the remaining chapters.

Notes

1. Paul Willis, *Learning to Labour: How Working Class Kids Get Working Class Jobs* (Westmead, England: Saxon House, 1977); and Howard London, *The Culture of a Community College* (New York: Praeger Publishers, 1978). Such comparisons must be made cautiously, however, especially in the case of Willis's "lads." The United States has had a less overt set of class antagonisms than Britain, and working class cultures will differ somewhat simply on that basis. In addition, the lads attend school by law whereas community college students attend by choice. Despite these caveats, the comparisons promote fruitful discussion about cultural form and its relationship to the economy.

2. Fathers of students typically hold such jobs as construction worker, longshoreman, telephone worker, fork-lift driver and industrial machinist. See Richard Edwards, *Contested Terrain* (New York: Basic Books, 1979) for a discussion of the Traditional Proletariat.

3. Periods of wagelessness are probably far more common now than they were at the time of Willis's study.

4. Willis, *Learning to Labour*, p. 19.

5. The pattern for females is different. London also suggests that "older" students do not exhibit these behavioral manifestations of lived cultural form.

6. London, *Culture*, especially chapter 3.

7. It is significant that Urban College students, in the final analysis, also hold *themselves* responsible for failure. I will discuss this at a later point.

8. See Willis, *Learning to Labour*, pp. 62–77 for a discussion of the teaching paradigm.

9. In point of fact the vast majority of the teachers are white. I will pursue this point further in chapter 3.

10. See Jean Anyon, "Social Class and School Knowledge," *Curriculum Inquiry* 11, 1(1981): 3–41; and Jean Anyon, "Social Class and the Hidden Curriculum of Work," *Journal of Education* 162, 1(Winter 1980): 67–92.

11. Willis, *Learning to Labour*, p. 26.

12. London suggests that absence from class is a "means of dissociating [oneself] from slavish adherence to official expectations." As such, it was defined positively. See London, *Culture*, p. 68.

13. This is an important element of the "hidden curriculum" and will be subject to more extended analysis in chapter 3.

14. If students attend regularly during the first three weeks, their name appears on the final class list and they receive grant checks whether they attend regularly after that point or not. Students are not necessarily aware of this, however. The discussion between two faculty members below is instructive here.

    1 February 1980*
    [informal discussion in the hall]
    Phil [a Mathematics instructor] had given a report to the faculty at yesterday's meeting. He argued that attendance did not "drop off" significantly after checks were issued. Indeed there had been large-scale drop-out *before* checks came out.
    Sam [a Business Administration instructor] wanted to point something out to Phil. He suggested that if students attended class consistently the first three weeks of school, they get their check anyway.
    Phil asked if the students knew this.
    Sam: "The sharpies do." He told Phil to check with the financial aids office to see whether this was the case. He said it took him a long time to find this out, but indeed it's true. He said Phil "might be right and might be wrong." It's something for him to think about.

15. The attendance policy allows two hours of absence for each hour of credit. This means that six absences are allowed for a three-credit course. Faculty reserve the right to count "lateness" as absence. This is the second semester 1979–80 policy; the first semester policy was somewhat different. See chapter 3.

16. Not all students receive BEOG and TAP monies. Some have EOP grants (Educational Opportunity Program) and others receive Veterans' benefits or social security payments. The main source of financial aid to students, however, is BEOG and TAP.

17. While there has been some attempt on the part of the administration to stop this practice, the attempt is not without its contradictory effects. Since faculty and ultimately administrative jobs depend upon student headcount in the state system, it may not be in the college's best interest to deny admission to students even if they engage in this practice.

18. In the 1979 graduation ceremony, only one black student received an Associate's degree in Radiologic Technology. Since many students go through the formal graduation when they have not in fact met all requirements, this is not generally a good source of graduation rates by race.

19. Diane is a white female, approximately 50 years old. I will explore white response to elements of black lived culture at the end of the chapter. It is also the case that older women, both black and white, are largely exempt from the group logic examined here.

20. It can be assumed, because of grant requirements, that these students have always taken a full load. At the time of this writing, Jerome had left Urban College (without completing the Associate's) and was taking courses at another local institution.

21. Urban College Task Force, *Student Enrollment, Retention and Placement*, 1976–81 Data Bank. These are estimates based on number of admits per given year and number of graduates two and three years later.

22. As noted earlier, individual faculty are free to develop their own policy with respect to lateness.

23. These are interesting comments in light of my earlier discussion of the relationship between the economy and the state. See chapter 1.

24. See Paul Corrigan, *Schooling the Smash Street Kids* (London: Macmillan, 1979).

25. "Horse" is heroin.

26. Faculty occasionally comment on this. Phil [a Mathematics instructor], for example, told me that a number of the students in his classes come stoned. One of the students even asked him how he kept from laughing at some of the "off the wall" questions. He said that indeed some of the questions "come from left field. They just seemed to come from nowhere; they were not related to any of the topics they were discussing in class."

27. My two research assistants and myself were approached on numerous occasions throughout the year by students and asked to "share a joint" with them.

28. Marijuana is more common in large part because it is relatively inexpensive.

29. The importance of an apartment and its relationship to selling drugs is expressed by Anthony, a Business Administration student, below.

It's getting harder to find a job. You don't want to stay home with your mom and pop once you are 19 and 20 years old, so you go out to the streets to get a job to take care of yourself. How do you get your money? It's beautiful, you know, the parents are there whenever you need them, but to call yourself an adult now, I want my own apartment, I want to go out, I want to party, I want to get me a car. And if you can't get a job to get any of these things, then how do you do it? How do you get these things? Sure, you can stay at home until you get 90 years old. But you reach a certain age, you want to be on your own. With the unemployment ratio being as great as it is, what do you turn to to get this money and get these things that you want to do? So if I can get enough money together to get my first quarter pound, or my first pound, I can go from there.

It is important to point out, however, that blacks, for the most part, do not control drug traffic in the United States. Drug sales in the ghetto are dependent upon the availability of drugs in the larger marketplace, which is not, in the final analysis, under black control. Bequai has argued persuasively that the structure of the illegal (or irregular) economy closely parallels that of the legal one, with high monopolistic earnings at the top, and low-paid, unstable, risky jobs at the bottom. As in the legal economy, blacks occupy positions in the illegal sector largely at the bottom. See A. Bequai, *Organized Crime: The Fifth Estate* (Lexington, Mass.: Lexington Books, 1979).

30. The essay is reproduced here exactly as written.

31. It is significant that students "share a joint" or otherwise engage in drug use collectively. It must be pointed out that the logic examined here is a group logic; it does not lie in any individual act. I will discuss this further in chapters 6 and 7.

32. See footnote 21.

33. A list was compiled of all Urban College graduates by curriculum from 1975–8 (Associate degree only). Student race was estimated on the basis of residence zip codes. Four zip codes are associated with black neighborhoods during 1975–8. While there are certainly some blacks who reside in white neighborhoods and vice versa, I am confident that the breakdown in Table 2.3 is reasonably accurate. The one neighborhood that is now "transitional" was almost totally white until 1978. Data presented in Table 2.3 may understate slightly the proportion of black graduates since blacks who live in white neighborhoods are likely to be of a higher status than those who live in ghetto neighborhoods and therefore more likely to graduate. Such individuals would not, of course, appear as "black" in these calculations.

34. General Studies implies no particular commitment to specific academic or vocational goals. Fewer credits transfer to four-year institutions, and it is commonly thought of as a "second class" curriculum. General Studies allows ten free electives whereas Liberal Arts, for example, allows six.

35. A new curriculum, Paralegal Assistant, also draws a high proportion of white students.

36. These data were obtained through questionnaires administered to all students in Day division English classes (see Appendix C). Questionnaires were administered by a carefully trained group of Urban College students in order to maximize accuracy in responses. Since forms were administered to students in English classes, results are skewed slightly toward newer students. Results are likely to be skewed slightly toward black students as well, since a relatively greater proportion of blacks take the required English course more than once.

37. Although I cannot substantiate this claim, it was alleged that, since Urban College was shifting location within the year (out of the ghetto), a greater proportion of whites attended the school during the academic year 1979–80 than during previous years.

38. An Urban College party, for example, held on 7 September 1979 at a local bar, drew approximately fifty black students and only a few white students. Frank, a Business Administration instructor, commented to me that only black students showed and that this always happens "whenever a party is on *this* side of street; if it were downtown, only white students would show." *While there is no overt hostility between black and white students in classes, "at the end of classes, they don't see each other at all."*

39. The majority of white students at the college are working class. It cannot be assumed, however, that white student cultural form in this predominantly black institution parallels that depicted by London. White lived culture in Urban College will be linked dialectically with urban black culture (as produced within the institution) as well as broader white working class cultural forms. Whites in the college take education more seriously, for example, than students in studies by London, Willis, or Corrigan. I suspect this represents an attempt on the part of whites to distance themselves from what they judge to be the "non-serious" nature of black students with respect to education. Some whites, however, are less enthusiastic about schooling than others. Jay, for example, is reminiscent of London's students.

    LW: You feel you can learn here [Urban College] if you really want to?

    Jay: Oh, definitely. Like if you have a good head. I feel that I have a good head, but like I say, my girlfriend and neighborhood it conflicts all the time. Striving for the best and then falling back and being a player. No responsibility, that's what it boils down to. (. . .) It's fun, living your life with no responsibility and then dying. But I like to be in the latest design clothes and the nicest car. I know you have to hit the books to get somewhere, but the way the world's going today, you don't know which way to go. Don't know what to do, where to go, what to learn, where to learn it. I think about going into the Air Force (. . .) every time I discuss it [the future]. When I think of my folks they're shot.

Most whites interviewed, however, talked less about personal dilemmas and more about how they differed from blacks.

40. Some black students, like Anthony and Belinda, blame the institution for not using better judgment with respect to admissions (see chapter 3). While Anthony and Belinda resent the attendance policy and feel that this effort to control their time is due in large part to poor admissions criteria, there is no comparable sense among black students that an individual's education suffers because of others' absence.

41. While I cannot provide exact figures, most white students receive some form of financial aid as well. The relative amount of such aid may be less, however.

42. Dick is very specific in his reference to "southern blacks." He states the following:

Dick: The RT [Radiologic Technology] was sort of a clique. (. . .) As far as the other students, considering that the majority of them were black—we really didn't associate with them. (. . .) Culturally they were behind us. There was a big cultural gap.

LW: What do you mean by cultural gap?

Dick: Well, I worked in California. The blacks there are highly civilized. When I came back here I found that the blacks were uncivilized. It was really kind of a surprise to me because I had been away from it for a number of years. The blacks out there I could relate to as a person. When I came back here it was sort of a cultural shock. (. . .) I've been back here for five years; I'm becoming sort of a bigot myself. The southern blacks came up here and brought up a lot of their culture. I find it very degrading. They're slow in action, slow in moves, and always lagging behind. The American thing is sort of to move up and improve yourself. Basically from what I see from the southern blacks, they don't care.

43. I will explore the relationship between student culture and the pace of learning more fully in chapter 4.

44. There was some hostility on the part of black women toward white women who dated black men. Paula, a Business Administration student, dated George for a period of time. She told me that a number of black women who knew George would not speak to her in the hall, even when she said "hello" to them first. Interracial dating was not common, however, and blacks and whites basically kept to themselves.

Academic Quality and the Choice of Suburban Community Colleges by City Students

WILLIAM E. MAXWELL

Variables from the college choice literature are examined in an analysis of the reasons students give for migrating from a city community college district to suburban district community colleges. A secondary analysis used a questionnaire survey administered to students at 3 suburban campuses (N = 1,868). Large numbers of students migrated. Previous research reports of the importance of proximity and low importance of academic quality for college choices were contradicted by this study's findings. The migrating students rated their specific courses and other academic issues as the most important factors in their choice of a suburban college. Safety was of moderate importance and proximity was of less importance. Although this student migration had been described by some as "white flight," there was substantial movement and similar attitudes by all major ethnic groups. The suggestion is made that stratification may explain these migrations along with racial conflict. Previous college choice research has conceptually treated community colleges as undifferentiated. However, the findings suggest the distinctiveness of various community colleges in a metropolis and the significance of academic quality in recruitment.

Public community colleges are pictured in the college choice research literature in a gray, faceless manner as if they all have essentially the same image of convenient distance, low cost, tolerant standards, and homogeneous academic reputation. This article presents evidence from a secondary analysis for another view. In examining why city students choose to migrate to suburban colleges, it is proposed that there is variation between community colleges and that many students in metropolitan areas choose to migrate to particular community colleges for academic purposes and quality.

Theory

The conceptualization of college choice has been limited mainly to lists of correlated variables, with little linkage to the relevant and more elaborated theories of the behavioral sciences (some exceptions are found in the more developed theories proposed by Hossler, 1985, and Jackson, 1982). Although some of the lists of these variables are lengthy (Chapman, 1981; Rossi & Coleman, 1964; Weiler, 1987; Zemsky & Oedel, 1983), the factors are summarized by Hartnett (1982) as involving cost, distance, and image.

Cost and Distance

Cost and distance are major factors affecting the decision to attend a community college (Bers & Smith, 1987; Chapman, 1981; Lavin, 1971; Office of Educational Planning and Resource Development, n.d.; Smith, 1990; Smith & Bers, 1989; Trent & Medsker, 1968). Estimates of the number of students for whom cost is the most important factor range between 15% to 65%. Trent and Medsker (1968) explained that proximity is so important because of the limited finances of the students. The percentage of students who rate proximity as the most crucial factor ranges from 45% to 80% in the various studies. Tinto (1973) observed that distance is especially important in the college choices of less academically talented students. This research literature typically concludes that academic motivation is of considerably less importance than cost and proximity for most community college students.

Image and College Differences

Image was introduced as a specific theoretical concept by Clark (1959) to designate an organization's reputation but is used by Hartnett (1982) to generally encompass almost all aspects of a student's attitudes about the differences between colleges. The interest in a particular courses and programs is cited by Chapman (1981; Lavin, 1971) as the factor most frequently emphasized by students in the selection of a 4-year college. Other factors frequently mentioned include concerns about academic reputation, quality of teaching, campus environment, social life, and friends (Cook & Zallocco, 1983; Hartnett, 1982; Lavin, 1971; Smith, 1990).

This article applies several of these 4-year college image variables to the study of distinctive features of community colleges chosen by students. The present study assumes that some of the same factors that differentiate bachelor's degree programs, such as the academic tradition, wealth, faculty, and students, also operate to distinguish public community colleges. Thus, in a large metropolitan area, there may be more than one type of community college. Distance and cost are major factors for many students at most public community colleges, yet it is possible that academic reputation and other image dimensions will affect the recruitment of significant numbers of students.

Race Relations

A remarkable feature of the college choice research literature is its almost complete omission of reference to the significance of racial and ethnic stratification despite the continuing ethnic tensions and considerable segregation in American higher education (for exceptions see Crosson, 1988; Oteri & Malaney, 1990). Thus, there are no well-developed theories of the effect of a college's ethnic image or the different college choices of various ethnic groups.

The notion of "white flight" has been posited to describe the movement of white school children from cities to private and suburban schools (Pettigrew & Green, 1976). More recent demographic analyses have observed that members of several middle-class ethnic groups, not just the white middle class, have moved to the suburbs for the latter's advantages over the inner city (Darden, 1986; Frey, 1984).

Method

This article examines the college choice attitudes of interdistrict students who elected to commute from the city across community college district boundaries to attend community colleges in any one of three suburbs of a large metropolis on the West Coast. The three suburban campuses were all older, well established, and well appointed, all having been founded in affluent districts before 1930. Although there was some significant distribution of ethnic groups within each suburban district and campus, a majority of these suburban district populations and college students were white. The metropolitan area involved a large city district with a centralized system of several community college campuses and 11 community college districts in the suburbs around the metropolis.

Most of the data for this study were obtained through a secondary analysis of a questionnaire survey administered by institutional researchers to students at the three suburban colleges. The questionnaire requested students to rate the importance of each of a variety of factors potentially affecting their decision to attend their college, including such issues as proximity, social relations, safety, and academic features. The initial items, and the majority, were identical on the survey used at each college. At two of the campuses, the questionnaire was extended slightly to include a few additional items concerning such matters as distance traveled and ethnic attitudes. Two of the colleges also added other student data from the college master student computer file. The reliability of the survey items was evidenced by a remarkable similarity in the results among each of the three colleges and by intercorrelations for each of the sets of items concerning academic quality and social factors.

After a pilot test of the instrument, at each campus a random sample of courses meeting on the campus on Wednesday at 10 a.m. and 7 p.m. was selected. The course instructors administered the instrument to their students during a class meeting. Although questionnaires were administered to all students in the selected classrooms, this study used only the questionnaires from the interdistrict students who resided outside the district of the suburban college that they were attending. By this procedure, usable responses were obtained from 1,868 interdistrict students.

Findings

Distance

Table 1 indicates that 68% of the students rated proximity of the college to their residence as being of moderate to extreme importance. Although distance and travel are not considered important as frequently by the interdistrict students as some other factors in their choice of a college, most of them have selected a suburban campus within a convenient distance of their home. The majority of these students reside within a relatively comfortable driving distance of approximately 5 to 12 miles. The importance of proximity is suggested, in the case of students who live near college district borders, by the fact that the suburban campus that they attend is actually closer to their residence than is the closest inner-city district community college.

However, a significant portion of the students chose to attend a suburban campus that is more distant than an adjacent inner-city campus. In the survey conducted at one of the suburban colleges, data were collected concerning the mileage between the students' homes and the campus. About one third of these students commuted more than 8 miles (24% traveled between 9 to 16 miles, and 8% traveled 17 miles or more).

Table 1
Rating of Various Reasons for Choosing to Attend a
Community College in a Suburban District (in Percentages)

Reason	Scale Range				
	5	4	3	2	1
Academic					
I can get the courses that I want and need here.	45	33	14	5	4
This college has a good program in my area of interest.	33	32	20	8	8
This college has a strong academic reputation.	27	30	24	9	9
This college has the best teachers.	24	36	24	9	7
Safety					
This is a safe campus.	23	24	24	13	17
Distance					
This college is close to where I live.	17	27	24	13	18
This college is close to my work.	8	14	18	11	49
Social					
Many of my friends go to this college.	6	8	15	17	54

Note: Number of interdistrict students — 1,868. 5 — very or extremely important; 4 — quite important; 3 — moderately important; 2 — slightly important; 1 — not important.

Race Relations

Some observers and college officials characterized the flow of students into the suburban colleges as white flight. Whites comprised the largest group (38%) of the students within the city district and were migrating to suburban community colleges in even larger proportions. Fifty-three percent of the outflow were white students, a fact that might be consistent with an interpretation of white flight. However, whites may have migrated more readily mainly because of the proximity to the suburban colleges.

The demographic data in Table 2 indicate that, rather than white flight, there is a general movement of many ethnic groups toward the suburbs. Whites do predominate in the migrations in both directions. Nevertheless, far greater numbers of all of the major groups including whites, Hispanics, blacks and Asians migrate *out* to suburban colleges than they do *into* city colleges. Eleven times as many students flowed into these three suburban campuses as entered the city district campuses.

The survey at one of the colleges included an item that asked whether students had chosen the campus because of its ethnic composition. Eleven percent of the students responded "yes." This supports the view that at least some of the migration to the suburbs is ethnically motivated flight away from the inner city yet it involves far less than a majority of the students.

Regarding the issue of safety, data in Table 1 indicate that, in their choice of a suburban campus, 71% of the students reported that safety was a factor of moderate to extreme importance. If this questionnaire item is interpreted as an indicator of covert racial fears, of fear about dangers that some of the students associate in their mind with high inner-city densities of poverty and oppressed races, this interpretation suggests that more than 11% of the students are leaving inner-city campuses in part for racial reasons. An alternative interpretation might be that inner-city campuses are viewed as unsafe in terms of crime simply because they are associated with poverty rather than racial images.

Table 2
Number of Students Migrating Between Colleges in City
District and Colleges in Three Suburban Districts by Ethnic Group

| Ethnic Group | Direction of Migration | |
	To City	To Suburbs
Asian	180	1,574
Black	213	1,610
Hispanic	199	2,465
White	789	10,134
Other	70	387

Further analysis indicates that students from all ethnic groups held similar images of campus safety. Table 3 indicates that the percentage of each student ethnic group who rated safety as an issue of moderate to extreme importance varies from 59% to 75%. The majority of each ethnic group considers safety concerns as having had moderate or greater impact on their choice of a suburban campus. Although these data might be interpretable as flight from inner city, they can hardly be construed simply as white racial flight.

Movement—particularly that which is ethnically inspired—to suburban campuses could involve more than just flight *away* from the inner city. The flow of students *to* the suburbs could also manifest a desire for relations with certain ethnic groups for purposes of friendship, social activities, marriage, and career networking. The questionnaire survey did not focus on measures indicative of these latter interests. However, two survey items are relevant: (a) that item cited previously concerning ethnic composition and (b) the fact that "many of my friends go to this college." Only 29% responded that having their friends at the college was of moderate to extreme importance in their choice of the college. A majority of the students, 54%, indicated that this aspect of social relations was not important for their choice. Although these types of measures are inconclusive, these data do not suggest that a large proportion of the flow to the suburbs was motivated primarily by flight from ethnic groups or the desire for social relations with particular ethnic groups.

Educational Purposes

Academic programs and quality were treated more often by the students as important in their choice of a suburban college than were any of the factors of proximity, safety, race, and social relations.

This emphasis on educational goals can be seen, especially in the questionnaire items in Table 1 concerning attending "the courses that I want and need" and "a good program in my area of interest." More than 90% of the students considered the courses they needed as moderately to extremely important in their choice of their college. Forty-five percent of the students rated access to needed courses as very or extremely important. Choosing a college for its courses was thus rated at that level of emphasis twice as frequently as campus safety and almost three times as frequently as proximity of residence.

Other features of these students also emphasized their interest in academic quality. The students migrating to the suburbs were younger on average than either the students who remained at inner-city colleges or the community college students who resided in the three suburban districts. The migrating students were also more likely to have the goal of transferring into a 4-year college program. Thus, more so than other students in the inner city, these migrants were academically ambitious. They were seeking good-quality academic preparation for transfer into full bachelor's programs.

The academic attitudes of several ethnic groups are presented in Table 4. These data display a high degree of similarity of academic interests between all four ethnic categories. Each of the ethnic groups generally manifested a strong academic motivation in choosing to attend a suburban community college. Rather than one or two groups attempting to flee from other racial groups, these data suggest that students from several groups migrated to the suburbs primarily for educational purposes.

Table 3
Importance of Campus Safety Rated by Ethnic Group

| Ethnic Group | Importance of Campus Safety | | |
	Moderate to Extreme Importance	Slight to No Importance	n
Asian	75%	25%	281
Black	59%	41%	118
Hispanic	75%	25%	175
White	66%	34%	745

Note: Data taken from surveys at two of the suburban colleges.

Further Discussion

The preceding findings, along with what is known about other campuses in the metropolis, suggest a complex system of several kinds of community colleges. There is more variation in the choices that lead to enrollment in different community colleges than has been recognized in the literature. The students who migrated from the suburbs into city community colleges tend to be older and less interested in ultimately transferring to a 4-year bachelor's program (Office of Educational Planning and Resource Development, 1984). Many of these students were attracted to the superior technical and vocational training programs of one of the city campuses. Of the suburban students commuting to a predominantly black student campus in the city, 94% of these migrants were themselves black. For the city students who attended city campuses, the reason most frequently cited for choosing these colleges was that they were "close to home" (Office of Educational Planning and Resource Development, n.d.).

Table 4
Percentage of Each Ethnic Group Rating
Academic Features as Quite Important to Extremely Important

Campus Academic Features	Ethnic Group			
	Asian	Black	Hispanic	White
Can get the courses that I				
want and need	75%	78%	79%	82%
A good program in				
my area of interest	71%	62%	70%	62%
Academic reputation	55%	62%	65%	57%
Has the best teachers	63%	49%	59%	58%
n	280	119	177	747

Note: Data taken from surveys at two of the suburban colleges.

Around the border of the city lay 11 suburban campuses. The three examined in this study were ethnically mixed, yet predominantly white, prosperous, and well-established. Their programs and image of academic quality attracted from the city sizable numbers of younger students who aspired to transfer ultimately into a 4-year bachelor's-degree institutions.

Two practical implications concern the importance of the academic programs and quality. First, the most important factor in the college choices of these students is the availability of desired courses and programs. Attention to specific student markets by offering desired courses continues to be a fundamental issue for college leaders. Second, if a community college seeks to maximize its recruitment of educationally ambitious students, it should nourish both the quality of its academic programs and their reputation. Young students with transfer goals who had the time and resources to travel to moderately distant campuses frequently chose these colleges for academic reasons. In a period of declining enrollments, these academically advantaged colleges benefited from their reputation.

Further Research

Research on college choice is in need of better theories. A typology identifying various kinds of community colleges would enhance college choice theories. Such a typology could begin by distinguishing colleges by the percentage of students aspiring to transfer to bachelor's-degree programs. Just as traditionally black or white liberal arts colleges must be distinguished from each other to make meaningful sense of choice processes, ethnic composition may be useful in classifying community colleges in relation to student choices. In general, the typologies should be linked with theories that have proved useful in classifying organizations in other areas of the social sciences.

The lower-than-expected frequency of ethnic flight motives and segregation observed at the suburban colleges in this study suggest that alternative interpretations of stratification be examined and that alternative measures be used. With respect to methods, the questionnaire used for this analysis focused on academic attitudes rather than on ethnic issues. More measures focused on ethnic attitudes might lead to evidence of larger effect of racial attitudes on college choice than indicated by this study.

Stratification issues such as these have generally been neglected in most of the recent decade of research on college choice and community college despite promising earlier work on these topics

(Clark, 1960; Collins, 1979; Karabel, 1986). Rather than escaping particular ethnic groups, the student migrants appear to be seeking the class and status advantages of the suburbs. There is, after all, a considerable mix of ethnic groups at most of the suburban colleges and among the migrants themselves. The emphasis on particular educational programs, academic quality, and transfer leading to the bachelor's degree is consistent with such an interpretation. The survey in this study did not collect evidence about stratification. The college records indicate that about 6% of the interdistrict students had qualified for financial aid. By contrast, among the students remaining in the city district, about 11% received financial aid. Although these statistics involved only a small fraction of all the students, they are consistent with the view that the migrants to the suburbs were more affluent and seeking to maintain or raise their status level.

Conclusions

Students migrating from a city district to suburban community colleges and surveyed in this study manifested both similarities and differences with previous research on college choices. In contrast to other research on community college students, these students rated other research on community college students, these students rated academic programs and quality most frequently as being of greatest importance in their choices. Similar to the choices of students attending 4-year colleges, these community college students emphasize, as the most important factor, the specific courses and programs they seek. Safety is mentioned moderately frequently as a concern. Similar to previous research on community colleges, proximity is also rated as important but much less than in other studies. Social relations with friends and ethnic group composition are less frequently mentioned as important.

These findings suggest the variation among public community colleges and the larger range of factors of affecting students' choices for attending community colleges beyond distance and cost.

Although there is evidence of some flight from the city to avoid racial integration on inner-city campuses, there is, in fact, significant migration to suburban community colleges and emphasis on academic quality by members of all major ethnic groups.

References

Bers, T.H. & Smith, K. (1987). College choice and the nontraditional student. *Community College Review, 15,* 39–45.

Bourdieu, P. & Passeron, J.C. (1977). *Reproduction.* Beverly Hills, CA: Sage Publications.

Bowles, S. & Gintis, H. (1976). *Schooling in capitalist America.* New York: Basic Books.

Chapman, D.W. (1981). A model of student college choice. *Journal of Higher Education, 52,* 490–505.

Clark, B.R. (1959). College and student selection. In Center for the Study of Higher Education, *Selection and educational differentiation: Proceedings* (pp. 155–168). Berkeley, CA: Center for the Study of Higher Education.

Clark, B.R. (1960). The "cooling-out" function in higher education. *American Journal of Sociology, 65,* 569–576.

Collins, R. (1979). *The credential society.* New York: Academic Press.

Cook, R.W. & Zallocco, R.L. (1983). Predicting university preference and attendance: applied marketing in higher education administration. *Research in Higher Education, 19,* 197–211.

Crosson, P.H. (1988). Four-year college and university environments for minority degree achievement. *Review of Higher Education 11*, 365–382.

Darden, J.T. (1986). Asians in metropolitan areas of Michigan: a retest of the social and spatial distance hypothesis. *Amerasia Journal, 19*, 365–382.

Frey, W.H. (1984). Lifecourse migration of metropolitan whites and blacks and the structure of demographic change in large central cities. *American Sociological Review, 49*, 803–827.

Hartnett, R.T. (1982). Admission to colleges and universities. In H.E. Mitzel (Ed.), *Encyclopedia of educational research* (5th ed., Vol. 1, pp. 59–67). New York: Free Press.

Hossler, D. (1985). *Studying student college choice: a three phase model and research agenda*. Paper presented at the meeting of the Chicago Conference on Enrollment Management, Chicago.

Jackson, G. (1982). Public efficiency and private choice in higher education. *Educational Evaluation and Policy Analysis, 4*, 237–247.

Karabel, J. (1986). Community colleges and social stratification. *New Directions for Community Colleges, 14*, 13–30.

Lavin, D.E. (1971). Selection processes for higher education. In L.C. Deighton (Ed.), *The encyclopedia of education* (4th ed., Vol. 3, pp. 181–188). New York: Free Press

Office of Educational Planning and Resource Development. (1984). *A preliminary reveiw of student migration patterns in the Los Angeles area*. Los Angeles: Los Angeles Community College District.

Office of Educational Planning and Resource Development. (n.d.). *The fall 1980 student survey*. Los Angeles: Los Angeles Community College District.

Oteri, L.A. & Malaney, G.D. (1990). Racism on campus—the negative impact on enrollment. *College and University, LXV*, 213–226.

Pettigrew, T.F. & Green, R.L. (1976). School desegregation in large cities: a critique of the Coleman "white flight" thesis. *Harvard Educational Review, 46*, 1–53

Rossi, P. & Coleman, J.S. (1964). *Determinants and consequences of college choice*. Chicago: National Opinion Research Center.

Smith, K. (1990). A comparison of the college decisions of two-year and four-year college students. *College and University, LXV*, 109–126.

Smith, K. & Bers, T.H. (1989). Parents and the college choice decisions of community college students. *College and University, LXIV*, 335–348.

Tinto, V. (1973). College proximity and rates of college attendance. *American Educational Research Journal, 10*, 277–293.

Trent, J.W. & Medsker, L.L. (1968). *Beyond high school: A psychosociological study of 10,000 high school graduates*. San Francisco: Jossey-Bass.

Weiler, W.C. (1987). An application of the nested multinomial logit model to enrollment choice behavior. *Research in Higher Education, 27*, 273–282.

Zemsky, R. & Oedel, P. (1983). *The structure of college choice*. New York: College Entrance Examination Board.

Success of Community College Students: Current Issues

Laura I. Rendon and Terri B. Mathews

As the educational entity characterized by open admissions and equal opportunity, the community college has attracted a disproportionate share of minority students, many of whom are on their way toward the baccalaureate. In 1984-85, about 54% of Hispanics enrolled in higher education attended two-year colleges. The comparable figure for blacks and Asians was 43% and for American Indians, 54% (El-Khawas et al., 1988). Yet these abundant cohorts exhibit the lowest retention rates and the highest transfer losses (Commission on the Higher Education of Minorities, 1982; Hayward, 1985; Lee, 1985). There is mounting concern that access and opportunity, the very elements on which community colleges were founded, may now be in jeopardy. Unless access can be made more meaningful for underrepresented minority student groups by the year 2000, it is likely that this nation will be one in which one-third of the population will be impoverished, disconnected from mainstream America, poorly educated, and unable to participate fully in positions of leadership authority and policymaking. Thus a most crucial problem for community colleges is not only how to facilitate the transfer process for minority students but also how to raise the number of students who successfully transfer far above historic levels. The trends are occurring at a time when large numbers of minority students are performing poorly and are dropping out of high school. Moreover, compared to their representation in the nation's schools systems fewer minorities are enrolling in two- and four-year colleges and even fewer are earning college degrees (Orfield and Paul, 1987; Commission on Minority Participation in Education and American Life, 1988, Wilson and Melendez, 1987). Consequently, America is now a nation where large academic and socioeconomic gaps separate majority and minority groups. Unless these inequities are quickly reduced, this country may be one in which one-third of the nation can become America's own Third World.

Numerous reports and research studies give ample and mounting evidence that the greatest losses of minority students are occurring as students pass through two points in the educational pipeline: (1) the precollege level, and (2) the community college level. For many minority students, full access to higher education is conditioned by high school graduation and transfer from a two- to a four-year college. Yet large numbers of minority students are leaking out of the educational pipeline at the precollege level, and of those who do make it to college, a disproportionate number enroll in community colleges where another rupture in the pipeline occurs. This leads to one clear point: Unless there is a dramatic increase in the number of minorities who graduate from high school and who transfer from community colleges to senior institutions, there will not be a significant change in the number of minority students earning undergraduate and graduate degrees. Thus it it important to understand what is happening to minorities at these two critical points in the educational pipeline.

The K-12 System

Racial and ethnic diversity is brimming in the nation's K-12 system. Between 1968 and 1986 the number of white children enrolled in public schools fell 16% while the number of blacks grew 5% and the number of Hispanics increased 103% (Orfield and Paul, 1987). Overall, some 12 million blacks, Hispanics, Asians, and American Indians were enrolled in schools in 1986—close to 30% of the total school population. Kindergartens are already approximately one-third minority and in many large cities much higher. In fact, when demographers look at the school population, they find minorities in the majority in schools in California, New Mexico, and Mississippi, with Texas and New York poised to join that list. Minority students are in the majority in all 25 of the largest systems in the nation (Massachusetts Institute of Technology, 1988). However, there is mounting concern that the quality of education available for these students is deteriorating.

Hearings conducted by the National Resource Group of the Carnagie Corporation's Quality Education for Minorities project, of which the principal author is a member, have related the poor condition of the nation's school system that feeds students to community colleges. According to testimony provided by school administrators, faculty, and policymakers, inner city schools are decaying and turning into places infected with drugs, violence, crime, and teachers who kill the hopes, dreams, and aspirations of minority students.

In Los Angeles, a policy analyst revealed a disturbing account of how minority students were educated in elementary schools. It was noted that in California schools a first grade teacher made a decision, as early as the first two or three weeks of school as to who was a fast or a slow learner. This critical decision was made not on comprehensive assessment, but on quick impression. Sometimes, youngsters who did not speak English were misdiagnosed as learning disabled. Once this decision was made, youngsters in slow groups were educated quite differently. While fast groups were given passages to read and opportunities to discuss, analyze, and write, children in the slow groups were given ditto sheets. They circled letters in dittos, and spent their time coloring dittos. This insidious practice resulted in tracking—in funneling children into or out of a quality education. The cumulative effects were devastating:

—In kindergarten, very few differences were noted among youngsters.

—By the third grade, the slow group was six months behind in math and reading.

—By the sixth grade, the slow group was one year behind in math and reading.

—By the eighth grade, the slow group was two years behind.

—By the twelfth grade, the slow group was three years behind.

Consequently, by the tenth grade, in California 48% of the blacks and 45% of Hispanics drop out of high school. But California is not alone in this dark scenario. In New York, San Antonio, Texas, and Chicago, the Carnegie Resource Group heard similar stories of schools that failed and pushed out students. For example, in Chicago more than five out of six students are minority. A recent study conducted at the University of Chicago (Orfield and Paul, 1987, 1988) documented differences in the quality of education between students attending segregated city schools and those attending suburban schools. Blacks and Hispanics in Chicago were attending segregated minority schools characterized by crowded classes, teachers with fewer advanced degrees and with degrees from less selective colleges. These schools also had fewer counseling resources, and there were wide differences in achievement test scores owing to differential tracking. Disproportionate numbers of minority students were in lower track programs where they were taught obedience, deference, routine, and mechanical learning. Students in the middle and upper tracks were socialized toward inquiry, creative thinking, and higher order precollegiate skills. In short, the country appears to have not one but two educational systems. In this dual system, one tier serves affluent students, mainly white, and prepares them diligently for the future. The other serves poorer students, chiefly minority, and prepares them for little if any role in the nation's economic destiny.

An open conversation among Carnegie Resource Group members and leaders of community-based organizations revealed the major reasons that minorities dropped out of high school. They included: (1) a lack of identification with counselors and teachers—people who add a human touch, who make the child feel welcome, and who accept the child's culture; (2) poor attitudes and low expectations from teachers—the mind-set is that minority students cannot learn so they are written off as dumb, ignorant, and unready; and (3) a lack of support systems. Early in school some teachers kill children's curiosity and spirit of learning through (4) unclear goals—not understanding the connection between what goes on in school and in real life (often youngsters come out of school with no skills, and others still in school see this and get disappointed); (5) feelings of failure—community leaders explained that students dropped out psychologically first, then they stopped trying; (6) undefined values—leading to drugs, gangs, and violence; (7) problems at home with parents, siblings, and peers; (8) uninvolved parents—while lip service is given to the need for parental involvement, generally schools have not made parents feel welcome or provided mechanisms to help them get involved; and (9) students being taught by new, inexperienced, and low-yield teachers, many of whom are teaching outside their fields.

The impact of these disturbing social trends on higher education is enormous. First, high dropout rates from high schools greatly reduce the number of minorities qualified to enter college. Second, differential tracking in junior high and high schools leads many minorities to enroll in vocational, commercial, or general education programs. Third, those minority students who do manage to graduate will usually have lower GPAs and achievement test scores. Fourth, because many of these students do not qualify for admission to four-year institutions, many of which recently tightened their admission standards, they will be left with only one alternative to initiate a college-based education: the community college. At this point, the community college becomes the minority student's last chance for college access.

The Community College System

There is evidence that community colleges have not been able to make higher education a reality for minority students. In California, the Carnegie Resource Group heard a state representative describe the three-tier system where community colleges are the access point to the California State University and the University of California systems as an unmitigated disaster. Another policymaker said, "Transfer is a state scandal—a major failure." Indeed, California policymakers noted that only about 5% of all community college students transferred. Nationally, the transfer rate ranges between 5% and 25%, even though studies document that nearly 75% of all community college entrants declare a transfer goal (Rendon and Nora, 1988, Richardson and Bender, 1987; Cohen et al., 1985). In Chicago, a policy analyst indicated that community colleges provided a fraudulent system of education, where students were made to feel as if they were in college, when they really were not. He cited that minority students exhibited low transfer rates, and of those who transferred, only one-fifth eventually earned college degrees. Other studies have documented high minority student attrition and low transfer rates. For example, studies have revealed that California black and Hispanic students exhibit low transfer rates and that the greatest transfer losses occurred in community colleges with high proportions of minority students (Mexican American Legal Defense and Education Fund, 1983; California State Postsecondary Education Commission, 1985; Hayward, 1985). In a survey taken two years after 1980 high school seniors enrolled in college, 48% of the blacks, 50% of Hispanics, and 48% of low SES whites were not enrolled in college (Lee, 1985). These student types are predominant in community colleges. According to the Commission on the Higher Education of Minorities (1982), one of the most important reasons that Chicanos, Puerto

Ricans, and American Indians are underrepresented in graduate programs is their greater than average attrition from undergraduate colleges, particularly community colleges. Further, a recent study (Rendon et al., 1988) substantiated that not only are community college students not transferring, they are not earning associate degrees. The study found that compared to each institution's total enrollment, the proportion of associate degrees awarded ranged from a low of 2.5% to a high of 7.9%. A number of studies have documented the factors that account for poor minority participation in transfer programs.

Barriers to Transfer

The factors associated with low transfer and associate degree completion may be student- and institution-related. Site visits to six community colleges with large Hispanic enrollments located along the United States/Mexico border in Texas, California, and Arizona (Rendon et al., 1988) documented some of the student-related factors influencing community college student achievement and transfer rates.

Student-Related Factors

According to community college administrators and faculty, minority students exhibited the following characteristics: (1) lack of motivation and academic preparation; (2) low intellectual self-concept; (3) unfamiliarity with what it takes to be college student; (4) financial pressures—many students work full- or part-time and feel pressure to send money home to help their families survive; (5) lack of family involvement in their education; (6) unwillingness to leave their community or families; (7) difficulties meeting time lines; (8) a tendency to start with small, seemingly attainable goals and/or to choose majors directly related to employment; (9) unfamiliarity with steps needed to achieve transfer goals; and (10) confusion about the options and benefits of higher education and/or naive about costs and expectations.

These student characteristics are very similar to those described in an earlier study that focused on urban community colleges and universities with high proportions of minority students enrolled (Richardson and Bender, 1987). This study, conducted during 1984-85 covered eight urban centers in eight different states and also made use of site visits and case studies to document its findings. According to this study, students enrolled in community colleges exhibited the following characteristics: low level of academic preparation; unfamiliarity with the higher education system—many of them are first-generation college students; financial pressures—job and family responsibilities; conflicting expectations of short-range occupational objectives with long-range baccalaureate aspirations; and poor concepts of time.

Institution-Related Factors

Institutional barriers were also outlined in the study on transfer education in southwest community colleges (Rendon et al., 1988). For example, community collage staff complained that high schools provided minorities with poor preparation in basic skills. In addition students did not take college preparatory courses in high school nor did they understand how taking a set level of courses would track them into a program of study. Further, it was evident that there were some problems inherent within community colleges. For example, there was (1) some facile resistance to advise students or meet with students outside the classroom; (2) a failure of programs to generate success; (3) some racism—lack of true understanding and acceptance of minorities; (4) some insensitive faculty who were reluctant to deal with unprepared students; (5) a lack of institutional research on retention, transfer, and achievement; (6) poor articulation with universities; (7) inadequate transfer information in college catalogs; (8) an inadequate number of transfer courses in comparison to developmental courses—remedial students took three to four years to earn an associate degree; and (9) channeling of students into vocational-technical tracks. Additional barriers were noted at senior institutions. These included: (1) costs such as application fees, transcript fees, moving, and tuition; (2) assessment policies; (3) impacted programs—limited space especially in business programs; (4) varying university general education patterns; (5) university faculty independence in determining curriculum and in being unwilling to discuss and negotiate curriculum changes; (6) poor articulation with community colleges; and (7) failure to send data about transfers back to community colleges.

Richardson and Bender's (1987) study of urban community colleges and universities also highlighted barriers to transfer at the community college level. They included inadequate offerings of sequential and prerequisite academic transfer courses, channeling minority students out of certain selective programs, poor articulation with universities, an emphasis on vocational career programs, and neglect of transfer programs. The same study outlined barriers at the senior institution level that included lack of approval and fiscal constraints in providing programs for transfers, poor articulation with community colleges, varying standards regarding acceptance of college-parallel courses, university faculty resistance to negotiate curriculum changes, and a tendency to emphasize a specialized, vertical curriculum.

Community College Student and Faculty Perspectives

The community college student experience is illuminated in a recent study of transfer students in six southwest community colleges (Rendon et al., 1988). Students' perspectives about their goals and experiences in community colleges were determined by a random sample of 422 Hispanics and 147 whites enrolled in English, math, history, and business courses. Students were asked a number of different questions related to transfer. Over half of the sample indicated that the main reason for college enrollment was to transfer. Most students aspired to professions requiring at least a bachelor's degree. Over one-half planned to transfer after earning an associate degree and one-fourth planned to transfer before earning an associate degree. Nearly three-fourths thought transferring was important. Over 60% felt that transferring was more important than getting a job. Nearly one-half of the students were talking about transferring with their friends, and about one-half felt that if they did not transfer they would feel disappointed. These affirmative responses strongly suggest that students are giving transfer very serious consideration. The critical issue raised is why minority students in transfer programs are not transferring.

Data from the student survey provided interesting information about why students might not be transferring. Only one-third of the students felt community college teachers had encouraged them to think seriously about transferring. On the other hand it was interesting to note that while students rated their academic and career preparation experiences very positively, felt that the community college offered excellent information on transfer opportunities, and knew they could get assistance about transferring from faculty and counselors, they were not taking advantage of college services. The vast majority did not participate in academic or career counseling or in meetings with four-year college recruiters. Further, about one-half never or rarely made appointments to meet with faculty, over 60% never or rarely asked faculty for advice, and over 50% never or rarely asked faculty for additional references or for help with writing skills. Few students participated in extracurricular activities, had informal conversations with faculty, or participated in freshman orientation. Further, few students sought information about transferring from the counseling office, community college faculty, or four-year institutions. Instead, it appeared that students were getting some assistance about transferring from friends who planned to transfer or who had already transferred. Moreover, students with low levels of commitment to attaining their goals and attending college exhibited low levels of transfer behaviors and perceptions. Similarly, students with less social and academic integration exhibited low levels of transfer behavior and perceptions (Rendon et al., 1988).

The same study involved a random sample of faculty, which determined that often faculty attitudes, policies, and practices did not facilitate transfer. For example, faculty appeared to be overreliant on quick-score, objective tests that measured student performance. Half of the faculty never required additional readings in outside reference materials or asked students to summarize extended prose. Few ever assigned a term paper. In addition, faculty reported to be only somewhat confident or not confident at all about students being able to summarize points from a book, learn on their own, or interpret charts and graphs. General disregard for higher-order thinking skills is substantiated in studies of community college teaching and learning issues (Richardson, 1983; Cohen et al., 1985; Roueche and Comstock, 1981). Further, about one-half of the faculty reported frequently meeting with students during office hours. Nonetheless, few faculty frequently discussed students' applications for transfer, advised students on course selection, or participated in orientation sessions. While most faculty appeared to be aware of comparable course content and textbooks in four-year colleges, most had not compared exams and assignments. Further, few had served as a member of articulation committees. Thus few community college faculty were actively involved in meeting with four-year faculty to compare assignments, exams, and practices, or serving on committees to develop articulation agreements with four-year institutions (Rendon et al., 1988).

Richardson and Bender's study (1987) further illuminates the minority student community college experience as well as how faculty influence the learning process for transfer students. Of the students entering the urban community colleges, 40-50% were reported to have transferring as a primary objective. However, the estimate of the number who might reach their goals ranged from 7% to 20%. According to the student survey and student essays, the number of students reporting that community college faculty and counselors were not an important influence on their decision to transfer ranged from 41% to 88%. More than one-half of the students turned to friends who had transferred for information. Only 10% of the students found orientation sessions useful. Even though most of the students rated their experiences at the community college positively, their favorable responses were concentrated in a relatively small number of programs scattered across the participating community colleges in the study. It was interesting to note that there was no systematic, coordinated effort to make community college environments and services more supportive for students aspiring to transfer. The largest category of improvements for community colleges recommended by students who had transferred to senior institutions focused on the need to expand counseling services and on the need for existing counselors to be more knowledgeable about transfer courses and policies.

Faculty attitudes and practices in some of the community colleges in the urban districts that were cited as not being facilitative to transfer included: (1) frequent use of "watered down courses"; (2) emphasis on students' liabilities rather than on students' potential—suggesting that minority students prepare for employment rather than transfer; (3) rigor of coursework not matching what is expected by university faculty; (4) permitting students without necessary reading and writing skills to enroll in college-parallel courses; and (5) tolerance of different standards for the same courses, and norm-referenced grading standards rather than defined, expected exit competencies.

At this point one is led to conclude that the rate of transfer is conditioned not so much by how many students express a desire to transfer but by what happens to students after they enroll in a transfer program of study. Clearly, if the transfer process is a barrier-filled maze, if few faculty interact with students, if mechanisms are not in place to ensure that students take advantage of college services, if faculty do not involve students in rigorous coursework, if faculty do not encourage students to transfer, and if little articulation exists between community colleges and high schools and between community colleges and senior institutions, students alone cannot be blamed for not transferring.

The consequences of multiple barriers to student achievement and transfer weigh very heavily on minority students. By the end of the pipeline, so many leaks have occurred that the number of minorities earning bachelor's degrees represents but a small trickle. In the 1984-85 academic year, Hispanics earned only 2.7% of all bachelor's degrees, blacks earned 5.9%, American Indians earned .4%, and Asians earned 2.6%. By comparison, whites earned 85% of all bachelor's degrees (Wilson and Melendez, 1987).

Recommendations

While the long range solutions to the critical problem of improving the quality of education for minority students surely lies in a massive effort to reform the K-12 system and the social and economic fabric of society, it is important to develop short-term and viable solutions that involve attention to the K-12 system, teaching and learning, intersegmental collaboration, student and academic support services, assessment, and financial aid.

We begin by presenting some unique interventions that are already being implemented in some school systems across the country, and by recommending that these interventions be adapted to other systems. One such intervention is the development of collaborative agreements that involve schools, colleges and universities, and the business community. Articulation between schools and colleges is crucial, but we now have evidence that partnerships with the business community are also important.

The Boston Compact is an example of a collaborative agreement initiated between the Boston school system and the city's business community, and then expanded to include local colleges and universities in 1983, and building-trade unions in 1984. The Boston School Committee agreed to work to improve attendance, reading and math scores, to reduce the dropout rate, and to increase the number of students who go on to college and get jobs. In return, the business community agreed to hire Boston public school students and graduates on a priority basis for summer jobs, part-time jobs during school, and entry-level career-track jobs upon graduation. Businesses also pledged to bolster support to school partnerships and to assist teachers with their professional development. Further, the Compact includes an industry council-sponsored dropout-prevention and career guidance counselors in all city high schools. Recently, San Antonio, Texas developed the San Antonio Education Partnership, which is based largely on the Boston Compact model. The lesson to be learned is that it is not a matter of what different sectors can do independently of one another, it is a matter of what they can do together (Loverude, 1988).

Another intervention that has proven to be successful in working with high-risk students is the middle college, modeled around the Middle College High School at La Guardia Community College in New York. The Middle College, an alternative high school at the two-year college, recruits only high-risk students. Students attend Middle College in the tenth grade and take the next three years of schooling at the college site. About 85% graduate and 75% go on to college at La Guardia or elsewhere. Components of this model include daily tutoring in every course, personal contact with counselors and teachers, opportunity to repeat a course so that nobody fails, opportunity to work outside the school on unpaid internships, and the option to go to high school on a college campus. The true success of this model indicates that at-risk students are capable of learning and can be helped to learn (La Guardia Community College, 1987).

We also make some recommendations that apply to community college faculty for faculty to shoulder the greatest responsibility for minority student achievement, retention, and transfer. These recommendations include: (1) believing minority students can learn; (2) revising course expectations and making them clear and specific to students; (3) initiating and maintaining articulation meetings with high school and university faculty to discuss expectations, curriculum, and content; (4) increasing contact with students—serving as advocates and mentors to motivate and support students; (5) participating in special programs to help students learn in effective teaching seminars and in the evaluation of curricular programs; (6) learning about the minority family and culture and including minority perspectives in the curriculum; (7) learning how to use and interpret assessment—students should have a clear understanding of what they learned from the beginning to the end of the class; (8) learning to teach critical thinking synthesis and analysis—inspiring students to read, write, and document; (9) knowing why students drop out of class; and (10) collecting data on student achievement, retention, and transfer.

Finally, we present a model to improve student retention and transfer in community colleges. The model is three-dimensional and conceptualizes student flow through the educational pipeline from community colleges to senior institutions.

1. *Bringing students in: opening the door of opportunity.* At the entry level, mechanisms that facilitate access into the educational system are needed. Many of them have already been designed by most colleges, recruitment, financial aid, orientation advisement and counseling, and registration. To these critical services we add the following:

   - Transfer faculty mentors. Students should be assigned to faculty who will advise them on every phase of the transfer process throughout the students', tenure at the institution.

   - Financial planning seminars. Topics such as how to budget financial aid opportunities, and selecting the best package of financial aid should be covered in monthly seminars.

   - Transfer ombudsman. A person assigned to provide information and assistance about transferring should be available to students.

   - Catalog/brochure/video. "All You Ever Wanted to Know About Transferring" might be an appropriate title for a video or document developed for transfer students.

   - Assessment of prior learning. Faculty/counselors should discuss entering student test scores and clearly explain their significance.

   - Amend mission statement and college catalog. Colleges should revise their mission statements to include a reference to transfer students and should identify in their catalogs a section that presents transfer information in a clear, concise, and organized way.

2. *Keeping students in: making access count.* Once students enroll in college, it will be necessary to design mechanisms that enhance institutional and academic integration as well as achievement and retention. To the range of student and academic support services already developed by most two-year colleges, such as counseling and advisement, tutorial centers, developmental studies, and extracurricular activities, we add the following practices.

   - Reserved sections of courses for transfer students. This includes courses such as human potential and general education courses in English, math, history, psychology, and political science, among others.

   - Special orientation for transfer students.

   - Incentive scholarship programs.

- Transfer honors programs. These should be patterned after cluster learning communities that are entered around a common theme, set high expectations, incorporate close student/faculty contact, and provide peer support and networking activities.

- Faculty orientation. Faculty should be sensitized to the characteristics, needs, and problems of transfer students.

- Faculty classroom research training. Faculty should develop assessment instruments to measure student learning and growth at entry, during, and at exit points of student enrollment. Also, faculty should evaluate the effectiveness of their own teaching.

- Intersegmental collaboration. Community college faculty should host meetings with high school and university faculty to compare texts, tests, syllabi, content, curricula, and expectations, as well as to arrive at means to mesh general education requirements.

3. *Moving students on: getting students beyond the open door.* The successful flow of students from two- to four-year colleges is critical to the transfer process. Often, community colleges devote less time to students near the end of their enrollment, even though it is a time that transfer students need support, encouragement, and follow-up as they experience the trauma of leaving one college to enter another. To facilitate student flow, we recommend the following:

  - Exit interview. Students should meet with either a counselor or a faculty mentor to ensure that students are armed with sufficient information to make the successful transition and have completed all course requirements and application forms.

  - Alumni advising. Former transfer students can be brought to community college campuses to inform students about housing, moving and expectations, among others.

  - Two- and four-year college articulation. The two tiers should be involved in comparing academic standards and expectations, exchanging student information, recruiting transfer students, and arranging student tours of four-year college campuses.

In summary, we feel it is important that institutions begin to address the transfer issue in a systemic manner, and we believe that our plan provides a preliminary model that can be incorporated in multiple community college settings.

Conclusion

For minority students, the community college is the most important vehicle of opportunity to attain a college-based education. Access and opportunity must be preserved by making systemic changes throughout the pipeline, for we cannot continue to let schools, community colleges, and universities become academic graveyards for minority students. The most critical challenge for community colleges in the next decade is to provide demonstrable evidence that the number of minorities transferring to senior institutions is significantly rising. This will require renewed attention to the collegiate function. Further, to maintain integrity of the collegiate function will require strong leadership on the part of state leaders, two- and four-year college presidents, and school principals and superintendents, faculty commitment to high standards of teaching and learning, openness to new ideas, and reallocation of funds and resources. Most colleges are trying to cope with the needs of diverse students, but trying is no longer enough, for we have reached a point where moving a small number of exceptions through the system is not enough. The challenge now is to move a large, growing, and critical mass of minority students through the educational pipeline.

It is time for a renewal of community colleges, for the reform of policies and practices designed to promote student achievement, retention, and transfer and for renewed, enforced commitment to the needs of minorities. At stake is far more than the colleges' integrity in the lineage of postsecondary institutions. To allow the excessive drainage of minority students is to create a dearth of human capital needed to help sustain the country's social, economic, and political future. To neglect abysmally low student retention and transfer rates is to contribute to the perpetuation of social injustice and inequity. To ignore the dramatic population shifts in the country is not only to cancel or defer the hopes and dreams of new groups of people, but to put access and opportunity in crisis. In short, from a political, academic, and moral perspective, the community colleges have no choice but to make access meaningful, to generate demonstrable student outcomes, and to provide a high-quality collegiate program of study for the students they were created to serve.

References

California Postsecondary Education Commission. (1985). Update of Community College Transfer Student Statistics: University of California and the California State University, Fall 1985. Report 86-11. Sacramento: Author.

Cohen, A., F. Brawer, and E. Bensimon. (1985). *Transfer Education in American Community Colleges*. Los Angeles: Center for the Study of Community Colleges.

Commission on Minority Participation in Education and American Life. (1988). *One-Third of a Nation*. Washington, DC: American Council on Education.

Commission on the Higher Education of Minorities. (1982). Final Report on the Higher Education of Minorities. Los Angeles: Higher Education Research Institute.

El-Khawas, E., D. J. Carter, and C. A. Ottinger. (1988). *Community College Fact Book*. Washington, DC: American Council on Education/Macmillan.

Hayward, G. (1985). Preparation and Participation of Hispanic and Black Students: A Special Report. Sacramento: California Community Colleges, Office of the Chancellor. (ERIC Document Reproduction Service No. ED 254–285)

La Guardia Community College (1987). La Guardia Community College awarded grant to replicate middle college high school. New York: La Guardia Community College/CUNY (news bulletin).

Lee, V. (1985). Access to Higher Education: The Experience of Blacks, Hispanics, Low Socio-Economic Status Whites. Washington, DC: American Council on Education.

Loverude, D. (1988). San Antonio education partnership. *San Antonio Light* p: A4.

Massachusetts Institute of Technology. (1988). Draft action plan to improve the quality of education for minorities. Quality Education for Minorities Project. Cambridge: Author. (unpublished)

Mexican American Legal Defense and Education Fund. (1983). Petition to Increase Minority Transfer from Community Colleges to State Four-Year Schools. San Francisco: Author.

Orfield, G. and F. Paul. (1987). Declines in minority access: a tale of five cities. *Educational Record*, 68, 4/69, 1: 56–62.

Rendon, L. and A. Nora. (1988). Hispanic students: stopping the leaks in the pipeline. *Educational Record*, 68, 4/69, 1: 79–85.

Rendon, L. M. Justiz, and P. Resta. (1988). *Transfer Education in Southwest Community Colleges.* Columbia: Univ. of South Carolina Press.

Richardson, R. C. (1983). *Literacy in the Open-Access College.* San Francisco: Jossey-Bass.

Richardson, R. C. and L. Bender. (1987). Fostering Minority Access and Achievement in Higher Education. San Francisco: Jossey-Bass.

Roueche, S. D. and V. N. Comstock. (1981). A Report on Theory and Method for the Study of Literacy Development in Community Colleges. Contract No. 400-780-600. Washington, DC: National Institute of Education. (ERIC Document Reproduction Service No. ED 182 465)

Wilson, R. and S. Melendez. (1987). *Minorities in Higher Education.* Washington, DC: American Council on Education.

Suggested Readings:
The Students

Brookfield, S. D. (1986). "Adult Learners" in Brookfield, Stephen D. (ed.), *Understanding and Facilitating Adult Learning.* San Francisco: Jossey-Bass.

Cloves, D. A., Smart, J. A. & Himble, D. (Nov/Dec 1986). "Enrollment Patterns in Post secondary Education: 1961–1982." *Journal of Higher Education,* 57 (2), 121–133.

Cross, K. P. (1968). *The Junior College Student: A Research Description.* Berkeley, University of California, American Association of Junior Colleges.

Maxwell, W. (July 1992). "Academic Quality and the Choice of Suburban Community Colleges by City Students." *Community-Junior College Quarterly of Research and Practice,* 16 (3), 239–50.

Parnell, D. (1986). *Neglected Majority.* Washington, D.C.: Community College Press.

Renden, L. and Matthews, T. (May 1989). "Success of Community College Students: Current Issues." *Education and Urban Society,* 21 (3), 312–327.

Rendon, L. I. (1993). "Eyes on the Prize: Students of Color and the Bachelor's Degree." *Community College Review,* 21(2), 3–13.

Richardson, R. C. and Bender, L. (1987). "Helping Minorities Achieve Degrees: Recommendations for Community Colleges, Universities, and State Boards" in Richardson et al. (eds.) *Fostering Minority Access and Achievement in Higher Education.* San Francisco: Jossey-Bass.

Turner, C. (Spring 1992). "It Takes Two To Transfer: Relational Networks and Educational Outcomes," *Community College Review,* 19 (4), 27–33.

Turner, C. (1990). "A California Case Study: Organizational Determinants of the Transfer of Hispanic Students form Two-to Four-year colleges in the Bay Area." *Metropolitan Education,* (6), 1–24.

Walleri, D. et al, (Feb/March, 1992). "What Do Students Want? How Student Intentions Affect Institutional Assessment." *Community, Technical and Junior College Journal,* 64 (4), 29–31.

Weis, L. (1985). "Without Dependence on Welfare for Life: Black Women in the Community College." *Urban Review,* 17 (4), 233–55.

THE PROFESSIONAL STAFF

The New Professoriate of Community Colleges

DENNIS MCGRATH AND MARTIN B. SPEAR

Everybody now recognizes the new student; hardly anybody notices the new faculty, but as community colleges evolved their distinctive pedagogical strategies, curricular forms, and academic culture, they evolved also a distinctive faculty consciousness and novel faculty culture. Now, the weak and disordered academic culture of community colleges finds its perfect analogue in a weak and disordered faculty intellectual culture.

Community college faculty routinely express difficulty understanding their students—that is a simple consequence of nontraditionality. But, they have trouble understanding themselves as well. The profession of community college instructor is new, its rules unclear. Community colleges have an ambiguous position within higher education, somewhere between high schools and four-year colleges. Indeed, for a long time, high school teachers provided the largest pool from which community college instructors were recruited (Weddington, 1976). For the faculty, institutional ambiguity translates into a role ambiguity that floats unsurely somewhere between high school teacher and university professor. This plays out in everyday life in ways both large and small (London, 1980) community college instructors have in common with high school faculty that they almost always are called "teachers," and those addressed as "Doctor" (a small minority in both settings) are thereby strongly distinguished from their colleagues. Both groups describe themselves as professional teachers or educators, and strongly disavow the university professor's strong identification with scholarship. Faculty members too publicly committed to research and publication, or displaying too much of the traditional professional style, very likely will face overt charges of "elitism," and be criticized by their colleagues for not "caring" for students, for not being sufficiently "student-centered" (Sledge, 1987; Seidman, 1985).

Community college professors are drawn into and reshaped by the culture of open access, but they seldom leave behind all traces of traditional academic styles and expectations. The image of the university professor lingers for them still, though it may beckon them far less than it threatens. Peter Buttenwieser noticed this among community college faculty members he interviewed as part of a project evaluation for the Ford foundation:

> While faculty members might not readily acknowledge it, they exhibit, almost to a person, a pronounced *inferiority complex*, which comes, I believe, from being one rung under college or university and in quest of doctorates, publishing in top-flight journals, giving papers at prestigious conferences, and gaining recognition for academic prowess. This was the most striking phenomenon in all the conversations I had, evidencing itself repeatedly and with considerable force (Buttenwieser, 1987; emphasis in original).

Buttenwieser has interviewed only liberal arts faculty. Teachers in vocational programs don't communicate the same sense of not having made it; quite the contrary, the profession of community college professor is experienced by them as a career advance, as success rather than failure (Caldwell, 1986).

Unlike the university professoriate, both high school and community college teachers work one-step careers, evaluated, if at all, by journeyman notions of competence. Typically, faculty have lengthy, even lifelong ties to one college. With neither upward nor parallel movement available to them, professional life looms as the teaching and reteaching of the same courses, maybe even in the same classrooms. Like high schools, community colleges have extremely flat occupational hierarchies, with only few and ill-defined distinctions among staff. Journeyman instructors have no official hierarchy of competence or excellence, and no public system of recognition or reward beyond initial admission to and permanent membership in the guild. In such a system, all teachers are thought to teach equally well, or mostly so. To suggest otherwise is a serious violation of the professional courtesy expected within an egalitarian organizational culture.

But, again, community colleges are ambiguous institutions. They characteristically retain at least some traditional collegiate forms; hardly any obliterate all traces of academic hierarchy. However, practices such as tenure and promotion, a system of academic rank, and formal recognition of distinction, where these exist at all, are unlikely to be linked explicitly to scholarly accomplishments, or even success in the classroom, since the former are thought irrelevant, and the latter impossible to evaluate. Public distinction is more likely bestowed for "service to the college," for longevity, or simply to guarantee roughly equal distribution of recognition among departments and divisions. To community college faculty, the whole concept of academic hierarchy that permeates the university seems to smack of the twin evils of arbitrariness and elitism.

The interesting and paradoxical corollary is that faculty at "teaching institutions" resist evaluation of teaching as inherently suspicious, as necessarily subjective and capricious, the first step on the slippery slope away from "academic freedom." Perhaps that resistance comes from a natural desire for autonomy or is just a fear of being found out; but it has deeper cultural sources in the code of the guild. The journeyman illusion is that all faculty members are created equal, be they part or full-time, Ph.D. or B.A., published or not—one might even say competent or not, since the defining feature of a journeyman system is that competence is entirely a matter of initial certification. A faculty so organized naturally splinters: toward isolated and autonomous jobbers with no professional future beyond maintenance of membership in the guild, toward loss of corporate identity.

Earl Seidman's *In the Words of the Faculty* (1985) sketches how faculty experience their work situations and career prospects in the face of the transformations that open admissions wrought within community colleges. He portrays community college teachers as beset by uncertainties and torn by ambiguities in a professional role that wavers somewhere between traditional college professor and traditional high school teacher. His picture is of frustration and isolation, of progressive detachment from graduate disciplines fostered by the elevation of teaching over research, and the Sisyphean struggle to satisfy the powerful community college imperative of "student centeredness."

For Seidman, the small daily crises of community college faculty and their more global role ambiguities and tensions are symptoms of institutional and political failures of higher education. Though community colleges took on the task of democratic education, endorsed in word but largely renounced in action by traditional institutions, the underside of open access has been that they remain at the bottom of the academic status hierarchy. Denied respect as academics, community college faculty self-define as teachers, rather than as sociologists or philosophers, and turn to a student service ethos to understand the nature of their profession. Thus, community college "professors" are pushed ever farther from the disciplines they originally professed.

Of course, role ambiguities hit teachers of the traditional liberal arts much harder than their colleagues in vocational programs. Many of the latter are drawn from vocational schools and industry; both socially and economically they experience their new positions as personal advance. Typically, they report high levels of job satisfaction, and low levels of dissonance. Partly, this is because they come with very different expectations about their role, which plays on one side of the dissonance, but, also their experience actually is very different. While liberal arts faculty typically see students for only one semester, perhaps teaching "service courses" for vocational students or introductory courses for which there are no corresponding advanced courses, their colleagues in career programs have much more sustained mentor-like relations with students. Within the structure of their programs they are able to experience student growth and success over time (Richardson et al., 1983; Caldwell, 1986).

However, for teachers of literature, psychology, philosophy, physics—for teachers of the traditional academic disciplines—a career line consists of introductory level courses, four or five, at some places even six per semester, taught over and over for twenty, thirty, or forty years. Joined with the tensions and dissonances of the new teaching role, the faculty's disengagement from disciplines spawns a progressive, if silent, academic drift—away from rigor, toward negotiated anemic practices. For any individual teacher, disciplinary concerns rather quickly recede under the pressure of classroom necessity, to be replaced by the approved professional concern with "teaching." If they share nothing else community college faculty members share that initiatory experience.

Thus, disarticulation and nontraditionality cut two ways. The new student now encounters a new professoriate. On that everybody is agreed. However, its newness is perhaps less a matter of being "student centered," or "exclusively committed to teaching," as in the reigning ideology, than a matter of the confused reshaping of traditional professional models, and the loss of corporate norms, identity, and mission. Still, the striking mismatch between traditionally-trained faculty and a nontraditional career has been long recognized almost everywhere. In response, community colleges have made routine staff development activities ever more ordinary, and more prominent, features of their institutional landscape.

"Developing" Individual Teachers

The problem of the academic culture is not a matter of the personal qualities of either students or faculty, whether individually or in sum. Similarly, what is distinctive, and disturbing, about the new professoriate is not so much their personal professional qualifications, predilections, abilities, and styles, than the social and cultural features of the new profession. However, just as we have seen the educational issues of community colleges always recast in terms of individual students, so ordinary staff development activities also are conceived as trying to influence teachers only individually, or, at best, in aggregate. Individual faculty members are the target: the intention to make them more informed or better teachers, even happier people. By now, that should be familiar as the way deep cultural issues can reappear, twisted and thrust into the heads of individual persons, in this case teachers. That kind of lens is bound to distort the cultural picture. Still, standard practices notice things worth noticing.

1. Workshops to Counter "Burnout." The last twenty years have seen an amazing proliferation of in-service activities with a strong therapeutic and social service orientation, designed to help faculty better understand and manage the normal transitions and stresses of career and personal life. The days of "T groups" and experiential workshops are now mostly behind us, but many workshops still are touted as offering sensitivity training, stress management, personal development, and so on. Additionally, in keeping with widespread corporate practice, colleges are now more frequently implementing Employee Assistance Programs featuring drug and alcohol intervention, counseling, and "wellness" workshops.

Such programs may focus directly on "burnout" (a feature of the one step career), or "middle-age crisis" (a concern primarily because of the so-called "graying of the faculty") or maybe just the teacher stress that flows from the unusually intense professional/client exchange demanded by "student centeredness" (Seidman, 1985). All implicitly recognize that deep tensions and ambiguities in the faculty role produce high levels of stress, dissatisfaction, and disengagement. But rather than encouraging a reflection on the nature of the role, [a social] and cultural matter, workshops inevitably redefine the issues as internal to the individual faculty member. The college faculty again is imagined to be an aggregate of independent journeyman, each individually to be addressed by therapeutic activities to improve his well-being.

Were faculty understood not so much from under the skin, but culturally, their real situation would be better displayed—the overall shape of their professional lives, how they understand their professional role, and the way they are influenced by the organizational culture they both share and shape. That would move the level of analysis from the aggregate psychological to the structural sociological and interpretive anthropological. If staff development "facilitators" were drawn from the ranks of organizational theorists rather than psychologists, there would be many more attempts to influence the faculty culture by affecting the intellectual and social environment, the structures within which faculty act.

2. Sending the Faculty Back to School. The traditional graduate training of community college faculty typically is much more limited than their university counterparts, and their continuing disciplinary identification is certainly very much weaker. Many fewer than twenty percent of community college faculty hold the doctoral degree, even in traditional liberal arts disciplines; few engage in scholarly research and publication. Although those demographic and social features of community college faculty are sometimes the consequences of consciously chosen administrative policies (Sledge, 1987), nevertheless, many community colleges offer incentives to their faculty to continue or return to graduate education. They may provide tuition remission or reimbursement for graduate coursework, released time or study leaves, perhaps even sabbaticals.

Since community college instructors have neither need nor opportunity to teach the fine details of their graduate specialities, the relevance of strong scholarly abilities and interests for their day-to-day work has always seemed dubious (London, 1980; Sledge, 1987). The tendency has been to think that disciplinary expertise roughly equivalent to a graduate teaching assistant's is sufficient for staffing the introductory level course—the staple of the community college general curriculum. Encouraging faculty "back to school" therefore seems a bit puzzling until it is recognized as expressing a minority report on the still unresolved issue of the relation of academics to the open-access classroom. Perhaps, some would say, we don't need journeyman experts who can be counted on to routinely teach the basics from a multicolored textbook. Perhaps the exact reverse is true, that extraordinary knowledge and understanding of disciplines is needed for effectively teaching in the community college.

At the university, lower-division introductory or survey courses have a clear and well-understood place in the curriculum. They entice students toward majors, or they provide a background in a discipline for students pursuing other majors, or are part of general education requirements. However, at open-access colleges, these avowed purposes have a somewhat hollow ring. Only a tiny percentage of students in any classroom will actually major in the discipline; perhaps nobody will. Most students will leave college before they have the opportunity to major in anything. That is the context for the informal renegotiation of course rigor and course content which is so familiar. Faculty members who are relatively undereducated in and professionally disconnected from their disciplines, and without ongoing research interest, are unlikely to be able to represent their discipline intelligibly to nontraditional students, to interpret its intellectual structures, theoretical models, and vocabulary, to locate its concerns relative to others, and so on.

Community college curricula need not be arranged as disciplinary matrices; the question of the relation of individual disciplines to curricula, and to student educational experience is hardly ever debated. And, staff development on the "back to school" model actually reinforces the tendency to think of disciplinary courses and disciplinary information as being at the heart of the community college curriculum.[1] However, for as long as the arrangement remains the norm, more powerful and quite different programs of disciplinary education and professional involvement seem necessary for strengthening the intellectual norms of the average classroom—though by themselves they are surely insufficient. For individual teachers, finishing degrees is certainly a worthwhile endeavor. However, the institutional impact of the relatively few is somewhat more problematic.

3. Developing "Effective Teachers." The proudest claim of community colleges has always been that they are student-centered teaching institutions. As community colleges were largely shaped by this vision, so also their faculties developed professional identities divorced from scholarship and disciplines, new identities as effective teachers, the vanguard of an instructional revolution. With this came a new notion of faculty development; the new profession was to be single-mindedly concerned with the improvement of instruction. In keeping with that orientation, the most common professional development activities at community colleges purport to help individual faculty members improve their teaching.

The new profession, "effective teacher," was made possible by the assumption that pedagogy can be meaningfully separated from the various disciplines, that teachers might be experts in teaching and learning understood generically. Cognitive psychology would provide the model for effective teaching. Members of the new profession typically are urged to respond to the special needs of nontraditional students by gaining expertise in the instructional process. In particular, teachers are told to learn such things as specifying objectives and organizing courses into carefully arranged sequences for mastery by students. Similarly, "learning packages" are endorsed, as is computer-assisted instruction and other forms of individualized learning. This had been the primary focus of in-service sessions and curriculum development workshops for the past twenty years.

By now it is a familiar line, drawn from the canonical model of education, and with it dependent on the epistemological and cognitive psychological assertion that the processes of teaching and learning can be independent objects of knowledge. On that assumption, the professional development staff really have something to teach faculty, and one would expect them to adopt a stance analogous to that of the faculty to the students (i.e., expert to novice, teacher to learner). However, hard-working, strong-willed, and battle-tested faculty so strongly resist claims to superior expertise from anyone who would teach them how to teach that staff development on this model is always fraught with tension and anxiety. Having to play on that court, staff developers characteristically adopt a softer pose: "facilitating" faculty growth, "sharing" expertise, "celebrating" diversity. But although that now seems to everyone the natural way to proceed, it is actually quite peculiar that at colleges that self-define as "teaching institutions," public claims to theoretical knowledge of teaching and learning can appear only so tentatively, so weakly, and so much in constant worry of being trumped by the everyday experience of individual classroom teachers: "practitioners."

The Spread of Practitioners' Culture

The familiar models of staff development all conceive community college faculties as aggregates of individual teachers, each independently struggling with the concerns and frustrations of his role. Staff development activities attempt to affect colleges by influencing individual classrooms, and that by changing individual teachers. The magnitude and audacity of that effort has always been daunting, and the likelihood of success a bit spare, but it has seemed the only route for really changing students' classroom experience. Unfortunately, just as the canonical account of education entirely ignores the social and cultural features of student transformation, the familiar staff development processes utterly disregard the sociocultural condition of the faculty. In fact, faculties are more than aggregates of individual teachers. The initiatory process of disengagement from disciplines, and reengagement through classroom practice, create a peculiar, but still recognizable form of professional culture.

"I am an independent contractor in my classroom," said one of our colleagues recently; "we are all independent contractors." His picture of a community college faculty was of an association of independent journeymen, each sovereign in his classroom, joined only by such informal agreements as such weak social arrangements are able to support. However, although community college faculty imagine themselves in the natural condition of a professoriate (our colleague's remark was enthusiastically endorsed by everybody present), their situation is actually quite novel, a consequence of the particular evolutionary path traversed by open-access institutions. The forces that have shaped the distinctive community college professoriate are often remarked upon, if the details inevitably vary from here to there: a typically large reliance on part-time teachers, faculty unionization, the drive for educational technology and "learning packages," the weakening, even the disappearance of courses beyond the introductory level, the geographical fragmentation of colleges into numerous community sites, and so on. Almost everything about their situation pushes community college teachers apart from their colleagues, and shatters their corporate identity.

Sharing a commitment to teaching, but without a shared notion of what effective teaching might be, with strong affective ties to one another, but without the intellectual guidance and constraint provided by disciplinary cultures, faculties take on the aspect of a "practitioners' culture." They come to undervalue intellectual exchange and mutual criticism, and to overvalue "sharing" as sources of professional and organizational development (North, 1987). For the institutions themselves, facing the most difficult job in higher education, the consequences are debilitating. Operating within the rules of practitioners' culture, colleges cannot bring their collegiate intellectual resources to bear on curricular or educational problems. In fact, since intellectual issues come to look like political issues that call only for political adjustments among contending parties within the society of journeyman equals, colleges effectively deny that they actually have corporate intellectual resources. They will be unable to conceive their problems at any level higher than the individual classroom. Thus, when colleges imagine themselves to be aggregates of individual teachers, their wishes will come true.

For people who have not lived within a practitioners' culture, it is hard to imagine; and no ethnographic research as yet adequately details the community college faculty culture. So we now offer two descriptions of faculty interaction, two stories really. Insiders will recognize the pattern, and outsiders will begin to get a sense of the malaise afflicting the community college professoriate.

The first story takes place within the walls of a single community college (Seymour, 1989); the second at a national conference among instructors who had never before met (McGrath and Spear, 1987).

In the first tale, an instructor had invited his colleagues to join in a series of workshops to engage one another in theoretical debate on the "the reasoning behind our methods" in remedial reading courses. The announced plan was for an initial presenter to focus on "the underlying philosophical assumptions which drive our teaching of Reading courses," and then have two respondents comment on that presentation.

However, the very first workshop departed from that plan in classic practitioner style. The presenter, Mary, began with a story that produced smiles and nods of approval among the dozen or so participants. Several years earlier, as a graduate teaching assistant assigned to teach her first reading course, Mary had expressed concern about her lack of training. She had been immediately assured by her faculty advisor "that teachers with graduate degrees in Reading don't know any more abut how to teach reading" than Mary did. She reported being told that a personal enjoyment of reading and a desire to get students to experience that enjoyment themselves were the real keys to good teaching of a reading course.

Mary then described her initiation into the ranks of community college reading teachers. From the start, she said, she had rejected standard reading textbooks that had students read paragraphs and answer questions about them. Instead, she adopted an impressive array of activities—geared to achieve basic reading skills, of course, but also aimed at developmental objectives. She listed them: students gaining familiarity with the library and learning basic research techniques, achieving self-awareness as well as cultural literacy, learning cooperation with other students and respect for ethnic diversity, gaining self-esteem, and more.

The first respondent, John, asked the moderator if he were really required to respond the Mary. The moderator replied that he was not. John then proceeded to describe in detail how he conducted his own reading courses. In other words, for John, discussing teaching meant "sharing"—a term never used lightly in practitioners' culture. The college, in his view, was just physical space, the faculty a collection of private practitioners. "I am an independent contractor. . . .allowed to use the classrooms [here] for my teaching," he claimed. The activities and objectives John listed were somewhat different than Mary's but within the sharing relationship; there was no way to pointedly formulate their relation—whether they were opposed or complementary, for instance. In fact, that issue did not seem important to John.

The second respondent took a somewhat different tack. Henry tried placing his own teaching in relation to that of the other speakers. John, he said, was at one end of a spectrum, trying to cultivate the students' inner voices. In contrast, Mary was in the middle and he, Henry, was on the opposite side from John, attempting to expose students to an "outside," to Western culture itself—in the form of Homer's *Odyssey*. Although he did not work it out in any detail, Henry's "spectrum" might have shaded from subjective to objective, or Romantic to Classic, or perhaps expressivist to social functionalist. The implication of his remarks seemed to be that very deep, if muted, theoretical conflicts existed among the three presenters which might have important educational implications. In any case, Mary's emphasis on academic routine, Henry's on reading the classics of Western literature, and John's on personal liberation do seem seriously at odds.

But Henry's attempt to construct a grid to map differences in practice onto differences in theory met with an extremely strong negative response from the audience. The first to speak set the tone. For all the apparent differences among Mary, John, and Henry, the similarities, he said, were really much stronger. All three established "comfort zones" for students, and all developed "customized approaches" appropriate for community college students. Immediately, other participants, including the presenters, rushed enthusiastically to assure everyone that the three accounts actually revealed far more similarities, what they called "commonalities," than differences. They listed some: all used reading aloud; all had their students copy material from books; and all emphasized questioning. That, as it turned out, was the end of the discussion devoted to theoretical issues about the teaching of reading. The rest of the time was spent telling classroom stories, success stories mostly, but occasionally cautionary tales about how impersonal institutional and social forces undermine students' efforts.

Perhaps it is natural that co-workers whose professional lives are spent in close proximity will develop social processes for defusing potentially explosive debates. So, our second story throws the net wider; it tells of community college teachers at a national conference. Each had been invited as an articulate spokesperson for a familiar approach to teaching reading and writing. They had never before met, nor, as far as we know, ever met again. The format of the conference was for several preliminary sessions in which each speaker would make a formal presentation, followed by a plenary session which would bring everyone together for debate.

Mostly, the speakers broke out along the lines uncovered in our previous chapters. One appealed for readings drawn from the cultural canon. Strangely, the reason given for this was from classical aesthetics, that apprehension of beauty is definitive of our humanity and therefore should not be denied to community college students. The second speaker insisted that texts and writing assignments should be chosen with a view to heightening students' personal, social, and, especially, political awareness. The reading and writing classrooms' claim to be "liberating" was offered quite literally. Students were portrayed as struggling, under the guidance of a politically aware faculty, to appreciate their own position as black, Hispanic, female, or working-class. Now although the speakers on this first panel were as opposed as right wing and left wing educational views can be, in the cross talk portion of the session they were content to deny their differences, actually claiming that they agreed about all important matters and were just pursuing alternative routes to the same goals.

The second set of speakers each went a different way. One argued that skills development, the traditional goal of remedial education, is best conceived as an exercise in linguistic anthropology. Students and teachers can be partners in research, the goal of which is the students' achieving competence in a new language community. This speaker joined in the polemic against "mechanical" methods, the explicit bogey of the earlier session, and stressed that literacy must be understood as embedded in a tacit tradition of textuality. Perhaps the existence of a common polemical opponent and the analysis of literacy as partly constituted by traditions of canonical texts masked the differences between this speaker and the others. But an account so self-consciously proceeding within a social-scientific framework ought to be at pains to distinguish itself from accounts coming from traditional aesthetics or from romantically conceived notions of personal liberation through political action. But alas, that was not to be.

The final presenter tried to understand the problem of remedial education using primarily literary categories. What, he asked, are the "stories we tell our students, and ourselves?" What narrative can find the personal, social, and moral meaning in an enterprise that the surrounding culture defines as failure? None of the approaches of the previous speakers seemed to him to touch this fundamental issue.

The plenary session was begun with remarks by a respondent who commented globally on the various speakers' relations to one another. The scene that followed is reminiscent of our earlier story, though on a larger scale. Very quickly, all rejected the characterization that they were in any real theoretical opposition at all, certainly not fundamental opposition. They began to tell stories about their colleges and their students, to find areas of commonality. The audience joined in. After a while the moderator thanked everyone present for sharing their experiences, and the session was adjourned.

These were all good and caring teachers, not deadwood, but among the best. All had gone far out of their way, in the second story hundreds or thousands of miles out of their way, ostensibly to argue, to debate, to make intellectual progress together on some of the most critical issues of their professional lives. Why is it that such important conversations short-circuited so quickly? The quick answer is that among community college faculties, unlike university faculties, social organization does not follow the academic/intellectual organization. The elevation of teaching over research or scholarship may have turned faculty into "generic teachers," but it also stripped away an intellectual norms that might bind them together. And so they search for commonalities, or in any event don't raise matters they see no rational way to resolve.

One by one, individual teachers are drawn from their disciplines and initiated into community college culture. Maintenance of disciplinary ties is extremely difficult; everyone notices that. Teachers are not expected to write; few do. More important is that exchanges among community college faculty are not characteristically written. They are spoken, experienced, shared. Put differently, teachers share what is primarily an *oral* culture. Paradoxically, although highly educated and literate, they are, relative to one another, "more comfortable in the person-to-person human life world than in a world of pure abstraction" (A. R. Luria; quoted in Ong, 1982:53). this is why community college faculty are such storytellers. As Walter Ong notes regarding oral cultures: "Oral cultures tend to use concepts in situational, operational frames of reference that are minimally abstract in the sense that they remain close to the living human lifeworld (1982:49)." Released from the intellectual norms and social constraints of writing practices, the faculty culture "concretizes." Teachers grow deeply suspicious of "abstract theory," and turn to experience, to classroom practice, as the only things really worth talking about.[2]

So the community college practitioners' culture provides but meager resources for persuasion; it accords only very weak status to theory, analysis, and debate. Inevitably, precedence is granted to anecdote over theory, and to informal classroom experience over rigorous method as sources of knowledge. Stephen North calls this form of knowledge "practitioners' lore" and describes the social rules governing it like this:

> Anything can become part of lore. The only requirement for entry is that the idea, notion, practice, or whatever be nominated: some number of the community must claim that it worked, or seems to work, or might work . . . contributions to it have to be framed in practical terms, as knowledge about what to do; if they aren't they will be changed (North, 1987: 24-25).[3]

Within a practitioners' culture the conscious link between theory and practice is broken. If and when theory is proposed, it is treated as something to be mined for practical suggestions, for what to do in class on Monday. Likewise, when a new course, a change in policy, or new curriculum is debated, anyone who says "I tried that in my class last week and it worked just fine—or didn't," cannot be meaningfully debated with, certainly not refuted. No public rules can decide among practitioner claims because they don't seem to compete; they seem instead to complement, or supplement one another. That is why lore just piles up in a way that disciplinary knowledge does not. Nothing can ever really be left behind; teachers just accumulate more and more techniques to choose from. Since the social demands of practitioners' culture are such that sharing is the approved mode of interacting—criticism being forbidden—nothing can stand against that ace of trump: the everyday classroom experience. Certainly theory cannot; that has to seem mere speculation, perhaps personal bias, at any rate far inferior to personal experience, and anecdotes about that experience.[4]

Toward a New Faculty Culture

Many recent calls for reforming secondary education have focused on the role of teachers in developing effective schools. The typical high school teacher has few opportunities for intellectual challenge and stimulation, support for professional growth, and little control over decisionmaking in the school. Advocates of "effective schools" argue that to improve public education schools should work to overcome the isolation of teachers by creating a collegial environment which provides opportunities for staff interaction, and helps teachers view their colleagues as sources of ideas and support (Lieberman, 1988). Studies suggest that schools characterized by high levels of staff interaction develop shared professional norms and have more faculty involvement in instructional planning and practice (Little, 1982; Van Maanen and Barley, 1984).

In comparison with the average high school, most community colleges appear to have a professional culture. Individual teachers exercise considerable autonomy in the classroom, and governance structures permit faculty significant influence over curricular and other academic matters. However, the comparison with high schools has tended to blind commentators to the peculiar academic culture which has developed in open-access institutions. The startling features of the professional culture of community colleges—the studied insistence on avoiding even the appearance of disagreement, the continuing search for areas of commonality, and the dread of irresolvable conflict within a society of equals—have no real analogue among either university professors or high school teachers.

The disordered academic culture of community college is the perfect expression of faculty that have become unable to sustain strong academic practices among themselves, whose professional culture is organized primarily along social rather than intellectual dimensions. A powerful academic culture can be created and sustained only by a faculty that is itself organized according to academic and intellectual rules of discourse and decision.

Since the institutional and social forces weakening the intellectual culture among faculty at community colleges are unlikely to lose their influence in the near future, community colleges should work seriously toward constructing activities which encourage and sustain academic practices among the faculty as a collegiate body. If the educational problem of open access is how to initiate nontraditional students into an academic culture, the first order of business has to be ensuring that a strong academic culture exists in the first place. Realistically, relatively little can be done to reengage faculty in their original disciplinary communities. But much can be done to help faculty reengage one another as intellectuals, as members of an academic community, to rediscover the excitement that once drove their own academic careers.

Schools cannot be fundamentally improved by trying to change faculty members one by one, by exhorting them to whatever teaching techniques happen to be approved by reigning educational theories. The more important point is that schools cannot even be changed that way, since that is their current condition: individual teachers struggling alone in the open-access classroom, taking teaching tips from wherever they may be found. It is not always easy to distinguish mature professional autonomy from finely honed eccentricity; but strengthening individual classrooms, the heart of students' academic experience, surely means strengthening the institutional academic culture in which they nestle. And that is something no "autonomous" teacher, however gifted and good-willed, has control over; the problem is ourselves together, the solution ourselves together.

Notes

1. Teachers returning to graduate school for further training may not be strengthening their disciplinary abilities at all. Many are "retooling" for teaching reading or writing to remedial students. Others pursue advanced degrees in education rather than their home disciplines. And, of course, there are now graduate programs specifically designed for community college teachers that are analogous to "teacher training" for elementary or high school.

2. Research on oral cultures has been almost completely concerned with preliterate cultures—archaic Greece, for instance—where it can be seen in pure form. But it would be a mistake to think of orality as something we've all left behind. Literate modes are not "wired into" the brain, nor even into societies. Both "literacy" and "orality" are not so much features of an individual person's brain, or consciousness, or cognitive structures, as they are particular social forms of cognitive organization; they are social performances.

3. North's description of practitioners' culture, on which we have drawn so heavily, is offered by him as a sketch of composition departments. We have expanded the range here to cover the community college faculty more generally, but, of course it is not irrelevant that those are so much dominated by composition teachers.

4. The frequent recent calls for teacher-conducted classroom research might be seen as making a virtue of necessity within a practitioners' culture (Goswami and Stillman, 1987; Cross, 1988). Although faculty may not have the resources to talk and reflect as a collegial body, at least "lore" can be strengthened by improving the ability of individual teachers to interpret their experience. Quite in consonance with the primarily social organization of faculties, advocates of "classroom research" urge that "teachers can serve each other as resources and consultants, sharing insights, observations and speculations" (Atwell, 1987:91).

References

Buttenwiser, Peter L. "Achieving Fundamental Change Within a Change-Resistant Environment: The Transfer Opportunities Program Experience in Community College of Philadelphia (1984–1987)." A report prepared for the Ford Foundation, August 1987.

Caldwell, Corrinne. "Implications of the One-Stage Career For Community College Faculty." *Ph.D. diss.*, University of Pennsylvania, 1985.

Lieberman, Ann, ed. *Building a Professional Culture in Schools.* New York: Teacher's College, 1988.

Little, J. W. "Norms of Collegiality and Experimentation: Workplace Conditions of School Success." *American Educational Research Journal*, 19 (1982): 325–340.

London, Howard. "In Between: The Community College Teacher." *Annals of the American Academy of Political and Social Science*, vol. 448 (1980).

McGrath, Dennis and Spear, Martin B. "The Humanities and Remedial Education: Reflections on the San Francisco Conference." *Community College Humanities Review*, 8 (1987): 77–82.

North, Stephen M. *The Making of Knowledge in Composition.* New Jersey: Boynton/Cook, 1987.

Ong, Walter J. *Orality and Literacy: The Technologizing of the Word.* London and New York: Methuen, 1982.

Richardson, Richard C., Jr., Fisk, Elizabeth A., and Okum, Morris A. *Literacy in the Open Access College.* San Francisco: Jossey-Bass, 1983.

Seidman, Earl. *In the Words of the Faculty: Perspectives on Improving Teaching and Educational Quality in Community Colleges.* San Francisco: Jossey-Bass, 1985.

Seymour, Evan. "How should reading courses be read?" Paper presented at Fall, 1989 Community College of Philadelphia English Department Workshops on Reading and Writing.

Sledge, Linda Ching. "The Community College Scholar." *Community College Humanities Review*, 8 (1987): 61–66.

Van Maanen, John and Barley, S. R. "Occupational Communities: Culture and Control in Organizations." In *Research in Organizational Behavior*, Barry M. Staw, ed. Greenwich, Conn: JAI, 1984.

Weddington, Doris. *Faculty Attitudes in Two Year College.* Los Angeles: Center for the Study of Community Colleges, 1976.

Minority Faculty Recruitment Programs at Two-Year Colleges

RONALD D. OPP AND ALBERT B. SMITH

Increasing the representation of minorities among full-time faculty is a particularly important issue at the two-year college level. In a current study from the U.S. Department of Education, two-year colleges were reported to enroll a disproportionate share of all minority students enrolled in higher education (*Chronicle of Higher Education Almanac*, 1991). Fifty-six percent of all Hispanics, 54 percent of all American Indians, and 42 percent of all African-Americans enrolled in higher education are attending two-year colleges.

Given the disproportionate number of minority students enrolled in two-year colleges, the need for adequate minority representation among full-time faculty in this sector is particularly critical. In a recent study, it was reported that minority students account for 19.2% of the nation's 13.7 million college students in 1990, up from 18.7% in 1980 (*Chronicle of Higher Education*, March 18, 1992). As minority students become a larger proportion of all higher education enrollments, finding ways to increase the recruitment and retention of minority college students is becoming an increasingly important concern in higher education. The significant presence of minority full-time faculty can help two-year colleges become more successful in recruiting and retaining minority students.

Minority faculty on two-year college campuses can also help increase the educational aspirations of minority students by providing positive role models of individuals with high levels of educational achievement. They can also help white students overcome prejudicial thoughts about the intellectual capabilities of people of color, and help white faculty gain a deeper understanding and appreciation for different cultural heritages (Linthicum, 1989). For all of these reasons, adequate representation of minority faculty is essential to excellence and equity in two-year colleges.

Federal data on the representation of minorities among full-time faculty in higher education are readily available. In a 1989–90 Equal Employment Opportunity Commission survey, it was reported that African-Americans represent 4.5%, Hispanics 1.9%, and American Indians .3% of all full-time faculty (*Chronicle of Higher Education Almanac*, 1991). The representation of these minority groups among full-time faculty is significantly less than their proportional representation in the overall U.S. population: African-Americans make up 12.1%, Hispanics make up 9.0% and American Indians make up .8% (*Chronicle of Higher Education Almanac*, 1991). Clearly, African-Americans, Hispanics and American Indians are significantly underrepresented in higher education compared to their representation in the general population.

Although Equal Employment Opportunity Commission (EEOC) data regarding the distribution of faculty by race/ethnicity are readily available, these data are typically not reported by *institutional type*. Thus, researchers interested in the distribution of faculty by race/ethnicity within two-year colleges have to rely on sources other than the EEOC for data. Most of the data about the racial/ethnic distribution of two-year college faculty comes from the work of individual researchers. In the most recent national study, based on a weighted sample of faculty in 89 community colleges, Astin found that about 9.8% of full-time faculty were minority (1991).

Purposes of the Study

One of the purposes of this study was to provide current *institutional* data on the number and percentage of underrepresented minorities among full-time faculty in two-year colleges. Unlike previous studies reporting data on minority two-year college faculty (Russell, 1991; Astin, 1991), this study was based on information gathered directly from two-year institutions rather than from faculty surveys. Thus, the number of minorities reported by institutions can be compared with the weighted estimates of the number of minority faculty derived from national faculty surveys.

Another purpose of the study was to examine empirically what academic administrators felt about a number of barriers to minority faculty recruitment. A number of researchers have posited attitudinal and structural factors which hinder the recruitment of minorities in four-year institutions (Smelser & Content, 1980; Reed, 1983; Menges & Exum, 1983; Exum, 1983; Exum et al. 1984; Reed, 1986; Banks, 1988; Bunzel, 1990; Mickelson & Oliver, 1991). This study was designed to test empirically whether these same factors are perceived as barriers to recruiting minority faculty at the two-year college level as well.

This study was also designed to examine empirically what institutions were *actually* doing to recruit minority faculty. Much of the existing literature on minority faculty recruitment consists of suggestions about what *should* be done to improve recruitment programs (Harris, 1989; Lessow-Hurley, 1989; Boyd, 1989). In only one recent national study was there an examination of what two-year colleges were *actually* doing to recruit minority faculty. That study contained a report on what *states* were doing to recruit minority faculty, but provided little information about what individual *institutions* were doing (Linthicum, 1989). This study complements that research on *state* programs by providing information on what is being done at the *individual campus* level to recruit minority faculty.

A final purpose of this study was to determine empirically what characterizes successful programs of minority faculty recruitment. Much of the existing literature has focused primarily on describing strategies for improving minority faculty recruitment, without testing empirically how successful these strategies actually are. In this study an analysis is provided about what strategies are related to having a high number of underrepresented minority full-time faculty. Hopefully, information about strategies which facilitate minority faculty recruitment can be utilized by two-year college administrators in designing more successful programs and practices.

Research Design

Definitions, sampling methodology, questionnaire design, data gathering procedures and response rates will be discussed in the sections that follow.

Definitions

In this study *underrepresented minorities* are defined as those minority groups whose presence among full-time faculty in higher education is not proportionate with their overall representation in the U.S. population. Using this definition of underrepresentation, the investigators focused on four different minority groups: African-Americans, Mexican-Americans, Puerto Rican-Americans, and American Indians. In this study *full-time faculty* were further defined as those individuals for whom teaching was their principal activity and who were considered full-time employees at their institution for at least nine months of the 1991–92 academic year.

Sampling Methodology

The researchers utilized individual two-year institutions as the unit of analysis, rather than college districts or state systems. Within each two-year institution, the vice president of academic affairs or a person in an equivalent position was surveyed to obtain information about the college's minority faculty recruitment program. Given the major responsibility that this administrator typically has for faculty recruitment, it was assumed that this individual would be knowledgeable both about the number of full-time minority faculty employed at the college, and about the college's minority faculty recruitment program.

The vice president of academic affairs at each two-year college was identified by using *Who's Who in Community, Technical and Junior Colleges* (AACJC, 1991). This particular reference guide was chosen because it is an authoritative source of recent information about administrative leaders at virtually every two-year institution in the country. A total of 1,293 vice presidents of academic affairs at individual two-year college campuses was identified through the use of this reference guide. In short, virtually every two-year college vice-president of academic affairs in the country was included in the sample for this study, with the exception of those vice-presidents at two-year campuses not listed in this AACJC reference guide.

Questionnaire Design

The questionnaire instrument was designed to test many of the assumptions found through a review of the literature on minority faculty recruitment. The questionnaire was field tested utilizing 34 community college faculty and administrators representing a number of community colleges in West Texas. As a result of this validation process, the questionnaire was revised to eliminate any questions which were found to be ambiguous or misleading. The final instrument which emerged was a four-page instrument divided into five sections.

Appendix A

A National Survey of Recruitment Practices for Minority Full-Time Faculty at Two-Year Colleges

Directions: Please answer each question by circling the appropriate number.
Example: This is a survey on minority faculty recruitment practices.

1	Yes	2	No

Part I: Demographic Background

1. Your sex:

1	Male	2	Female

2. Racial/ethnic group (Circle *all* that apply):

1	White/Caucasian	5	Mexican-American
2	Black/African-American	6	Puerto Rican-American
3	American Indian	7	Other
4	Asian-American		

3. How old will you be on December 31 of this year? _____

4. What is the highest degree that you have earned?

1	Bachelor's	4	Ed.d.
2	Master's	5	Ph.D.
3	Ed. Specialist	6	Other Degree

5. What is the highest level of education reached by your mother?

1	Grammar school or less	5	Some college
2	Some high school	6	College degree
3	High school graduate	7	Some graduate school
4	Postsecondary school other than college	8	Graduate degree

6. What is the highest level of education reached by your father?

1	Grammar school or less	5	Some college
2	Some high school	6	College degree
3	High school graduate	7	Some graduate school
4	Postsecondary school other than college	8	Graduate degree

7. Number of years of two-year college administration experience: _____

How much contact do you have with each of the following groups:

1 = Extensive
2 = Some
3 = None at all

8. Minority students 1   2   3

9. Minority faculty 1   2   3

10. Minority administrators 1   2   3

Part II: Campus Demographics

11. How many *full-time* African-American faculty do you have?_____

12. How many *full-time* Mexican-American faculty do you have? _____

13. How many *full-time* Puerto Rican-American faculty do you have? _____

14. How many *full-time* American Indian faculty do you have? _____

15. How many *full-time* faculty do you have? _____

16. In recruiting minority *full-time* faculty in the 1980s, this college:

1	made progress	3	lost ground
2	stayed about the same		

17. How much gain (if any) do you expect to make in recruiting minority *full-time* faculty during the 1990s?

1	substantial	3	little
2	moderate	4	none

Part III: Barriers to Recruiting Minority Faculty

Below are some statements about your current college. Indicate the extent to which you agree or disagree with each of the following: (Circle one response for each item)

>   1 = Agree Strongly
>   2 = Agree Somewhat
>   3 = Disagree Somewhat
>   4 = Disagree Strongly

18. Current economic constraints make it difficult to hire
    additional minority faculty here 1   2   3   4

19. Affirmative action requirements significantly raise
    the costs of faculty searches here 1   2   3   4

20. Minority faculty are hired at this college primarily to
    staff ethnic studies programs 1   2   3   4

21. Attempts to influence departments here to hire minority
    faculty evoke the red flag of interference with
    faculty prerogatives 1   2   3   4

22. Departments/divisions here avoid the issue of hiring minority
    faculty by arguing that there are few minorities in their field 1   2   3   4

23. Minority faculty would have difficulty fitting in socially
    with the community here 1   2   3   4

24. Minority faculty are not available for positions here
    in arts and science fields 1   2   3   4

25. Minority faculty are not available for positions here
    in technical and occupational fields 1   2   3   4

26. Women and minorities are competing with each other
    at this college for the same faculty positions 1   2   3   4

27. Prospective minority faculty prefer employment
    in business and industry to employment here 1   2   3   4

Part IV: Minority Faculty Recruitment Strategies

Which of the following strategies for recruiting minority faculty has your institution used?
    (Circle one response for each item).

1 = Yes
    2 = No
    3 = Not Applicable

28. Advertising in media outlets used by minorities 1   2   3

29. Inviting minority professionals for guest lectures.................................1   2   3

30. Inviting minority professionals for part-time
    adjunct assignments 1   2   3

31. Recruiting minorities in private enterprise jobs with the
support of their employers to teach part-time 1   2   3

32. Encouraging faculty to make contact with minority scholars
in their fields to publicize available positions 1   2   3

33. Including faculty from diverse cultural backgrounds
on search committees 1   2   3

34. Including minority community members on search committees 1   2   3

35. Having minorities serve on college advisory boards
to remind institutions of their commitments to minorities 1   2   3

36. Having minorities serve on the board of trustees
to remind institutions of their commitments to minorities 1   2   3

37. Having college representatives meet with minority
representatives of civic organizations 1   2   3

38. Having college representatives meet with minority
representatives of churches...1   2   3

39. Having college representatives meet with minority
representatives of businesses 1   2   3

40. Having college representatives attend conferences held by
professional organizations concerned with minority issues 1   2   3

41. Funding teaching internships for minority graduate
students at two-year colleges 1   2   3

42. Creating faculty exchange programs between two-year
colleges and predominantly minority four-year colleges 1   2   3

43. Conducting staff development sessions and workshops
about affirmative action 1   2   3

44. Utilizing an applicant tracking system of resumes
and applications of minorities 1   2   3

45. Asking deans or department chairs to justify
nonminority hires 1   2   3

46. Rewarding departments with an extra position
for each minority hire 1   2   3

47. Filling on a temporary basis positions where minority
candidateshave not been recruited into the applicant pool 1   2   3

48. Cancelling positions where minority candidates have not
been recruited into the applicant pool 1   2   3

49. Hiring a high level campus affirmative action officer
to enforce campus affirmative action policies 1   2   3

50. Making affirmative action part of collective bargaining 1   2   3

Part V: Description of Minority Faculty Recruitment Program

Please briefly describe below your minority faculty recruitment program (or send under separate cover material that describes your college's policies and practices and success in this area).

The first section contained a number of questions related to the respondents' personal backgrounds, including their age, sex, race, and educational level. Also included in this first section was a question on the number of years of respondents' two-year college administrative experience, and the amount of contact the respondents had with minority students, faculty, and administrators. In the second section, respondents provided information on the number of minority faculty and total full-time faculty at their institutions, and whether their institutions expected to make progress in hiring minority faculty in the 1990s. In the third section, respondents were asked to indicate the degree to which they agreed or disagreed with a number of statements about attitudinal and structural barriers to recruiting minority faculty. The fourth section consisted of questions designed to determine which strategies institutions had actually utilized in recruiting minority faculty. The final section contained questions that asked respondents to briefly describe their minority faculty recruitment program, or to send material that described their college's policies, practices, and success in this area.

Data Gathering Procedures

The first wave of the questionnaire was mailed out in mid-February, 1992 to 1,293 vice-presidents of academic affairs listed in *Who's Who in Community, Technical and Junior Colleges* (AACJC, 1991). The first-wave packet contained a cover letter explaining the purpose of the study, a sheet defining underrepresented minorities and full-time faculty, the questionnaire, and a self-addressed, business-reply envelope. After a three-week interval, a second wave packet was mailed out in early March to all non-respondents to the first-wave. This paper is based on a preliminary analysis of data received up to this point.

Responses

Out of the 1,293 questionnaires mailed out with the first wave, a total of 391 surveys were received, for a response rate of 30.4%. Out of the additional 902 questionnaires mailed out in the second wave, 222 additional questionnaires have been received to date, for a response rate of 24.6%. Thus, at present, the overall response rate for the survey after two waves is 47.4%. The final response rate is expected to exceed 50% when all second wave questionnaires are received.

Discussion of Results

Results will be discussed in the following sections: characteristics of the sample, percentages of underrepresented minority faculty, barriers to minority faculty recruitment, recruitment strategies, and the prediction of minority faculty recruitment success.

Characteristics of the Sample

The vice-presidents of academic affairs who responded to this survey tended to be white males, 51 years of age, with either an Ed.D. or Ph.D., and 13 years of community college experience. Slightly more than one-quarter of the respondents were female, and slightly more than one-tenth were members of a minority group. This profile of respondents is quite similar to findings by Hankin (1985) that 29.8% of two-year college administrators were female and 13.4% were minority. In short, the respondents to this study have demographic backgrounds similar to community college administrators nationally.

Table 1
Characteristics of Sample

Demographic Characteristics	Percentage or Mean	Number of Respondents
Sex		
Female	27.4%	167
Male	72.6%	442
Race		
White	88.3%	542
Black	6.8%	42
American Indian	2.1%	13
Asian-American	.7%	4
Mexican-American	2.9%	18
Puerto Rican-American	.2%	1
Other	.5%	3
Educational Background		
Bachelors	1.8%	11
Masters	26.4%	160
Ed.D.	31.9%	193
Ph.D.	37.9%	229
Other	2.0%	12
Average Age	51 years	607
Average Number of Years of Community College Experience	13 years	

Percentages of Minority Faculty

Percentages of minority faculty were calculated by dividing the number of a particular minority group by the number of full-time faculty to be found within the total sample of institutions. Separate percentages were calculated for African-American, American Indian, Mexican-American, and Puerto Rican-American faculty, as well as for the percentage of all of these minority groups combined. There were a total of 53,628 full-time faculty across the 616 institutions included in this study, which represents 60.7% of the 88,252 full-time faculty found in the two-year college sector (Astin, 1991).

Table 2
Percentage of Underrepresented Minority
Faculty at Two-Year Colleges (in percentages)

Institutional Minority Group	Astin[1] Self-Report	NCES[2] Study	Study
African-Americans	5.1	4.0	3
American Indians	1.4	1.2	1
Mexican-Americans	1.7	1.7	—
Puerto Rican-Americans	.3	.2	—
Total	8.5	7.1	—

[1]Percentages obtained from *National Norms for the 1989–90 HERI Faculty Survey*, A. W. Astin et. al, 1991.

[2]Percentages obtained from *Profiles of Faculty in Higher Education Institutions, 1988*, NCES. Data are for public two-year colleges only.

There was a total of 3,103 full-time African-American faculty reported, or 5.1% of all full-time faculty. This figure is one percentage point higher than the percentage reported in either of the two recent national faculty studies. There was a total of 1,075 Mexican-American faculty reported, or 1.7% of all full-time faculty. This figure exactly coincides with the percentage of Mexican-American faculty reported in the national study by Astin. Similar data were not available from NCES, since they reported aggregated data for Hispanics, rather than disaggregated data for Mexican-Americans and Puerto Rican-Americans. There was a total of 125 Puerto Rican-American faculty reported, or 0.3% of all full-time faculty. This figure is again slightly above the percentage reported in the study by Astin. Finally, the percentage of American Indians is slightly above the percentages reported in the two national faculty studies.

Comparing the minority data gathered from this study with the data from the two recent national faculty studies indicates that there is considerable agreement in the percentages of minority full-time two-year college faculty across all three studies. With the exception of the percentage of Mexican-American faculty, there is a trend for the institutional self-reported data to be slightly higher than the weighted data gathered from faculty samples. There might be several reasons for these differences in the percentages of minority full-time faculty across studies. One possible reason is that minority faculty may be less likely to respond to faculty surveys than their nonminority counterparts. This underrepresentation of minority faculty respondents may have had an effect on the weighting schemes used by Astin and NCES to estimate the total full-time faculty population from their faculty samples. For example, Astin's weighting scheme took into account *gender* and *rank* nonresponse bias within institutions, but did not address nonresponse bias by *minority status*. Another possible reason is that the institutions who reported to this study may not have been representative of the total population of two-year institutions with regards to their percentage of minority faculty. Vice presidents of academic affairs at institutions with a higher percentage of underrepresented minorities may have been more likely to respond to this survey than those at institutions with a lower percentage. In short, *between-institution* nonresponse bias may account for the differences between these studies.

Barriers to Minority Faculty Recruitment

Respondents were asked to indicate the extent to which they agreed or disagreed with a list of statements regarding barriers to minority faculty recruitment at their college. In order to shorten the presentation, only the top nine barriers are displayed in Table 3.

Table 3
Percent Agreeing or Strongly Agreeing
with Barriers to Minority Faculty Recruitment

Recruitment Barrier	Number of Institutions (n=616)	Percentage of Institutions
Economic constraints make it difficult to hire additional minority faculty	422	68.5
Minority faculty are not available in technical and occupational fields	339	55.0
Minorities prefer jobs in business and industry	308	50.0
Minority faculty are not available in arts and science fields	285	46.3
Women and minorities are competing with each other	246	39.9
Affirmative action significantly raises the cost of recruitment	196	31.8
Departments argue that there are few minorities in their fields	185	30.0
Minorities would have difficulty fitting in socially with community	151	24.5
Minority recruitment interferes with faculty prerogatives	133	21.6

Over two-thirds of the 616 respondents indicated that current economic constraints make it difficult to hire additional minority faculty at their institution. In a period of tight state budgets across the country, it is perhaps not surprising that two-year colleges administrators mentioned finances as their biggest barrier in hiring more minority faculty. The large percentage who agreed with this barrier underscores the difficulty many two-year institutions are having in achieving their minority faculty recruitment goals given the condition of their state and local economies. There may be little improvement in the number of underrepresented minority full-time faculty at two-year colleges until this economic situation improves.

Another set of structural barriers mentioned by a large number of respondents is the unavailability of minority faculty in both technical and occupational as well as arts and science fields. A number of researchers have noted the uneven distribution of academic majors among minority students (Astin, 1982; Garza, 1988; Blackwell, 1988). African-Americans, Mexican-Americans, Puerto Rican-Americans and American Indians are much more likely to pursue advanced degrees in education and the social sciences than degrees in such fields as mathematics, sciences, and languages and literature. Given the severity of this maldistribution, it is very difficult to recruit minority full-time faculty for a number of arts and science as well as occupational and technical fields. One of the reasons for this maldistribution of academic majors is minority students' lack of adequate preparation in mathematics and science at the secondary level. Clearly, two-year college faculty and administrators interested in increasing the representation of minority groups among full-time faculty need to collaborate with elementary and secondary schools in increasing minority student interest in and preparation for science and math-related areas.

The other structural barrier to minority faculty recruitment mentioned by a majority of the respondents is that prospective minority faculty prefer employment in business and industry to employment in two-year colleges. A number of researchers have noted that academic salaries rank far below salaries in business and industry (Bowen and Schuster, 1986; Bunzel, 1990). There are several approaches that two-year college administrators might use to compete with business and industry for prospective minority candidates. One possible recruitment approach is to stress the intrinsic satisfactions involved in a two-year college academic career. These intrinsic motivators include the considerable personal and professional autonomy of an academic career and the critical role that two-year college faculty play in educating minority students in higher education. A second possible approach is to try to recruit minorities in private enterprise jobs to teach part-time with the support of their employers. This study provides evidence that having minorities from private enterprise teach part-time is a particularly successful strategy for increasing the number of minority full-time faculty. One possible reason for the success of this strategy is that teaching part-time at a two-year college may provide minorities with a better sense of the intrinsic satisfactions of a full-time academic career.

Recruitment Strategies

A comparison of recruitment strategies between institutions with high versus low percentages of underrepresented minority faculty is presented in Table 4. In order to shorten the presentation, only those recruitment strategies where there was a difference of 12 or more percent between high and low percentage institutions are displayed.

A high percentage of underrepresented minority faculty was defined as 5 or more percent, while a low percentage was defined as less than 5 percent. Institutions with higher percentages of minority faculty are much more likely than those with lower percentages to include minority faculty and community members on search committees, and to have minorities serve on college advisory boards and on boards of trustees. These findings provide evidence that minorities on search committees and governance bodies of two-year college facilitate the recruitment of minority faculty. One possible explanation for this finding is that an institution's commitment to diversity is demonstrated to prospective minority candidates through this recruitment strategy. Another possible explanation is that minorities on search committees and governing bodies may serve as institutional or departmental advocates for the need for greater faculty diversity. Such advocacy would be expected to lead to higher numbers of minority faculty.

Institutions with a high percentage of underrepresented minority faculty are more likely than other institutions to have faculty make contact with minority faculty to recruit minorities in private enterprise to teach part-time, to cancel positions that have not attracted minorities in the applicant pool, and to have college representatives attend conferences held by professional organizations concerned with minority issues. These strategies hold in common a proactive stance to the recruitment of minority faculty. These findings provide evidence that proactive recruitment strategies facilitate the recruitment of minority faculty. One possible explanation for the success of these recruitment strategies is that they all tend to enlarge the pool of potential minority applicants for faculty positions. Such an enlarging of the pool would be expected to increase the number of minority faculty ultimately hired. Another possible explanation is that these proactive strategies also serve as concrete demonstrations of the institution's commitment to diversity. As a consequence, more minority candidates may be encouraged to apply for faculty positions at these institutions.

Table 4
A Comparison of Recruitment Strategies between Institutions
with High versus Low Percentages of Underrepresented Minority Faculty

Recruitment Strategy	Low Percentage (Less than 5%)	High Percentage (5% or more)	Difference
Have minorities serve on board of trustees	59.7	86.6	26.9
Include minority community members on search committees	23.4	50.2	26.8
Include minority faculty on search committees	66.7	92.9	26.2
Have faculty make contact with minority faculty	46.6	66.1	19.5
Recruiting minorities to teach part-time	48.1	29.6	18.5
Have minorities serve on college advisory boards	72.0	90.2	18.2
Canceling positions without minority applicants	7.1	24.1	17.0
Attend conferences concerned with minority issues	70.0	87.0	17.0
Meet with minority business representatives	64.3	80.9	16.6
Hire minorities as part-time adjunct faculty	75.1	91.6	16.5
Filling positions on a temporary basis	13.9	30.2	16.3
Meet with minority civic organizations	71.2	83.8	12.6
Funding teaching internships for minority graduate students	8.0	20.9	12.0

Predicting Minority Faculty Recruitment Success

The results of a regression analysis predicting the percentage of underrepresented minority faculty are displayed in Table 5.

Table 5
Prediction of the Percentage of Underrepresented Minority Faculty

Step	Variable	Zero r	Step Beta	Final Step Beta	F Ratio*
1	African-American	.36	.36	.33	57.9
2	Amount of contact with minority students	.29	.24	.11	44.6
3	Mexican-American	.18	.18	.15	36.4
4	Fitting in socially within the community	-.33	-.26	-.17	33.3
5	Amount of progress recruiting in the 1980s	.22	.15	.12	30.4
6	Minority faculty not available in arts/sciences	-.25	-.13	-.12	28.0
7	Interfering with faculty prerogatives	-.05	-.12	-.14	25.8
8	Minorities on board of trustees	.24	.14	.11	24.7
9	Recruiting minorities in private industry	.24	.10	.10	23.0
10	Cancelling positions without minority applicants	.19	.10	.10	21.7

*F-Ratio greater than 1.81 significant at the .05 level.
Multiple R=62 Adjusted R^2=.36
Mean=8.1 S.D.=12.2
Number of cases=402

In this analysis, it was found that being an African-American or Mexican-American vice president of academic affairs are positive predictors of the percentage of underrepresented minority faculty. There are several possible explanations for this positive influence for racial background. One possible explanation is that minority chief academic administrators may serve as strong advocates for the need for greater minority representation at their institutions. Such advocacy would be expected to lead to an increase in the number of minority faculty hired. Another possible explanation is that having a minority in such a highly visible position sends a positive message to prospective minority faculty about the institution's commitment to diversity. Because of this commitment, more minority candidates may be encouraged to apply for faculty positions.

The amount of contact with minority students is also a positive predictor of the percentage of minority faculty. The more contact the chief academic administrator has with minority students, the greater the percentage of underrepresented minority faculty at the institution. The positive influence of contact with minority students has several possible explanations. One possible explanation is that contact with minority students simply serves as a proxy measure for institutions with a high percentage of minority students. Such institutions might be expected to have a vigorous minority faculty recruitment program. Another possible explanation is that extensive contact with minority students serves to make the chief academic administrator more aware of the needs of minority students. As a consequence of this greater awareness of minority student needs, the chief academic administrator might be more motivated to recruit more minorities for faculty openings.

Three of the barriers to minority faculty recruitment were negative predictors of the percentage of minority faculty. The greatest barrier was the difficulty in having minorities fit in socially with the community. The more strongly respondents agreed with this statement, the lower was the percentage of minority faculty at the institution. There are several possible explanations for the negative influence of this finding. One possible explanation is that two-year institutions may not actively recruit minority faculty because of the difficulties they anticipate with minorities fitting in socially with the community. Without an active recruitment program, institutions would be expected to have a low percentage of minority faculty. Another possible explanation is that minority faculty may simply not apply to institutions in communities where they expect to have difficulty fitting in socially. In short, minority candidates may self-select themselves from applying to these two-year institutions.

Another barrier to minority faculty recruitment which was a negative predictor was the unavailability of minority faculty for arts and science positions. The more strongly the respondents agreed with this statement, the lower the percentage of minority faculty at the institution. One possible explanation for this finding is that there are simply not enough prospective minority faculty in a number of arts and science fields. This shortage may be the result of the maldistribution of academic majors among minority students. Such a maldistribution would be expected to lower the number of minority faculty available to be hired. Another possible explanation is that chief academic officers who strongly agree with this statement may not actively recruit minority faculty because of their perception that few, if any, prospective minority faculty are available. In short, this lack of minority faculty recruitment may result in a self-fulfilling prophecy.

Attempts to influence departments to hire minority faculty evoke the red flag of interference with faculty prerogatives was another negative predictor. The more strongly respondents agreed with this statement, the lower was the percentage of minority faculty at the institution. One possible explanation for this finding is that academic administrators may not attempt to actively recruit minority faculty in order to "maintain normative consensus and collegial relationships. . ." (Exum, 1983, p. 390). The absence of active minority recruiting would be expected to lead to low numbers of minority faculty. Another possible explanation is that academic administrators may actively recruit minority faculty applicants, but these applicants may be rejected by faculty as threats to their prerogatives. The rejection by faculty of all minority candidates recruited by administrators would be expected to lead to lower numbers of minority faculty.

Finally, three recruitment strategies served as positive predictors of the percentage of minority faculty. Of these three recruitment strategies, having minorities serve on boards of trustees was the most influential predictor. Institutions that used this recruitment strategy were more likely to have a higher percentage of underrepresented minority faculty. One possible explanation for this finding is that such a minority presence serves as a concrete demonstration of an institutional commitment to diversity for prospective minority faculty. More minority candidates may be encouraged to apply for faculty positions at these institutions. Another possible explanation is that minorities on the board serve as advocates for improving the diversity on campus. Such advocacy would be expected to lead to more minority faculty being hired.

Another recruitment strategy which served as a positive predictor was recruiting minorities in private enterprise jobs to teach part-time with the support of their employers. Institutions which used this strategy were more likely to have a high percentage of underrepresented minority faculty. One possible explanation for this finding is that institutions using this strategy are more aware of qualified minority applicants when positions became available. Such an awareness would be expected to lead to more minority faculty being hired. Another possible explanation is that minority faculty teaching part-time may be more likely to apply for full-time faculty positions when they become available. Any increase in the number of minority candidates applying for faculty jobs would be expected to lead to an increased number of minorities eventually being hired.

The final recruitment strategy which served as a positive predictor was cancelling positions where minority candidates had not been recruited into the applicant pool. Institutions that utilized this recruitment strategy were more likely to have a higher percentage of underrepresented minority faculty. One possible explanation for this finding is that institutions that utilize this recruitment strategy motivate departments to widely disseminate information about faculty job openings to prospective minority candidates. Such an active recruitment process would be expected to increase the number of minority faculty eventually hired. Another possible explanation is that canceling positions without minority candidates serves as a concrete demonstration to prospective minority faculty of the institution's commitment to diversity. Such a demonstration of commitment would be expected to motivate more prospective minority candidates to apply for faculty positions at these institutions.

Policy Implications and Conclusions

In this study evidence is provided that African-American, American Indian, Mexican-American, and Puerto Rican-American full-time faculty at two-year colleges are significantly underrepresented compared to the proportional representation of these minority groups in the U.S. population. Clearly, two-year colleges administrators need to address this issue of equity in their full-time faculty hiring.

The underrepresentation of minority faculty is also an issue of excellence as well as equity. Astin has argued that institutions of higher education cannot have excellence without promoting the cause of equity (Astin, 1985). Minority full-time faculty on two-year campuses serve to more fully develop the talents and cultural sensitivity of both minority and white students. Minority faculty not only play a vital role as positive role models for minority students, but also help white students overcome prejudicial thoughts about the intellectual capabilities of people of color. Minority faculty also help white faculty gain a deeper understanding and appreciation for different cultural heritages (Linthicum, 1989). In short, minority full-time faculty promote both the cause of excellence as well as equity within two-year institutions.

In this study it was shown that many of the attitudinal and structural barriers which hinder the recruitment of minority full-time faculty at four-year institutions also serve as barriers at two-year institutions as well. Structural barriers were found to be much greater hindrances to minority faculty recruitment than attitudinal barriers within institutions. The most influential structural barrier for a majority of two-year institutions is the economic constraints which prevent hiring additional minority full-time faculty. Given the current economic situation facing many two-year colleges, individual institutions may have few resources to hire *any* full-time faculty. This is a problem which probably needs to be addressed at the state, rather than at the local level. A state incentive program targeting additional funds for each minority full-time faculty hired at two-year colleges would provide the resources two-year college administrators need to enhance their minority recruitment programs.

The other set of structural barriers mentioned by a majority of respondents is the unavailability of prospective minority faculty for many arts and science as well as technical and occupational fields. A large part of this problem is due to a maldistribution of majors, with minority students tending to avoid majors in math and science-related fields because of their lack of preparation in these subjects at the secondary level. Clearly, two-year college faculty and administrators need to collaborate with elementary and secondary schools in increasing minority student interest in and preparation for these math and science-related areas. One possible collaboration is for two-year colleges to sponsor science fairs for elementary and secondary students in their catchment area. Another possible approach is for two-year institutions to offer summer programs for elementary and secondary students focusing on science, math, and technology-related areas. It is clearly in the best interest of two-year colleges to develop early outreach programs to try to interest and prepare minority students for faculty positions in math, science, and technology-related areas at their institutions.

Two of the most important variables in the prediction of the percentage of underrepresented minority faculty were being an African-American or Mexican-American vice president of academic affairs. These findings provide evidence that having minorities in highly visible positions of leadership facilitates the recruitment of minority faculty. Many two-year institutions might argue that they already have an administrator, often a minority, responsible for affirmative action. Slightly under one-half of the respondents reported that they had just such an affirmative action officer. However, having such an officer responsible for affirmative action was found not to be significantly related to the number of minority faculty at an institution. This finding underscores the importance of hiring minorities for highly visible administrative positions. In summary, the single most important step that an institution can take to increase the number of underrepresented minority full-time faculty is to hire a minority as the chief academic administrator.

Three recruitment strategies were also found to be positively related with the percentage of underrepresented minority full-time faculty. The most influential of these recruitment strategies is having minorities on the board of trustees. Minorities on the board of trustees serve as advocates promoting the cause of equity in full-time faculty hiring. They also remind the institution of its commitment to equity and to the community that it represents. Perhaps most importantly, the institution's commitment to diversity is clearly demonstrated by having minorities on the board of trustees. Additional minority candidates for faculty positions may be attracted to the institution because of this commitment. In short, appointing minorities to the board of trustees is a successful means of increasing the number of underrepresented minority full-time faculty at an institution.

Another recruitment strategy which is positively related to an institution's percentage of underrepresented minorities is recruiting minorities in private enterprise jobs to teach part-time with the support of their employers. One of the important structural barriers mentioned by a majority of two-year respondents is the fact that careers in business and industry tend to pay far more than careers in academe. One way to effectively compete with business and industry for minority candidates is to hire minorities for part-time teaching assignments. This strategy serves to make institutions more aware of minority candidates when full-time positions become available. It also serves to make minorities more aware of the intrinsic satisfactions of a career as a two-year college faculty member. Although two-year college administrators may not be able to outbid business and industry for prospective minority candidates, they may be able to woo them away from business and industry with intrinsic rather than extrinsic motivators. In summary, hiring minorities as part-time teachers is another successful recruitment strategy for increasing the number of underrepresented minorities.

A final recruitment strategy which is positively related to the number of underrepresented minorities is cancelling positions where minority candidates have not been recruited into the candidate pool. Institutions that utilize this strategy tend to have a high number of minority faculty. Interestingly, less than 15% of respondents reported using this particular recruitment strategy. One might expect that chief academic administrators would have some reluctance in using this strategy, given that it often evokes among faculty the red flag of interference with their prerogatives. Despite potential opposition from faculty, this recruitment strategy is a particularly effective means of increasing the number of underrepresented minority full-time faculty. Many more two-year college administrators should consider utilizing this strategy in addressing the issue of equity in faculty hiring.

References

American Association of Community and Junior Colleges (1991). *Who's Who in Community, Technical, and Junior Colleges 1991*. Washington: Author.

Astin, A. W. (1982). *Minorities in American Higher Education*. San Francisco: Jossey-Bass.

Astin, A. W. (1985). *Achieving Educational Excellence*. San Francisco: Jossey-Bass.

Astin, A. W.; Korn, W. S. & Dey, E. L. (1991). *The American College Teacher*. Los Angeles: Higher Education Research Institute.

Banks, W. M. (1984). Afro-American scholars in the university. *American Behavioral Scientist.* Vol. 27, No. 3, 325–338.

Blackwell, J. E. (1988). Faculty issues: the impact on minorities. *The Review of Higher Education*, Vol. 11, No. 4, 417–434.

Boyd, W. M. (1989). Affirmative action: a way to win. *AGB Reports*, Vol. 31, No. 4, 22–25.

Bunzel, J. H. (1990). Faculty hiring: problems and practices. *American Scholar*, Vol. 59, No. 1, 39–52.

Exum, W. H. (1983). Climbing the crystal stair: values, affirmative action, and minority faculty. *Social Problems*, Vol. 30, No. 4, 383–399.

Exum, W. H.; Menges, R. J.; Watkins, B. & Berglund, P. (1984). Making it at the top. *American Behavioral Scientist*, Vol. 27, No. 3, 301–324.

Garza, H. (1988). The "barriorization" of Hispanic faculty. *Educational Record*, Vol. 68, No. 4, 122–124.

Hankin, J. N. (1984). Where the (affirmative) action is: the status of minorities and women among the faculty and administrators of public two-year colleges. *Journal of College and University Personnel Association*, Vol. 35, No. 4, 36–39.

Harris, P. G. (1989). Almost 50 ways. . . . *AGB Reports*, Vol. 31, No. 4, 32–33.

Lessow-Hurley, J. (1989). Recruitment and retention of minority faculty. *CUPA Journal*, Vol. 40, No. 3, 22–26.

Linthicum, D. S. (1989). *The Dry Pipeline: Increasing the Flow of Minority Faculty*. Washington: National Council of State Directors of Community and Junior Colleges.

Menges, R. J. & Exum, W. H. (1983). Barriers to the progress of women and minority faculty. *Journal of Higher Education*, Vol. 54, No. 2, 123–144.

Mickelson, R. A. & Oliver, M. L. (1991). The demographic fallacy of the Black academic: does quality rise to the top? in W. R. Allen; E. G. Epps; & N. Z. Haniff, ed. *College in Black and White*. Albany: State University of New York Press.

Moore, W. (1988). Black faculty in white colleges: a dream deferred. *Educational Record*, Vol. 68, No. 4, 116–121.

Reed, R. J. (1983). Affirmative action in higher education: is it necessary? *Journal of Negro Education*. Vol. 52, No. 3, 332–349.

Reed, R. J. (1986). Faculty diversity: an educational and moral imperative in search of institutional commitment. *Journal of Educational Equity and Leadership*, Vol. 6, No. 4, 274–294.

Russell, S. H.; Fairweather, J. S.; Hendrickson, R. M. & Zimbler, L. J. (1991). *Profiles of Faculty in Higher Education Institutions, 1988*. Washington: National Center for Education Statistics.

Smelser, N. J. & Content, R. (1980). *The Changing Academic Market*. Berkeley: University of California Press.

The Chronicle of Higher Education (1991). *The Chronicle of Higher Education Almanac*, Washington, D.C.: Author.

The Chronicle of Higher Education. (1992, March 18), 1.

The Scholarly Activities of
Community College Faculty:
Findings of a National Survey

JAMES C. PALMER

How active are community college faculty members in scholarly work outside of classroom teaching? Few national surveys have addressed this question, and those that do usually analyze scholarship from the perspective of research and publication. For example, Cohen and Brawer (1977) assessed, among other constructs, the "Research orientation" of community college humanities faculty, determining that only a minority had published at some point during their careers or had applied for research grants from outside agencies. A more recent survey conducted by the Carnegie Foundation for the Advancement of Teaching (1989) came to the predictable finding that four-year college faculty were more likely than two-year college faculty to view research (rather than teaching) as their primary interest and to have received research grants over the past twelve months. The U.S. Department of Education provided corroborating evidence in its 1988 survey of faculty, noting that four-year college faculty spend considerably more time per week on research than two-year college faculty; the latter, however, spend more time per week on teaching than the former (Russell and others, 1990). Finally, a national survey conducted during the 1989–90 academic year by UCLA's Higher Education Research Institute found that two-year college faculty were less likely than four-year college faculty to publish and to view research as an essential or important part of their work (Astin and others, 1991).

These findings reflect the negligible role assigned to published research in the community college mission. But they say little about the contributions community college faculty make within the broader framework of scholarship posited by Vaughan at the beginning of this monograph. Though it may be conceded that relatively few community college faculty are published researchers, little is known about the degree to which faculty produce other scholarly products that are rooted in the knowledge of one's discipline and that are open to the criticism of others.

In order to understand faculty scholarship within this broader context, George Mason University's Center for Community College Education, with assistance from the National Council for Instructional Administrators, an AACJC-affiliated council, surveyed a national sample of faculty members at public community, technical, and junior colleges. Conducted in the spring of 1991, the survey solicited information related to five questions:

- What proportion of the faculty engage in scholarly projects along the broad lines defined by Vaughan?

- What types of projects are faculty most likely to engage in?

- In carrying out these projects, what support do faculty receive, if any, from their institutions and their colleagues?

- In the opinion of faculty members, what are the factors that limit their ability to work on these projects?

- How do faculty feel about the role out-of-class scholarship plays in their professional lives?

The survey methodology (detailed in the appendix to this monograph) was designed to oversample full-time faculty and those teaching the liberal arts and sciences (as opposed to those teaching vocational or technical fields). Usable responses were received from 840 randomly selected faculty members at 101 randomly selected colleges (See Table 1 for a profile of the respondents). The following pages outline major findings and conclude with a discussion of implications for college leaders seeking to create an institutional culture that encourages faculty in their scholarly endeavors.

Table 1
Characteristics of Survey Respondents (n=840)

	Full-Time Respondents	Part-Time Respondents
Gender		
Male	65%	52%
Female	35%	48%
Age		
Under 30	3%	7%
30–44	35%	44%
45–54	42%	24%
55–64	19%	17%
65 or over	1%	7%
Highest Degree Earned		
Associate	2%	2%
Bachelor's	8%	20%
Master's	67%	61%
Ph.D.	16%	9%
Ed.D.	4%	4%
Other	4%	3%
Subject of Highest Degree		
Arts and Sciences	54%	48%
Education	22%	15%
Vocational/Technical	24%	33%
Other	0%	4%
Years Teaching at the Community College Level		
Less than One Year	2%	12%
1–2 Years	5%	18%
3–4 Years	9%	18%
5–10 Years	20%	24%
11–20 Years	33%	19%
Over 20 Years	29%	8%

Note: 75 percent of the respondents were full-time faculty members; 25 percent were part-time faculty members.

Faculty Involvement in Scholarship

Adhering to the broad definition of scholarship proposed by Vaughan (1988), the survey instrument listed a wide array of products that may be shared with others and that ostensibly require those who produce them to have a solid grounding in their fields of study. Respondents to the survey were asked to indicate how many of each they had completed during the past two years. These products can be placed in seven broad categories:

- *Conference papers*

- *Publications*, including books, journal articles, published reviews of creative works, editorials or op-ed pieces, chapters in edited volumes, and published textbooks

- *Instructional materials*, including instructional software and unpublished textbooks or learning guides that are used by colleagues (and not simply in one's own classes)

- *Research or technical reports* that are disseminated internally to the college or to other clients

- *Community informational materials*, such as brochures or pamphlets that are designed for the general public or to help area businesses improve operations

- *Exhibits or performances in the fine arts*

- *Technical innovations*, such as a patented invention, a new technology for use in the operation of a business or industry, or computer software designed for noninstructional purposes

- *Other products* (the respondents were asked to describe other scholarly products they have completed but that do not fall into any of the categories listed above)

Given the wide array of products listed on the survey instrument, most respondents found at least one that applied to their own scholarly work. Eighty-six percent of the full-time respondents and 75 percent of the part-time respondents indicated that they had produced at least one of these products during the past two years. Among full-timers, the median number of products completed per faculty member was five; among part-timers, the median number was six.

What is the nature of this work? Because respondents were not asked to describe the scholarly products they completed, the survey provides only a rough picture of the types of scholarly work community college faculty engage in. The products most often completed by the respondents are the traditional standbys of academe: papers delivered at professional conferences (completed by 55 percent of the full-time faculty and 51 percent of the part-time faculty) and publications (completed by 36 percent of the full-timers and 29 percent of the part-timers). Instructional materials to be used by colleagues were a close third (34 percent of the full-timers and 23 percent of the part-timers), followed by research or technical reports (28 percent of the full-timers and 14 percent of the part-timers), community informational materials (23 percent of the full-timers and 20 percent of the part-timers), exhibits or performances in the fine arts (16 percent of the full-timers and 20 percent of the part-timers), and technical innovations (12 percent of the full-timers and 15 percent of the part-timers).

Are some faculty members more likely than others to engage in scholarly work outside of the classroom? Not if one looks across the broad categories of products listed on the survey instrument (Table 2). For example, the proportion of full-time faculty indicating that they have completed at least one of these products hovers at approximately 85 to 90 percent regardless of teaching field (liberal arts or vocational/technical fields), highest degree earned (master's or doctorate), the subject area of that degree (liberal arts, education, or vocational/technical fields), the year in which the degree was earned, the number of years teaching experience at the community college level, gender, or age.

Table 2
Proportion of Full-Time Faculty Completing at
Least One Scholarly Product, by Selected Characteristics

	% Completing	
	At Least One	None
All Faculty	86%	14%
By Teaching Field		
Liberal Arts & Sciences	85%	15%
Vocational/Technical	87%	13%
By Highest Degree Earned		
Master's	85%	15%
Doctorate	90%	10%
By Field of Highest Degree		
Liberal Arts & Sciences	85%	15%
Education	85%	15%
Vocational/Technical	88%	12%
By Year Highest Degree Was Earned		
1974–1991	87%	13%
1973 or Earlier	85%	15%
By Years Teaching Experience at the Community College Level		
0–10 Years	83%	17%
11 or More Years	87%	13%
By Gender		
Male	86%	14%
Female	84%	16%
By Age		
Under 30	85%	15%
30–44	85%	15%
45–54	88%	12%
55–64	82%	18%
65 or Older	90%	10%

Yet, when one looks within categories, it becomes evident that some faculty are more likely to produce certain types of scholarly products than others. These variances are quite predictable. For example, data in Table 3 suggest that those teaching the liberal arts and sciences are more likely to have published (41 percent) than those teaching in vocational/technical fields (28 percent). Vocational/technical faculty, however, are much more likely than their colleagues in the arts and sciences to have worked on instructional materials (43 percent versus 30 percent) or technical innovations (21 percent versus 7 percent). A similar pattern emerges when one contrasts the scholarly work of those who hold degrees in the liberal arts and sciences on the one hand and those who hold degrees in education or in vocational/technical areas on the other (Table 4). The former are more likely to publish and less likely to work on educational materials, technical innovations, and community informational materials. Finally, the type of degree one holds also comes into play (Table 5). Almost 50 percent holding a doctorate have published, compared to only 36 percent of

Table 3
Percent of Full-Time Respondents
Completing One or More Scholarly Products During
the Past Two Years, by Teaching Field and Type of Product

% Who Have Completed	Full-Time Faculty Who Teach:	
	Liberal Arts and Sciences	Vocational/ Technical Fields
Any Scholarly Product	85%	87%
Conference Papers	57%	51%
Publications	41%	28%
Instructional Materials	30%	43%
Research/Technical Reports	27%	29%
Community Informational Materials	20%	29%
Exhibits, Performances in Fine Arts	20%	8%
Technical Innovations	7%	21%
Other Products	19%	18%

Table 4
Percent of Full-Time Respondents Completing
One or More Scholarly Products During the Past Two
Years, by Subject of Highest Degree and Type of Product

% Who Have Completed	Subject of Highest Degree Held		
	Liberal Arts and Sciences	Education	Vocational/ Technical
Any Scholarly Product	85%	85%	88%
Conference Papers	58%	55%	46%
Publications	41%	28%	32%
Instructional Materials	30%	42%	38%
Research/Technical Reports	28%	29%	27%
Community Informational Materials	19%	27%	26%
Exhibits, Performances in Fine Arts	18%	15%	9%
Technical Innovations	9%	14%	17%
Other Products	18%	19%	19%

those holding the master's degree. In addition, doctoral degreeholders are more likely to have produced research or technical reports than master's degreeholders. Those holding the master's degree, on the other hand, are more likely than those holding the doctorate to work on instructional materials or community informational materials.

Other variances emerged when findings were compared by gender (Table 6). For example, women are less likely than men to publish but more likely than men to attend conferences. The reasons for these variances are a matter of speculation. Part of the explanation for the variance in the rate of publication may lie in the fact that women are less likely than men to hold a doctorate (14 percent versus 22 percent, respectively). But this seems to be counterbalanced by the fact that men

Table 5
Percent of Full-Time Respondents
Completing One or More Scholarly Products
During the Past Two Years, by Level of Highest Degree Held and Type of Product

	Highest Degree Held	
% Who Have Completed	Master's	Doctorate
Any Scholarly Product	85%	90%
Conference Papers	56%	61%
Publications	36%	49%
Instructional Materials	37%	29%
Research/Technical Reports	29%	38%
Community Informational Materials	26%	17%
Exhibits, Performances in Fine Arts	18%	7%
Technical Innovations	12%	9%
Other Products	17%	26%

Table 6
Percent of Full-Time Respondents
Completing One or More Scholarly Products
During the Past Two Years, by Gender and Type of Product

% Who Have Completed	Men	Women
Conference Papers	52%	60%
Publications	40%	30%
Instructional Materials	36%	32%
Research/Technical Reports	30%	24%
Community Informational Materials	23%	23%
Exhibits, Performances in Fine Arts	18%	12%
Technical Innovations	14%	9%
Other Products	18%	20%

are more likely to teach vocational/technical subjects than women (59 percent versus 49 percent respectively). Perhaps family commitments come into play; 34 percent of the women responding to the survey, as opposed to 21 percent of the men, indicated that time required for family responsibilities was a factor that limited their scholarly work.

But whatever the reasons, academic factors remain important variables. The differences emerging in the types of scholarly products completed by those with a doctorate and those with a master's degree and by those in the liberal arts and sciences and those in vocational/technical fields apply to both men and women (See Tables 7 and 8). Among men teaching on a full-time basis, for example, those who had published were more likely to hold a doctorate or to teach in the liberal arts and sciences than those who did not. On the other hand, men who taught vocational/technical fields or who held the master's degree as the highest credential were more likely to have worked on instructional materials. The same pattern holds for women. Regardless of gender, the traditions of one's academic background and teaching discipline help guide scholarly work, differentiating, particularly, between those who are more likely to publish on the one hand and those who are

Table 7
Percent of Full-Time, Male Respondents
Completing One or More Scholarly Products
During the Past Two Years, by Selected Characteristics

By Teaching Field		
	Liberal Arts and Sciences	Vocational/ Technical
Conference Papers	54%	49%
Publications	44%	32%
Instructional Materials	30%	45%
Research/Technical Reports	30%	32%
Community Informational Materials	21%	28%
Exhibits, Performances in Fine Arts	21%	12%
Technical Innovations	7%	24%
Other Products	19%	17%

By Level of Highest Degree		
	Doctorate	Master's
Conference Papers	59%	54%
Publications	48%	40%
Instructional Materials	30%	37%
Research/Technical Reports	40%	29%
Community Informational Materials	18%	17%
Exhibits, Performances in Fine Arts	8%	21%
Technical Innovations	10%	15%
Other Products	21%	17%

By Subject of Highest Degree			
	Liberal Arts and Sciences	Education	Vocational/ Technical
Conference Papers	65%	49%	46%
Publications	44%	28%	39%
Instructional Materials	30%	42%	43%
Research/Technical Reports	29%	29%	34%
Community Informational Materials	22%	25%	25%
Exhibits, Performances in Fine Arts	19%	20%	12%
Technical Innovations	10%	15%	20%
Other Products	20%	14%	16%

more likely to engage in less traditional scholarly work, such as the development of instructional materials or technical innovations.

Support Received by Faculty

The questionnaire also asked respondents to check off, from a list of several items, the types of support that they received from their institutions while working on out-of-class scholarly projects (Table 9). Twenty-seven percent of the full-time faculty and 50 percent of the part-time faculty who had completed one or more scholarly products indicted that they received no support at all. When

Table 8
Percent of Full-Time, Female Respondents
Completing One or More Scholarly Products
During the Past Two Years, by Selected Characteristics

By Teaching Field		
	Liberal Arts and Sciences	Vocational/ Technical
Conference Papers	62%	56%
Publications	36%	22%
Instructional Materials	29%	38%
Research/Technical Reports	22%	27%
Community Informational Materials	17%	34%
Exhibits, Performances in Fine Arts	18%	5%
Technical Innovations	6%	14%
Other Products	20%	20%

By Level of Highest Degree		
	Doctorate	Master's
Conference Papers	70%	60%
Publications	50%	29%
Instructional Materials	24%	35%
Research/Technical Reports	30%	22%
Community Informational Materials	14%	25%
Exhibits, Performances in Fine Arts	4%	13%
Technical Innovations	7%	8%
Other Products	40%	17%

By Subject of Highest Degree			
	Liberal Arts and Sciences	Education	Vocational/ Technical
Conference Papers	63%	63%	49%
Publications	34%	27%	27%
Instructional Materials	30%	41%	27%
Research/Technical Reports	26%	30%	15%
Community Informational Materials	15%	31%	31%
Exhibits, Performances in Fine Arts	16%	8%	6%
Technical Innovations	7%	12%	10%
Other Products	26%	27%	23%

faculty did receive support, it was more likely to be in the form of collegial assistance rather than monetary outlay. For example, the items most frequently checked off by full-time faculty were encouragement from faculty colleagues (37 percent), encouragement from the division chair (37 percent), and encouragement from the dean (33 percent); 18 percent cited encouragement from the president. More tangible support, though less frequently cited, was also received by the faculty: computer time and equipment (a category checked off by 18 percent of the full-time faculty members); release time or sabbatical leave (16 percent); financial support, excluding salary (15 percent); student assistants (9 percent); and help from the institutional research office (5 percent).

Table 9
Institutional Support Received by Faculty for Work on Scholarly Products

	Full-Time Faculty	Part-Time Faculty
% Indicating that They Have Received:		
Encouragement from Faculty Colleagues	37%	26%
Encouragement from Division Chair	37%	25%
Encouragement from Dean	33%	12%
Encouragement from President	18%	6%
Computer Time or Equipment	18%	9%
Release Time or Sabbatical	16%	3%
Financial Support (Excluding Salary)	15%	6%
Student Assistant	9%	2%
Other	6%	5%
Help from Institutional Research Office	5%	4%
No Help at All	27%	50%

Note: Percentages refer only to those respondents who indicated that they had produced at least one scholarly product during the past two years.

These findings are encouraging, suggesting that collegial relationships have the potential to compensate—at least partially—for the lack of resources available to support faculty scholarship. This collegiality was underscored by the penciled-in comments of some respondents who noted that although they had received no support from the institution for their scholarly work, they were sure that some support would have been forthcoming had they only asked for it. On the other hand, others didn't feel they were working in a collegial environment at all. One respondent scribbled, "This college doesn't give a damn!" Similar sentiments were expressed by others, though in a less bitter vein. For example, one respondent wrote that "administrators place no value on independent scholarly research, writing, or publication; creativity or initiative are not important or encouraged at my institution." The fact remains that some faculty members feel their institutions welcome their scholarly work, while others feel their institutions are indifferent or hostile to it.

Barriers to Faculty Scholarship

The survey instrument also asked respondents to check off, from a list of several items, the factors that pose the most formidable barriers to the completion of out-of-class scholarly products at the community college. Some of these items dealt with time constraints due to teaching loads, family commitments, or outside job or volunteer responsibilities (items 1, 3, 5, 6, and 8 in Table Ten). Others dealt with remuneration, that is, with the way colleges reimburse faculty and—more importantly—for what (items 2, 4, 7, and 9 in Table Ten). Thus, this part of the questionnaire was designed to answer the following question: Do faculty view constraints on their time as the most formidable barrier to work on scholarship, or do they view the limited financial support their colleges provide for these activities and the limited extent to which colleges reward these activities as the most formidable barriers?

The respondents indicated that both were problems, though limited time was an overriding concern. Most of the full-time faculty (61 percent) cited the obvious: "Teaching takes up too much time." Part-timers were more likely to cite the time constraints posed by obligations outside of the college; 44 percent of the part-time respondents cited the time required by other jobs, and 36 percent cited the time constraints caused by family commitments. Interestingly, the more scholarly prod-

Table 10
Faculty Opinions Concerning Factors that Limit Ability to Work on Scholarly Products

	Full-Time Faculty	Part-Time Faculty
% Indicating:		
1) Teaching Takes Up Too Much Time	61%	30%
2) College Provides Little or No Financial Help	45%	41%
3) Advising/Work with Students Outside of Class Takes Up Too Much Time	32%	12%
4) Scholarship Outside of Teaching Will Not Improve My Rank or Salary	31%	24%
5) Administrative/Committee Work Takes Up Too Much Time	28%	7%
6) Family Commitments Take Up Too Much Time	26%	36%
7) Administrators Do Not Encourage or Recognize Scholarship	22%	16%
8) Work Outside of College Takes Up Too Much Time	9%	44%
9) Union Contract Does Not Make Provision for Scholarly Work	8%	3%

ucts the respondent had completed, the less likely he or she was to cite time as a problem and the more likely he or she was to cite remuneration policies and the expectations of the college. For example, of the full-time respondents who checked off two or more items related to remuneration, 46 percent had published at least once during the past two years. But of those full-time respondents who checked no items related to remuneration and who cited time constraints exclusively, only 26 percent had published during the past two years. Obviously, those who have found time to work on scholarly products are less likely to see time as a problem; and, having invested quite a bit of their time in scholarly work, they are probably more keenly aware of the extent to which that work has or has not been rewarded by the college.

Though some faculty manage to maintain a productive schedule of scholarly work outside of teaching, others find that the time constraints posed by heavy teaching loads take their toll. In unsolicited comments, many respondents emphasized the imposing burdens born by teachers who face 150 or more students per semester, many of whom have deficiencies in the basic skills. Some commented that the work-a-day grind is intellectually debilitating. For example, a philosophy instructor with several years' experience wrote that "the problem with the community college is we teach too much—repeat ourselves too often and don't have enough time and energy to refuel." Another respondent noted that after years of teaching five courses per term, including summers, he had "gotten out of the habit of being scholarly." For many faculty members, though not all, time constraints posed by heavy teaching loads stifled intellectual life, making it more difficult for faculty to remain active scholars as they progress through their careers.

Faculty Attitudes Toward Scholarship

Finally, how do the faculty feel about the role out-of-class scholarship plays in their professional lives? In the survey, respondents were asked to indicate their agreement or disagreement with the following statement: "Working on scholarly products such as those listed earlier in this survey instrument will improve my teaching effectiveness." Of the full-time respondents, 73 percent agreed, 15 percent disagreed, and 11 percent indicated that they weren't sure. Responses were similar for part-timers: 72 percent agreed; 14 percent disagreed; and 11 percent indicated that they weren't sure. Another item asked the respondents to indicate their agreement or disagreement with the statement that "community college faculty should not be required by their colleges to work on scholarly products such as those listed earlier in this questionnaire." Responses to this question were not so lopsided: 48 percent disagreed; 33 percent agreed; and 17 percent responded that they were not sure. Responses from part-timers were reversed: 30 percent disagreed with the statement; 49 percent agreed; and 16 percent were not sure. Though the faculty recognize the value of remaining active in scholarship, many—especially full-time instructors—are reluctant to view it as a collective, professional responsibility or as a requisite of employment. Several of the respondents noted in the margins that though their institutions should encourage faculty work on scholarly products, such works should not be required.

The view of scholarship as a personal and optional endeavor rather than as a professional requisite was emphasized in the respondents' written comments. For example, one instructor with a lengthy publications record indicated that while "lack of recognition from the college 'hurts,'. . . I'm doing all this writing for the very best reason (I want to), and neither tenure, rank, nor salary is dependent upon publication." To this respondent, the time constraints and fiscal limitations that come with work at a community college were irrelevant as far as his scholarship was concerned. The implication was that while he valued the importance of scholarship, he also valued his freedom from the publish-or-perish atmosphere of the university. This freedom, he implied, made scholarship at the community college a labor of love and not a matter of coercion.

The distinction between voluntary scholarship and the forced production of scholarship was highlighted by the comments of another respondent who expressed dismay at the little regard his college has for faculty efforts to publish. "Active hostility [toward publication]," he wrote, "is found not only within the administration, but also among faculty members who seem to associate research and publication with all that is evil in the university system." The ideal institutional culture, he continued, would be one that encouraged faculty publication without demanding it: "I would not like to be forced to publish, but I am very angry at the lack of toleration for those who do."

Implications

A brief survey cannot do full justice to the topic of scholarship and the ways faculty view their scholarly lives. The comments that some faculty respondents wrote on the questionnaire showed that the survey barely scratched the surface of a tempestuous issue. Some faculty feel strongly that they should be more involved in the production of scholarly products and that community colleges should encourage this work. One respondent, conceding that "teaching is our main function at the community college," deplored the limited support and recognition he received from his college for his scholarly efforts: "I think it is dangerous—almost anti-intellectual—to not support written or other work that has been adjudicated by outside publishers and sources." Other faculty are leery of calls for attention to out-of-class scholarship, fearful that their contributions as teachers will be undervalued. For example, a political science instructor noted that ". . . the obvious must be stated: the principal mission of a two-year community college is *to teach*. I am here in large part because I consider that mission to be valid, important, and satisfying." Another respondent concurred, seeing in the survey an endorsement of the publish-or-perish philosophy:

> The gist of your instrument rubs at a sore in my educational philosophy. Your stated items equate "scholarly" with publishing, be it software, papers, books, etc. This represents the traditional "publish-or-perish" syndrome. Somewhere in your research it must be recognized [and] factored into your results that our scholarly activities are directed toward other ends. For years on end I have reviewed books to use as texts. Many are just plain bad. Many are outrageously priced if they are good. This is what has forced me into writing [and] publishing the materials that I have for classroom use. The objective, however, is what will help my students vs. my publishing something.

Clearly, scholarship at the community college is a touchy issue. No survey can capture all nuances of this topic, and much more needs to be done to understand the professional roles community college faculty play as scholars. Nonetheless, the survey findings, however limited, lead to several tentative conclusions.

First, if scholarship is defined broadly along the lines suggested by Vaughan, and not limited solely to original research, then it appears that most community college faculty—perhaps 80 percent of those employed on a full-time basis—are actively engaged in the production of works that are of *potential* scholarly value. What these works are precisely and how they complement teaching are questions that cannot be answered through a brief questionnaire. It is not possible, for example, to determine if the products developed by the survey respondents were actually subject to the criticism of peers or if the development of these products required the systematic application of a substantial body of knowledge. Nonetheless, the survey findings suggest that college efforts to encourage faculty scholarship can be built on what faculty are already doing. This can be accomplished by providing forums that allow faculty to share the results of their scholarly work and that provide the college with a mechanism for recognizing and rewarding this work.

Second, college leaders need to articulate a broad definition of scholarship and assure faculty that an institutional emphasis on scholarship will not be constructed within a publish-or-perish framework and will not compete with classroom teaching. Despite the wide variety of scholarly products listed in the survey instrument, many respondents reacted negatively to it, equating calls for scholarship with demands that faculty maintain a strong publications record. This reaction is understandable, given the long association of scholarship with original research undertaken at the university. But unless faculty understand that publishable research is simply one form of scholarship, they may resent and resist efforts to encourage scholarly work. Scholarship will not flourish if it is not understood.

Third, it should be recognized that work on scholarly products will not take the same form for all faculty members. Some will write for publication, while others will concentrate on less traditional projects. Much will depend on one's academic background and teaching discipline. College efforts to encourage scholarship should be structured at the departmental level with input from division chairs and faculty. Though all can be held to the same standard of excellence, each should be free to pursue a wide variety of projects. This is consistent with the broad definition of scholarship put forward by Vaughan.

Fourth, encouragement and support among colleagues is an extremely important determinant of faculty work on scholarly products at community colleges. While university faculty look to professional encouragement from colleagues across the country who specialize in the same subject areas, this is not usually the case for community college instructors, who must often seek collegial support from within the institution. While many respondents indicated that they had received such support, especially from fellow instructors, the division chair, and the academic dean, others indicated that they received no support at all. Clearly, college leaders and faculty themselves have a role to play in assessing the degree to which scholarship is welcome and encouraged within their institutional cultures.

Finally, the task of bringing scholarship foursquare into the professional lives of faculty will not be accomplished by simply adding the development of scholarly products to the list of things faculty have to do. Many faculty will resent this, especially if additional compensation is not forthcoming. Scholarship is not a matter for the personnel office. It is a function of the institutional culture and will flourish best if that culture helps faculty pursue scholarship as a labor of love. While the issues of workload and compensation cannot be ignored, much can be accomplished by encouraging, recognizing, and valuing the scholarly work community college faculty already do.

References

Astin, A. W., Korn, W. S., and Dey, E. L. *The American College Teacher: National Norms for the 1989–90 HERI Faculty Survey.* Los Angeles: Higher Education Research Institute, University of California, 1991.

Carnegie Foundation for the Advancement of Teaching. *The Condition of the Professoriate: Attitudes and Trends, 1989.* Princeton, N.J.: Carnegie Foundation for the Advancement of Teaching, 1989.

Cohen, A. M., and Brawer, F. B. *The Two-Year College Instructor Today.* New York: Praeger, 1977.

Russell, S. H., Cox, R. S., Williamson, C., Boismier, J., Javitz, H., and Fairweather, J. *Faculty in Higher Education Institutions, 1988.* Contractor Report. NCES 90-365. Washington, D.C.: United States Department of Education, Office of Educational Research and Improvement, 1990.

Vaughan, G. B. "Scholarship and Community Colleges: The Path to Respect." *Educational Record,* 1988, *69* (2), 26–31.

Scholarship, the Transformation of Knowledge, and Community College Teaching

JAMES L. RATCLIFF

Community college educators take pride in their commitment to teaching. They view the ideal faculty member as a concerned, dedicated, and effective teacher. The emphasis of this vision is on how teaching takes place, not on what is taught. Indeed, the teacher's expertise in a discipline's subject matter has until recently been trivialized, glossed over, and even treated with hostility by those writing about community college education.

The emphasis on method rather than content developed with the best of intentions. But the result has been a static vision of teaching, a diminished view of the transformation of subject expertise into ways of knowing for students, and a slighting of scholarship as a source of renewal and reinvigoration for community college faculty. Much of this oversight and antipathy originated during the second great growth period of community colleges (1955–1975) when many of today's community college faculty were hired. During this time, college leaders often expressed open hostility toward scholarship and the role of subject matter expertise in the pre-service education of two-year college teachers. For example, Garrison (1967) argued that preparation for scholarship is not the same as preparation for teaching. O'Banion (1972) concurred, viewing scholarship and subject matter expertise as potentially negative forces that may cause faculty to enter community college teaching with "academic biases which seem to conflict abruptly with their responsibility for teaching the common man" (p. 21).

Even where no open hostility to scholarship existed, there was no clear vision of how faculty members should sustain an intellectual engagement with their teaching fields. Although the American Association of Community and Junior Colleges (1969) called for rigorous graduate preparation in subject matter, the association provided no indication of what such graduate preparation should entail, why it was important, or what kind of scholarly activity might be desirable for faculty after attaining the master's degree. The leaders of community college in-service and graduate preparation programs, usually housed in the education schools of universities, were no more articulate. While they agreed that a master's degree was the appropriate minimum preparation for those teaching college-parallel courses, they provided no clear indication of how subject matter expertise and scholarship might contribute to the renewal and continued professional development of faculty (Vaughan, 1989). As a result, the master's degree became the standard credential for admission to the profession. But the contribution of subject matter expertise, beyond that of fodder for transmission of information to students, remained obscure. A common underlying assumption was that if the faculty member was competent in conveying the subject matter and in understanding the specific learning needs, interests, and abilities of students, good teaching would take place. Little heed was given to the nature of the subject matter to be taught or to changes in the content and modes of inquiry in one's field of study.

As community colleges move into the twenty-first century, the essential link between disciplinary expertise and teaching effectiveness must be acknowledged. This chapter examines the nature of the relationship between the two and concludes with a discussion of implications for faculty development within an institution dedicated to learning and scholarly inquiry.

The Curriculum as Knowledge

That which is taught in college is of necessity based on some body of knowledge (Squires, 1990). This basic though often forgotten premise is at the heart of what mediates scholarship, faculty renewal, and effective teaching. Consider, for example, the following questions:

- How do you clearly convey ideas to students?
- How do you clearly convey ideas about the causes of the American Civil War to students?

The questions are fundamentally different. The second question inserts a body of knowledge (American history) and a mode of inquiry (historical research) into the formulation of effective teaching. Similarly, "How do you clearly convey ideas about the causes of the American Civil War?" is different from "How do you clearly convey the ideas of pitch and tone in playing the violin?" The body of knowledge adds dimension, complexity, and elegance to the task of teaching and to the talents required of its practitioners. The vision of teaching without reference to what is to be taught stultifies and oversimplifies the teaching process (Shulman, 1990). More importantly, it denies the importance of scholarship in good teaching.

Despite the critical intersection between instructional methods and the knowledge base, previous writers on community college instruction have portrayed teaching as transferring knowledge (Cohen and Brawer, 1972; Gleazer, 1968; O'Banion, 1972). It became popular in the 1960s and 1970s to use Bloom's (1954) *Taxonomy of Educational Objectives* to place what is to be learned on a linear plane from simple recall and understanding of facts to the analysis, synthesis, and evaluation of knowledge, skills, and abilities. See, for example, the League for Innovation's 1981 monograph, *Teaching in the Community College.* This view of instruction as knowledge transfer cast most curricula as a static set of facts to be consumed, understood, and recalled by students. The role of the discipline in mediating instruction went unmentioned.

Several attributes of the curriculum are ignored when teaching is viewed as the transmission of knowledge. First, collegiate studies, be they in physics or Spanish literature, involve the conceptualization and explanation of people, phenomena, and ideas, not simply the memorization of facts. Second, each college-level subject area has its own mode of inquiry and its own way of organizing knowledge. Biologists learn a way of examining phenomena that is quite different from the methods used by psychologists. These modes of inquiry and analysis are not simply abstract qualities; they are valued by students, employers, and faculty as the hallmarks of the intellectual contribution of the field of study to society as a whole. Third, the knowledge base of a discipline does not remain static; it is cumulative or developmental in nature. Why is it that microeconomics, macroeconomics, and quantitative methods of analysis are common core subjects in the field of economics? Why does chemistry typically include organic and inorganic courses? The answer to these questions is partly attributable to the unique way in which the content and method of these disciplines are organized to produce cumulative and developmental effects on students. Teachers do not impart discrete facts; they help students develop—on a step-by-step basis—a knowledge base that will enable them to employ specific modes of inquiry in interpreting and conceptualizing the world around them.

Recognition of the theoretical or conceptual complexities of a subject, its modes of inquiry and organization, and its cumulative or developmental nature elevates the enterprise of teaching; those who would understand this enterprise need more than teaching tips leading to the effective transmission of information. The teacher's task is to use the appropriate mode of inquiry to represent the concepts, terms, and ideas of the knowledge base. It is through this process of transforming the knowledge base that learning occurs (Shulman 1990). Students acquire more than the salient dates and events pertaining to the Civil War; they also learn the major social, economic, and political interpretations of how the war came about and how different historians arrive at the various conclusions regarding its origins. In short, students learn not only facts, but also ways of framing and conceptualizing those facts.

The transformation of knowledge, using concepts and modes of inquiry that help students learn, is a challenging and worthy lifelong profession. Such transformation, where the discipline mediates the pedagogy, elevates teaching beyond the repeated transmission of knowledge that faculty members learned while they were graduate students. It suggests a new and vital role for faculty development and faculty scholarship—scholarship that involves sustained reflection, dialogue, and inquiry. Viewed in this light, teaching becomes more intellectually challenging than research, in which modes of inquiry are applied to a discrete part of the knowledge base in order to produce or test a new understanding, insight, or set of findings. The teacher requires broader skills; he or she must devise representations of knowledge, concepts, and means of inquiry so that students can comprehend, apply, and begin to utilize the range of perspectives, frames of reference, and ways of problem solving that are attendant to specific disciplines. This view of teaching calls for continued intellectual engagement in the field of study and suggests a clear link between subject matter scholarship and faculty vitality.

The Role of Difficult Concepts in Scholarship and Teaching

Once one acknowledges that the field of study mediates and adds definition to the teaching-learning process, then it follows that not all ideas and skills within a field are equally easy to learn. For example, a recent focus group of history faculty determined that while it was relatively easy to teach particular events in history, it is more difficult to lead students to an understanding of the concept of time itself and to an understanding of how events can be placed in a historical context (Ratcliff, 1991b). Shulman (1990) has suggested that the history of a field of study reveals which concepts may be more demanding for students to grasp. For example, the history of the development of mathematics over the centuries reveals that the concepts of zero and negative numbers evolved over relatively long periods of time, reflecting the fact that they are—in relation to other, more concrete concepts—more difficult to understand. Is it no wonder that students usually have more difficulty comprehending negative numbers or the concept of zero than the principles of multiplication or division?

If some concepts are more difficult for students to grasp than others, it follows that faculty will have more difficulty teaching certain topics and concepts than others. The ability to teach relatively difficult concepts depends not only on the instructional methods used, but also on the insights gained through scholarly inquiry into the evolution of those concepts. This does not mean that community college faculty should imitate university faculty; scholarship may or may not involve experimental research and publication. But regardless of the form scholarship takes, it should be driven by an inquiry into how difficult concepts may be represented and transformed in ways that make them understandable and meaningful to students. This is a logical, challenging, and critical role for faculty whose primary role is teaching students in the first two years of college.

The Role of Socially Troublesome Topics

Troublesome topics also pose challenges to the classroom teacher. Here society, rather than the field of knowledge itself, has created circumstances in which study of a topic takes on new meaning, motivating new scholarship and inquiry (Ratcliff, 1991a). It is the crucible-like nature of the curriculum to place before students and scholars the unresolved issues of our society—be they civil rights, abortion, or war—and subject them to scrutiny outside the political and social contexts in which they exist. College curricula have always taken up the politically charged issues of the era. With their close ties to the community, two-year colleges are particularly adept in serving as forums for issues of social ferment.

Study of the Vietnam War is a good example of a socially troubling topic. Here disciplines such as history or political science render an order to the examination of an issue that is otherwise charged with emotion. Pike (1985), for example, urges the use of objective social science inquiry to weigh the conflicting interpretations of the war. In the wake of new historical information that vastly revises much of what anyone—left, right, or center—knew about the war, he urges faculty to engage in scholarly reflection on this new information and to apply their conclusions to how the war is conceptualized and taught in the classroom. Similarly, Wilcox (1988) advocates the use of primary sources in teaching about the Vietnam War. This approach, he maintains, encourages student questioning and discussion of issues surrounding the war within a framework of discipline-guided inquiry. Within this framework, the task of teaching is not merely to provide a foundation of knowledge about the war, but also to help students employ an academic discipline's tools as a means of generating thinking, interpretation, and analysis.

Troublesome topics bring excitement, imagination, and motivation to the faculty and students who study them. In stimulating disciplinary scholarship they foster the evolution of the curriculum, shaping its transitional nature and underscoring the key relationship between curriculum and inquiry. Subjects or topics sanguine for one generation of students may not be for the next. The coursework embodying troublesome topics may enter the curriculum from the extracurriculum; these topics may reside in the curriculum for a decade or more and then may wane or disappear as the topic's salience subsides. Ultimately a course on a socially troubling topic may be discontinued for lack of student demand or may migrate to the secondary school curriculum as examination of the topic becomes more widespread.

Toward an Enhanced Vision of Teaching and Scholarship

Clearly, academic disciplines play a vital role in scholarly inquiry. They teach people ways of knowing and ways of examining issues, events, and phenomena. Faculty who learn a discipline learn more than facts; they learn the values, norms, and modes of inquiry attendant to a particular field of study (Biglan, 1973a, 1973b). From this perspective, there is much that is literal about the term "discipline." Disciplines habituate and order our thinking; they provide frames of reference for viewing problems. Most importantly, they guide how we transform our knowledge of the field of study into representations that students can understand and from which they can learn different ways of viewing a situation. Disciplines provide us with the knowledge base and the tools for critical review and analysis. These tools are particularly important in understanding and teaching topics that are relatively difficult to comprehend or that raise particularly troublesome social issues.

Recognizing the key role of the discipline leads to a recognition of the symbiotic relationship between teaching and scholarship. As Vaughan (1988) reminds us, scholarship and teaching are inseparable: "The discipline and thinking required to be a scholar sharpens the critical skills of the individual. It is only through critical review and analysis that we as colleges and as individuals can formulate positions on the issues of the day and in turn interpret these issues to our students" (p. 9).

Through scholarship we come to recognize that what we teach is based on a body of knowledge with theoretical and conceptual elements. These facets of the knowledge base sustain both the interest in and the importance of the discipline or field of study. They also shape the act of teaching itself.

The importance of discipline-specific scholarship, however, is rarely recognized by community college leaders, who continue to structure in-service education for faculty around campus-based workshops on instructional techniques or "the community college philosophy" (Cohen and Brawer, 1989). This is contrary to the real needs of faculty, who want professional development in their teaching fields. It also turns a blind eye to the important role disciplinary debates play in collegiate life. Rather than viewing disciplinary scholarship as a threat to the role of the community college teacher, administrators should embrace the notion of scholarship and embody the expectation of continuous professional renewal in the subject matter within the ethic of the learning community. Several steps can be taken to accomplish this:

- Those planning professional development programs should recognize that difficult concepts and socially troubling topics have a direct bearing on teaching effectiveness. Teacher evaluation forms and student ratings of instruction need to be revised accordingly. Faculty dialogue, development, and scholarship need to give focus to the concepts, issues, and topics most difficult for students to learn.

- A department or division can schedule a monthly seminar, with faculty suggesting the topic. Because the interaction of faculty and students outside the classroom contributes to retention (Pascarella and Terenzini, 1991), these seminars should be open to students as well.

- Divisions structured around related disciplines (rather than single-discipline departments) will also help. Such configurations are ideal for ferreting out the different frames of reference each discipline brings to the understanding of concepts, phenomena, and issues.

- Finally, a certain proportion of faculty development funds should be set aside for participation in discipline-based professional meetings. Because content mediates pedagogy in effective teaching, faculty need the opportunity and encouragement to engage the field of study, to explore the emerging paradigms of inquiry within their field, and to learn what their colleagues are thinking and how they are teaching in other institutional environments.

Faculty involvement in disciplinary associations will be particularly difficult to achieve. Such disciplinary associations tend to be dominated by research university faculty, and the programs often focus on research rather than teaching. This will always be the case until community college faculty are enabled to be full and active participants in associations representing the fields of study they teach. Each community college should set a goal of having several faculty members in leadership positions in disciplinary associations. These organizations can be used to enrich the college curriculum, faculty development, and the quality and currency of instruction.

Conclusion

The field of study plays a fundamental role in the renewal of community college faculty. New knowledge is not necessarily generated from research alone. It comes from new syntheses and analyses of the knowledge base of the field of study. By thinking about the teaching process and how to convey, represent, and explore difficult concepts and troublesome topics, we generate new ideas, conceptualizations, and approaches within the field of study. Engagement in the literature of the discipline enriches teaching and stimulates a culture of inquiry that we so desperately seek in our college classrooms.

References

American Association of Community and Junior Colleges. *Preservice Training of Two-Year College Instructors.* Washington, D.C.: American Association of Community and Junior Colleges, 1969.

Biglan, A. "The Characteristics of Subject Matter in Different Academic Areas." *Journal of Applied Psychology*, 1973a, *57* (3), 195–203.

Biglan, A. "Relationships Between Subject Matter Characteristics and the Structure and Output of University Departments." *Journal of Applied Psychology*, 1973b, *57* (3), 204–213.

Bloom, B. S. (Ed.). *The Taxonomy of Educational Objectives: Cognitive Domain.* New York: Longmans, Green, 1954.

Cohen, A. M., and Brawer, F. B. *Confronting Identity: The Community College Instructor.* Englewood Cliffs, N.J.: Prentice-Hall, 1972.

Cohen, A. M., and Brawer, F. B. *The American Community College.* 2nd Ed. San Francisco: Jossey-Bass, 1989.

Garrison, R. *Junior College Faculty: Issues and Problems.* Washington, D.C.: American Association of Community and Junior Colleges, 1967.

Gleazer, E. J., Jr. *This is the Community College.* New York: Houghton Mifflin, 1968.

League for Innovation in the Community College. *Teaching in the Community College.* New York: HBJ Media Systems, 1981.

O'Banion, T. *Teachers for Tomorrow: Staff Development in the Community Junior College.* Tucson, Ariz.: University of Arizona Press, 1972.

Pascarella, E. T. and Terenzini, P. T. *How College Affects Students.* San Francisco: Jossey-Bass, 1991.

Pike, D. "Teaching the Vietnam Experience as a Whole Course." *Teaching Political Science*, 1985, *12* (4), 144–151.

Ratcliff, J. L. "Undergraduate Curriculum." In B. R. Clark and G. Neave (Eds.), *Encyclopedia of Higher Education.* New York: Pergamon Press, 1991a.

Ratcliff, J. L. Notes from a focus group on teaching difficult concepts in history, Asheville Institute on General Education, Association of American Colleges, June 9, 1991b.

Shulman, L. "The Transformation of Knowledge: A Model of Pedagogical Reasoning and Action." Paper presented at the annual meeting of the American Educational Research Association, Boston, Mass., April 1990.

Squires, G. *First Degree: The Undergraduate Curriculum.* Buckingham, England: Society for Research into Higher Education/Open University Press, 1990.

Vaughan, G. B. "Scholarship in Community Colleges: The Path to Respect." *Educational Record*, 1988, *69* (2), 26–31.

Vaughan, G. B. *Scholarship: The Community College's Achilles Heel.* Occasional Papers Series, No. 1. Wyers Cave, Va.: Virginia Community College Association, 1989.

Wilcox, F. A. "Pedagogical Implications of Teaching 'Literature of the Vietnam War'." *Social Education*, 1988, *52* (1), 39–40.

Suggested Readings:
The Professional Staff

Keim, M. C. (1989). "Two-Year College Faculty: A Research Update." *Community College Review,* 17 (3), 34–43.

Kempner, K. (1990). "Faculty Culture in the Community College: Facilitating or Hindering Learning?" *The Review of Higher Education,* 13 (2), 215–235.

Seidman, E. (1987). "Merging Access and Excellence: The Work of Community College Faculty." *Community, Technical, and Junior College Journal,* 57 (4), 43–45.

Seidman, E. (1985). *In the Words of the Faculty: Perspectives on Improving Teaching and Educational Quality in Community Colleges.* San Francisco: Jossey-Bass.

*L*EADERSHIP

New Leadership
Considerations for Old Realities

DONALD W. BRYANT

A current major concern in community college circles is focused on leadership at the institutional or local college level. The American Association of Community and Junior Colleges, as well as selected universities, are devoting increased attention to leadership development for America's community and junior colleges. One of the main concerns seems to be the overly autocratic inclinations of community college administrators. A related problem is that community colleges, as opposed to universities, have no history of shared governance. University history is rich and varied and provides a philosophical basis for the place of faculty in higher education governance. Community colleges are young by comparison and have no such heritage of faculty involvement. As a consequence, community college leaders could learn from university governance models to pay more attention to those functional areas that have always been the province of faculty: curricula, subject matter content, methods of instruction, faculty status, and aspects of student life related to the educational process. The article suggests several points that bear consideration in order to embellish new leadership considerations. It concludes with several suggestions, the implementation of which could well develop more responsive community college leadership.

One of the major areas of concern in current community college circles focuses upon leadership at the institutional or local college level. Consequently, there is a heavy emphasis on leadership development. There have been countless observations that something is amiss in community college leadership training. A February 13, 1990 issue of "The Community and Junior College Times" (Eddy, 1990, p. 2) relates, "We need to find ways not only to enhance the current leadership at our colleges but to foster strong and informed administrators at the mid-level, who are ready to play leadership roles in their current positions and to move into positions with greater responsibilities." The 1990 Public Policy Agenda of the American Association of Community and Junior Colleges listed *leadership development* as an area of priority and in February, the Professional Administrators Development Institute (PADI) was launched by AACJC. According to Carrole Wolin in an article about future leaders written for "The Community and Junior College Times" (1990, p. 12), "The institute is aimed at 'broadening the leadership vision' of executive, senior, and mid-level administrators at the nation's community, technical, and junior colleges, ..."

In addition, university programs to develop community college leadership are receiving renewed attention. This attention stems from recognition that there are some serious problems with the current state of community college leadership on the local or college level. For example, the University of California at Berkeley has recently initiated a "Program in Higher Education" with an emphasis on community college leadership. One of the strong points of the California program is on the ability to do practical research—research applicable to the community college setting. For the students who select this program, there is a focus on "learning how to learn," or better put, "learning how to stay current" by engaging in practical research and applying that research to the institutional setting. Along with this concentration upon research, the program entails an internship and a practice-oriented dissertation. Hence, there is a unique blend of practicality and research. As the program brochure indicates, it is "... a doctoral program to prepare a new generation of leaders for America's premier institutions of teaching and learning" (1989, p.1).

There have also been several fairly current studies concerning the leadership problem. The problem has two dimensions: a quantitative one and a qualitative one. The quantitative dimension is much more simple to address. In a nutshell, there are many reports that indicate that about 40 percent of current community college administrators and faculty will retire by the year 2000. Simply put, there are going to be many replacements needed. However, the long-term problem is not with the quantitative issue, but the qualitative one. One of the more recent cites that deals with the qualitative issue is in *Building Communities*, which is a report of the Commission on the Future of Community Colleges initiated by the American Association of Community and Junior Colleges. It (1988, p. 41) cited a Carnegie Foundation survey revealing that "over 60 percent of community college faculty rated their administrators 'fair or poor,' and 66 percent said the administrator at their institution is 'autocratic.'"

There are studies to support the contention that autocratic behavior is a kind of self-fulfilling prophecy. One report (Wofford, 1989, p.1) indicates that if one has certain expectations of people and acts towards them according to those expectations, they are more likely to behave as expected. If the autocrat behaves, as he or she often does, as if people are "bad," he or she operates from a position of mistrust. Subordinates then exhibit behavior that substantiate that mistrust.

There is a related issue that feeds the problem of autocratic behavior as far as community college administrators is concerned. As opposed to universities, there is no history of shared governance in American community colleges. Since medieval times, university faculty have had traditional control over selected aspects of college or university governance. These areas include curriculum, instruction, and areas related to instruction such as equipment and text selection.

Faculty were free to teach and conduct their classes in any reasonable way. Moreover, faculty have always been a part of the governance tradition of higher education. Much has been made over the years about collegial governance as opposed to other forms of governance, especially bureaucratic governance. The collegial tradition was started in 1637 at Harvard College in Massachusetts. At Harvard there were actually two boards, an external board of overseers and an internal body politic. The same structure took place in 1693 at William and Mary in Virginia. However, the structure at Yale in 1701, more than the structure at the other two colleges, became the governance prototype for postsecondary education in the United States. A charter granted by the Connecticut Legislature to Yale recognized the president and trustees as the legal corporation. The university was to be governed by a single body of external trustees and the university president. The concept of shared governance came to mean over time the interconnected governance responsibilities of the president and board. Yet, it has always been a much broader concept in university circles.

European traditions formulated a conceptual base for faculty governance or governance by masters. In both Bologna and Paris, masters were given a great deal of latitude to teach and license others to become a part of the guild. Oxford followed the Parisian tradition, and it was the masters who formulated the university. European universities were corporations of masters, not trustees. Lay trusteeship is a concept of American origin. Nevertheless, faculty have conceptually always been an integral part of that governance tradition as far as universities are concerned. In return for their loyalty, teachers were surrounded by an institutional framework that supported their pride and security as men of learning and offered them a vigorous defense against interference. Indeed, in great crisis the positions even of such heretics as Wycliff and Huss were for a time strengthened by powerful support given them within their universities. Yet, through hundreds of years the question of governance continued to be debated. In 1957, however, the United States Supreme Court once again affirmed the place of faculty in the governance structure. According to a report by the Carnegie Foundation for the Advancement of Teaching, the Court affirmed, in Sweezy v. New Hampshire (1982, p. 4), "the four essential freedoms of a university: to determine for itself on academic grounds who may teach, what may be taught, how it shall be taught, and who may be admitted to study."

The seeds of that governance responsibility had been in place since university formation in Europe; however, the actual role of faculty in governance had been slow to develop. The earliest teachers in America were young tutors who were vastly different in educational background, aspiration, and motivation from the professionalized faculties of the present. However, in the last quarter of the 1800s, universities became much more complex than they had been previously, and their professoriate was professionalized. Faculty was recognized as having a specific role in campus governance. In 1966 the American Association of University Professors (AAUP), the American Council on Education (ACE), and the Association of Governing Boards of Universities and Colleges (AGB) issued a *Statement on Government of Colleges and Universities* which said,

> The faculty has primary responsibility for such fundamental areas as curriculum, subject matter and methods of instruction, research, faculty status, and those aspects of student life which relate to the educational process. On these matters the power of review or final decision lodged in the governing board or delegated by it to the president should be exercised adversely only exceptional circumstances and for reasons communicated to the faculty. (AAUP, 1977, p. 43)

The AAUP statement, however, transcended individual or departmental considerations to indicate that faculty had a campus-wide responsibility. "Agencies for faculty participation in the government of the college or university should be established at each level where faculty responsibility is present. An agency should exist for the presentation of the views of the whole faculty" (AAUP, 1977, pp. 43–47).

Despite the long history of shared governance in university circles, there is no such history regarding community colleges. The place of faculty in the governance process has been evolving since 1636. Most community colleges, however, were started in the 1960s, and were generated "as teenagers if not adults" in the chronological growth process. There was no evolution of a governance concept. It was and is an instant governance concept, and does not involve the faculty. It was recently related in Community College Week that, "community colleges have not embraced nor are they characterized by the shared governance models that have traditionally been integral to the university. As a result of their research, Gunne and Mortimer found that community colleges reflected administrative dominance in the decision-making process to a greater extent than did four-year institutions" (Stoddard, 1989, p.12).

This is not to advocate "giving away the store." Community college leaders could learn from university governance models to give more heed to those functional areas that have always been the province of faculty: curriculum, subject matter content, methods of instruction, faculty status, and aspects of student life related to the educational process.

There are several points that need to be emphasized in order to embellish new leadership considerations.

Understand The Concept of Delegation

Many community college administrators take the concept of delegation for granted. The approach is "Oh, I aready know how to do that!" In reality, however, many do a poor job with delegation. Some delegate very little; others delegate only mundane matters; and others do delegate functions but retain widespread "veto control." They in essence give lip service to the process.

Delegation involves the sharing of power and authority. If one delegates the employment function to a committee structure, it makes little sense to frequently countermand the committee. It is true that one cannot delegate responsibility and occasionally one must invoke the power to override; however, to do so frequently disembowels the concept of delegation. The administrator must feel at ease in giving others the opportunity to do on his or her behalf even though he or she knows the responsibility has not passed.

Understand Historic Place of Faculty in Academic Areas

Based upon the historic role of faculty in the university governance structure, administrators should learn more of what to delegate. Involve faculty on committees that make recommendations regarding employment of their peers; support, based upon objective verification, faculty input or recommendations regarding faculty contract renewals or dismissals; give substantial latitude regarding subject matter content and methods of instruction; involve faculty in the initiation of new curricula; allow faculty to alter prior-approved curricula as long as curricula standards approved by some higher education authority are followed; and permit faculty to set testing and other standards which relate student life to the educational process. In short, community college leaders should allow faculty to participate in the governance process in those areas that have historically been the prerogative of faculty. A new model of governance is needed, and the administrative leadership must be trained to take charge in this process. The faculty do not have the power, and lay trustees do not have the perspective to generate the needed framework.

Understand New Parameters of Faculty Participation in Total College Governance

The process of faculty participation in governance must be extended further than participation in academic affairs. Community college leaders should recognize the campus-wide emphasis of faculty participation. This translates into allowing faculty input or a voice in administrative council meetings, meetings of the board or trustees or other forums where decisions that are made have a bearing upon faculty interests.

For example, giving a faculty representative the opportunity to attend administrative council meetings does not mean that channels of authority are short circuited. It simply means that faculty can receive a direct, first-hand report on council action and can have immediate input on decisions that affect faculty welfare.

Open Channels of Communication Between Faculty and Board

Just as the governance models at Harvard and William and Mary involved faculty, even if by a separate group or board, a community college governance model needs to be developed that involves faculty. Faculty should play a role in governance and should have some access to the Board. Many colleges allow the student government and their faculty, through their respective organizations, to make a report at each board meeting. This does not involve letting these groups circumvent administrators on policy issues, but does serve to keep communication channels open. Others arrange for socials where faculty, staff, and the board can communicate in an informal fashion.

Allow the Affirmative Action Process to Really Work in Employment

This point is perhaps more related to the first point about delegation, but many administrators act as if they lack confidence in their organizations. If a college has a strong employment process and personnel office, and the office is allowed to operate without interference in the execution of board personnel policy, there is a likelihood that competent people will always be employed. Pay-offs and political favors will be avoided, and the college will be assured of quality performance. There will be less concern about delegation.

The following are several suggestions the implementation of which could well develop more responsive community college leadership.

Address the New Leadership Considerations at the University Education Level

Programs in community college leadership similar to the one at the University of California should address such considerations in a formal educational setting and involve future leaders in the kinds of educational endeavors that will allow them to develop a concept of educational leadership applicable to the present educational market. This involves viable concepts of delegation, governance, faculty involvement in governance, communication, and affirmative action, and the ability to complete and apply practical research concerning those matters.

Identify Model Institutions

Identify colleges that can serve as models where faculty have been adequately involved in the governance process and where delegation is truly practiced. These colleges should be highlighted in some of this practical research to see what makes them productive, quality-oriented institutions.

Identify Mentors

Identify administrators that excel in such a system of governance. These individuals could serve a leadership role at seminars where leadership development is the goal. They could also serve as lecturers at universities where leadership is taught.

In conclusion, new leadership considerations to address autocratic behavior inclinations by community college administrators are in order. Special attention must be paid to address the issue of faculty involvement in college governance. Such involvement is an old reality for the university, but has never been fully addressed by community colleges. In the report of the Commission of the Future of the American Association of Community and Junior Colleges, it was related, "It is our conviction that, if a spirit of a community is to be built, the relationship between faculty and president must be strong (1988, p. 41)." In order to make it strong, community college administrators must share more governance responsibility with faculty, and this system of governance must be internalized by more administrators.

References

AACJC Launching Institute to Develop Future Leaders. (1990, February 13). *The Community, Technical, and Junior College Times*. 12.

American Association of Community and Junior Colleges. (1990). Public policy agenda. *Community and Junior College Journal, 60* (4), 46.

American Association of University Professors. (1977). *Policy Documents and Reports*. Washington, D.C.: Author.

Cohen, Arthur M. & Brawer, Florence B. (1982). *The American Community College*. San Francisco: Jossey-Bass.

Commission on the Future of Community Colleges. (1988). *Building communities: A vision for a new century*. Washington, D.C.: American Association of Community and Junior Colleges.

Division of Education Administration. (1989). *Program in higher education*. Berkeley, CA: University of California.

Eddy, Nancy. (1990). Developing the next generation of college leaders. *The Community, Technical, and Junior College Times*. 1

O'Banion, Terry. (19xx). Retaining a peak performing president: A special challenge for trustees of outstanding colleges. *Trustee Quarterly*, 7–11.

Stoddard, Lucille T. (1989, October 16). Shared governance. *Community College Week*, 12.

The Carnegie Foundation for the Advancement of Teaching. (1982). *The control of the campus*. Lawrenceville, NY: Princeton University Press.

Wofford, David. (1989, September 26). Changing behavior can prevent a second heart attack professor says. *Winston-Salem Journal*, A-1.

Dilemmas of Leadership: Decision Making and Ethics in the Community College

George B. Vaughan

If community college leaders are to avoid the ethical dilemmas that ensnare many of their colleagues, the campus climate must be one in which ethical considerations are a part of the decision-making process. Although talk of punishment is anathema to many academics, they can nevertheless, while tolerating and indeed encouraging differences of opinion as to the specifics of rules and regulations, agree on what constitutes unethical behavior. And they must punish those who violate the rules, even their professional colleagues.

How can leaders of community colleges weave the debate on ethical issues into the fabric of campus activities and thus arrive at practical solutions to the many ethical issues faced by members of every campus community? Before exploring this question, a brief discussion of ethics and higher education is in order.

Ethics and Higher Education

Higher education, in general, has played its role of ethical arbitrator rather well. Its leaders have generally taken the high road in dealing with ethical behavior. However, leadership from the academic community in solving ethical issues at the national and international levels has been scant, with the exception of leadership on a few "big ticket" issues such as divestiture in South Africa. Nevertheless, for every professor who misuses graduate students, there are hundreds who give of themselves and of their knowledge in order that students may grow in wisdom and in stature. For every Nobel laureate who has been caught plagiarizing, there are thousands of professors who document their work to the smallest detail. For every "fusion in a bottle" fiasco, researchers take giant strides in the search for a cure for cancer.

Can leaders in higher education, then, be unconcerned with ethical issues? Are the cases that make the headlines the only ones requiring attention? No, for higher education today does not exist in an ivory tower, if it ever did—certainly community colleges never did. Academics are not immune to the temptations that afflict the rest of society.

Higher education, then, has not ignored the need for maintaining ethical standards among its members, although there is little evidence to suggest that these standards are universal or even accepted by much of the academic community. Nevertheless, in 1968, Eric Ashby, a master of Clare College in Cambridge, England, and former vice-chancellor of the University of Cambridge, called for a "Hippocratic oath" for the academic profession.

A decade later, Ashby noted that "at the moment there is no declared code of professional practice to which academics have subscribed. . . . If we had such a code, it would stabilize what I fear is a schizophrenic and disintegrating profession, and it would provide a basis of authority and example to the students" (1977, p. 273). Ashby's Hippocratic oath would require the scholar to subscribe to a rigorous code of ethics that would prohibit a blurring of the facts in any way, for scholarship, Ashby feels, has "an inherent morality" (p. 275).

Ashby offers advice that applies equally to all professionals, including community college leaders. He notes that often there are any number of conflicting views on what is good and what is bad for society. "Someone has to make a balanced judgment between these two sets of factors, and you can't make balanced judgments of values without working out your own sets of values" (1977, p. 282). Certainly, if community college presidents, trustees, and others are to promote ethical values on campus, they must work out their own sets of values and make balanced judgments among competing values, thus setting a moral tone that others will accept and emulate.

Clark Kerr, in a speech given at the twentieth anniversary meeting of Harvard University's Institute for Educational Management, picks up on Ashby's phrase "a disintegrating profession" in describing ethics and university teachers. Kerr (1989) notes that academics are quite willing to study ethics in general and are especially prone to write about medical and legal ethics. Kerr also notes the dearth of literature on academic ethics and believes that this lack of literature hinders the advancement of academic ethics. Indeed, Kerr could have turned to a report by Paul N. Ylvisaker, former dean of the Harvard Graduate School of Education, for support regarding the scarcity of literature on ethics in higher education. Ylvisaker studied 206 codes of ethics of various professions and discovered that while such fields as psychology and engineering have extensive codes of ethics, there is no generic code for educators (Ylvisaker, 1983, pp. 30–32).

Some segments of higher education have developed codes of ethics for some of their members. For example, in 1988, the American Association of State Colleges and Universities issued a policy statement entitled "Ethical Practices for College Presidents." In 1978, the Association of California Community College Administrators adopted a code called "Statement of Ethics: Professional Standards for Community College Administrators" (revised in 1981, 1986, and 1989). Currently, the Presidents Academy of the American Association of Community and Junior Colleges is considering a code of ethics for community college presidents. More will be said about this code in a subsequent chapter.

These codes, which some people see as a step in the right direction, nevertheless fail to provide an umbrella code (or generic code, to use Ylvisaker's phrase) of ethics covering all members of the college community. Indeed, if the codes are to become a part of an institution's culture, they must be incorporated into its mission statement, where they can serve as guideposts to ethical decision making rather than as inflexible boundaries that prescribe actions to be taken.

Joining the call for a code of ethics for academics, Kerr believes that such codes might be designated "derivative ethics" because they can only exist if they are effective. "They seek to set forth what each person should expect in the conduct of others, and what each person in return owes in his own conduct toward others, to make relations over the longer term more effective" (Kerr, 1989, p. 141). While pointing out that in the past higher education has handled its ethical responsibilities rather well, Kerr ends his discussion on a somewhat pessimistic note: "I conclude, regretfully, that the academic profession may, in fact, be disintegrating slowly in some aspects of its ethical conduct. I also conclude that the academic profession should not practice evaluative neutrality about its own ethical values any more than should the medical or legal professions" (p. 156). Community college leaders who wish to create a campus climate and a culture that embrace and promote decision making based on accepted concepts of right and wrong and who promote institutional effectiveness and leadership simply cannot remain neutral on institutional values. As we argue, community college leadership has an ethical dimension.

Other academics also have commented on the need for academic leaders to be concerned with ethical values. Harold L. Enarson, president emeritus of Ohio State University, asks and answers the question, What are the ethical dimensions of a college or university presidency? Enarson, like Ashby and Kerr, bemoans the lack of concern for the ethical dimension of academic leadership. He believes that college and university presidents should operate according to consistent values applied consistently. For example, he believes that to define institutional purpose is to define the values of the organization, to manage an institution of higher education is to strive to ensure that administrative decisions reflect the values and mission of the institution, and to lead a college or university is to transform it over time so that it better reflects the values of society (Enarson, 1984, p. 25).

The test of integrity, Enarson believes, is whether or not the institution lives by its own rules. Enarson, after his many years in the administrative trenches, understands as only someone who has been there can understand that it is easy for presidents with good intentions and good character to look the other way as "subtle signs of corruption appear. . . . The avoidance of wrongdoing is, of course, the easiest of the moral imperatives. Indeed, this is the bare minimum required of leaders who prize both personal and institutional integrity. Beyond is the more important and difficult imperative of promoting the highest values of the institution, the self, and the society" (1984, p. 25). Enarson says that "there is not a single code of ethics to follow" (p. 26). Although Enarson is perhaps correct in his lament regarding the lack of a code of ethics, this problem does not alter the need for community college leaders to set a moral standard for the institution that is in concert with the institutional mission.

In addition to established leaders such as Enarson, Kerr, and Ashby, any number of institutions and higher education leaders are currently looking at the role of ethics in the curriculum. For example, reforms in college sports, although being made slowly, are nevertheless occurring.

The spring 1989 issue of *Educational Record*, published by the American Council on Education, focuses on moral leadership in higher education. In one article, the president of an urban university discusses the role of the president in establishing a moral tone on campus. Another article discusses academic politics and presidential leadership. A higher education scholar entitles his article "The Moral Message of the University." In a similar vein, a community college dean of instruction entitled his remarks to a group of community college faculty members and administrators "Community Colleges and Civic Literacy: The Quest for Values, Ethics, and College Renewal." A community college faculty member examined ethics and administration in America's community colleges and concluded that community college administrators must define ethical standards of conduct for themselves and for future leaders if the community college is to serve its constituents (Whisnant, 1988).

Leaders in higher education, then, have not been blind to ethical issues, although, as Kerr points out, they have been reluctant to deal with these issues. It now seems to be the time for leaders in all segments of higher education to heed Kerr's advice (1988, p. 141) and "seek to set forth what each person should expect in the conduct of others, and. . . in return owes in his own conduct toward others." These leaders must realize that much that occurs on campus ultimately penetrates into society as graduates assume their roles as teachers, doctors, nurses, lawyers, legal assistants, business leaders, and technicians.

All leaders in higher education are subject to temptations. Community college leaders, positioned in that middle ground on the academic continuum where the community intersects with the college in ways not found in much of the rest of higher education and committed to serving all segments of society, are certainly no exception. Indeed, community college leaders are constantly subjected to the song of the Lorelei, ever luring them to cross the line of ethical misconduct only to be broken apart on rocks masquerading as easy solutions to ever-present funding and image problems.

Noting the almost blind commitment on the part of some community college leaders to achieving what they perceive to be the mission of their school, one community college faculty member reminds us that "the important note to keep in mind is that unethical behavior may not always be the result of an individual's quest for personal gain. Rather, unethical behavior may result from what the administrator views as institutionally necessary decisions or interpretations of policy" (Whisnant, 1988, p. 244).

One example serves to illustrate how blind adherence to the perceived mission of a college raises a number of ethical issues. In this situation, a community college was committed to serving the coal mining industry. The mining company required a flexible class schedule for its workers because they worked various shifts. The company preferred that classes be taught on site at company headquarters. One of the college's students—an employed miner—when asked whether he preferred to take classes on campus or at the mine site, responded that he preferred the classes held at the mine. (The purpose of the question was to determine if the miners took pride in coming to the campus and blending in with the other students.) When asked why he preferred to take classes at the mine, he replied that he got three more hours of credit with no additional work if he took the class at the mine site. Further questioning revealed that his work at the mine was viewed as a cooperative learning experience, although it required no additional work on his part.

What are the ethical implications inherent in this situation other than the obvious one of compromised academic integrity? First, the student has a distorted view of what should be required to obtain a college degree. Second, the image of the college from this student's perspective (and probably from a number of other perspectives) was one of "anything goes" rather than one of promoting ethical principles. Third, the college received funds from the state and tuition costs from the mining company for "void" college credits, a serious legal as well as ethical lapse. Fourth, the funding formula based upon student enrollment, not academic or fiscal integrity, was the driving force in the decision-making process of the leaders of the college. The decision to pad the enrollment figures was not an evil decision on the part of the college leadership; rather, it was a decision that did not take into consideration the ethical dimensions of leadership.

Knowing When to Say No

Community college presidents, as is true with all leaders, must learn to say no to any number of requests but must do so without losing constituent support. Indeed, saying no is an art that the successful leader practices daily. But does the art of saying no have an ethical base?

The following brief case studies illustrate how three community college presidents said no and lived to lead another day. The first case is personal: the situation is as vivid in my memory today as it was on that day almost two decades ago when I stood in the office of the board chair and faced my first ethical dilemma as president. The second case describes a situation faced by James Hudgins, president of Midlands Technical College, and the third illustration comes from Richard Greenfield, current community college leader and former president of three community colleges, including the St. Louis Community College District.

Case One

I had been in my first presidency for only three weeks (my spouse was still packing for the move) when I received a call from the board chair asking if I could come to his office for a brief meeting. Of course, I volunteered to meet with him at his convenience. His "convenience" was two hours after I received the call.

When I arrived at the chair's office, I was met by him and another member of the board. After we exchanged cordial greetings, the chair said, "Dr. Vaughan, here are the names of three people I want to see appointed to the college faculty."

Suddenly it all came back to me. The college was located in the most political section of the state: even the janitor's position at the courthouse in the chair's home district was up for grabs at election time, and the janitor regularly changed with a change in the party. How could I say no to a chair who lived and died by the political code of his district?

I took the three names and looked the board chair in the eye and said, "Thank you for the names. Let me assure you that they will get every consideration. If they come to the top of the stack they will be employed. If they don't, they won't. But I promise you one thing: the fact that you recommended them *will not* be held against them." I politely excused myself, returned to my motel, and called my wife. I suggested that she stop packing since I had probably concluded my tenure as president after an inglorious three weeks. As a new president, I had obviously not learned the art of saying no. I did, however, know where I had drawn my compromise line and was not about to cross it.

Thus my dilemma was not in deciding whether to accept political appointments to the college faculty; I had decided long before becoming president that I would never do so. My ethical dilemma was in making sure that the three applicants favored by the chair were treated like all other applicants. As it turned out, I kept my promise while remaining true to myself. One of the three applicants was employed, an outstanding choice I should add, and the other two applicants lost out to more qualified candidates.

Case Two

Midlands Technical College depends on two counties, Richland and Lexington, for its local budget. The local budget is approved by council members who are elected from single-member districts. During the previous four years, the college had enjoyed the support of a large majority of the eleven-member Richland County Council. One major exception was a council member who had strong negative feelings toward the college based on a bad experience with the college that occurred several years ago.

I visited him twice to seek a reconciliation between him and the college. He was courteous but refused the offer. During the previous two years, he had served as chair of the county council. On three occasions in 1990, he had used his authority to reduce or deny funding for the college.

In the fall of 1990, he was in a close race for his council seat. A member of his opponent's party informed a newspaper reporter that he had not acted in the best interest of education, especially Midlands Technical College. The reporter called me three days before the election and asked me to comment on the relationship between the council member and the college. I possessed information that would have been damaging to his campaign.

Although I personally opposed his candidacy and desired, for the benefit of the college, his defeat at the polls, I concluded that revealing this information in a time frame that would give him no opportunity to respond would not be ethical. I declined the request.

On the same weekend, I received a call from his opponent, a former student of the college who expressed his intent to support the college if elected. He offered me a similar opportunity to provide information damaging to his opponent. When I explained my intent to keep the college out of the political campaign and asked for his understanding, he courteously withdrew his request.

The story has a happy ending. The council member's challenger was elected, and since the campaign, he has reaffirmed his intention to support the college.

Case Three

After years in the presidency, at least some incumbents realize that there are many roads to Jerusalem and that their ideas of right and wrong are not necessarily absolute. With age comes caution and a sense of relativity, tempered by a growing awareness of vulnerability and the need to protect one's flanks if one is to survive in the face of internal as well as external community pressures. After age fifty to fifty-five, few incumbent presidents can move readily into another presidency. For most, any shift to a "lesser" position, other than perhaps to a professorship at a university, signifies a great loss of status, a punctured ego, and consignment to limbo. Hence, at least some aging presidents may be willing to compromise their ethical standards in the interest of job security. Ironically, in doing so, they often undermine the very security that they seek since ultimately their weakness is perceived, and a compromised president frequently becomes a former president.

The case I relate occurred fairly early in my presidential career, while I was in my early forties. As founding president of a new community college, I was in the midst of building an entire campus as well as expanding the size of the faculty and support staff to meet surging demand and rapid growth in student enrollments. Blessed with an outstanding and prestigious appointed board of trustees, the college enjoyed great community support and experienced no overt political interference or attempts at improper influence during the first few years of its existence. Personnel and business decisions were made on the basis of appropriate criteria, policies, and procedures.

However, at some point, those people involved in local government, which sponsored the college and supported it with tax dollars, came to realize that they might be able to influence the appointment of staff or the awarding of contracts. I was contacted by a person who was very powerful in local politics and government and who had been a key supporter of the college in the course of its establishment and early development, including during the appointment of the blue-ribbon founding board of trustees. I was not asked to do anything illegal but was asked to consider certain people for appointments for various positions and to favor certain firms in making business decisions where bidding laws were not involved.

I was tempted to consider ways of pleasing this very powerful person and the forces he represented by cooperating, but I felt that personnel appointment policies and procedures had to be protected and business decisions had to be made on an impartial basis to foster the best interests of the college in the long run. At the same time, I was aware of the possibility that any refusal on my part could jeopardize this local support and perhaps my own job security.

I decided to have a private meeting with the person involved. At this meeting, I explained that the college would welcome inquiries or recommendations concerning any aspect of college operations from any source, but that as an appointed official with a public trust, I had to make sure that everyone, whether job applicant or vendor, would be treated impartially and fairly. Decisions would be made with the future of the college in mind and not with the idea of the college becoming a part of local government or local politics.

Of course, I was greatly concerned over his reaction to my views for the future of the college and myself. Fortunately, my reassurance of fair treatment and the genuine pride in the progress of the college exhibited by the official led him to back down and to agree that my decision (supported completely by the college's board of trustees) was one he could live with. He and his colleagues continued to be good supporters of the college in the years ahead and to refrain from attempting to control the operation of the institution.

The Role of the President

The central question to be answered by this book is, What can be done on our campuses to strengthen the commitment to ethical values? This chapter introduces the question and provides some answers. The remaining chapters also deal with the question, and the concluding chapter offers a road map to ethical decision making.

I believe the answer to this question lies, in part, in the desire and ability of community college leaders to create a framework on campus in which ethical values can evolve and be examined, a framework that will result in a campus climate in which decisions are considered and made from the perspective of what is ethically right. Implicit in creating such a campus climate is the belief that the rules, regulations, and standards of conduct of the college must be in concert with the mission of the college.

Although it would be impossible and impractical to codify accepted ethical behavior for all possible situations or decisions on campus, it is possible to create at least a basic code or pattern of behavior. This "code of integrity," if you will, should bind all members of the academic community and hold them responsible for their behavior and decisions. And although all members of an academic community may not be able to agree upon set rules and regulations regarding ethical behavior, one would hope that they could distinguish between ethical and unethical behavior, between acting with integrity and acting dishonorably. If people in the college community view decisions from the perspective of ethical behavior, the campus climate evolves to the point where ethical considerations become a part of the culture of the institution, a culture with roots in the past that extend into the future. I believe that institutional decisions based on those ethical values that are in concert with the college mission will effectively meet societal, institutional, and individual needs by maintaining integrity in all aspects of the college's operation.

Who should take the lead in establishing a climate on campus based upon accepted concepts of right and wrong? I believe the leader in this goal must be the college president. Just as Nixon had the responsibility to set the moral climate for his administration, so the president of a college has the responsibility for setting the moral climate for the campus. However, community college presidents cannot and should not act alone in establishing and maintaining this campus climate.

The president occupies a unique position on campus and is the person with the greatest potential to see that members of the campus community take ethics seriously. The president is the person most likely to influence the campus climate and ultimately the campus culture. And the president is the one person on campus who cannot say, "Ethical behavior at this institution is not my problem." The final responsibility for ethics does indeed rest with the president, whether the president chooses to promote ethical conduct or run the risk of ignoring ethical misconduct.

Community college presidents must not fail, as Nixon did with the White House, to set a moral tone on campus that causes members of the college community to think, judge, and act with integrity. To fail to set this moral tone is to court the disaster that ultimately befalls leaders in our society who violate the rules. These leaders limit their own accomplishments and the accomplishments of those they are morally bound to lead. If U.S. democracy and its proud offspring, our higher education system, are to be successful, leaders at all levels must be able to distinguish right from wrong, to act on what is right, and to deal with breaches of ethical conduct.

Ethics and Institutional Culture

In literally thousands of conversations with community college leaders, I have rarely heard anyone discuss institutional culture. Institutional cultures evolve over many years and sometimes over several centuries and are often documented, in part, in extensive institutional histories. When this long-term evolution is contrasted with the short history of community colleges (most community college histories consist of a page in the college catalogue), one can understand why institutional culture has rarely been a topic of discussion among community college leaders at professional meetings, in the literature, or on campus.

In a parallel argument, and one that supports the need to make ethics a part of the community college culture, one author argues that the brief history of the community college increases the chances that community college administrators will make ethically questionable decisions. Pointing out that most community colleges are less than three decades old, the author notes, "This stage of development means that the community college does not have a reserve of experience or tradition from which to draw in times of difficult decision making. Community college administrators do not have generations of predecessors having left a legacy to follow" (Whisnant, 1988, p. 246). Whether having a legacy on which to base their ethical decisions would enhance the ability of community college administrators to make ethical decisions is debatable. What is not debatable is that all organizations, including community colleges, have a culture (Birnbaum, 1988; Kuh and Whitt, 1988). If community colleges are to serve as an important avenue for promoting ethical behavior, consistent ethical conduct must become a recognized part of their institutional culture.

How can institutional culture be used to promote rules of conduct based on a standard of ethics? Perhaps before answering this question, we should examine institutional culture and its relationship to the community college.

Definitions of the term *institutional culture* abound. Kuh and Whitt (1988) note that over thirty-five years ago, two scholars reported 164 different definitions of culture. Peterson and his colleagues point out that ambiguity exists regarding what constitutes organizational culture and note that "the definition of organizational culture is neither precise nor consensual" (Peterson and others, 1986, p. 11). They believe that the attributes of culture—values, beliefs, and assumptions—distinguish the concept of culture from the concept of climate. They observe that the institutional climate consists of individual attitudes and perceptions and that these may change much more quickly than the values, beliefs, and assumptions that make up the institutional culture. The distinction between climate and culture is relevant to this discussion and will be alluded to below.

Culture grows out of past and present actions (process) and results in shared values, beliefs, and assumptions about an institution (product). Institutional image and culture have a symbiotic relationship; one constantly feeds and shapes the other.

Institutional culture changes slowly. For example, outmoded attitudes toward race have dominated the culture of some institutions, outmoded attitudes toward religion others, and outmoded attitudes toward gender still others. The domination of these attitudes often inhibits the development of students and faculty members whose values are in conflict with the existing culture.

Although understanding a culture is a rational process, appreciating an institution's culture can be an emotional process, one that demands sensitivity to what has gone before and what may happen in the future. This sensitivity often evokes chills and even tears when one sings a certain song or visits a certain place on campus. Culture consists of those things that make an institution distinct: its history, traditions, values, interaction with the larger environment, ceremonies, renewal process—including recruitment and selection of personnel—and evaluation process, including assessment of its ethical values.

Any discussion of institutional culture raises a number of questions. Do members of the college community generally agree upon concepts of ethical behavior and integrity to such a degree that these concepts are an inherent part of the institutional culture? Or is the culture one that says "anything goes," for example, winning football games at any cost or padding enrollment figures in order to generate full-time-equivalent students (FTEs)? Is the culture one that encourages, indeed rewards, taking a stand on institutional values? Is the culture in tune with the times, especially in relationship to women and minorities, both on campus and in society? How do we know when to let parts of our culture die or when to kill them?

Open access, an important aspect of the culture of a community college, is itself a value statement. Admitting students who have academic deficiencies and not dealing with those deficiencies, however, is ethically wrong. Myths, legends, and stories of the founding of the college and of early institutional leaders are part of institutional culture; they contribute to a sense of history and community and inspire loyalty to the institution. The culture of an institution influences how the institution is perceived by members of the college community and by the community at large.

The effective leader understands and is sensitive to the culture of an institution. The leader respects and preserves the good things of the past but always leads in shaping the present and planning for the future. The effective leader, and especially the effective president, understands when and where to try to change an institution's culture and when to let go of past values that are no longer acceptable in society or as a part of the institutional mission. The effective leader discusses the institutional culture in ways that can be understood by much of the public, often using metaphors with which the audience identifies. Indeed, the highly successful president becomes one with the culture, as its interpreter and as the symbol of the institution. The president absorbs and is absorbed by the institutional culture and ultimately becomes an integral part of that culture, often after passing from the scene.

The importance of leaders, especially presidents, in influencing the campus climate and ultimately shaping institutional culture helps to answer in part the question posed earlier: what can be done on our campuses to strengthen the commitment to ethical values? The answer, in the broadest sense, is that the president and other campus leaders working with the governing board can shape the institutional culture in ways that assure that members of the college community examine and live by the rules and values of the college and that these rules and values are instilled as a permanent part of the campus culture.

Actions for Shaping Institutional Culture

Changing the culture of an institution is extremely difficult and somewhat risky if the changes depart dramatically from accepted and revered practices. Nevertheless, changing the culture of the institution is an important way for community college leaders to shape institutional values.

Assuring that ethical values occupy a prominent role in the decision-making process on campus should not rend the cultural fabric of most campuses or even be seen as a challenge to the existing culture. Rather, by emphasizing values in the decision-making process and by encouraging members of the college community to ask if a decision or an act is right or wrong, community college leaders tap into those institutional values normally associated with effective institutions of higher education. Therefore, the leaders are not perceived as inventing or imposing new values. They can subtly but effectively change the institutional culture without creating chaos or hostility among members of the college community.

In the rest of this section, I offer suggestions for shaping the culture of a community college in ways that enhance the commitment of the institution to doing the right thing, regardless of the issue at hand. The suggestions take into consideration that each institution is unique and has its own unique culture.

A first, and perhaps most important, step for shaping the culture of institutions based on ethical values is for presidents to be sensitive to the ethical dimension of leadership. Once presidents step forward and insist that decisions be made from an ethical base, students, faculty members, staff members, and trustees will be more inclined to view their roles from the perspective of ethical behavior or at least to think about and perhaps debate the ethical dimensions of their decisions. All members of the college community can then sense that the campus climate is one in which debating of ethical issues is valued and encouraged. Thus the process of placing ethics at the center of the campus culture begins. It is at this point that the president begins to influence the campus climate in a positive way, at least as far as placing emphasis upon institutional values (influencing the culture takes longer).

How can presidents bring an ethical dimension to their leadership without giving the appearance of having just descended from Mount Sinai, hoisting high a faculty handbook filled with rules and regulations, the breaking of which will bring forth harsh moral judgments? This is very difficult. But effective presidents realize that a sure way to alienate the college community is to become preachy or moralistic, regardless of whether the subject is conserving energy, serving students, or maintaining ethical standards.

Probably the most effective way for presidents to bring an ethical approach to their leadership is to be above reproach in their own professional and personal actions. It is good to remember that the incumbent is president twenty-four hours a day, seven days a week, three hundred and sixty-five days a year. Serving as a role model extends into the president's personal life in ways not experienced by other members of the college community, and few things are off limits when considering the conduct of the president. By serving as an example of good ethical conduct, the president becomes a role model and symbol for other members of the college community. Leading by example, then, is the first step presidents can take to establish a climate on campus that embraces values built upon a sense of right and wrong.

Next, presidents must use the many opportunities available almost daily to exhibit ethical behavior, thereby weaving their own behavior into the fabric (and ultimately the culture) of the institution. The president may present day-to-day issues and problems that are ethical dilemmas to the college community and ask for help in finding a resolution that is in concert with the values of the institution. Ethical decision making thus becomes a part of the daily activities of the campus. As one president, my friend and colleague Robert Templin, is fond of saying, by using current situations to emphasize ethics, the president is a "teacher and not a preacher."

Once the president engages in a decision-making process based upon the accepted values of the institution, and especially if other members of the campus are involved, the college community can reflect upon the actions taken. By "doing ethics" the president can encourage all members of the college community to discuss the ethical dimensions of leadership and decision making. The discussions may, however, become little more than philosophical wanderings that devour a great deal of time and energy but yield few useful results, especially if no mechanism is available to test ethical concepts in a way that produces a product.

To provide an anchor for the discussions and to encourage a product at the end of the process, the president should build discussions around applying ethical practices to existing issues. For example, one approach might be for members of a campus community to examine the rules and regulations governing the college and to use this examination to focus the debate on values. They might ask, Are the rules fair? Do any of them discriminate against women or ethnic or racial minorities? Although few members of the college community are interested in discussing rules and regulations in isolation, using rules and regulations as the bridge to a discussion of ethics in a broader context might be useful on some campuses.

Once the discussion on the fairness of rules and regulations has served its purpose, the more difficult question of whether the rules and regulations are applied consistently and fairly to all members of the college community can lead the discussion of ethics to a higher level. The discussion of rules and regulations may generate a list of issues that a later definition or later concepts of ethics can be applied to or tested against.

A similar but more interesting and creative way of broaching the subject of ethics on a community college campus is one used at Brookdale Community College. After polling members of the campus community regarding what they viewed as ethical concerns on campus, campus leaders held a series of nine seminars to discuss the issues. Using case studies based upon real situations at the college (past or present), the organizer of the seminars assigned various roles to those who were willing to act out the cases. No attempt was made to find the right answers; rather, "the participants came up with a set of tentative guidelines to distinguish morally acceptable from morally unacceptable behavior" (Mellert, 1990, p. 1). All the participants thought the discussions were worthwhile, and those in attendance learned from the process and were able to relate the ethical issues discussed to their own campus responsibilities.

Once members of the campus community have discussed ethics and have had time to reflect and to draw some conclusions about what is meant by the ethical dimensions of leadership, the governing board of the college must be actively brought into the process. The board should be aware of the debates taking place on campus regarding ethics, especially if rules and regulations are being examined. If the institutional culture is to reflect ethical values, the board must be involved in both the processes and products that will shape that culture. The board should be brought into the process carefully, for the board members must not see themselves as arbitrators for ethical conduct. On the other hand, the board has a right and responsibility to help determine campus values.

At this stage, the president can exert leadership in helping the board members to understand their role in assuring ethical conduct among themselves and among members of the college community. (In working with the board, the president's role must once again be to teach and not preach.) The board members must, however, avoid taking a moralistic stance, especially in raising questions related to activities that have little to do with how individuals perform as board members or as members of the college community. They must resist the temptation to peek into the personal lives of individuals. (Here, again, the president is something of an exception.) The board members should thoroughly discuss the meaning of the terms *institutional ethics* and *institutional culture*, yet resist the temptation to offer an official definition of either at this stage. But the board should make clear its interest in helping shape the institution's understanding of ethics and should recognize that the ultimate goal is to make ethics an even more important part of the culture of the college.

Once the board and president agree on the direction the discussion of the ethical dimensions of leadership should take in general, a committee should be established consisting of representatives from the board and from all segments of the college community. The committee's task and deadline should be clearly defined. For example, the committee may be asked to define ethics in the context of the institutional mission within six months.

The committee should be charged with applying the rule of reason when discussing its task because, again, not all statements of ethical behavior can or should be listed in the policy manual. Rather, the committee can propose a framework for discussing ethical values or, as at Brookdale Community College, establish a set of guidelines to distinguish morally acceptable from morally unacceptable behavior. A way of keeping the president involved and of assuring support from that office is to have the president chair the committee and present the report of the committee to both the board and to the college community.

All members of the college community and all members of the governing board should have the opportunity to debate the issues raised in the report and to offer recommendations for revision. The committee should then revise its report based upon the recommendations and submit the report to the governing board (assuming the president chairs the committee) with a recommendation for adoption.

The governing board should then issue its statement on ethics as official college policy. The statement should provide for periodic review and revision as required, for as Enarson (1984, p. 26) reminds us, "there is not a single code of ethics to follow," and there certainly is not one code for all people for all times. The college community should then apply the ethical principles to the daily activities of the college, incorporating appropriate portions of the policy statement into all publications, including the college catalogue, recruitment brochures, course syllabi, the annual report, fundraising material, and other appropriate publications.

Conclusion

This chapter, in setting the stage for the remainder of the book, has attempted to offer some practical advice for incorporating into the institutional culture standards of ethical conduct that are understood and accepted by members of the academic community. Although I do not call for a formal code of ethical conduct as advocated by Ashby and others (a topic that will be dealt with more fully in a later chapter), I believe that if the culture of an institution incorporates debates on standards of right and wrong, the culture will ultimately be shaped by the debates. And thus the community of the institution will be more willing to take a stand on ethical issues and may issue a formal statement, approved by the governing board, that outlines the stand of the college on the ethical dimensions of leadership. The statement should follow a rule of reason rather than attempt to answer all ethical (and legal) questions for all times.

As Ylvisaker (1983) observes, "We arrive at an ethical decision and what ethics are, not by power, not by politics, not by the market mechanism. . . and not by compromise, but by some moral touchstone that is not identical with the law, nor even a code of ethics, or religion, or custom. It's a standard that is constantly evolving. There's a growth in our consciousness of what is ethical behavior. It's a sense that drives us to want to act nobly, to act in the general interest as well as in our own" (p. 31). Once the college community commits itself to a decision-making process based upon ethical values and applies these values in the general interest of all concerned, the college will be well on its way to creating a culture that inculcates these values and that judges its processes and products based upon these values.

References

Ashby, E. "A Hippocratic Oath for the Academic Profession." In G. R. Urban (ed.), *Hazards of Learning*. La Salle, Ill.: Open Court, 1977.

Birnbaum, R. *How Colleges Work: The Cybernetics of Academic Organization and Leadership*. San Francisco: Jossey-Bass, 1988.

Brockett, R. G. "Ethics and the Adult Educator." In R. G. Brockett (ed.), *Ethical Issues in Adult Education*. New York: Teachers College, Columbia University, 1988.

Enarson, H. L. "The Ethical Imperative of the College Presidency." *Educational Record*, Spring 1984, pp. 24–26.

Kerr, C. "The Academic Ethic and University Teachers: A 'Disintegrating Profession'?" *Minerva*, Summer–Fall 1989, pp. 139–156.

Kuh, G. D., and Whitt, E. J. *The Invisible Tapestry: Culture in American Colleges and Universities*. Washington, D.C.: ERIC Clearinghouse for Higher Education, George Washington University, 1988.

Magner, D. K. "Can't Fire Professor for Ethical Lapses, Rutgers Told." *Chronicle of Higher Education*, Aug. 15, 1990, p. A2.

Mellert, R. B. "Ethics in Higher Education." *Innovation Abstracts*, 1990, 12 (30), 1–2.

Nixon, R. "I Could See No Reason to Live." *Time*, Apr. 2, 1990, pp. 34–49.

Peterson, M. W., and others. *The Organizational Context for Teaching and Learning: A Review of the Literature*. Ann Arbor: University of Michigan Press, 1986.

Shea, G. F. *Practical Ethics*. New York: American Management Association, 1988.

Whisnant, W. T. "Ethics and Administration in America's Community Colleges." *Community/Junior College Quarterly of Research and Practice*, 1988, 12 (3), 243–249.

Ylvisaker, P. N. "Ethical Problems in Higher Education." *AGB Reports*, Jan.–Feb. 1983, pp. 28–35.

Proven Techniques—
The Use and Impact
of Major Management
Concepts in Community Colleges

WILLIAM L. DEEGAN

Management may be more art than science, but there is still much to be learned from the study of management theory and practice. In the past 25 years increased competition in business and concerns about declining quality in education have produced an unparalleled interest in management in both the corporate and noncorporate worlds. In business, the loss of both foreign and domestic market share to Japan and Germany, the emergence of Third World countries as new competitors, and the dramatic shift in America from a manufacturing economy to a service economy have stimulated a major search for better ways for American companies to manage. Similarly, higher education has seen a shift away from the era of freedom in the 1960s and the era of accountability in the 1970s to a new emphasis on quality, productivity, standards, and institutional effectiveness through the 1980s and into the 1990s.

The search for more effective management and leadership has produced a number of distinctive concepts and theories that have shaped the way organizations of all kinds are managed today. As part of the research to conduct the study reported here, a review was made of the major management books that have been influential in shaping management practice over the past 25 years. In addition, a series of studies was begun at the University of Miami in 1986 and continued in 1990 to establish a baseline of management concepts that have evolved in the past three decades and to chart the changing use and impact of those concepts in American community colleges.

Based on a review of the management literature of the past 25 years and on interviews with leaders in higher education, we developed a comprehensive questionnaire and conducted a national survey of community college presidents in the spring of 1990 to determine which management concepts are being used—and which are most effective—in these institutions. Three hundred and eleven surveys were mailed, and 167 usable responses were returned, a response rate of 54 percent. The respondents' colleges were generally representative of American community colleges in terms of enrollments: there were no statistically significant differences between the sample and institutions listed by enrollment category in the AACJC membership directory.

Dividing management concepts into the five categories of planning, organizing, budgeting, staffing, and evaluation, the survey examined more than 50 key concepts. Presidents were asked to name the concepts they were presently using and to rate the success of those concepts on a five-

431

point scale ranging from very successful to moderately successful to not successful at all. This article reports on the concepts labeled very successful in each of the five categories.

Planning

As Table 1 shows, the most widely used planning concepts were strategic planning institutionwide (89 percent), formal needs assessment conducted by college staff (77 percent), expansion of the institutional research office to gather planning data (69 percent), and use of business leaders as one of the primary planning advisory groups (64 percent). The least-used concept was the creation of futures task forces in departments or divisions. Concepts rated most successful by the presidents were the use of business leaders as one of the primary planning advisory groups (42 percent), strategic planning (34 percent), and management by objectives (34 percent). The least successful concept was the creation of future task forces in departments or divisions (18 percent).

The data uncovered several interesting trends and issues. First, while strategic planning is the most widely used concept, there appears to be a significant gap between the amount of strategic planning going on institutionwide (89 percent) and the amount of strategic planning going on in the departments (39 percent). One has to wonder to what extent a strategic plan is really carried out if there is a relatively low level of follow-up at the department level. Compared to data from the 1986 study, there is now a much greater emphasis on research and data gathering, including the use of such concepts as needs assessment and expansion of the institutional research office to gather outcome data. The final trend suggested by the data on planning concepts and reflected throughout the study is the increased use of entrepreneurial management concepts such as more inclusion of business leaders in planning or, we shall see later, contract training or college foundations.

Table 1
Planning Concepts

	Percentage Using The Concept	Percentage Rated Very Successful
Strategic planning (institutionwide)	89	34
Formal needs assessment conducted by college staff	77	26
Expansion of the institutional research office to gather planning data	69	31
Use of business leaders as one of the primary planning advisory groups	64	42
Use of management by objectives systems	44	34
Use of "futures" task forces (collegewide)	41	28
Use of strategic planning in dept. (decentralized planning)	39	29
Formal needs assessment conducted by *outside* consultants	26	32
Use of "futures" task forces (dept./divisions)	20	18

Table 2
Organizing Concepts

	Percentage Using The Concept	Percentage Rated Very Successful
Increased decentralization of decision making	77	26
Used special units for innovative ideas to be developed or tried	57	54
Decreased the number of people reporting directly to you	37	35
Increased the number of people reporting directly to you	26	25
Use of matrix organization (collegewide)	18	27
Increased centralization of decision making	14	22
Used quality circles	10	35
Created "cluster" colleges or academic units organized around themes	8	31
Use of matrix organization models (within units/divisions)	7	17
Used job rotation programs within units	6	10
Used job rotation programs between units	5	22

Organizing

Two concepts emerged as clearly the most widely used organizing concepts in community colleges: increased decentralization of decision making (77 percent); and creating special units for innovative ideas to be developed or tried (57 percent) (see Table 2). The concept rated most successful by the presidents by far was the creation of special units for innovation (54 percent), followed by, surprisingly, quality circles (35 percent), and decreasing the number of people reporting directly to them (35 percent). Compared with data from a 1986 study, there is a decrease in 1990 in the use of a number of Japanese management concepts, such as matrix organization, job rotation, and quality circles, although quality circles had a fairly high success rate where it was used.

Budgeting Finance

While much of the management literature has focused on topics such as strategic planning, vision, or leadership, the survey found that budgeting concepts are some of the most used and most successful in the college presidents' repertoire (see Table 3). The most-used concepts were creating a college foundation (74 percent), increased risk capital for contract training (69 percent), incremental budgeting (59 percent), and program budgeting (54 percent). As previously stated, the impact of a number of the budgeting concepts was rated very high by the presidents.

Concepts receiving the highest rating include contract training (52 percent), improved auditing procedures (50 percent), creation of special funds for innovation (47 percent), and creation of a college foundation (45 percent).

Several of the newer budgeting concepts that evolved in the 1970s presented an interesting pattern in the study. Incremental budgeting (an old concept) has high use (59 percent), but it has a very low rating in terms of impact (13 percent). The more recent concept of program budgeting, on the other hand, has high use (54 percent) and a much higher rating on impact (31 percent) Zero-based budgeting seems to have become a concept whose time has passed at many colleges. It is down significantly in use from previous studies (from 31 percent in 1986 to 17 percent in 1990), but interestingly its impact rating is up (from 14 percent in 1986 to 41 percent in 1990).

Obviously, those colleges still using zero-based budgeting are finding it highly successful.

Table 3
Budgeting/Finance Concepts

	Percentage Using The Concept	Percentage Rated Very Successful
Use of a college foundation to raise funds	74	45
Began or expanded a contract training program with business and industry	69	52
Incremental budgeting	59	13
Program budgeting	54	31
Use of a special fund for internal innovations	45	47
Hired more staff to write grants on a full-time basis	34	37
Used internal staff to improve auditing procedures	31	50
Used outside staff to improve auditing procedures	28	52
Zero-based budgeting	17	41

Staffing

As outlined in Table 4, four concepts emerged as the most widely used in the staffing area: creating a health, wellness, or counseling program for staff (53 percent); increasing the percentage of full-time faculty (49 percent); creating a formal staff development program with a part-time director (46 percent); and initiating an early retirement system (43 percent). The top three staffing concepts that the presidents rated as most successful were creating a staff development program with a full-time director (60 percent), creating new reward systems (45 percent), and increasing the percentage of full-time faculty (43 percent). The concept rated as least successful was merit pay (20 percent), which also scored low in the 1986 survey.

A final issue concerned the concept of contracting for services with vendors from outside the college rather than using college staff. This concept has received a good deal of attention in the literature. Twenty-nine percent of the presidents reported using this approach, and 38 percent of those using it rated the concept as very successful.

Evaluating

Almost all evaluation concepts have increased in use since the 1986 study, perhaps due to the growing emphasis on the importance of evaluation, accountability, and institutional effectiveness throughout the 1980s along with a greater emphasis on generating "outcome data" (see Table 5). The most highly used evaluation concept was increased curriculum review (80 percent), which perhaps reflects the impact of a number of major national reports that have called for curriculum review, followed by expanded computer feedback of information to staff (68 percent), creating systems to better gather outcome data (62 percent), and expanding computer-generated feedback of data to faculty (6I percent). The most successful concepts involved providing feedback, including feedback to students (41 percent), feedback to staff (35 percent), and feedback to faculty (32 percent). Interestingly, the least successful concepts as rated by the presidents were an increased emphasis on formal staff evaluation for administrators (20 percent) and an increased emphasis on formal staff evaluation for tenured faculty (20 percent).

Problems

A final part of the survey asked presidents to list the top three problems facing them. While they cited a wide range of problems, there was a clear consensus about four general problem areas.

Inadequate Resources of All Kinds. The top priority problem cited was the lack of resources of all kinds—funding, physical resources, staff and equipment, and a feeling of falling behind developments in technology. Respondents admitted a general concern that many community colleges have reached a point where they cannot accomplish the objectives they have been asked to achieve with current resources.

Staff Relations and Morale. The second cluster of problems concerns staff relationships and morale, especially faculty morale. Many presidents cited a growing tension between administrators and faculty, especially in relationships with senior faculty. Several presidents described senior faculty who are not only resistant to change, but who in some cases actively work to undermine college initiatives. Burn-out of both faculty and administrators seems exacerbated by declining resources, demands for greater productivity, and a growing number of interventions by staff agencies.

Difficulty of Management and Leadership. The third problem, obviously related to staff relations, is the growing difficulty of management and leadership in community colleges. Many presidents expressed frustration with the lack of planning data, increasing litigation, and the general "unpleasantness" of many relationships between administrators and faculty. A large number of presidents also cited worries about the difficulty of currently recruiting effective administrators and faculty, as well as recruiting, training, and developing both faculty and administrators in the years ahead.

Increased Demands from Outside Agencies. A final cluster of problems concerns the growing accountability demands from outside agencies (both state and accrediting). Many presidents expressed concern about the excessive accountability, overwhelming intrusion, and general waste of time resulting from many studies and demands for data. While acknowledging the need for reasonable accountability, many presidents complained about duplication of studies, the general lack of understanding of issues by many state bureaucrats, and the time and effort that reporting demands make on limited college staff. A number of presidents cited the need for outside agencies to "get their own act together" by streamlining their reporting requirements to eliminate some of the duplication and waste of resources. The need to write multiple reports for a variety of agencies when "one coherent report might serve all" was a particularly frustrating problem.

Perspectives on the Future

While the data suggest a wide range of problems, issues, and trends, certain issues emerged as most predominant. First, the data uncovered a wide gap between the amount and impact of strategic planning conducted institutionwide as compared with strategic planning activities in college departments. This finding calls into question the extent to which a strategic plan will be effective if there is such a relatively low level of follow-up at the department level.

Entrepreneurial concepts are emerging as important management strategies. Concepts such as contract training programs with business and industry, creating college foundations, or creating special units within the college for innovation and entrepreneurship are on the rise from the 1986 study. Entrepreneurship is increasing in both internal and external activities, generally with high ratings of success. This emergence of entrepreneurship in community colleges is part of the effort to "de-institutionalize" large organizations that is taking place throughout American society.

Table 4
Staffing Concepts

	Percentage Using The Concept	Percentage Rated Very Successful
Created a health/wellness or counseling program for staff	53	31
Increased the percentage of full-time faculty	49	43
Used a formal staff development program with a part-time director	46	33
Initiated an early retirement program	43	34
Increased the percentage of part-time faculty	38	30
Conducted a review of staffing needs for the decade ahead	37	23
Contracted for services with vendors from outside the college	29	38
Used a merit pay system	27	20
Used new reward systems to encourage staff initiative	17	45
Used a formal staff development system with a full-time director	12	60

Table 5
Evaluation Concepts

	Percentage Using The Concept	Percentage Rated Very Successful
Increased curriculum review	80	32
Expanded computer-generated feedback of information to staff	68	35
Crested or expanded systems to better gather "outcome" data	62	25
Expanded computer-generated feedback of information to faculty	61	32
Increased emphasis on formal staff evaluation procedures for administrators	54	20
Increased emphasis on formal staff evaluation procedures for tenured faculty	51	20
Increased emphasis on formal staff evaluation procedures for non-tenured faculty	50	24
Provided training programs to increase evaluation skills of staff	39	22
Expanded computer-generated feedback of information to students	31	41

The survey also found a decreased use of a number of Japanese management organizational concepts such as matrix management, quality circles, and job rotation, although the success of quality circles was rated higher than many other management concepts.

Incremental budgeting remains the primary budgeting technique, but program budgeting and zero-based budgeting had much higher ratings of success. Presidents also reported a growing interest in effective staff development, and the use of both full-time and part-time administrators to lead staff development programs is increasing.

The level of activity in research and evaluation of all kinds has significantly increased. Much of this activity is an outgrowth of the recent national reports that have been published in the past few years. Activity ranged from extensive curriculum review to outcome studies conducted by college staff or by outside agencies. A final trend is the increased emphasis and effort to use data to provide feedback to faculty, staff, and students. Major problems cited by the presidents present a disturbing picture of management at many community colleges. Many of the colleges were characterized as having serious problems of inadequate resources and an overevaluation by both internal and external evaluators. Tension caused by these problems have led to a decline in staff morale, administrator and faculty burn-out, and a general unpleasantness in many faculty-administration relationships.

There will be no simple management fix for the issues facing community colleges in the 1990s. While management on an individual campus remains an art, it is hoped this review of the use and impact of management concepts used at community colleges, and the discussion of issues and problems cited by community college presidents, will present a useful perspective on current management and a focus for analysis and change as community college leaders consider management concepts for the decade ahead.

What We Know About Women in Community Colleges

SUSAN B. TWOMBLY

Introduction

A majority of all community college students are women, and approximately 60 percent of its part-time students are women. In fact, much of the growth in community college enrollments can be attributed to increased participation by women[63]. There have been parallel gains in the share of administrative and faculty positions held by women[3, 28, 43]. In 1987 there were 101 female two-year college presidents, more than double the number of women presidents in 1975[3]. These gains are significant, and compared to most other types of postsecondary institutions, community colleges appear to be hospitable to women at all levels. However, historian Barbara Solomon [55] cautions that equity in numbers has not assured equality for women in higher education, and community colleges would appear to be no exception. Billie Dziech [18] writes, "In reality, the story of women in 'the people's college' is an account of success and failure, of hope and despair" [18, p. 55]. She goes on to say, "The statistics [on the percentage of administrative positions held by women] remind women staff that although on the surface the community college has been a good place for them, it has not always been good enough. Not good enough to recruit them, pay them, promote them, or tenure them equitably. . . . Not good enough to challenge academic traditions and build an environment in which men and women can work as equals" (p. 61).

The ambivalence of the community college attitude toward women is dramatically demonstrated by two pieces of writing, published more than ten years apart. In the mid-1970s the editors of the *Junior College Journal* created a fictitious author, C. M. Pegg, who wrote a supposedly satirical piece about the progress of women in community colleges [45]. Pegg, a "modern man," rails against the recently formed American Association of Women in Community and Junior Colleges and affirmative action legislation; community colleges have done quite well without Washington's help he insists. Further, he warns against the dangers of women advancing into places for which their temperament is not suited, namely administration. The reader is left to ponder just what the editors were intending to satirize: Pegg's attitudes or women's concerns.

This "fictitious" article can be dismissed relatively easily as being time-bound or light-hearted, but the second is not so easily ignored. In his most recent book on the community college presidency, Vaughan [61] includes a chapter entitled "Women Who Are Presidents" in an attempt to compensate for the fact that most treatises on the college presidency are written as if all presidents were men. And this chapter makes an important contribution. However, while discussing the search process, Vaughan makes a very revealing statement. He says, "Although women encounter certain difficulties that men do not when seeking the presidency, to assume that being female caused failure to be selected for a given presidency is to greatly oversimplify the presidential selection process. . . . Trustees are obligated to determine the right fit, or chemistry for a college at a particular time and location. There are some cases when the right fit requires a white male president and other cases when it requires a female president" (p. 76). He makes a similar statement about minority presidents. So while lamenting the difficulties faced by women (and minorities), he, perhaps unintentionally, reinforces stereotypes that certain characteristics and skills needed in the presidency are primarily associated with one's sex. If the situation for women in community colleges had really changed, Vaughan might have written instead that certain attributes are required for the community college presidency in the 1990s and that these can be found in either men or women of any racial or ethnic background.

These two examples reinforce ambivalence toward women faculty and administrators in community colleges; however, the same ambivalence is also evident toward students. Gittell [26] notes that it is in the area of the curriculum that community colleges do the most damage to women students. This is borne out by recent studies that show continued gender stereotyping in community college occupational programs [15, 39, 40]. Furthermore, entrance to a community college is frequently reported to reduce one's chances of completing a bachelor's degree for those who aspire to such a level [for example, 7, 12]. This effect may be of particular importance for women, who by virtue of their numbers, may stand to gain or lose the most by participation in community colleges.

In light of the increasing importance of the community college, especially for women, the economically disadvantaged, and minorities, it is critical to understand how these constituencies are conceptualized within the context of this specific educational setting. The purpose of this study is to examine two decades of community college research on women as one means of identifying how women have been conceptualized in this important segment of higher education. In focusing on the community college literature on women, this study shares Boxer's [in 5] belief in the importance of changing what is studied and known about women and the potential for changing women's and men's lives. This line of thinking is based on the belief that knowledge—for Boxer, women's studies; for this study, the published literature—directly or indirectly affects women's lived experience and the possibilities for changing existing patterns of gender relations. Elizabeth Minnich [38] and Cynthia Epstein [21] both emphasize this point from somewhat different perspectives. Minnich employs a philosopher's keen sense of argument to "dissect the errors underlying patriarchal thought" [38, p. 10]. Transforming knowledge, according to Minnich, involves changing what and how we think and leads us "to begin to change who and how we are in the world we share" (p. 80). The world will not change, she notes, because a few people change their minds, "but it is also true that unless we change our minds as well as our actions and our institutions, no lasting transformation will be possible" (p. 2). Thinking about thinking, examining familiar concepts—even feminist discourse—with new insights are key to the transformative process. Minnich emphasizes that changing the liberal arts curriculum, her main concern, is not enough to bring about transformation: "The conceptual blocks to the comprehension and full inclusion of women that we find in familiar scholarly theories and arguments, as in their institutional expressions in organizations and systems, political and economic and legal, are at root the same blocks that are to be found within the curriculum" (p. 12). In short, uncovering institutional conceptualizations and knowledge about women is essential to transforming those conceptualizations and ultimately women's and men's lives.

Epstein [21], from the perspective of a social scientist, shares at least some of Minnich conclusions. After reviewing results of literally hundreds of studies undertaken in recent decades in a wide range of fields, Epstein concludes, "The overwhelming evidence created by the past decade of research on gender supports the theory that gender differentiation—as distinct, of course, from sexual differentiation—is best explained as a social construction rooted in hierarchy, not in biology or in internalization, either through early experiences, as described by psychoanalysts, or through socialization, as described by psychologists and sociologists" (p. 15). She bases this conclusion on the fact that hundreds of studies have either found no or few gender differences, and for every study that does there seem to be others that report contradictory findings. Despite all of this seemingly contradictory evidence, research findings are often used to maintain the division of the world by sex. Epstein says, "The studies. . . bring to light the processes by which the powerful contrive to create, emphasize, and maintain gender differences. From the knowledge generated by such research we can expect the realities of men's and women's lives to emerge, superseding the stereotyped perceptions of the past. Although people manage reality and make imagined things real, scholars and activists are discovering a non-dichotomous reality that may one day put an end to the self-fulfilling prophecy of differences between men and women" (p. 240). In undertaking this study, I made the assumption that institutional conceptualizations of women are in part created and maintained through the appropriate scholarly literature. This scholarly literature both constitutes our knowledge, reflecting values and biases, and contributes in turn to social constructions of gender and what and how we think about gender. For these reasons the literature merits close investigation. This particular study used the literature published during the last two decades as one means of obtaining insight into the dominant modes of thinking about women in community colleges.[1] Feminist phase theory, a scheme for classifying evolution in thought about women in traditional disciplines and the college curriculum, provided the basis for examining the ways in which women have been conceptualized in the community college literature.

Study Objectives

More specifically, this study employed a review of the published scholarship on sex/gender[2] in two-year colleges published between 1970 and 1989 to: (1) provide general descriptive information: number of articles, nature of articles (for example, research study, program description), sex of authors, trends in topics, which groups of women are the focus of studies, trends in research methods, and types of journals; and most importantly to (2) identify phases in thinking about women in community colleges and whether there have been changes in thinking over time; (3) assess the utility of feminist phase theory for evaluating thinking about women in community colleges. The findings of the study are presented in four sections: First, the data source and method of analysis are described. Second, general descriptive information on the literature is presented. This analysis is important in setting the context for the second part of the article. Phase theory is presented in the third section, and the community college literature is analyzed according to the various stages of phase theory. Finally, conclusions and implications of the findings are discussed.

Literature Source and Method of Analysis

Literature published in education and social science journals from 1971 to March 1989 that identified women/gender in community/two-year colleges as a major or minor descriptor was reviewed for this study. The *Educational Research Information Clearinghouse* (ERIC) citation retrieval system was used to identify relevant journal articles published during the period in question. The following descriptors were used in conjunction with the descriptor two-year/community colleges to identify articles: women, females, sex, women's education, sex differences, women faculty, sex stereotypes, sex discrimination, feminism, women's studies, women administrators and female students. A few additional articles were located through Social Sciences Citation Index.

A cautionary note. Published literature is just one measure of thinking about women (or any other topic) in community colleges. As Minnich [38] says, "Books and articles are by no means the only or even the primary sources of ideas that change us" (p. xiii). There is also a large body of unpublished materials on women available through Resources in Education (RIE). Published literature was chosen as the medium of choice for this article for several reasons: it potentially creates and mirrors its field [52], has gone through some form of editorial or peer review process, and is also more public. Unless information on a specific topic is needed, RIE materials are not as accessible as articles in regularly read journals despite the fact that they probably represent a broader spectrum of information. And finally, the published literature was of manageable size. In the future, it would be revealing to compare the findings reported here with a similar review of information contained in RIE, because one of the strengths of published articles is also a potential weakness: publishing involves gatekeepers—either editors or reviewers—who have power to reject or accept an article and shape it in certain ways. Unfortunately, merit is not always the major factor in determining what and who gets published [38]. The implications for this article are that "mainstream" viewpoints might be overrepresented and "radical" viewpoints underrepresented. Finally, stages of thinking about women as revealed in the literature do not necessarily reflect the everyday lives of women at any one community college today.

The findings of the study are reported in two sections. First the literature is described according to authorship, type of journal, years of publication, groups of women, and type of article. This discussion is important for creating a context for the subsequent analysis and discussion of feminist phase theories as applied to the community college literature. The method for categorizing articles for each research task is reported in the appropriate section.

Description of the Literature

One hundred and seventy-four articles were identified between 1970 and 1989 that used descriptors of two-year/community colleges and the sex/gender related descriptors identified earlier. Articles were analyzed and coded to provide descriptive information such as journal, year of publication, type of article, group of women, author, and sex of author. For some of the articles unavailable through local libraries or interlibrary loan, it was possible to identify basic descriptive data from the ERIC abstract. However, no attempt was made to make judgments about phases in thinking about women in these cases.

Author. One hundred and eleven of the identified articles (64 percent) were first-authored by women while men were first authors of the remaining 63 (36 percent). For those individuals interested in the relationship between sex and publication rates, it should be noted that 84 (75.3 percent) of women-first-authored articles had a single author, whereas 44 (69 percent) of the male first authors wrote by themselves. When women collaborated with others (27) they tended to write with both women (16 or 59.3 percent) and men (11 or 40.7 percent). The 19 men who collaborated with others were more likely to collaborate with other men (15 to 79 percent). Overall, a substantial proportion of the writing about sex or gender in community colleges is by women. These results substantiate other research on the relationship between gender and publication: women are more likely than men to write alone, whereas men are likely to collaborate, and when they do so it is with other men [for example, 8, 41]. Whether it is isolation or choice which results in women writing alone cannot be determined from this study.

Because research and scholarship tend not to be a determinant of promotion, tenure, or merit salary increases in community colleges, there is little attention to authorship issues among community college writers. Given differences between faculty expectations and interests, existing research on this topic based on four-year college and university faculty may be of limited value in explaining publication trends in community colleges. However, the concerns about authorship extend not only to the relationship between publication and promotion, tenure, and salary increases but to issues of who does the writing and what topics and perspectives are evidenced in the literature. In a recent article Amey and Twombly [4] suggested that more attention needs to be paid to who does the writing about leadership because of the specific images communicated through the literature and of the potential of these images to be exclusionary. The same can be said for the scholarship on women.

One tentative conclusion to be drawn from the percentages reported above is that women participate fully in creating the scholarship about women in community colleges. Whether these writers pursue feminist agendas is the question to which the present study is addressed. What we do not know from this study is what proportion of the total writing on community colleges is by women or whether women authors are disproportionately represented in writing about women compared with other topics. That is, do women in this sector tend to write predominantly about women and not about other topics such as governance or curriculum?

Type of journal. Nearly two-thirds of the articles (113, or 64.9 percent) used in this study appeared in community college journals including *Community, Junior and Technical College Journal, Community College Frontiers, Community College Review, Community/Junior College Quarterly of Research and Practice, New Directions for Community Colleges,* and *The Journal of the American Association of Women in Community and Junior Colleges.* Another 24 percent were found in other education journals such as the *Journal of College Student Personnel* and *Initiatives: Journal of NAWDAC.* Only 12 articles were published in psychological or sociological journals. On the one hand this pattern is expected, but it has both positive and negative implications. When gender issues in community and junior colleges are being studied, they are reported in appropriate outlets where those most likely to benefit will have access to them. However, many of the articles published in the mainstream community college journals, such as *Community, Junior and Technical College Journal, New Directions for Community Colleges,* and *Community College Frontiers,* were program descriptions. The research-oriented journals, such as *Community College Review* and *Community/Junior College Quarterly of Research and Practice,* tended to publish studies in which women and men were compared on some variable(s). Occasionally *Initiatives* and primarily the *Journal of the American Association of Women in Community and Junior Colleges* publish articles that call into question the ways in which gender is studied and constructed in community colleges and argue for changes in the very structures of the organizations themselves. The danger is that unless one reads these different types of journals, any one reader may not be exposed to different phases of thinking. On the "down side," despite their social consequences, articles on two-year colleges appear relatively infrequently in "mainstream" disciplinary journals.

Publication dates. As indicated earlier, this study involved articles published between 1970, the generally recognized beginning of the most recent feminist movement, and 1989. Slightly fewer than one-half of the identified articles (83 or 47.7 percent) were published between the years 1970 and 1979. To gain a sense of continued emphasis on women's issues, the decade of the 80s was divided into two periods: 1980–84 and 1985 to the present. Sixty-eight articles or 39 percent of the total were published between 1980 and 1984. Only 19 percent of the total, or 33 articles were published since 1985, suggesting that interest in the issue has waned, that the topic is no longer important in the eyes of reviewers or editors, or that "problems" or special needs no longer exist. The recent indexing of *The Journal of the American Association of Women in Community and Junior Colleges*[3] added substantially to the number of articles published since 1985. This journal is currently only available to members of the association and is held by few libraries.

Subjects: What group of women. Students were the focus of the vast majority of the articles—116 or 66 percent.[4] Administrators have drawn much less attention and were the subject of 18.4 percent (32) of the articles while only 6 percent (11) were primarily about faculty. The remainder focused on all women, trustees, classified employees, the college environment, curriculum, and other issues. Five articles were not classifiable. There were only a half-dozen or so articles that dealt in any substantial way with race or ethnicity of students. Clearly, studies or articles that focus on issues of gender in the administrative or faculty ranks are vastly underrepresented in the literature. This is particularly troublesome because 38 percent of two-year college faculty are women; a substantially larger proportion than of any type of four-year institution (liberal arts colleges have the highest percent of women faculty—29 percent) [60]. Relatively speaking, community college faculty do not seem to study and write about themselves to the same extent as women administrators in community colleges or faculty in the four-year sector do. The relatively high percentage of women faculty members in two-year colleges provides opportunity for a wide range of research topics, but to date the women of the two-year college faculty have been largely ignored.

One can only speculate why there are so few articles that deal comprehensively with gender, race, ethnicity, and class. One possible explanation is that feminist scholars have only recently recognized their error in focusing on predominantly white middle-class women to the exclusion of women of color and different social classes. As higher education is dependent on traditional disciplines for many of its theories and concepts, one might expect a lag before the community college literature will reflect attention to issues of race, ethnicity, and class. A second explanation is that in the absence of any profile of who does the writing on community colleges, it is not known to what extent members of minority groups are represented among the writers. It is reasonable to hypothesize that there were few minorities who, until recently, have been in positions to contribute to the community college literature; and because minority women may face a double set of barriers, it is even less likely that minority women have had the luxury of engaging in scholarly work by writing about their own experiences or bringing their perspectives to bear on other ethnic groups or social classes. Assuming that much writing on community colleges is by college faculty and administrators for whom scholarship is not a job responsibility or criterion for rewards, it is to be expected that few would have the time to engage in the sophisticated research necessary to capture the relationship of race, class, and gender in community colleges. On the other hand, the lack of focus on class, ethnicity, and race in a sector of higher education that serves so many women and members of minority groups is inexcusable.

Type of article. Three major types of articles emerged. The first and most prevalent type was "research." Any article that was based on a systematic collection and analysis of data was classified as research. The methods employed in these articles include quasi-experimental design, survey, literature review, and to a lesser extent, case study, ethnography, and other forms of qualitative research. Approximately one out of every two classifiable articles was based on research (93, or 51.5 percent). "Program description" emerged as the second most frequent type of article, comprising 21.9 percent (37) of the 169 classifiable articles. The authors of these articles typically described a support or remedial program or a special effort to attract women into non-traditional occupational curricula. There were many fewer descriptions of women's studies curricula. Seldom did these descriptions include more than one program or college. The third type of article was labeled "opinion." These 28 (16.5 percent) articles included personal reflection, opinions, and development of a position on some topic related to sex/gender issues. An "other" category captured 16 articles that did not fit in the three major categories and did not have enough representatives to constitute a separate category. For example, four bibliographies are included in this category.

There were no great variations in type of articles that were most common for different groups of women. The majority of articles for students, faculty, and administrators were research based. One-quarter of the articles on students were descriptions of programs, and, as indicated earlier, most program descriptions were of the support-remedial type.

Feminist Phase Theory Applied to the Community College Literature

The framework used to analyze the community college literature on gender was derived from Tetreault's [58] phases of feminist scholarship. The notion of feminist phase theory has emerged during the past fifteen years as a "classification scheme of evolution in thought about the incorporation of women's traditions, history, and experiences into selected disciplines" [58, p. 364].

Tetreault and other feminist scholars [Lerner in 5, 37, 51, 63] proposed phase theories for assessing the ways and degrees to which women were conceptualized and incorporated in undergraduate curricula and in the disciplines themselves. Phase theories "provide a conceptual outline of transformations in our thinking about women" [5, p. 48]. Not intended to represent rankings or hierarchies, phase theories demonstrate how knowledge and curricula in some disciplines evolve from simply adding women to more fundamental reconstructions of concepts, methods, and theories [5]. Mary Kay Tetreault specifically proposed phase theory as a basis "to build an evaluation model sensitive enough to measure curricular change, cognitive learning in women's studies, and changes in how faculty conceptualize including women in their courses and research" [58, p. 364]. The model explicated by Tetreault provides a potentially useful framework to analyze thinking about women in higher education more generally and specifically in institutions such as community colleges. The phase theories of McIntosh [37], Schuster and Van Dyne [51], and Warren [63] were also helpful in order to reflect stages in thinking about women in community colleges more accurately. The characteristics of the stages described below were used to categorize each of the articles. In some cases, articles reflected ideas of more than one phase.

Tetreault [58] argues that there are five phases of thinking about women commonly reflected in scholarship: (1) male scholarship, (2) compensatory scholarship, (3) bifocal scholarship, (4) feminist scholarship, and (5) multifocal or relational scholarship. These phases are described more fully below in relation to the literature. However, in labeling the various phases as they do, phase theorists risk suggesting that earlier scholarship, such as compensatory, was not feminist, when in fact, authors of biographies of famous or lesser-known women or investigators who compared the careers of male and female administrators would most certainly argue that their work was done in the feminist tradition. In short, the feminist agenda has many equally valuable foci and the value of application of phase theories is that it permits these varying perspectives to come to the fore. Yet another concern about feminist phase theory is that it tends to view disciplines on which the theories were based as homogeneous and to overlook the interdisciplinary nature of much of feminist scholarship.

In order to determine the stage or phase of feminist thinking reflected in community college literature, a coding scheme based on Tetreault's [58] phase theory was developed to guide the content analysis of the literature. This process is described more fully in conjunction with the subsequent analysis. For this study, the primary focus of each article determined its resulting category. For example, a study whose primary objective was to compare men and women on some variable such as mathematics performance was determined to be an example of bifocal scholarship. A study or article that counted women administrators or described those who have become college presidents was categorized as representative of compensatory scholarship. A study that focused on understanding women's experiences in two-year colleges was considered to be an example of feminist scholarship. Feminist phase theory and the resulting coding process are discussed more fully below. Although this study sought to apply feminist phase theory to the literature on community college women, it also sought to evaluate the applicability of feminist phase theory as it has been applied in traditional disciplines to a more heterogeneous literature stemming not from a disciplinary but from an institutional orientation. Consequently an inductive approach was also taken in which the characteristics of the literature were used to expand interpretations of the various phases. The present study may help to validate the utility of feminist phase theory for future use.

Feminist Phases in the Community College Literature

The first phase described by Tetreault is *male* or *womanless*. In this phase the male experience is assumed to be universal and the absence of women is not noted. Furthermore, knowledge about the male experience is unquestioned. For example, authors who write about community college presidents often note the small percentage of presidents who are women, and these authors then go on to discuss their findings as if all the presidents were men. As expected, because of selecting literature with gender or female as a basis, there were few male or womanless articles in this study.

The second phase in Tetreault's scheme is *compensatory* scholarship. This stage has variously been labeled "women in" [37], "search for missing women" [51], or "women worthies" [Lerner in 5]. Literature representative of this phase seeks to overcome the lack of attention to women by identifying outstanding or great women. The standard by which "women worthies" are judged is that of great men. However, as Tetreault notes, "When women present different descriptions and explanations of the world, it is seen not as a problem of theory but as a problem of women's development or of women's inferiority" [58, p. 373]. This type of literature was particularly prevalent about women administrators in community colleges, although the focus was somewhat different than in a discipline such as history. In fact, there were two types of compensatory articles identified in the community college literature. First there was literature that identified and described "women who had made it" to top level positions. For example, Pfiffner [47] provides a profile of the characteristics of women who were successful in attaining presidencies rather than stories of specific individuals. The purpose of these articles was in some cases to celebrate specific lives. Smith and West's [54] biographical sketch of Charlotte Hawkins Brown, founder of Palmer Institute, home to a short-lived junior college program fit this pattern. In other cases, successful women administrators were profiled in order to determine their characteristics in relation to successful male administrators [for example, 13].

A second form of compensatory scholarship emerged in this body of literature: that of counting women, or census-taking. For example Hankin's [28] article on affirmative action counted women to determine what proportion of faculty and administrative posts were held by women. In another example, the American Association of Community and Junior Colleges [1] reported on the status of women in occupational education programs. Women were counted and their numbers noted in order to track the movement of women into positions, but the implications of their numbers were typically not discussed (except, in this case, as an indication of whether affirmative action was working). This type of article sought to compensate for lack of attention to women by noting their prevalence (or lack thereof) in important positions or in certain academic programs. One might also argue that because these articles often noted the absence of women (oppression) in important positions that they were also examples of the next stage reinforcing the transitional nature of scholarship and resulting difficulties in placing some scholarship in only one category. On the whole, compensatory scholarship accepted male standards as universal. When women differ from men, the differences are translated as deficiencies. In one example, Edsall [19] determined that over half of all community college librarians were women and that only one-third of library directors were women. The data were then discussed as if sex or gender did not matter.

Of the total 148 classifiable articles, one in four (37, or 25 percent) fit the compensatory phase. Some of these articles also fit other phases as well. For example, the Edsall article just mentioned also might be considered male in focus because sex or gender differences in librarians are not discussed. Paul et al. [44] noted the number of male and female administrators in Massachusetts' community colleges and then compared them on a variety of personal and educational characteristics—an example of an article that fits both compensatory and bifocal thinking.

The *bifocal* phase proved most problematic for this analysis because it, as explicated by Tetreault, seemingly encompasses two different foci. For this reason the thinking and terminology employed by other phase theorists were helpful. Tetreault argues that "three factors are common to thinking about women at phase three, bifocal scholarship" [58, p. 373]. One of these factors is the conceptualization of men and women as separate, equal, and complementary sexes. For example, scholarship of this type views women and men as having separate spheres, different ways of knowing and making moral judgments, different developmental paths, and different values.

Women's ways are not better or worse than men's—just different. Another example of this aspect of bifocal scholarship which might be found in psychology, according to Tetreault, asks how the nature and significance of women's achievement motivation differs from men's. The objective of this type of scholarship is to overcome women's previous status as deficient to men's by providing equally valued alternative models or paradigms. Unfortunately, representative scholarship of this type tends to view women as a homogeneous group having universally different characteristics from men. As a result women are often treated as a homogeneous group and differences are overlooked and new stereotypes emerge to replace the old ones. Although the objective of this stage is to suggest that women's lives provide an alternative "paradigm" and to illuminate that paradigm for all to see, Tetreault notes a resulting "tendency to slip back into thinking of women as inferior and subordinate" [58, p. 373].

In the community college literature the three foci of the bifocal phase manifested themselves in two particularly distinct types of literature: comparisons of men and women and descriptions of remedial programs designed to prepare women to compete with men. It was relatively easy to identify literature, particularly research, that seemed on the surface at least to conceptualize men and women as separate sexes. These articles generally compared men and women or used sex as an independent variable, implying as Epstein [21] says, that men and women have specific biologically defined characteristics and attributes that matter. Examples of this type of literature include an examination of the cognitive differences between male and female administrators [17], differences between men and women on mathematics competencies [56], comparison of women's and men's learning styles [11], and career self-efficacy [50]. Articles written in this vein, especially those based on research, did not in *any* case critique the theoretical models guiding research or the inventories or scales used in data collection for their appropriateness to populations of women. On the one hand these articles represent bifocal scholarship because they sought to compare men and women, theoretically viewing men and women as separate but equal. However, the use of resulting comparisons varied greatly as will be discussed below.

A second emphasis in literature of this phase, according to Tetreault, is the oppression of women and the different forms oppression takes including explorations of sexism, discrimination, and other factors resulting in disadvantage for women. The third theme found at this stage is attention to women's efforts to overcome oppression. McIntosh [37] and Schuster and Van Dyne [51] conceptualize stage three in feminist thinking as "women as a problem" or "women as a subordinate group," respectively. Schuster and Van Dyne [51] explain this stage as arising from the often frustrating search for "missing women." For example, questions become focused on why so few women enroll in non-traditional programs or hold administrative positions. Many articles in this study fit this later category. Most of the articles classified as fitting this aspect of bifocal scholarship described programs to overcome deficiencies or disadvantages in women such as women's exclusion from leadership positions (women's oppression) attributable to a variety of factors. For example, Foulkes and Taines' [24] "Teaching Composition to Re-Entry Women" describes a program that seeks to develop skills so that women can compete. Smith's [53] attempt to combat "The Cinderella Syndrome" in order to "educate women for today's world" is another example of an article reporting efforts to overcome women's deficiencies in order that they may compete in "today's world" (read male). In other examples, Taylor [57] and Jones [33] describe programs that exist to help potential administrators to overcome skill deficiencies and to develop networks as part of an overall strategy to help women to obtain top-level administrative posts. Tuckman and Tuckman [59] examined sex-discrimination among part-time faculty. Brown-Turner [14] reported on efforts to knock down barriers to employment for women once they have completed community college programs.

Authors who view men and women as equal, complementary groups seek to overcome women's perceived deficiency according to male standards by demonstrating that women have their own sphere and make their own important contributions, albeit different ones from men.

Others focus on women as an oppressed group and how that oppression can be overcome. In the community college literature these emphases were represented by two types of articles: (1) articles in which sex was used as an independent variable or in which men and women were compared on some identified variable(s), and (2) articles that recognized women's unequal status and recommended strategies for overcoming this status. Generally speaking no attempt was made by authors of the first type of articles to suggest different or separate spheres for women. In the strictest interpretation of Tetreault's phases, some might argue these articles more appropriately fit the compensatory stage because their authors were attempting to account for women, to see if they differed from men. However, it was clear that at least some of the authors were genuinely concerned about identifying differences between women and men. And it is perhaps best to view these articles as indicative of the transitional nature of scholarship and the inability of any classification scheme to take account of this variation. As for the second type of article, the goal of most remedial programs was to prepare women to compete adequately according to male standards of success.

Out of 158 articles in which phase was classifiable, 93 (58.9 percent) fit one of these types and thus were considered to represent bifocal thinking. A finer-grained analysis suggests that approximately one-half compared men and women or implied comparison by using sex as an independent variable, and one-half fit the second type.

An interesting contradiction emerged in the bifocal literature. First, many authors used (abused?) sex as a convenient independent or control variable, but then did not report findings of their studies by sex. In fact, few of the research articles that used sex as a control variable had any theoretical reason to believe that there might be differences between women and men on the variables of interest. Neither were researchers interested in identifying women's separate sphere. Second, many of the studies that looked at sex differences found *no* or few significant differences between men and women. In fact, Beckerman and Fontana [10] almost apologize for finding no differences in aspirations of men and women business students. Actually, the lack of substantial sex differences in many of these studies supports Epstein's [21] recent argument that social construction of gender roles is a far more influential factor in "creating" reported differences between women and men than real biological or psychological differences. Herein lies the contradiction: despite the lack of evidence of significant sex differences, dozens of remedial programs for women have been organized around assumed differences (interpreted deficiencies). Only one of the articles about re-entry students even acknowledged that men might have similar problems returning to school as do women. The literature leaves the reader feeling that it is one's gender that makes re-entry difficult, not going back to school. Of the authors who write about "remedial" programs for potential administrators Adickes [2] and more recently Ravekes and Cross [49] are among the few to ask whether women *have* to manage like men.

Tetreault and other stage theorists agree that the next stage is *feminist* thinking or "women as" [37] "women studied on their own terms" [51]. In this stage, women's experiences are valued in and of themselves and women's activities are the focus of attention. Feminist authors ask questions such as, "what are women's experiences?," and importantly "what are the historical and cultural contexts of these experiences?" Furthermore, recent feminist literature recognizes diversity of women by race/ethnicity, sexual orientation, and class. Answers to these questions provide the basis for new frameworks that accommodate women's history and traditions. Weis's [64] article "Without Dependence on Welfare for Life: Black Women in the Community College" is an excellent example of feminist thinking. Weis explores the reasons why black urban women attended community college and seeks to understand what they expect to gain from the experience. Weis was concerned with how the urban context and racial background of the women in her study affected their experiences. As another excellent representative of this stage, Moore [41] examined the ways in which women are "cooled out" of occupational programs. Seventeen percent or a total of 26 articles out of 158 classifiable articles were primarily feminist in orientation. It must be noted that articles classified as either compensatory or bifocal often had a feminist flavor. Many of the "remedial" programs discussed earlier as representative of bifocal scholarship were about women's experiences, and as such they too were feminist, although not representing the ideal of this stage.

Stage 5 is variously described as multifocal [58], (a discipline) redefined or relational. Defining characteristics of this stage include a focus on how men and women relate to each other and conceptualizations of human experience as a continuum rather than in dualistic male and female terms. McIntosh [37] notes that this stage is difficult to describe fully because it is so unrealized. Warren [63] argues that the gendered phase (here equivalent to Tetreault's multifocal stage) will not be reached until an equivalent to the feminist stage is developed in which the variety of men's experiences are explored as experienced by men. Only when knowledge of both men's and women's experiences exists can truly inclusive knowledge and practice be achieved. Only a few of the articles included in this study came close to fitting the ideal of the multifocal phase. For example, Averill [9] suggests that the community college curriculum can be made more fully human through the contributions of women. Harper's [29] interview with Peter Pelham, president of a two-year college for women, provides a vision of how a college that truly responds to women can be very different from the traditional college.

In summary, and as noted in table 1, the major focus on women, sex, and gender in community colleges has been bifocal in nature. It has sought to compare women and men or to describe programs and activities designed to help women overcome their unequal status. Few studies have identified and described "women worthies," taken censuses, or examined women's experiences in and of themselves. Very few of the authors challenged the status quo in any serious way. Sadly, only Harper's [29] description of the unique contributions of a two-year college for women provides clues to a vision of how community colleges might be different kinds of organizations that are inclusive or relational as suggested by Warren [63].

Changes in Thinking About Women Over Time

The phase theories used in this study imply progression and evolution in thought even though hierarchy or ranking is not intended. Consequently, we can ask whether feminist thinking has been more highly represented in recent years and, conversely, whether compensatory is more representative of earlier years? An analysis of phases by three time periods is presented in table 1. The somewhat surprising finding from this analysis is that feminist literature is more prevalent in the literature of the 1970s than of 1980s. Since 1980 only 11 percent of the 91 identified articles had a feminist orientation, and the only reason the proportion exceeds 10 percent is because of articles concentrated in the *Journal of the American Association of Women in Community and Junior Colleges*. So, while the total number of articles having sex or gender as a descriptor published during each decade is approximately the same, the percentage having a feminist perspective declined in the 80s. If phase theories generally are intended to represent progression in thinking about women, such is not the case in the literature on women in the community college. When the 80s are further divided into two time periods, we note an overall decline in the number of articles published on the topic, but a slight increase in percentage of feminist articles among the 1985 to present group. Perhaps this slight increase signals a new trend; however, much of the increase can be attributed to recent issues of the *AAWCJC Journal*.

Table 1
Phases in Thinking about Community College Women by Time Period

	Year			
Phase	1970–79	1980–84	1985–present	Total
		—percent (number)—		
Bifocal	48.2 (40)	60.3 (35)	54.5 (18)	53.4 (93)
Compensatory	22.9 (19)	22.8 (13)	15.2 (5)	21.3 (37)
Feminist	19.3 (16)	5.3 (3)		21.2 (7)
Male	1.2 (1)			6.0 (1)
Multifocal		1.8 (1)		0.6 (1)
Not Classifiable	8.4 (7)	10.5 (6)	9.1 (3)	9.2 (16)
Total	100 (83)	100 (58)	100 (33)	174
	50.6	35.4	14.0	100

Conclusion

This review strongly suggests that thinking about women in the community colleges has largely been compensatory and bifocal and only to a lesser extent feminist thinking, in which women's experiences are valued in their own right. Neither has thinking about women changed much during the nearly twenty years encompassed by this study. Researchers have counted women, developed profiles, compared women and men on various characteristics, and to a much lesser extent, written about "women worthies." This is necessary scholarship. It helps to define and locate problems (of numbers at least), to describe the characteristics of leaders, and to point out gaps in information. For example, little is known about the lives of heroines in the community college movement. Who were they? In the early years of the junior college movement, the dean of women was viewed as the second most important administrator in these new colleges [23]. Who were the women who held these positions? What role did they play in their institutions and in the lives of their students, and what influence did they have in shaping the ideas that would become the modern comprehensive community colleges? At present only the "fathers" of the community college movement are known. The value of counting and profiling has its limits in bringing about change, because neither method typically questions male-defined norms or proposes new ways of thinking about the organizations in which women work and study.

As interpreted for this study, a bifocal approach to women in community colleges was most common in the literature. Men and women students have been compared on such diverse variables as mathematics abilities, aspirations, learning styles, and career-related characteristics. Sex has been used as an independent variable frequently without apparent reason or subsequent analysis, only to learn that there were relatively few significant differences between men and women on variables tested. The other aspect of the bifocal phase, women (usually students and to a lesser extent administrators and faculty) as a subordinate group in need of special services, programs and remediation, was equally common in the literature. This is not to say that the programs themselves and their published descriptions do not serve a real and important need.

There are, however, at least three problems with this concentration on bifocal thinking in the research and writing about women. First, overemphasis on women's oppression tends to portray women as passive respondents to a sexist society—as victims. This results in reinforcing sex stereotypes and does not help women to move beyond their own oppression [58]. This is evidenced in the community college's propensity to develop "special" programs for women—a group in need of help. Second, although recent authors such as Ravekes and Cross [49] suggest a separate and unique approach to leadership for women administrators based on the work of Gilligan, little community college literature takes this road. The identified bifocal literature did not, for the most part, seek to create knowledge about men's and women's separate, complementary spheres in the community college. Much of the literature reporting efforts to overcome women's disadvantaged status through remediation results in negative stereotypes. Third, special programs, support groups, and other services offered as solutions to problems or difficulties posed by women are viewed as add-ons. Providing services and programs for special populations is a common mode of response for community colleges. One wonders whether programs still exist, whether they were (are) effective, whether they perpetuate the attitude that women are a "special group" that is not central to the function of the community college, and whether institutions have changed to accommodate the special needs of all who attend them. The other factor that became apparent was how little attention was given to the diversity of men or women, particularly diversity defined as "ethnicity, race, and class." The types of diversity most recognized were reentry versus traditional, remedial versus non-remedial, traditional occupations versus non-traditional; that is, diversity as defined by institutional categories.

Skill building and support groups provide necessary services for women. Women need skills, but this emphasis has been guided largely by an assumed objective (male) standard of excellence rather than a vision based on an understanding of the female experience. The small body of feminist thinking gives hope for the future, but more of this type of scholarship, as well as research on men's experiences, needs to be conducted. In particular, articles published recently by the *Journal of the American Association of Women in Community and Junior Colleges* and the work of the National Institute for Leadership Development's leadership training program give hope of better things to come. However, the journal has limited distribution, and the leadership training programs are predominantly based on a model of gender developed by Gilligan [29], and as such they risk creating stereotypes of women. In addition, these models tend to focus on individual development rather than on the organizational context of leadership.

Application of phases theories, as developed by Tetreault and others, to the literature on community college revealed a declining interest in topics of gender in general, and specifically in articles written from a feminist perspective. If, as feminist scholars suggest, thinking about women in a particular area progresses through various stages and the feminist stage represents a more "advanced" stage than either bifocal or compensatory, the literature reviewed for this study gives cause for concern. Not only has literature that uses sex or gender as a descriptor dropped off sharply in recent years, the percentage of articles written from a feminist perspective declined overall during the decade of the 1980s, even though it has increased slightly during the last five years, due largely to the impact of a single journal. Bifocal thinking, on the other hand, remains the dominant mode of thinking about women in this sector. Scholars are left to ponder (1) why the interest in sex/gender-related issues has dropped off, (2) why faculty in the community college have received so little scholarly attention, and (3) what the implications of a continued emphasis on the bifocal approach to women are.

In general, feminist phase theory proved to be a useful tool for examining the ways in which women have been conceptualized in the community college literature. However, as noted in the discussion, this literature suggested some modifications in phases. The major difficulty in classifying the community college literature occurred primarily at the compensatory and bifocal stages. Difficulties arose because articles often encompassed ideas of two or more stages at once, emphasizing the transitional nature of scholarship more appropriately captured by a horizontal continuum rather than discrete categories implied by phase theory. A second problem arises with Tetreault's attempt to include three foci in the bifocal stage. A better strategy might be to break the bifocal stage into two separate categories: recognition of and attempts to overcome oppression and development of separate, equal, and complementary spheres for women and men. Incorporating the recommendations of Warren [63] to include a male stage, the resulting theory might include seven phases: womanless, women worthies or compensatory, women's oppression, bifocal (separate spheres), feminist, male, gendered, or relational. Existing feminist phase theories did not deal very well with studies of which the objective was to compare women and men on some variable(s) but which did not extend analysis to portrayal of women and men as different but equal and complementary. Perhaps inability to fit this literature into existing phase theories points to a characteristic problem with the community college literature with respect to women—frequent comparison of men and women with seeming failure to develop conceptualizations of women and men as complementary groups, each with its own set of valued truths. Another problem seemingly ignored by phase theory is the assumed homogeneity of traditional disciplinary knowledge at all but the multifocal or relational phase. Traditional disciplines often reflect different, sometimes contradictory, theories and methods in addition to the fact that feminist research, even at compensatory and bifocal stages, has an interdisciplinary flavor.

As those who study higher education become more educated in what has become very sophisticated language of feminist theory we may hope for renewed interest in gender issues in the community college. In the 70s feminist researchers in higher education compared men and women. Many of these researchers recognized that in order to change the status quo, women had to gain access to positions of power. One way to accomplish this goal was to discover how their male counterparts and exemplary women did it. Unfortunately, having comparable knowledge and skills has not paved the way for great gains for women in community colleges. Biases are deeply ingrained, as Epstein [21] suggests, and as Vaughan [61] in his statement about presidential searches confirms. Moving beyond compensatory and bifocal conceptualizations to feminist and male and then to gendered perspectives that take into account women's and men's experiences on their own merit is necessary in order to create truly inclusive colleges for the future.

Notes

1. A decision was made by the author to make gender the main focus of this research. Although recent feminist scholars emphasize the necessity of noting women's differences as well as commonalities, ethnicity was included in this study only as it emerged in the literature having gender as a main focus. Unfortunately, there were few examples of such studies.

2. For the purposes of this article the terms sex and gender will be used in the following ways: sex refers to attributes created by biological differences, and gender refers to socially and culturally created differences between men and women [21].

3. The first appearance of this journal in ERIC is 1988. The whole volume and not individual articles are indexed.

4. Program descriptions were classified as being about students because of their primary focus on special needs for students. The exception was descriptions of programs for administrators and faculty members.

References

1. AACJC. "AACJC Study: Women in Occupational Education." *Community and Junior College Journal*, 47 (1977), 28–30.

2. Adickes, S. "Leadership Styles: Do Women Have to Act Like Men?" *Community College Frontiers*, 5 (1977), 12–15.

3. American Council on Education. *Fact Book on Higher Education.* New York: ACE/Macmillan, 1989.

4. Amey, M. J., and S. B. Twombly. "Re-visioning Leadership in Community Colleges." *Review of Higher Education,* 15 (1992), 125–50.

5. Andersen, M. "Changing the Curriculum in Higher Education." In *Reconstructing the Academy,* edited by E. Minnich, J. O'Barr, and R. Rosenfeld. Chicago: The University of Chicago Press, 1988. Originally published in *Signs,* 12 (1987).

6. Archer, J. A. "Developmental Mathematics: An Ex-Post Facto Study." *Community/Junior College Research Quarterly,* 3 (1978), 75–86.

7. Astin, A. *Four Critical Years.* San Francisco: Jossey-Bass, 1977.

8. Astin, H. "Factors Affecting Women's Scholarly Productivity." In *The Higher Education of Women: Essays in Honor of Rosemary Park,* edited by H. Astin and Werner Hirsch. New York: Praeger Publishers, 1978.

9. Averill, L. "How Can Women Influence Humanities Education." *New Directions for Community Colleges,* 9 (1981), 23–31.

10. Beckerman, A., and L. Fontana. "Perceptions and Aspirations of Community College Business Students: Does Gender Make a Difference?" *Community College Review,* 15 (1987), 51–58.

11. Brainard, S., and J. Ommen. "Men, Women and Learning Styles." *Community College Frontiers,* 5 (1977), 32–36.

12. Brint, S. and J. Karabel. *The Diverted Dream: Community Colleges and the Promise of Educational Opportunity in America, 1900–1985.* New York: Oxford University Press, 1989.

13. Brooks, G., and J. Avila. "A Profile of Student Personnel Workers in Junior and Community Colleges." *Journal of College Student Personnel,* 14 (1973), 532–36.

14. Brown-Turner, A. "Knocking Down the Barriers to Education and Employment for Women." *Community and Junior College Journal,* 51 (1981), 4–6.

15. Cohen, A., and F. Brawer. *The American Community College,* 2nd ed. San Francisco: Jossey-Bass, 1989.

16. Desjardins, C. "Gender Issues and Community College Leadership." *Journal of American Association of Women in Community and Junior Colleges* (1989), 5–10.

17. Doyle, R., and B. Mueller. "Cognitive Differences of Male and Female Administrators." *Journal of American Association of Women in Community and Junior Colleges* (1989), 17–19.

18. Dziech, B. W. "Changing Status of Women." In *Issues for Community Colleges Leaders in a New Era,* edited by George Vaughan. San Francisco: Jossey-Bass, 1983.

19. Edsall, S. "The Community College Librarian." *Community and Junior College Journal,* 46 (1976), 32–33.

20. Eells, W. C. *The Junior College.* Boston: Houghton Mifflin, 1931.

21. Epstein, C. *Deceptive Distinctions: Sex, Gender, and the Social Structure.* New Haven, Conn.: Yale University Press, and New York: Russell Sage Foundation, 1988.

22. Feurs, S. "Shortening the Odds." *Community and Junior College Journal,* 52 (1981), 6, 10–12.

23. _____. "The Pepperdine Conference: Women in Community College Administration." *Community and Junior College Journal*, 52 (1981), 8–9.

24. Foulkes, N., and B. Taines. "Teaching Composition to Re-Entry Students." *Community College Frontiers*, 6 (1978), 8–12.

25. Gilligan, C. *In a Different Voice: Psychological Theory and Women's Development.* Cambridge, Mass.: Harvard University Press, 1982.

26. Gittell, M. "A Place for Women?" *New Directions for Community Colleges*, 14 (1986), 71–79.

27. Glogowski, D., and W. Lanning. "The Relationships among Age, Category, Curriculum, Selected and Work Values for Women in a Community College." *Vocational Guidance Journal*, 25 (1976), 119–24.

28. Hankin, J. "Where the (Affirmative) Action Is: The Status of Minorities and Women Among Faculty and Administrators of Public Two-Year Colleges, 1983–84." *Journal of CUPA*, 35 (1984), 36–39.

29. Harper, W. "The 'Liberating' College: An Interview with Peter Pelham." *Community and Junior College Journal*, 46 (1976), 27–31.

30. Healy, C. et al. "Age and Grade Differences in Career Development among Community College Students." *Review of Higher Education*, 10 (1987), 247–58.

31. Hemming, R. "Women in Community College Administration: A Progress Report." *Journal of NAWDAC*, 46 (1982), 3–8.

32. Isenberg, J. "The Role of Collaboration in Scholarly Writing: A National Study." Paper presented at the annual meeting of the American Educational Research Association, Washington, D.C., 1987.

33. Jones, S. "Moving Up: Advancement Strategies for Women in Higher Education." *Journal of American Association of Women in Community and Junior Colleges* (1988), 3–6.

34. Kuznik, A. "Women in Agriculture in a Two-Year College." *Agricultural Education Magazine*, 47 (1975), 275–76.

35. Lerner, G. "To Think Ourselves Free." Review of *Transforming Knowledge* by Elizabeth Minnich. *Women's Review of Books*, 3 (October, 1990), 10–11.

36. McDonald, S. "A Writer's Workshop for Women: Its Pleasures and Its Problems." *Teaching English in the Two-Year College*, 7 (1981), 129–32.

37. McIntosh, P. "Interactive Phases of Curricular Re-Vision: A Feminist Perspective." Working Paper Series, no. 124. Wellesley, Mass.: Wellesley College Center for Research on Women, 1983.

38. Minnich, E. K. *Transforming Knowledge.* Philadelphia: Temple University Press, 1990.

39. Monk-Turner, E. "Sex, Educational Differentiation, and Occupational Status: Analyzing Occupational Differences for Community and Four-Year Entrants." *The Sociological Quarterly*, 24 (1983), 393–404.

40. _____. "Sex Differences in Type of First College Entered and Occupational Status: Changes Over Time." *Social Science Journal*, 22 (1985), 89–97.

41. Moore, K. M. "The Cooling Out of Two-Year College Women." *Personnel and Guidance Journal*, 53 (1975), 578–83.

42. Morgan, G. "Journals and the Control of Knowledge: A Critical Perspective." In *Publishing in the Organizational Sciences*, edited by L. L. Cummings and P. J. Frost. Homewood, Ill.: Richard D. Irwin, Inc., 1985.

43. Palmer, J. "Sources and Information: The Social Role of the Community College." *New Directions for Community Colleges*, 14 (1986), 101–13.

44. Paul, C., R. Sweet, and N. Brigham. "Personal, Educational, and Career Characteristics of Male and Female Community College Administrators in Massachusetts." *Journal of NAWDAC*, 44 (1980), 14–18.

45. Pegg, M. C. "A Modest Man's Proposal." *Community and Junior College Journal*, (December/January 1976), 11–13.

46. Perry-Miller, M. "Why, What and Where To? Title IX, Educational Amendment of 1972." *Community College Frontiers*, 5 (1977), 23–26.

47. Pfiffner, V. "Composite Profile of a Top-Level California Community College Woman Administrator." *Journal of NAWDAC*, 40 (1976), 16–17.

48. Price, R. "Women of the Faculty." *New Directions for Community Colleges*, 9 (1981), 13–21.

49. Ravekes, J., and C. Cross. "Leadership in a Different Voice." *Journal of American Association of Women in Community and Junior Colleges* (1990), 7–14.

50. Rotberg, H. et al. "Career Self-Efficacy Expectations and Perceived Range of Career Options in Community College Students." *Journal of Counseling Psychology*, 34 (1987), 164–70.

51. Schuster, M., and S. VanDyne (eds.). *Women's Place in the Academy: Transforming the Liberal Arts Curriculum.* Totowa, N.J.: Rowman & Allanheld, 1985.

52. Silverman, R. "How We Know What We Know." *Review of Higher Education*, 11 (1987), 39–59.

53. Smith, A. "Combating the Cinderella Syndrome: How to Educate Women for Today's World." *Community College Review*, 3 (1975), 6–13.

54. Smith, S., and E. West. "Charlotte Hawkins Brown." *Journal of Negro Education*, 51 (1982), 191–206.

55. Solomon, B. *In the Company of Educated Women.* New Haven: Yale University Press, 1985.

56. Stones, I. et al. "Sex-Related Differences in Mathematical Competencies of Pre-Calculus College Students." *School Science and Mathematics*, 82 (1982), 295–99.

57. Taylor, E. "Women Community College Presidents." *New Directions for Community Colleges*, 9 (1981), 1–12.

58. Tetreault, M. K. "Feminist Phase Theory." *Journal of Higher Education*, 56 (July/August 1976), 363–84.

59. Tuckman, B., and H. Tuckman. "Part-Timers, Sex Discrimination, and Career Choice at Two-Year Institutions: Further Findings from the AAUP Survey." *Academe: Bulletin of the AAUP*, 66 (1980), 71–76.

60. U.S. Department of Education. "Full-Time Regular Instructional Faculty in Institutions of Higher Education by Selected Characteristics and Type of Control of Institution: Fall 1987." *Digest of Education Statistics*, 1991.

61. Vaughan, G. *Leadership in Transition: The Community College Presidency.* New York: ACE/Macmillan, 1989.

62. Warren, J. "The Changing Characteristics of Community College Students." In *Renewing the American Community College*, edited by W. Deegan and D. Tillery. San Francisco: Jossey-Bass, 1985.

63. Warren, K. "Rewriting the Future: The Feminist Challenge to the Malestream Curriculum." *Feminist Teacher*, 4 (1989), 46–52.

64. Weis, L. "Without Dependence on Welfare for Life: Black Women in the Community College." *Urban Review*, 17 (1985), 233–55.

SOCIAL ROLE AND
FUTURE PERSPECTIVES

Community, Technical, and Junior Colleges: Are They Leaving Higher Education?

Darrel A. Clowes and Bernard H. Levin

Introduction

In 1981 this journal published an article by Cross which described America's community colleges as "on the plateau" [7]; in 1983 a follow-up article by McCartan [16] attempted to identify the community colleges' current mission and to predict the future mission for the community college [6] and Tillery and Deegan identified a "fifth generation" of community colleges [26]. This article continues that re-examination of community college mission.

Ample evidence exists to support the fact of change in the function and mission of community, technical, and junior colleges, but the direction of that change is not clear nor has a clear consensus on current or future mission emerged. While change in mission is occurring, the debate over mission has been slow to develop. We believe continued debate on mission would be constructive. We also believe that the weight of the available evidence indicates a drift or evolution of that mission in a direction with potentially significant consequences for all of higher education. We propose to identify the direction of drift and to indicate areas of concern. We hope to further stimulate the discussion of mission for the community college so that planned change, not institutional drift or mission erosion, will determine the future mission(s) of the community, technical, and junior college.

Change has been a constant in the landscape of American higher education, and no segment of higher education has changed as much or as rapidly as the junior college—then community/junior college, now community, technical, and junior college. Higher education continues to respond to social, demographic, and economic shifts. Notably recent responses have been the evolution from more to less academic emphasis [20] and from less to more occupational emphasis [8, 24]. Responses have been less pronounced in the core institutions of higher education—the research universities and selective admissions liberal arts colleges—and more pronounced in the nonselective institutions, especially the regional public universities; nonselective liberal arts colleges; community, technical, and junior colleges; and post secondary proprietary institutions. One result of these developments has been a reduced differentiation among nonselective institutions and consequently an increased potential for competition.

Mission Drift

Recent work by others as well as our own research have led us to a line of reasoning and to tentative conclusions about the direction and impact of social, demographic, and economic changes upon the nonselective sector of higher education generally and the community, technical, and junior college (hereafter called the community college) particularly. First, the stability in baccalaureate institution enrollments in the face of declining student cohorts has been reported but not fully explained [8, 19]. We propose that this stability is a consequence of four interdependent factors: the academically oriented student has shifted increasingly to the baccalaureate-granting institution and is bypassing the academic transfer programs of the community college; the academic transfer program at the community college is atrophying; the curriculum at all nonselective institutions—both baccalaureate and associate degree granting—is becoming increasingly occupationally and technically oriented; and, when it survives, the transfer function of the community college is increasingly a transfer from an occupational curriculum to an occupational curriculum.

The gradual shift of the academically oriented student to the four-year institution is reflected in the shrinking proportion of head-count enrollment students who transfer and the stabilized if not declining numbers of actual transfer students so clearly documented by Cohen and Brawer [5]. The gradual shrinkage of the collegiate or academic transfer curriculum is reflected in the marked decline in the range of academic courses offered and in the limited availability of sophomore-level courses, especially those with prerequisites [5]. The occupational curriculum has dominated the community college curriculum since the mid-sixties [10, 14]. A similar phenomenon in slightly different form has occurred within baccalaureate-granting institutions and especially among the less selective institutions. This is demonstrated in the shifting pattern of degrees conferred shown in government reports and in various efforts to explain [9] or justify [22] the phenomenon. Finally, the emergence of the occupational/transfer curriculum in the community college is a recent but recognized development. Hunter and Sheldon [11] were among the first to identify this occurrence in their longitudinal study of California community college students; it is now an accepted reality [5]. Although no data or literature exists to document the emergence of the occupational/transfer curriculum and the student as the dominant transfer vehicle, we believe the trends in both two- and four-year colleges are strongly in support of this configuration, and we see it as the dominant transfer pattern for the future.

The second step in this line of argument is to consider the stability of community college enrollments in the face of declining student cohorts. We identify at least four interdependent factors that contribute to this phenomenon: the community college curriculum is aggressively marketed through horizontal partnerships with business, industry, and government and vertical partnerships with secondary schools and baccalaureate-granting institutions; the curriculum is increasingly dominated by occupational courses and programs; the course offerings are increasingly directed toward a non-academic and off-campus clientele; and the clientele is increasingly older, female, and part-time [5].

Third, the literature has implied a competition for students between the community college and the postsecondary proprietary institutions [1, 18, 25]. Although data on proprietary institutions and their students are very unreliable, the proprietary market share also has appeared to remain at least stable if not slightly increased. A recent study using data from the National Longitudinal Study of the High School Class of 1972 provides our best information to date and finds no evidence of direct competition between these two purveyors in the higher education marketplace [13].

Fourth, higher education has been called upon to advance the egalitarian principle in American society through increased access. The nonselective sector of higher education has met that call. The selective sector, however, has maintained restricted access, high levels of academic quality, and the established functions of higher education, that is, maintaining the collegiate model, conducting and publishing research, and preparing students for privileged positions in the society. Now questions are being raised about the quality of education provided by nonselective institutions, about which institutions actually provide access for minorities, women, and older students, and about the desirability of continuing open-access higher education. Richarson and his colleagues (20) raised serious and yet unanswered questions about negative consequences of open-access upon the college curriculum. Olivas [17] found a strong role for the community college in providing access to higher education for minorities and other traditionally underrepresented, but a more recent study [3] reported that baccalaureate institutions (probably non-selective) serve greater proportions of recent high-school graduates who are minorities, women, and of low socioeconomic status than do community colleges. Commission reports urge renewed attention to academic quality, and the wave of community college curriculum reform calls into question the maintenance of the open-access model as we knew it in the sixties (see 4,5,15, and 23).

The generally accepted niche of the community college within American higher education has been "to provide low-cost, degree-credit and non-credit programs in hometown settings for low-ability, part-time, minority-group, and low income students who probably would not have otherwise participated in higher education" [5, p. 10]. In this context "programs" refers to the 1960's comprehensive community colleges' mission of providing collegiate/transfer, career, remedial, and community service education. We conclude that community colleges generally are losing significant components of their mission (specifically, collegiate/transfer and career education) to other nonselective institutions in higher education. Because we find little or no evidence for competition for students between community colleges and proprietary schools [13], we place the competition between community colleges and nonselective four-year institutions. Community colleges have maintained their enrollments by delivering a career-oriented curriculum aimed at older, employed students and by reducing expectations for degree completion or for transfer. With this drift a curriculum has evolved that is oriented to intermittent course taking rather than degree or program completion, to career-related coursework rather than general education, to remediation rather than advanced basic skills or integrative coursework, and to continuing or community education. As this curriculum evolves, the community college is drifting toward a position outside the existing system of graded education, which links primary, secondary, and higher education.

We argue that the collegiate/ transfer function has been diminished while the career education function has been challenged and in part co-opted by the nonselective senior institutions. The remedial and community service education functions have also been co-opted and are not now, if they ever were, unique or defining characteristics of the community college. Remediation and community service were never functions that could stand alone as core functions of any higher educational institution; they always existed on the margin of the institution and were dependent upon other core functions providing identity and justification for the institution and its place in higher education. When a core function is in place and institutional identity established, then and only then can marginal functions like remediation and community service become viable. Studies by Richardson and Leslie [12] and Breneman and Nelson [2] speak to the failure of these marginal functions to generate the needed political and financial support, and each argues for the identification of a core function of functions for the community college. More specifically, each argues that one or more core functions must be established and the institution structured around that core to survive within higher education. We agree. But what core is viable?

Mission Redefined—A Proposal

Several courageous and visionary writers have argued for a mission based on a redefinition of collegiate/academic transfer education and have urged that the community college be restructured about this core function. Cohen has argued long and eloquently for this position [12], and Miami-Dade Community College under President McCabe's leadership has demonstrated that, in the appropriate environment, it can be done [23]. However, there is little evidence that other institutions or leaders have followed that lead; instead, the data show a pronounced swing away from the collegiate/transfer function. The argument justifying the community colleges' transfer function from the social mission of providing access to higher education has been compromised by the emergence of the nonselective senior institutions as primary providers in this area. A related argument justifies the continuation of collegiate/transfer education as a core function of community colleges necessary to justifying the community colleges' claim to a place within higher education. That argument, however, falls before the charge of self-interest and the evidence of declining collegiate/transfer enrollments.

We conclude that the only viable core function for most community colleges is career education. This is a function the society needs and supports, it is a function the institution can and does provide, and it can serve as the essential element, the core function—the *élan vital* about which community colleges may be restructured for a viable future. Cross urges the community college leaders to consider vertical and horizontal linkages or partnerships in any restructuring [6]. We agree and believe that career education as the core function would provide a solid base for that restructuring. Vertical linkages occur within the system of graded education. Linkages with secondary schools are already in vogue and concentrate around career education [27]. From such linkages come programs ranging from low level occupational skills training through general service-related programs in business to high level technical training. These programs can attract a viable traditional-age student body for the community college while still maintaining its appeal to the older student. These programs also establish the critical mass of students and courses essential to career education as a core function.

Under this proposal, most students would take only a few courses at the community college and, with their immediate goals met, would to continue further. Others would want further education. Additional vertical linkages should be forged between the community colleges and the senior institutions offering complementary programs in service and technical areas. Such linkages would provide a basis for reestablishing the transfer function in modified form and would provide a service for the student. This modified transfer function would be primarily a technical/transfer function, but it would serve to maintain place within graded education and higher education. This technical/transfer function would also serve to sustain at least a vestigial social mission (ensuring access to higher education for those who might otherwise not attend). Horizontal linkages already occur with service agencies, business, and industry. These linkages or partnerships connect the core career education function with the adult population and with the local community. Although much of the instruction would continue to be in specialized courses taught off-campus to a variety of client groups, bringing all of these activities under the banner of career education as the core function should provide greater direction and focus for the college. Performing within its core function should strengthen the individual community college by restricting its mission and not dissipating its energies over multiple functions with imprecise focuses and indifferent support.

Summary

The community, technical, and junior college must identify a core function and restructure itself around that core function. We believe career education is the viable choice and perhaps the only possible choice given the inroads other institutions have made in the historic roles of the community college. A modified transfer and collegiate function could develop from this core and could provide the basis for maintaining some position within higher education. The remaining functions could become satellites to the core of career education: remedial education would be a necessary and appropriate support activity, and local conditions would indicate when a community service function would be appropriate and when some variety of the traditional academic transfer education should be provided.

Is the community, technical, and junior college leaving higher education? We believe it is very close to assuming a role in post secondary education that is outside graded education and at the penumbra of higher education. Leaving higher education would belie the "college" in the community college and would be a serious blow to the role and significance of the institution for its students, faculty, and communities. We foresee a long-term negative effect upon political and ultimately financial support if this shift is perceived to occur.

Therefore we conclude that the community college must identify a viable core function and restructure its mission from that core. We see career education as that core. Career education and its support functions (remediation and community service) would be sufficient to sustain a place within postsecondary education. A revitalized career education focus, including a career/transfer function, is necessary to provide the connection to graded education, to maintain the connection with the collegiate tradition and curriculum, and ultimately to maintain place within higher education.

References

1. Braden, P., and K. Paul. "Vocational Education and Private Schools," in *Contemporary Concepts in Vocational Education*, edited by G. Law, pp. 200-204. Washington, D.C.: American Vocational Association, 1971.

2. Breneman, D., and S. Nelson. *Financing Community Colleges: An Economic Perspective*. Washington, D.C.: Brookings Institute, 1981.

3. Clowes, D., D. Hinkle, and J. Smart. "Enrollment Patterns in Higher Education: 1960-1980." *Journal of Higher Education*, 57 (March/April 1986), 121-33.

4. Cohen, A. "The Community College in the American Educational System," in *Contexts for Learning: The Major Sectors of American Higher Education*, edited by The Study Group on the Conditions of Excellence in American Higher Education, pp. 1-16. Washington, D.C.: National Institute for Education, 1985.

5. Cohen, A. M., and F. B. Brawer. *The American Community College*. San Francisco: Jossey-Bass, 1982.

6. Cross, K. P. "Determining Missions and Priorities for the Fifth Generation," in *Renewing the American Community College* edited by W. Deegan and D. Tillery, pp. 34-50. San Francisco: Jossey-Bass, 1985.

7. _____. "Community Colleges on the Plateau." *Journal of Higher Education*, 52 (March/April 1981), 113-23.

8. Dearman, N., and V. Plisko. *The Condition of Education: Statistical Report*. Washington, D.C: National Center for Educational Statistics, 1982.

9. Geigre, R. "The College Curriculum and the Marketplace." *Change*, 12 (November/December 1980), 17-23, 53-54.

10. Harris, N. C., and J. F. Grebe. *Career Education in Colleges: A Guide for Planning Two- and Four-Year Occupational Programs for Successful Employment*. San Francisco: Jossey-Bass, 1977.

11. Hunter, R., and M. S. Sheldon. *Statewide Longitudinal Study: Report on Academic Year 1979-80. Part III: Fall Results*. Woodland Hills, Calif.: Los Angeles Pierce College. (ED 180 530)

12. Kettlewell, G. "Arthur M. Cohen: Benevolent Critic of the Community College—a Literature Review." *Community/Junior College Quarterly of Research and Practice*, 10 (1986), 73-86.

13. Levin, B. H., and D. A. Clowes. "Competition between Community Colleges and Postsecondary Proprietary Schools: Reality or Myth?" *Journal of Studies in Technical Careers*, 9 (1988), 317-23.

14. Lombardi, J. *Resurgence of Occupational Education*. Topical Paper Number 65. Los Angeles: ERIC Clearinghouse for Junior Colleges, 1978.

15. McCabe, R., and S. Skidmore. "New Concepts for Community Colleges," in *Issues for Community College Leaders in a New Era,* edited by G. Vaughan, pp. 232-48. San Francisco: Jossey-Bass Publishers, 1983.

16. McCartan, A-M. "The Community College Mission: Present Challenges and Future Visions." *Journal of Higher Education,* 54 (November/December 1983), 676-92.

17. Olivas, M. *The Dilemmas of Access: Minorities in Two-Year Colleges.* Washington, D.C: Howard University Press, 1979.

18. Peterson, J. "Community College and Proprietary School Relationships Within the Educational Marketplace," in *New Directions for Community Colleges: Improving Articulation and Transfer Relationships,* edited by F. C. Kintzer, no. 39, pp. 51–57. San Francisco: Jossey-Bass, September 1982.

19. Petrovich, J. "Enrollment in Higher Education: Have Projected Declines Occurred?" *Educational Record,* 65 (Fall 1984), 58-59.

20. Richardson, R.,E. Fiske, and M. Okum. *Literacy in the Open-Access College.* San Francisco: Jossey-Bass, 1983.

21. Richardson, R., and L. Leslie. *The Impossible Dream? Financing Community Colleges' Evolving Mission.* Horizons Issue Monograph Series. Washington, D.C.: American Association of Community and Junior Colleges: Los Angeles: ERIC Clearinghouse for Junior Colleges, 1980.

22. Roemer, R. "Technical Studies and the Curriculum in Higher Education." *Curriculum Inquiry,* 10 (1980), 293-302.

23. Roueche, J., and G. Baker. *Access & Excellence: The Open Door College.* Washington, D.C.: The Community College Press, 1987.

24. Rudolph, F. "The Power of Professors: The Impact of Specialization and Professionalism on the Curriculum." *Change,* 16 (1984), 12-17.

25. Shoemaker, E. "The Challenge of Proprietary Schools." *Change,* 5 (Summer, 1973), 71-72.

26. Tillery, D., and W.L. Deegan. "The Evolution of Two-Year Colleges Through Four Generations," in *Renewing the American Community College,* edited by W. L. Deegan and D. Tillery, pp. 3-33. San Francisco: Jossey-Bass, 1985.

27. Parnell, D. *The Neglected Majority.* Washington, D.C.: The Community College Press, 1985.

The Community College at the Crossroads: The Need for Structural Reform

KEVIN J. DOUGHERTY

Community colleges offer many students an alternative route to achieving a baccalaureate degree. In this article, Kevin Dougherty analyzes data on these institutions to see how effective they are in helping students transfer to and succeed in four-year colleges. After controlling for differences in family background, high school record, and educational aspirations of students entering two- and four-year colleges, the author finds that community college entrants receive fewer bachelor's degrees. While finding a strong case for reform, Dougherty argues that present reformers need to keep in mind the comprehensive nature of the community college and be sure that their reform proposals will preserve rather than diminish the services it offers students. Dougherty then discusses two sweeping reforms: transforming community colleges into four-year colleges, and converting them into two-year branches of state universities.

The community college today is middle-aged. The ideals that motivated its spectacular growth and change in the 1960s and 1970s—equal access to college and responsiveness to the needs of all students—are now matters of routine. The idealistic manifestos of the community college's pioneers have given way to five-year master plans, which in turn have gotten yearly progress reports based on data spewed forth by management information systems (Cross, 1981).

Having reached a plateau in enrollments, the community college is now facing the consequences of its earlier choice. Community college officials, scholars, and policymakers are reflecting on how far the institution has come and how far it should go. New journals devoted to studying the community college have appeared, such as the *Community and Junior College Quarterly of Research and Practice* and the *Community College Review*. National and state commissions on its future have proliferated (see, for example, American Association of Community and Junior Colleges, 1988: California Legislature, 1987; and Commission on the Future of the North Carolina Community College System, 1989). This examination has been made sharper by the realization that a new millennium is but a few years away (McCartan, 1983; Cohen & Brawer, 1989, pp. 365–366, 378).

Many of those evaluating the community college conclude that it needs little change. They project a future that is largely a continuation of its present as an institution that emphasizes vocational education. This view can be seen in the annual public policy agendas of the American Association of Community and Junior Colleges (AACJC). Despite the great current concern among many scholars and government officials about reviving transfer education—that is, programs

465

preparing community college students for baccalaureate programs at four-year colleges—the AACJC's 1990 statement of its public-policy agenda says nothing about transfer, and its 1989 statement has only this one statement: "The Association will foster the development of strong college curricula by: . . . identifying and disseminating information on two-year/four-year curriculum coordination and transfer arrangements in every state" (American Association of Community and Junior Colleges, 1989, 1990).

But this essentially status-quo attitude is being challenged from many different quarters. Arguing that the community college is in crisis and subject to increasingly tough scrutiny, many scholars and policymakers proclaim that it must sharply redefine its goals and modes of operation. In particular, they have focused on the rapid attenuation of transfer education throughout the 1960s and 1970s, as vocational education has risen to overshadow it. But beyond this common under-standing, the critics of the status quo are in little agreement. Some, whom we might call the noncollegiate reformers, believe that the community college should accelerate its drift away from transfer education by explicitly deciding to replace it with noncollegiate education, especially vocational education (Breneman & Nelson, 1981; Clowes & Levin, 1989). Others, whom we might call the collegiate reformers, forcefully reject this policy, calling instead for a major renewal of the community college's commitment to transfer and general academic education (Brint & Karabel, 1989; Cohen & Brawer, 1989; Pincus & Archer, 1989).[1]

This article has two purposes. First, I examine whether the reformers are right in their assertion that the community college is in crisis and needs to be reformed. After reviewing the evidence on the educational success of community college students, I find that there is a compelling case for reform. Entering a community college seriously hampers the educational success of baccalaureate aspirants, apart from any effect that results from community college students having, on average, lower test scores and aspirations than comparable four-year college entrants. This negative *institutional* effect is particularly distressing since the community college has become the main gateway into higher education for minority and working-class students (U.S. Bureau of the Census, 1988, pp. 71–72; U.S. National Center for Education Statistics, 1990). More of these students enter higher education through community colleges than through four-year colleges. As a result, in the past fifteen years community colleges have played a major role in the declining proportion of Blacks receiving baccalaureates (Orfield & Paul, 1987–1988, p. 62).

Once the need for reform is made clear, I will address this article's second purpose: to examine the main proposals that have been advanced to revamp the community college. I conclude that the recommendations of the noncollegiate reformers would seriously injure many students because they neglect the fact that a vocationalized community college would still attract many baccalaureate aspirants. While the policies of the collegiate reformers are preferable because they recognize the need to maintain and revamp the transfer program, they are also insufficient. The collegiate reformers suggest operational changes that mitigate the obstacles encountered by baccalaureate aspirants, but do not drastically reduce or eliminate them. Their reforms do not address the fact that the obstacles baccalaureate aspirants encounter in the community college are rooted in the very *structure* of the community college as a vocationally oriented, two-year commuter institution that is separate from the four-year colleges to which is baccalaureate aspirants must eventually transfer. Hence, I conclude by weighing the advantages and disadvantages of two "structural" reforms that aim to modify not just how community colleges operate, but also their very structure and place in the system of higher education: transforming community colleges into four-year colleges, and converting community colleges into two-year branches of the state universities.

Does the Community College Need Reform?

While the reformers base their calls for change on various factors, the most important is a perceived deterioration in the quality of baccalaureate preparation of community college students. They note the disappearance of many traditional transfer courses, particularly post-introductory humanities courses (Clowes & Levin, 1989, p. 350; Cohen & Brawer, 1989, pp. 288–296). They find that the proportion of students transferring to universities has been steadily declining (Brint & Karabel, 1989, pp. 120, 129; Clowes & Levin, 1989, p. 350; Cohen & Brawer, 1989, p. 53). And, most controversially, many have argued that baccalaureate aspirants entering community colleges today are much less likely to eventually receive a bachelor's degree than students with similar characteristics entering four-year colleges (Bernstein, 1986; Breneman & Nelson, 1981, p. 209; Brint & Karabel, 1989, p. 226; Cohen & Brawer, 1989, pp. 51-58; Dougherty, in press; Pincus & Archer, 1989, pp. 13–15). David Breneman and Susan Nelson have stated:

> Even after controlling for a wide range of background characteristics, including educational aspirations, enrolling in a community college [is] a significant—and negative—factor in determining bachelor's degree completion. . . . [A] majority of students would have a better chance of earning a bachelor's degree if they started at a four-year rather than a two-year college. (1981, p 209)

More recently, Steven Brint and Jerome Karabel (1989, p. 226) have declared: "The very fact of attending a two-year rather than a four-year institution lowers the likelihood that a student will obtain a bachelor's degree."

Evaluating the Rationale for Reform: The Tenuous Transfer Function

A careful review of the evidence supports the reformers' claim that transfer education weakened considerably during the 1960s and 1970s, so that baccalaureate aspirants now fare much better if they enter a four-year rather than a community college. But before reviewing that evidence, we need to establish that, despite the headlong rush toward vocational education in the last thirty years, baccalaureate aspirants remain a significant constituency of the community college. In fact, baccalaureate aspirants still make up 30 percent to 40 percent of all community college entrants (Cohen & Brawer, 1989, pp. 49–52; Dougherty, 1987, p. 87; Pincus & Archer, 1989, pp. 10–11).[2]

Reformers are correct that baccalaureate aspirants entering the community college face great difficulty. Far fewer eventually receive baccalaureates than students with similar characteristics entering four-year colleges. Surveys routinely find a large gap between community college entrants and four-year college entrants in rates of attaining a bachelor's degree. Three different national surveys have found that, on average, 70 percent of four-year college entrants had received a baccalaureate degree when followed up four to fourteen years later, while only 26 percent of public two-year college entrants had done so (Astin, Astin, Green, Kent, McNamara, & Williams, 1982; Bayer, Royer, & Webb, 1973; Velez, 1985). In addition, Anderson (1984) found that on average, four-year college entrants complete one half-year more of higher education than two-year entrants.

Community college defenders have responded that this "baccalaureate gap" is largely rooted in the fact that community college students differ greatly from four-year college entrants in family background, high school academic record, and educational aspirations (Cohen & Brawer, 1989, p. 44; Vaughan, 1980, pp. 11–12). This difference in student characteristic does indeed exist. On average, community college students are poorer, more often non-White, less academically prepared, and less ambitious than four-year college students (Cohen & Brawer, 1989, pp. 31–51). For example, compared to four-year college students, public two-year college students more often are non-White (21% versus 15% in 1984), have family incomes below $30,000 (49% versus 35% in 1986), and have families headed by persons with high school diploma or less (53% versus 40% in 1986) (U.S. Bureau of the Census, 1988, pp. 71–72; U.S. National Center for Education Statistics, 1990).

Nonetheless, the fact that a greater proportion of community college students comes from disadvantaged backgrounds than four-year college students only partly explains their disparity in educational attainment. This gap is not attributable to student characteristics alone; it arises as well from the nature of the institution they are entering. Even when we restrict our analysis to baccalaureate aspirants of similar background and ability, those entering two-year colleges are significantly less likely to attain a bachelor's degree. This is a difficult finding to accept, so let us carefully examine the studies from which it emerges.

Several different studies using different samples and methods have found that students entering community college receive 11 percent to 19 percent fewer bachelor's degrees and average one-eighth to one-fourth-year less higher education than students of comparable background, ability, and ambition entering four-year colleges. Using the National Longitudinal Survey of the High School Class of 1972 (NLS-72), Charlene Nunley and David Braneman (1988) examined the educational records of *baccalaureate aspirants* who entered college in October 1972 and were followed up in October 1979. They found that those entering community college received 11.5 percent fewer bachelor's degrees and averaged 0.16 fewer years of education than those entering four-year colleges, even after controlling for differences between the two sets of students and family background, high school record, and educational aspirations (pp. 80-81). These finding were replicated in two other studies that also used the NLS-72 1979 follow-up data, but focused instead on students who entered the *academic* programs of community colleges and four-year colleges in the fall of 1972. William Velez (1985) found that, even after controlling for various pre- and post-matriculation differences between the student bodies, community college entrants still received 18.7 percent fewer baccalaureate degrees than comparable four-year college entrants (Velez, 1985, p. 199). Kristine Anderson (1984), meanwhile, found that students who entered community colleges secured 13.4 percent fewer bachelor's degrees and 0.25 fewer years of education than comparable students who entered four-year state colleges (Anderson, 1984, pp. 33–34).

It could be argued that these findings are peculiar to the NLS-72. But an analysis of an entirely separate national survey discovered the same pattern. In 1980, Alexander Astin and his colleagues conducted a follow-up study of freshmen surveyed in 1971 as part of the American Council for Education's national survey of full-time freshmen. Concentrating on those aspiring to bachelor's degree, they found that nine years later, the two-year college entrants had less often attained a baccalaureate degree than had four-year college entrants, even after controlling for their differing personal characteristics.[3]

The poorer outcomes encountered by baccalaureate aspirants who entered community colleges compared to four-year colleges cannot be attributed solely to the community college entrants' less advantaged backgrounds, poorer academic preparation, and lower aspirations. When we compare students with similar traits, we find that baccalaureate aspirants are still significantly less likely to realize their hopes if they enter a community college than a four-year college. There is quite sizable *institutional* effect, over and above the effect of differences in student characteristics.

Explaining the Baccalaureate Gap

If the critics have been correct in their claim that community colleges hinder their baccalaureate aspirants, they have been less clear about what precise institutional features of community college account for this. To address this issue, I have collected and analyzed a broad range of research on the community college and on colleges in general, and conclude that baccalaureate aspirants in the community college encounter institutional obstacles at three stages: surviving in the community college; transferring to a four-year college; and persisting the four-year college. Let us examine the vicissitudes encountered at each of these stages in baccalaureate aspirants' pilgrimages toward their desired degree.[4]

The first challenge that community college entrants face is survival in the difficult first years of college. Unfortunately, community college entrants are 10 percent to 18 percent more likely to drop out in the first two years than four-year college entrants of similar background, ability, and aspirations (Astin, 1975; Pascarella & Chapman, 1983). Moreover, the dropout rates are highest for students who are non-White and from low socioeconomic backgrounds (Astin, 1975; Olivas, 1979, p. 44; U.S. National Center for Education Statistics, 1977b, pp. 22, 135–136, 150; 1990a, pp. 19–28). The key institutional causes of this high drop out rate are lack of financial aid and the failure of the community college to integrate students sufficiently into the academic and social life of the institution.

Community college students receive less financial aid than students at public four-year colleges, despite their being considerably less well-off (Orfield et al., 1984). The 1987 National Postsecondary Student Aid Study found that only 28.5 percent of public two-year college students receive student aid of any kind in 1986, while the comparable percent for students of public universities was 46.8 percent (U.S. National Center for Education Statistics, 1990b, p. 286).

Further, community colleges are less able than four-year colleges to integrate their students socially. One of the most important reasons for this is their lack of that potent integrating device: dormitories and campus life. Campus residence powerfully contributes to retention by fostering greater participation in extracurricular activities, wider social contact with faculty and fellow students, and deeper satisfaction with campus life (Astin, 1975, pp. 91–92, 165–168; Tinto, 1987; Velez, 1985, pp. 196–199).

Finally, community colleges are less able to integrate their students academically. Their lower academic selectivity tends to lead faculty to have diminished expectations for student success. These low expectations not only hamper good teaching, they also reinforce the considerable doubts among working-class and minority students about the value and possibility of attaining a baccalaureate degree (Astin et al., 1982, pp. 101–102; London, 1978, chaps. 2–5; Weis, 1985, pp. 84–93, 134–137, 153–154).

If baccalaureate aspirants survive the first one or two years of community college, they face a second obstacle: transferring to a four-year college in order to pursue their degree. Unfortunately, community college entrants continue on to the junior and senior year of four-year colleges at a lower rate than comparable four-year college entrants.[5] An estimate has been made that only about 15 percent of community college entrants eventually transfer to a four-year college (Brint & Karabel, 1989, p. 129; Cohen & Brawer, 1989, p. 53; Pincus & Archer, 1989, pp. 11–13). This reflects in part the greater proportion of students in the community college with lower academic preparation, lower ambition, and lower socioeconomic backgrounds. Yet even when we control for these differences, we still find that community college entrants are at a disadvantage relative to four-year entrants. An analysis of the National Longitudinal Survey of the High School Class of 1972 found that, among baccalaureate aspirants who survive the first two years of college, only 49.3 percent of the community college entrants reached the junior year at a four-year college, compared to 96.2 percent of the four-year college entrants.

This transfer gap arises in part because community college entrants try less often to move on to the last two years of college than do four-year entrants. Transferring to a four-year college requires them to move to a new and foreign institution. This hesitation, clearly, needs to be overcome by strong encouragement on the part of the community college, but several studies have found that far too many community colleges provide at best cursory and haphazard encouragement and advice for their transfer aspirants (Bernstein, 1986, p. 37; Cohen & Brawer, 1987, pp. 180–181; Rendon & Matthews, 1989, pp. 317–321; Richardson & Bender, 1987, p. 152). For example, a recent nationwide survey of community college faculty found that only a small number had frequent meetings with students to discuss transfer, and only one-third had information on their students' transfer intentions (Cohen, Brawer, & Bensimon, 1985, p. 90). In fact, community colleges often inadvertently dampen students' interest in transferring by drawing them into their occupational programs, which are much more attractively packaged and more vigorously publicized than transfer programs (Richardson & Bender, 1987, p. 41). But while occupational education is no longer an absolute barrier to transfer, it has still been found to pose an obstacle. For example, community college students in the City University of New York who enrolled in the vocational curriculum were 13 percent less likely to eventually receive a baccalaureate degree than those who enrolled in the liberal arts, even with controls for background, aspirations, and lower-division achievement (Crook & Lavin, 1989). In addition, it has been found that the more vocationally oriented a community college is, the lower its transfer rate is, all other things being equal (California Community Colleges, 1984, pp. 17–19).

Even if they attempt to transfer, community college entrants continue to encounter institutional obstacles. Many four-year colleges are still reluctant to take transfers, accepting them only if they cannot fill their classes with freshmen (Richardson & Bender, 1987, p. 81; Willingham & Findikyan, 1969, pp. 5–6, 25–26; Zwerling, 1976, pp. 246–249). Even institutions that are committed to accepting transfer students, such as the California state universities, turn them away because of insufficient room (California Postsecondary Education Commission, 1989, pp. 7–8). In addition, would-be transfers secure less financial aid than do four-year college entrants (U.S. National Center for Education Statistics, 1977b, p. 34). The financial aid gap is probably smaller today, yet there is still no federal program specifically for transfer students, and many states have taken little initiative in this area. This shortfall in financial aid clearly undermines transfer. A study of transfer applicants to the University of California who were accepted but did not matriculate (19% of those accepted) found that a major reason was finances (Baratta & Apodaca, 1984, p. 6). Furthermore, a survey of minority transfers with high grade-point averages (GPAs) found that one-third could not have transferred if they had not received a scholarship (Pincus & Archer, 1989, p. 34).

Finally, if community college entrants do succeed in transferring to a four-year college, they find it harder to survive the junior and senior years for reasons that are traceable to their community college experience. Community college transfer students drop out more often than comparable four-year college entrants. Around one-third of students who transferred to the California State University System and the Florida public universities drop out of the upper division within the next three to five years, while the rate for juniors in four-year colleges is approximately one-fifth (California Community Colleges, 1984; Florida State Department of Education, 1983, p. 12).

While student deficiencies play a role in this attrition, institutional factors are clearly also at work, hindering the academic and social integration of transfer students. Many four-year colleges make little effort to incorporate them socially through special orientation programs. Moreover, transfers are hindered by inadequate financial aid. Lacking money, they have to work and thus cannot mix as well socially (Astin, 1975, pp. 154, 168; Richardson & Bender, 1987, pp. 56–57, 82–83, 112, 161).

Meanwhile, the academic integration of community college transfers is impeded by frequent loss of credit in the transfer process and by inadequate academic preparation in the community college for university work. A recent study of community college transfers at nine urban universities across the country found that 58 percent reported losing credits in transferring, with 29 percent reporting losing 10 or more credits (Richardson & Bender, 1987, p. 148). Similarly, a recent study of transfer students from Maryland community colleges found that 6 percent lost thirteen or more credit hours, this is, at least one semester (Maryland State Board for Community Colleges, 1983, p. 12). As a result of this credit loss, transfer students progress more slowly toward their degrees, making them less likely to finish. They are more likely to run out of funds, time, or motivation.

Even if all their credits are accepted, transfer students often find that they are inadequately prepared for university work. In many community colleges, programs ostensibly designed to prepare students for eventual transfer to four-year colleges have become essentially open-door programs with virtually no entry or exit requirements. Consequently, transfer courses are often not up to university standards of instruction (Bernstein, 1986, p. 38; Bowles, 1988, pp. 32–35; Cohen & Brawer, 1987, p. 100; Orfield et al., 1984, pp. 210, 213, 226–228). Moreover, community college instructors often do not communicate and enforce high academic expectations for their students. They more often grade relative to the class norm (rather than to an abstract standard) than do university instructors. They cover less material in class. They also assign fewer difficult readings and essay exams (Bernstein, 1986, pp 36–37; Richardson & Bender, 1987, pp. 27–28, 34–36, 46–48). A national survey of community college instructors found that only 27 percent allocated more than a quarter of the final course grade to essay exams (Cohen et al., 1985, p. 90). Moreover, community college students are required to write papers in only one-fourth of their humanities courses and one-tenth of their science courses (Cohen & Brawer, 1982, p. 156). The result is poor preparation for the academic demands of the university. In a 1977 survey of community college transfers to UCLA, only one-third reported that in the community college they frequently had to write papers integrating ideas from various parts of a course; yet two-thirds stated that at UCLA they had to do this frequently (Lara, 1981, pp. 2, 8–9).

In summary, the case for reform is strong. Baccalaureate aspirants are less likely to succeed if they enter a community college rather than a four-year college. This baccalaureate gap is only partially explained by the different characteristic of the two student bodies. It also arises from various institutional characteristics of the community college that produce lower rates of persistence in the lower division, of transfer to the upper division, and of persistence in the upper-division than is the case for four-year colleges. The need for reform is made all the more imperative by the fact that the community college has become the main point of entry into higher education for working-class and minority students. Consequently, it plays a significant role in the fifteen-year decline in the number of Blacks receiving baccalaureate degrees (Orfield & Paul, 1987–1988, p. 62).

What Form Should Reform Take?

Although the need for reform is evident, we face much less certainty about what direction reform should take. Reformers are in sharp disagreement about possible solutions. Hence we need to weigh their proposals against the evidence. In doing so, we find that the two main sets of proposals advanced so far—which I have labeled the noncollegiate and collegiate reforms—are both deeply flawed. Therefore, once I have discussed these two reform proposals, I will advance a third set of proposals to transform the community college, which I dub "structural" changes.

The Noncollegiate Program

The noncollegiate reformers argue that community colleges should address the apparent deterioration of transfer education by largely eliminating it from the curriculum and instead playing to their strength in noncollegiate education: vocational education, adult and community education, and remedial education. Breneman and Nelson (1981) made this argument in a study commissioned by the American Association of Community and Junior Colleges from the Brookings Institution:

> The demands of an era of limited growth and retrenchment in higher education will force state policymakers to consider institutional performance carefully in allocating limited resources for education. One area within the community college that is likely to be examined critically is the educational performance and productivity of academic transfer programs . . . . The performance data in many states are troubling. . . . One way to approach this question is to consider those areas in which a particular type of institution may have an educational comparative advantage over others. . . . We favor an educational division of labor among institutions . . . that would result in the community colleges enrolling fewer full-

time academic transfer students of traditional college age and retaining a dominant position in those activities that four-year institutions have not undertaken traditionally and are likely to do less well. (pp. 209, 211)

Similar sentiments have been expressed by many prominent community college commentators and officials, including Darrel Clowes and Bernard Levin (1989), K. Patricia Cross (1985), Edmund Gleazer (1980), Clark Kerr (1980), and the Carnegie Council on Policy Studies in Higher Education (1979).

For the noncollegiate school, the central program within a transformed community college would be vocational education, with remedial, adult, and community education as key adjuncts (Carnegie Council on Policy Studies in Higher Education, 1979, p. 25; Clowes & Levin, 1989, p. 353; Cross, 1985, pp. 41–42, 46; Gleazer, 1980, pp. 4–5, 10, 16; Kerr, 1980, pp. 8–9). Darrel Clowes and Bernard Levin (1989) put this pithily:

> The only viable core function for most community colleges is career education. This is a function the society needs and supports, it is a function the institution can and does provide, and it can serve as the essential element, the core function—the *élan vital* about which community colleges may be restructured for a viable future. . . . Career Education is . . . perhaps the only possible choice given the inroads other institutions have made in the historic roles of the community college. A modified transfer and collegiate function could develop from this core and could provide the basis for maintaining some position within higher education. The remaining functions could become satellites to the core of career education. (Clowes & Levin, 1989, p. 353; emphasis in original)

Evaluation: These Reforms Would Exacerbate the Problem. The noncollegiate program has merit in that it recognizes that the community college's attempt to balance academic, vocational, adult, and remedial education has created a host of contradictions and difficulties. In trying to be a jack-of-all-trades, the community college has often ended up being master of none. As we have seen, the community college has failed to provide lower-division baccalaureate preparation of equal quality to that of four-year colleges.

Unfortunately, the wish of noncollegiate reformers to bring coherence to the community college by closing down its baccalaureate preparation program would leave many baccalaureate aspirants homeless. As noted above, over a third of community college students today aspire to a baccalaureate degree. What would happen to them if the community college recenters itself around vocational education? Noncollegiate reformers evasion that baccalaureate aspirants would largely circumvent the community college and go directly to four-year schools (Breneman & Nelson, 1981), and those that remain would have a fallback path to the baccalaureate through the transfer of vocational credits:

> This modified transfer function would primarily be a technical/transfer function, but it would serve to maintain a place within graded education and higher education. This technical/transfer function would also serve to sustain at least a vestigial social mission (ensuring access to higher education for those who might otherwise not attend). (Clowes & Levin, 1989, p. 353)

Unfortunately, this scenario breaks down in the face of obdurate reality.[6]

The hope that most baccalaureate aspirants will simply sidestep the community college ignores the fact that four-year colleges are much less accessible than community colleges. Leland Medsker and James Trant (1964) studied college access in sixteen cities in the Midwest and California with different kinds of college opportunities. The five cities possessing only community colleges had higher college attendance rates than the four cities with only state colleges, the four with extension centers of state universities, the one with a mixture of institutions, and the two with no college of any kind.[7] Furthermore, W. Norton Grubb (1989) found that in the fall of 1979, states that ranked high in the proportion of their college-age population enrolled in community college tended also to rank high in the proportion of males, but not females, going to college. This effect held even after controlling for differences between states in social composition, educational structure, and labor market conditions.

Several features of four-year colleges make them less accessible than community colleges to baccalaureate aspirants. Typically, they are farther away, and often located in distant rural areas. Moreover, they are more expensive to attend, if only because they are farther away, so that one has to pay not only tuition but also room and board charges. They are usually more selective academically, being less willing to take "nontraditional" students, such as vocational students, high school dropouts, and the academically deficient.

Even if it is true that baccalaureate aspirants will have to continue going to community colleges in significant numbers, could they still transfer from vocationally centered community colleges? Clearly, this is unlikely if a major purpose of shifting the community college in a noncollegiate direction is to get it out of the business of transfer education. Even more to the point, there is a great deal of evidence against the hope that a large vocational-transfer track will really emerge. As we have seen above, the presence of a strong vocational education program hinders the transfer even of baccalaureate aspirants.[8]

In sum, the noncollegiate reform program should be rejected. The amputation of the transfer program in the name of a more coherent mission for the community college will leave many baccalaureate aspirants stranded.

The Collegiate Reformers

The collegiate reformers have reacted to the travails of transfer education by calling not for its amputation, but rather for its amplification (Astin, 1983; Bernstein, 1986; Brint & Karabel, 1989; Cohen & Brawer, 1989; Orfield et al., 1984; McCabe, 1981; Pincus & Archer, 1989; Richardson & Bender, 1987). In a recent report by the College Board and the Academy of Educational Development, Fred Pincus and Elayne Archer declare:

> Prior to the 1960s,. . . prebaccalaureate education was the primary role of two-year colleges. We believe that low-income and minority students, both male and female, deserve the same opportunities today. . . . Strong prebaccalaureate programs should be the foundation upon which vocational, adult, and continuing education programs are developed. (1989, p. 3)

The collegiate reformers make a wide variety of proposals for improving transfer education. To reduce attrition in the community college, they have proposed strengthening students' academic and social integration into college life through such means as providing more jobs on campus, holding more campus events, and encouraging greater interaction between faculty and students through formal conferences and informal contact (Astin, 1983, pp. 132–133; Center for the Study of Community Colleges, 1988, pp. 100–102; Cohen & Brawer, 1987, p. 182; Pincus & Archer, 1989, p. 4).

Transfer rates could be increased, according to collegiate reformers, by better transfer advising, by familiarizing would-be transfer students with four-year colleges through campus visits, and by providing more financial aid tailored to transfer students' special needs. Transfer advising in particular could be improved by clearly labeling transfer courses, establishing centers at community colleges to centralize and disseminate transfer information, and creating computerized systems to track student progress and indicate how well students are meeting transfer requirements (Astin, 1983, pp. 132–133; Bernstein, 1986, p. 37; Center for the Study of Community Colleges, 1988, pp. 99–102; Cohen & Brawer, 1987, pp. 180–181; Orfield et al., 1984, pp. 332–334; Pincus & Archer, 1989, pp. 3, 7; Richardson & Bender, 1987, pp. 38–39, 108–109, 173–174, 206–213, 219; Zwerling, 1976, pp. 240–246.

Finally, post-transfer retention could be promoted through more and better financial aid, greater social integration of transfer students, more rigorous pre-transfer academic preparation, and greater acceptance of credits. Regarding financial aid, more should be provided, especially in the form of scholarships rather than loans. Pre-transfer academic preparation could be improved by familiarizing community college teachers with the universities' academic expectations for students, by testing students more rigorously when they enter the community college, and not allowing them to enter transfer courses until they are functioning at a collegiate level of preparation. Credit transfer could be eased by a better exchange of information between community colleges and four-year colleges about transferability, creating common course numbers across two- and four-year colleges, having state governments require public four-year colleges to give full credit to general education courses taken in the community college, and reducing the obstacles to transfer of vocational credits by establishing more "capstone" or "inverted major" programs, in which students receive their technical training at the community college and their general education at the senior college (Center for the Study of Community Colleges, 1988, pp. 99–101; Cohen & Brawer, 1987, pp. 19, 160–161, 179–181; Orfield et al., 1984, p. 333; Pincus & Archer, 1989, pp. 3–5, 7, 40–41, 44; Rendon & Matthews, 1989, pp. 323–324; Richardson & Bender, 1987, pp. 56–57, 82–83, 112, 147, 169–170, 184–185, 207–218). The proposals of the collegiate reformers are systematic and sensible. They target many of the obstacles faced by baccalaureate aspirants in their odyssey toward their degree: attrition in the lower division, difficulty in transferring to four-year colleges, and lack of success in the upper division. Despite these strengths, however, the collegiate reform program is also insufficient. Let us evaluate its strengths and weaknesses.

Evaluation: These Reforms Are Necessary but Insufficient The collegiate reformers have been heeded by many. The twenty-four community colleges participating in the Urban Community College Transfer Opportunity Program (UCCTOP) of the Ford Foundation have implemented many parts of the collegiate reform program (Center for the Study of Community Colleges, 1988; Pincus & Archer, 1989). Moreover, the state of California has provided funds for twenty community college districts to establish Transfer Centers. Florida has established a system of mandatory testing upon entry to community college to ensure that students get needed remedial education, and it has funded the development of a computerized student advisement system. Some states have mandated common course numbering and required their senior colleges to provide full transfer credit for general-education courses meeting certain requirements. For example, Florida has established a system where community college and four-year college courses of equivalent content and difficulty carry the same course number (California Postsecondary Education Commission, 1989, pp. 7–8; Florida State Board for Community Colleges, 1988, pp. 7–11, 21, 52–53; Jaschik, 1988, p. A24).

This pledge of faith in the collegiate reform program seems warranted. Its recommendations directly address the multiple perils faced by baccalaureate aspirants. Moreover, there is some empirical evidence that the reforms are having an effect. Miami-Dade Community College, a UCCTOP participant that has pursued the collegiate program with particular energy, has found that a higher proportion (19%) of its new, full-time "degree-seeking" students graduate three years later with an associate's degree or certificate than at several comparable community colleges: Mercer County, NJ (17%), Kapiolani, Hawaii (17%), and New York City (15%) (Morris & Losak, 1986, p. 14). Moreover, an evaluation of experimental transfer advice and preparation programs at two California community colleges found that 22 percent of the forty-six students participating said that they were planning to transfer because of these programs (California Postsecondary Education Commission, 1983, pp. 15, 19).

Nonetheless, the programs of the collegiate reformers, though useful, are too limited. While the baccalaureate gap has been mitigated, it has by no means been eliminated. Even Miami-Dade Community College has encountered obstacles. The number of students transferring from its North campus to four-year colleges dropped from 2,121 in 1982–1983 to 1,192 in 1985–1986.[9] In fact, other UCCTOP community colleges have also experienced similar declines during the same period. The Community Colleges of Philadelphia saw their transfers decline in number from 402 in 1982–83 to

338 in 1985–86; and Cuyahoga Community College in Cleveland experienced a drop from 1,337 to 1,063 over the same three-year period (Center for the Study of Community Colleges, 1988, pp. 108, 110, 144, 146, 156, 160). Statewide transfer rates from Florida, California, and New York present a similarly discouraging picture. In Florida, the number of community college transfers to the nine state university campuses dropped from 9,217 in fall 1984 to 7,983 in fall 1987 (State University System of Florida, 1986, p. 45; 1989, p. 20). In California, the number of community college students transferring to the University of California and the California State University System dropped from a yearly average of 39,411 students in the 1970s to 34,784 in the 1980s. In fact, despite that state's energetic efforts to encourage transfer, the number of students transferring in 1988 was actually somewhat lower than it was in 1980 (35,327 versus 35,913) (California Postsecondary Education Commission, 1989, p. 4). Finally, in New York, another bellwether state, the number of students transferring from the community colleges to the senior colleges and universities of the State University of New York dropped from an average of 6,697 for the years 1975–1979 to 6,466 for the years 1980–1988 (Baden-Borel, 1984, pp. 165, 170–171; State University of New York, 1984–1989).[10] How do we explain these disappointing results? Clearly, many factors are at work, but let us consider the limitations of the collegiate reform program.

The collegiate reform program has been limited by the fact that it has focused on revamping how the community college operates while largely ignoring the need to change its very structure and position within the higher education system. As long as the community college remains a two-year, commuter institution that is structurally separate from the four-year colleges that baccalaureate aspirants must eventually enter, its baccalaureate aspirants will encounter major obstacles to their success.

As long as community colleges remain commuter institutions, they will never be able to integrate their students academically and socially to the same degree as four-year colleges, which are more often residential. Devices such as arranging more events on campus and requiring faculty to interact more with students enhance social cohesion, but they are pale reflections of the success of college residential life in involving students in the life of a four-year college (Astin, 1977; Tinto, 1987). As long as community colleges remain two-year institutions, their baccalaureate aspirants will have to overcome the psychological obstacle that, in order to pursue their degree, they have to transfer to a new and foreign institution. Even if the university is in the same city, it remains a separate institution, with its own culture and organizational routines (Richardson & Bender, 1987). After all, one has to apply to it and be accepted; it is not a matter of just moving from your sophomore to your junior year by registering for new courses. As a result, many students will still choose not to brave the chasm between the institutions.

Furthermore, as long as community colleges remain organizationally separate from universities, preparation for upper-division studies will always be difficult. Because they are not members of the same institutions, university and community college faculty find it hard to keep up with each others' academic expectations. As a result, community college faculty often do not know if they are pitching their transfer courses at a level that university faculty find acceptable (Richardson & Bender, 1987). This gulf can be partially bridged by the faculty visits and exchanges proposed by the collegiate reformers, but these cannot substitute for the regular contact that occurs between teachers of upper-division and lower-division courses within a single institution. A few faculty acting as messengers between two different worlds cannot replace the experience of living within the same organizational milieu.

Finally, as long as community colleges remain institutions separate from universities, credit transfer will always be a difficult process. State mandates that universities accept community college credits—for example, in general education—can smooth the transfer of credits. But these mandates will not make transfer friction free. Despite their commitment to accepting transfer students, the campuses of the University of California often have to refuse entry into specific programs for lack of space (California State Postsecondary Education Commission, 1989). Moreover, even if space is available, university faculties often respond to demands to accept community college credits by imposing tight restrictions on counting them toward majors. In a survey of community college students entering nine urban universities, 25 percent reported that even when the university gave them credit for certain courses, those credits were not counted towards their majors. For 11 percent, this loss of major credit involved ten or more credits. To get elective as well as major credit, students frequently have to pass validation exams or earn high grades in courses that follow the ones for which they wish credit (Bowles, 1988, pp. 28–30; Richardson & Bender, 1985, pp. 39–40; 1987, p. 148).

The Structural Reformers

The limitations of the nonstructural reform program of the collegiate reformers suggest the need for a new reform program that would change the very structure, and not just the operations, of the community college. The aim of this structural reform would be to overcome the institutional separation between community colleges and four-year colleges that exists at the root of many of the obstacles faced by baccalaureate aspirants in community colleges. One such structural reform— transforming community colleges into four-year colleges—although mentioned now and again, has been conspicuously absent in the current debate over the future of the community college. As I will show, this reform has much to offer, but it also has notable liabilities. Hence, I would like to bring attention to another structural reform that has great promise but has gone unmentioned: the conversion of community colleges into two-year university branches.

Transforming Community Colleges into Four-Year Colleges

This idea has been raised now and again in debates over the community college, with the most notable recent proponent being L. Steven Zwerling (1976, pp. 251–252). This is a highly controversial recommendation, one that has been denounced by commentators on the community college ranging from Burton Clark (1980, p. 23) to the Carnegie Commission on Higher Education (1970). Yet Zwerling's (1976) proposal deserves careful consideration, for its benefits would be great.

As four-year colleges, community colleges could make it much easier for students to move between the lower and upper divisions, without any of the difficulties and repercussions attendant today with transfer between community college and senior college. In moving from the lower to the upper division in a senior college, students would not be crossing the chasm between separate institutions, but rather traversing a barely discernible line within the same institution. They would take their financial aid and credits with them, since the same student-assistance and registration systems are involved. Their lower-division academic preparation would be much better attuned to the demands of upper-division courses, because the faculty in the two divisions would usually be the same. And if they were to take any vocational courses, these would usually be creditable toward their baccalaureate degree.

Many objections, have been raised against this proposal. Some observers argue that converting the community college into a four-year institution would not change its position in the higher education prestige hierarchy. Whether two-year or four-year, community colleges would still be at the bottom (Karabel, 1972, p. 557). This objection ignores, however, that students are judged as much by the level of their degree as by the institution that grants it. A baccalaureate degree from a very indifferent four-year college is almost always of higher repute than an associate's degree from a good community college. Once armed with the ability to confer baccalaureate degrees, many community colleges would pull ahead of the many mediocre four-year colleges that are less well known and have poorer resources. While even the best community colleges, such as the Miami-Dade or Los Angeles community colleges, would be unlikely to shoot to the top or even the middle of the college prestige hierarchy, they would probably race past many four-year colleges.

A second objection that might be made is that converting the larger community colleges into four-year colleges would be horrendously expensive, requiring major expenditures to hire liberal arts faculty and stock libraries. But on examination it is not clear that, especially in the case of the larger community colleges, this would be a major problem. Most have well-stocked libraries and, if anything, a surplus of liberal arts faculty eager to teach traditional four-year college courses.

A narrower criticism is that many community colleges are too small to be turned into efficient and effective four-year colleges. They would never have enough staff to offer effective four-year courses. However, this objection could be met by allowing only community colleges above a certain size, say 2,000 students, to become four-year colleges.

The question might be raised: would the newly minted four-year colleges be content to remain four-year colleges, or would they push to develop graduate programs, following the well-worn path of the academic revolution trod by the teachers' colleges (Jencks & Riesman, 1968)? The cost of such a wholesale academic revolution would be insupportable, but it is questionable whether this specter would materialize. State coordinating boards and commissions are much stronger today than they used to be, and thus much better able to contain any major push for institutional social mobility. Hence, newly minted four-year colleges would unlikely to be successful in any push to become universities.

A fourth objection raised by observers is that the transformed community colleges would produce too many baccalaureates, thus fueling educational inflation and overeducation (Clark, 1980; Karabel, 1972, p. 557). This may indeed happen. But it prompts the question of whether it is indeed best to equilibrate the demand for and supply of the limited number of good, "college level" jobs by diverting many baccalaureate aspirants into pursuing sub-baccalaureate degrees, rather than explicitly confronting the excess of demand over supply by increasing the supply of good college-level jobs (Carnoy & Shearer, 1980; Carnoy & Levin, 1985; Levin, 1984; Zwerling, 1976, pp. 252–255). And if in the short run many baccalaureates are unable to get college-level jobs, they will still have gained much in cultural and political sophistication from their college experiences (Bowen, 1977).

Even if the previous objections may be set aside, there are two that are much less easily dismissed. A four-year community college is unlikely to adequately meet the needs of the 60 to 70 percent of community college entrants who are not baccalaureate aspirants, but rather are looking for vocational education, remedial education, or adult recreational education (Clark, 1980, p. 23). To be sure, many four-year colleges have provided vocational, developmental, and adult education for many years, and more are adding programs in these areas as they try to cope with declines in the numbers and abilities of traditional college students. Moreover, as a matter of tradition, community colleges transformed into four-year colleges are likely to retain a good part of their nonbaccalaureate programs. Furthermore, some retraction in vocational education would be desirable, because there is evidence that community colleges produce more vocational education graduates in various fields than the economy can absorb (Grubb, 1988; Mitchell et al., 1986). Still, in becoming four-year institutions, community colleges may retract their nonbaccalaureate programs too much, given the historically weaker commitment of four-year colleges to vocational and adult education.

In addition, the idea of transforming community colleges into four-year schools simply may be impracticable politically (R. Richardson, personal communication, 1989). It is likely to attract the obdurate, and perhaps fatal, opposition of existing four-year colleges and even many community colleges (Brint & Karabel, 1989, p. 229). Many community colleges would be opposed because they are committed to the present structure and may be afraid that change will bring loss of power, prestige, and funds for the institution and for its officials. Meanwhile, many selective universities and four-year colleges would be opposed because they have historically seen the community college as protecting selective university admissions by diverting away less able college students (Brint & Karabel, 1989; Dougherty, 1988, 1991). Four-year community colleges might reawaken students' appetite for traditional university education, leading many more to seek admittance to a university.

The concerns raised above may indicate that the idea of transforming community colleges into four-year institutions may be premature, if not mistaken. But there is another alternative, one largely ignored, that also addresses the need for a change in the structure of the community college and its relation to four-year colleges. It is the conversion of community colleges into two-year branches of the state universities. While going entirely unmentioned in current debates over the community college, it seems to provide most of the benefits and avoid most of the problems of transforming community colleges into four-year colleges.

Converting Community Colleges into Two-Year University Branches

Although the community college has become the norm for two-year colleges, other types of two-year education also exist. One is the two-year state university branches that are found in several states: Alaska, Connecticut, Hawaii, Kentucky, Louisiana, New Mexico, Ohio, Pennsylvania, and South Carolina (Cohen & Brawer, 1989, p. 103).

Converting community colleges into components of the university branch systems could accrue many of the same benefits, but largely avoid the costs, of transforming community colleges into four-year colleges. While usually housed separately from four-year campuses, university branches apparently make it easier to transfer than do community colleges. Moreover, university branches would be less likely to catalyze the opposition of the state universities than would new independent four-year colleges.

Several features of the branch campuses make them better conduits to the baccalaureate than community colleges. First, branch students are less likely to be diverted from their baccalaureate aspirations by the allure of vocational education leading to immediate employment. University branches usually put less emphasis on vocational education than community colleges, and thus are less likely to entice or pressure students to enter these programs. This is not to say that university branches lack vocational education. Although some are entirely academic, as in the case of the regional campuses of the University of Connecticut (L. Katz, personal communication, 1987), the branch systems in Alaska, Hawaii, Kentucky, and New Mexico maintain strong vocational programs.[11] This presence of vocational education is good—it addresses the argument that the community college must meet the needs of nonbaccalaureate aspirants as well as baccalaureate aspirants (Beckes, 1964; Medsker, 1960). At the same time, vocational education in the branches is not so strong as to become the obstacle to the pursuit of the baccalaureate that it is in the contemporary community college. Some may criticize this lesser commitment of university branches to vocational education on the grounds that it would starve the labor market's demand for middle-level workers. However, several studies show that the highly vocationalized community college is often *over-shooting* labor market demand for middle-level workers (Grubb, 1988; Mitchell et al., 1986; Pincus, 1980)[12]

The second way in which university branches improve on community colleges in facilitating pursuit of the baccalaureate is by making it easier to gain admission and transfer credits to the universities. Branches are usually treated by their parent universities as integral parts of one system. In its statement of the general principles and assumptions guiding the organization and operation of its Commonwealth system of two-year branches, Pennsylvania State University states: "The University functions as one institution and not as a collection of separate campuses or program delivery systems. . . . The concept [is] of one university, one academic program, and one faculty" (Pennsylvania State University, 1983, p. 3). Therefore, university-branch students are treated not as foreigners, but as members of the university, with movement to the central campus being typically regarded more as a matter of changing campuses than of applying for admission. As the University of South Carolina at Columbia puts it, "movement between USC campuses [which include several two-year branches] is not considered transfer by the university" (South Carolina Commission on Higher Education, 1979, p. 54). Students are able to transfer their credits more easily because the parent universities are more committed to accepting them. This commitment is often based on the fact that the parent university must approve the branch courses in advance (New Mexico Governor's State Task Force on Higher Education Reform, 1986, p. 31; Pennsylvania State University, 1983, p. 7; University of Connecticut, 1987, p. 81). In New Mexico, new programs and course offerings at the university branches "must be routed through the approval process of parent institutions. . . . A benefit of this lengthy process is that the course is generally transferable from a branch to the parent institution" (New Mexico Governor's Task Force on Higher Education Reform, 1986, p. 31). In fact, branch courses often have the same content and catalog numbers as central campus lower-division courses (University of Connecticut, 1987, p. 81).[13]

Finally, university branch students encounter fewer difficulties after transfer than do community college entrants. They are more likely to receive financial aid, because several university systems operate a unified student aid program that includes the branches (Katz, 1987). Moreover, branch students are more likely to be prepared for upper-division courses. Because of the course approval system, branch lower-division courses are much closer to main campus lower-division courses than community college courses typically are. As the University of Connecticut (1987, p. 81) puts it, "courses offered there [at the local branches] are identical to those offered at the main campus and occupy the same place in the university's curriculum as those offered at Storrs." Moreover, branch faculty are likely to be better apprised of the academic standards and concerns of main-campus faculty than are traditional community college faculty because they usually are appointed by the central administration and often are members of university-wide departments (Pennsylvania State University, 1983, pp. 3, 4, 8).

A number of studies of student degree attainment reinforce the impression that university branches better facilitate the attainment of baccalaureate degrees. Trent and Medsker (1968) found that, nationwide, a higher proportion of university extension-center students than community college students eventually transferred to, and graduated from, four-year colleges. They followed 241 university-branch students and 1,104 community college students in 16 different communities nationwide who entered college full-time in the fall of 1959. By June 1963, 54 percent of the branch students had transferred to a four-year college, while only 42 percent of the community college entrants had done so. Moreover, 17 percent of the branch entrants had received a bachelor's degree compared to only 11 percent of the community college entrants. More recent studies show a similar pattern. A study of 1,528 students entering the four two-year branches of Ohio University in the fall of 1966 found that by fall 1971, 48 percent had transferred either to the main campus in Columbus or to another accredited four-year or two-year college (Vaughan, 1971, p. 111). This transfer percentage is far higher than the 15 percent typical for community colleges. Furthermore, university branch attendees seem to have a better record of persistence in college than community college attendees. A study comparing 238 community college students transferring to the main campus of Kent State University in the fall of 1985 against 292 students transferring the same year from the university's seven regional two-year campuses found that the latter were much more likely to persist to graduation. By the summer of 1990, 64.1 percent of the regional-branch transfers, but only 43.3 percent of the community college transfers, had graduated with a baccalaureate degree (Knight, 1990).

It is important to note that these studies are by no means conclusive. They do not control for the known differences between the student populations of university branches and community colleges on such factors as family background, high school record, and educational and occupational aspirations. University-branch students tend to have more advantaged families, higher test scores, and better grades than community college students (Knight, 1990; Vaughan, 1971, pp. 81–85, 116). Controlling for these differences undoubtedly would reduce the university-branch advantage, but these studies raise the real possibility that university branches may better facilitate baccalaureate attainment than do community colleges.

While approximating the benefits of transforming community colleges into four-year colleges in one area (facilitating baccalaureate success), the conversion of community colleges into two-year branches has a decided advantage in a second area. State universities, long the arbiters of state higher educational policy, are much more likely to favor the conversion of community colleges into university branches. In fact, universities in many states have sponsored the formation of two-year branches while remaining opposed to the multiplication of four-year colleges. One only has to think of the branch systems established by Kent State University, Ohio State University, Pennsylvania State University and the Universities of Alaska, Connecticut, Kentucky, Ohio, and South Carolina. To be sure, some universities might oppose the conversion of community colleges into branches out of fear that it would increase their administrative load and force open their doors to many more students. But on the whole, universities would probably prefer to have community colleges converted into university branches rather than four-year colleges, because the former would be under university control while the latter would most likely be independent and competing institutions.

Summary and Conclusions

The community college is in crisis. Strong empirical evidence shows that its many baccalaureate aspirants are significantly hindered in their pursuit of a bachelor's degree by entering a community college rather than a four-year college. But if the crisis of the community college is clear, the solutions are less obvious. The discovery that baccalaureate aspirants encounter many *institutional* obstacles on their way to success has prompted a wide variety of reform proposals, ranging from recasting the community college as an essentially noncollegiate institution to vigorously reviving its original commitment to collegiate education.

Both empirical evidence and our nation's political values oppose the noncollegiate program, which would virtually amputate transfer education in favor of organizing the community college around vocational education. A wholesale emphasis on noncollegiate education would leave homeless the one-third of community college students who aspire to a baccalaureate degree.

The goals of the collegiate reformers should be given preference instead. Their recommendations directly acknowledge the needs of baccalaureate aspirants, and target several of the key obstacles they face. Still, while valuable and eminently worth implementing, the collegiate reforms do not address the fact that these obstacles are rooted, not just in how the community college operates, but also in its very *structure*. Even if its operation is revamped, its structure as a vocationally oriented, two-year commuter institution separate from the four-year colleges will always place substantial obstacles in the path of its baccalaureate aspirants.

We need therefore to consider structural reforms that try to span the institutional chasm between community colleges and four-year colleges. Two policies in particular have been discussed: transforming community colleges into four-year colleges, a recommendation that has surfaced in policy discussions on the future of the community college; and converting community colleges into two-year branches of the state universities, a policy that has not been raised in those discussions. Though not without defects, each policy merits serious consideration. In fact, the ratio of benefits to costs seems particularly good in the case of conversion into two-year branches. Although our evidence on both these structural reforms is still tentative and inconclusive, it is strong enough to indicate that we should vigorously explore these two possible futures for the community college.

In the end, we may want to think of the reform of the community college as an open-ended experiment. At the very least, the nonstructural changes suggested by the collegiate reformers should be implemented, for they promise significant benefits, are fairly noncontroversial, and will not preclude further structural reforms. If circumstances allow, and further research supports it, community colleges should be brought under the aegis of the state universities in order to help overcome the structural barriers that will still remain after the nonstructural reforms are implemented. Finally, it may be possible to think of transforming the larger community colleges into four-year colleges if conditions are favorable and if the objections raised against this transformation can be met. With all these changes, it is important that the comprehensive nature of the community college be preserved and its mission to provide pre-baccalaureate, vocational, and general adult education respected. Too many students want and benefit from its many services for them to be eliminated.

Notes

1. See the thoughtful review by McCartan (1983) of these "college for community" and "community college as college" positions.

2. A frequently stated mis-estimate of the number of baccalaureate aspirants is that they run as high as two-thirds to three-quarters of all community college students. The mistake derives from basing the estimate on figures in the annual freshman survey of the American Council on Education. This survey questions only full-time students, who make up only 58 percent of community college entrants and tend to have higher aspirations than part-time students (Dougherty, 1987, p. 87; Sheldon, 1982; U.S. Bureau of the Census, 1989, p. 53).

3. Astin et al. (1982) compared the results of entering a community college versus entering one of four different four-year institutions (public or private university, and public or private college) for five different racial/ethnic groups: Whites, Blacks, Chicanos, Native Americans, and Puerto Ricans. The *partial correlation* (after controlling for social background, aspirations, and high school experiences) between community college entrance and achieving a bachelor's degree was -0.14 for Whites, -0.06 for Blacks, -0.20 for Chicanos, -0.10 for Native Americans, and +0.01 for Puerto Ricans. On the other hand, for all groups except Puerto Ricans, the partial correlations between entrance to a four-year institution and baccalaureate attainment were more favorable (either being positive or less negative than the community college correlations).

4. For reasons of space, the following discussion is quite condensed. A much fuller treatment can be found in Dougherty (1991, in press).

5. Moreover, these transfer problems are greater for students who are female, non-White, and low in socioeconomic status than for students with the obverse characteristics (Lee & Frank, 1990; U.S. National Center for Education Statistics, 1977a, pp. 8, 11, 13, 28, 32, 70, 73; Velez & Javalgi, 1987).

6. The material following is drawn from Dougherty (1991).

7. These differences held not only in the aggregate but also across different kinds of students: for those high and medium in socioeconomic status (SES); those high, medium, and low in ability; and six of nine combined SES by ability categories. Tinto (1974) conducted a similar study that may contradict Medsker and Trent's (1964) findings. However, its research design precludes reaching any definitive judgment. He regressed college attendance rates of Illinois and North Carolina high school graduates in the 1966 School to College: Opportunities for Postsecondary Education (SCOPE) survey on type of college locally available, student ability, and family background (parents' education and occupation). Unfortunately, he had to exclude Chicago from his analysis, a key omission given the fact that it contains a very high proportion of Illinois's population and has a notably large community college system.

8. This can be seen in the record of postsecondary vocational schools, which resemble the *very* highly vocationalized community colleges envisioned by the noncollegiate reformers. Using the 1979 followup of the National Longitudinal Survey of the High School Class of 1972, Nunley and Breneman (1988) found that *baccalaureate aspirants* entering postsecondary vocational-technical schools received 31 percent fewer bachelor's degrees and averaged 0.88 fewer years of education than comparable community-college

entrants, even with extensive controls for socioeconomic background, academic aptitude, and educational aspirations.

9. In fact, among new, full-time "degree-seeking" students who entered Miami-Dade's doors between 1980 and 1982, only 25 percent transferred to a state university and only 8 percent received a bachelor's degree by January 1988. Even among students who entered the community college already eligible to attend a state university immediately, the percentages were not much better: 41 percent and 17 percent, respectively (Belcher, 1989, pp. 9, 38).

10. These declines are not explicable in terms of shifts in the number of community college students. In fact, when we divide the number of transfers by the number of students enrolled the previous year, the resulting proportions show the same pattern of decline. In the case of Florida, the number of transfers as a percentage of the fall enrollment in the previous year declined from 4.2 percent in 1984 to 3.3 percent in 1987. For California, the same ratio dropped from 4.4 percent in the 1970s to 3.3 percent in the 1980s.

11. The vocational proportion of their enrollments is 39 percent in Alaska (fall 1986 FTEs), 39 percent in New Mexico (1979–1980 FTEs), 40 percent in Kentucky (fall 1986 FTEs), and 47 percent in Hawaii (fall 1983 headcount) (Hauselman & Tudor, 1987, pp. 1–2, 29; New Mexico State Board of Education Finance, 1980, pp. 3, 26; Polk, 1984, pp. 8, 31; University of Alaska, 1987, pp. 18–31; University of Hawaii, 1986).

12. In Washington State, for example, the community college system trains large numbers of people in several occupations in which the supply of vocational graduates exceeds the demand by at least 200 percent: auto mechanics, diesel engine repair, computer programming and analysis, food production, welding, and electrical and electronic technology. In fact, in food production, the community college system alone graduates three times as many people as the field can employ (Mitchell et al., 1986). This overproduction of vocational graduates may also be evidenced by the repeated finding that on the average, only about 50 percent to 70 percent of community college vocational graduates find jobs directly related to their training (Cohen & Brawer, 1989, p. 213; Maryland State Board for Community Colleges, 1990, p. 100; Pincus, 1980, p. 348).

13. This is not to say that transferring from a branch to the main campus is frictionless. Transfers from the University of Alaska's community colleges to its four-year campuses have found that, while their community college credits are fully accepted toward the total needed for a baccalaureate, they often do not receive full credit for courses in their *major* (Alaska State Commission on Postsecondary Education, 1985, p. 107). In New Mexico, students at the branch campus of one state university have had difficulty moving to another state university (New Mexico Governor's Task Force on Higher Education Reform, 1986, p. 31; Richardson, 1989).

References

Alaska State Commission on Postsecondary Education. (1985). *Alaska postsecondary education, 1986–1990: A statewide plan.* Juneau: Author. (ERIC Document Reproduction Service No. ED 265 898)

American Association of Community and Junior Colleges. Commission on the Future of Community Colleges. (1988). *Building community colleges: A vision for a new century.* Washington, DC: Author. (ERIC Document Reproduction Service No. ED 293 578)

American Association of Community and Junior Colleges. Commission on the Future of Community Colleges. (1989). Mission statement. *Community and Junior College Journal, 59*(4), 19–26.

American Association of Community and Junior Colleges. Commission on the Future of Community Colleges. (1990). 1990 public policy agenda. *Community and Junior College Journal, 60*(4), 45–47.

Anderson, K. (1984). *Institutional differences in college effects.* Boca Raton: Florida Atlantic University. (ERIC Document Reproduction Service No. ED 256 204)

Astin, A. (1975). *Preventing students from dropping out*. San Francisco: Jossey-Bass.

Astin, A. (1977). *Four critical years*. San Francisco: Jossey-Bass.

Astin, A. (1983). Strengthening transfer education. In G. Vaughan (Ed.), *Issues for community college leaders in a new era* (pp. 122–138). San Francisco: Jossey-Bass.

Astin, A., Astin, H. S., Green, K. C., Kent, L., McNamara, P. R., & Williams, M. R. (1982). *Minorities in American higher education*. San Francisco: Jossey-Bass.

Baden-Borel, P. (1984). *Compilation of statistical data concerning the community colleges of the State University of New York, 1983–84*. Albany: State University of New York. (ERIC Document Reproduction Service No. ED 253 280)

Baratta, F., & Apodaca, E. (1984). *A profile of California community college transfer students at the University of California*. Berkeley: University of California. (ERIC Document Reproduction Service No. ED 260 754)

Bayer, A. E., Royer, J. T., & Webb, R. M. (1973). *Four years after college entry* (American Council on Education Research Reports 8[1]). Washington, DC: U.S. Government Printing Office. (ERIC Document Reproduction Service No. ED 077 329)

Beckes, I. (1964). The case for community junior colleges. *Junior College Journal, 34*(7), 24, 26–28.

Belcher, M. (1989). *Institutional effectiveness of Miami-Dade Community College*. Miami: Miami-Dade Community College. (ERIC Document Reproduction Service No. ED 311 962)

Bernstein, A. (1986). The devaluation of transfer. In L. S. Zwerling (Ed.), *The community college and its critics* (New Directions for Community Colleges No. 54) (pp. 31–40). San Francisco: Jossey-Bass. (ERIC Document Reproduction Service No. ED 271 169)

Bowen, H. (1977). *Investment in learning*. San Francisco: Jossey-Bass.

Bowles, D. (1988). Transferability in the liberal arts and sciences. In C. Prager (Ed.), *Enhancing articulation and transfer* (New Directions for Community Colleges No. 61) (pp. 27–38). San Francisco: Jossey-Bass.

Breneman, D. W., & Nelson, S. C. (1981). *Financing community colleges*. Washington, DC: Brookings Institution.

Brint, S., & Karabel, J. (1989). *The diverted dream*. New York: Oxford University Press.

California Community Colleges. (1984). *Transfer education*. Sacramento: Author. (ERIC Document Reproduction Service No. ED 250 025)

California Legislature. Joint Committee for Review of the Master Plan for Higher Education. (1987). *California's community college reform: Final report*. Sacramento: Author. (ERIC Document Reproduction Service No. ED 282 587)

California Postsecondary Education Commission. (1989). *Update of community college transfer student statistics, 1988–1989*. Sacramento: Author. (ERIC Document Reproduction Service No. ED 313 073)

Carnegie Commission on Higher Education. (1970). *The open door colleges*. New York: McGraw-Hill.

Carnegie Council on Policy Studies in Higher Education. (1979). *Giving youth a better chance*. San Francisco: Jossey-Bass.

Carnoy, M., & Shearer, D. (1980). *Economic democracy*. White Plains, NY: M. E. Sharpe.

Carnoy, M., Shearer, D., & Levin, H. M. (1985). *School and work in the democratic state.* Stanford, CA: Stanford University Press.

Center for the Study of Community Colleges. (1988). *An assessment of the Urban Transfer Opportunity Program. The Ford Foundation's Second Stage Transfer Opportunity Awards. Final report.* Los Angeles: University of California at Los Angeles. (ERIC Document Reproduction Service No. ED 293 573)

Clark, B. (1980). The "cooling out" function revisited. In G. Vaughan (Ed.), *Questioning the community college role* (New Directions for Community Colleges No. 32) (pp. 15–31). San Francisco: Jossey-Bass.

Clowes, D. A., & Levin, B. H. (1989). Community, technical, and junior colleges: Are they leaving higher education? *Journal of Higher Education, 60,* 349–355.

Cohen, A. M., & Brawer, F. B. (1982). *The American community college* (1st ed.), San Francisco: Jossey-Bass.

Cohen, A. M., & Brawer, F. (1987). *The collegiate function of the community college.* San Francisco: Jossey-Bass.

Cohen, A. M., & Brawer, F. (1989). *The American community college* (2nd ed.). San Francisco: Jossey-Bass.

Cohen, A. M., Brawer, F. B., & Bensimon, E. (1985). *Transfer education in American community colleges.* Los Angeles: University of California at Los Angeles. (ERIC Document Reproduction Service No. ED 255 250)

Commission on the Future of the North Carolina Community College System. (1989). *Gaining the competitive edge: The challenge to North Carolina's community colleges.* Chapel Hill, NC: MDC.

Crook, D., & Lavin, D. (1989). *The community college effect revisited: The long-term impact of community college entry on baccalaureate attainment.* Paper presented to the annual meeting of the American Educational Research Association, San Francisco.

Cross, K. P. (1981). Community colleges on the plateau. *Journal of Higher Education, 52,* 113–123.

Cross, K. P. (1985). Determining missions and priorities for the fifth generation. In W. Deegan & D. Tillery (Eds.), *Renewing the American community college.* San Francisco: Jossey-Bass.

Dougherty, K. (1987). The effects of community colleges: Aid or hindrance to socioeconomic attainment? *Sociology of Education, 60,* 86–103.

Dougherty, K. (1988). The politics of community college expansion: Beyond the functionalist and class-reproduction theories. *American Journal of Education, 96,* 351–393.

Dougherty, K. (1991). *The contradictory college: The political origins, current impact, and likely future of the community college.* Unpublished manuscript, Department of Sociology, Manhattan College, New York.

Dougherty, K. (in press). Community colleges and baccalaureate preparation. *Journal of Higher Education.*

Florida State Board for Community Colleges. (1988). *The role of Florida's community colleges in articulation.* Tallahassee: Author. (ERIC Document Reproduction Service No. ED 300 042)

Florida State Department of Education. (1983). *A longitudinal study comparing university native and community college transfer students in the state university system of Florida.* Tallahassee: Author. (ERIC Document Reproduction Service No. ED 256 405)

Gleazer, E. J. (1980). *Community colleges: Values, vision, and vitality.* Washington, DC: American Association of Community and Junior Colleges.

Grubb, W. N. (1984). The bandwagon once more: Vocational preparation for high technology occupations. *Harvard Educational Review, 54,* 429–451.

Grubb, W. N. (1988). Vocationalizing higher education: The causes of enrollment and completion in public two-year colleges, 1970–1980. *Economics of Education Review, 7,* 301–319.

Grubb, W. N. (1989). The effects of differentiation on educational attainment: The case of community colleges. *The Review of Higher Education, 12*(4), 349–374.

Hauselman, A. J., & Tudor, D. (1987). *Compendium of selected characteristics: University of Kentucky Community College System, 1986–1987.* Lexington: University of Kentucky. (ERIC Document Reproduction Service No. ED 289 543)

Holderman, K. (1964). The case for university branch campuses. *Junior College Journal, 34*(7), 25, 28–30.

Jaschik, S. (1988, September 7). California legislature passes a "historic" measure to reorganize the state's two year college system. *Chronicle of Higher Education,* pp. A17, 24.

Jencks, C., & Riesman, D. (1968). *The academic revolution.* New York: Doubleday.

Karabel, J. (1972). Community colleges and social stratification. *Harvard Educational Review, 42,* 521–562.

Kerr, C. (1980). Changes and challenges ahead for community colleges. *Community and Junior College Journal, 50*(8), 4–10.

Knight, W. (1990). *GPA and attrition information for students relocating to the Kent Campus of Kent State University from four two-year colleges and from the KSU regional campuses.* Unpublished report, Kent State University, Kent, OH.

Lara, J. (1981). *Differences in quality of academic effort between successful and unsuccessful community college transfer students.* Paper delivered at the annual meeting of the American Educational Research Association, Los Angeles. (ERIC Document Reproduction Service No. ED 201 359)

Lee, V., & Frank, K. (1990). Student characteristics that facilitate the transfer from two-year to four-year colleges. *Sociology of Education, 63,* 178–193.

Levin, H. (1984, October). Jobs: A changing workforce, a changing education? *Change Magazine,* pp. 32–37.

London, H. (1978). *The culture of a community college.* New York: Praeger.

Maryland State Board for Community Colleges. (1983). *The role of community colleges in preparing students for transfer to four-year colleges and universities.* Annapolis: Author. (ERIC Document Reproduction Service No. ED 230 255)

Maryland State Board for Community Colleges. (1990). *Databook and annual report.* Annapolis: Author. (ERIC Document Reproduction Service No. ED 315 136)

McCabe, R. (1981). Now is the time to reform the American community college. *Community and Junior College Journal, 51*, 6–10.

McCartan, A. (1983). The community college mission: Present challenges and future visions. *Journal of Higher Education, 54*, 676–692.

Medsker, L. L. (1960). *The junior college.* New York: McGraw-Hill.

Medsker, L. L., & Trent, J. (1964). *The influence of different types of public higher education institutions on college attendance from varying socioeconomic and ability levels.* Berkeley: University of California, Center for the Study of Higher Education. (ERIC Document Reproduction Service No. ED 002 875)

Mitchell, M., Postlewaite, B., Short, C., Wilson, S. M., & Wolfe, R. O. (1986). *Change and the future of vocational education.* Olympia: Washington State Vocational Directors Council. (ERIC Document Reproduction Service No. ED 268 284)

Morris, C., & Losak, J. (1986). *Student success at Miami-Dade Community College.* Miami: Miami-Dade Community College. (ERIC Document Reproduction Service No. ED 305 123)

New Mexico State Board of Educational Finance. (1980). *Factbook on New Mexico public two-year community colleges and vocational schools, 1979–1980.* Santa Fe: Author. (ERIC Document Reproduction Service No. ED 198 886)

New Mexico Governor's Task Force on Higher Education Reform. (1986). *Excellence and accountability.* Santa Fe: New Mexico Commission on Postsecondary Education. (ERIC Document Reproduction Service No. ED 272 079)

Nunley, C. R., & Breneman, D. W. (1988). Defining and measuring quality in community college education. In J. Eaton (Ed.), *Colleges of choice* (pp. 62–92). New York: Macmillan.

Olivas, M. (1979). *The dilemma of access: Minorities in two-year colleges.* Washington, DC: Howard University Press.

Orfield, G., Mitzel, H., Austin, T., Bentley, R., Bice, D., Dwyer, M., Gedlow, L., Herschensohn, J., Hibino, B., Kelly, T., Kuhns, A., Lee, M., Rabinowitz, C., Spoerl, J., Vosnos, A., & Wolf, J. (1984). *The Chicago study of access and choice in higher education.* Chicago: University of Chicago, Committee on Public Policy. (ERIC Document Reproduction Service No. ED 249 929)

Orfield, G., & Paul, F. (1987–1988). Declines in minority access: A tale of five cities. *Educational Record, 68*(4), *69*(1).

Pascarella, E., & Chapman, D. W. (1983). A multi-institutional, path analytic validation of Tinto's model of college withdrawal. *American Educational Research Journal, 20*, 87–102.

Pennsylvania State University. (1983). *Statement of policies, procedures, and guidelines for the Commonwealth educational system.* University Park: Author.

Pincus, F. L. (1980). The false promises of community colleges. *Harvard Educational Review, 50*, 332–361.

Pincus, F. L., & Archer, E. (1989). *Bridges to opportunity? Are community colleges meeting the transfer needs of minority students?* New York: The College Board.

Polk, B. (1984). *Hawaii's community colleges: New directions for the 80s.* Honolulu: University of Hawaii. (ERIC Document Reproduction Service No. ED 266 820)

Rendon, L., & Matthews, T. (1989). Success of community college students. *Education and Urban Society, 21*, 312–327.

Richardson, R., & Bender, L. (1985). *Students in urban settings: Achieving the baccalaureate degree* (ASHE/ERIC Higher Education Report No. 6). Washington, DC: Association for the Study of Higher Education/ERIC Clearinghouse on Higher Education. (ERIC Document Reproduction Service No. ED 265 798)

Richardson, R., & Bender, L. (1987). *Fostering minority access and achievement in higher education.* San Francisco: Jossey-Bass.

Sheldon, S. (1982). *Statewide longitudinal study. Report on academic years, 1978–1981. Part 5: Final report.* Sacramento: California Community Colleges. (ERIC Document Reproduction Service No. ED 217 917)

South Carolina Commission on Higher Education. (1979). *Policies of South Carolina senior colleges and universities concerning transfer from two-year colleges.* Columbia: Author. (ERIC Document Reproduction Service No. ED 177 994)

State University of New York. 1984–1989). *Application and enrollment patterns of transfer students.* Albany: Author. (ERIC Document Reproduction Service Nos. ED 254 122, 260 775, 273 341, 289 529, 302 108, 310 702)

State University System of Florida. (1986). *Fact book, 1984–85.* Tallahassee: Author. (ERIC Document Reproduction Service No. ED 312 937)

State University System of Florida. (1989). *Fact book, 1987–88.* Tallahassee: Author. (ERIC Document Reproduction Service No. ED 312 939)

Tinto, V. (1974). *Public junior colleges and the substitution effect in higher education.* Unpublished paper, Teachers College, Columbia University, New York. (ERIC Document Reproduction Service No. ED 089 808)

Tinto, V. (1987). *Leaving college.* Chicago: University of Chicago Press.

Trent, J., & Medsker, L. L. (1968). *Beyond high school.* San Francisco: Jossey-Bass.

U.S. Bureau of the Census. (1988). *School enrollment — Social and economic characteristics of students: October 1986* (Current Population Reports, Series P-20, No. 429). Washington, DC: Government Printing Office.

U.S. National Center for Education Statistics. (1977a). *Transfer students in institutions of higher education* (ASI 1977 4586-1.19). Washington, DC: Government Printing Office.

U.S. National Center for Education Statistics. (1977b). *Withdrawal from institutions of higher education* (ASI 1978 4586-1.26). Washington, DC: Government Printing Office.

U.S. National Center for Education Statistics. (1990a). *Patterns and trends of stopping out from postsecondary education: 1972, 1980, 1982 high school graduates* (ASI 1990 4842-41). Washington, DC: Government Printing Office.

U.S. National Center for Education Statistics. (1990b). *Digest of educational statistics, 1990.* Washington, DC: Government Printing Office.

University of Alaska. (1987). *Statistical abstract, 1987.* Fairbanks: University of Alaska. (ERIC Document Reproduction Service No. ED 292 437)

University of Connecticut. (1987). *Bulletin, 1986–87.* Storrs, CT: Author.

University of Hawaii. (1986). *Factbook, 1985. University of Hawaii Community Colleges.* Honolulu: University of Hawaii. (ERIC Document Reproduction Service No. ED 266 819)

Vaughan, G. (Ed.) (1980). Introduction. In *Questioning the community college role* (New Directions in Community Colleges No. 32). San Francisco: Jossey-Bass.

Vaughan, J. (1971). *A longitudinal study of the retention, attrition, and transfer of students at the regional campuses of the Ohio State University.* Unpublished master's thesis, Ohio State University, Columbus, OH.

Velez, W. (1985). Finishing college: The effects of college type. *Sociology of Education, 58,* 191–200.

Velez, W., & Javalgi, R. G. (1987). Two-year college to four-year college: The likelihood of transfer. *American Journal of Education, 96,* 81–94.

Weis, L. (1985). *Between two worlds: Black students in an urban community college.* Boston: Routledge and Kegan Paul.

Willingham, W., & Findikyan, N. (1969). *Patterns of admission for transfer students.* New York: College Entrance Examination Board.

Zwerling, L. S. (1976). *Second best: The crisis of the junior college.* New York: McGraw-Hill.

Insiders, Outsiders, and the Community College: A Sociology of Knowledge Perspective

Mark Oromaner

It is proposed that a more comprehensive view of the community college would emerge if a sociology of knowledge perspective toward analyses of that institution were adopted. Robert K. Merton's discussion of "insiders" and "outsiders" is applied to the often conflicting images of the role of the community college found in analyses of those affiliated with that institution (insiders) and those who view it from the vantage of the university (outsiders). It is suggested that a synthesis of insider and outsider perspectives is possible.

Insiders and Outsiders in the domain of knowledge, unite. You have nothing to lose but your claims. You have a world of understanding to win. (Merton, 1972, p. 44)

Researchers, commentators, defenders, critics, and theoreticians have increasingly approached the community college as an institution worthy of serious analysis (Vaughan, 1979, 1980; Oromaner, 1981-82; Cohen and Brawer, 1982). The present discussion does not look directly at the community college, but rather at those who write about it and their conceptions of it. The discussion is set in the tradition of the sociology of knowledge. Scholars from Karl Marx, Max Weber, and Emile Durkheim to Karl Mannheim, C. Wright Mills, Robert K. Merton, and Alvin W. Gouldner have contributed to this tradition. My central thesis is that biases, defined as "limited, partial, or distorted perspective(s)" (Meyers, 1981, pp. 165-166), exist in many analyses of the community college and that these biases can be understood on the basis of the backgrounds and current statuses of those who produce them. This is true for the Insiders, as well as for the Outsiders.[1] If the former are affiliated with the community college movement and usually defend it, the latter are likely to be affiliated with research universities and to be critical of the community college movement.[2]

Although a sociology of knowledge perspective cannot settle questions of truth, goodness, and beauty, it can contribute to an understanding of why particular views are produced and accepted by particular groups at particular times. The beginning of this understanding, I suggest, can be found in Marx's contention that "It is not the consciousness of men that determines their being, on the contrary, their social being determines their consciousness." We must realize that researchers are social beings (Gouldner, 1970) who approach their subject with background assumptions, interests, and values, and that these can be related to the social structures in which they are socialized, work, and live.

In his call for a sociology of knowledge approach to the study of social and economic development, Gunnar Myrdal made the following observation:

> A "disinterested" social science has never existed and never will exist. For logical reasons, it is impossible. A view presupposes a viewpoint. Research, like every other rationally pursued activity, must have a direction. The viewpoint and the direction are determined by our interest in a matter. Valuations enter into the choice of approach, the selection of problems, the definition of concepts, and the gathering of data, and are by no means confined to the practical or political inferences drawn from theoretical findings. (1968, p. 32)

Finally, in a sociology of knowledge analysis closer to our concerns, C. Wright Mills examined the theoretical, methodological, and political orientations presented in textbooks in the field of social disorganization. He found similar orientations in various texts and explained this on the basis of the social characteristics of the authors. Mills' hypothesis was:

> If members of an academic profession are recruited from similar contexts and if their backgrounds and careers are relatively similar, there is a tendency for them to be uniformly set for some common perspective. . . . The common conditions of their profession often seem more important in this connection than similarity of extraction. (1943, p. 167)

Individual and group biases are to be explained not on the basis of conscious distortions or conspiracies, but rather on the basis of the fact that common educational and work experiences lead to common viewpoints.

A sociology of knowledge approach might help in modifying the response of many members of the community college sector to criticisms of that sector. Vaughan suggests that while many community college leaders were trained in disciplines which emphasized the role of criticism, "yet when it comes to the community college movement and especially to the role a single college plays in that movement, a certain paranoia seems to emanate from community college leaders (1980, p. 13). Steven Zwerling, author of *Second Best: The Crisis of the Community College* (1976) was greeted at the 1979 meeting of the American Association of Community and Junior Colleges with a reaction that was "mostly defensive and even hostile, one administrator rising to say publicly at the close of the session, 'I think Mr. Zwerling is second best'" (cited in Johnston, 1980, p. 43). Although an understanding of the theoretical perspectives and conceptual bases of the work of those who analyze the community college would contribute to a better appreciation of these analyses (Oromaner, 1981-82), the development of a sociology of knowledge perspective would enable one to place the analyses within social rather than personal contexts.

In a review of a number of the critiques of the role of the community colleges, Vaughan suggests that "It will perhaps also be of interest to note that of the four critics quoted here, only one has worked in a community college" (1979, p. 10). This is certainly of interest in light of Mills' emphasis on the relationship between common professional experiences and the development of common perspectives. Two of Vaughan's critics were affiliated with the University of California—one at Berkeley and one at Los Angeles—and the third was affiliated with Harvard. In a somewhat more systematic examination of the associations, sponsorship, and affiliations of community college critics, Zwerling proposes that the major critics can be placed into four categories (1976, pp. 279–290): official critics, left official critics, anti-university group, and radicals. Once again, a number of the critics were affiliated with prestigious research universities. Studies in the sociology of higher education and science indicate that individuals affiliated with research universities are likely to have undergone a common socialization experience at such universities and to work in settings in which colleagues share common values, expectations, and rewards. They are particularly subject to pressure associated with the "publish or perish" phenomenon. They experience internal pressure as a result of professional socialization and external pressure from colleagues and employers. The internal pressure involves self-esteem; the external pressure involves the achievement of tenure, promotion, income, status, and prestige.

Vaughan has recognized that the community college has provided the "revisionists" with "a fertile field for research that often results in a proliferation of articles and books" (1979, p. 11). I assume that he restricted this observation to revisionists because, at present, many of the outsiders are critical of the role of the community college. The community college has also provided a fertile field for insiders who defend it.

Although a number of outsiders and insiders have been attracted to the community college as a research site, Cohen and Brawer commented "Few serious scholars have been concerned with the community colleges . . ."(1982, p. 342). I am not sure how one would identify serious scholars. However, I do believe that few outsiders have been attracted to the study of the community college and that this phenomenon deserves explanation. I would suggest that a partial explanation is that, to some extent, the professional reputation of a researcher is influenced by the class, status, and power of his/her subject. The community college is not an institution in the higher circles of American society, nor is it near the top of the stratification system within the structure of American higher education. Why study the community college if more influential and prestigious undergraduate, graduate, and professional schools are available? The class background of students in such schools, as compared with that of students in the community college, contributes to the attractiveness of these organizations as research sites.[3]

I also hypothesize that if the community college is not highly valued as a research site by university-based colleagues, "serious" outsiders who work in this area may be predisposed to be critical in their analyses. Researchers frequently fear the accusation that they have "gone native" or that they have become too involved with their subjects. These accusations are likely to arise when one views the world from the insider's perspective or produces an analysis that conflicts with the taken-for-granted wisdom of one's professional circle and peers. One can escape professional criticism of this type by maintaining a critical stance vis-à-vis the community college and its role in society. The least that one can do is to support the present wisdom. I suggest that the present wisdom among university-based researchers is that the community college is at best second best. Research should be conducted on the attitudes and perceptions of university-based faculty concerning the role of the community college, the nature of community college education, the quality of community college faculty and students, and the nature and quality of the work of those researchers who study the community college.[4]

The impact of the expectations of one's colleagues, professional socialization, and pressure to publish in the "right" journals (e. g., *Sociology of Education* and the *Harvard Educational Review* rather than *Community and Junior College Journal* and the *Community College Review*) largely account for the critical analyses of the outsiders. These same social forces do, I propose, help to account for the exaggerated claims made by a number of insiders. For insiders, the community college journals are the right journals.[5] These journals provide an important formal channel of communication with one's colleagues. It is not unfair to assume that potential authors believe that the editors of these journals are more receptive to positive rather than negative analyses of the community college. An examination of the insiders' perceptions of the interests of these gatekeepers would make a contribution to our understanding of the role played by journals in the selection of research questions and the analyses of these questions by insiders. At the same time, an analysis of the actual interests of gatekeepers should be conducted. It is possible that insiders are working in a situation of pluralistic ignorance in which each assumes that the other expects positive analyses to be produced. Colleagues, administrators, and gatekeepers may be more receptive to criticism from insiders than is generally expected. Perceptions and beliefs may become self-fulfilling prophecies. For example, insiders believe that community college journals will publish only positive analyses and therefore submit only positive analyses for publication consideration. Since no critical work is submitted, no critical work is published. Insiders who read these journals conclude that since no critical work is published, such work will not be published. Why waste one's time on work that will not be rewarded? The fact that Vaughan's stimulating paper, "The Challenge of Criticism" (1979) appeared in *Community and Junior College Journal* may have some impact on this phenomenon. He challenged insiders to "produce significant works on the role of the community college" and not "to turn their research and writing responsibilities over to university-based professors. . . ."

Vaughan's challenge raises the long-standing issue of the comparative advantages and disadvantages of insiders and outsiders. If we are to be concerned with whether insiders or outsiders analyze the community college, we must assume that an advantage or disadvantage is associated with each position. If such an advantage or disadvantage does not exist, then from the perspective of our understanding of that institution, who conducts the analysis is irrelevant. I am, of course, assuming that both insiders and outsiders are technically competent to conduct such an analysis. [6]

Merton has presented the insider-outsider issue in structural terms, that is, as "the problem of patterned differentials among social groups and strata in access to certain types of knowledge" (1972, p. 11). The insider doctrine can be expressed in the statement "You have to be one to know one." The insider has a monopolistic or privileged access to knowledge, while the outsider is excluded from this direct knowledge. Access or exclusion is based on one's group membership or social position. Since the outsider has not been socialized in the group nor experienced the daily activities of the group, he or she cannot develop an understanding of what it means to be a group member. This is a strong version of the insider doctrine and is not applicable to the issues under examination in this discussion. However, I would argue that the weaker version of the doctrine does aid in our understanding of current analyses of the community college. This version suggests that insiders and outsiders will have slightly different "foci of interest." Since they are members of different groups and occupy different positions in the social structure, they have different interests and raise different questions. In Merton's words:

> Unlike the stringent version of the doctrine which maintains that Insiders and Outsiders must arrive at different (and presumably incompatible) findings and interpretations even when they do examine the same problems, this weaker version argues only that they will not deal with the same questions and so will simply talk past one another. (1972, p. 16)

An example of the situation in which insiders and outsiders, vis-à-vis the community college, talk past one another involves the analysis of the role of that institution in the class system. Since insiders are likely to be exposed daily to the lives of community college students, one might expect that they would be aware of the successes and failures of individual students. Insiders are likely to be proud of the successes and to attribute these to the impact of the community college experience. To quote an insider:

> One can point to a number of areas where community college leaders can challenge the critics and thus further enlighten scholars, community college professionals and the public regarding the contributions community colleges have made to society, including that of providing an avenue of educational opportunity and upward social mobility for many Americans. (Vaughan, 1979, p. 11)

The contact that insiders have with students should influence them to raise questions about the impact of the college experience on the students' lives. These are legitimate questions that should be addressed. On the other hand, outsiders are less likely to have direct and prolonged contact with individual students and are more likely to raise questions concerning a structural or group level of analysis. For instance, one of the most prominent outsiders, Karabel, has argued: "To observe that educational expansion has not resulted in fundamental change in the American class structure is in no way to deny that it *has* been critical in providing upward mobility for many individuals" (1972, p. 526). The basic issue for Karabel and many outsiders is one of the structure of the American class system, and not of individual mobility within that system (Oromaner, 1981-82). The existence of a difference in emphasis on individual mobility (insiders) and group mobility (outsiders) has been recognized by Cohen and Brawer, who argue that "the critics' fundamental flaw is that *they have attempted to shift the meaning of educational equality from individual to group mobility*" (1982, p. 352). My analysis would lead me to propose that the critics (outsiders) have a different focus of interest than do insiders. Once this is understood, it may be easier for insiders and outsiders to stop talking past one another.

The strong version of the insider doctrine—and its assumption that the insider has an advantage—has its counterpart in the outsider doctrine and its associated tradition. The basic point of this tradition is that there is a corrupting influence of group membership and loyalties on one's ability to understand the group. In place of the insider doctrine one substitutes an outsider doctrine, which claims a special advantage for the outsider. The argument here is that as the outsider has not been socialized in the group and has not experienced the daily activities of the group, he or she is in a better position than is the insider to provide an "objective" view of the reality of the group. What are considered virtues from the insiders' perspective are considered sins from the outsiders' perspective. Merton cites a number of well-known research projects based on the assumptions of the outsider doctrine. Tocqueville's *Democracy in America* is probably the classic example. Merton quotes Tocqueville's statement that "there are certain truths which Americans can only learn from strangers." A second example involves the selection by the Carnegie Foundation for the Advancement of Teaching of Abraham Flexner to investigate the condition of medical schools. According to Merton, this was done after Flexner had admitted that he had never been inside a medical school. Gunnar Myrdal's *The American Dilemma* provides a third example of a study based on the assumptions of the outsider doctrine. When the Carnegie Corporation searched for an individual to examine the status of race relations in the United States, a Swedish economist was identified. Merton quotes Myrdal's observation that he "had never been subject to the strains involved in living in a black-white society."[7]

Although Vaughan challenges his insider colleagues to engage in serious analysis of the community college, he also argues that "there appear to be certain advantages associated with viewing a movement from the vantage point of the university" (1980, p. 11). These are: (1) that the university professor is unlikely to be caught up in the day-to-day operation of the community college and is therefore unlikely to become as emotionally involved, (2) that it is easier to be objective when one does not have a vested interest in the success or failure of an institution, and (3) although being university based does not guarantee good research, more emphasis is placed on research than would be normally in a community college. While the third point is certainly true, it is not directly related to the issue of the perspectives or biases present in analyses of the community college. The first two points are, however, based on the outsider doctrine. Again, I would argue that the advantage possessed by the outsider is that he/she has a different focus of interest than that of the insider and therefore raises different questions.[8] In Merton's words: "We no longer ask whether it is the Insider or Outsider who has monopolistic or privileged access to social truth; instead, we begin to consider their distinctive and interactive roles in the process of truth seeking" (1972, p. 36).

I have argued that the distinctive roles of the insider and outsider involve the perspectives brought by each to the study of the community college. The fact that each has a somewhat different perspective does not mean that one cannot communicate across perspectives and thus develop a more comprehensive understanding. The ability of insiders and outsiders to interact and influence one another is greatly enhanced by the fact that, in the present context, they are each members of a larger academic/scholarly community. Individuals do not occupy one status at a time. If our researchers are influenced by their affiliation with community colleges or universities, they are also influenced by other achieved and ascribed statuses. Most prominent among the former is the status of academic/scholar. The norms associated with the role of academic/scholar require the application of universalistic standards in the evaluation of ideas. Although this norm may be violated by a reliance on particularistic criteria—e. g., professional and personal characteristics—it is still a norm and, as such, plays a significant role in the academic/scholarly community. Merton has expressed the general point in the following terms: "The acceptance of criteria of craftsmanship and integrity in science and learning cuts across differences in the social affiliations and loyalties of scientists and scholars" (1972, p. 42).

The mere existence of the potential for syntheses of insider and outsider perspectives is not sufficient to guarantee the development of such syntheses. This development may be inhibited by the organizational, institutional, and professional forces described. In order to take advantage of this potential, a number of modifications in the academic reward/research/publication system should be instituted. Researchers could, for instance, take a lead from Myrdal and include both insiders and outsiders as collaborators.[7] However, if cross-disciplinary collaboration is difficult to achieve, one might anticipate even greater problems in cross-sectoral collaboration. One approach may be to engage in a more informal rather than formal collaboration. Insiders and outsiders could use one another as "trusted assessors" of their work at each stage in its development. It is current practice to circulate a draft of one's work before it is submitted for publication. My suggestion would require that this practice be incorporated into the design stage and not left until the research has been designed and the data collected and analyzed. An effort should also be made to incorporate different biases or perspectives. This is a more radical suggestion than the traditional one concerning the inclusion of a number of research techniques (triangulation).

Independent of the issue of insider-outsider collaboration, each should attempt to reach an audience comprised of members of the other group. The major benefit of this is that insider and outsider audiences would be exposed to perspectives and analyses that might challenge their taken-for-granted conceptions of the community college. At present, outsiders are not likely to receive rewards for publishing in community college journals. One way to change this is to have outsiders publish in these journals. If this were to occur, the status of these journals would increase among outsiders. At the same time, insiders are not likely to publish in outsider journals. This may reflect a reluctance to submit manuscripts for publication consideration. In each of these cases, gatekeepers of appropriate journals could have an impact if they were to solicit manuscripts from members of the other group.

These recommendations are based on the assumption that academics/scholars are influenced by ideas. This, I suggest, is an assumption that is equally valid for insiders and outsiders.

Notes

1. From the perspective of this essay, the structural perspective, "Insiders are members of specified groups and collectivities or occupants of specified social statuses; Outsiders are the nonmembers" (Merton, 1972, p. 21).

2. Although in this essay insiders and outsiders are distinguished on the basis of an achieved status—professional affiliation—Merton's (1972) examples are based principally on ascribed statuses—e.g., race, sex, religion, and ethnicity.

3. Bowles and Gintis have suggested that the status of organizations within the stratification system of higher education "reflects both the social status of the families of the students and the hierarchy of work relationships into which each type of student will move after graduation" (1976, p. 209).

4. The interests of sponsoring agencies should also be examined. In a critique of Daniel Bell's postindustrial society thesis concerning the preeminence of professional and technical strata, Coser argues that Bell does not seem seriously to entertain the notion that the employers and funding agencies, both public and private who employ them or contract for their work, may in fact direct their activities much more than they themselves are directed by them" (1975, p. 218). Agencies that have sponsored analyses of the community college include the Carnegie Commission on Higher Education, the American Association of Junior

Colleges, the Educational Testing Service, the College Entrance Examination Board, and the erstwhile Department of Health, Education, and Welfare (Zwerling, 1976, p. 280).

5. The fact that community college faculty are likely to publish in different journals than those utilized by their four-year college and university colleagues is one manifestation of their academic isolation (London, 1980).

6. The ability of community college insiders to examine their own institutions critically has been questioned by Cohen and Brawer (1982, p. 365).

7. Merton makes the interesting point that while Myrdal might have been an outsider, a number of his associates were insiders (Americans) engaged in the study of race relations.

8. The assessment of the social value of the community college provides an example of an area in which insiders and outsiders might ask different questions. The following comments provide an indication of the conflicting perspectives in this area:

> The traditional method of measuring the worth of a school has been to gauge the value it adds to its students. Measures of what the students know when they enter and of what they know when they leave are the classic assessment strategies.... But many community college people are convinced that their institution should no longer be assessed in that way. They feel they have moved into another sphere, one in which the institution is less concerned with traditional teaching and learning than with providing access, credentials, and connections. Accordingly, when Astin suggested that the two-year colleges were detrimental to students' passage through the system toward the baccalaureate degree, the college spokespersons reacted uproariously. (Cohen and Brawer, 1982, pp. 362–363)

The Astin referred to is the U.C.L.A. Professor of Higher Education Alexander W. Astin.

References

Bowles, S., and Gintis, H. *Schooling in Capitalist America.* New York: Basic Books, 1976.

Cohen, A. M., and Brawer, F. B. *The American Community College.* San Francisco: Jossey-Bass, 1982.

Coser, L. A. Structure and conflict. In P. M. Blau (Ed.), *Approaches to the Study of Social Structure.* New York: Free Press, 1975.

Gouldner, A. W. *The Coming Crisis of Western Sociology.* New York: Basic Books, 1970.

Johnston, J. R. Community colleges: Alternative to elitism in higher education. In G. B. Vaughan (Ed.), *New Directions For Community Colleges: Questioning the Community College Role, 32.* San Francisco: Jossey-Bass, 1980.

Karabel, J. Community colleges and social stratification. *Harvard Educational Review,* 1972, *42,* 521–562.

London, H. B. In between: The community college teacher. *The Annals,* 1980, *448,* 62–73.

Merton, R. K. Insiders and outsiders: A chapter in the sociology of knowledge. *American Journal of Sociology,* 1972, *78,* 9–47.

Meyers, W. R. *The Evaluation Enterprise.* San Francisco: Jossey-Bass, 1981.

Mills, C. W. The professional ideology of social pathologists. *American Journal of Sociology,* 1943, *49,* 165–180.

Myrdal, G. *Asian Drama: An Inquiry Into the Poverty of Nations, Vol. I* New York: Pantheon, 1968.

Oromaner, M. Community colleges and the class structure: A dialectical perspective. *Community College Review*, 1981–82, *9*, 50–55.

Vaughan, G. B. The challenge of criticism. *Community and Junior College Journal*, 1979, *50*, 8–11.

Vaughan, G. B. Critics of the community college: An overview. In G. B. Vaughan (Ed.), *New Directions For Community Colleges: Questioning the Community College Role, 32*. San Francisco: Jossey-Bass, 1980.

Zwerling, L. S. *Second Best: The Crisis of the Community College.* New York: McGraw-Hill, 1976. Received April 13, 1984.

The Path to Respect

George B. Vaughan

I believe that community colleges will achieve their full potential as institutions of higher education only when scholarship occupies a prominent place in the community college philosophy. As institutional leaders continue to evaluate and define the role community colleges play in the nation's system of higher education, they must realize that the failure to include scholarship as an important element in the community college philosophy is a flaw that erodes the image, indeed erodes the status, of these institutions among other institutions of higher education. The failure of community college leaders to address the relationship between scholarship and effective teaching is the community college's Achilles' heel. As institutions dedicated to outstanding teaching, community colleges can never achieve their full potential without a commitment to scholarship, nor can they assume a legitimate place as members of the higher education community.

This article explores this thesis and suggests ways community college faculty members and administrators might change their attitudes and practices relating to scholarship. The discussion centers around four questions.

1. Are scholarship and research different from each other, and if so, how?

2. Why do community colleges give so little attention to scholarship?

3. Should community college faculty members and administrators pay more attention to scholarship?

4. What can be done to enhance scholarship in the community college?

Defining Terms

In order to place the roles of scholarship and research in their proper perspectives in the community college philosophy, we must begin by defining the terms.

> Scholarship is the systematic pursuit of a topic, an objective, rational inquiry that involves critical analysis. It requires the precise observation, organization, and recording of information in the search for truth and order. Scholarship is the umbrella under which research falls, for research is but one form of scholarship. Scholarship results in a product that is shared with others and that is subject to the criticism of individuals qualified to judge the product. The product may take the form of a book review, an annotated bibliography, a lecture, a review of existing research on a topic, a speech that is a synthesis of the thinking of a topic. Scholarship requires that one have a solid foundation in one's professional field and that one keep up with the developments in that field.

Research is a systematic, objective search for new knowledge or a new application of existing knowledge. It results in knowledge that is verifiable based on empirical data, consensus in the field, or rules of logic. Others must be able to replicate the results of the research by following the same procedures. Research is not simply the act of gathering information or collecting data in a vacuum; it builds upon previous scholarly efforts and involves the understanding of relationships among data. One must be able to draw conclusions, interpretations, or more powerful generalizations as a result of the research process.

While research is a legitimate undertaking for selected community college professionals, I believe that the great majority of community college faculty and administrators should concern themselves with scholarship rather than research. All community college professionals should be scholars, for through scholarship a discipline love for learning manifests itself. It is this love, this passion for learning that sustains effective teaching.

Why Scholarship Is Neglected

I believe there are five reasons why scholarship is not part of the community college culture. Examining and questioning these reasons should help reshape the culture.

1. *Community colleges have failed to link scholarship to teaching.* We in community colleges rightfully pride ourselves on being committed to teaching. (So do almost all liberal arts colleges, state colleges, and undergraduate schools at our leading research universities.) Indeed, to describe community colleges as "teaching institutions" has become something of a cliché. As with most clichés, we use this one without thinking about what it means, *or* if it means anything.

In their zeal to call attention to the community college as a teaching institution, its supporters have failed to make the vital connection between teaching and scholarship. They have failed to acknowledge that outstanding teaching requires constant learning and intellectual renewal, and cannot exist without these essential elements of scholarship. In fact, some of our leaders seem to take perverse pleasure in proclaiming that community colleges are not research institutions and, therefore (one assumes), are not concerned with scholarship. Yet effective, inspirational teaching demands continual replenishing of the mind and spirit through scholarship and, in turn, bringing new knowledge and inspiration to one's teaching.

Faculty and administrators should not be excused from engaging in scholarship simply because community colleges are not research institutions. Indeed, since the intellectual stimulation and satisfaction that often accompanies research is missing for most community college faculty, it is imperative that they engage in scholarship as a means of professional renewal.

2. *Community colleges have failed to reward scholarship.* Historically, scholarship has been kept in the closets of our minds because we have been unwilling to recognize and reward scholarly activities. Rarely is scholarship even mentioned in the faculty promotion and retention process, much less viewed as a vital consideration.

While much of the blame for the failure to reward scholarship falls on the shoulders of administrators, faculty members must share the guilt. As a matter of fact, on some campuses if a faculty member or administrator becomes too scholarly (a contradiction in terms, one hopes), and especially if the results of that activity are published, that individual is likely to end up as something of an academic outcast. Earl Seidman, in his study of community college faculty, discovered that "the conditions of community college teaching reflect an absence of shared assumptions about its intellectual nature."[1] For example, one faculty member who participated in the study believes that in order to teach well he must devote time to scholarship. He found, however, that his colleagues reacted ambivalently toward the time he spent in preparation and study for his teaching and jokingly referred to him as the "guy who reads all the time."[2] David Reisman, in personal correspondence, commented briefly on this aspect of scholarship, which pervades all of academe. He writes,

> In all but a very small number of colleges and universities, there is very little scholarship and less research. When in these settings . . . people go beyond the peer group and do scholarly work, they are likely to be punished. In most of American academia . . . it is 'teach or perish' rather than 'publish or perish.'

We in the community college have not recognized the relationship between effective teaching and scholarship. As a result, we have not rewarded scholarly activities.

3. *Community college presidents fail to engage in scholarship.* Closely related to the rewards system is the failure of community college presidents to emphasize and promote scholarly activities for themselves. Partly as a result of the pragmatic nature of their position, and partly as a result of the climate on campus (a climate for which the president must assume major responsibility), community college presidents place little importance on scholarship, especially scholarship that results in publications. Indeed, when community college leaders identified 18 skills and abilities that would be required of the successful president, they ranked the ability to produce scholarly publications at the bottom of the scale. Further, they considered scholarly publications of little importance for those who report to the president, including the academic dean.[3] Consequently, president who do not hold scholarly activity as central to their own role are unlikely to see it as essential for others.

4. *Community college faculty and administrators have a misplaced sense of professional obligations.* Many community college faculty and administrators have failed to make the necessary connection between their obligations to the job and their obligations to the profession. There are some good reasons why obligations to the job overshadow a commitment to scholarship. Teaching faculty members are usually required to teach 15 to 18 credit hours a week (on campuses where they are paid for overloads, they often teach even more), to hold office hours, to serve on committees, and to engage in a number of other activities that go along with their employment. The administrator's schedule is just as hectic.

As a result of job requirements, a sort of "I can't do any more than I'm doing" attitude develops among faculty and administrators. This attitude can be especially difficult to overcome where tightly drawn union contracts permit certain activities and prohibit others, blurring the line between what can be expected of faculty members as professionals and what can be required of them as employees. (Unions could improve college teaching and their own image in the academic world if they made the pursuit of scholarship a priority for faculty.) Thinking in terms of the job rather than of the profession results in neglect of our scholarship, in part, because we are rebelling against doing any more than we are required to do, a serious mistake and one that is deadening to us as professionals.

5. *Many community college professionals neglect scholarship because they have been drawn into the debate, intellectually and emotionally, of teaching versus research.* This debate has little relevance to the community college, as I will explain further below.

Why Engage in Scholarship?

Critical to an understanding of the relationship between scholarship and the community college philosophy is the recognition that the community college is first and foremost an institution of higher education. The lifeblood of *any* such institution *must be* scholarship, for teaching alone is not enough.

Nancie L. Gonzales, professor of anthropology at the University of Maryland, College Park, argues that professors ". . . should do more than merely 'teach-'—worthy though that profession may be in and of itself. 'To profess' is to present one's *own* data, synthesis, or way of viewing the world. 'To profess' is to exercise intellectual leadership."[4] Teaching without scholarship is the brokering of information, not the providing of intellectual leadership.

Scholarship, then, is the avenue through which we stay in touch with the academic enterprise; it constantly pulls us back to learning, back to the college's mission, back to the core of the enterprise. Scholarship, perhaps more than any other characteristic, distinguishes teaching in an institution of higher education as a unique profession in our society, a profession that cannot settle for a snapshot of current or past knowledge but views knowledge as dynamic and views effective teaching as requiring constant inquiry, constant learning, and constant interacting with new and existing knowledge.

While many professionals outside the academic community engage in what often is referred to as lifelong learning, few pursue knowledge with an emphasis not just upon learning, but upon the interpretation of knowledge, upon teaching, and upon critical analysis. Scholarship gives us legitimacy in the world of higher education, the world we have chosen as our own. Scholarship in academia is truly the coin of the realm for without it, we might as well be working with the local bank or a department store.

These reasons for engaging in scholarship are largely philosophical. They may not appear relevant to much of what we do daily in the community college, but as Frank H.T. Rhodes, president of Cornell University has noted, "Even pragmatists need some light by which to live. . . ." Nevertheless, most community college professionals are justly proud of their pragmatic approach to their profession. As pragmatists, then, we need more then philosophy on which to build our house of the intellect.

There are as many practical as well as philosophical reasons for engaging in scholarship. As Ernest Boyer observes,

> Scholarship is not an esoteric appendage; it is at the heart of what the profession is all about. All faculty, throughout their careers, should, themselves, remain students. As scholars, they must continue to learn and be seriously and continuously engaged in the expanding intellectual world.[5]

Even the most pragmatic among us can see that the discipline and thought required to be a scholar sharpen the critical skills of the individual. Only through critical review and analysis can our colleges and we as individuals formulate positions on the issues of the day and in turn interpret them in that way that has meaning to us, our disciplines, our students, and ultimately to society. Critical review and analysis of the issues of the day are required if we are to receive adequate community support, funding, and ultimately students. Through scholarship we can ask and answer the difficult questions we face now and the ones we will face in the future.

Moreover, from a practical point of view, scholarship will enhance our standing as professionals in a profession that reveres scholarship if not always practice, certainly in theory. Scholarship functions to produce not only competence in the individual teacher but also respectability among peers both inside and outside of the community college field, a respect that is essential to membership in one's profession.

Sparring in the Wrong Debate

I suggested above that one of the reasons we in the community college do not emphasize scholarship is because we have been sidetracked by the debate on teaching versus research, a debate that might have been challenging while we were in graduate school but that is not relevant to those of us who work in a community college today.

Of course, we devote most of our time to teaching, for many of us chose the community college because it placed a high value on teaching. Most of us do almost no research in the traditional sense of the word, for many of us chose the community college because it did not require its faculty and administrators to conduct research. However, the debate of teaching versus research must not be used as a smokescreen for those administrators and faculty members who think that the lack of emphasis on research excuses them from pursing scholarship. *The debate for the community college professional is not one of the teaching versus research but rather one of the community college faculty member as teacher and scholar versus as teacher only. Every faculty member must face the question: Can one be an effective teacher or administrator without being a scholar?* Once we view the debate in this context, it takes on new dimensions and is not only relevant to our roles as community college professionals but may indeed also be critical to our success in the future, especially if we are to be viewed as legitimate members of the academic community.

Enhancing Scholarship

The most obvious way of enhancing scholarship is to make it an important part of the community college philosophy. This can only be done by incorporating scholarship in the rewards system. In those colleges with tenure and rank, scholarship should be an important consideration in granting tenure or a promotion in rank. Admittedly, there is some danger in this approach. The community college must not fall into a "scholarship or perish" syndrome. When scholarship is used in the tenure and promotion process, it must be one more important way of viewing faculty performance.

Including scholarship in the promotion and tenure process will emphasize its importance and encourage faculty members and administrators to take it into account as they perform their daily tasks. Thus they will see themselves as scholars and will act, one hopes, accordingly. Including scholarship in the process will make it impossible to separate scholarship from the faculty member's role as teacher and, therefore, make it impossible to separate scholarship from the community college philosophy.

Each community college should institute a forum devoted to scholarship whereby faculty and administrators demonstrate their commitment to and accomplishments in scholarly activities. These forums are especially important in the more than 500 small and often rural community colleges that suffer from the provincialism that results, in part, from their location. The forum, which can be an exhilarating form of renewal for faculty and administrators, should be conducted in the best academic tradition, with discussion, criticism, and questions following each presentation. Community college faculty and administrators could be the leaders in an approach to scholarship that cuts across disciplines, for rarely would the scholarly forum be conducted for just members of a single discipline, as is often the case on university campuses and at most professional meetings; rather, all faculty members who are interested would be encouraged to attend and participate in the forum.

Released time, summer employment and study, and other avenues should be available for scholarly pursuits. Faculty should devote such time to something other than the seemingly endless task of course restructuring. In the best of all worlds, course revision leads to new and exciting courses that call upon the scholarly abilities of faculty members; too often, however, course revision results in noting more than old wine in new bottles, and in many cases, old bottles with new packaging. Too often, course revision becomes an end, not the means for reading, for thinking, for synthesizing, for scholarship.

The president must lead the way in establishing a climate on campus that promotes scholarship. To do so, the president must be a scholar. As Clark Kerr and Marian Gade note in *The Many Lives of Academic Presidents,* all presidents are less involved today than in the past in the institution's academic life. They believe that presidents must have a personal concern for and familiarity with what is happening in the world of knowledge and that these are gained from reading and talking with people about where the intellectual world is going, and about new developments in research and instruction.[6]

Kerr and Gade are advocating, then, that presidents be scholars. The authors quote Richard M. Cyert on the intellectual role—the scholarly role—of the president:

> In the '80s, presidents must again become educational leaders in their institutions. Even fund-raising activities may have to take a back seat to the necessity of having the president function as an intellectual leader. In their actions and in their utterances, the presidents must embody the search [for] excellence that they want and need in faculty members. . . . The president will need to write more and speak more to the faculty in small and large groups. . . . Without the president at the end of the line, the faculty will not follow.[7]

Community college presidents must synthesize their thoughts on the subjects at hand, define problems, offer solutions, share their thoughts in open forums (either written or spoken), and be ready and willing to subject their thoughts to critical analysis by the faculty and other administrators. Community college presidents, then, must lead the way if community colleges are to devote significant time, attention, and energy to scholarship. They must realize that the era of growth has ended and that now is the time for a renaissance in learning, that new tensions and new agendas exist. The president must be the institution's educational leader; as educational leader, the president must understand that the keystone to educational leadership is scholarship.

Finally, community college faculty and administrators must get over the feeling that they are second-best in the higher education community. Once scholarship becomes a part of the everyday scene on campus, community college professionals will find that they are not only as capable of doing scholarly work as their four-year counterparts but they—community college professionals— are bringing that same pragmatic approach to scholarship that they have brought to so much else; they are *doing* scholarship as well as talking about it. This alone might be unique enough in higher education to warrant the attention of all academics who are engaged in the pursuit of truth and knowledge. But until community college leaders change current expectations, attitudes, and practices toward scholarly activities, scholarship will remain the community colleges' Achilles' heel.

Notes

1. Seidman, Earl *In the Words of the Faculty*. San Francisco: Jossey-Bass, 1985, p. 253.

2. Ibid, p. 254.

3. Vaughan, George B. *The Community College Presidency*. New York: American Council on Education/ Macmillan Publishing Co., 1986, pp. 189, 192.

4. Gonzales, Nancie L. "The Professor as Researcher." *National Forum*, Winter 1987, p. 7.

5. Boyer, Ernest L. *College: The Undergraduate Experience in America*. New York: The Carnegie Foundation for the Advancement of Teaching/Harper and Row Publishers, 1987, p. 131.

6. Kerr, Clark and Marian L. Gade. *The Many Lives of Academic Presidents: Time, Place and Character*. Washington, D.C.: Association of Governing Boards, 1986, p. 109.

7. Ibid, p.89.

Suggested Readings:
Social Role and Future Perspectives

Clowes, D. A. and Levin, B. H. (July/August, 1989). "Community, Technical, and Junior Colleges: Are They Leaving Higher Education?" *Journal of Higher Education*, 60 (3): 349–355.

Cohen, A. M. (1985). "Student Access and the Collegiate Function in Community Colleges." *Higher Education*, 14 (2), 149–63.

Dougherty, K. J. (August 1991). "The Community College at the Crossroads: The Need for Structural Reform." *Harvard Educational Review*, 61 (3), 311-36.

Dougherty, K. J. (1987). "The Effects of Community Colleges: Aid or Hindrance to Socioeconomic Attainment?" *Sociology of Education*, 60 (2), 86–103.

Eaton, J. (Jan. 1992). "The Coming Transformation of Community Colleges." *Planning for Higher Education*, 21 (1), 1–7.

Hlavna, D. P. (Spring 1992). "Economic Development, Human Capital Theory, and the Community College." *Community College Review*, 19 (4), 47–51.

Kopecek, R. J. (Fall 1991). "Assuming a Leadership Role in Community Economic Development." *New Directions for Community Colleges*, 19 (3), 41–46.

Richardson, R. C. (1988). "The Presence of Access and the Pursuit of Achievement," in Judith S. Eaton (ed.), *Colleges of Choice*, New York: Collier MacMillan Publishers.

Vaughan, G. B. (Sum. 1984). "Forging the Community College Mission." *Educational Record*, 65 (3), 24–29.

Vaughan, G. B. (Fall 1992). "Review Essay: The Community College Mission and The Diverted Dream." *The Review of Higher Education*, 16 (1),107–123.

Vaughan, G. B. (1988). "Scholarship in Community Colleges." *Educational Record*, 69 (2), 26–31.